# VW Beetle
# Service and Repair Manual

## by Bob Henderson, Martynn Randall and Andy Legg

**Models covered**

*(3798-1AR2-352)*

VW Beetle Hatchback, including special/limited editions
**Petrol:**   1.4 litre (1390cc), 1.6 litre (1595cc), 1.8 litre (1781cc) turbo & 2.0 litre (1984cc)
**Diesel:**   1.9 litre (1896cc) turbo, inc. PD

*Also covers major mechanical features of Cabriolet models*
*Does NOT cover 2.3 litre V5 engine or Tiptronic transmission*

© Haynes Group Limited 2012

A book in the **Haynes Service and Repair Manual Series**

ISBN **978 0 85733 654 5**

**British Library Cataloguing in Publication Data**
A catalogue record for this book is available from the British Library.

**Haynes Group Limited**
**Haynes North America, Inc**

www.haynes.com

# Contents

## LIVING WITH YOUR VW BEETLE

## MAINTENANCE

# Contents

The New Beetle combines current Volkswagen mechanical and technical details with an all new body, styled like the famous air-cooled original Beetle, or 'Bug'.

The chassis layout is conventional by today's standards, with the engine mounted at the front and the wheels driven through either a 5-speed or 6-speed manual transmission, or a 4-speed or 6-speed automatic transmission, via independent driveshafts.

These models feature independent front suspension with coil springs and MacPherson struts. At the rear, all models have a torsion beam axle supported by coil springs and shock absorbers.

The power-assisted steering is rack-and-pinion, mounted behind the engine.

All models have a power assisted brake system with disc brakes at the front and either disc or drum brakes at the rear. An Anti-lock Brake System (ABS) is optional.

## Acknowledgements

Technical writers who contributed to this project include Eric Godfrey, Jeff Kibler, Jay Storer and Larry Warren.

Working on your car can be dangerous. This page shows just some of the potential risks and hazards, with the aim of creating a safety-conscious attitude.

# General hazards

### Scalding

• Don't remove the radiator or expansion tank cap while the engine is hot.
• Engine oil, automatic transmission fluid or power steering fluid may also be dangerously hot if the engine has recently been running.

### Burning

• Beware of burns from the exhaust system and from any part of the engine. Brake discs and drums can also be extremely hot immediately after use.

### Crushing

• When working under or near a raised vehicle, always supplement the jack with axle stands, or use drive-on ramps. *Never venture under a car which is only supported by a jack.*

• Take care if loosening or tightening high-torque nuts when the vehicle is on stands. Initial loosening and final tightening should be done with the wheels on the ground.

### Fire

• Fuel is highly flammable; fuel vapour is explosive.
• Don't let fuel spill onto a hot engine.
• Do not smoke or allow naked lights (including pilot lights) anywhere near a vehicle being worked on. Also beware of creating sparks (electrically or by use of tools).
• Fuel vapour is heavier than air, so don't work on the fuel system with the vehicle over an inspection pit.
• Another cause of fire is an electrical overload or short-circuit. Take care when repairing or modifying the vehicle wiring.
• Keep a fire extinguisher handy, of a type suitable for use on fuel and electrical fires.

### Electric shock

• Ignition HT voltage can be dangerous, especially to people with heart problems or a pacemaker. Don't work on or near the ignition system with the engine running or the ignition switched on.

• Mains voltage is also dangerous. Make sure that any mains-operated equipment is correctly earthed. Mains power points should be protected by a residual current device (RCD) circuit breaker.

### Fume or gas intoxication

• Exhaust fumes are poisonous; they often contain carbon monoxide, which is rapidly fatal if inhaled. Never run the engine in a confined space such as a garage with the doors shut.
• Fuel vapour is also poisonous, as are the vapours from some cleaning solvents and paint thinners.

### Poisonous or irritant substances

• Avoid skin contact with battery acid and with any fuel, fluid or lubricant, especially antifreeze, brake hydraulic fluid and Diesel fuel. Don't syphon them by mouth. If such a substance is swallowed or gets into the eyes, seek medical advice.
• Prolonged contact with used engine oil can cause skin cancer. Wear gloves or use a barrier cream if necessary. Change out of oil-soaked clothes and do not keep oily rags in your pocket.
• Air conditioning refrigerant forms a poisonous gas if exposed to a naked flame (including a cigarette). It can also cause skin burns on contact.

### Asbestos

• Asbestos dust can cause cancer if inhaled or swallowed. Asbestos may be found in gaskets and in brake and clutch linings. When dealing with such components it is safest to assume that they contain asbestos.

# Special hazards

### Hydrofluoric acid

• This extremely corrosive acid is formed when certain types of synthetic rubber, found in some O-rings, oil seals, fuel hoses etc, are exposed to temperatures above 400ºC. The rubber changes into a charred or sticky substance containing the acid. *Once formed, the acid remains dangerous for years. If it gets onto the skin, it may be necessary to amputate the limb concerned.*
• When dealing with a vehicle which has suffered a fire, or with components salvaged from such a vehicle, wear protective gloves and discard them after use.

### The battery

• Batteries contain sulphuric acid, which attacks clothing, eyes and skin. Take care when topping-up or carrying the battery.
• The hydrogen gas given off by the battery is highly explosive. Never cause a spark or allow a naked light nearby. Be careful when connecting and disconnecting battery chargers or jump leads.

### Air bags

• Air bags can cause injury if they go off accidentally. Take care when removing the steering wheel and/or facia. Special storage instructions may apply.

### Diesel injection equipment

• Diesel injection pumps supply fuel at very high pressure. Take care when working on the fuel injectors and fuel pipes.

⚠ *Warning: Never expose the hands, face or any other part of the body to injector spray; the fuel can penetrate the skin with potentially fatal results.*

# Remember...

## DO

• Do use eye protection when using power tools, and when working under the vehicle.

• Do wear gloves or use barrier cream to protect your hands when necessary.

• Do get someone to check periodically that all is well when working alone on the vehicle.

• Do keep loose clothing and long hair well out of the way of moving mechanical parts.

• Do remove rings, wristwatch etc, before working on the vehicle – especially the electrical system.

• Do ensure that any lifting or jacking equipment has a safe working load rating adequate for the job.

## DON'T

• Don't attempt to lift a heavy component which may be beyond your capability – get assistance.

• Don't rush to finish a job, or take unverified short cuts.

• Don't use ill-fitting tools which may slip and cause injury.

• Don't leave tools or parts lying around where someone can trip over them. Mop up oil and fuel spills at once.

• Don't allow children or pets to play in or near a vehicle being worked on.

## Its purpose

The purpose of this manual is to help you get the best value from your vehicle. It can do so in several ways. It can help you decide what work must be done, even if you choose to have it done by a dealer service department or a garage; it provides information and procedures for routine maintenance and servicing; and it offers diagnostic and repair procedures to follow when trouble occurs.

We hope you use the manual to tackle the work yourself. For many simpler jobs, doing it yourself may be quicker than arranging an appointment to get the vehicle into a shop and making the trips to leave it and pick it up. More importantly, a lot of money can be saved by avoiding the expense the shop must pass on to you to cover its labour and overhead costs. An added benefit is the sense of satisfaction and accomplishment that you feel after doing the job yourself.

## Using the manual

The manual is divided into Chapters. Each Chapter is divided into numbered Sections, which are headed in bold type between horizontal pipes. Each Section consists of consecutively numbered paragraphs.

The reference numbers used in illustration captions pinpoint the pertinent Section and the paragraph within that Section. That is, illustration 3.2 means the illustration refers to Section 3 and paragraph (or Step) 2 within that Section.

Procedures, once described in the text, are not normally repeated. When it's necessary to refer to another Chapter, the reference will be given as Chapter and Section number. Cross references given without use of the word 'Chapter' apply to Sections and/or paragraphs in the same Chapter. For example, 'see Section 8' means in the same Chapter.

References to the left or right side of the vehicle assume you are sitting in the driver's seat, facing forward.

This manual is not a direct reproduction of the vehicle manufacturer's data, and its publication should not be taken as implying any technical approval by the vehicle manufacturers or importers.

**We take great pride in the accuracy of information given in this manual, but vehicle manufacturers make alterations and design changes during the production run of a particular vehicle of which they do not inform us. No liability can be accepted by the authors or publishers for loss, damage or injury caused by errors in, or omissions from, the information given.**

### NOTE

A **Note** provides information necessary to properly complete a procedure or information which will make the procedure easier to understand.

### CAUTION

A **Caution** provides a special procedure or special steps which must be taken while completing the procedure where the Caution is found. Not heeding a Caution can result in damage to the assembly being worked on.

### WARNING

A **Warning** provides a special procedure or special steps which must be taken while completing the procedure where the Warning is found. Not heeding a Warning can result in personal injury.

Modifications are a continuing and unpublicised process in vehicle manufacturing. Since spare parts manuals and lists are compiled on a numerical basis, the individual vehicle numbers are essential to correctly identify the component required.

The Vehicle Identification Number (VIN), which appears on the Vehicle Registration Document, is also embossed on a plate located on the upper left corner of the dashboard, near the windscreen **(see illustration)**. The VIN tells you when and where a vehicle was manufactured, its country of origin, make, type, passenger safety system, line, series, body style, engine and assembly plant. The VIN is also located on the right side of the floor, under the rear seat cushion.

The model year can be determined by examining the Vehicle Identification Number (VIN). The 10th character of the VIN represents the model year:

X 1999
Y 2000
1 2001
2 2002
3 2003
4 2004
5 2005

The engine code can be found in several places. The code is stamped into the left-hand end of engine block, on the forward facing edge of the flange where the engine block is joined to the transmission. The code can also be found on a sticker on the timing

**The VIN plate is located on the luggage compartment floor**

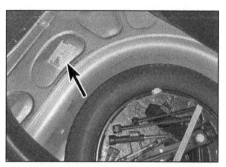

**The Vehicle Data Sticker is located on the left-hand side of the spare wheel well in the rear of the vehicle**

belt upper cover **(see illustration)**, and on the fourth row of the Vehicle Data Plate located on the left in the spare wheel recess **(see illustration)**.

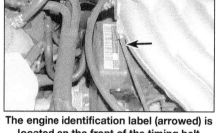

**The engine identification label (arrowed) is located on the front of the timing belt upper cover – a stamped number is located on the forward facing edge of the flange where the engine block is joined to the transmission**

**Typical transmission identification number location (arrowed) – manual transmission shown, automatic transmission similar**

The transmission identification number can be found stamped into a machined pad on the front side of the transmission **(see illustration)**.

# Anti-theft audio system

## General information

**1** All models are equipped with a stereo that has an anti-theft feature that will render the stereo inoperative if stolen or if the battery is disconnected. If the power source to the stereo is cut, the stereo will be inoperative. Even if the power source is immediately re-connected, the stereo will not function.

**2** Do not disconnect the battery, remove the stereo or disconnect related components unless you have the individual ID (code) number for the stereo.

## Unlocking the stereo after a power loss

**3** When the power is restored to the stereo, the stereo won't operate. Enter your ID code to reactivate it, using the following Steps.

**4** Turn the radio ON. The lower display window (where radio stations are displayed) should show 'SAFE'. After a few seconds, the SAFE message should go out and the numerals '1000' should display.

**5** At the bottom of the radio, the numbered buttons used to pre-set stations are used to enter your anti-theft code.

**6** Press the number 1 pre-set button repeatedly until the first number of your four-digit code is displayed, then enter the second

number of your code on button No.2, and so on until all four code numbers are displayed.

**7** Press the SEEK button until you hear a sound from the radio. The display will read 'LSM' if you've entered the correct code.

**8** If you have entered the wrong code during the above procedure, the display will read 'SAFE,' and you have one more try. If the second code is incorrect, the radio will stay locked for one hour, at which time two more code attempts can be made. Leave the radio on for an hour (while it is locked) and the key in the ignition switch, then try again.

**9** You should have the code written down in a secure place, for use in unlocking the anti-theft feature.

## Introduction

A selection of good tools is a fundamental requirement for anyone contemplating the maintenance and repair of a motor vehicle. For the owner who does not possess any, their purchase will prove a considerable expense, offsetting some of the savings made by doing-it-yourself. However, provided that the tools purchased meet the relevant national safety standards and are of good quality, they will last for many years and prove an extremely worthwhile investment.

To help the average owner to decide which tools are needed to carry out the various tasks detailed in this manual, we have compiled three lists of tools under the following headings: *Maintenance and minor repair, Repair and overhaul,* and *Special.* Newcomers to practical mechanics should start off with the *Maintenance and minor repair* tool kit, and confine themselves to the simpler jobs around the vehicle. Then, as confidence and experience grow, more difficult tasks can be undertaken, with extra tools being purchased as, and when, they are needed. In this way, a *Maintenance and minor repair* tool kit can be built up into a *Repair and overhaul* tool kit over a considerable period of time, without any major cash outlays. The experienced do-it-yourselfer will have a tool kit good enough for most repair and overhaul procedures, and will add tools from the *Special* category when it is felt that the expense is justified by the amount of use to which these tools will be put.

## Maintenance and minor repair tool kit

The tools given in this list should be considered as a minimum requirement if routine maintenance, servicing and minor repair operations are to be undertaken. We recommend the purchase of combination spanners (ring one end, open-ended the other); although more expensive than open-ended ones, they do give the advantages of both types of spanner.

- [ ] *Combination spanners:*
  *Metric - 8 to 19 mm inclusive*
- [ ] *Adjustable spanner - 35 mm jaw (approx.)*
- [ ] *Spark plug spanner (with rubber insert) - petrol models*
- [ ] *Spark plug gap adjustment tool - petrol models*
- [ ] *Set of feeler gauges*
- [ ] *Brake bleed nipple spanner*
- [ ] *Screwdrivers:*
  *Flat blade - 100 mm long x 6 mm dia*
  *Cross blade - 100 mm long x 6 mm dia*
  *Torx - various sizes (not all vehicles)*
- [ ] *Combination pliers*
- [ ] *Hacksaw (junior)*
- [ ] *Tyre pump*
- [ ] *Tyre pressure gauge*
- [ ] *Oil can*
- [ ] *Oil filter removal tool (if applicable)*
- [ ] *Fine emery cloth*
- [ ] *Wire brush (small)*
- [ ] *Funnel (medium size)*
- [ ] *Sump drain plug key (not all vehicles)*

## Repair and overhaul tool kit

These tools are virtually essential for anyone undertaking any major repairs to a motor vehicle, and are additional to those given in the *Maintenance and minor repair* list. Included in this list is a comprehensive set of sockets. Although these are expensive, they will be found invaluable as they are so versatile - particularly if various drives are included in the set. We recommend the half-inch square-drive type, as this can be used with most proprietary torque wrenches.

The tools in this list will sometimes need to be supplemented by tools from the *Special* list:

- [ ] *Sockets to cover range in previous list (including Torx sockets)*
- [ ] *Reversible ratchet drive (for use with sockets)*
- [ ] *Extension piece, 250 mm (for use with sockets)*
- [ ] *Universal joint (for use with sockets)*
- [ ] *Flexible handle or sliding T "breaker bar" (for use with sockets)*
- [ ] *Torque wrench (for use with sockets)*
- [ ] *Self-locking grips*
- [ ] *Ball pein hammer*
- [ ] *Soft-faced mallet (plastic or rubber)*
- [ ] *Screwdrivers:*
  *Flat blade - long & sturdy, short (chubby), and narrow (electrician's) types*
  *Cross blade - long & sturdy, and short (chubby) types*
- [ ] *Pliers:*
  *Long-nosed*
  *Side cutters (electrician's)*
  *Circlip (internal and external)*
- [ ] *Cold chisel - 25 mm*
- [ ] *Scriber*
- [ ] *Scraper*
- [ ] *Centre-punch*
- [ ] *Pin punch*
- [ ] *Hacksaw*
- [ ] *Brake hose clamp*
- [ ] *Brake/clutch bleeding kit*
- [ ] *Selection of twist drills*
- [ ] *Steel rule/straight-edge*
- [ ] *Allen keys (inc. splined/Torx type)*
- [ ] *Selection of files*
- [ ] *Wire brush*
- [ ] *Axle stands*
- [ ] *Jack (strong trolley or hydraulic type)*
- [ ] *Light with extension lead*
- [ ] *Universal electrical multi-meter*

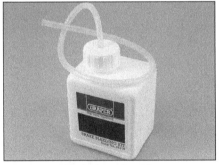

**Sockets and reversible ratchet drive**

**Brake bleeding kit**

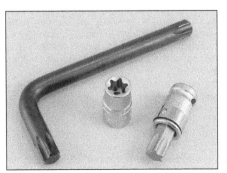

**Torx key, socket and bit**

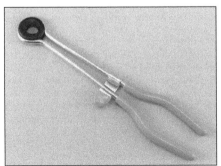

**Hose clamp**

**Angular-tightening gauge**

## Special tools

The tools in this list are those which are not used regularly, are expensive to buy, or which need to be used in accordance with their manufacturers' instructions. Unless relatively difficult mechanical jobs are undertaken frequently, it will not be economic to buy many of these tools. Where this is the case, you could consider clubbing together with friends (or joining a motorists' club) to make a joint purchase, or borrowing the tools against a deposit from a local garage or tool hire specialist.

The following list contains only those tools and instruments freely available to the public, and not those special tools produced by the vehicle manufacturer specifically for its dealer network. You will find occasional references to these manufacturers' special tools in the text of this manual. Generally, an alternative method of doing the job without the vehicle manufacturers' special tool is given. However, sometimes there is no alternative to using them. Where this is the case and the relevant tool cannot be bought or borrowed, you will have to entrust the work to a dealer.

☐ Angular-tightening gauge
☐ Valve spring compressor
☐ Valve grinding tool
☐ Piston ring compressor
☐ Piston ring removal/installation tool
☐ Cylinder bore hone
☐ Balljoint separator
☐ Coil spring compressors (where applicable)
☐ Two/three-legged hub and bearing puller
☐ Impact screwdriver
☐ Micrometer and/or vernier calipers
☐ Dial gauge
☐ Tachometer
☐ Fault code reader
☐ Cylinder compression gauge
☐ Hand-operated vacuum pump and gauge
☐ Clutch plate alignment set
☐ Brake shoe steady spring cup removal tool
☐ Bush and bearing removal/installation set
☐ Stud extractors
☐ Tap and die set
☐ Lifting tackle

## Buying tools

Reputable motor accessory shops and superstores often offer excellent quality tools at discount prices, so it pays to shop around.

Remember, you don't have to buy the most expensive items on the shelf, but it is always advisable to steer clear of the very cheap tools. Beware of 'bargains' offered on market stalls, on-line or at car boot sales. There are plenty of good tools around at reasonable prices, but always aim to purchase items which meet the relevant national safety standards. If in doubt, ask the proprietor or manager of the shop for advice before making a purchase.

## Care and maintenance of tools

Having purchased a reasonable tool kit, it is necessary to keep the tools in a clean and serviceable condition. After use, always wipe off any dirt, grease and metal particles using a clean, dry cloth, before putting the tools away. Never leave them lying around after they have been used. A simple tool rack on the garage or workshop wall for items such as screwdrivers and pliers is a good idea. Store all normal spanners and sockets in a metal box. Any measuring instruments, gauges, meters, etc, must be carefully stored where they cannot be damaged or become rusty.

Take a little care when tools are used. Hammer heads inevitably become marked, and screwdrivers lose the keen edge on their blades from time to time. A little timely attention with emery cloth or a file will soon restore items like this to a good finish.

## Working facilities

Not to be forgotten when discussing tools is the workshop itself. If anything more than routine maintenance is to be carried out, a suitable working area becomes essential.

It is appreciated that many an owner-mechanic is forced by circumstances to remove an engine or similar item without the benefit of a garage or workshop. Having done this, any repairs should always be done under the cover of a roof.

Wherever possible, any dismantling should be done on a clean, flat workbench or table at a suitable working height.

Any workbench needs a vice; one with a jaw opening of 100 mm is suitable for most jobs. As mentioned previously, some clean dry storage space is also required for tools, as well as for any lubricants, cleaning fluids, touch-up paints etc, which become necessary.

Another item which may be required, and which has a much more general usage, is an electric drill with a chuck capacity of at least 8 mm. This, together with a good range of twist drills, is virtually essential for fitting accessories.

Last, but not least, always keep a supply of old newspapers and clean, lint-free rags available, and try to keep any working area as clean as possible.

**Micrometers**

**Dial test indicator ("dial gauge")**

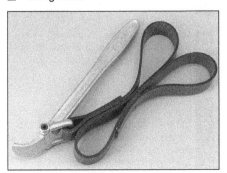

**Oil filter removal tool (strap wrench type)**

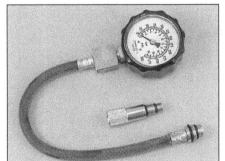

**Compression tester**

**Bearing puller**

# Jump starting

When jump-starting a car using a booster battery, observe the following precautions:

✔ Before connecting the booster battery, make sure that the ignition is switched off.

✔ Ensure that all electrical equipment (lights, heater, wipers, etc) is switched off.

✔ Take note of any special precautions printed on the battery case.

✔ Make sure that the booster battery is the same voltage as the discharged one in the vehicle.

✔ If the battery is being jump-started from the battery in another vehicle, the two vehicles MUST NOT TOUCH each other.

✔ Make sure that the transmission is in neutral (or PARK, in the case of automatic transmission).

**1** Connect one end of the red jump lead to the positive (+) terminal of the flat battery

**2** Connect the other end of the red lead to the positive (+) terminal of the booster battery.

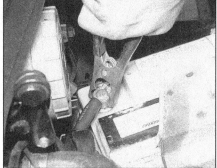

**3** Connect one end of the black jump lead to the negative (-) terminal of the booster battery

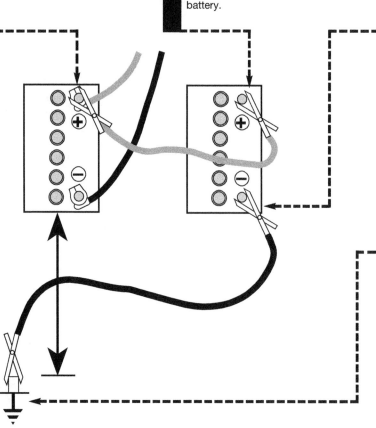

**4** Connect the other end of the black jump lead to a bolt or bracket on the engine block, well away from the battery, on the vehicle to be started.

**5** Make sure that the jump leads will not come into contact with the fan, drive-belts or other moving parts of the engine.

**6** Start the engine using the booster battery and run it at idle speed. Switch on the lights, rear window demister and heater blower motor, then disconnect the jump leads in the reverse order of connection. Turn off the lights etc.

## Jacking

*Warning: The jack supplied with the vehicle should only be used for changing a tyre or placing axle stands under the frame. Never work under the vehicle or start the engine while this jack is being used as the only means of support.*

The vehicle should be parked on level ground with the wheels blocked, the handbrake applied and the transmission in Park (automatic) or Reverse (manual). If the vehicle is parked alongside the roadway, or in any other hazardous situation, turn on the emergency hazard flashers. If a tyre is to be changed, loosen the wheel bolts one-half turn before raising the vehicle off the ground.

Place the jack under the vehicle in the indicated position **(see illustrations)**. Operate the jack with a slow, smooth motion until the wheel is raised off the earth. Remove the wheel bolts, pull off the wheel, refit the spare and thread the wheel bolts back on. Tighten the wheel bolts snugly, lower the vehicle until some weight is on the wheel, tighten the wheel bolts completely in a criss-cross pattern and remove the jack.

## Towing

As a general rule, the vehicle should be towed with the front (drive) wheels off the ground.

Vehicles equipped with an automatic transmission can be towed from the front with all four wheels on the ground, provided that speeds don't exceed 30 mph and the distance is not over 40 miles. Also, check the transmission lubricant to make sure it is up to the proper level.

*Caution: Never tow a vehicle with an automatic transmission from the rear with the front wheels on the ground.*

When towing a vehicle equipped with a manual transmission with all four wheels on the ground, be sure to place the gearchange lever in neutral and release the handbrake, and turn the ignition key to the first position to unlock the steering wheel. If towed on a dolly from the rear, the ignition key must be in the ACC position, since the steering lock mechanism isn't strong enough to hold the front wheels straight while towing. The tow truck operator will attach a purpose-built steering wheel holder suitable for towing conditions. Also, check the transmission lubricant to make sure it is up to the proper level.

Equipment specifically designed for towing should be used. It should be attached to the main structural members of the vehicle, not the bumpers or brackets.

Safety is a major consideration when towing and all applicable laws must be obeyed.

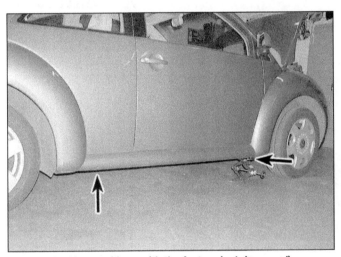

Jacking positions with the factory jack (arrowed)

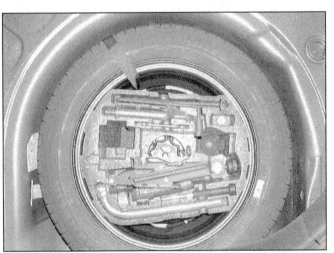

The jack and factory tools are located in a tray above the spare wheel

# Buying parts

Renewal parts are available from many sources, which generally fall into one of two categories - authorised dealer parts departments and independent retail motor factors. Our advice concerning these parts is as follows:

## Retail motor factors

Good motor factors will stock frequently needed components which wear out relatively fast, such as clutch components, exhaust systems, brake parts, tune-up parts, etc. These stores often supply new or reconditioned parts on an exchange basis, which can save a considerable amount of money. Discount motor factors are often very good places to buy materials and parts needed for general vehicle maintenance such as oil, grease, filters, spark plugs, belts, touch-up paint, bulbs, etc. They also usually sell tools and general accessories, have convenient hours, charge lower prices and can often be found not far from home.

## Authorised dealer parts department

This is the best source for parts which are unique to the vehicle and not generally available elsewhere (such as major engine parts, transmission parts, trim pieces, etc).

## Warranty information

When the vehicle is new, it should be serviced by a dealer service department (or other workshop recognised by the vehicle manufacturer as providing the same standard of service) in order to preserve the warranty. The vehicle manufacturer may reject warranty claims if you are unable to prove that servicing has been carried out as and when specified, using only original equipment parts or parts certified to be of equivalent quality.

To be sure of obtaining the correct parts, have engine and chassis numbers available and, if possible, take the old parts along for positive identification.

This is a guide to getting your vehicle through the MOT test. Obviously it will not be possible to examine the vehicle to the same standard as the professional MOT tester. However, working through the following checks will enable you to identify any problem areas before submitting the vehicle for the test.

It has only been possible to summarise the test requirements here, based on the regulations in force at the time of printing. Test standards are becoming increasingly stringent, although there are some exemptions for older vehicles.

An assistant will be needed to help carry out some of these checks.

*The checks have been sub-divided into four categories, as follows:*

**1** Checks carried out **FROM THE DRIVER'S SEAT**

**2** Checks carried out **WITH THE VEHICLE ON THE GROUND**

**3** Checks carried out **WITH THE VEHICLE RAISED AND THE WHEELS FREE TO TURN**

**4** Checks carried out on **YOUR VEHICLE'S EXHAUST EMISSION SYSTEM**

---

**1** Checks carried out **FROM THE DRIVER'S SEAT**

### Handbrake (parking brake)

☐ Test the operation of the handbrake. Excessive travel (too many clicks) indicates incorrect brake or cable adjustment.
☐ Check that the handbrake cannot be released by tapping the lever sideways. Check the security of the lever mountings.

☐ If the parking brake is foot-operated, check that the pedal is secure and without excessive travel, and that the release mechanism operates correctly.
☐ Where applicable, test the operation of the electronic handbrake. The brake should engage and disengage without excessive delay. If the warning light does not extinguish when the brake is disengaged, this could indicate a fault which will need further investigation.

### Footbrake

☐ Depress the brake pedal and check that it does not creep down to the floor, indicating a master cylinder fault. Release the pedal, wait a few seconds, then depress it again. If the pedal travels nearly to the floor before firm resistance is felt, brake adjustment or repair is necessary. If the pedal feels spongy, there is air in the hydraulic system which must be removed by bleeding.

☐ Check that the brake pedal is secure and in good condition. Check also for signs of fluid leaks on the pedal, floor or carpets, which would indicate failed seals in the brake master cylinder.
☐ Check the servo unit (when applicable) by operating the brake pedal several times, then keeping the pedal depressed and starting the engine. As the engine starts, the pedal will move down slightly. If not, the vacuum hose or the servo itself may be faulty.

### Steering wheel and column

☐ Examine the steering wheel for fractures or looseness of the hub, spokes or rim.
☐ Move the steering wheel from side to side and then up and down. Check that the steering wheel is not loose on the column, indicating wear or a loose retaining nut. Continue moving the steering wheel as before, but also turn it slightly from left to right.

☐ Check that the steering wheel is not loose on the column, and that there is no abnormal movement of the steering wheel, indicating wear in the column support bearings or couplings.
☐ Check that the ignition lock (where fitted) engages and disengages correctly.
☐ Steering column adjustment mechanisms (where fitted) must be able to lock the column securely in place with no play evident.

### Windscreen, mirrors and sunvisor

☐ The windscreen must be free of cracks or other significant damage within the driver's field of view. (Small stone chips are acceptable.) Rear view mirrors must be secure, intact, and capable of being adjusted.

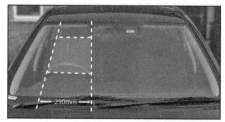

☐ The driver's sunvisor must be capable of being stored in the "up" position.

## Seat belts and seats

**Note:** *The following checks are applicable to all seat belts, front and rear.*

☐ Examine the webbing of all the belts (including rear belts if fitted) for cuts, serious fraying or deterioration. Fasten and unfasten each belt to check the buckles. If applicable, check the retracting mechanism. Check the security of all seat belt mountings accessible from inside the vehicle, ensuring any height adjustable mountings lock securely in place.

☐ Seat belts with pre-tensioners, once activated, have a "flag" or similar showing on the seat belt stalk. This, in itself, is not a reason for test failure.

☐ The front seats themselves must be securely attached and the backrests must lock in the upright position.

## Doors

☐ Both front doors must be able to be opened and closed from outside and inside, and must latch securely when closed.

## Bonnet and boot/tailgate

☐ The bonnet and boot/tailgate must latch securely when closed.

## 2 Checks carried out WITH THE VEHICLE ON THE GROUND

## Vehicle identification

☐ Number plates must be in good condition, secure and legible, with letters and numbers correctly spaced – spacing at (A) should be 33 mm and at (B) 11 mm. At the front, digits must be black on a white background and at the rear black on a yellow background. Other background designs (such as honeycomb) are not permitted.

☐ The VIN plate and/or homologation plate must be permanently displayed and legible.

## Electrical equipment

☐ Switch on the ignition and check the operation of the horn.

☐ Check the windscreen washers and wipers, examining the wiper blades; renew damaged or perished blades. Also check the operation of the stop-lights.

☐ Check the operation of the sidelights and number plate lights. The lenses and reflectors must be secure, clean and undamaged.

☐ Check the operation and alignment of the headlights. The headlight reflectors must not be tarnished and the lenses must be undamaged.

☐ Switch on the ignition and check the operation of the direction indicators (including the instrument panel tell-tale) and the hazard warning lights. Operation of the sidelights and stop-lights must not affect the indicators - if it does, the cause is usually a bad earth at the rear light cluster. Indicators should flash at a rate of between 60 and 120 times per minute – faster or slower than this could indicate a fault with the flasher unit or a bad earth at one of the light units.

☐ Check the operation of the rear foglight(s), including the warning light on the instrument panel or in the switch.

☐ The ABS warning light must illuminate in accordance with the manufacturers' design. For most vehicles, the ABS warning light should illuminate when the ignition is switched on, and (if the system is operating properly) extinguish after a few seconds. Refer to the owner's handbook.

## Footbrake

☐ Examine the master cylinder, brake pipes and servo unit for leaks, loose mountings, corrosion or other damage. If ABS is fitted, this unit should also be examined for signs of leaks or corrosion.

☐ The fluid reservoir must be secure and the fluid level must be between the upper (**A**) and lower (**B**) markings.

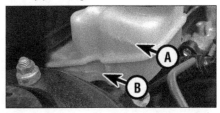

☐ Inspect both front brake flexible hoses for cracks or deterioration of the rubber. Turn the steering from lock to lock, and ensure that the hoses do not contact the wheel, tyre, or any part of the steering or suspension mechanism. With the brake pedal firmly depressed, check the hoses for bulges or leaks under pressure.

## Steering and suspension

☐ Have your assistant turn the steering wheel from side to side slightly, up to the point where the steering gear just begins to transmit this movement to the roadwheels. Check for excessive free play between the steering wheel and the steering gear, indicating wear or insecurity of the steering column joints, the column-to-steering gear coupling, or the steering gear itself.

☐ Have your assistant turn the steering wheel more vigorously in each direction, so that the roadwheels just begin to turn. As this is done, examine all the steering joints, linkages, fittings and attachments. Renew any component that shows signs of wear or damage. On vehicles with power steering, check the security and condition of the steering pump, drivebelt and hoses.

☐ Check that the vehicle is standing level, and at approximately the correct ride height.

## Shock absorbers

☐ Depress each corner of the vehicle in turn, then release it. The vehicle should rise and then settle in its normal position. If the vehicle continues to rise and fall, the shock absorber is defective. A shock absorber which has seized will also cause the vehicle to fail.

## Exhaust system

☐ Start the engine. With your assistant holding a rag over the tailpipe, check the entire system for leaks. Repair or renew leaking sections.

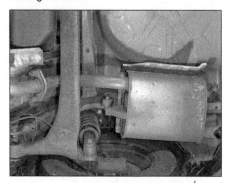

**3** Checks carried out **WITH THE VEHICLE RAISED AND THE WHEELS FREE TO TURN**

*Jack up the front and rear of the vehicle, and securely support it on axle stands. Position the stands clear of the suspension assemblies. Ensure that the wheels are clear of the ground and that the steering can be turned from lock to lock.*

## Steering mechanism

☐ Have your assistant turn the steering from lock to lock. Check that the steering turns smoothly, and that no part of the steering mechanism, including a wheel or tyre, fouls any brake hose or pipe or any part of the body structure.
☐ Examine the steering rack rubber gaiters for damage or insecurity of the retaining clips. If power steering is fitted, check for signs of damage or leakage of the fluid hoses, pipes or connections. Also check for excessive stiffness or binding of the steering, a missing split pin or locking device, or severe corrosion of the body structure within 30 cm of any steering component attachment point.

## Front and rear suspension and wheel bearings

☐ Starting at the front right-hand side, grasp the roadwheel at the 3 o'clock and 9 o'clock positions and rock gently but firmly. Check for free play or insecurity at the wheel bearings, suspension balljoints, or suspension mount-ings, pivots and attachments.
☐ Now grasp the wheel at the 12 o'clock and 6 o'clock positions and repeat the previous inspection. Spin the wheel, and check for roughness or tightness of the front wheel bearing.

☐ If excess free play is suspected at a component pivot point, this can be confirmed by using a large screwdriver or similar tool and levering between the mounting and the component attachment. This will confirm whether the wear is in the pivot bush, its retaining bolt, or in the mounting itself (the bolt holes can often become elongated).

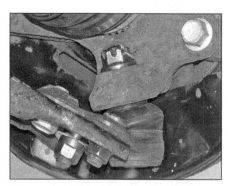

☐ Carry out all the above checks at the other front wheel, and then at both rear wheels.

## Springs and shock absorbers

☐ Examine the suspension struts (when applicable) for serious fluid leakage, corrosion, or damage to the casing. Also check the security of the mounting points.
☐ If coil springs are fitted, check that the spring ends locate in their seats, and that the spring is not corroded, cracked or broken.
☐ If leaf springs are fitted, check that all leaves are intact, that the axle is securely attached to each spring, and that there is no deterioration of the spring eye mountings, bushes, and shackles.

☐ The same general checks apply to vehicles fitted with other suspension types, such as torsion bars, hydraulic displacer units, etc. Ensure that all mountings and attachments are secure, that there are no signs of excessive wear, corrosion or damage, and (on hydraulic types) that there are no fluid leaks or damaged pipes.
☐ Inspect the shock absorbers for signs of serious fluid leakage. Check for wear of the mounting bushes or attachments, or damage to the body of the unit.

## Driveshafts (fwd vehicles only)

☐ Rotate each front wheel in turn and inspect the constant velocity joint gaiters for splits or damage. Also check that each driveshaft is straight and undamaged.

## Braking system

☐ If possible without dismantling, check brake pad wear and disc condition. Ensure that the friction lining material has not worn excessively, (A) and that the discs are not fractured, pitted, scored or badly worn (B).

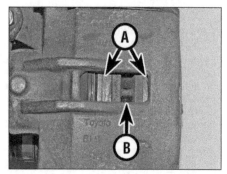

☐ Examine all the rigid brake pipes underneath the vehicle, and the flexible hose(s) at the rear. Look for corrosion, chafing or insecurity of the pipes, and for signs of bulging under pressure, chafing, splits or deterioration of the flexible hoses.
☐ Look for signs of fluid leaks at the brake calipers or on the brake backplates. Repair or renew leaking components.
☐ Slowly spin each wheel, while your assistant depresses and releases the footbrake. Ensure that each brake is operating and does not bind when the pedal is released.

□ Examine the handbrake mechanism, checking for frayed or broken cables, excessive corrosion, or wear or insecurity of the linkage. Check that the mechanism works on each relevant wheel, and releases fully, without binding.

□ It is not possible to test brake efficiency without special equipment, but a road test can be carried out later to check that the vehicle pulls up in a straight line.

## Fuel and exhaust systems

□ Inspect the fuel tank (including the filler cap), fuel pipes, hoses and unions. All components must be secure and free from leaks. Locking fuel caps must lock securely and the key must be provided for the MOT test.

□ Examine the exhaust system over its entire length, checking for any damaged, broken or missing mountings, security of the retaining clamps and rust or corrosion.

## Wheels and tyres

□ Examine the sidewalls and tread area of each tyre in turn. Check for cuts, tears, lumps, bulges, separation of the tread, and exposure of the ply or cord due to wear or damage. Check that the tyre bead is correctly seated on the wheel rim, that the valve is sound and properly seated, and that the wheel is not distorted or damaged.

□ Check that the tyres are of the correct size for the vehicle, that they are of the same size and type on each axle, and that the pressures are correct.

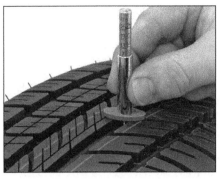

□ Check the tyre tread depth. The legal minimum at the time of writing is 1.6 mm over the central three-quarters of the tread width. Abnormal tread wear may indicate incorrect front wheel alignment or wear in steering or suspension components.

□ If the spare wheel is fitted externally or in a separate carrier beneath the vehicle, check that mountings are secure and free of excessive corrosion.

## Body corrosion

□ Check the condition of the entire vehicle structure for signs of corrosion in load-bearing areas. (These include chassis box sections, side sills, cross-members, pillars, and all suspension, steering, braking system and seat belt mountings and anchorages.) Any corrosion which has seriously reduced the thickness of a load-bearing area (or is within 30 cm of safety-related components such as steering or suspension) is likely to cause the vehicle to fail. In this case professional repairs are likely to be needed.

□ Damage or corrosion which causes sharp or otherwise dangerous edges to be exposed will also cause the vehicle to fail.

## Towbars

□ Check the condition of mounting points (both beneath the vehicle and within boot/hatchback areas) for signs of corrosion, ensuring that all fixings are secure and not worn or damaged. There must be no excessive play in detachable tow ball arms or quick-release mechanisms.

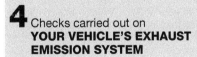
**4** Checks carried out on **YOUR VEHICLE'S EXHAUST EMISSION SYSTEM**

## Petrol models

□ The engine should be warmed up, and running well (ignition system in good order, air filter element clean, etc).

□ Before testing, run the engine at around 2500 rpm for 20 seconds. Let the engine drop to idle, and watch for smoke from the exhaust. If the idle speed is too high, or if dense blue or black smoke emerges for more than 5 seconds, the vehicle will fail. Typically, blue smoke signifies oil burning (engine wear);

black smoke means unburnt fuel (dirty air cleaner element, or other fuel system fault).

□ An exhaust gas analyser for measuring carbon monoxide (CO) and hydrocarbons (HC) is now needed. If one cannot be hired or borrowed, have a local garage perform the check.

## CO emissions (mixture)

□ The MOT tester has access to the CO limits for all vehicles. The CO level is measured at idle speed, and at 'fast idle' (2500 to 3000 rpm). The following limits are given as a general guide:

*At idle speed* – Less than 0.5% CO
*At 'fast idle'* – Less than 0.3% CO
*Lambda reading* – 0.97 to 1.03

□ If the CO level is too high, this may point to poor maintenance, a fuel injection system problem, faulty lambda (oxygen) sensor or catalytic converter. Try an injector cleaning treatment, and check the vehicle's ECU for fault codes.

## HC emissions

□ The MOT tester has access to HC limits for all vehicles. The HC level is measured at 'fast idle' (2500 to 3000 rpm). The following limits are given as a general guide:

*At 'fast idle'* – Less then 200 ppm

□ Excessive HC emissions are typically caused by oil being burnt (worn engine), or by a blocked crankcase ventilation system ('breather'). If the engine oil is old and thin, an oil change may help. If the engine is running badly, check the vehicle's ECU for fault codes.

## Diesel models

□ The only emission test for diesel engines is measuring exhaust smoke density, using a calibrated smoke meter. The test involves accelerating the engine at least 3 times to its maximum unloaded speed.

**Note:** *On engines with a timing belt, it is VITAL that the belt is in good condition before the test is carried out.*

□ With the engine warmed up, it is first purged by running at around 2500 rpm for 20 seconds. A governor check is then carried out, by slowly accelerating the engine to its maximum speed. After this, the smoke meter is connected, and the engine is accelerated quickly to maximum speed three times. If the smoke density is less than the limits given below, the vehicle will pass:

*Non-turbo vehicles:* 2.5m-1
*Turbocharged vehicles:* 3.0m-1

□ If excess smoke is produced, try fitting a new air cleaner element, or using an injector cleaning treatment. If the engine is running badly, where applicable, check the vehicle's ECU for fault codes. Also check the vehicle's EGR system, where applicable. At high mileages, the injectors may require professional attention.

A number of automotive chemicals and lubricants are available for use during vehicle maintenance and repair. They include a wide variety of products ranging from cleaning solvents and degreasers to lubricants and protective sprays for rubber, plastic and vinyl.

## Cleaners

*Carburettor cleaner and choke cleaner* is a strong solvent for gum, varnish and carbon. Most carburettor cleaners leave a dry-type lubricant film which will not harden or gum up. Because of this film it is not recommended for use on electrical components.

*Brake system cleaner* is used to remove grease and brake fluid from the brake system, where clean surfaces are absolutely necessary. It leaves no residue and often eliminates brake squeal caused by contaminants.

*Electrical cleaner* removes oxidation, corrosion and carbon deposits from electrical contacts, restoring full current flow. It can also be used to clean spark plugs, carburettor jets, voltage regulators and other parts where an oil-free surface is desired.

*Moisture dispersant* removes water and moisture from electrical components such as alternators, voltage regulators, electrical connectors and fuse blocks. They are non-conductive and non-corrosive.

*Degreasers* are heavy-duty solvents used to remove grease from the outside of the engine and from chassis components. They can be sprayed or brushed on and, depending on the type, are rinsed off either with water or solvent.

## Lubricants

*Motor oil* is the lubricant formulated for use in engines. It normally contains a wide variety of additives to prevent corrosion and reduce foaming and wear. Motor oil comes in various weights (viscosity ratings) from 0 to 50. The recommended weight of the oil depends on the season, temperature and the demands on the engine. Light oil is used in cold climates and under light load conditions. Heavy oil is used in hot climates and where high loads are encountered. Multi-viscosity oils are designed to have characteristics of both light and heavy oils and are available in a number of weights from 5W-15 to 20W-50.

*Gear oil* is designed to be used in differentials, manual transmissions and other areas where high-temperature lubrication is required.

*Chassis and wheel bearing grease* is a heavy grease used where increased loads and friction are encountered, such as for wheel bearings, balljoints, track rod ends and universal joints.

*High-temperature wheel bearing grease* is designed to withstand the extreme temperatures encountered by wheel bearings in disc brake equipped vehicles. It usually contains molybdenum disulphide (moly), which is a dry-type lubricant.

*White grease* is a heavy grease for metal-to-metal applications where water is a problem. White grease stays soft under both low and high temperatures (usually from –70 to 90°C), and will not wash off or dilute in the presence of water.

*Assembly lubricant* is a special extreme pressure lubricant, usually containing moly, used to lubricate high-load parts (such as main and big-end bearings and cam lobes) for initial start-up of a new engine. It lubricates the parts without being squeezed out or washed away until the engine oiling system begins to function.

*Silicone lubricants* are used to protect rubber, plastic, vinyl and nylon parts.

*Graphite lubricants* are used where oils cannot be used due to contamination problems, such as in locks. The dry graphite will lubricate metal parts while remaining uncontaminated by dirt, water, oil or acids. It is electrically conductive and will not foul electrical contacts in locks such as the ignition switch.

*Moly penetrants* loosen and lubricate seized, rusted and corroded fasteners and prevent future rusting or freezing.

*Heat-sink grease* is a special electrically non-conductive grease that is used for mounting electronic ignition modules where it is essential that heat is transferred away from the module.

## Sealants

*RTV sealant* is one of the most widely used gasket compounds. Made from silicone, RTV is air curing, it seals, bonds, waterproofs, fills surface irregularities, remains flexible, doesn't shrink, is relatively easy to remove, and is used as a supplementary sealer with almost all low and medium temperature gaskets.

*Anaerobic sealant* is much like RTV in that it can be used either to seal gaskets or to form gaskets by itself. It remains flexible, is solvent resistant and fills surface imperfections. The difference between an anaerobic sealant and an RTV-type sealant is in the curing. RTV cures when exposed to air, while an anaerobic sealant cures only in the absence of air. This means that an anaerobic sealant cures only after the assembly of parts, sealing them together.

*Thread and pipe sealant* is used for sealing hydraulic and pneumatic fittings and vacuum pipes. It is usually made from a Teflon compound, and comes in a spray, a paint-on liquid and as a wrap-around tape.

## Chemicals

*Anti-seize compound* prevents seizing, galling, cold welding, rust and corrosion in fasteners. High-temperature anti-seize, usually made with copper and graphite lubricants, is used for exhaust system and exhaust manifold bolts.

*Anaerobic locking compounds* are used to keep fasteners from vibrating or working loose and cure only after refitting, in the absence of air. Medium strength locking compound is used for small nuts, bolts and screws that may be removed later. High-strength locking compound is for large nuts, bolts and studs which aren't removed on a regular basis.

*Oil additives* range from viscosity index improvers to chemical treatments that claim to reduce internal engine friction. It should be noted that most oil manufacturers caution against using additives with their oils.

*Petrol additives* perform several functions, depending on their chemical makeup. They usually contain solvents that help dissolve gum and varnish that build up on carburettor, fuel injection and intake parts. They also serve to break down carbon deposits that form on the inside surfaces of the combustion chambers. Some additives contain upper cylinder lubricants for valves and piston rings, and others contain chemicals to remove condensation from the fuel tank.

## Miscellaneous

*Brake fluid* is specially formulated hydraulic fluid that can withstand the heat and pressure encountered in brake systems. Care must be taken so this fluid does not come in contact with painted surfaces or plastics. An opened container should always be resealed to prevent contamination by water or dirt.

*Weatherstrip adhesive* is used to bond weatherstripping around doors, windows and boot lids. It is sometimes used to attach trim pieces.

*Underseal* is a petroleum-based, tar-like substance that is designed to protect metal surfaces on the underside of the vehicle from corrosion. It also acts as a sound-deadening agent by insulating the bottom of the vehicle.

*Waxes and polishes* are used to help protect painted and plated surfaces from the weather. Different types of paint may require the use of different types of wax and polish. Some polishes utilise a chemical or abrasive cleaner to help remove the top layer of oxidised (dull) paint on older vehicles. In recent years many non-wax polishes that contain a wide variety of chemicals such as polymers and silicones have been introduced. These non-wax polishes are usually easier to apply and last longer than conventional waxes and polishes.

This section provides an easy reference guide to the more common problems that may occur during the operation of your vehicle. These problems and their possible causes are grouped under headings denoting various components or systems, such as Engine, Cooling system, etc. They also refer you to the chapter and/or section that deals with the problem.

Remember that successful troubleshooting is not a mysterious black art practised only by professional mechanics. It is simply the result of the right knowledge combined with an intelligent, systematic approach to the problem. Always work by a process of elimination, starting with the simplest solution and working through to the most complex - and never overlook the obvious. Anyone can run the fuel tank dry or leave the lights on overnight, so don't assume that you are exempt from such oversights.

Finally, always establish a clear idea of why a problem has occurred and take steps to ensure that it doesn't happen again. If the electrical system fails because of a poor connection, check the other connections in the system to make sure that they don't fail as well. If a particular fuse continues to blow, find out why - don't just renew one fuse after another. Remember, failure of a small component can often be indicative of potential failure or incorrect functioning of a more important component or system.

# Engine

## 1 Engine will not rotate when attempting to start

1 Battery terminal connections loose or corroded (Chapter 1).
2 Battery discharged or faulty (Chapter 1).
3 Automatic transmission not completely engaged in Park (Chapter 7B) or clutch pedal not completely depressed (Chapter 8).
4 Broken, loose or disconnected wiring in the starting circuit (Chapters 5 and 12).
5 Starter motor pinion jammed in flywheel ring gear (Chapter 5).
6 Starter solenoid faulty (Chapter 5).
7 Starter motor faulty (Chapter 5).
8 Ignition switch faulty (Chapter 12).
9 Starter pinion or flywheel teeth worn or broken (Chapter 5).
10 Transmission Range (TR) switch malfunctioning (Chapter 7B).

## 2 Engine rotates but will not start

1 Fuel tank empty.
2 Battery discharged (engine rotates slowly) (Chapter 5).
3 Battery terminal connections loose or corroded (Chapter 1).
4 Leaking fuel injector(s), faulty fuel pump, pressure regulator, etc. (Chapter 4).
5 Broken or stripped timing belt (Chapter 2).
6 Ignition components damp or damaged (Chapter 5).
7 Worn, faulty or incorrectly gapped spark plugs (Chapter 1).
8 Broken, loose or disconnected wiring in the starting circuit (Chapter 5).
9 Broken, loose or disconnected wires at the ignition coils or faulty coils (Chapter 5).
10 Defective MAF sensor (see Chapter 6).
11 Broken, loose or disconnected wires at the fuel shutoff solenoid (diesel) (Chapter 4B).
12 Defective fuel injection pump or fuel injector (diesel) (Chapter 4B).
13 Incorrect fuel injection pump timing (diesel) (Chapter 4B).
14 Contaminated fuel.

## 3 Engine hard to start when cold

1 Battery discharged or low (Chapter 1).
2 Malfunctioning fuel system (Chapter 4).
3 Faulty coolant temperature sensor or intake air temperature sensor (Chapter 6).
4 Injector(s) leaking (Chapter 4B).
5 Faulty ignition system (Chapter 5).
6 Defective MAF sensor (see Chapter 6).

7 Defective fuel injection pump or fuel injector (diesel) (Chapter 4B).
8 Incorrect fuel injection pump timing (diesel) (Chapter 4B).

## 4 Engine hard to start when hot

1 Air filter clogged (Chapter 1).
2 Fuel not reaching the fuel injection system (Chapter 4).
3 Corroded battery connections, especially ground (Chapter 1).
4 Faulty coolant temperature sensor or intake air temperature sensor (Chapter 6).
5 Low cylinder compression (Chapter 2).
6 Defective fuel injection pump or fuel injector (diesel) (Chapter 4B).
7 Incorrect fuel injection pump timing (diesel) (Chapter 4B).

## 5 Starter motor noisy or excessively rough in engagement

1 Pinion or flywheel gear teeth worn or broken (Chapter 5).
2 Starter motor mounting bolts loose or missing (Chapter 5).

## 6 Engine starts but stops immediately

1 Loose or faulty electrical connections at distributor, coil or alternator (Chapter 5).
2 Insufficient fuel reaching the fuel injector(s) (Chapters 1 and 4).
3 Vacuum leak at the gasket between the intake manifold/plenum and throttle body (Chapters 1 and 4).
4 Intake air leaks, broken vacuum pipes (see Chapter 4).
5 Defective fuel injection pump or fuel injector (diesel) (Chapter 4B).
6 Contaminated fuel.

## 7 Oil puddle under engine

1 Sump gasket and/or sump drain bolt washer leaking (Chapter 2).
2 Oil pressure sending unit leaking (Chapter 2).
3 Valve covers leaking (Chapter 2).

4 Engine oil seals leaking (Chapter 2).
5 Oil pump housing leaking (Chapter 2).

## 8 Engine 'lopes' while idling or idles erratically

1 Vacuum leakage (Chapters 2 and 4).
2 Leaking EGR valve (Chapter 6).
3 Air filter clogged (Chapter 1).
4 Fuel pump delivering insufficient fuel to the fuel injection system (Chapter 4).
5 Leaking head gasket (Chapter 2).
6 Timing belt and/or sprockets worn (Chapter 2).
7 Camshaft lobes worn (Chapter 2).
8 Defective fuel injection pump or fuel injector (diesel) (Chapter 4B).
9 Incorrect fuel injection pump timing (diesel) (Chapter 4B).

## 9 Engine misses at idle speed

1 Spark plugs worn or not gapped properly (Chapter 1).
2 Faulty HT leads (Chapter 1).
3 Vacuum leaks (Chapters 2 and 4).
4 Uneven or low compression (Chapter 2).
5 Problem with the fuel injection system (Chapter 4).
6 Faulty ignition coils (Chapter 5).
7 Defective fuel injection pump or fuel injector (diesel) (Chapter 4B).
8 Incorrect fuel injection pump timing (diesel) (Chapter 4B).

## 10 Engine misses throughout driving speed range

1 Fuel filter clogged and/or impurities in the fuel system (Chapter 1).
2 Low fuel output at the fuel injector(s) (Chapter 4).
3 Faulty or incorrectly gapped spark plugs (Chapter 1).
4 Defective HT leads (Chapters 1 or 5).
5 Faulty emission system components (Chapter 6).
6 Low or uneven cylinder compression pressures (Chapter 2).
7 Weak or faulty ignition system (Chapter 5).
8 Vacuum leak in fuel injection system, throttle body, intake manifold or vacuum hoses (Chapter 4).
9 Defective fuel injection pump or fuel injector (diesel) (Chapter 4B).
10 Incorrect fuel injection pump timing (diesel) (Chapter 4B).

# Engine (continued)

## 11 Engine stumbles on acceleration

1 Spark plugs fouled (Chapter 1).
2 Problem with fuel injection system (Chapter 4).
3 Fuel filter clogged (Chapters 1 and 4).
4 Intake manifold leak (Chapters 2 and 4).
5 EGR system malfunction (Chapter 6).

## 12 Engine surges while holding accelerator steady

1 Intake air/vacuum leak (Chapter 4).
2 Problem with fuel injection system (Chapter 4).
3 Problem with the emissions control system (Chapter 6).

## 13 Engine stalls

1 Idle speed incorrect (Chapter 4).
2 Fuel filter clogged and/or water and impurities in the fuel system (Chapters 1 and 4).
3 Faulty emissions system components (Chapter 6).
4 Faulty or incorrectly gapped spark plugs (Chapter 1).
5 Faulty HT leads (Chapter 1).
6 Vacuum leak in the fuel injection system, intake manifold or vacuum hoses (Chapters 2 and 4).
7 Defective fuel injection pump or fuel injector (diesel) (Chapter 4B).

## 14 Engine lacks power

1 Faulty HT leads or coils (Chapters 1 and 5).
2 Faulty or incorrectly gapped spark plugs (Chapter 1).
3 Problem with the fuel injection system (Chapter 4).
4 Plugged air filter (Chapter 1).
5 Brakes binding (Chapter 9).
6 Automatic transmission fluid level incorrect (Chapter 1).
7 Clutch slipping (Chapter 8).
8 Fuel filter clogged and/or impurities in the fuel system (Chapters 1 and 4).
9 Emission control system not functioning properly (Chapter 6).
10 Low or uneven cylinder compression pressures (Chapter 2).
11 Obstructed exhaust system (Chapters 2 and 4).
12 Defective fuel injection pump or fuel injector (diesel) (Chapter 4B).
13 Incorrect fuel injection pump timing (diesel) (Chapter 4).
14 Defective turbocharger or wastegate (diesel or petrol-turbo) (Chapter 4B).

## 15 Engine backfires

1 Emission control system not functioning properly (Chapter 6).
2 Faulty spark plug lead or coils (Chapters 1 and 5).
3 Problem with the fuel injection system (Chapter 4).

4 Vacuum leak at fuel injector(s), intake manifold, air control valve or vacuum hoses (Chapters 2 and 4).
5 Valves sticking (Chapter 2).

## 16 Pinking or knocking engine sounds during acceleration or uphill

1 Incorrect grade of fuel.
2 Ignition timing incorrect (Chapter 5).
3 Fuel injection system faulty (Chapter 4).
4 Improper or damaged spark plugs or leads (Chapter 1).
5 EGR valve not functioning (Chapter 6).
6 Vacuum leak (Chapters 2 and 4).
7 Knock sensor malfunctioning (Chapter 6A).

## 17 Engine runs with oil pressure light on

1 Low oil level (Chapter 1).
2 Idle rpm below specification (Chapter 4).
3 Short in wiring circuit (Chapter 12).
4 Faulty oil pressure sender (Chapter 2).
5 Worn engine bearings and/or oil pump (Chapter 2).

## 18 Engine continues to run after switching off

1 Excessive engine operating temperature (Chapter 3).
2 Excessive carbon deposits on valves and pistons (Chapter 2).
3 Fuel shut-off valve malfunctioning (diesel) (Chapter 4B).

# Engine electrical system

## 19 Battery will not hold a charge

**1** Auxiliary drivebelt defective or not adjusted properly (Chapter 1).
**2** Battery electrolyte level low (Chapter 1).
**3** Battery terminals loose or corroded (Chapter 1).
**4** Alternator not charging properly (Chapter 5).
**5** Loose, broken or faulty wiring in the charging circuit (Chapter 5).
**6** Short in vehicle wiring (Chapter 12).
**7** Internally defective battery (Chapters 1 and 5).

## 20 Alternator light fails to go out

**1** Faulty alternator or charging circuit (Chapter 5).
**2** Auxiliary drivebelt defective or out of adjustment (Chapter 1).
**3** Alternator voltage regulator inoperative (Chapter 5).

## 21 Alternator light fails to come on when key is turned on

**1** Warning light bulb defective (Chapter 12).
**2** Fault in the printed circuit, dash wiring or bulb holder (Chapter 12).

# Fuel system

## 22 Excessive fuel consumption

**1** Dirty or clogged air filter element (Chapter 1).
**2** Engine management problem (Chapter 6).
**3** Emissions system not functioning properly (Chapter 6).
**4** Fuel injection system not functioning properly (Chapter 4).
**5** Low tyre pressure or incorrect tyre size (Chapter 1).

## 23 Fuel leakage and/or fuel odour

**1** Leaking fuel feed or return pipe (Chapters 1 and 4).
**2** Tank overfilled.
**3** Problem with the evaporative emissions control system (Chapters 6).
**4** Problem with the fuel injection system (Chapter 4).

# Cooling system

## 24 Overheating

1 Insufficient coolant in system (Chapter 1).
2 Water pump defective (Chapter 3).
3 Radiator core blocked or grille restricted (Chapter 3).
4 Thermostat faulty (Chapter 3).
5 Electric coolant fan inoperative or blades broken (Chapter 3).
6 Expansion tank cap not maintaining proper pressure (Chapter 3).
7 Blown head gasket (Chapter 2).
8 Coolant temperature sender inoperative (Chapter 3)

## 25 Overcooling

1 Faulty thermostat (Chapter 3).
2 Inaccurate temperature gauge sender unit (Chapter 3)

## 26 External coolant leakage

1 Deteriorated/damaged hoses; loose clamps (Chapters 1 and 3).
2 Water pump defective (Chapter 3).
3 Leakage from radiator core or coolant reservoir tank (Chapter 3).
4 Cylinder head gasket leaking (Chapter 2).

## 27 Internal coolant leakage

1 Leaking cylinder head gasket (Chapter 2).
2 Cracked cylinder bore or cylinder head (Chapter 2).

## 28 Coolant loss

1 Too much coolant in system (Chapter 1).
2 Coolant boiling away because of overheating (Chapter 3).
3 Internal or external leakage (Chapter 3).
4 Faulty expansion tank cap (Chapter 3).

## 29 Poor coolant circulation

1 Defective water pump (Chapter 3).
2 Restriction in cooling system (Chapters 1 and 3).
3 Thermostat sticking (Chapter 3).

# Clutch

## 30 Pedal travels to floor - no pressure or very little resistance

1 Hydraulic release system leaking or air in the system (Chapter 8).
2 Broken release bearing or fork (Chapter 8).

## 31 Unable to select gears

1 Faulty transmission (Chapter 7).
2 Faulty clutch disc or pressure plate (Chapter 8).
3 Faulty release lever or release bearing (Chapter 8).
4 Faulty gearchange lever assembly or cables (Chapter 8).
5 Faulty clutch release system.

## 32 Clutch slips (engine speed increases with no increase in vehicle speed)

1 Clutch plate worn (Chapter 2 and 8).
2 Clutch plate is oil soaked by leaking rear main seal (Chapter 2 and 8).

3 Clutch plate not seated (Chapter 8).
4 Warped pressure plate or flywheel (Chapter 8).
5 Weak diaphragm spring in pressure plate (Chapter 8).
6 Clutch plate overheated. Allow to cool.
7 Piston stuck in bore of clutch slave cylinder, preventing clutch from fully engaging (Chapter 8).

## 33 Grabbing (juddering) as clutch is engaged

1 Oil on clutch plate lining, burned or glazed facings (Chapter 8).
2 Worn or loose engine or transmission mounts (Chapters 2 and 7).
3 Worn splines on clutch plate hub (Chapter 8).
4 Warped pressure plate or flywheel (Chapter 8).
5 Burned or smeared resin on flywheel or pressure plate (Chapter 8).

## 34 Transmission rattling (clicking)

1 Release fork loose (Chapter 8).
2 Low engine idle speed (Chapter 1).

## 35 Noise in clutch area

Faulty bearing (Chapter 8).

## 36 Clutch pedal stays on floor

1 Broken release bearing or fork (Chapter 8).
2 Hydraulic release system leaking or air in the system (Chapter 8).
3 Over-centre spring in clutch pedal assembly broken (Chapter 8).

## 37 High pedal effort

1 Piston binding in bore of slave cylinder (Chapter 8).
2 Pressure plate faulty (Chapter 8).

# Manual transmission

### 38 Knocking noise at low speeds

Worn driveshaft constant velocity (CV) joints (Chapter 8).

### 39 Noise most pronounced when turning

Differential gear noise (Chapter 7A).*

### 40 Clunk on acceleration or deceleration

**1** Loose engine or transmission mountings (Chapters 2 and 7A).
**2** Worn differential pinion shaft in case.*
**3** Worn or damaged driveshaft inboard CV joints (Chapter 8).

### 41 Clicking noise in turns

Worn or damaged outboard CV joint (Chapter 8).

### 42 Vibration

**1** Rough wheel bearing (Chapter 10).
**2** Damaged driveshaft (Chapter 8).
**3** Out-of-round tyres (Chapter 1).
**4** Tyre out of balance (Chapters 1 and 10).
**5** Worn CV joint (Chapter 8).

### 43 Noisy in neutral with engine running

**1** Damaged input gear bearing (Chapter 7A).*
**2** Damaged clutch release bearing (Chapter 8).

### 44 Noisy in one particular gear

**1** Damaged or worn constant mesh gears (Chapter 7A).*
**2** Damaged or worn synchronisers (Chapter 7A).*
**3** Bent reverse fork (Chapter 7A).*
**4** Damaged fourth speed gear or output gear (Chapter 7A).*
**5** Worn or damaged reverse idler gear or idler bush (Chapter 7A).*

### 45 Noisy in all gears

**1** Insufficient lubricant (Chapter 7A).
**2** Damaged or worn bearings (Chapter 7A).*
**3** Worn or damaged input gear shaft and/or output gear shaft (Chapter 7A).*

### 46 Slips out of gear

**1** Worn or improperly adjusted linkage (Chapter 7A).
**2** Gearchange linkage does not work freely, binds (Chapter 7A).
**3** Input gear bearing retainer broken or loose (Chapter 7A).*
**4** Worn gearchange fork (Chapter 7A).*

### 47 Leaks lubricant

**1** Driveshaft seals worn (Chapter 7A).
**2** Excessive amount of lubricant in transmission (Chapters 1 and 7A).
**3** Loose or broken input gear shaft bearing retainer (Chapter 7A).*
**4** Input gear bearing retainer O-ring and/or lip seal damaged (Chapter 7A).*
**5** Selector rod seal leaking (Chapter 7A).
**6** Vehicle speed sensor O-ring leaking (Chapter 7A).

### 48 Hard to gearchange

Gearchange cable(s) worn (Chapter 7A).

*Although the corrective action necessary to remedy the symptoms described is beyond the scope of this manual, the above information should be helpful in isolating the cause of the condition so that the owner can communicate clearly with a professional mechanic.*

# Automatic transmission

**Note:** *Due to the complexity of the automatic transmission, it is difficult for the home mechanic to properly diagnose and service this component. For problems other than the following, the vehicle should be taken to a dealer or transmission specialist.*

### 49 Fluid leakage

1 Automatic transmission fluid is a deep red colour. Fluid leaks should not be confused with engine oil, which can easily be blown onto the transmission by air flow.

2 To pinpoint a leak, first remove all built-up dirt and grime from the transmission housing with degreasing agents and/or steam cleaning. Then drive the vehicle at low speeds so air flow will not blow the leak far from its source. Raise the vehicle and determine where the leak is coming from. Common areas of leakage are:
a) *Pan (Chapters 1 and 7B).*
b) *Dipstick tube (Chapters 1 and 7B).*
c) *Transmission oil pipes (Chapter 7B).*
d) *Speed sensor (Chapter 7B).*
e) *Driveshaft oil seals (Chapter 7B).*

### 50 Transmission fluid brown or has a burned smell

Transmission fluid overheated (Chapter 1).

### 51 General gearchange mechanism problems

1 Chapter 7, Part B, deals with checking and adjusting the gearchange cable on automatic transmissions. Common problems that may be attributed to poorly adjusted cable are:
a) *Engine starting in gears other than Park or Neutral.*
b) *Indicator on selector lever pointing to a gear other than the one actually being used.*
c) *Vehicle moves when in Park.*
2 Refer to Chapter 7B for the gearchange cable adjustment procedure.

### 52 Transmission will not downshift with accelerator pedal pressed to the floor

The transmission is electronically controlled. This type of problem - which is caused by a malfunction in the control unit, a sensor or solenoid, or the circuit itself - is beyond the scope of this book. Take the vehicle to a dealer service department or a competent automatic transmission specialist.

### 53 Engine will start in gears other than Park or Neutral

Transmission Range (TR) switch malfunctioning (Chapter 7B).

### 54 Transmission slips, shifts roughly, is noisy or has no drive in forward or reverse gears

There are many probable causes for the above problems, but the home mechanic should be concerned with only one possibility - fluid level. Before taking the vehicle to a garage, check the level and condition of the fluid as described in Chapter 1. Correct the fluid level as necessary or change the fluid and filter if needed. If the problem persists, have a professional diagnose the cause.

# Driveshafts

## 55 Clicking noise in turns

Worn or damaged outboard CV joint (Chapter 8).

## 56 Shudder or vibration during acceleration

1 Excessive toe-in (Chapter 10).
2 Incorrect spring heights (Chapter 10).
3 Worn or damaged inboard or outboard CV joints (Chapter 8).
4 Sticking inboard CV joint assembly (Chapter 8).

## 57 Vibration at motorway speeds

1 Out-of-balance front wheels and/or tyres (Chapters 1 and 10).
2 Out-of-round front tyres (Chapters 1 and 10).
3 Worn CV joint(s) (Chapter 8).

# Brakes

**Note:** *Before assuming that a brake problem exists, make sure that:*
*a) The tyres are in good condition and properly inflated (Chapter 1).*
*b) The front end alignment is correct (Chapter 10).*
*c) The vehicle is not loaded with weight in an unequal manner.*

## 58 Vehicle pulls to one side during braking

1 Incorrect tyre pressures (Chapter 1).
2 Front end out of alignment (have the front end aligned).
3 Front, or rear, tyre sizes not matched to one another.
4 Restricted brake pipes or hoses (Chapter 9).
5 Malfunctioning caliper assembly (Chapter 9).
6 Loose suspension parts (Chapter 10).
7 Loose calipers (Chapter 9).
8 Excessive wear of pad material or disc on one side.

## 59 Noise (high-pitched squeal when the brakes are applied)

Front and/or rear disc brake pads worn out (Chapter 9).

## 60 Brake roughness or chatter (pedal pulsates)

1 Excessive lateral runout (Chapter 9).
2 Uneven pad wear (Chapter 9).
3 Defective disc (Chapter 9).

## 61 Excessive brake pedal effort required to stop vehicle

1 Malfunctioning brake servo (Chapter 9).
2 Partial system failure (Chapter 9).
3 Excessively worn pads (Chapter 9).
4 Piston in caliper stuck or sluggish (Chapter 9).
5 Brake pads contaminated with oil or grease (Chapter 9).
6 Brake disc grooved and/or glazed (Chapter 1).
7 New pads fitted and not yet seated. It will take a while for the new material to seat against the disc or drum.
8 Vacuum pump not operating properly (diesel) (Chapter 9).

## 62 Excessive brake pedal travel

1 Partial brake system failure (Chapter 9).
2 Insufficient fluid in master cylinder (Chapters 1 and 9).
3 Air trapped in system (Chapters 1 and 9).

## 63 Dragging brakes

1 Master cylinder pistons not returning correctly (Chapter 9).
2 Restricted brakes pipes or hoses (Chapters 1 and 9).
3 Incorrect handbrake adjustment (Chapter 9).
4 Seized caliper (Chapter 9).

## 64 Grabbing or uneven braking action

1 Malfunction of proportioning valve (Chapter 9).
2 Malfunction of brake servo unit (Chapter 9).
3 Binding brake pedal mechanism (Chapter 9).

## 65 Brake pedal feels spongy when depressed

1 Air in hydraulic pipes (Chapter 9).
2 Master cylinder mounting bolts loose (Chapter 9).
3 Master cylinder defective (Chapter 9).

## 66 Brake pedal travels to the floor with little resistance

1 Little or no fluid in the master cylinder reservoir caused by leaking caliper piston(s) (Chapter 9).
2 Malfunctioning master cylinder (Chapter 9).
3 Loose, damaged or disconnected brake pipes (Chapter 9).

## 67 Handbrake does not hold

Handbrake linkage improperly adjusted (Chapters 1 and 9).

# Suspension and steering systems

**Note:** *Before attempting to diagnose the suspension and steering systems, perform the following preliminary checks:*

*a) Tyres for wrong pressure and uneven wear.*
*b) Steering universal joints from the column to the rack-and-pinion for loose connectors or wear.*
*c) Front and rear suspension and the rack-and-pinion assembly for loose or damaged parts.*
*d) Out-of-round or out-of-balance tyres, bent rims and loose and/or rough wheel bearings.*

## 68 Vehicle pulls to one side

1 Mismatched or uneven tyres (Chapter 10).
2 Broken or sagging springs (Chapter 10).
3 Wheel alignment out of specifications (Chapter 10).
4 Front brake dragging (Chapter 9).

## 69 Abnormal or excessive tyre wear

1 Wheel alignment out of specifications (Chapter 10).
2 Sagging or broken springs (Chapter 10).
3 Tyre out-of-balance (Chapter 10).
4 Worn strut damper or shock absorber (Chapter 10).
5 Overloaded vehicle.

## 70 Wheel makes a thumping noise

1 Blister or bump on tyre (Chapter 10).
2 Improper strut damper or shock absorber action (Chapter 10).

## 71 Shimmy, shake or vibration

1 Tyre or wheel out-of-balance or out-of-round (Chapter 10).
2 Loose or worn wheel bearings (Chapters 1, 8 and 10).
3 Worn track rod ends (Chapter 10).
4 Worn balljoints (Chapters 1 and 10).
5 Excessive wheel runout (Chapter 10).
6 Blister or bump on tyre (Chapter 10).

## 72 Hard steering

1 Defective balljoints, track rod ends or rack-and-pinion assembly (Chapter 10).

2 Front wheel alignment out of specifications (Chapter 10).
3 Low tyre pressure(s) (Chapters 1 and 10).
4 Power steering system defective (Chapter 10).

## 73 Poor self-centring

1 Defective balljoints or track rod ends (Chapter 10).
2 Binding in steering gear or column (Chapter 10).
3 Lack of lubricant in steering gear assembly (Chapter 10).
4 Front wheel alignment out of specifications (Chapter 10).

## 74 Abnormal noise at the front end

1 Defective balljoints or track rod ends (Chapters 1 and 10).
2 Damaged strut mounting (Chapter 10).
3 Worn control arm bushings or track rod ends (Chapter 10).
4 Loose stabiliser bar (Chapter 10).
5 Loose wheel bolts (Chapter 1 Specifications).
6 Loose suspension bolts (Chapter 10).

## 75 Wander or poor steering stability

1 Mismatched or uneven tyres (Chapter 10).
2 Defective balljoints or track rod ends (Chapters 1 and 10).
3 Worn strut assemblies (Chapter 10).
4 Loose stabiliser bar (Chapter 10).
5 Broken or sagging springs (Chapter 10).
6 Wheels out of alignment (Chapter 10).

## 76 Erratic steering when braking

1 Wheel bearings worn (Chapter 10).
2 Broken or sagging springs (Chapter 10).
3 Defective caliper (Chapter 10).
4 Warped discs (Chapter 10).
5 Front end alignment incorrect.

## 77 Excessive pitching and/or rolling around corners or during braking

1 Loose stabiliser bar (Chapter 10).
2 Worn strut dampers, shock absorbers or mountings (Chapter 10).

3 Broken or sagging springs (Chapter 10).
4 Overloaded vehicle.
5 Front end alignment incorrect.

## 78 Suspension bottoms

1 Overloaded vehicle.
2 Worn strut dampers or shock absorbers (Chapter 10).
3 Incorrect, broken or sagging springs (Chapter 10).

## 79 Excessive tyre wear on outside edge

1 Inflation pressures incorrect (Chapter 1).
2 Excessive speed in turns.
3 Front end alignment incorrect (excessive toe-in). Have professionally aligned.
4 Suspension arm bent or twisted (Chapter 10).

## 80 Excessive tyre wear on inside edge

1 Inflation pressures incorrect (Chapter 1).
2 Front end alignment incorrect (toe-out). Have professionally aligned.
3 Loose or damaged steering components (Chapter 10).

## 81 Tyre tread worn in one place

1 Tyres out-of-balance.
2 Damaged wheel. Inspect and renew if necessary.
3 Defective tyre (Chapter 1).

## 82 Excessive play or looseness in steering system

1 Wheel bearing(s) worn (Chapter 10).
2 Track rod end loose or worn (Chapter 10).
3 Steering gear loose or worn (Chapter 10).
4 Worn or loose steering intermediate shaft (Chapter 10).

## 83 Rattling or clicking noise in steering gear

1 Steering gear loose or worn (Chapter 10).
2 Steering gear defective.

## Length (distance)

| | | | | | |
|---|---|---|---|---|---|
| Inches (in) | x 25.4 | = Millimetres (mm) | x 0.0394 | = Inches (in) |
| Feet (ft) | x 0.305 | = Metres (m) | x 3.281 | = Feet (ft) |
| Miles | x 1.609 | = Kilometres (km) | x 0.621 | = Miles |

## Volume (capacity)

| | | | | | |
|---|---|---|---|---|---|
| Cubic inches (cu in; in³) | x 16.387 | = Cubic centimetres (cc; cm³) | x 0.061 | = Cubic inches (cu in; in³) |
| Imperial pints (Imp pt) | x 0.568 | = Litres (l) | x 1.76 | = Imperial pints (Imp pt) |
| Imperial quarts (Imp qt) | x 1.137 | = Litres (l) | x 0.88 | = Imperial quarts (Imp qt) |
| Imperial quarts (Imp qt) | x 1.201 | = US quarts (US qt) | x 0.833 | = Imperial quarts (Imp qt) |
| US quarts (US qt) | x 0.946 | = Litres (l) | x 1.057 | = US quarts (US qt) |
| Imperial gallons (Imp gal) | x 4.546 | = Litres (l) | x 0.22 | = Imperial gallons (Imp gal) |
| Imperial gallons (Imp gal) | x 1.201 | = US gallons (US gal) | x 0.833 | = Imperial gallons (Imp gal) |
| US gallons (US gal) | x 3.785 | = Litres (l) | x 0.264 | = US gallons (US gal) |

## Mass (weight)

| | | | | | |
|---|---|---|---|---|---|
| Ounces (oz) | x 28.35 | = Grams (g) | x 0.035 | = Ounces (oz) |
| Pounds (lb) | x 0.454 | = Kilograms (kg) | x 2.205 | = Pounds (lb) |

## Force

| | | | | | |
|---|---|---|---|---|---|
| Ounces-force (ozf; oz) | x 0.278 | = Newtons (N) | x 3.6 | = Ounces-force (ozf; oz) |
| Pounds-force (lbf; lb) | x 4.448 | = Newtons (N) | x 0.225 | = Pounds-force (lbf; lb) |
| Newtons (N) | x 0.1 | = Kilograms-force (kgf; kg) | x 9.81 | = Newtons (N) |

## Pressure

| | | | | | |
|---|---|---|---|---|---|
| Pounds-force per square inch (psi; lbf/in²; lb/in²) | x 0.070 | = Kilograms-force per square centimetre (kgf/cm²; kg/cm²) | x 14.223 | = Pounds-force per square inch (psi; lbf/in²; lb/in²) |
| Pounds-force per square inch (psi; lbf/in²; lb/in²) | x 0.068 | = Atmospheres (atm) | x 14.696 | = Pounds-force per square inch (psi; lbf/in²; lb/in²) |
| Pounds-force per square inch (psi; lbf/in²; lb/in²) | x 0.069 | = Bars | x 14.5 | = Pounds-force per square inch (psi; lbf/in²; lb/in²) |
| Pounds-force per square inch (psi; lbf/in²; lb/in²) | x 6.895 | = Kilopascals (kPa) | x 0.145 | = Pounds-force per square inch (psi; lbf/in²; lb/in²) |
| Kilopascals (kPa) | x 0.01 | = Kilograms-force per square centimetre (kgf/cm²; kg/cm²) | x 98.1 | = Kilopascals (kPa) |
| Millibar (mbar) | x 100 | = Pascals (Pa) | x 0.01 | = Millibar (mbar) |
| Millibar (mbar) | x 0.0145 | = Pounds-force per square inch (psi; lbf/in²; lb/in²) | x 68.947 | = Millibar (mbar) |
| Millibar (mbar) | x 0.75 | = Millimetres of mercury (mmHg) | x 1.333 | = Millibar (mbar) |
| Millibar (mbar) | x 0.401 | = Inches of water (inH₂O) | x 2.491 | = Millibar (mbar) |
| Millimetres of mercury (mmHg) | x 0.535 | = Inches of water (inH₂O) | x 1.868 | = Millimetres of mercury (mmHg) |
| Inches of water (inH₂O) | x 0.036 | = Pounds-force per square inch (psi; lbf/in²; lb/in²) | x 27.68 | = Inches of water (inH₂O) |

## Torque (moment of force)

| | | | | | |
|---|---|---|---|---|---|
| Pounds-force inches (lbf in; lb in) | x 1.152 | = Kilograms-force centimetre (kgf cm; kg cm) | x 0.868 | = Pounds-force inches (lbf in; lb in) |
| Pounds-force inches (lbf in; lb in) | x 0.113 | = Newton metres (Nm) | x 8.85 | = Pounds-force inches (lbf in; lb in) |
| Pounds-force inches (lbf in; lb in) | x 0.083 | = Pounds-force feet (lbf ft; lb ft) | x 12 | = Pounds-force inches (lbf in; lb in) |
| Pounds-force feet (lbf ft; lb ft) | x 0.138 | = Kilograms-force metres (kgf m; kg m) | x 7.233 | = Pounds-force feet (lbf ft; lb ft) |
| Pounds-force feet (lbf ft; lb ft) | x 1.356 | = Newton metres (Nm) | x 0.738 | = Pounds-force feet (lbf ft; lb ft) |
| Newton metres (Nm) | x 0.102 | = Kilograms-force metres (kgf m; kg m) | x 9.804 | = Newton metres (Nm) |

## Power

| | | | | | |
|---|---|---|---|---|---|
| Horsepower (hp) | x 745.7 | = Watts (W) | x 0.0013 | = Horsepower (hp) |

## Velocity (speed)

| | | | | | |
|---|---|---|---|---|---|
| Miles per hour (miles/hr; mph) | x 1.609 | = Kilometres per hour (km/hr; kph) | x 0.621 | = Miles per hour (miles/hr; mph) |

## Fuel consumption*

| | | | | | |
|---|---|---|---|---|---|
| Miles per gallon, Imperial (mpg) | x 0.354 | = Kilometres per litre (km/l) | x 2.825 | = Miles per gallon, Imperial (mpg) |
| Miles per gallon, US (mpg) | x 0.425 | = Kilometres per litre (km/l) | x 2.352 | = Miles per gallon, US (mpg) |

## Temperature

Degrees Fahrenheit = (°C x 1.8) + 32          Degrees Celsius (Degrees Centigrade; °C) = (°F - 32) x 0.56

*It is common practice to convert from miles per gallon (mpg) to litres/100 kilometres (l/100km), where mpg x l/100 km = 282*

# Chapter 1
# Routine maintenance and servicing

## Contents

## Degrees of difficulty

| **Easy,** suitable for novice with little experience  | **Fairly easy,** suitable for beginner with some experience  | **Fairly difficult,** suitable for competent DIY mechanic  | **Difficult,** suitable for experienced DIY mechanic  | **Very difficult,** suitable for expert DIY or professional |

## Recommended lubricants and fluids

**Note:** *Listed here are manufacturer recommendations at the time this manual was written. Manufacturers occasionally upgrade their fluid and lubricant specifications, so check with your local auto parts store for current recommendations.*

**Engine (petrol)**

Standard (distance/time) service interval . . . . . . . . . . . . . . . . . . . . . . . Multigrade engine oil, viscosity SAE 5W/40 to 20W/50
VW engine oil VW 501 01, 502 00, 504 00 or better

LongLife (variable) service interval . . . . . . . . . . . . . . . . . . . . . . . . . . . VW LongLife engine oil
VW 503 00, 504 00 or better*

**Engine (diesel)**

Standard (distance/time) service interval . . . . . . . . . . . . . . . . . . . . . . . Multigrade engine oil, viscosity SAE 5W/40 to 20W/50
VW 505 01 or better

LongLife (variable) service interval . . . . . . . . . . . . . . . . . . . . . . . . . . . VW LongLife engine oil
VW 506 01, 507 00 or better*

**Manual transmission** . . . . . . . . . . . . . . . . . . . . . . . . . . . . . . . . . . . . Synthetic gear oil, viscosity SAE 75W/90, VW G50

**Automatic transmission fluid** . . . . . . . . . . . . . . . . . . . . . . . . . . . . . VW automatic transmission fluid

**Differential (automatic transmissions)** . . . . . . . . . . . . . . . . . . . . SAE 75W90 synthetic gear oil

**Power steering fluid** . . . . . . . . . . . . . . . . . . . . . . . . . . . . . . . . . . . . VW hydraulic oil

**Brake & clutch fluid** . . . . . . . . . . . . . . . . . . . . . . . . . . . . . . . . . . . DOT 4 brake fluid

**Engine coolant** . . . . . . . . . . . . . . . . . . . . . . . . . . . . . . . . . . . . . . . VW additive G12 only (antifreeze and corrosion protection)

*A maximum of 0.5 litres of standard VW oil may be used for topping-up when LongLife oil is unobtainable*

## Capacities*

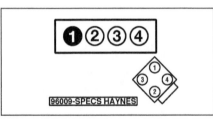

Engine oil (including filter)
   1.4L petrol engine . . . . . . . . . . . . . . . . . . . . . . . . . . . . . . . . . . . . . 3.2 litres
   1.6L and 1.8L petrol engines
      To 2000 . . . . . . . . . . . . . . . . . . . . . . . . . . . . . . . . . . . . . . . . . 4.2 litres
      2001 to 2003 . . . . . . . . . . . . . . . . . . . . . . . . . . . . . . . . . . . . . . 4.5 litres
      2004-on . . . . . . . . . . . . . . . . . . . . . . . . . . . . . . . . . . . . . . . . . 4.2 litres
   2.0L petrol engines . . . . . . . . . . . . . . . . . . . . . . . . . . . . . . . . . . . 4.2 litres
   Diesel engine . . . . . . . . . . . . . . . . . . . . . . . . . . . . . . . . . . . . . . . 4.5 litres
Manual transmission
   O2J . . . . . . . . . . . . . . . . . . . . . . . . . . . . . . . . . . . . . . . . . . . . . 2.0 litres
   O2M . . . . . . . . . . . . . . . . . . . . . . . . . . . . . . . . . . . . . . . . . . . . . 2.3 litres
Automatic transmission
   O1M 4-speed . . . . . . . . . . . . . . . . . . . . . . . . . . . . . . . . . . . . . . . 3.0 litres
   09G 6-speed . . . . . . . . . . . . . . . . . . . . . . . . . . . . . . . . . . . . . . . Filled for life with
approximately 7.0 litres

   02E 6-speed direct shift . . . . . . . . . . . . . . . . . . . . . . . . . . . . . . . . 5.2 litres
Differential lubricant, O2M and O1M models . . . . . . . . . . . . . . . . . . . 0.75 litre

Cooling system
   Petrol engines . . . . . . . . . . . . . . . . . . . . . . . . . . . . . . . . . . . . . . 5.0 litres
   Diesel engine . . . . . . . . . . . . . . . . . . . . . . . . . . . . . . . . . . . . . . 5.7 litres

*All capacities approximate. Add as necessary to bring to appropriate level.*

Engine cylinder location and coil terminal
number (1.6L and 2.0L code AQY petrol
engines)

## Brakes

Disc brake pad wear limit (including backing plate) . . . . . . . . . . . . . . . 7 mm

## Ignition system

Spark plug type
   1.4L engine . . . . . . . . . . . . . . . . . . . . . . . . . . . . . . . . . . . . . . . VW/Audi 101 000 033
   1.6L engine . . . . . . . . . . . . . . . . . . . . . . . . . . . . . . . . . . . . . . . VW/Audi 101 000 033 AA (BKUR 6 ET-10)
   1.8L engine . . . . . . . . . . . . . . . . . . . . . . . . . . . . . . . . . . . . . . . VW/Audi 101 000 063 AA (PFR 6Q)
   2.0L engine . . . . . . . . . . . . . . . . . . . . . . . . . . . . . . . . . . . . . . . VW/Audi 101 000 033 AA (BKR 6 ET-10)
Spark plug gap
   1.4L engine . . . . . . . . . . . . . . . . . . . . . . . . . . . . . . . . . . . . . . . 0.9 to 1.1 mm
   1.6L engine . . . . . . . . . . . . . . . . . . . . . . . . . . . . . . . . . . . . . . . 0.9 to 1.1 mm
   1.8L engine . . . . . . . . . . . . . . . . . . . . . . . . . . . . . . . . . . . . . . . 0.8 mm
   2.0L engine . . . . . . . . . . . . . . . . . . . . . . . . . . . . . . . . . . . . . . . 0.9 to 1.1 mm
Firing order . . . . . . . . . . . . . . . . . . . . . . . . . . . . . . . . . . . . . . . . . 1-3-4-2

## Torque specifications

| | Nm | Ft-lbs |
|---|---|---|
| Glow plugs . . . . . . . . . . . . . . . . . . . . . . . . . . . . . . . . . . . . . . . | 15 | 11 |
| Spark plugs . . . . . . . . . . . . . . . . . . . . . . . . . . . . . . . . . . . . . . | 30 | 22 |
| Wheel bolts . . . . . . . . . . . . . . . . . . . . . . . . . . . . . . . . . . . . . . | 120 | 89 |

## Engine compartment components (1.6L petrol model)

1 Engine oil filler cap
2 Engine oil dipstick
3 Coolant expansion tank
4 Windscreen/headlight washer fluid reservoir
5 Ignition coils and spark plugs (beneath lower inlet manifold)
6 Fuel rail and injectors (beneath lower inlet manifold)
7 Fuel pressure regulator
8 Secondary air injection pump
9 Power steering fluid reservoir
10 Air filter housing
11 Brake master cylinder fluid reservoir
12 Inlet manifold (upper)
13 Air mass meter
14 Throttle control assembly
15 Secondary air injection combi-valve
16 Battery and fusebox (beneath cover)
17 Alternator
18 Auxiliary drivebelt
19 Charcoal (EVAP) canister purge valve

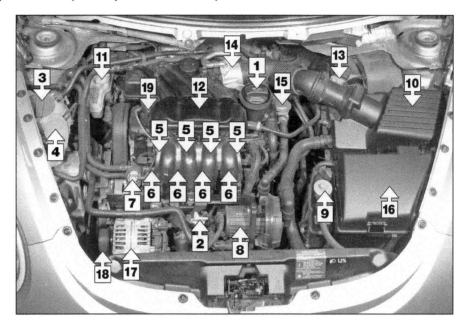

## Engine compartment components (2.0L petrol model)

1 Engine oil dipstick
2 Coolant expansion tank pressure cap
3 Oil filler cap
4 Air filter housing
5 Upper radiator hose
6 Auxiliary drivebelt
7 Power steering fluid reservoir
8 Windscreen washer fluid reservoir
9 Battery
10 Under bonnet fuse box

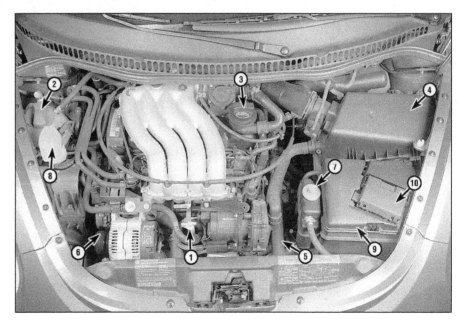

## Engine compartment components (1.9L diesel model)

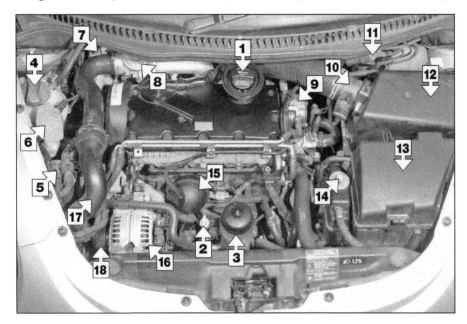

1 Engine oil filler cap
2 Engine oil dipstick
3 Oil filter
4 Coolant expansion tank
5 Fuel filter
6 Windscreen/headlight washer fluid reservoir
7 Master cylinder brake fluid reservoir
8 EGR valve
9 Tandem pump (combined fuel lift pump and brake vacuum pump)
10 Air mass meter
11 EGR vacuum-solenoid valve
12 Air cleaner housing
13 Battery (fuseholder beneath cover)
14 Power steering fluid reservoir
15 Vacuum reservoir (for EGR and turbo control solenoid valve)
16 Alternator
17 Air duct from the intercooler to the inlet manifold
18 Auxiliary drivebelt

## Engine compartment underside components (1.6L petrol model shown, others similar)

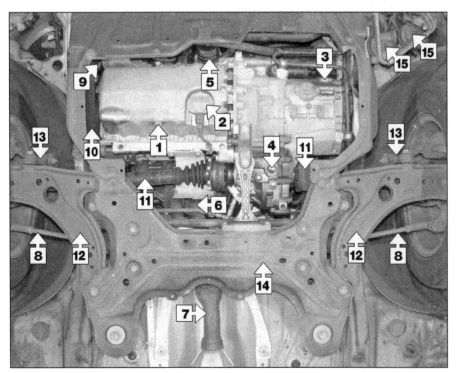

1 Sump drain plug
2 Oil level/temperature sensor
3 Manual transmission filler/level plug
4 Manual transmission drain plug
5 Engine oil filter
6 Exhaust manifold
7 Exhaust front pipe
8 Steering track rods
9 Air conditioning compressor
10 Auxiliary drivebelt
11 Driveshafts
12 Front suspension lower arms
13 Front anti-roll bar
14 Crossmember
15 Horns

## Typical rear underside components

1 Shock absorber
2 Coil spring
3 Brake caliper
4 Rear axle assembly
5 Fuel tank
6 Fuel filter (petrol models)
7 Handbrake cable
8 Silencer

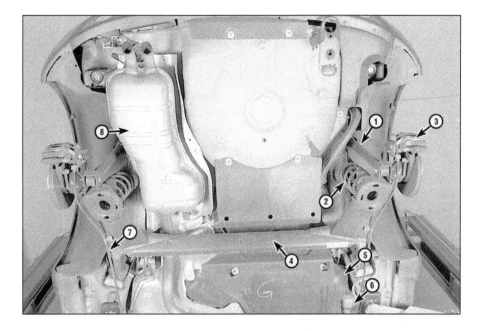

# Maintenance schedule

The following maintenance intervals are based on the assumption that the vehicle owner will be doing the maintenance or service work, as opposed to having a dealer service department do the work. These are the minimum maintenance intervals recommended by the factory for vehicles that are driven daily. If you wish to keep your vehicle in peak condition at all times, you may wish to perform some of these procedures even more often. Because frequent maintenance enhances the efficiency, performance and resale value of your car, we encourage you to do so. If you drive in dusty areas, tow a caravan, idle or drive at low speeds for extended periods, or drive for short distances (less than four miles), shorter intervals are also recommended.

When the vehicle is new, it should be serviced by a dealer service department, in order to preserve the factory warranty.

All VW Beetle models are equipped with a service interval display indicator in the instrument panel. Every time the engine is started the panel will illuminate for approximately 20 seconds with service information. With the standard display (fitted to models manufactured up to and including

model year 1999) the service interval is strictly in accordance with the mileage (or km) coverage or time elapsed. With the display fitted to models manufactured from model year 2000, the service interval is variable according to the number of starts, length of journeys, vehicle speeds, brake pad wear, bonnet opening frequency, fuel consumption, oil level and oil temperature, although the vehicle must be serviced at least every two years. At a distance of 2000 miles (3000 km) before the next service is due, 'Service in 2000 miles' (or '3000 km') will appear at the bottom of the speedometer, and this figure will reduce in steps of 100 units as the vehicle is used. Once the service interval has been reached, the display will flash 'Service' or 'Service Now'.

After completing a service, VW technicians use a special instrument to reset the service display to the next service interval, and a print-out is put in the vehicle service record. The display can be reset by the owner as described in Section 2, but note that for models manufactured from model year 2000 using the 'variable' interval, the procedure will automatically reset the display to a 'distance/time' interval (i.e. 10 000 miles/

15 000 km). To have the display reset to the 'variable' interval, it is necessary to take the vehicle to a VW dealer who will use a special instrument to encode the on-board computer.
**Note:** *If the vehicle is operated under severe conditions, perform all maintenance indicated with an asterisk (\*) at half the indicated intervals. Severe conditions exist if you mainly operate the vehicle:*
● *in dusty areas.*
● *towing a caravan.*
● *idling for extended periods.*
● *driving at low speeds when outside temperatures remain below freezing and most trips are less than four miles long.*
***Caution 1: These models are equipped with an anti-theft radio. Before performing a procedure that requires disconnecting the battery, make sure you have the proper activation code.***
***Caution 2: Disconnecting the battery can cause driveability problems that require a scan tool to remedy. See Chapter 5, Section 1, for the use of an auxiliary voltage input device (or 'Memory-saver') before disconnecting the battery.***

# Models using distance/time intervals

* See **Note** in *Maintenance schedule*.

## Every 250 miles (400 km) or weekly, whichever comes first
- ☐ Check the engine oil level (Section 3)
- ☐ Check the coolant level (Section 4)
- ☐ Check the windscreen washer fluid level (Section 5)
- ☐ Check the brake and clutch fluid levels (Section 6)
- ☐ Check the tyres and tyre pressures (Section 7)

## Every 6000 miles (10 000 km) or 6 months, whichever comes first
- ☐ Check the seat belts (Section 8)
- ☐ Inspect the windscreen wiper blades (Section 9)
- ☐ Check and service the battery (Section 10)
- ☐ Check the auxiliary drivebelt (Section 11)
- ☐ Inspect under bonnet hoses (Section 12)
- ☐ Check the cooling system (Section 13)
- ☐ Drain the water separator (diesel models) (Section 14)

## Every 10 000 miles (15 000 km) – 'Service OIL' on display
- ☐ Renew the engine oil and filter (Section 15)

**Note:** *Frequent oil and filter changes are good for the engine. We recommend changing the oil at less than the mileage specified here, or at least twice a year.*
- ☐ Check the timing belt on diesel engines (Section 16)
- ☐ Reset the service interval display (Section 2)

## Every 12 months – 'Service INSP' on display
**Note:** *For vehicles covering less than 20 000 miles (30 000 km) a year, the following work is carried out at the 12 month interval.*
- ☐ Check the brake system (Section 17)*
- ☐ Check the power steering fluid level (Section 18)
- ☐ Check the operation of all external and interior lights, warning lights and horn.
- ☐ Check the exhaust system (Section 19)
- ☐ Check the fuel system (Section 20)
- ☐ Check the steering, suspension and driveshaft boots (Section 21)
- ☐ Check for trouble codes in the on-board computer (See Chapter 6)
- ☐ Lubricate all hinges and locks
- ☐ Reset the service interval display (Section 2)

## Every 20 000 miles (30 000 km) – 'Service INSP' on display
- ☐ Renew the pollen filter (Section 22)*
- ☐ Check the headlight alignment (See Chapter 12)
- ☐ Check the manual transmission lubricant level (Section 23)
- ☐ Reset the service interval display (Section 2)

## Every 24 months (regardless of mileage)
- ☐ Renew the brake fluid (Section 24)
- ☐ Renew the coolant (Section 25)

**Note:** *This work is not included in the VW schedule and should not be required if the recommended VW G12 LongLife coolant antifreeze/inhibitor is used. However, if standard antifreeze/inhibitor is used, the work should be carried out at the recommended interval.*

## Every 40 000 miles (60 000 km) or 48 months, whichever comes first
- ☐ Check the differential lubricant level (automatic transmissions) (Section 26)
- ☐ Check the automatic transmission fluid level (Section 27)
- ☐ Renew the spark plugs (Section 28)
- ☐ Renew the air filter (Section 29)*
- ☐ Renew the fuel filter (diesel models) (Section 30)
- ☐ Renew the timing belt and tensioner (diesel models) (Chapter 2C)

## Every 60 000 miles (90 000 km) or 48 months, whichever comes first
- ☐ Renew the timing belt and tensioning roller (petrol models) (Chapter 2A or 2B)

**Note:** *VW specify timing belt inspection after the first 60 000 miles (90 000 km) and then every 20 000 miles (30 000 km). However, if the vehicle is used mainly for short journeys, we recommend that this renewal interval is adhered to. Belt renewal interval is very much up to the individual owner but, bearing in mind the severe engine damage will result if the belt breaks in use, we recommend the shorter interval.*

## Every 60 000 miles (90 000 km) or 72 months, whichever comes first
- ☐ Renew the fuel filter (petrol models) (Section 31)

# Models using 'LongLife' variable intervals

**Note:** *The following service intervals are only applicable to models with a PR number of QG1 (on the data sticker in the luggage compartment, next to the spare wheel). This schedule must only be used by vehicles using VW LongLife engine oil specification (see 'Recommended lubricants and fluids'). Failure to do so may result in severe engine damage. The distance/time interval of the service on the display unit will depend on how the vehicle is being used (number of starts, length of journeys, vehicle speeds, brake pad wear, bonnet opening frequency, fuel consumption, oil level and oil temperature).*

\* See **Note** in *Maintenance schedule.*

## Every 250 miles (400 km) or weekly, whichever comes first
- [ ] Check the engine oil level (Section 3)
- [ ] Check the coolant level (Section 4)
- [ ] Check the windscreen washer fluid level (Section 5)
- [ ] Check the brake and clutch fluid levels (Section 6)
- [ ] Check the tyres and tyre pressures (Section 7)

## Every 6000 miles (10 000 km) or 6 months, whichever comes first
- [ ] Check the seat belts (Section 8)
- [ ] Inspect the windscreen wiper blades (Section 9)
- [ ] Check and service the battery (Section 10)
- [ ] Check the auxiliary drivebelt (Section 11)
- [ ] Inspect under bonnet hoses (Section 12)
- [ ] Check the cooling system (Section 13)
- [ ] Drain the water separator (diesel models) (Section 14)

## 'Service' on display
**Note:** *Under 'moderate' driving conditions as defined by the on-board computer, this service may occur at or near 20 000 miles (30 000 km) or 24 months. Under 'extreme' driving conditions, it may occur at 10 000 miles (15 000 km) or 12 months.*
- [ ] Renew the engine oil and filter (Section 15)

**Note:** *Frequent oil and filter changes are good for the engine. We recommend changing the oil at least twice a year.*
- [ ] Check the timing belt on diesel engines (Section 16)
- [ ] Check the brake system (Section 17)\*
- [ ] Check the power steering fluid level (Section 18)
- [ ] Check the operation of all external and interior lights, warning lights and horn
- [ ] Check the exhaust system (Section 19)

## 'Service' on display (continued)
- [ ] Check the fuel system (Section 20)
- [ ] Check the steering, suspension and driveshaft boots (Section 21)
- [ ] Check for trouble codes in the on-board computer (See Chapter 6)
- [ ] Lubricate all hinges and locks
- [ ] Renew the pollen filter (Section 22)\*
- [ ] Check the headlight alignment (See Chapter 12)
- [ ] Check the manual transmission lubricant level (Section 23)
- [ ] Reset the service interval display (Section 2)

## Every 24 months (regardless of mileage)
- [ ] Renew the brake fluid (Section 24)
- [ ] Renew the coolant (Section 25)

**Note:** *This work is not included in the VW schedule and should not be required if the recommended VW G12 LongLife coolant antifreeze/inhibitor is used. However, if standard antifreeze/inhibitor is used, the work should be carried out at the recommended interval.*

## Every 40 000 miles (60 000 km)
**Note:** *Many dealers perform these tasks with every second 'Service'*
- [ ] Check the differential lubricant level (automatic transmissions) (Section 26)
- [ ] Check the automatic transmission fluid level (Section 27)
- [ ] Renew the spark plugs (Section 28)
- [ ] Renew the air filter (Section 29)\*
- [ ] Renew the fuel filter (diesel models) (Section 30)
- [ ] Renew the timing belt and tensioner (diesel models) (Chapter 2C)

## Every 60 000 miles (90 000 km) or 48 months, whichever comes first
- [ ] Renew the timing belt and tensioning roller (petrol models) (Chapter 2A or 2B)

**Note:** *VW specify timing belt inspection after the first 60 000 miles (90 000 km) and then every 20 000 miles (30 000 km). However, if the vehicle is used mainly for short journeys, we recommend that this renewal interval is adhered to. Belt renewal interval is very much up to the individual owner but, bearing in mind the severe engine damage will result if the belt breaks in use, we recommend the shorter interval.*

## Every 60 000 miles (90 000 km)
- [ ] Renew the fuel filter (petrol models) (Section 31)

## 1 Introduction

This Chapter is designed to help the home mechanic maintain the Volkswagen New Beetle vehicle with the goals of maximum performance, economy, safety and reliability in mind.

Included is a master maintenance schedule, followed by procedures dealing specifically with each item on the schedule. Visual checks, adjustments, component renewal and other helpful items are included. Refer to the accompanying illustrations of the engine compartment and the underside of the vehicle for the locations of various components.

Servicing your vehicle in accordance with the mileage/time/display maintenance schedule and the step-by-step procedures will result in a planned maintenance program that should produce a long and reliable service life. Keep in mind that it's a comprehensive plan, so maintaining some items but not others at the specified intervals will not produce the same results.

As you service your vehicle, you will discover that many of the procedures can – and should – be grouped together because of the nature of the particular procedure you're performing or because of the close proximity of two otherwise unrelated components to one another. For example, if the vehicle is raised for chassis lubrication, you should inspect the exhaust, suspension, steering and fuel systems while you're under the vehicle. Finally, let's suppose you have to borrow or rent a torque wrench. Even if you only need it to tighten the spark plugs, you might as well check the torque of as many critical fasteners as time allows.

The first step in this maintenance program is to prepare yourself before the actual work begins. Read through all the procedures you're planning to do, then gather up all the parts and tools needed. If it looks like you might run into problems during a particular job, seek advice from a mechanic or an experienced do-it-yourselfer.

## 2 Servicing – general information

The term servicing is used in this manual to represent a combination of individual operations rather than one specific procedure that will maintain an engine in proper tune.

If, from the time the vehicle is new, the routine maintenance schedule is followed closely and frequent checks are made of fluid levels and high wear items, as suggested throughout this manual, the engine will be kept in relatively good running condition and the need for additional work will be minimised.

More likely than not, however, there may be times when the engine is running poorly due to lack of regular maintenance. This is even more likely if a used vehicle, which has not received regular and frequent maintenance checks, is purchased. In such cases, an engine service will be needed outside of the regular routine maintenance intervals.

The first step in any service or diagnostic procedure to help correct a poor-running engine is a cylinder compression check. A compression check (see Chapter 2C) will help determine the condition of internal engine components and should be used as a guide for tune-up and repair procedures. If, for instance, the compression check indicates serious internal engine wear, a conventional service won't improve the performance of the engine and would be a waste of time and money. Because of its importance, the compression check should be done by someone with the right equipment and the knowledge to use it properly.

The following procedures are those most often needed to bring a generally poor-running engine back into a proper state of tune.

### Minor service

- Check all engine related fluids (Sections 3 and 4)
- Clean, inspect and test the battery (Section 10)
- Check and adjust the auxiliary drivebelt (Section 11)
- Check all under bonnet hoses (Section 12)
- Check the cooling system (Section 13)
- Renew the spark plugs (Section 28)
- Clean the air filter (Section 29)
- Inspect the HT leads

### Major service

All items listed under Minor tune-up, plus:
- Renew the air filter (Section 29)
- Renew the HT leads
- Check the ignition system (Chapter 5)
- Check the charging system (Chapter 5)

### To reset the service display

On vehicles up to and including 1999 model year, switch off the ignition, then press and hold down the trip reset button at the bottom of the speedometer. Switch on the ignition and release the button, and note that the service type will appear in the display. Pressing the reset button briefly will change the display from 'OIL' to 'INSP'. Holding down the button for at least 10 seconds will change the display from one service type to the other, and reset the display.

On vehicles from model year 2000, switch off the ignition, then press and hold down the trip reset button at the bottom of the speedometer. Switch on the ignition and release the button, and note that the display will read 'Service'. Press down the reset button for approximately 10 seconds and the display 'Service' will be erased. The procedure will automatically reset the display to a 'distance/time' interval (i.e. 10 000 miles/ 15 000 km). To have the display reset to the variable/LongLife interval, it is necessary to take the vehicle to a VW dealer who will use a special instrument to encode the on-board computer.

# Every 250 miles (400 km) or weekly, whichever comes first

## 3 Engine oil level check

**Note:** *Regardless of intervals, be alert to fluid leaks under the vehicle, which would indicate a fault to be corrected immediately.*

**1** Fluids are an essential part of the lubrication, cooling, brake, clutch and windscreen washer systems. Because the fluids gradually become depleted and/or contaminated during normal operation of the vehicle, they must be periodically replenished. See *Recommended lubricants and fluids* at the beginning of this Chapter before adding fluid to any of the following components. **Note:** *The vehicle must be on level ground when fluid levels are checked.*

**2** The engine oil level is checked with a dipstick that extends through a tube and into the sump at the bottom of the engine **(see illustration)**.

**3** The oil level should be checked before the vehicle has been driven, or about 5 minutes after the engine has been shut off. If the oil is checked immediately after driving the vehicle, some of the oil will remain in the upper engine components, resulting in an inaccurate reading on the dipstick.

**3.2 The engine oil dipstick (arrowed) is clearly marked**

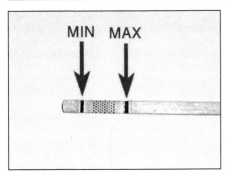

**3.4 The oil level must be maintained between the marks at all times – it takes approximately one litre of oil to raise the level from the MIN to MAX mark**

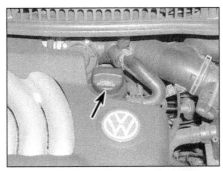

**3.6 Oil is added to the engine after unscrewing the oil filler cap (arrowed) – always make sure the area around the opening is clean before removing the cap to prevent dirt from contaminating the engine**

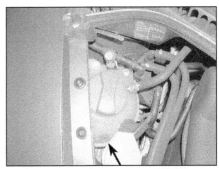

**4.3 The coolant expansion tank is located on the right-hand side – keep the level near the MAX mark (arrowed) or MIN mark on the side of the tank, depending on engine temperature**

4 Pull the dipstick out of the tube and wipe all the oil from the end with a clean rag or paper towel. Insert the clean dipstick all the way back into the tube, then pull it out again. Note the oil at the end of the dipstick. Add oil as necessary to keep the level in the shaded area on the dipstick **(see illustration)**.

5 Do not overfill the engine by adding too much oil since this may result in oil-fouled spark plugs, catalytic converter failure, oil leaks or oil seal failures.

6 Oil is added to the engine after unscrewing a cap from the valve cover **(see illustration)**. A funnel may help to reduce spills.

7 Checking the oil level is an important preventive maintenance step. A consistently low oil level indicates oil leakage through damaged seals, defective gaskets or past worn rings or valve guides. If the oil looks milky or has water droplets in it, the cylinder head gasket may be blown or the head or block may be cracked. The engine should be checked immediately. The condition of the oil should also be checked. Whenever you check the oil level, slide your thumb and index finger up the dipstick before wiping off the oil. If you see small dirt or metal particles clinging to the dipstick, the oil should be changed (see Section 15).

## 4  Engine coolant level check

*Warning: Do not allow antifreeze to come in contact with your skin or painted surfaces of the vehicle. Rinse off spills immediately with plenty of water. Antifreeze is highly toxic if ingested. Never leave antifreeze lying around in an open container or in puddles on the floor; children and pets are attracted by its sweet smell and may drink it. Check with local authorities on disposing of used anti-freeze. Many communities have collection centres that will see that antifreeze is disposed of safely.*

***Caution: Never mix standard anti-freeze and red-coloured silicate-free VW G12 coolant because doing so will destroy the efficiency of the red coolant.***

**Note:** *Regardless of intervals, be alert to fluid leaks under the vehicle, which would indicate a fault to be corrected immediately.*

1 Fluids are an essential part of the lubrication, cooling, brake, clutch and windscreen washer systems. Because the fluids gradually become depleted and/or contaminated during normal operation of the vehicle, they must be periodically replenished. See *Recommended lubricants and fluids* at the beginning of this Chapter before adding fluid. **Note:** *The vehicle must be on level ground when fluid levels are checked.*

2 All vehicles covered by this manual are equipped with a coolant expansion tank, located at the right side of the engine compartment, and connected by hoses to the radiator and cooling system.

3 The coolant level in the expansion tank should be checked regularly. The level of coolant in the expansion tank varies with the temperature of the engine. When the engine is cold, the coolant level should be at or slightly above the MIN mark on the tank **(see illustration)**. Once the engine has warmed up, the level should be at or near the MAX mark. If it isn't, add coolant to the expansion tank. To add coolant simply twist open the cap and add a 50/50 mixture of red-coloured VW G12 coolant and water.

*Warning: Do not remove the pressure cap to check the coolant level when the engine is warm.*

4 Drive the vehicle and recheck the coolant level. If only a small amount of coolant is required to bring the system up to the proper level, water can be used. However, repeated additions of water will dilute the antifreeze and water solution. In order to maintain the proper ratio of antifreeze and water, always top up the coolant level with the correct mixture.

5 If the coolant level drops consistently, there may be a leak in the system. Inspect the radiator, hoses, filler cap, drain plugs and

water pump (see Section 13). If no leaks are noted, have the pressure cap tested by a service facility.

6 If you have to remove the pressure cap, wait until the engine has cooled completely, then wrap a thick cloth around the cap and unscrew it slowly. If coolant or steam escapes, let the engine cool down longer, then remove the cap.

7 Check the condition of the coolant as well. It should be relatively clear. If it is brown or rust coloured, the system should be drained, flushed and refilled.

## 5  Windscreen washer fluid level check

**Note:** *Regardless of intervals, be alert to fluid leaks under the vehicle, which would indicate a fault to be corrected immediately.*

1 Fluids are an essential part of the lubrication, cooling, brake, clutch and windscreen washer systems. Because the fluids gradually become depleted and/or contaminated during normal operation of the vehicle, they must be periodically replenished.

2 Fluid for the windscreen washer system is located in a plastic reservoir in the right side of engine compartment **(see illustration)**.

3 In milder climates, plain water can be used

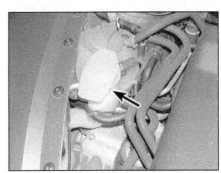

**5.2 Flip open the cap (arrowed) to check the fluid level in the windscreen washer reservoir**

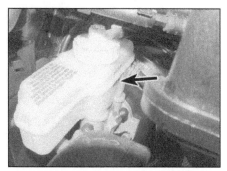

**6.3 Never let the brake fluid level drop below the MIN mark (arrowed)**

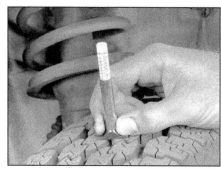

**7.2 Use a tyre tread depth gauge to monitor tyre wear – they are available from most automotive parts stores and service stations**

in the reservoir, but it should be kept no more than 2/3 full to allow for expansion if the water freezes. In colder climates, use windscreen washer system antifreeze, available at any auto parts store, to lower the freezing point of the fluid. Mix the antifreeze with water in accordance with the manufacturer's directions on the container.

*Caution: Don't use cooling system antifreeze – it will damage the vehicle's paint.*

4 To help prevent icing in cold weather, warm the windscreen with the defroster before using the washer.

## 6 Brake and clutch fluid level check

**Note:** *Regardless of intervals, be alert to fluid leaks under the vehicle, which would indicate a fault to be corrected immediately.*

1 Fluids are an essential part of the lubrication, cooling, brake, clutch and windscreen washer systems. Because the fluids gradually become depleted and/or contaminated during normal operation of the vehicle, they must be periodically replenished. See *Recommended lubricants and fluids* at the beginning of this Chapter before adding fluid. **Note:** *The vehicle must be on level ground when fluid levels are checked.*

2 The brake master cylinder is mounted on the upper left of the engine compartment bulkhead. The clutch master cylinder on manual transmission vehicles is mounted at the clutch pedal assembly, but receives its hydraulic fluid directly from the brake master cylinder reservoir, via a hose. Checking the fluid at the brake master cylinder reservoir effectively checks the level of brake and clutch fluid.

3 The translucent plastic reservoir allows the fluid inside to be checked without removing the cap **(see illustration)**. Be sure to wipe the top of the reservoir cap with a clean

rag to prevent contamination of the brake and/or clutch system before removing the cover.

4 When adding fluid, pour it carefully into the reservoir to avoid spilling it on surrounding painted surfaces. Be sure the specified fluid is used, since mixing different types of brake fluid can cause damage to the system.

⚠️ *Warning: Brake fluid can harm your eyes and damage painted surfaces, so use extreme caution when handling or pouring it. Do not use brake fluid that has been standing open or is more than one year old. Brake fluid absorbs moisture from the air. Moisture in the system can cause a dangerous loss of brake performance.*

5 At this time, the fluid and master cylinder can be inspected for contamination. The system should be drained and refilled if deposits, dirt particles or water droplets are seen in the fluid.

6 After filling the reservoir to the proper level, make sure the cap is on tight to prevent fluid leakage.

7 The brake fluid level in the master cylinder will drop slightly as the pads at the front wheels wear down during normal operation. If the master cylinder requires repeated additions to keep it at the proper level, it's an indication of leakage in the brake system or clutch release system, which should be corrected immediately. Check all brake pipes and connections (see Section 17 for more information). Inspect the clutch release system, too (see Chapter 8).

8 If, upon checking the master cylinder fluid level, you discover the reservoir empty or nearly empty, the brake system should be bled and thoroughly inspected (see Chapter 9). Inspect the clutch release system, too (see Chapter 8).

## 7 Tyre and tyre pressure checks

1 Periodic inspection of the tyres may spare you the inconvenience of being stranded with a flat tyre. It can also provide you with vital information regarding possible problems in the steering and suspension systems before major damage occurs.

2 The original tyres on this vehicle are equipped with 12 mm wide wear bands that will appear when tread depth reaches 1.6 mm, at which point the tyres can be considered worn out. Tread wear can be monitored with a simple, inexpensive device known as a tread depth indicator **(see illustration)**.

3 Note any abnormal tread wear **(see illustration)**. Tread pattern irregularities such as cupping, flat spots and more wear on one side than the other are indications of front end alignment and/or balance problems. If any of these conditions are noted, take the vehicle to

**UNDERINFLATION**

**CUPPING**

Cupping may be caused by:
- Underinflation and/or mechanical irregularities such as out-of-balance condition of wheel and/or tire, and bent or damaged wheel.
- Loose or worn steering tie-rod or steering idler arm.
- Loose, damaged or worn front suspension parts.

**OVERINFLATION**

**INCORRECT TOE-IN OR EXTREME CAMBER**

**FEATHERING DUE TO MISALIGNMENT**

**7.3 This chart will help you determine the condition of the tyres and the probable cause(s) of abnormal wear**

a tyre specialist or service station to correct the problem.

**4** Look closely for cuts, punctures and embedded nails or tacks. Sometimes a tyre will hold air pressure for a short time or leak down very slowly after a nail has embedded itself in the tread. If a slow leak persists, check the valve stem core to make sure it's tight **(see illustration)**. Examine the tread for an object that may have embedded itself in the tyre or for a 'plug' that may have begun to leak (radial tyre punctures are repaired with a plug that's fitted in a puncture). If a puncture is suspected, it can be easily verified by spraying a solution of soapy water onto the puncture area **(see illustration)**. The soapy solution will bubble if there's a leak. Unless the puncture is unusually large, a tyre specialist or service station can usually repair the tyre.

**5** Carefully inspect the inner sidewall of each tyre for evidence of brake fluid leakage. If you see any, inspect the brakes immediately.

**6** Correct air pressure adds miles to the lifespan of the tyres, improves mileage and enhances overall ride quality. Tyre pressure cannot be accurately estimated by looking at a tyre, especially if it's a radial. A tyre pressure gauge is essential. Keep an accurate gauge in the vehicle. The pressure gauges attached to the nozzles of air hoses at gas stations are often inaccurate.

**7** Always check tyre pressure when the tyres are cold. Cold, in this case, means the vehicle has not been driven over a mile in the three hours preceding a tyre pressure check.

**8** Unscrew the valve cap protruding from the wheel or hubcap and push the gauge firmly onto the valve stem **(see illustration)**. Note the reading on the gauge and compare the

**7.4a If a tyre loses air on a steady basis, check the valve stem core first to make sure it's tight (special inexpensive tool are available from most automotive parts stores)**

**7.8a To extend the life of the tyres, check the air pressure at least once a week with an accurate gauge (don't forget the spare)**

figure to the recommended tyre pressure shown on the sticker on the fuel filler flap **(see illustration)**. Be sure to refit the valve cap to keep dirt and moisture out of the valve stem mechanism. Check all four tyres and, if

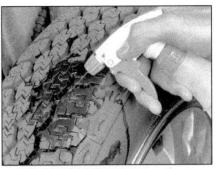

**7.4b If the valve stem core is tight, raise the corner of the vehicle with the low pressure tyre and spray a soapy water solution onto the tread as the tyre is turned slowly – leaks will cause small bubbles to appear**

**7.8b The tyre pressure chart is located on the fuel filler lid**

necessary, add enough air to bring them up to the recommended pressure.

**9** Don't forget to keep the spare tyre inflated to the specified pressure (refer to your owner's manual or the tyre sidewall).

# Every 6000 miles (10 000 km) or 6 months, whichever comes first

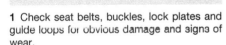

## 8  Seat belt check

**1** Check seat belts, buckles, lock plates and guide loops for obvious damage and signs of wear.

**2** Where the seat belt receptacle bolts to the floor of the vehicle, check that the bolts are secure.

**3** See if the seat belt reminder light comes on when the key is turned to the Run or Start position.

 *Warning: The lap and shoulder belt adjusters incorporate a small explosive device that is triggered by the airbag system. The adjusters automatically tighten up the seat belts in case of a collision sufficient to set off the airbags. Do not use a hammer or impact driver of any kind near the seat belt*

*or airbag module unless the airbag system has been disabled (see Chapter 12).*

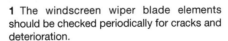

## 9  Wiper blade inspection and renewal

**1** The windscreen wiper blade elements should be checked periodically for cracks and deterioration.

**2** Lift the wiper blade assembly away from the glass.

**3** Press the release lever and slide the blade assembly out of the hook in the end of the wiper arm **(see illustration)**.

**4** Squeeze the two rubber prongs at the end of the blade element, then slide the element out of the frame. **Note:** *These elements can be replaced by hand, without pliers.*

**5** Compare the new element with the old for length, design, etc. Some renewal elements

come in a three-piece design (two metal strips, one on either side of the rubber) that is held together by several small plastic sleeves. Keep the sleeves in place on this design until you start sliding the element into the frame.

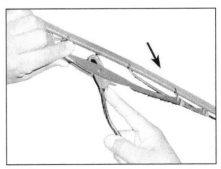

**9.3 Depress the release lever (finger is on it here) and slide the wiper assembly down the wiper arm and out of the hook in the end of the arm**

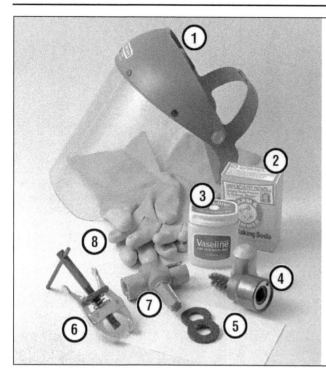

**10.1 Tools and materials required for battery maintenance**

1 *Face shield/safety goggles* – When removing corrosion with a brush, the acidic particles can easily fly up into your eyes
2 *Baking soda* – A solution of baking soda and water can be used to neutralise corrosion
3 *Petroleum jelly* – A layer of this on the battery terminals will help prevent corrosion
4 *Battery terminal/clamp cleaner* – This wire brush cleaning tool will remove all traces of corrosion from the battery terminals and cable clamps
5 *Treated felt washers* – Placing one of these on each terminal, directly under the clamps, will help prevent corrosion
6 *Puller* – Sometimes the clamps are very difficult to pull off the terminals, even after the nut/bolt has been completely loosened. This tool pulls the clamp straight up and off the terminal without damage
7 *Battery terminal/clamp cleaner* – Here is another cleaning tool that is a slightly different version of Number 4 above, but it does the same thing
8 *Rubber gloves* – Another safety item to consider when servicing the battery; remember that's acid inside the battery!

Remove each of the plastic sleeves as needed when they reach the frame.
6 Slide the new element into the frame, notched end last and secure the clips into the notches of the frame.
7 Refit the blade assembly on the arm, wet the windscreen and test for proper operation.

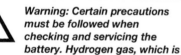

## 10 Battery check, maintenance and charging

⚠️ *Warning: Certain precautions must be followed when checking and servicing the battery. Hydrogen gas, which is highly flammable, is always present in the battery cells, so keep lighted tobacco and all other naked flames and sparks away from the battery. The electrolyte inside the battery is actually dilute sulphuric acid, which will cause injury if splashed on your skin or in your eyes. It will also ruin clothes and painted surfaces. When removing the battery cables, always detach the negative cable first and reconnect it last.*
*Caution 1: These models are equipped with an anti-theft radio. Before performing a procedure that requires disconnecting the battery, make sure you have the proper activation code.*
*Caution 2: Disconnecting the battery can cause driveability problems that require a scan tool to remedy. See Chapter 5, Section 1, for the use of an auxiliary voltage input device (a 'Memory-saver') before disconnecting the battery.*

1 A routine preventive maintenance program for the battery in your vehicle is the only way to ensure quick and reliable starts. But before performing any battery maintenance, make sure that you have the proper equipment necessary to work safely around the battery (see illustration).
2 There are also several precautions that should be taken whenever battery maintenance is performed. Before servicing the battery, always turn the engine and all accessories off and disconnect the cable from the negative terminal of the battery.
3 The battery produces hydrogen gas, which is both flammable and explosive. Never create a spark, smoke or light a match around the battery. Always charge the battery in a ventilated area.
4 Electrolyte contains poisonous and corrosive sulphuric acid. Do not allow it to get in your eyes, on your skin or on your clothes. Never ingest it. Wear protective safety glasses when working near the battery. Keep children away from the battery.
5 Note the external condition of the battery. If the positive terminal and cable clamp on your vehicle's battery is equipped with a rubber protector, make sure that it's not torn or damaged. It should completely cover the terminal. Look for any corroded or loose connections, cracks in the case or cover or loose hold-down clamps. Also check the entire length of each cable for cracks and frayed conductors (see illustration).
6 If corrosion, which looks like white, fluffy deposits is evident, particularly around the terminals, the battery should be removed for cleaning. Loosen the cable bolts with a spanner, being careful to remove the earth

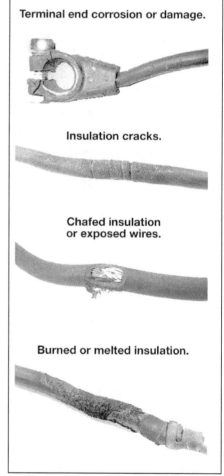

Terminal end corrosion or damage.

Insulation cracks.

Chafed insulation or exposed wires.

Burned or melted insulation.

**10.5 Typical battery cable problems**

10.7a  A tool like this one is used to clean the battery terminals

10.7b  Use the brush side of the tool to clean the inside of the cable clamps

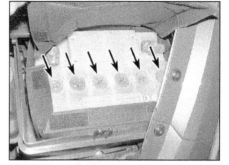

10.20  Lift up the battery cover and remove the screwed in caps (arrowed) to check the battery electrolyte level

cable first, and slide them off the terminals. Refer to Chapter 5 for specific battery removal procedures.

7  Clean the cable ends thoroughly with a battery brush or a terminal cleaner and a solution of warm water and baking soda. Wash the terminals and the battery case with the same solution but make sure that the solution doesn't get into the battery. When cleaning the cables, terminals and battery case, wear safety goggles and rubber gloves to prevent any solution from coming in contact with your eyes or hands. Wear old clothes too – even diluted, sulphuric acid splashed onto clothes will burn holes in them. If the terminals have been corroded, clean them up with a terminal cleaner **(see illustrations)**. Thoroughly wash all cleaned areas with plain water.

8  Make sure that the battery tray is in good condition and the hold-down clamp bolts are tight. If the battery is removed from the tray, make sure no parts remain in the bottom of the tray when the battery is reinstalled. When reinstalling the hold-down clamp bolts, do not overtighten them.

9  Any metal parts of the vehicle damaged by corrosion should be covered with a zinc-based primer, then painted.

10  Information on removing and refitting the battery can be found in Chapter 5. Information on jump starting can be found at the front of this manual.

## Charging

**Warning: When batteries are being charged, hydrogen gas, which is very explosive and flammable, is produced. Do not smoke or allow naked flames near a charging or a recently charged battery. Wear eye protection when near the battery during charging. Also, make sure the charger is unplugged before connecting or disconnecting the battery from the charger.**

Note: *The manufacturer recommends the battery be removed from the vehicle for charging because the gas that escapes during this procedure can damage the paint. Fast charging with the battery cables*

connected can result in damage to the *electrical system.*

11  Slow-rate charging is the best way to restore a battery that's discharged to the point where it will not start the engine. It's also a good way to maintain the battery charge in a vehicle that's only driven a few miles between starts. Maintaining the battery charge is particularly important in the winter when the battery must work harder to start the engine and electrical accessories that drain the battery are in greater use.

12  It's best to use a one or two-amp battery charger (sometimes called a 'trickle' charger). They are the safest and put the least strain on the battery. They are also the least expensive. For a faster charge, you can use a higher amperage charger, but don't use one rated more than 1/10th the amp/hour rating of the battery. Rapid boost charges that claim to restore the power of the battery in one to two hours are hardest on the battery and can damage batteries not in good condition. This type of charging should only be used in emergency situations.

13  The average time necessary to charge a battery should be listed in the instructions that come with the charger. As a general rule, a trickle charger will charge a battery in 12 to 16 hours.

14  Remove all the cell caps (if applicable) and cover the holes with a clean cloth to prevent spattering electrolyte. Disconnect the negative battery cable and connect the battery charger cable clamps to the battery posts (positive to positive, negative to negative), then plug in the charger. Make sure it is set at 12-volts if it has a selector switch.

15  If you're using a charger with a rate higher than two amps, check the battery regularly during charging to make sure it doesn't overheat. If you're using a trickle charger, you can safely let the battery charge overnight after you've checked it regularly for the first couple of hours.

16  If the battery has removable cell caps, measure the specific gravity with a hydrometer every hour during the last few hours of the charging cycle. Hydrometers are available inexpensively from motor factors – follow the instructions that come with the

hydrometer. Consider the battery charged when there's no change in the specific gravity reading for two hours and the electrolyte in the cells is gassing (bubbling) freely. The specific gravity reading from each cell should be very close to the others. If not, the battery probably has a bad cell(s).

17  Some batteries with sealed tops have built-in hydrometers on the top that indicate the state of charge by the colour displayed in the hydrometer window. Normally, a bright-coloured hydrometer indicates a full charge and a dark hydrometer indicates the battery still needs charging.

18  If the battery has a sealed top and no built-in hydrometer, you can connect a digital voltmeter across the battery terminals to check the charge. A fully charged battery should read 12.5 volts or higher.

19  Further information on the battery and jump starting can be found in Chapter 5 and at the front of this manual.

## Battery electrolyte

20  These vehicles are equipped with a battery which has a translucent plastic case. You should be able to read the electrolyte level by looking at the side of the case, and comparing the level to the Minimum and Maximum markings on the case, but most models have the battery mounted in a black plastic box. Instead, read the fluid level by removing the screw-in plastic caps on top of the battery **(see illustration)**. This check is most critical during the warm summer months. Add only distilled water to any battery, and fill only to the ledge below the filler caps. Note: *The filler caps are equipped with O-rings. Make sure the O-rings are in place when reinstalling the caps.*

## 11  Auxiliary drivebelt check, adjustment and renewal

1  A serpentine auxiliary drivebelt is located at the front of the engine and plays an important role in the overall operation of the engine and its components. Due to its function and material make up, the belt is prone to wear

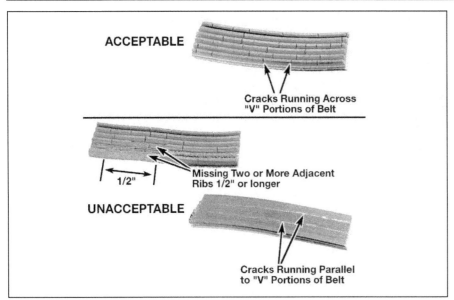

11.2 Check auxiliary belts for signs of wear like these – if it looks worn, replace it

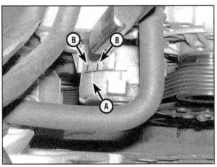

11.4 The indexing mark (A) on the belt tensioner must remain between the marks (B) on the tensioner assembly

11.5a On petrol models, the belt tensioner (arrowed) is accessed from above – use a long 15mm spanner is order to rotate it for belt removal

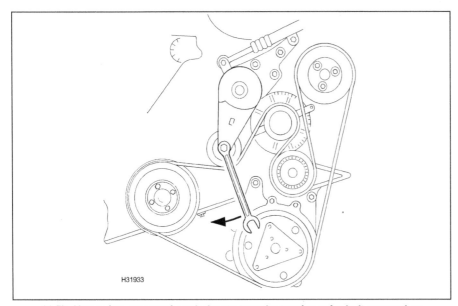

11.5b Use a ring spanner from below to turn the tensioner for belt removal on diesel models

and should be periodically inspected. The serpentine belt drives the alternator, power steering pump, and air conditioning compressor, if applicable.

2 With the engine off, open the bonnet and use your fingers (and an electric torch, if necessary), to move along the belt checking for cracks and separation of the belt plies. Also check for fraying and glazing, which gives the belt a shiny appearance (see illustration). Both sides of the belt should be inspected, which means you will have to twist the belt to check the underside.

3 Check the ribs on the underside of the belt. They should all be the same depth, with none of the surface uneven.

4 The tension of the belt is maintained by a spring-loaded tensioner assembly and isn't adjustable. The belt should be replaced when the indexing arrow is outside the range of the indexing marks on the tensioner assembly (see illustration).

5 To renew the belt, rotate the tensioner to release belt tension (see illustrations). On petrol models, the tensioner can be locked in the released position by inserting a drill bit through the hole at the top of the tensioner. Note: On diesel engines, access to the drivebelt tensioner is from below, and you may have to remove the pipe between the intercooler and turbocharger (see Chapter 4B).

6 Remove the belt from the tensioner and auxiliary components and slowly release the tensioner.

7 Route the new belt over the various pulleys, again rotating the tensioner to allow the belt to be fitted, then release the belt tensioner.

### Tensioner renewal

8 To renew a tensioner that doesn't fall into the proper tension range, even with a new belt, or that exhibits binding, remove the two mounting bolts. On diesel models, remove two bolts to remove the tensioner assembly (see illustration 11.5b).

9 Refitting is the reverse of the removal procedure.

## 12 Under bonnet hose check and renewal

### General

 Warning: Renewal of air conditioning hoses must be left to a dealer service department or air conditioning specialist that has the equipment to depressurise the system safely and recover the refrigerant. Never remove air conditioning components or hoses until the system has been depressurised.

1 High temperatures in the engine compartment can cause the deterioration of the rubber and plastic hoses used for engine, accessory and emission systems operation. Periodic inspection should be made for

cracks, loose clamps, material hardening and leaks. Information specific to the cooling system hoses can be found in Section 13.

2 Some, but not all, hoses are secured to their fittings with clamps. Where clamps are used, check to be sure they haven't lost their tension, allowing the hose to leak. If clamps aren't used, make sure the hose has not expanded and/or hardened where it slips over the fitting, allowing it to leak.

## Vacuum hoses

3 It's quite common for vacuum hoses, especially those in the emissions system, to be colour-coded or identified by coloured stripes moulded into them. Various systems require hoses with different wall thickness, collapse resistance and temperature resistance. When replacing hoses, be sure the new ones are made of the same material.

4 Often the only effective way to check a hose is to remove it completely from the vehicle. If more than one hose is removed, be sure to label the hoses and fittings to ensure correct refitting.

5 When checking vacuum hoses, be sure to include any plastic T-fittings in the check. Inspect the fittings for cracks and the hose where it fits over the fitting for distortion, which could cause leakage.

6 A small piece of vacuum hose (8 mm inside diameter) can be used as a stethoscope to detect vacuum leaks. Hold one end of the hose to your ear and probe around vacuum hoses and fittings with the other end, listening for the 'hissing' sound characteristic of a vacuum leak.

 *Warning: When probing with the vacuum hose stethoscope, be very careful not to come into contact with moving engine components such as the drivebelt, cooling fan, etc.*

## Fuel hose

 *Warning: Fuel is extremely flammable, so take extra precautions when you work on any part of the fuel system. Don't smoke or allow naked flames or bare light bulbs near the work area, and don't work in a garage where a gas-type appliance (such as a water heater or clothes dryer) is present. Since fuel is carcinogenic, wear latex gloves when there's a possibility of being exposed to fuel, and, if you spill any fuel on your skin, rinse it off immediately with soap and water. Mop up any spills immediately and do not store fuel-soaked rags where they could ignite. When you perform any kind of work on the fuel system, wear safety glasses and have a Class B type fire extinguisher on hand. The petrol fuel system is under pressure, so if any pipes must be disconnected, the pressure in the system must be relieved first (see Chapter 4A for more information).*

7 Check all rubber fuel pipes for deterioration

and chafing. Check especially for cracks in areas where the hose bends and just before fittings, such as where a hose attaches to the fuel filter and fuel injection unit.

8 High quality fuel line, specifically designed for high-pressure fuel injection applications, must be used for fuel line renewal. Never, under any circumstances, use regular fuel line, unreinforced vacuum line, clear plastic tubing or water hose for fuel pipes.

9 Spring-type (pinch) clamps are commonly used on fuel pipes. These clamps often lose their tension over a period of time, and can be 'sprung' during removal. Renew all spring-type clamps with screw clamps whenever a hose is replaced.

## Metal pipes

10 Sections of metal pipe may be routed along the chassis, between the fuel tank and

**Check for a chafed area that could fail prematurely.**

**Check for a soft area indicating the hose has deteriorated inside.**

**Overtightening the clamp on a hardened hose will damage the hose and cause a leak.**

**Check each hose for swelling and oil-soaked ends. Cracks and breaks can be located by squeezing the hose.**

**13.4 Hoses, like drivebelts, have a habit of failing at the worst possible time – to prevent the inconvenience of a blown radiator or heater hose, inspect them carefully as shown here**

the engine. Check carefully to be sure the pipe has not been bent or crimped and no cracks have started in the pipe.

11 If a section of metal fuel pipe must be replaced, only seamless steel tubing should be used, since copper and aluminium tubing don't have the strength necessary to withstand normal engine vibration.

12 Check the metal brake pipes where they enter the master cylinder and brake proportioning unit for cracks in the pipes or loose fittings. Any sign of brake fluid leakage calls for an immediate and thorough inspection of the brake system.

## 13 Cooling system check

*Caution: Never mix standard anti-freeze and red-coloured silicate-free VW G12 coolant because doing so will destroy the efficiency of the red coolant.*

1 Many major engine failures can be attributed to a faulty cooling system. If the vehicle is equipped with an automatic transmission, the cooling system also cools the transmission fluid and thus plays an important role in prolonging transmission life.

2 The cooling system should be checked with the engine cold. Do this before the vehicle is driven for the day or after it has been shut off for at least three hours.

3 Remove the pressure cap on the expansion tank by slowly turning it anti-clockwise. If you hear any hissing sounds (indicating there is still pressure in the system), wait until it stops. Thoroughly clean the cap, inside and out, with clean water. Also clean the filler neck on the tank. All traces of corrosion should be removed. The coolant inside the tank should be relatively transparent. If it is rust-coloured, the system should be drained, flushed and refilled (see Section 25). If the coolant level is not up to the top, add additional anti-freeze/coolant mixture (see Section 4).

4 Carefully check the large upper and lower radiator hoses along with any smaller diameter heater hoses that run from the engine to the bulkhead. Inspect each hose along its entire length, replacing any hose that is cracked, swollen or shows signs of deterioration. Cracks may become more apparent if the hose is squeezed (see illustration).

5 Make sure all hose connections are tight. A leak in the cooling system will usually show up as white or rust-coloured deposits on the areas adjoining the leak. If wire-type clamps are used at the ends of the hoses, it may be wise to renew them with more secure, screw-type clamps.

6 Use compressed air or a soft brush to remove bugs, leaves, etc, from the front of the radiator or air conditioning condenser. Be careful not to damage the delicate cooling fins or cut yourself on them.

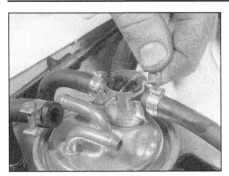

**14.4a Release the clip . . .**

**14.4b . . . and lift out the control valve, leaving the fuel hoses attached to it**

**7** Every other inspection, or at the first indication of cooling system problems, have the cap and system pressure tested. If you don't have a pressure tester, most gas stations and garages will do this for a minimal charge.

## 14 Fuel filter draining (diesel engines)

*Warning: Diesel fuel isn't as volatile as petrol, but it is flammable, so take extra precautions when you work on* *any part of the fuel system. Don't smoke or allow naked flames or bare light bulbs near the work area. Don't work in a garage or other enclosed space where there is a gas-type appliance (such as a water heater or clothes dryer). Finally, when you perform any work on the fuel system, wear safety glasses, latex gloves and have a Class B type fire extinguisher on hand. If you spill any diesel fuel on your skin, rinse it off immediately with soap and water. Caution: Keep a container handy below the work area, since spilled diesel fuel can ruin asphalt pavement. Diesel fuel can also deteriorate rubber hoses, so clean up* *spills immediately if it gets on coolant or brake hoses.*

**1** Water collects frequently in diesel fuel tanks, but since water is heavier than diesel fuel, it will separate at the fuel filter/separator. Regular draining at the fuel filter will keep the water from getting to the engine.

**2** Raise the vehicle and support it securely on axle stands.

**3** The fuel filter is mounted in the engine compartment, on the right side in front of the windscreen washer tank.

**4** Use pliers to pull the retaining clip that secures the control valve to the top of the filter assembly **(see illustrations)**. Pull up the control valve and its hoses, away from the filter.

**5** At the bottom of the fuel filter, loosen the drain plug, while holding a container underneath the filter to catch the diesel fuel and water. **Note:** *Have spare rags or a small container to catch or wipe up extra fuel that will spill from the filter assembly.*

**6** The water will come out first. When you have drained some of fuel/water, twist the drain plug closed. Pour a some fresh diesel fuel in the top of the filter.

**7** Use a new O-ring when reattaching the control valve to the filter top.

**8** When the vehicle is running, inspect for any leaks around the filter assembly.

# Every 10 000 miles (15 000 km), 'Service OIL' or 'Service' on display

## 15 Engine oil and filter change

**Note:** *If a vehicle originally filled with 'LongLife' oil is filled with oil other than that recommended by VW, the service interval must be reset to the standard 'distance/time' interval.*

**1** Frequent oil changes are the most important preventive maintenance procedures that can be done by the home mechanic. As engine oil ages, it becomes diluted and contaminated, which leads to premature engine wear.

**2** Although some sources recommend oil filter changes every other oil change, we feel that the minimal cost of an oil filter and the relative ease with which it is fitted dictate that a new filter be fitted every time the oil is changed.

**3** Gather together all necessary tools and materials before beginning this procedure **(see illustration)**.

**4** You should have plenty of clean rags and newspapers handy to mop up any spills. Access to the under side of the vehicle may be improved if the vehicle can be lifted on a hoist, driven onto ramps or supported by axle stands.

*Warning: Do not work under a vehicle which is supported only by a hydraulic or scissors-type jack.*

**5** If this is your first oil change, familiarise yourself with the locations of the oil drain plug and the oil filter.

**6** Warm the engine to normal operating

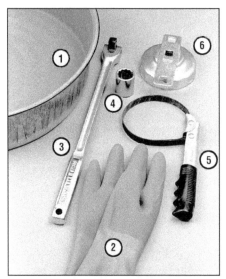

**15.3 These tools are required when changing the engine oil and filter**

| | |
|---|---|
| 1 Drain pain | 4 Socket |
| 2 Rubber gloves | 5 Filter wrench |
| 3 Breaker bar | 6 Filter wrench |

temperature. If the new oil or any tools are needed, use this warm-up time to gather everything necessary for the job. The correct type of oil for your application can be found in *Recommended lubricants and fluids* at the beginning of this Chapter.

**7** With the engine oil warm (warm engine oil will drain better and more built-up sludge will be removed with it), raise and support the vehicle. Make sure it's safely supported.

**8** Remove the splash shield under the engine **(see illustration)**.

**9** Move all necessary tools, rags and newspapers under the vehicle. Set the drain

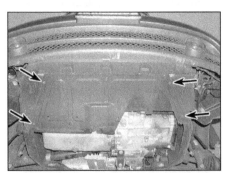

**15.8 Remove the screws (arrowed) and lower the engine splash shield to access the oil filter**

15.10 Use the proper size ring spanner or socket to remove the oil drain plug to avoid rounding it off

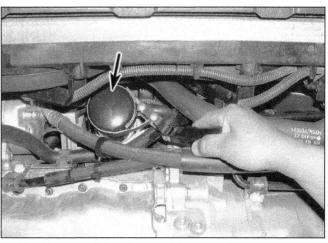

15.15a Since the oil filter (arrowed) is on very tight, you'll need oil filter removal tool – DO NOT use the tool to tighten the new filter (petrol model shown)

pan under the drain plug. Keep in mind that the oil will initially flow from the pan with some force; position the pan accordingly.

**10** Being careful not to touch any of the hot exhaust components, use a spanner to remove the drain plug near the bottom of the sump **(see illustration)**. Depending on how hot the oil is, you may want to wear gloves while unscrewing the plug the final few turns.

**11** Allow the oil to drain into the pan. It may be necessary to move the pan as the oil flow slows to a trickle.

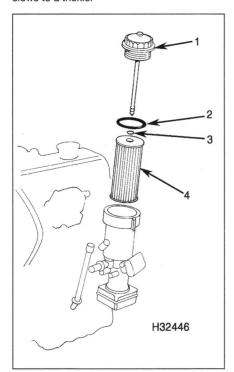

H32446

15.15b On diesel engines, unscrew the filter top (1) and remove the filter element (4) – when installing the new filter, use new rubber seals (2 and 3)

**12** After all the oil has drained, wipe off the drain plug with a clean rag. Small metal particles may cling to the plug and would immediately contaminate the new oil.

**13** Clean the area around the drain plug opening and refit the plug. Tighten the plug securely with the spanner.

**14** Move the drain pan into position under the oil filter.

**15** Use the oil filter spanner to loosen the oil filter **(see illustrations)**.

**16** Completely unscrew the old filter. Be careful; it's full of oil. Empty the oil inside the filter into the drain pan, then lower the filter. In order to ensure that all the old oil is removed, puncture the 'dome' of the filter in two places, and allow the oil to drain from the filter completely.

**17** Compare the old filter with the new one to make sure they're the same type.

**18** Use a clean rag to remove all oil, dirt and sludge from the area where the oil filter mounts to the engine. Check the old filter to make sure the rubber gasket isn't stuck to the engine. If the gasket is stuck to the engine (use an electric torch if necessary), remove it.

**19** Apply a light coat of clean oil to the rubber gasket on the new oil filter **(see**

15.19 Lubricate the oil filter gasket with clean engine oil before installing the filter on the engine

**illustration)**, or on diesel engines, apply oil to the O-rings.

**20** Attach the new filter to the engine, following the tightening directions printed on the filter canister or packing box (petrol engines). Most filter manufacturers recommend against using a filter spanner due to the possibility of overtightening and damage to the seal.

**21** Remove all tools, rags, etc, from under the vehicle, being careful not to spill the oil in the drain pan, refit the splash shield, then lower the vehicle.

**22** Move to the engine compartment and locate the oil filler cap.

**23** Pour the fresh oil through the filler opening. A funnel may be helpful.

**24** Refer to the engine oil capacity in this Chapter's Specifications and add the proper amount of fresh oil into the engine. Wait a few minutes to allow the oil to drain into the pan, then check the level on the oil dipstick (see Section 3 if necessary). If the oil level is above the hatched area, start the engine and allow the new oil to circulate.

**25** Run the engine for only about a minute and then shut it off. Immediately look under the vehicle and check for leaks at the sump drain plug and around the oil filter.

**26** With the new oil circulated and the filter now completely full, recheck the level on the dipstick and add more oil as necessary.

**27** During the first few trips after an oil change, make it a point to check frequently for leaks and proper oil level.

**28** The old oil drained from the engine cannot be reused in its present state and should be disposed of. Check with your local auto parts store, waste disposal facility or environmental agency to see if they will accept the oil for recycling. After the oil has cooled it can be drained into a container for transport to one of these disposal sites. Don't dispose of the oil by pouring it on the ground or down a drain.

### 16 Timing belt check (diesel engines)

1 Refer to Chapter 2B, Section 5, for the procedure to remove the upper timing belt cover.
2 Check the timing belt for wear, especially on the thrust side of the teeth **(see illustration)**.
3 Look for cracks, missing teeth, splits, fraying, or any sign that oil or diesel fuel has got onto the belt. If at all in doubt about the condition of the belt, renew it (see Chapter 2B).
4 Using a vernier caliper, measure the width of the belt in several places. If any section of the belt has reached 22mm, the belt has reached its wear limit and must be replaced (Chapter 2B).

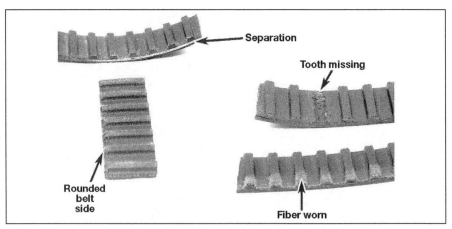

**16.2 Timing belt defects**

# Every 12 months, 'Service INSP' or 'Service' on display

### 17 Brake system check

⚠ *Warning : The dust created by the brake system is harmful to your health. Never blow it out with compressed air and don't inhale any of it. An approved filtering mask should be worn when working on the brakes. Do not, under any circumstances, use petroleum-based solvents to clean brake parts. Use brake system cleaner only. Try to use non-asbestos renewal parts whenever possible.* **Note:** *For detailed photographs of the brake system, refer to Chapter 9.*

1 In addition to the specified intervals, the brakes should be inspected every time the wheels are removed or whenever a defect is suspected.
2 Any of the following symptoms could indicate a potential brake system defect: The vehicle pulls to one side when the brake pedal is depressed; the brakes make squealing or dragging noises when applied; brake pedal travel is excessive; the pedal pulsates; or brake fluid leaks, usually onto the inside of the tyre or wheel.

3 Loosen the wheel bolts.
4 Raise the vehicle and place it securely on axle stands.
5 Remove the wheels (see *Jacking and towing* at the front of this book, or your owner's manual, if necessary).
6 There are two pads (an outer and an inner) in each caliper. The pads are visible with the wheels removed. All vehicles covered by this manual have disc brakes front and rear. **Note:** *On 2001 and later models, there are wear indicators in the pads, and a brake pad wear warning light on the instrument panel.*
7 Check the pad thickness by looking at each end of the caliper and through the inspection window in the caliper body **(see illustrations)**. If the thickness of the lining material and backing plate is less than that listed in this Chapter's Specifications, renew the pads.
8 If it is difficult to determine the exact thickness of the remaining pad material by the above method, or if you are at all concerned about the condition of the pads, remove the caliper(s), then remove the pads from the calipers for further inspection (refer to Chapter 9).
9 Once the pads are removed from the calipers, clean them with brake cleaner and re-measure them with a ruler or a vernier caliper.

10 Measure the disc thickness with a micrometer to make sure that it still has service life remaining. If any disc is thinner than the specified minimum thickness, renew it (refer to Chapter 9). Even if the disc has service life remaining, check its condition. Look for scoring, gouging and burned spots. If these conditions exist, remove the disc and have it resurfaced (see Chapter 9).
11 Before refitting the wheels, check all brake pipes and hoses for damage, wear, deformation, cracks, corrosion, leakage, bends and twists, particularly in the vicinity of the rubber hoses at the calipers **(see illustration)**. Check the clamps for tightness and the connections for leakage. Make sure that all hoses and pipes are clear of sharp edges, moving parts and the exhaust system. If any of the above conditions are noted, repair, reroute or renew the pipes and/or fittings as necessary (see Chapter 9).

### Brake servo check

12 Sit in the driver's seat and perform the following sequence of tests.
13 With the brake fully depressed, start the engine – the pedal should move down a little when the engine starts.

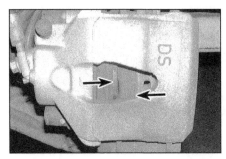

**17.7a With the wheel off, check the thickness of the pads (arrowed) through the inspection hole (front caliper shown, rear caliper similar)**

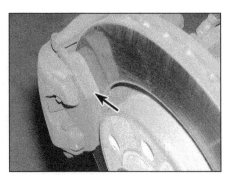

**17.7b The outer pad (arrowed) is more easily checked at the edge of the caliper**

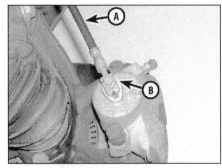

**17.11 Check along the brake hoses (A) and at each fitting (B) for deterioration, cracks and leakage**

**14** With the engine running, depress the brake pedal several times – the travel distance should not change.

**15** Depress the brake, stop the engine and hold the pedal in for about 30 seconds – the pedal should neither sink nor rise.

**16** Restart the engine, run it for about a minute and turn it off. Then firmly depress the brake several times – the pedal travel should decrease with each application.

**17** If your brakes do not operate as described, the brake servo has failed. Refer to Chapter 9 for the renewal procedure.

### Handbrake

**18** The handbrake cables operate the rear calipers mechanically, and there is no adjustment needed at the rear brakes unless cables or other parts are being replaced. One method of checking the handbrake is to park the vehicle on a steep hill with the handbrake set and the transmission in Neutral (stay in the vehicle for this check). If the handbrake cannot prevent the vehicle from rolling, it's in need of adjustment (see Chapter 9).

## 18 Power steering fluid level check

**1** Unlike manual steering, the power steering system relies on fluid which may, over a period of time, require replenishing.

**2** On all models, the fluid reservoir for the power steering pump is located on the pump body at the front of the engine compartment, next to the battery **(see illustration)**.

**3** For the check, the front wheels should be pointed straight ahead and the engine should be off.

**4** Use a clean rag to wipe off the reservoir cap and the area around the cap. This will help prevent any foreign matter from entering the reservoir during the check.

**5** Twist off the cap and check the temperature of the fluid at the end of the dipstick with your finger.

**6** Wipe off the fluid with a clean rag, reinsert the dipstick, then withdraw it and read the fluid level. The fluid should be at the proper

**18.2 The power steering fluid dipstick (arrowed) is located in the power steering pump reservoir – turn the cap anti-clockwise to remove it**

level, depending on whether it was checked hot or cold **(see illustration)**. Never allow the fluid level to drop below the lower mark on the dipstick.

**7** If additional fluid is required, pour the specified type directly into the reservoir, using a funnel to prevent spills.

**8** If the reservoir requires frequent fluid additions, all power steering hoses, hose connections, steering gear and the power steering pump should be carefully checked for leaks.

## 19 Exhaust system check

**1** With the engine cold (at least three hours after the vehicle has been driven), check the complete exhaust system from the manifold to the end of the tailpipe. Be careful around the catalytic converter, which may be hot even after three hours. The inspection should be done with the vehicle on a hoist to permit unrestricted access. If a hoist isn't available, raise the vehicle and support it securely on axle stands.

**2** Check the exhaust pipes and connections for signs of leakage and/or corrosion indicating a potential failure. Make sure that all brackets and rubbers are in good condition and tight **(see illustrations)**.

**3** Inspect the underside of the body for holes,

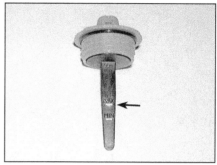

**18.6 The power steering fluid dipstick has marks on it so the fluid level can be checked hot (arrow at MAX) or cold (MIN)**

corrosion, open seams, etc, which may allow exhaust gasses to enter the passenger compartment. Seal all body openings with silicone sealant or body putty.

**4** Rattles and other noises can often be traced to the exhaust system, especially the rubbers, mountings and heat shields. Try to move the pipes, silencers and catalytic converter. If the components can come in contact with the body or suspension parts, secure the exhaust system with new brackets and rubbers.

## 20 Fuel system check

⚠ *Warning: Fuel is extremely flammable, so take extra precautions when you work on any part of the fuel system.*
*Don't smoke or allow naked flames or bare light bulbs near the work area, and don't work in a garage where a gas-type appliance (such as a water heater or clothes dryer) is present. Since fuel is carcinogenic, wear latex gloves when there's a possibility of being exposed to fuel, and, if you spill any fuel on your skin, rinse it off immediately with soap and water. Mop up any spills immediately and do not store fuel-soaked rags where they could ignite. When you perform any kind of work on the fuel system, wear safety glasses and have a Class B type fire extinguisher on hand. The petrol fuel system is under constant pressure, so, before any pipes are disconnected, the fuel system pressure must be relieved (see Chapter 4A). Diesel fuel is only slightly less dangerous than petrol, so take the same precautions when dealing with diesel fuel.*

**1** If you smell fuel while driving or after the vehicle has been sitting in the sun, inspect the fuel system immediately.

**2** Remove the fuel filler cap and inspect if for damage and corrosion. The gasket should have an unbroken sealing imprint. If the gasket is damaged or corroded, refit a new cap.

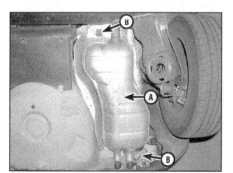

**19.2a Inspect the silencer (A) for signs of deterioration, and all rubbers (B)**

**19.2b Inspect all flanged joints (arrow indicates front exhaust pipe joint) for signs of exhaust gas leakage**

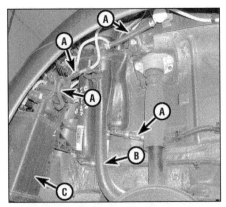

**20.7 Inspect the fuel tank mounting straps, the various fuel and vapour pipes (A), the plastic filler hose (B), and the evaporative emissions canister (C)**

**3** Inspect the fuel feed and return pipes for cracks. Make sure that the connections between the fuel pipes and the fuel injection system are tight.

**4** If the fuel injectors are visible, look for signs of fuel leakage (wet spots) around any of the injectors, they may need new O-rings (see Chapter 4A).

**5** Since some components of the fuel system – the fuel tank and part of the fuel feed and return pipes, for example – are underneath the vehicle, they can be inspected more easily with the vehicle raised on a hoist. If that's not possible, raise the vehicle and support it on axle stands.

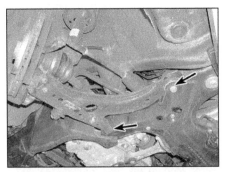

**21.9a Examine the mounting points (arrowed) for the lower control arms on the front suspension subframe**

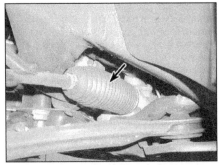

**21.9c Inspect the steering gear boots (arrowed) for signs of cracking or lubricant leakage**

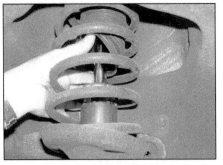

**21.6 Check for signs of fluid leakage at this point on the struts and shock absorbers (front strut shown)**

**6** With the vehicle raised and safely supported, inspect the fuel tank and filler neck for punctures, cracks and other damage. The connection between the filler neck and the tank is particularly critical. Inspect all fuel tank mounting brackets and straps to be sure that the tank is securely attached to the vehicle.

 **Warning: Do not, under any circumstances, try to repair a fuel tank (except rubber components).**

**7** Carefully check all rubber hoses and nylon pipes leading away from the fuel tank **(see illustration)**. Check for loose connections, deteriorated hoses, crimped pipes and other damage. Repair or renew damaged sections as necessary (see Chapter 4A).

**8** The evaporative emissions control system

**21.9b Inspect the track rod ends (A), the lower ball joints (B), and anti-roll bar link bushes (C)**

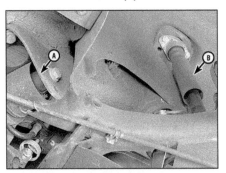

**21.9d At the rear suspension, check the rear axle pivot bushes (A) and the shock absorbers (B)**

can also be a source of fuel odours. The function of the system is to store fuel vapours from the fuel tank in a charcoal canister until they can be routed to the intake manifold where they mix with incoming air before being burned in the combustion chambers.

**9** The most common symptom of a faulty evaporative emissions system is a strong odour of fuel. If a fuel odour has been detected, and you have already checked the areas described above, check the charcoal canister, and the hoses connected to it **(see illustration 20.7)**. The rear wheel arch liner must be removed for access (see Chapter 11, Section 13).

## 21 Suspension, steering and driveshaft boot check

**Note:** *The steering linkage and suspension components should be checked periodically. Worn or damaged suspension and steering components can result in excessive and abnormal tyre wear, poor ride quality and vehicle handling and reduced fuel economy. For detailed illustrations of the steering and suspension components, refer to Chapter 10.*

### Strut/shock absorber check

**1** Park the vehicle on level ground, turn the engine off and set the handbrake. Check the tyre pressures.

**2** Push down at one corner of the vehicle, then release it while noting the movement of the body. It should stop moving and come to rest in a level position within one or two bounces.

**3** If the vehicle continues to move up-and-down or if it fails to return to its original position, a worn or weak strut or shock absorber is probably the reason.

**4** Repeat the above check at each of the three remaining corners of the vehicle.

**5** Raise the vehicle and support it securely on axle stands.

**6** Check the struts and shock absorbers for evidence of fluid leakage **(see illustration)**. A light film of fluid is no cause for concern. Make sure that any fluid noted is from the struts or shocks and not from some other source. If leakage is noted, renew the struts or shocks as a set (front or rear).

**7** Check the struts and shocks to be sure that they are securely mounted and undamaged. Check the upper mounts for damage and wear. If damage or wear is noted, renew the struts and shocks as a set (front or rear).

**8** If the struts or shocks must be replaced, refer to Chapter 10 for the procedure.

### Steering and suspension check

**9** Visually inspect the steering and suspension components (front and rear) for damage and distortion. Look for damaged seals, boots and bushes and leaks of any kind. Examine the bushes where the control arms meet the chassis **(see illustrations)**.

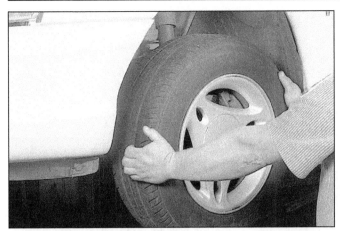

**21.11 With the steering wheel in the locked position and the vehicle raised, grasp the front tyre as shown and try to move it back-and-forth if any play is noted, check the steering rack mountings and track rod ends for looseness**

**21.14 Inspect the inner and outer driveshaft boots for loose clamps, cracks or signs of leaking lubricant (inner boot shown)**

10 Clean the lower end of the steering knuckle. Have an assistant grasp the lower edge of the tyre and move the wheel in-and-out while you look for movement at the steering knuckle-to-control arm balljoint. If there is any movement the suspension balljoint(s) must be replaced.

11 Grasp each front tyre at the front and rear edges, push in at the front, pull out at the rear and feel for play in the steering system components. If any freeplay is noted, check the rack mounts and the track rod ends for looseness (see illustration).

12 Additional steering and suspension system information and illustrations can be found in Chapter 10.

### Driveshaft boot check

13 The driveshaft boots are very important because they prevent dirt, water and foreign material from entering and damaging the constant velocity (CV) joints. Oil and grease can cause the boot material to deteriorate prematurely, so it's a good idea to wash the boots with soap and water. Because it constantly pivots back and forth following the steering action of the front hub, the outer CV boot wears out soonest and should be inspected regularly.

14 Inspect the boots for tears and cracks as well as loose clamps (see illustration). If there is any evidence of cracks or leaking lubricant, they must be replaced as described in Chapter 8.

# Every 20 000 miles (30 000 km), 'Service INSP' or 'Service' on display

## 22 Pollen filter renewal

1 The pollen filter is located on the bulkhead, in front of the windscreen – on RHD models it is on the left-hand side, and on LHD models it is on the right-hand side.
2 Ease off the rubber seal and undo the four screws, then pull up and withdraw the cover. The cover may be quite tight and the use of a wooden wedge or suitable lever may be required to release it from the bulkhead panel.
3 Release the clips and withdraw the filter frame, then remove the element from the frame (see illustration).
4 Locate the frame into the end laminations of the new element, then fit to the housing, making sure that the lugs engage with the recesses.
5 Refit the cover and secure with the screws, then press down the rubber seal.

## 23 Manual transmission lubricant level check

1 The manual transmission has a filler plug which must be removed to check the lubricant level. If the vehicle is raised to gain access to the plug, be sure to support it safely on axle stands – DO NOT crawl under a vehicle that is supported only by a jack. Be sure the vehicle is level or the check may be inaccurate.
2 Using the appropriate spanner, unscrew the plug from the transmission; most models require a 17mm Allen spanner (see illustration).
3 Use your little finger to reach inside the housing to feel the lubricant level. The level should be at or near the bottom of the plug hole. If it isn't, add the recommended lubricant through the plug hole with a syringe or squeeze bottle.
4 Refit and tighten the plug. Check for leaks after the first few miles of driving.

**22.3 Removing the pollen filter**

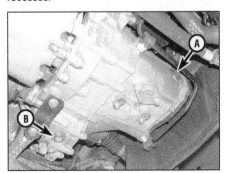

**23.2 The manual transmission check/filler plug (A) is located at the front side of the transmission – (B) is the drain plug**

# Every 24 months (regardless of mileage)

### 24 Brake fluid renewal

![warning]  *Warning: Brake fluid can harm your eyes and damage painted surfaces, so use extreme caution when handling or pouring it. Do not use brake fluid that has been standing open or is more than one year old. Brake fluid absorbs moisture from the air. Excess moisture can cause a dangerous loss of braking effectiveness.*

1 At the specified intervals, the brake fluid should be drained and replaced. Since the brake fluid may drip or splash when pouring it, place plenty of rags around the master cylinder to protect any surrounding painted surfaces.

2 Before beginning work, purchase the specified brake fluid (see *Recommended lubricants and fluids* at the beginning of this Chapter).

3 Remove the cap from the master cylinder reservoir.

4 Using a hand suction pump or similar device, withdraw the fluid from the master cylinder reservoir.

5 Add new fluid to the master cylinder until it rises to the line indicated on the reservoir.

6 Bleed the brake system as described in Chapter 9 at all four brakes until new and uncontaminated fluid is expelled from each bleed screw. Be sure to maintain the fluid level in the master cylinder as you perform the bleeding process. If you allow the master cylinder to run dry, air will enter the system.

7 As the brake master cylinder also supplies the clutch hydraulic system, the clutch hydraulic fluid should be changed at the same time. Bleed the clutch system as described in Chapter 8 until new uncontaminated fluid is expelled from the bleed screw.

8 Refill the master cylinder with fluid and check the operation of the brakes. The pedal should feel solid when depressed, with no sponginess.

![warning]  *Warning: Do not operate the vehicle if you are in doubt about the effectiveness of the brake system.*

### 25 Cooling system servicing (draining, flushing and refilling)
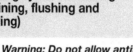

![warning]  *Warning: Do not allow antifreeze to come in contact with your skin or painted surfaces of the vehicle. Rinse off spills immediately with plenty of water. Antifreeze is highly toxic if ingested. Never leave antifreeze lying around in an open container or in puddles on the floor; children and pets are attracted by its sweet smell and may drink it. Check with local authorities on disposing of used antifreeze. Many communities have collection centres that will see that antifreeze is disposed of safely. Caution: Never mix standard ethylene glycol anti-freeze and red-coloured silicate-free VW G12 coolant because doing so will destroy the efficiency of the red coolant.*

#### Draining

1 Periodically, the cooling system should be drained, flushed and refilled to replenish the antifreeze mixture and prevent formation of rust and corrosion, which can impair the performance of the cooling system and cause engine damage. When the cooling system is serviced, all hoses and the radiator cap should be checked and replaced if necessary.

2 Apply the handbrake and block the wheels.

![warning]  *Warning: If the vehicle has just been driven, wait several hours to allow the engine to cool down before beginning this procedure.*

3 Move a large container under the radiator drain to catch the coolant. The drain plug is located on the lower left side of the radiator, at the lower radiator hose **(see illustration)**.

Attach a 10 mm diameter hose to the drain fitting to direct the coolant into the container, then open the drain fitting (a pair of pliers may be required to turn it). Remove the coolant expansion tank cap.

4 After coolant stops flowing out of the radiator, move the container under the engine oil cooler **(see illustration)**. Remove the hose and allow the coolant in the block to drain.

5 While the coolant is draining, check the condition of the radiator hoses, heater hoses and clamps (refer to Section 13 if necessary).

6 Renew any damaged clamps or hoses. Reconnect the hoses, replacing the spring-type clamps with screw-type ones if necessary to get a tight connection.

#### Flushing

7 Once the system is completely drained, remove the thermostat from the engine (see Chapter 3). Then refit the thermostat housing without the thermostat. This will allow the system to be thoroughly flushed.

8 Refit the lower hose on the oil cooler and tighten the radiator drain plug. Turn your heating system controls to Hot, so that the heater core will be flushed at the same time as the rest of the cooling system.

9 Disconnect the upper radiator hose, then place a garden hose in the upper radiator inlet and flush the system until the water runs clear at the upper radiator hose.

10 In severe cases of contamination or clogging of the radiator, remove the radiator (see Chapter 3) and have a radiator repair facility clean and repair it if necessary.

11 Many deposits can be removed by the chemical action of a cleaner available at motor factors. Follow the procedure outlined in the manufacturer's instructions. **Note:** *When the coolant is regularly drained and the system refilled with the correct antifreeze/water mixture, there should be no need to use chemical cleaners or descalers.*

#### Refilling

12 To refill the system, refit the thermostat and reconnect any radiator hoses.

13 Place the heater temperature control in the maximum heat position.

14 Make sure to use the proper coolant listed in this Chapter's Specifications. Slowly fill the expansion tank with the recommended mixture of antifreeze and water until it reaches the MIN mark. Wait five minutes and recheck the coolant level in the tank, adding if necessary.

15 Leave the expansion tank cap off and run the engine in a well-ventilated area until the thermostat opens (coolant will begin flowing through the radiator and the upper radiator hose will become hot).

16 Turn the engine off and let it cool. Add more coolant mixture to bring the level back up to the MIN level on the expansion tank.

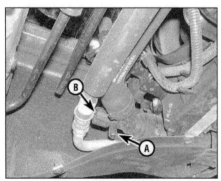

**25.3 Attach a hose to the drain (A), then turn the cooling system drain knob (B), located at the lower radiator hose**

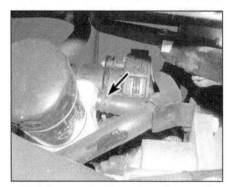

**25.4 Remove the lower hose (arrowed) from the engine oil cooler to drain the cylinder block (seen here from below)**

17 Squeeze the upper radiator hose to expel air, then add more coolant mixture if necessary. Refit the expansion tank cap.

18 Place the heater temperature control and the blower motor speed control to their maximum setting.

19 Start the engine, allow it to reach normal

operating temperature and check for leaks.

20 Let the engine cool, then recheck the coolant level, adding as necessary to bring the level just above the MIN mark.

# Every 40 000 miles (60 000 km) or 48 months, whichever comes first

## 26 Differential lubricant level check (automatic transmissions)

**Note:** *On manual transmission models, the differential lubricant is not separated from the transmission lubricant; filling the transmission fills the differential, too (see Section 23). The differential has a separate filler, and different lubricant, on automatic transmission models.*

1 If the vehicle is raised to perform this procedure, be sure to support it safely on axle stands – DO NOT crawl under the vehicle when it's supported only by the jack. Be sure the vehicle is level or the check may not be accurate.

2 Refer to Chapter 6A and remove the Vehicle Speed Sensor (VSS) from the transmission. Using a spanner, remove the speedometer driveshaft from the transmission **(see illustration).**

3 The speedometer driveshaft is used as a dipstick for the differential lubricant **(see illustration).** If the level is too low, use a pump or squeeze bottle to add the recommended lubricant until it just starts to run out of the opening.

4 Refit the driveshaft securely and refit the VSS.

## 27 Automatic transmission fluid level check

1 The automatic transmission fluid level should be carefully maintained. Low fluid level can lead to slipping or loss of drive, while overfilling can cause foaming and loss of fluid. **Note:** *Checking the fluid on the New Beetle isn't easy. The transmission is considered by the manufacturer to be a 'sealed' unit, to which fluid doesn't need to be added unless a leak is evident. There is no conventional dipstick in the engine compartment, but rather a fill plug and a level-inspection plug accessible only from below the transmission. Make sure you have a new seal for each plug before you begin.*

2 Transmission fluid expands as it warms up, and the fluid check should only be begun on a cold drivetrain. The transmission fluid must only be checked at a transmission temperature of 35 to 45°C. With the handbrake set, start the engine, then move the gearchange lever through all the gear

ranges, ending in Park. The fluid level must be checked with the vehicle level.

3 When the transmission temperature reaches 35 to 45°C, remove the level-check plug **(see illustration).** If fluid just comes out of the hole as drips, the fluid level is OK. If more fluid comes out, the transmission may have been overfilled.

4 If no fluid comes out at 45°C, remove the filler plug and add a small amount of fluid, until it just drips out of the level-check hole **(see illustration).**

5 When the correct level is achieved at the specified temperature, refit new seals on the level-check plug and screw it in, and refit the fill plug with a new seal. The cap over the fill plug is easily damaged during removal, so have a new one of these on hand as well.

6 The condition of the fluid should also be checked along with the level. If the fluid is a dark reddish-brown colour, or if it smells burned, it should be changed. If you are in doubt about the condition of the fluid, purchase some new fluid and compare the two for colour and smell. **Note:** *When the*

*work is done at a dealership, the factory scan tool is used to read the transmission fluid temperature. To perform the job at home, you may need a cooking or darkroom thermometer that has a long probe, which you can insert in the level-check hole to read the fluid temperature.*

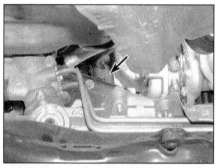

**26.2 Remove the vehicle speed sensor (arrowed) from the top of the speedometer driveshaft on the differential, then remove the driveshaft**

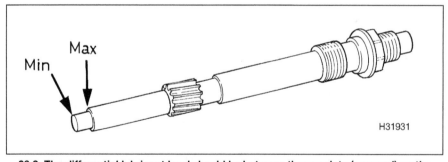

**26.3 The differential lubricant level should be between these points (arrowed) on the speedometer driveshaft**

**27.3 Location of the level-check plug (arrowed) on automatic transmissions**

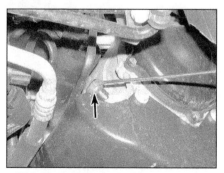

**27.4 Use a large screwdriver to pry the automatic transmission filler plug (arrow) out of the transmission from below**

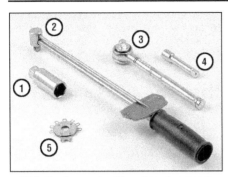

**28.2 Tools required for changing spark plugs**

1 *Spark plug socket* – *This will have special padding inside to protect the spark plugs porcelain insulator*
2 *Torque wrench* – *Using this tool is the best way to ensure the plugs are tightened properly*
3 *Ratchet* – *Standard hand tool to fit the spark plug socket*
4 *Extension* – *Depending on model and accessories, you may need special extensions and universal joints to reach one or more of the plugs*
5 *Spark plug gap gauge* – *This gauge for checking the gap comes in a variety of styles*

## 28 Spark plug renewal

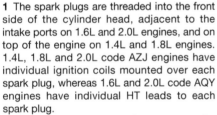

1 The spark plugs are threaded into the front side of the cylinder head, adjacent to the intake ports on 1.6L and 2.0L engines, and on top of the engine on 1.4L and 1.8L engines. 1.4L, 1.8L and 2.0L code AZJ engines have individual ignition coils mounted over each spark plug, whereas 1.6L and 2.0L code AQY engines have individual HT leads to each spark plug.
2 In most cases, the tools necessary for spark plug renewal include a spark plug socket which fits onto a ratchet (spark plug sockets are padded inside to prevent damage to the porcelain insulators on the new plugs),

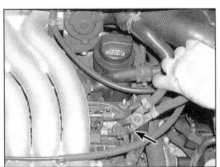

**28.6a A tool like this one (arrowed) makes the job of removing the spark plug boot easier – twist it back-and-forth and pull only on the boot**

**28.4 Remove the plastic plugs (arrowed) with a small screwdriver to access three screws retaining the engine cover**

various extensions and a gap gauge to check and adjust the gaps on the new plugs **(see illustration)**. A special plug boot removal tool is available for separating the wire boots from the spark plugs. On 1.4L, 1.8L and 2.0L code AZJ engines, VW technicians use tool T10094 or T10112 to pull out the ignition coils, however, a length of welding rod bent to hook under the connectors may be used instead. Note on engine 1.8L code AVC each coil is secured with two bolts. A torque spanner should be used to tighten the new plugs.
3 The best approach when replacing the spark plugs is to purchase the new ones in advance, adjust them to the proper gap and renew them one at a time. When buying the new spark plugs, be sure to obtain the correct plug type for your particular engine. This information can be found in your owner's manual and the Specifications at the front of this Chapter.
4 Allow the engine to cool completely before attempting to remove any of the plugs. Remove the plastic cover at the top of the engine for access **(see illustration)**. While you're waiting for the engine to cool, check the new plugs for defects and adjust the gaps.
5 The gap is checked by inserting the proper-thickness gauge between the electrodes at the tip of the plug **(see illustration)**. The gap between the electrodes should be the same as the one specified in this Chapter's Specifications. The gauge should just slide between the electrodes. If the gap is

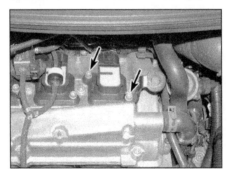

**28.6b On 1.8L code AVC models, remove the two screws (arrowed) securing each individual ignition coil . . .**

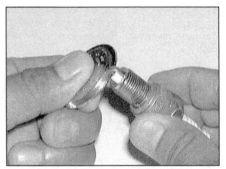

**28.5a Spark plug manufacturers recommend using a tapered thickness gauge when checking the gap – slide the thin side into the gap and turn until the gauge just fills the gap, then read the thickness on the gauge – do not force the tool into the gap or use the tapered portion to widen a gap**

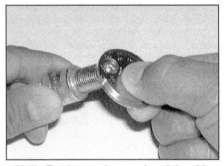

**28.5b To change the gap, bend the side electrode only, using the adjuster hole in the tool, and be very careful not to crack or chip the porcelain insulator surrounding the centre electrode**

incorrect, use the adjuster on the gauge body to bend the curved side electrode slightly until the proper gap is obtained **(see illustration)**. If the side electrode is not exactly over the centre electrode, bend it with the adjuster until it is. Check for cracks in the porcelain insulator (if any are found, the plug should not be used). **Note:** *Manufacturers recommend using a tapered thickness gauge when checking platinum-type spark plugs. Other types of gauges may scrape the thin platinum*

**28.6c . . . then pull the coil/boot up and off the spark plug**

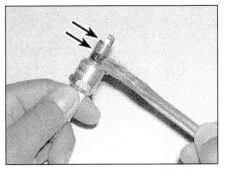

28.8 Use a socket and extension to unscrew the spark plugs – various length extensions and perhaps a universal joint may be required to reach some plugs

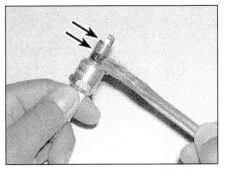

28.9 Apply a thin coat of anti-seize compound to the spark plug threads, being careful not to get any near the lower threads

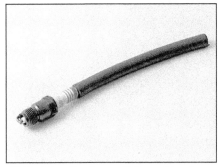

28.10 A length of snug-fitting rubber hose will save time and prevent damaged threads when installing the spark plugs

*coating from the electrodes, thus dramatically shortening the life of the plugs.*

6 On 1.6L and 2.0L code AQY engines, remove the HT lead from one spark plug. If available, use a plug lead removal tool, and pull only on the boot at the end of the lead (do not pull on the lead) **(see illustrations)**. Note you will have to reach around the intake plenum to remove the number 2 and 3 plug wires and plugs. To extract the number 2 plug, you may have to disconnect the electrical connector at the injector nearest it, and swivel it to provide more working room. On 1.8L engines, unbolt the vacuum reservoir and place it to one side without disconnecting

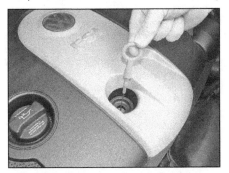

29.1 Remove the engine oil dipstick . . .

the lines, then on 1.4L, 1.8L and 2.0L code AZJ engines remove one ignition coil (see paragraph 2). Note on engine 1.8L code AVC the coil is secured with two bolts, whereas on engine code 1.8L code AWU it is pressed into position by hand.

7 If compressed air is available, use it to blow any dirt or foreign material away from the spark plug hole. The idea here is to eliminate the possibility of debris falling into the cylinder as the spark plug is removed.

8 Place the spark plug socket over the plug and remove it from the engine by turning it in a anti-clockwise direction **(see illustration)**.

9 Before fitting the new plugs, it is a good idea to apply a thin coat of anti-seize compound to the threads **(see illustration)**. Don't get any on the bottom threads or it could run (during hot engine operation) down onto the porcelain or electrodes and potentially ruin the plug.

10 Thread one of the new plugs into the hole until you can no longer turn it with your fingers, then tighten it with a torque spanner (if available) or the ratchet. Where plugs are harder to reach, it might be a good idea to slip a short length of rubber hose over the end of the plug to use as a tool to thread it into place **(see illustration)**. The hose will grip the plug well enough to turn it, but will start to slip if the plug begins to cross-thread in the hole – this

will prevent damaged threads and the accompanying repair costs.

11 Attach the plug lead to the new spark plug, again using a twisting motion on the boot until it's seated on the spark plug. On 1.4L, 1.8L and 2.0L code AZJ engines, refit the ignition coil and, where applicable, tighten the two bolts.

12 Repeat the procedure for the remaining spark plugs, replacing them one at a time to prevent mixing up the HT leads. Finally, on 1.8L models, refit the vacuum reservoir and tighten the bolts.

## 29 Air filter renewal

### *Engine code BCA*

1 The air cleaner is incorporated in the engine top cover. First, remove the engine oil dipstick **(see illustration)**.

2 Release each corner of the engine top cover by pulling sharply upwards. This will also release the air cleaner housing from the throttle valve module/housing **(see illustration)**.

3 Disconnect the wiring from the inlet air temperature sensor **(see illustration)**.

4 Disconnect the crankshaft ventilation hose

29.2 . . . lift the engine top cover/air cleaner . . .

29.3 . . . then disconnect the wiring from the inlet air temperature sensor . . .

29.4 . . . and disconnect the crankcase ventilation hose from the camshaft housing

29.5a Remove the rubber grommet . . .

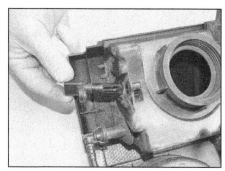

29.5b . . . and air temperature sensor

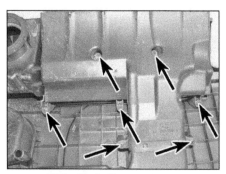

29.6a Undo the screws . . .

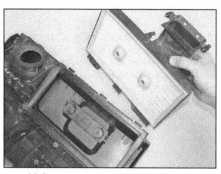

29.6b . . . separate the air cleaner housing . . .

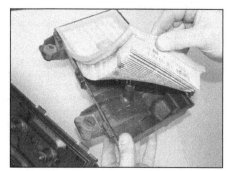

29.6c . . . then remove the filter element

from the air cleaner housing or camshaft housing, and lift the assembly from the engine **(see illustration)**.

**5** With the assembly inverted on the bench, if necessary remove the rubber grommet, then undo the screw and remove the air temperature sensor **(see illustrations)**.

**6** Undo the screws and separate the air cleaner housing from the top cover, then remove the filter element **(see illustrations)**.

**7** Fit the new filter element using a reversal of the removal procedure.

### All other engine codes

**8** The air filter is housed in a black plastic box mounted on the inner wing on the left side of the engine compartment. Where applicable, also disconnect the hose between the air intake and the air filter housing cover.

**9** Disconnect the Mass Airflow Sensor connector, remove the screws and pull the air filter housing cover up, then lift the air filter element out of the housing **(see illustrations)**. Wipe out the inside of the air filter housing

with a clean rag. **Note:** *There is some 'wrestling' involved in getting the air filter cover out, since it has to come away from the air induction hose and away from the wing at almost the same time.*

**10** While the cover is off, be careful not to drop anything down into the air filter housing.

**11** Place the new filter element in the air filter housing. Make sure it seats properly in the groove of the housing.

**12** Fit the new filter element using a reversal of the removal procedure.

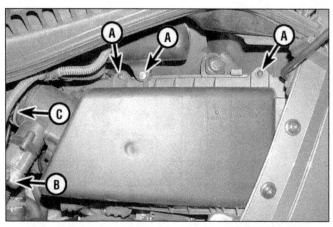

29.9a Remove the screws (A), disconnect the MAF sensor connector (B), release the clamp (C) and lift out the air filter housing cover

29.9b Set the cover aside and pull out the filter element

## 30 Fuel filter renewal (diesel engines)

**Warning: Diesel fuel isn't as volatile as petrol, but it is flammable, so take extra precautions when you work on any part of the fuel system. Don't smoke or allow naked flames or bare light bulbs near the work area. Don't work in a garage or other enclosed space where there is a gas-type appliance (such as a water heater or clothes dryer). Finally, when you perform any work on the fuel system, wear safety glasses, latex gloves and have a Class B type fire extinguisher on hand. If you spill any diesel fuel on your skin, rinse it off immediately with soap and water.**

*Caution: Keep a container handy below the work area, since spilled diesel fuel can ruin asphalt pavement. Diesel fuel can also deteriorate rubber hoses, so clean up spills immediately if it gets on coolant or brake hoses.*

**1** Disconnect the fuel control valve from the top of the filter **(see illustrations 14.4a and 14.4b)**.

**2** Mark the other two fuel pipes with tape and disconnect them. **Note:** *The pipes may be secured with crimp-type clamps, which may have to be cut off with wire-cutting pliers to remove the hoses.*

**3** Remove the fasteners and take the filter and mounting bracket from the vehicle. Loosen the bracket and remove the filter.

**4** Fill a new filter with fresh diesel fuel and refit it in the bracket, then reattach the bracket to the vehicle. Attach the control valve with a

**30.4 Reconnect the fuel supply and delivery hoses**

new O-ring and secure the hoses with screw-type clamps **(see illustration)**.

**5** When the vehicle is running, inspect for any leaks around the filter assembly.

# Every 60 000 miles (90 000 km) or 72 months, whichever comes first

## 31 Fuel filter renewal (petrol engines)

**Warning: Petrol is extremely flammable, so take extra precautions when you work on any part of the fuel system.**
*Don't smoke or allow naked flames or bare light bulbs near the work area, and don't work in a garage where a gas-type appliance (such as a water heater or clothes dryer) is present. Since fuel is carcinogenic, wear latex gloves when there's a possibility of being exposed to fuel, and, if you spill any fuel on your skin, rinse it off immediately with soap and water. Mop up any spills immediately and do not store fuel-soaked rags where they could ignite. When you perform any kind of work on the fuel system, wear safety glasses and have a Class B type fire*

*extinguisher on hand. The fuel system is under pressure, so if any pipes must be disconnected, the pressure in the system must be relieved first (see Chapter 4A for more information).*

**1** The fuel filter is located under the rear of the vehicle, at the front of the fuel tank.

**2** The manufacturer does not give a renewal interval, but our suggested interval is based on experience with many other vehicles. The fuel filter is not expensive, so replacing it is like inexpensive insurance.

**3** Raise the vehicle and support it securely on axle stands.

**4** Use compressed air or carburettor cleaner to clean any dirt surrounding the fuel inlet and outlet pipe fittings.

**5** There are quick-connect fittings at each end of the filter **(see illustration)**. Depress the tab on each fitting to release them, then pull them off the filter. **Note:** *Have spare rags or a small container to catch or wipe up extra fuel that will spill from the filter.*

**6** Loosen the screw-clamp and remove the filter.

**7** Refitting is the reverse of removal. Makes sure the arrow on side of the new filter is pointing toward the engine side of the fuel system, and check for leaks after running the vehicle.

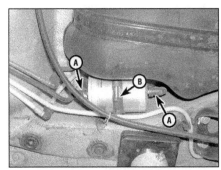

**31.5 Detach the fittings (A) at the fuel filter, then loosen the clamp (B) to remove the filter**

# Chapter 2 Part A:
## 1.4L petrol engine in-car repair procedures

## Contents

## Degrees of difficulty

| | | |
|---|---|---|
| **Easy,** suitable for novice with little experience  | **Fairly easy,** suitable for beginner with some experience  | **Fairly difficult,** suitable for competent DIY mechanic 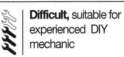 |

**Difficult,** suitable for experienced DIY mechanic

**Very difficult,** suitable for expert DIY or professional

## Specifications

### General

| | |
|---|---|
| Displacement ............................................ | 1390 cc |
| Manufacturer's engine code* ............................. | BCA |
| Maximum power output .................................... | 55 kW (74 bhp) at 5000 rpm |
| Maximum torque output .................................. | 128 Nm at 3300 rpm |
| Bore ................................................... | 76.5 mm |
| Stroke ................................................. | 75.6 mm |
| Compression ratio ...................................... | 10.5 : 1 |
| Compression pressures | |
|    Minimum compression pressure ........................ | Approximately 7.0 bar |
|    Maximum difference between cylinders .................. | Approximately 3.0 bar |
| Firing order ........................................... | 1 – 3 – 4 – 2 |
| No 1 cylinder location ................................. | Timing belt end |

**\* Note:** *See 'Vehicle identification numbers' at the beginning of this manual for the location of engine code markings.*

### Camshafts

| | |
|---|---|
| Camshaft endfloat ...................................... | 0.40 mm |
| Camshaft bearing running clearance ..................... | N/A |
| Camshaft run-out ....................................... | N/A |

### Lubrication system

| | |
|---|---|
| Oil pump type .......................................... | Rotor type, driven directly from crankshaft |
| Oil pressure (oil temperature 80°C) | |
|    At idling .............................................. | No figure specified |
|    At 2000 rpm ............................................ | 2.0 bar |
|    In excess of 2000 rpm .................................. | 7.0 bar maximum |

## Torque wrench settings

| | Nm | Ft-lbs |
|---|---|---|
| Ancillary (alternator, etc) bracket mounting bolts . . . . . . . . . . . . . . . . . | 50 | 37 |
| Auxiliary drivebelt tensioner securing bolt | | |
|   M8 bolt | | |
|     Step 1 . . . . . . . . . . . . . . . . . . . . . . . . . . . . . . . . . . . . . . . . | 20 | 15 |
|     Step 2 . . . . . . . . . . . . . . . . . . . . . . . . . . . . . . . . . . . . . . . . | Angle-tighten a further 90° | |
|   M10 bolt | 45 | 33 |
| Big-end bearing caps bolt/nuts* | | |
|   Step 1 . . . . . . . . . . . . . . . . . . . . . . . . . . . . . . . . . . . . . . . . | 30 | 22 |
|   Step 2 . . . . . . . . . . . . . . . . . . . . . . . . . . . . . . . . . . . . . . . . | Angle-tighten a further 90° | |
| Camshaft carrier bolts* | | |
|   Step 1 . . . . . . . . . . . . . . . . . . . . . . . . . . . . . . . . . . . . . . . . | 10 | 7 |
|   Step 2 . . . . . . . . . . . . . . . . . . . . . . . . . . . . . . . . . . . . . . . . | Angle-tighten a further 90° | |
| Camshaft sealing cap bolts . . . . . . . . . . . . . . . . . . . . . . . . . . . . . . | 10 | 7 |
| Camshaft sprocket bolts* | | |
|   Step 1 . . . . . . . . . . . . . . . . . . . . . . . . . . . . . . . . . . . . . . . . | 20 | 15 |
|   Step 2 . . . . . . . . . . . . . . . . . . . . . . . . . . . . . . . . . . . . . . . . | Angle-tighten a further 90° | |
| Clutch pressure plate/driveplate mounting bolts* | | |
|   Step 1 . . . . . . . . . . . . . . . . . . . . . . . . . . . . . . . . . . . . . . . . | 60 | 44 |
|   Step 2 . . . . . . . . . . . . . . . . . . . . . . . . . . . . . . . . . . . . . . . . | Angle-tighten a further 90° | |
| Crankcase breather/oil separator bolts . . . . . . . . . . . . . . . . . . . . . . | 10 | 7 |
| Crankshaft left-hand oil seal housing bolts . . . . . . . . . . . . . . . . . . . | 10 | 7 |
| Crankshaft pulley/sprocket bolt* | | |
|   Old type (without drilled head) | | |
|     Step 1 . . . . . . . . . . . . . . . . . . . . . . . . . . . . . . . . . . . . . . . . | 90 | 66 |
|     Step 2 . . . . . . . . . . . . . . . . . . . . . . . . . . . . . . . . . . . . . . . . | Angle-tighten a further 90° | |
|   New type (with drilled head) | | |
|     Step 1 . . . . . . . . . . . . . . . . . . . . . . . . . . . . . . . . . . . . . . . . | 150 | 111 |
|     Step 2 . . . . . . . . . . . . . . . . . . . . . . . . . . . . . . . . . . . . . . . . | Angle-tighten a further 180° | |
| Cylinder head bolts* | | |
|   Step 1 . . . . . . . . . . . . . . . . . . . . . . . . . . . . . . . . . . . . . . . . | 30 | 22 |
|   Step 2 . . . . . . . . . . . . . . . . . . . . . . . . . . . . . . . . . . . . . . . . | Angle-tighten a further 90° | |
|   Step 3 . . . . . . . . . . . . . . . . . . . . . . . . . . . . . . . . . . . . . . . . | Angle-tighten a further 90° | |
| Engine-to-automatic transmission bolts | | |
|   M12 bolts . . . . . . . . . . . . . . . . . . . . . . . . . . . . . . . . . . . . . . . | 80 | 59 |
|   M10 cylinder block-to-transmission bolts . . . . . . . . . . . . . . . . . . . . | 60 | 44 |
|   M10 sump-to-transmission bolts . . . . . . . . . . . . . . . . . . . . . . . . . | 25 | 18 |
| Engine-to-manual transmission bolts | | |
|   M10 bolts . . . . . . . . . . . . . . . . . . . . . . . . . . . . . . . . . . . . . . . | 40 | 30 |
|   M12 bolts . . . . . . . . . . . . . . . . . . . . . . . . . . . . . . . . . . . . . . . | 80 | 59 |
| Engine-to-manual transmission cover plate bolts . . . . . . . . . . . . . . | 10 | 7 |
| Engine mountings | | |
|   Left-hand mounting-to-body bolts | | |
|     Large bolts* | | |
|       Step 1 . . . . . . . . . . . . . . . . . . . . . . . . . . . . . . . . . . . . . . . . | 40 | 30 |
|       Step 2 . . . . . . . . . . . . . . . . . . . . . . . . . . . . . . . . . . . . . . . . | Angle-tighten a further 90° | |
|     Small bolts . . . . . . . . . . . . . . . . . . . . . . . . . . . . . . . . . . . . . . . | 25 | 18 |
|   Left-hand mounting-to-engine bracket bolts . . . . . . . . . . . . . . . . | 100 | 74 |
|   Right-hand mounting-to-body bolts* | | |
|     Step 1 . . . . . . . . . . . . . . . . . . . . . . . . . . . . . . . . . . . . . . . . | 40 | 30 |
|     Step 2 . . . . . . . . . . . . . . . . . . . . . . . . . . . . . . . . . . . . . . . . | Angle-tighten a further 90° | |
|   Right-hand mounting plate bolts (small bolts) . . . . . . . . . . . . . . . | 25 | 18 |
|   Right-hand mounting-to-engine bracket bolts . . . . . . . . . . . . . . . | 100 | 74 |
|   Right-hand mounting bracket-to-engine bolts . . . . . . . . . . . . . . . | 50 | 37 |
|   Rear engine/transmission mounting | | |
|     Bracket-to-subframe bolts* | | |
|       Step 1 . . . . . . . . . . . . . . . . . . . . . . . . . . . . . . . . . . . . . . . . | 20 | 15 |
|       Step 2 . . . . . . . . . . . . . . . . . . . . . . . . . . . . . . . . . . . . . . . . | Angle-tighten a further 90° | |
|     Bracket-to-transmission bolts* | | |
|       Step 1 . . . . . . . . . . . . . . . . . . . . . . . . . . . . . . . . . . . . . . . . | 40 | 30 |
|       Step 2 . . . . . . . . . . . . . . . . . . . . . . . . . . . . . . . . . . . . . . . . | Angle-tighten a further 90° | |
| Exhaust manifold nuts . . . . . . . . . . . . . . . . . . . . . . . . . . . . . . . . . | 25 | 18 |
| Exhaust pipe-to-manifold nuts . . . . . . . . . . . . . . . . . . . . . . . . . . . | 40 | 30 |
| Oil cooler securing nut . . . . . . . . . . . . . . . . . . . . . . . . . . . . . . . . . | 25 | 18 |
| Oil drain plug . . . . . . . . . . . . . . . . . . . . . . . . . . . . . . . . . . . . . . . | 30 | 22 |
| Oil level/temperature sender-to-sump bolts . . . . . . . . . . . . . . . . . . | 10 | 7 |
| Oil pick-up pipe securing bolts . . . . . . . . . . . . . . . . . . . . . . . . . . . | 10 | 7 |

## Torque wrench settings (continued)

| | Nm | Ft-lbs |
|---|---|---|
| Oil pressure warning light switch | 25 | 18 |
| Oil pump securing bolts* | 12 | 9 |
| Sump | | |
| Sump-to-cylinder block bolts | 13 | 10 |
| Sump-to-transmission bolts | 45 | 33 |
| Timing belt idler pulley bolt | 50 | 37 |
| Timing belt outer cover bolts | | |
| Small bolts | 10 | 7 |
| Large bolts | 20 | 15 |
| Timing belt rear cover bolts | | |
| Small bolts | 10 | 7 |
| Large bolt (water pump bolts) | 20 | 15 |
| Timing belt tensioner | | |
| Main timing belt tensioner bolt | 20 | 15 |
| Secondary timing belt tensioner bolt | 20 | 15 |
| Water pump bolts | 20 | 15 |

**\* Note:** *Use new bolts*

## 1 General information

### How to use this Chapter

This Part of Chapter 2 describes those repair procedures that can reasonably be carried out on the engine while it remains in the vehicle. If the engine has been removed from the vehicle and is being dismantled as described in Part D, any preliminary dismantling procedures can be ignored.

Note that while it may be possible physically to overhaul certain items while the engine is in the vehicle, such tasks are not usually carried out as separate operations, and usually require the execution of several additional procedures (not to mention the cleaning of components and of oilways); for this reason, all such tasks are classed as major overhaul procedures, and are described in Part D of this Chapter.

*Caution: The crankshaft must not be removed on these engines – just loosening and retightening the main bearing bolts will render the cylinder block unserviceable. If the crankshaft or bearings are excessively worn or damaged, the complete cylinder block must be renewed.*

### Engine description

The engines are water-cooled, double overhead camshaft, in-line four-cylinder units. All engines have an aluminium-alloy cylinder head and block. All engines are mounted transversely at the front of the vehicle, with the transmission bolted to the left-hand end of the engine.

The crankshaft is of five-bearing type, and thrustwashers are fitted to the centre main bearing to control crankshaft endfloat.

The crankshaft and main bearings are matched to the alloy cylinder block, and it is not possible to reassemble the crankshaft and

cylinder block once the components have been separated. If the crankshaft or bearings are worn, the complete cylinder block/crankshaft assembly must be renewed.

The inlet camshaft is driven by a toothed belt from the crankshaft sprocket, and the exhaust camshaft is driven from the inlet camshaft by a second toothed belt. The camshafts are located in a camshaft carrier, which is bolted to the top of the cylinder head.

The valves are closed by coil springs, and run in guides pressed into the cylinder head. The camshafts actuate the valves by roller rockers and hydraulic tappets. There are four valves per cylinder; two inlet valves and two exhaust valves.

The oil pump is driven directly from the front of the crankshaft. Oil is drawn from the sump through a strainer, and then forced through an externally-mounted, renewable filter. From there, it is distributed to the cylinder head, where it lubricates the camshaft journals and hydraulic tappets, and also to the crankcase, where it lubricates the main bearings, connecting rod big-ends, gudgeon pins and cylinder bores. A coolant-fed oil cooler is fitted to most engines.

On all engines, engine coolant is circulated by a pump, driven by the main timing belt. For details of the cooling system, refer to Chapter 3.

### Operations with engine in car

The following operations can be performed without removing the engine:
a) Compression pressure – testing.
b) Camshaft carrier – removal and refitting.
c) Crankshaft pulley – removal and refitting.
d) Timing belt covers – removal and refitting.
e) Timing belt – removal, refitting and adjustment.
f) Timing belt tensioner and sprockets – removal and refitting.
g) Inlet camshaft timing belt, sprockets and tensioner – removal and refitting.
h) Inlet camshaft adjuster mechanism – removal and refitting.
i) Camshaft oil seals – renewal.

j) Camshafts and hydraulic tappets – removal, inspection and refitting.
k) Cylinder head – removal and refitting.
l) Cylinder head and pistons – decarbonising.
m) Sump – removal and refitting.
n) Oil pump – removal, overhaul and refitting.
o) Crankshaft oil seals – renewal.
p) Engine/transmission mountings – inspection and renewal.
q) Flywheel – removal, inspection and refitting.

**Note:** *It is possible to remove the pistons and connecting rods (after removing the cylinder head and sump) without removing the engine. However, this is not recommended. Work of this nature is more easily and thoroughly completed with the engine on the bench, as described in Chapter 2D.*

## 2 Compression test – description and interpretation

**Note:** *A suitable compression tester will be required for this test. See also Chapter 2D.*
*Caution: The following work may insert fault codes in the engine management ECU. These fault codes must be cleared by a VW dealer.*

1 When engine performance is down, or if misfiring occurs which cannot be attributed to the ignition or fuel systems, a compression test can provide diagnostic clues as to the engine's condition. If the test is performed regularly, it can give warning of trouble before any other symptoms become apparent.

2 The engine must be fully warmed-up to normal operating temperature, the battery must be fully-charged and the spark plugs must be removed. The aid of an assistant will be required.

3 Disable the ignition and fuel injectors by removing fuses SB6 and SB29 from the fusebox.

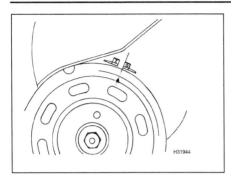

**3.4a Crankshaft pulley timing mark aligned with TDC mark on timing belt cover**

**3.4b Timing mark scribed on inner flange of pulley aligned with TDC mark on timing belt cover**

**3.5 Crankshaft sprocket tooth with chamfered edge aligns with cast arrow on oil pump**

4 Fit a compression tester to the No 1 cylinder spark plug hole. The type of tester that screws into the plug thread is preferred.

5 Have the assistant hold the throttle wide open and crank the engine for several seconds on the starter motor. **Note:** *The throttle will not operate until the ignition is switched on.* After one or two revolutions, the compression pressure should build-up to a maximum figure and then stabilise. Record the highest reading obtained.

6 Repeat the test on the remaining cylinders, recording the pressure in each.

7 All cylinders should produce very similar pressures. Any difference greater than that specified indicates the existence of a fault. Note that the compression should build-up quickly in a healthy engine. Low compression on the first stroke, followed by gradually increasing pressure on successive strokes, indicates worn piston rings. A low compression reading on the first stroke, which does not build-up during successive strokes, indicates leaking valves or a blown head gasket (a cracked head could also be the cause). Deposits on the undersides of the valve heads can also cause low compression.

8 If the pressure in any cylinder is reduced to the specified minimum or less, carry out the following test to isolate the cause. Introduce a teaspoonful of clean oil into that cylinder through its spark plug hole and repeat the test.

9 If the addition of oil temporarily improves the compression pressure, this indicates that bore or piston wear is responsible for the pressure loss. No improvement suggests that leaking or burnt valves, or a blown head gasket, may be to blame.

10 A low reading from two adjacent cylinders is almost certainly due to the head gasket having blown between them and the presence of coolant in the engine oil will confirm this.

11 If one cylinder is about 20 percent lower than the others and the engine has a slightly rough idle, a worn camshaft lobe could be the cause.

12 If the compression reading is unusually high, the combustion chambers are probably coated with carbon deposits. If this is the case, the cylinder head should be removed and decarbonised.

13 On completion of the test, refit the spark plugs and the fuses.

14 Have any fault codes cleared by a VW dealer.

## 3 Engine assembly and valve timing marks – general information and usage

### General information

1 TDC is the highest point in the cylinder that each piston reaches as it travels up-and-down when the crankshaft turns. Each piston reaches TDC at the end of the compression stroke and again at the end of the exhaust stroke, but TDC generally refers to piston position on the compression stroke. No 1 piston is at the timing belt end of the engine.

2 Positioning No 1 piston at TDC is an essential part of many procedures, such as timing belt removal and camshaft removal.

3 The design of the engines covered in this Chapter is such that piston-to-valve contact may occur if the camshaft or crankshaft is turned with the timing belt removed. For this reason, it is important to ensure that the camshaft and crankshaft do not move in relation to each other once the timing belt has been removed from the engine.

4 The crankshaft pulley has a marking which, when aligned with a corresponding reference marking on the timing belt cover, indicates that No 1 piston (and hence also No 4 piston) is at TDC. Note that on some models, the crankshaft pulley timing mark is located on the outer flange of the pulley. In order to make alignment of the timing marks easier, it is advisable to remove the pulley (see Section 4) and, using a set-square, scribe a corresponding mark on the inner flange of the pulley **(see illustrations)**.

5 There is also a timing mark which can be used with the crankshaft sprocket – this is useful if the crankshaft pulley and timing belt have been removed. When No 1 piston is at TDC, the crankshaft sprocket tooth with the chamfered inner edge aligns with a cast arrow on the oil pump **(see illustration)**.

6 The camshaft sprockets are equipped with TDC positioning holes. When the positioning holes are aligned with the corresponding holes in the camshaft carrier, No 1 piston is at TDC on the compression stroke **(see illustration)**.

7 Additionally, the flywheel/driveplate has a TDC marking, which can be observed by

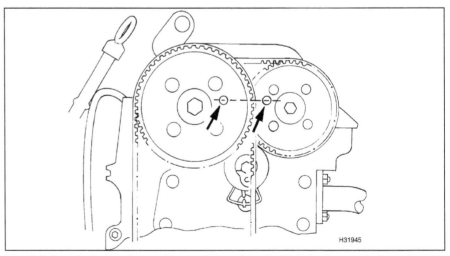

**3.6 Camshaft sprocket positioning holes aligned with holes in camshaft carrier (No 1 piston at TDC)**

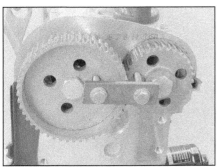

**3.16 Improvised tool used to lock camshaft sprockets in position at TDC (viewed with engine removed, and timing belt removed from engine)**

unscrewing a protective plastic cover from the transmission bellhousing. The mark takes the form of a notch in the edge of the flywheel on manual transmission models, or an O marking on automatic transmission models. Note that it is not possible to use these marks on all models due to the limited access available to view the marks.

### Setting No 1 cylinder to TDC

**Note:** *Suitable locking pins will be required to lock the camshaft sprockets in position during this procedure. On some engines, it may be necessary to use a small mirror to view the timing marks from under the wheel arch.*

**8** Before starting work, make sure that the ignition and all electrical consumers are switched off.
**9** Remove the engine top cover, and remove the air cleaner assembly as described in Chapter 4A.
**10** If desired, to make the engine easier to turn, remove all of the spark plugs as described in Chapter 1.
**11** Apply the handbrake, then jack up the front of the vehicle and support on axle stands (see *Jacking and towing*). Remove the right-hand front roadwheel, then remove the securing screws and/or clips, and remove the appropriate engine undershields and wheel arch liner to enable access to the crankshaft pulley.
**12** Remove the upper timing belt cover as described in Section 5.
**13** Turn the engine clockwise, using a spanner

on the crankshaft pulley bolt, until the TDC mark on the crankshaft pulley or flywheel/driveplate is aligned with the corresponding mark on the timing belt cover or transmission casing, and the locking pin holes in the camshaft sprockets are aligned with the corresponding holes in the camshaft carrier.
**14** If necessary, to give sufficient clearance for the camshaft locking tool to be engaged with the camshaft sprockets, unbolt the air cleaner support bracket from the engine mounting.
**15** A suitable tool will now be required to lock the camshaft sprockets in the TDC position. A special VW tool is available for this purpose, but a suitable tool can be improvised using two M8 bolts and nuts, and a short length of steel bar. With the camshaft sprocket positioned as described in Step 13, measure the distance between the locking pin hole centres, and drill two corresponding 8 mm clearance holes in the length of steel bar. Slide the M8 bolts through the holes in the bar, and secure them using the nuts.
**16** Slide the tool into position in the holes in the camshaft sprockets, ensuring that the pins (or bolts) engage with the holes in the camshaft carrier **(see illustration)**. The engine is now locked in position, with No 1 piston at TDC on the firing stroke.

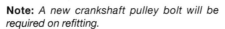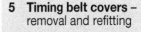

### 4 Crankshaft pulley – removal and refitting

**Note:** *A new crankshaft pulley bolt will be required on refitting.*

### Removal

**1** Switch off the ignition and all electrical consumers and remove the ignition key.
**2** For improved access, jack up the front of the vehicle, and support securely on axle stands (see *Jacking and towing*). Remove the right-hand front roadwheel.
**3** Remove the securing screws and/or release the clips, and withdraw the relevant engine undershield and wheel arch liner to enable access to the crankshaft pulley.
**4** If necessary (for any later work to be carried out), turn the crankshaft using a socket or

spanner on the crankshaft pulley bolt, until the relevant timing marks align (see Section 3).
**5** Remove the auxiliary drivebelt, as described in Chapter 1.
**6** To prevent the crankshaft from turning as the pulley bolt is slackened, a suitable tool can be used. Engage the tool with two of the slots in the pulley **(see illustration)**.
**7** Counterhold the pulley, and slacken the pulley bolt (take care – the bolt is very tight) using a socket and a suitable extension.
**8** Unscrew the bolt, and remove the pulley **(see illustration)**.
**9** Refit the crankshaft pulley securing bolt, with a spacer washer positioned under its head, to retain the crankshaft sprocket.

### Refitting

**10** Unscrew the crankshaft pulley/sprocket bolt used to retain the sprocket, and remove the spacer washer, then refit the pulley to the sprocket. Ensure that the locating pin on the sprocket engages with the corresponding hole in the pulley.
**11** Oil the threads of the new crankshaft pulley bolt. Prevent the crankshaft from turning as during removal, then fit the new pulley securing bolt, and tighten it to the specified torque, in the two Steps given in the Specifications.
**12** Refit and tension the auxiliary drivebelt as described in Chapter 1.
**13** Refit the engine undershield and wheel arch liner.
**14** Refit the roadwheel and lower the vehicle to the ground.

### 5 Timing belt covers – removal and refitting

### Upper outer cover

**1** Remove the air cleaner assembly as described in Chapter 4A.
**2** Release the two securing clips, and lift the cover from the engine **(see illustration)**.
**3** Refitting is a reversal of removal.

### Lower outer cover

**4** Remove the crankshaft pulley, as described in Section 4.

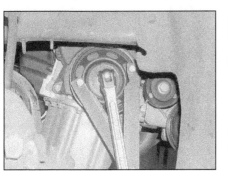

**4.6 Counterhold the crankshaft pulley using a tool similar to that shown**

**4.8 Removing the crankshaft pulley**

**5.2 Removing the upper outer timing belt cover**

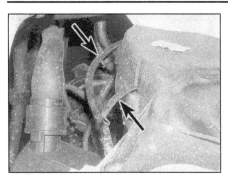

5.5a Release the two securing clips . . .

5.5b . . . then unscrew the two lower securing bolts . . .

5.5c . . . and the single bolt securing the cover to the engine mounting bracket . . .

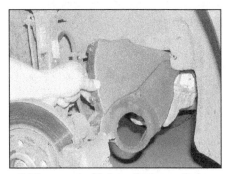

5.5d . . . and withdraw the lower timing belt cover

**6 Timing belt(s) –** removal and refitting

5 Release the two cover securing clips, located at the rear of the engine, then unscrew the two lower securing bolts, and the single bolt securing the cover to the engine mounting bracket. Withdraw the cover downwards from the engine **(see illustrations)**.
6 Refitting is a reversal of removal, but refit the crankshaft pulley with reference to Section 4.

### *Rear timing belt cover*

**Note:** *As the rear timing belt cover securing bolts also secure the water pump, it is advisable to drain the cooling system (see Chapter 1) before starting this procedure, and to renew the water pump seal/gasket (see*

5.8 Removing the idler pulley/bracket assembly (viewed with engine removed)

*Chapter 3) before refitting the cover. Refill the cooling system with reference to Chapter 1.*
7 Remove the timing belt as described in Section 6.
8 Unbolt the timing belt idler pulley/bracket assembly **(see illustration)**.
9 Unscrew the rear timing belt cover securing bolt located next to the right-hand engine lifting eye **(see illustration)**.
10 Unscrew the two securing bolts, and remove the rear timing belt cover. Note that the bolts also secure the water pump **(see illustration)**.
11 Refitting is a reversal of removal, but tighten the timing belt idler pulley/bracket bolt to the specified torque, and refit the timing belt as described in Section 6.

## *Main timing belt*

### Removal

1 The engine in this Chapter has two timing belts; the main timing belt drives the inlet camshaft from the crankshaft, and the secondary timing belt drives the exhaust camshaft from the inlet camshaft.
2 Switch off the ignition and all electrical consumers and remove the ignition key.
3 Remove the air cleaner assembly as described in Chapter 4A.
4 Release the two securing clips and remove the upper outer timing belt cover.
5 Turn the crankshaft to position No 1 piston at TDC on the firing stroke, and lock the camshaft sprockets in position, as described in Section 3.
6 Remove the crankshaft pulley as described in Section 4. Refit the crankshaft pulley securing bolt, with a spacer washer positioned under its head, to retain the crankshaft sprocket.
7 Remove the lower outer timing belt cover, as described in Section 5.
8 Where applicable, on models with air conditioning, unscrew the securing bolt, and remove the auxiliary drivebelt idler pulley.
9 Similarly, unscrew the two securing screws,

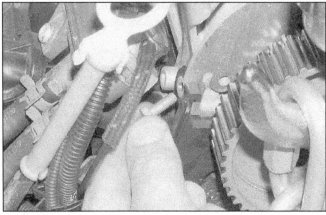

5.9 Unscrew the rear timing belt cover securing bolt located next to the right-hand engine lifting eye

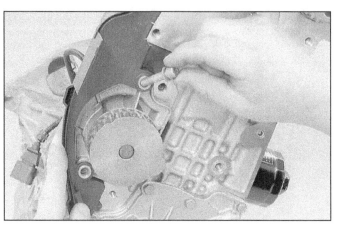

5.10 Removing the rear timing belt cover (viewed with engine removed)

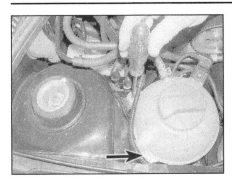

6.9a Unscrew the securing screws . . .

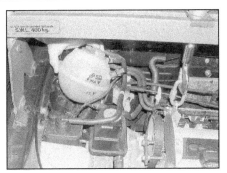

6.9b . . . and move the coolant expansion tank clear of the working area

6.14 Slacken the tensioner bolt and lever the tensioner anti-clockwise using an Allen key, then retighten the tensioner bolt

and move the coolant expansion tank clear of the working area **(see illustrations)**.

**10** Attach a hoist and lifting tackle to the right-hand (timing belt end) engine lifting bracket, and raise the hoist to just take the weight of the engine.

**11** Remove the complete right-hand engine mounting assembly, as described in Section 17.

**12** Unscrew the four securing bolts, and remove the right-hand engine mounting bracket from the engine.

**13** If either of the timing belts are to be refitted, mark their running directions to ensure correct refitting.

**14** Engage a suitable Allen key with the hole in the main timing belt tensioner plate, then slacken the tensioner bolt, lever the tensioner anti-clockwise using the Allen key (to release the tension on the belt), and retighten the tensioner bolt **(see illustration)**.

**15** Temporarily remove the camshaft sprocket locking tool, then slide the main timing belt from the sprockets, noting its routing **(see illustration)**. Refit the camshaft sprocket locking tool once the timing belt has been removed.

**16** Turn the crankshaft a quarter-turn (90°) anti-clockwise to position Nos 1 and 4 pistons slightly down their bores from the TDC position. This will eliminate any risk of piston-to-valve contact if a camshaft is turned whilst the timing belt is removed.

**Refitting**

**17** Where applicable, reposition the crankshaft

at TDC (see Step 20) and ensure that the secondary drivebelt has been refitted and tensioned. Temporarily remove the camshaft sprocket locking tool, and fit the main timing belt around the sprockets. Work in an anti-clockwise direction, starting at the water pump, followed by the tensioner roller, crankshaft sprocket, idler roller, inlet camshaft sprocket and the second idler roller. If the original belt is being refitted, observe the running direction markings. Once the belt has been refitted, refit the camshaft sprocket locking tool.

**18** Ensure that the tensioner bolt is slack, then engage an Allen key with the hole in the tensioner plate, and turn the plate clockwise until the tension indicator pointer is aligned with the centre of the cut-out in the backplate. Tighten the tensioner securing bolt to the specified torque.

**19** Remove the camshaft sprocket locking tool.

**20** Using a spanner or socket on the crankshaft pulley bolt, turn the engine through two complete turns in the normal direction of rotation, until the crankshaft sprocket tooth with the chamfered inner edge is aligned with the corresponding mark on the oil pump housing. Check that the locking tool can again be fitted to lock the camshaft sprockets in position – if not, one or both of the timing belts may have been incorrectly fitted.

**21** With the crankshaft timing marks aligned, and the camshaft sprockets locked in position, check the tension of the timing belts. The secondary and main tension indicators

should be positioned as described in Steps 38 and 18 respectively – if not, repeat the appropriate tensioning procedure, then recheck the tension.

**22** When the belt tension is correct, refit the right-hand engine mounting bracket, and tighten the securing bolts to the specified torque.

**23** Refit the complete right-hand engine mounting assembly, as described in Section 17.

**24** Disconnect the hoist and lifting tackle from the engine lifting bracket.

**25** Refit the coolant reservoir.

**26** Where applicable, refit the auxiliary drivebelt idler pulley.

**27** Refit the lower outer timing belt cover, with reference to Section 5 if necessary.

**28** Refit the crankshaft pulley as described in Section 4.

**29** Refit the upper outer timing belt cover.

**30** Refit the air cleaner assembly then refit the engine top cover.

### *Inlet camshaft timing belt*
#### Removal

**31** Once the main timing belt has been removed, to remove the secondary timing belt, proceed as follows.

**32** Engage a suitable Allen key with the hole in the secondary timing belt tensioner plate, then slacken the tensioner bolt, and lever the tensioner clockwise using the Allen key (to release the tension on the belt). Unscrew the securing bolt, and remove the secondary timing belt tensioner **(see illustrations)**.

6.15 Removing the main timing belt

6.32a Slacken the secondary timing belt tensioner bolt, and lever the tensioner clockwise using an Allen key . . .

6.32b . . . then unscrew the securing bolt and remove the tensioner

6.33 Removing the secondary timing belt

6.34 Crankshaft sprocket tooth with chamfered edge aligned with cast arrow on oil pump

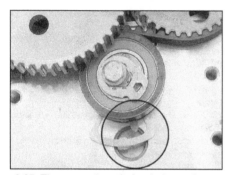

6.37 The secondary timing belt tensioner pointer should be positioned on the far right of the tensioner backplate, and the lug on the backplate should be engaged with the core plug hole

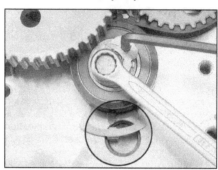

6.38 Turn the tensioner anti-clockwise until the tensioner pointer aligns with the lug on the tensioner backplate, with the lug positioned against the left-hand stop in the core plug hole

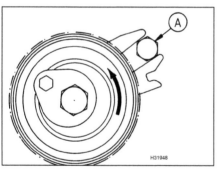

7.3 Turn the tensioner anti-clockwise to the position shown before fitting. Note that the cut-out engages with the bolt (A) on the cylinder block when fitting

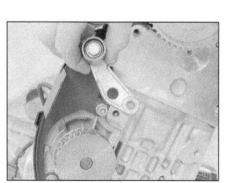

7.8a Removing the smaller . . .

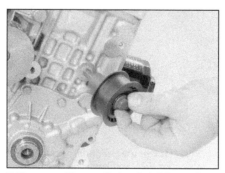

7.8b . . . and larger timing belt idler pulleys

33 Temporarily remove the camshaft sprocket locking tool, and slide the secondary timing belt from the sprockets (see illustration). Refit the sprocket locking tool once the belt has been removed.

### Refitting

34 Check that the camshaft sprockets are still locked in position by the locking pins, then turn the crankshaft a quarter-turn (90°) clockwise to reposition Nos 1 and 4 pistons at TDC. Ensure that the crankshaft sprocket tooth with the chamfered inner edge is aligned with the corresponding mark on the oil pump housing (see illustration).

35 Temporarily remove the camshaft sprocket locking tool, and fit the secondary timing belt around the camshaft sprockets.

Make sure that the belt is as tight as possible on its top run between the sprockets (but note that there will be some slack in the belt). If the original belt is being refitted, observe the running direction markings. Refit the camshaft sprocket locking tool once the belt has been fitted to the sprockets.

36 Check that the secondary timing belt tensioner pointer is positioned on the far right of the tensioner backplate.

37 Press the secondary timing belt up using the tensioner, and fit the tensioner securing bolt (if necessary turn the tensioner with an Allen key until the bolt hole in the tensioner aligns with the bolt hole in the cylinder head). Make sure that the lug on the tensioner backplate engages with the core plug hole in the cylinder head (see illustration).

38 Use the Allen key to turn the tensioner anti-clockwise until the tensioner pointer aligns with the lug on the tensioner backplate, with the lug positioned against the left-hand stop in the core plug hole (see illustration). Tighten the tensioner bolt to the specified torque.

## 7 Timing belt tensioner and sprockets – removal and refitting

### Main timing belt tensioner

1 Remove the main timing belt as described in Section 6.

2 Unscrew the main timing belt tensioner bolt, and remove the tensioner from the engine.

3 Engage an Allen key with the hole in the tensioner plate, and turn the tensioner anti-clockwise to the position shown (see illustration).

4 Refit the tensioner to the engine, ensuring that the cut-out in the tensioner backplate engages with the bolt on the cylinder block. Refit the tensioner securing bolt, and tighten by hand.

5 Refit and tension the main timing belt as described in Section 6.

### Inlet camshaft timing belt tensioner

6 Removal and refitting of the tensioner is described as part of the timing belt removal procedure in Section 6.

### Main timing belt idler pulleys

7 Remove the timing belt as described in Section 6.

8 Unscrew the securing bolt and remove the relevant idler pulley. Note that the smaller pulley (the idler pulley nearest the inlet manifold side of the engine) can be removed complete with its mounting bracket (unbolt the mounting bracket bolt, leaving the pulley attached to the bracket) (see illustrations).

9 Refit the relevant idler pulley and tighten the securing bolt to the specified torque. Note

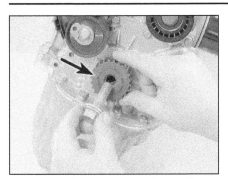

**7.13 Refitting the crankshaft sprocket. Pulley locating pin must be outermost**

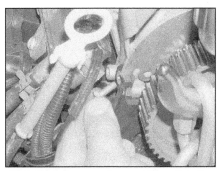

**7.18 Refit the sprocket, ensuring that the lug (1) on the sprocket engages with the notch (2) in the end of the camshaft**

**7.19 Tighten the sprocket securing bolt using a suitable tool to hold the sprocket stationary**

that if the smaller idler pulley has been removed complete with its bracket, ensure that the bracket locates over the rear timing belt cover bolt on refitting.

10 Refit and tension the main timing belt as described in Section 6.

### Crankshaft sprocket

11 Remove the main timing belt as described in Section 6.

12 Unscrew the crankshaft pulley bolt, and the washer used to retain the sprocket, and withdraw the sprocket from the crankshaft.

13 Commence refitting by positioning the sprocket on the end of the crankshaft, noting that the pulley locating pin must be outermost **(see illustration)**. Temporarily refit the pulley securing bolt and washer to retain the sprocket.

14 Refit the main timing belt as described in Section 6.

### Camshaft sprockets

**Note:** *A new camshaft sprocket securing bolt must be used on refitting.*

15 Remove the main and secondary timing belts as described in Section 6. Ensure that the crankshaft has been turned a quarter-turn (90°) anti-clockwise to position Nos 1 and 4 pistons slightly down their bores from the TDC position. This will eliminate any risk of piston-to-valve contact if a camshaft is turned whilst the timing belt is removed.

16 The relevant camshaft sprocket bolt must now be slackened. The camshaft must be prevented from turning as the sprocket bolt is unscrewed – **do not** rely solely on the sprocket locking tool for this. To hold the sprocket, make up a tool and use it to hold the sprocket stationary by means of the holes in the sprocket.

17 Unscrew the camshaft sprocket bolt, and withdraw the sprocket from the end of the camshaft, noting which way round it is fitted.

18 Commence refitting by offering the sprocket up to the camshaft, ensuring that lug on the sprocket engages with the notch in the end of the camshaft. If both camshaft sprockets have been removed, note that the double sprocket (for the main and secondary timing belts) should be fitted to the inlet camshaft, and note that the exhaust camshaft sprocket must be fitted first **(see illustration)**.

19 Fit a new sprocket securing bolt, then use the tool to hold the sprocket stationary, as during removal, and tighten the bolt to the specified torque, in the two Steps given in the Specifications **(see illustration)**.

20 Refit the secondary and main timing belts as described in Section 6.

### Water pump sprocket

21 The water pump sprocket is integral with the water pump. Refer to Chapter 3 for details of water pump removal.

## 8 Camshaft carrier – removal and refitting

**Note:** *New camshaft carrier securing bolts must be used on refitting. Suitable sealant (VW AMV 188 003, or equivalent) will be required, and two M6 studs (approximately 70 mm long) will be required – see text.*

### Removal

1 Switch off the ignition and all electrical consumers and remove the ignition key.

2 Remove the main and secondary timing belts, as described in Section 6.

3 Remove the ignition HT coils as described in Chapter 5.

4 Unbolt the coil wiring earth lead from the top of the camshaft cover, then release the coil wiring from the clips on the camshaft cover, and move the wiring clear of the camshaft cover.

5 Disconnect the breather hose from the rear of the cylinder head.

6 Disconnect the inlet camshaft position sensor wiring connector **(see illustration)**.

7 Disconnect the wiring plug from the oil pressure warning light switch, located at the front left-hand corner of the camshaft carrier. Release the wiring harness from the clip on the end of the camshaft carrier, and move the wiring to one side **(see illustrations)**.

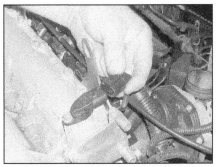

**8.6 Disconnect the wiring connector from the inlet camshaft position sensor**

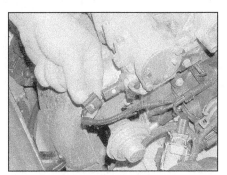

**8.7a Disconnect the oil pressure warning light switch wiring plug . . .**

**8.7b . . . then release the wiring from the clip on the end of the camshaft carrier**

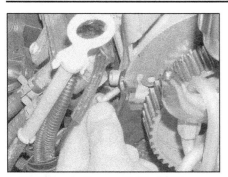

8.8 Remove the rear timing belt cover securing bolt located next to the right-hand engine lifting eye

8.9 Remove the camshaft carrier securing bolts . . .

8.10 . . . then lift the camshaft carrier from the cylinder head

8 Remove the rear timing belt cover securing bolt, located next to the right-hand engine lifting eye (see illustration).

9 Working progressively from the centre out, in a diagonal sequence, slacken and remove the camshaft carrier securing bolts (see illustration).

10 Carefully lift the camshaft carrier from the cylinder head (see illustration). The camshafts can be removed from the carrier, as described in Section 9.

### Refitting

11 Commence refitting by thoroughly cleaning all traces of old sealant, and all traces of oil and grease, from the mating faces of the cylinder head and camshaft carrier. Ensure that no debris enters the cylinder head or camshaft carrier.

12 Ensure that the crankshaft is still positioned a quarter-turn (90°) anti-clockwise from the TDC position, and that the camshafts are locked in position with the locking tool, as described in Section 3.

13 Check that the valve rockers are correctly located on the valves, and securely clipped into position on the hydraulic tappets.

14 Apply a thin, even coat of sealant (VW AMV 188 003, or equivalent) to the cylinder head mating face of the camshaft carrier (see illustration). Do not apply the sealant too thickly, as excess sealant may enter and block the oilways, causing engine damage.

15 Carefully lower the camshaft carrier onto the cylinder head, until the camshafts rest on the rockers. Note that the camshaft carrier locates on dowels in the cylinder head; if desired, to make fitting easier, two guide studs can be made up as follows:
  a) Cut the heads off two M6 bolts, then cut slots in the top of each bolt to enable the bolt to be unscrewed using a flat-bladed screwdriver.
  b) Screw one bolt into each of the camshaft carrier bolt locations at opposite corners of the cylinder head.
  c) Lower the camshaft carrier over the bolts to guide it into position on the cylinder head.

16 Fit new camshaft carrier securing bolts, and tighten them progressively, working from the centre out, in a diagonal sequence (ie, tighten all bolts through one turn, then tighten all bolts through a further turn, and so on). Ensure that the camshaft carrier sits squarely on the cylinder head as the bolts are tightened, and make sure that the carrier engages with the cylinder head dowels. Where applicable, once the camshaft carrier contacts the surface of the cylinder head, unscrew the two guide studs, and fit the two remaining new camshaft carrier securing bolts in their place.

17 Tighten the camshaft carrier securing bolts to the specified torque, in the two

Steps given in the Specifications (see illustration).

18 Leave the camshaft carrier sealant to dry for approximately 30 minutes before carrying out any further work on the cylinder head or camshaft carrier.

19 Once the sealant has been allowed to dry, refit the rear timing belt cover bolt.

20 Reconnect the oil pressure warning light switch wiring plug, and clip the wiring into position on the end of the camshaft carrier.

21 Reconnect the camshaft position sensor wiring connector.

22 Refit the ignition coils with reference to Chapter 5.

23 Refit the secondary and main timing belts, as described in Section 6.

### 9  Camshafts – removal, inspection and refitting

### Removal

1 Remove the camshaft carrier as described in Section 8.

2 Remove the camshaft sprockets, with reference to Section 7.

3 If the inlet camshaft is to be removed, unscrew the securing bolt, and remove the inlet camshaft position sensor (see illustration).

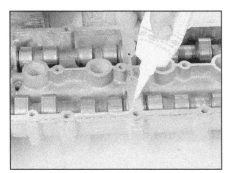

8.14 Apply a thin, even coat of sealant to the cylinder head mating face of the camshaft carrier

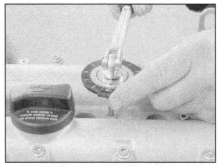

8.17 Tightening a camshaft carrier bolt through the specified Step 2 angle

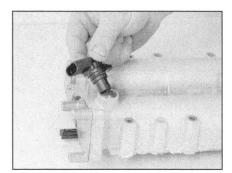

9.3 Remove the inlet camshaft position sensor

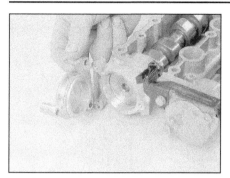

**9.4 Remove the camshaft carrier endplate**

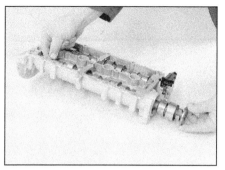

**9.5 Withdraw the camshaft from the endplate end of the camshaft carrier**

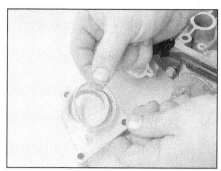

**9.10 Renew the camshaft carrier endplate O-ring**

**4** Remove the relevant camshaft carrier endplate **(see illustration)**.

**5** Carefully withdraw the relevant camshaft from the endplate end of the camshaft carrier, taking care not to damage the bearing surfaces of the camshaft and housing as the camshaft is withdrawn **(see illustration)**.

### Inspection

**6** Visually inspect the camshafts for evidence of wear on the surfaces of the lobes and journals. Normally their surfaces should be smooth and have a dull shine; look for scoring, erosion or pitting and areas that appear highly polished, indicating excessive wear. Accelerated wear will occur once the hardened exterior of the camshaft has been damaged, so always renew worn items. **Note:** *If these symptoms are visible on the tips of the camshaft lobes, check the corresponding rocker, as it will probably be worn as well.*

**7** If the machined surfaces of the camshaft appear discoloured or blued, it is likely that it has been overheated at some point, probably due to inadequate lubrication. This may have distorted the shaft, so check the run-out as follows: place the camshaft between two V-blocks and, using a DTI gauge, measure the run-out at the centre journal. No maximum run-out figure is quoted by the manufacturers, but it should be obvious if the camshaft is excessively distorted.

**8** To measure camshaft endfloat, temporarily refit the relevant camshaft to the camshaft carrier, and refit the endplate to the rear of the camshaft carrier. Anchor a DTI gauge to the timing belt end of the camshaft carrier and

align the gauge probe with the camshaft axis. Push the camshaft to one end of the camshaft carrier as far as it will travel, then rest the DTI gauge probe on the end of the camshaft, and zero the gauge display. Push the camshaft as far as it will go to the other end of the camshaft carrier, and record the gauge reading. Verify the reading by pushing the camshaft back to its original position and checking that the gauge indicates zero again.

**9** Check that the camshaft endfloat measurement is as listed in the Specifications. Wear outside of this limit may be cured by renewing the relevant camshaft carrier endplate, although wear is unlikely to be confined to any one component, so renewal of the camshafts and camshaft carrier must be considered.

### Refitting

**10** Refitting is a reversal of removal, bearing in mind the following points.

a) *Before refitting the camshaft, renew the camshaft oil seal, with reference to Section 11.*

b) *Lubricate the bearing surfaces in the camshaft carrier, and the camshaft lobes before refitting the camshaft(s).*

c) *Renew the sealing O-ring on each camshaft carrier endplate (see illustration).*

d) *Refit the camshaft sprocket(s) with reference to Section 7, noting that if both sprockets have been removed, the exhaust camshaft sprocket must be fitted first.*

e) *Refit the camshaft carrier as described in Section 8.*

## 10 Rockers and tappets – removal, inspection and refitting

### Removal

**1** Remove the camshaft carrier, as described in Section 8.

**2** As the components are removed, keep them in strict order, so that they can be refitted in their original locations.

**3** Unclip the rockers from the hydraulic tappets, and lift them from the cylinder head **(see illustration)**.

**4** Carefully lift the tappets from their bores in the cylinder head. It is advisable to store the tappets (in order) upright in an oil bath whilst they are removed from the engine.

### Inspection

**5** Check the cylinder head bore contact surfaces of the tappets for signs of scoring or damage. Similarly, check the tappet bores in the cylinder head for signs of scoring or damage. If significant scoring or damage is found, it may be necessary to renew the cylinder head and the complete set of tappets.

**6** Inspect the hydraulic tappets for obvious signs of wear or damage, and renew if necessary. Check that the oil holes in the tappets are free from obstructions.

**7** Check the valve, tappet, and camshaft contact faces of the rockers for wear or damage, and also check the rockers for any signs of cracking. Renew any worn or damaged rockers.

**8** Inspect the camshaft lobes, as described in Section 9.

### Refitting

**9** Oil the tappet bores in the cylinder head, and the tappets themselves, then carefully slide the tappets into their original bores **(see illustration)**.

**10** Oil the rocker contact faces of the tappets, and the tops of the valve stems, then refit the rockers to their original locations, ensuring that the rockers are securely clipped onto the tappets.

**11** Check the endfloat of each camshaft, as described in Section 9, then refit the camshaft carrier as described in Section 8.

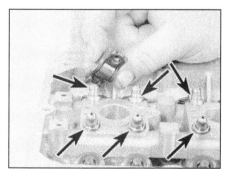

**10.3 Removing a rocker (hydraulic tappets arrowed)**

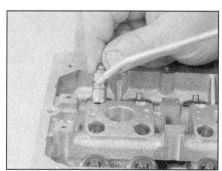

**10.9 Oil the tappets before fitting**

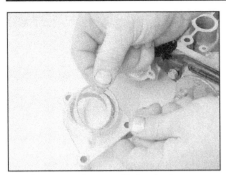

**11.12 Locate the new O-ring in the groove in the endplate**

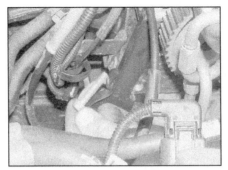

**12.4 Disconnect the radiator hoses from the coolant housing at the transmission end of the cylinder head**

**12.7 A suitable engine lifting bracket can be bolted to the cylinder block using a long bolt screwed into the hole located next to the water pump**

## 11 Camshaft oil seals – renewal

### Right-hand oil seals

**1** Remove the main and secondary timing belts as described in Section 6.

**2** Remove the relevant camshaft sprocket as described in Section 7.

**3** Drill two small holes into the existing oil seal, diagonally opposite each other. Take great care to avoid drilling through into the seal housing or camshaft sealing surface. Thread two self-tapping screws into the holes and, using a pair of pliers, pull on the heads of the screws to extract the oil seal.

**4** Clean out the seal housing and the sealing surface of the camshaft by wiping it with a lint-free cloth. Remove any swarf or burrs that may cause the seal to leak.

**5** Lubricate the lip and outer edge of the new oil seal with clean engine oil, and push it over the camshaft until it is positioned above its housing. To prevent damage to the sealing lips, wrap some adhesive tape around the end of the camshaft.

**6** Using a hammer and a socket of suitable diameter, drive the seal squarely into its housing. **Note:** *Select a socket that bears only on the hard outer surface of the seal, not the inner lip which can easily be damaged.*

**7** Refit the relevant camshaft sprocket with reference to Section 7.

**8** Refit and tension the secondary and main timing belts as described in Section 6.

### Left-hand oil seals

**9** The camshaft oil seals take the form of O-rings located in the grooves in the camshaft carrier endplates.

**10** Unscrew the securing bolts, and remove the relevant camshaft endplate.

**11** Prise the old O-ring from the groove in the endplate.

**12** Lightly oil the new O-ring, and carefully locate it in the groove in the endplate **(see illustration)**.

**13** Refit the endplate and tighten the bolts securely.

## 12 Cylinder head – removal, inspection and refitting

**Note:** *The cylinder head must be removed with the engine cold. New cylinder head bolts, a new cylinder head gasket, new inlet manifold O-rings, and a new exhaust manifold gasket will be required on refitting.*

### Removal

**1** Switch off the ignition and all electrical consumers and remove the ignition key.

**2** Drain the cooling system as described in Chapter 1.

**3** Remove the air cleaner assembly, complete with the air trunking, as described in Chapter 4A.

**4** Release the hose clips, and disconnect the two radiator hoses from the coolant housing at the transmission end of the cylinder head **(see illustration)**. Similarly, release the hose clips and disconnect the remaining three small coolant hoses from the rear of the coolant housing.

**5** Remove the main and secondary timing belts as described in Section 6.

**6** As the engine is currently supported using a hoist attached to the engine lifting brackets bolted to the cylinder head, it is now necessary to attach a suitable bracket to the cylinder block, so that the engine can still be supported as the cylinder head is removed.

**7** A suitable bracket can be bolted to the cylinder block using spacers, and a long bolt

screwed into the hole located next to the water pump **(see illustration)**. Ideally, attach a second set of lifting tackle to the hoist, adjust the lifting tackle to support the engine using the bracket attached to the cylinder block, then disconnect the lifting tackle attached to the bracket on the cylinder head. Alternatively, temporarily support the engine under the sump using a jack and a block of wood, then transfer the lifting tackle from the bracket on the cylinder head to the bracket bolted to the cylinder block.

**8** Remove the camshaft carrier, rockers and tappets, with reference to Sections 8 and 10.

**9** Unscrew the bolt securing the oil level dipstick tube bracket to the cylinder head, then lift the dipstick tube, and turn it to one side, to clear the working area **(see illustration)**. Release the wiring harnesses from the clip on the dipstick tube bracket. Note that the dipstick tube bracket bolt also secures the inlet manifold.

**10** Disconnect the fuel supply line located next to the coolant expansion tank. Squeeze the button to do this.

**11** Disconnect the hose from the charcoal canister to the inlet manifold.

**12** Disconnect the hose from the brake servo to the inlet manifold.

**13** Disconnect the wiring from the following:

a) *Knock sensor on the rear of the engine.*

b) *Inlet manifold pressure sender and air temperature sender.*

c) *Engine speed sender.*

d) *Coolant temperature sender **(see illustration)**.*

**12.9 Unscrew the bolt securing the oil level dipstick tube bracket to the cylinder head**

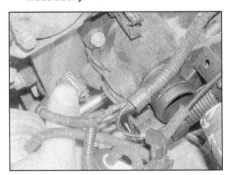

**12.13 Disconnect the coolant temperature sender wiring plug**

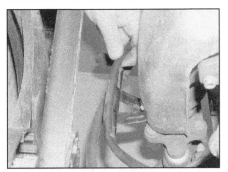

**12.14a  Unclip the wiring from the bracket on the exhaust heat shield . . .**

**12.14b  . . . then remove the heat shield**

**12.18  Lift the inlet manifold back from the engine**

e) *Oil pressure switch.*
f) *Throttle valve control module.*
g) *Injectors.*
h) *Heated vacuum valve on oil separator.*
i) *Crankcase breather on inlet manifold.*

**14** Unclip the wiring from the bracket attached to the exhaust heat shield, then unscrew the securing bolts (two upper bolts and one lower bolt), and remove the heat shield **(see illustrations)**.

**15** Disconnect the exhaust front section from the manifold. If desired, the exhaust manifold can be removed completely.

**16** Unscrew and remove the bolt securing the timing belt inner cover to the cylinder head (located near the right-hand engine lifting eye).

**17** Unbolt and remove the timing belt idler bracket.

**18** Unscrew the six securing bolts (three upper and three lower) and lift the inlet manifold back from the engine **(see illustration)**. Ensure that the inlet manifold is adequately supported in the engine compartment, and take care not to strain any wires, cables or hoses. Recover the O-rings if they are loose.

**19** Progressively slacken the cylinder head bolts in order, then unscrew and remove the bolts **(see illustrations)**.

**20** With all the bolts removed, lift the cylinder head from the block **(see illustration)**. If the

cylinder head is stuck, tap it with a soft-faced mallet to break the joint. **Do not** insert a lever into the gasket joint. As the cylinder head is lifted off, release the water pump pipe from the thermostat housing on the cylinder head.

**21** Lift the cylinder head gasket from the block.

### Inspection

**22** Dismantling and inspection of the cylinder head is covered in Part D of this Chapter. Additionally, check the condition of the water pump pipe-to-thermostat housing O-ring, and renew if necessary.

### Refitting

**23** The mating faces of the cylinder head and block must be perfectly clean before refitting the head. Use a scraper to remove all traces of gasket and carbon, also clean the tops of the pistons. Take particular care with the aluminium surfaces, as the soft metal is easily damaged. Make sure that debris is not allowed to enter the oil and water passages – this is particularly important for the oil circuit, as carbon could block the oil supply to the camshaft and crankshaft bearings. Using adhesive tape and paper, seal the water, oil and bolt holes in the cylinder block. To prevent carbon entering the gap between the pistons and bores, smear a little grease in the gap. After cleaning a piston, rotate the

crankshaft to that the piston moves down the bore, then wipe out the grease and carbon with a cloth rag. Clean the other piston crowns in the same way.

**24** Check the head and block for nicks, deep scratches and other damage. If slight, they may be removed carefully with a file. More serious damage may be repaired by machining, but this is a specialist job.

**25** If warpage of the cylinder head is suspected, use a straight-edge to check it for distortion, as described in Part D of this Chapter.

**26** Ensure that the cylinder head bolt holes in the crankcase are clean and free of oil. Syringe or soak up any oil left in the bolt holes. This is most important in order that the correct bolt tightening torque can be applied, and to prevent the possibility of the block being cracked by hydraulic pressure when the bolts are tightened.

**27** Ensure that the crankshaft has been turned to position Nos 1 and 4 pistons slightly down their bores from the TDC position (see Section 6). This will eliminate any risk of piston-to-valve contact as the cylinder head is refitted. Also ensure that the camshaft sprockets are locked in the TDC position using the locking tool, as described in Section 3.

**28** Ensure that the cylinder head locating dowels are in place in the cylinder block, then fit a new cylinder head gasket over the dowels, ensuring that the part number is uppermost. Where applicable, the OBEN/TOP

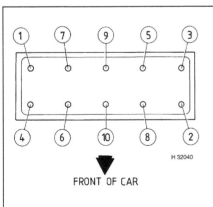

**12.19a  Cylinder head bolt slackening sequence**

FRONT OF CAR

H 32040

**12.19b  Slackening the cylinder head bolts**

**12.20  Removing the cylinder head**

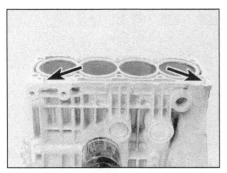

**12.28a  Ensure that the dowels are in place in the cylinder block**

**12.28b  Ensure that the part number and OBEN/TOP markings on the cylinder head gasket are uppermost**

marking should also be uppermost **(see illustrations)**. Note that VW recommend that the gasket is only removed from its packaging immediately prior to fitting.

**29** Lower the cylinder head into position on the gasket, ensuring that it engages correctly over the dowels. As the cylinder head is lowered into position, ensure that the water pump pipe engages with the thermostat housing (use a new O-ring if necessary).

**30** Fit the new cylinder head bolts, and screw them in as far as possible by hand.

**31** Working progressively, in sequence, tighten all the cylinder head bolts to the specified Step 1 torque **(see illustration)**.

**32** Again working progressively, in sequence, tighten all the cylinder head bolts through the specified Step 2 angle.

**33** Finally, tighten all the cylinder head bolts, in sequence, to the specified Step 3 angle.

**34** Reconnect the lifting tackle to the right-hand engine lifting bracket on the cylinder head, then adjust the lifting tackle to support the engine. Once the engine is adequately supported using the cylinder head bracket, disconnect the lifting tackle from the bracket bolted to the cylinder block, and unbolt the improvised engine lifting bracket from the cylinder block. Alternatively, remove the trolley jack and block of wood from under the sump.

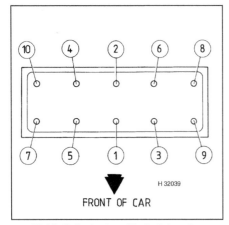

**12.31  Cylinder head bolt tightening sequence**

**35** Refit the rockers and tappets, and camshaft carrier as described in Sections 10 and 8.

**36** Further refitting is a reversal of removal, bearing in mind the following points.
  a) Renew gaskets and O-rings as required.
  b) Ensure that all wires, pipes and hoses are correctly reconnected and routed, as noted before removal.
  c) Tighten all fixings to the specified torque, where given.
  d) On completion, refill the cooling system as described in Chapter 1.

## 13  Sump – removal and refitting

**Note:** VW sealant (D 176 404 A2 or equivalent) will be required to seal the sump on refitting.

### Removal

**1** Apply the handbrake, then jack up the front of the vehicle and support securely on axle stands (see Jacking and towing).

**2** Remove the securing screws and withdraw the engine undershield(s).

**3** Detach the exhaust front pipe from the exhaust manifold and support to one side. Recover the gasket.

**4** Drain the engine oil as described in Chapter 1.

**5** Where fitted, disconnect the wiring connector from the oil level/temperature sender in the sump.

**6** Unscrew and remove the bolts securing the sump to the cylinder block, then withdraw the sump. If necessary, release the sump by tapping with a soft-faced hammer.

### Refitting

**7** Begin refitting by thoroughly cleaning the mating faces of the sump and cylinder block. Ensure that all traces of old sealant are removed.

**8** Ensure that the cylinder block mating face of the sump is free from all traces of old sealant, oil and grease, and then apply a 2.0 to 3.0 mm thick bead of silicone sealant (VW D 176 404 A2 or equivalent) to the sump. Note

that the sealant should be run around the inside of the bolt holes in the sump. The sump must be fitted within 5 minutes of applying the sealant.

**9** Offer the sump up to the cylinder block, then refit the sump-to-cylinder block bolts, and lightly tighten them by hand, working progressively in a diagonal sequence. **Note:** If the sump is being refitted with the engine and transmission separated, make sure that the sump is flush with the flywheel/driveplate end of the cylinder block. If necessary, temporarily screw two M6 studs into the block to act as guides.

**10** Refit the sump-to-block bolts, and tighten them lightly, using a socket.

**11** Working in a diagonal sequence, progressively tighten the sump-to-cylinder block bolts to the specified torque.

**12** Refit the exhaust front pipe together with a new gasket.

**13** Refit the wiring connector to the oil level/temperature sender (where fitted), then refit the engine undershield(s), and lower the vehicle to the ground.

**14** Allow at least 30 minutes from the time of refitting the sump for the sealant to dry, then refill the engine with oil, with reference to Chapter 1.

## 14  Oil pump – removal, inspection and refitting

**Note:** New oil pump securing bolts, a new oil pump gasket, a new oil pick-up pipe gasket, and a new crankshaft oil seal will be required on refitting.

### Removal

**1** Remove the main timing belt, as described in Section 6.

**2** Refit the crankshaft pulley securing bolt, with a spacer washer positioned under its head, to retain the crankshaft sprocket.

**3** Turn the crankshaft a quarter-turn (90°) clockwise to reposition Nos 1 and 4 pistons at TDC. Ensure that the crankshaft sprocket tooth with the chamfered inner edge is aligned with the corresponding mark on the oil pump housing (see Section 3).

**4** Turn the crankshaft to move the crankshaft sprocket three teeth anti-clockwise away from the TDC position. The third tooth to the right of the tooth with the ground down outer edge must align with the corresponding mark on the oil pump housing. This procedure positions the crankshaft with one of the polygon cams pointing upwards to enable correct oil pump refitting.

**5** Remove the main timing belt tensioner, as described in Section 7.

**6** Remove the sump as described in Section 13.

**7** Unscrew the securing bolts and remove the oil pick-up pipe from the oil pump and

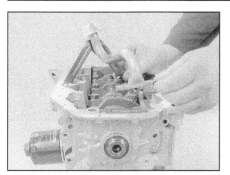

**14.7  Removing the oil pick-up pipe**

**14.9  Removing the oil pump**

**14.11  Lifting off the oil pump rear cover**

cylinder block **(see illustration)**. Recover the gasket.

**8** Remove the crankshaft sprocket, noting which way round it is fitted.

**9** Unscrew the securing bolts, noting their locations to ensure correct refitting, and remove the oil pump **(see illustration)**. Recover the gasket.

### Inspection

**10** No spare parts are available for the oil pump, and if worn or faulty, the complete pump must be renewed.

**11** To inspect the oil pump rotors, remove the securing screws, and lift off the oil pump rear cover **(see illustration)**.

**12** Note that the rotors fit with the punched dots on the edges of the rotors facing the oil pump cover **(see illustration)**.

**13** Lift out the rotors, and inspect them for

wear and damage. If there are any signs of wear or damage, the complete oil pump assembly must be renewed.

**14** Lubricate the contact faces of the rotors with clean engine oil, then refit the rotors to the pump, ensuring that the punched dots on the edges of the rotors face the pump cover.

**15** Refit the pump cover, and tighten the screws securely.

**16** Using a flat-bladed screwdriver, prise the crankshaft oil seal from the oil pump, and discard it **(see illustration)**.

**17** Thoroughly clean the oil seal seat in the oil pump.

**18** Press or drive a new oil seal into position in the oil pump, using a socket or tube of suitable diameter **(see illustration)**. Ensure that the seal seats squarely in the oil pump. Ensure that the socket or tube bears only on the hard outer ring of the seal, and take care

not to damage the seal lips. Press or drive the seal into position until it is seated on the shoulder in the housing. Make sure that the closed end of the seal is facing outwards.

### Refitting

**19** Commence refitting by cleaning all traces of old gasket and sealant from the mating faces of the cylinder block and oil pump.

**20** Wind a length of tape around the front of the crankshaft to protect the oil seal lips as the oil pump is slid into position.

**21** Fit a new oil pump gasket over the dowels in the cylinder block **(see illustration)**.

**22** Turn the inner oil pump rotor to align one of the drive cut-outs in the edge of the inner rotor with the line on the oil pump rear cover **(see illustration)**.

**23** Lightly oil the four tips of the oil pump drive cam on the end of the crankshaft.

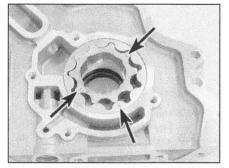

**14.12  Note that the rotors fit with the punched dots facing the oil pump cover**

**14.16  Prise the crankshaft oil seal from the oil pump**

**14.18  Driving a new oil seal into the oil pump using a socket**

**14.21  Fit a new gasket over the dowels in the cylinder block**

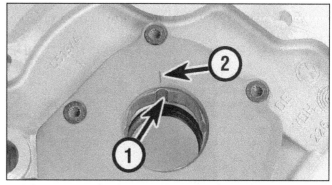

**14.22  Align one of the drive cut-outs (1) in the edge of the rotor with the line (2) on the oil pump rear cover**

**14.25 Slide the oil pump over the end of the crankshaft. Note the tape used to protect the oil seal**

**14.26 Fit the new oil pump securing bolts to the locations noted before removal**

**14.28 Fit a new oil pick-up pipe gasket**

**24** Coat the lips of the crankshaft oil seal with a thin film of clean engine oil.

**25** Slide the oil pump into position over the end of the crankshaft until it engages with the dowels, taking care not to damage the oil seal, and ensuring that the inner rotor engages with the drive cam on the crankshaft **(see illustration)**.

**26** Fit new oil pump securing bolts, to the locations noted before removal, and tighten them to the specified torque **(see illustration)**.

**27** Remove the tape from the end of the crankshaft, then refit the crankshaft sprocket, noting that the pulley locating pin must be outermost. Temporarily refit the securing bolt and washer to retain the sprocket.

**28** Refit the oil pick-up pipe, using a new gasket, and tighten the securing bolts to the specified torque **(see illustration)**.

**29** Refit the sump as described in Section 13.

**30** Refit the main timing belt tensioner as described in Section 7.

**31** Refit the main timing belt as described in Section 6.

### 15 Flywheel/driveplate – removal, inspection and refitting

**Note:** *New flywheel/driveplate securing bolts will be required on refitting.*

#### Removal

**1** On manual transmission models, remove the gearbox (see Chapter 7A) and clutch (see Chapter 8).

**2** On automatic transmission models, remove the automatic transmission as described in Chapter 7B.

**3** The flywheel/driveplate bolts are offset to ensure correct fitment. Unscrew the bolts while holding the flywheel/driveplate stationary. Temporarily insert a bolt in the cylinder block, and use a screwdriver to hold the flywheel/driveplate, or make up a holding tool.

**4** Lift the flywheel/driveplate from the crankshaft. If removing a driveplate, note the location of the shim (where applicable – between the driveplate and the crankshaft), and

the spacer under the securing bolts. Recover the engine-to-transmission plate if it is loose.

#### Inspection

**5** Check the flywheel/driveplate for wear and damage. Examine the starter ring gear for excessive wear to the teeth. If the driveplate or its ring gear are damaged, the complete driveplate must be renewed. The flywheel ring gear, however, may be renewed separately from the flywheel, but the work should be entrusted to a VW dealer. If the clutch friction face is discoloured or scored excessively, it may be possible to regrind it, but this work should also be entrusted to a VW dealer.

#### Refitting

**6** Refitting is a reversal of removal, bearing in mind the following points.

a) *Ensure that the engine-to-transmission plate is in place before fitting the flywheel/driveplate.*

b) *On automatic transmission models temporarily refit the driveplate using the old bolts tightened to 30 Nm (22 Ft-lbs), and check that the distance from the rear machined face of the cylinder block to the torque converter mounting face on the driveplate is between 19.5 and 21.1 mm. The measurement is most easily made through one of the holes in the driveplate, using vernier calipers. If necessary, remove the driveplate, and fit a shim between the driveplate and the crankshaft to achieve the correct dimension.*

c) *On automatic transmission models, the raised pip on the spacer under the securing bolts must face the torque converter.*

d) *Use new bolts when refitting the flywheel or driveplate, and coat the threads of the bolts with locking fluid before inserting them. Tighten the bolts securely.*

### 16 Crankshaft oil seals – renewal

#### Timing belt end oil seal

**1** Remove the main timing belt as described

in Section 6, and the crankshaft sprocket with reference to Section 7.

**2** To remove the seal without removing the oil pump, drill two small holes diagonally opposite each other, insert self-tapping screws, and pull on the heads of the screws with pliers.

**3** Alternatively, the oil seal can be removed with the oil pump, as described in Section 14.

**4** Thoroughly clean the oil seal seating in the oil pump.

**5** Wind a length of tape around the end of the crankshaft to protect the oil seal lips as the seal is fitted.

**6** Fit a new oil seal to the oil pump, pressing or driving it into position using a socket or tube of suitable diameter. Ensure that the socket or tube bears only on the hard outer ring of the seal, and take care not to damage the seal lips. Press or drive the seal into position until it is seated on the shoulder in the oil pump. Make sure that the closed end of the seal is facing outwards.

**7** Refit the crankshaft sprocket with reference to Section 7, and the main timing belt as described in Section 6.

#### Flywheel/driveplate end oil seal

**8** The crankshaft left-hand oil seal is integral with the housing, and must be renewed as an assembly, complete with the crankshaft speed/position sensor wheel. The sensor wheel is attached to the oil seal/housing assembly, and is a press-fit on the crankshaft flange. VW special tool T10134 is required to fit this assembly and, in the workshop, we found that there is no means of accurately aligning the sensor wheel on the crankshaft without the tool (there is no locating key, and there are no alignment marks). If the sensor wheel is not precisely aligned on the crankshaft, the crankshaft speed/position sensor will send incorrect TDC signals to the engine management ECU, and the engine will not run correctly (the engine may not run at all). As the appropriate special tool is only available to VW dealers, there is no alternative but to have the new assembly fitted by a VW dealer.

## 17 Engine/transmission mountings – inspection and renewal

### Inspection

**1** If improved access is required, jack up the front of the vehicle, and support it securely on axle stands (see *Jacking and towing*). Remove the engine top cover which also incorporates the air filter, then remove the engine undershield(s).

**2** Check the mounting rubbers to see if they are cracked, hardened or separated from the metal at any point; renew the mounting if any such damage or deterioration is evident.

**3** Check that all the mountings are securely tightened; use a torque wrench to check if possible.

**4** Using a large screwdriver or a crowbar, check for wear in the mounting by carefully levering against it to check for free play. Where this is not possible, enlist the aid of an assistant to move the engine/transmission back-and-forth, or from side-to-side, whilst you observe the mounting. While some free play is to be expected, even from new components, excessive wear should be obvious. If excessive free play is found, check first that the fasteners are correctly secured, then renew any worn components as described in the following Steps.

### Renewal

#### Right-hand mounting

**Note:** *New mounting securing bolts will be required on refitting.*

**5** Attach a hoist and lifting tackle to the engine lifting brackets on the cylinder head, and raise the hoist to just take the weight of the engine. Alternatively the engine can be supported on a trolley jack under the engine. Use a block of wood between the sump and the head of the jack, to prevent any damage to the sump.

**6** For improved access, unbolt the coolant reservoir and move it to one side, leaving the coolant hoses connected.

**7** Where applicable, move any wiring harnesses, pipes or hoses to one side to enable removal of the engine mounting **(see illustration)**.

**8** Unbolt the bracket for the charcoal canister from the mounting.

**9** Unscrew the bolts securing the mounting to the engine, then unscrew the bolts securing it to the body. Also, unbolt the movement limiter. Withdraw the mounting from the engine compartment.

**10** Refitting is a reversal of removal, bearing in mind the following points.
 a) Use new securing bolts.
 b) Tighten all fixings to the specified torque.

#### Left-hand mounting

**Note:** *New mounting bolts will be required on refitting (there is no need to renew the smaller mounting-to-body bolts).*

**11** Remove the engine top cover which also incorporates the air filter.

**12** Attach a hoist and lifting tackle to the engine lifting brackets on the cylinder head, and raise the hoist to just take the weight of the engine and transmission. Alternatively the engine can be supported on a trolley jack under the transmission. Use a block of wood between the transmission and the head of the jack, to prevent any damage to the transmission.

**13** Remove the battery, as described in Chapter 5, then disconnect the main starter motor feed cable from the positive battery terminal box.

**14** Release any relevant wiring or hoses from the clips on the battery tray, then unscrew the four securing bolts and remove the battery tray.

**15** Unscrew the bolts securing the mounting to the transmission, and the remaining bolts securing the mounting to the body, then lift the mounting from the engine compartment.

**16** Refitting is a reversal of removal, bearing in mind the following points:
 a) Use new mounting bolts.
 b) Tighten all fixings to the specified torque.

#### Rear mounting (torque arm)

**Note:** *New mounting bolts will be required on refitting.*

**17** Apply the handbrake, then jack up the front of the vehicle and support securely on axle stands (see *Jacking and towing*). Remove the engine undershield(s) for access to the rear mounting (torque arm).

**18** Support the rear of the transmission

beneath the final drive housing. To do this, use a trolley jack and block of wood, or alternatively wedge a block of wood between the transmission and the subframe.

**19** Working under the vehicle, unscrew and remove the bolt securing the mounting to the subframe.

**20** Unscrew the two bolts securing the mounting to the transmission, then withdraw the mounting from under the vehicle **(see illustration)**.

**21** Refitting is a reversal of removal, but use new mounting securing bolts, and tighten all fixings to the specified torque.

## 18 Oil pressure relief valve – removal, inspection and refitting

**1** The oil pressure relief valve is an integral part of the oil pump. The valve piston and spring are located to the side of the oil pump rotors and can be inspected once the oil pump has been removed from the engine and the rear cover has been removed (see Section 14). If any sign of wear or damage is found the oil pump assembly will have to be renewed; the relief valve piston and spring are not available separately.

## 19 Oil pressure warning light switch – removal and refitting

### Removal

**1** The oil pressure warning light switch is fitted to the front of the cylinder head, on its left-hand end. To gain access to the switch, remove the engine top cover.

**2** Disconnect the wiring connector and wipe clean the area around the switch **(see illustration)**.

**3** Unscrew the switch from the cylinder head and remove it along with its sealing washer. If the switch is to be left removed from the engine for any length of time, plug the hole in the cylinder head.

**17.7  Right-hand engine mounting**

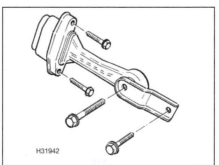

**17.20  Engine/transmission rear mounting components**

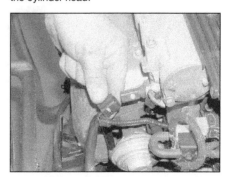

**19.2  Disconnect the oil pressure switch wiring connector**

**20.1 Oil level/temperature sender**

## Refitting

4 Examine the sealing washer for signs of damage or deterioration and if necessary renew.

5 Refit the switch, complete with washer, and tighten it to the specified torque.

6 Securely reconnect the wiring connector then refit the engine cover. Check and, if necessary, top-up the engine oil.

## 20 Oil level/temperature sender – removal and refitting

### Removal

1 The oil level/temperature sender is fitted to bottom of the sump **(see illustration)**.

2 Drain the engine oil as described in Chapter 1.

3 Disconnect the wiring connector and wipe clean the area around the sender.

4 Undo the three retaining bolts and remove the sender.

### Refitting

5 Examine the sealing washer for signs of

**21.8a  Loosening the intake manifold mounting bolts**

damage or deterioration and if necessary renew.

6 Refit the switch and tighten the retaining bolts to the specified torque.

7 Securely reconnect the wiring connector then refill the engine with oil, with reference to Chapter 1.

8 On completion, check and, if necessary, top-up the engine oil.

## 21 Intake manifold – removal and refitting

### Removal

1 The engine is fitted with a one-piece inlet manifold. The fuel rail is attached to and injects into the inlet manifold.

2 Disconnect the battery negative lead and position it away from the terminal. **Note:** Refer to 'Battery disconnection' in Chapter 5 first.

3 With reference to Chapter 4A, remove the throttle control module from the inlet manifold.

4 Disconnect the vacuum hoses for the fuel pressure regulator, and (if not already removed) for the brake servo. Note how the hoses are routed, for use when refitting.

5 On low pressure injection systems only, remove the fuel rail and injectors. However, if the manifold is being removed as part of another procedure (such as cylinder head or engine removal), the fuel rail can be left in place.

6 Disconnect the wiring plug from the inlet air temperature/pressure sensor.

7 Where fitted, unbolt and remove the manifold support bracket from the engine block, then unbolt the mounting bracket for the secondary air inlet valve from the front of the manifold.

8 Progressively loosen the bolts/nuts and withdraw the manifold from the cylinder head **(see illustrations)**. Recover the gasket or the

**21.8b  Removing the intake manifold from the cylinder head**

four seals as applicable – all should be renewed when refitting the manifold.

### Refitting

9 Refitting is a reversal of removal. Use a new gasket or seals, as applicable, and tighten the retaining bolts/nuts securely. It is most important that there are no air leaks at the joint.

## 22 Exhaust manifold – removal and refitting

### Removal

1 Apply the handbrake, then jack up the front of the vehicle and support it on axle stands (see *Jacking and towing*).

2 The exhaust manifold is located on the front of the cylinder head. For access to it, first remove the engine top cover, then move the lock carrier to its 'service' position as follows, leaving the air conditioning refrigerant lines connected to the compressor:

 a) Remove the front bumper (Chapter 11).
 b) Disconnect the bonnet release cable over the right-hand headlight (Chapter 11).
 c) Where necessary, remove the horn (Chapter 12).
 d) Support the lock carrier, then unscrew the mounting bolts and substitute them with one threaded rod on each side of the car.
 e) Carefully pull the lock carrier forwards approximately 10 cm to provide access to the front of the engine.

3 Under the car, unbolt the exhaust front pipe/catalytic converter front mounting from the subframe and from the rear of the engine, then unscrew the nuts securing the front pipe/catalytic converter flange to the bottom of the exhaust manifold, and lower it until clear of the manifold studs. Recover the gasket. Support the front pipe on an axle stand taking care not to strain the oxygen sensor wiring as applicable.

4 Remove the rubber bellows, then unbolt the hot-air shroud from the exhaust manifold, noting the cable guide bracket on the lower bolts.

5 Unscrew the nuts and withdraw the exhaust manifold from the cylinder head. Discard the nuts as new ones must be used on refitting. Also, recover the gasket and discard.

### Refitting

6 Refitting is a reversal of the removal procedure, but fit new gaskets and tighten all nuts and bolts to the specified torque where given.

# Chapter 2  Part B: 1.6, 1.8 and 2.0L petrol engine in-car repair procedures

## Contents

## Degrees of difficulty

| | | | | |
|---|---|---|---|---|
| **Easy,** suitable for novice with little experience  | **Fairly easy,** suitable for beginner with some experience  | **Fairly difficult,** suitable for competent DIY mechanic  | **Difficult,** suitable for experienced DIY mechanic  | **Very difficult,** suitable for expert DIY or professional |

## Specifications

### General

Engine codes
  1.6L . . . . . . . . . . . . . . . . . . . . . . . . . . . . . . . . . . . . . . . . . . . .  AWH
  1.6L (with roller rocker arms) . . . . . . . . . . . . . . . . . . . . . . . . . . . .  AYD and BFS
  1.8L (turbo-petrol) . . . . . . . . . . . . . . . . . . . . . . . . . . . . . . . . . . . .  AVC and AWU
  2.0L . . . . . . . . . . . . . . . . . . . . . . . . . . . . . . . . . . . . . . . . . . . . . .  AQY and AZJ
Displacement
  1.6L . . . . . . . . . . . . . . . . . . . . . . . . . . . . . . . . . . . . . . . . . . . . . .  1596 cc
  1.8L . . . . . . . . . . . . . . . . . . . . . . . . . . . . . . . . . . . . . . . . . . . . . .  1781 cc
  2.0L . . . . . . . . . . . . . . . . . . . . . . . . . . . . . . . . . . . . . . . . . . . . . .  1984 cc
Bore and stroke
  1.6L . . . . . . . . . . . . . . . . . . . . . . . . . . . . . . . . . . . . . . . . . . . . . .  81.01 x 77.40 mm
  1.8L . . . . . . . . . . . . . . . . . . . . . . . . . . . . . . . . . . . . . . . . . . . . . .  81.01 x 86.38 mm
  2.0L . . . . . . . . . . . . . . . . . . . . . . . . . . . . . . . . . . . . . . . . . . . . . .  82.51 x 92.78 mm
Cylinder numbers . . . . . . . . . . . . . . . . . . . . . . . . . . . . . . . . . . . . .  1-2-3-4 (drivebelt end-to-transmission end)
Firing order . . . . . . . . . . . . . . . . . . . . . . . . . . . . . . . . . . . . . . . . . .  1-3-4-2

### Camshaft

Endfloat
  1.6L . . . . . . . . . . . . . . . . . . . . . . . . . . . . . . . . . . . . . . . . . . . . . .  0.1 mm
  1.8L . . . . . . . . . . . . . . . . . . . . . . . . . . . . . . . . . . . . . . . . . . . . . .  0.2 mm
  2.0L . . . . . . . . . . . . . . . . . . . . . . . . . . . . . . . . . . . . . . . . . . . . . .  0.15 mm
Journal diameter . . . . . . . . . . . . . . . . . . . . . . . . . . . . . . . . . . . . . .  N/A
Journal oil clearance (in cylinder head) . . . . . . . . . . . . . . . . . . . . .  0.1 mm
Lobe lift . . . . . . . . . . . . . . . . . . . . . . . . . . . . . . . . . . . . . . . . . . . . .  N/A
Runout . . . . . . . . . . . . . . . . . . . . . . . . . . . . . . . . . . . . . . . . . . . . . .  0.01 mm

| Torque specifications | Nm | Ft-lbs |
|---|---|---|
| Camshaft bearing cap bolts/nuts | | |
|     1.6L engines | 20 | 15 |
|     1.8L engine | 10 | 7 |
|     2.0L engine | 20 | 15 |
| Camshaft drive chain tensioner/adjuster (1.8L engine) | 10 | 7 |
| Camshaft sprocket bolt | | |
|     1.6L engines | 100 | 74 |
|     1.8L engine | 65 | 48 |
|     2.0L engine | 100 | 74 |
| Crankshaft drive sprocket bolt* | | |
|     Step one | 90 | 66 |
|     Step two | Angle-tighten a further 90-degrees | |
| Crankshaft oil seal housing | 15 | 11 |
| Crankshaft pulley bolts | | |
|     Bolts marked 8.8 | 25 | 18 |
|     Bolts marked 10.9 | 40 | 30 |
| Cylinder head bolts* **(see illustration 10.26a)** | | |
|     Step one | 40 | 30 |
|     Step two | Angle-tighten a further 90-degrees | |
|     Step three | Angle-tighten a further 90-degrees | |
| EGR pipe to manifold union | 60 | 44 |
| EGR pipe to throttle valve control assembly | 10 | 7 |
| EGR valve nuts | 25 | 18 |
| Engine mountings* | | |
|     Mounting-to-body bolts | | |
|         Step one | 40 | 30 |
|         Step two | Angle-tighten a further 90-degrees | |
|     Mounting-to-engine or transmission bolts | | |
|         Models to 2004 | | |
|             Step one | 60 | 44 |
|             Step two | Angle-tighten a further 90-degrees | |
|         Models from 2005-on | 100 | 74 |
|     Mounting/bracket-to-body bolt | 24 | 18 |
| Exhaust manifold nuts* | 24 | 18 |
| Flywheel/driveplate bolts* | | |
|     Step one | 60 | 44 |
|     Step two | Angle-tighten a further 90-degrees | |
| Intake manifold bolts/nuts | | |
|     1.6L engines | 15 | 11 |
|     1.8L engine | 10 | 7 |
|     2.0L engine | 20 | 15 |
| Lower torque strut | | |
|     Strut-to-subframe bolts* | | |
|         Models to 2004 | | |
|             Step one | 20 | 15 |
|             Step two | Angle-tighten a further 90-degrees | |
|         Models from 2005-on | | |
|             Step 1 | 25 | 18 |
|             Step 2 | Angle-tighten a further 90-degrees | |
|     Strut-to-bracket bolt | | |
|         Models to 2004 | 40 | 30 |
|         Models from 2005-on | 50 | 37 |
|     Strut-to-strut bracket/bellhousing bolts* | | |
|         Models to 2004 | | |
|             Step one | 40 | 30 |
|             Step two | Angle-tighten a further 90-degrees | |
|         Models from 2005-on | 50 | 37 |
| Oil pump cover bolts | 10 | 7 |
| Oil pump drive chain tensioner bolt | 15 | 11 |
| Oil pump driven sprocket bolt | | |
|     1.6L engines | 20 | 15 |
|     1.8L and 2.0 L engines | 24 | 18 |
| Oil pump mounting bolt | 15 | 11 |
| Oil pump pick-up tube | 15 | 11 |

## Torque specifications (continued)

| | Nm | Ft-lbs |
|---|---|---|
| Sump | | |
| To bellhousing bolts | | |
| 1.6L engine | 25 | 18 |
| 1.8L engine | N/A | |
| 2.0L engines | 45 | 33 |
| To engine block bolts | 15 | 11 |
| Timing belt cover-to-block bolts | 10 | 7 |
| Timing belt tensioner | | |
| 1.6L engines | 20 | 15 |
| 1.8L engine | | |
| Damper-to-engine block bolts | 20 | 15 |
| Tensioner roller-to-cylinder head retaining bolt | 27 | 20 |
| 2.0L engine | | |
| Tensioner roller retaining nut | 20 | 15 |
| Valve cover-to-cylinder head nuts | 10 | 7 |

*\* Renew with new bolt/nut(s)*

## 1  General information

*Caution 1: Avoid disconnecting the battery whenever possible! Disconnecting the battery can cause severe driveability problems that require a special scan tool to remedy. See Chapter 5, Section 1, for the use of an auxiliary power source before disconnecting the battery.*
*Caution 2: These models are equipped with an anti-theft radio. Before performing a procedure that requires disconnecting the battery, make sure you have the proper activation code.*
Note: *The engine cover must removed before performing many of the procedures in this Chapter (see illustration 4.1).*

This Part of Chapter 2 is devoted to in-vehicle repair procedures for the 1.6L, 1.8L and the 2.0L four-cylinder petrol engines. These engines utilise cast-iron engine blocks with aluminium cylinder heads. The 1.8L 20-valve engine is turbocharged and utilises dual overhead camshafts with five valves per cylinder (3 inlet valves and 2 exhaust valves) – engine code AWU has variable inlet valve timing, where valve timing is varied by altering the tension on the drive chain using an electronically-actuated mechanical tensioner instead of the standard tensioner fitted to engine code AVC. The 1.6L and 2.0L engines are normally-aspirated and utilise a single overhead camshaft. Hydraulic followers are used to actuate the valves on all engines except the 1.6L engine codes AYD and BFS; the valves of this engine are actuated by rocker arms equipped with rollers which act upon the camshaft lobes, whilst the other end of the rocker arm is supported by hydraulic clearance compensators. On all engines, the aluminium cylinder heads are equipped with pressed-in valve guides and hardened valve seats. The oil pump is mounted at the timing belt end of the engine and is driven by a chain from the crankshaft.

To positively identify these engines, locate the sticker on the timing cover, or the engine code stamped into the front side of the engine block where the engine joins the transmission.

All information concerning engine removal and refitting and engine block and cylinder head overhaul can be found in Part D of this Chapter.

The following repair procedures are based on the assumption that the engine is fitted in the vehicle. If the engine has been removed from the vehicle and mounted on a stand, many of the steps outlined in this Part of Chapter 2 will not apply.

The Specifications included in this Part of Chapter 2 apply only to the procedures contained in this Part. Part D of Chapter 2 contains the Specifications necessary for cylinder head and engine block rebuilding.

## 2  Repair operations possible with the engine in the vehicle

Many major repair operations can be accomplished without removing the engine from the vehicle.

Clean the engine compartment and the exterior of the engine with some type of degreaser before any work is done. It will make the job easier and help keep dirt out of the internal areas of the engine.

Depending on the components involved, it may be helpful to remove the bonnet to improve access to the engine as repairs are performed (refer to Chapter 11 if necessary). Cover the wings to prevent damage to the paint. Special pads are available, but an old bedspread or blanket will also work.

If vacuum, exhaust, oil or coolant leaks develop, indicating a need for gasket or seal renewal, the repairs can generally be made with the engine in the vehicle. The intake and exhaust manifold gaskets, sump gasket, crankshaft oil seals and cylinder head gasket are all accessible with the engine in place.

Exterior engine components, such as the intake and exhaust manifolds, the sump, the oil pump, the water pump, the starter motor, the alternator and the fuel system components can be removed for repair with the engine in place.

Since the cylinder head can be removed without pulling the engine, camshaft and valve component servicing can also be accomplished with the engine in the vehicle. Renewal of the timing belt and sprockets is also possible with the engine in the vehicle.

In extreme cases caused by a lack of necessary equipment, repair or renewal of piston rings, pistons, connecting rods and big-end bearings is possible with the engine in the vehicle. However, this practice is not recommended because of the cleaning and preparation work that must be done to the components involved.

## 3  Top Dead Centre (TDC) for number one piston – locating

1 Top Dead Centre (TDC) is the highest point in the cylinder that each piston reaches as it travels up-and-down when the crankshaft turns. Each piston reaches TDC on the compression stroke and again on the exhaust stroke, but TDC generally refers to piston position on the compression stroke. The timing marks on the vibration damper/crankshaft pulley fitted on the crankshaft are referenced to the number one piston at TDC.
2 Positioning the piston(s) at TDC is an essential part of procedures such as timing belt and sprocket renewal.
3 In order to bring any piston to TDC, the crankshaft must be turned using one of the methods outlined below. When looking at the timing belt end of the engine, normal crankshaft rotation is clockwise.

 *Warning: Before beginning this procedure, be sure to place the transmission in Park or Neutral, set the handbrake and remove the ignition key.*

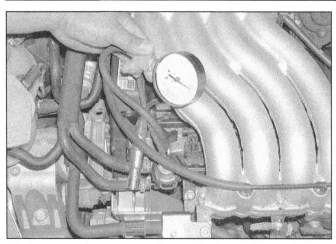

3.5  A compression gauge can be used in the number on plug hole to assist in finding TDC

3.6  Align the notch on the crankshaft drivebelt pulley with the mark on the timing belt cover (arrowed)

a) *The preferred method is to turn the crankshaft with a large socket and breaker bar attached to the large bolt threaded into the centre of the crankshaft pulley.*

b) *If an assistant is available to turn the ignition switch to the Start position in short bursts, you can get the piston close to TDC. Use a socket and breaker bar as described in Step a) to complete the procedure.*

**4** Disable the ignition system by disconnecting the primary electrical connectors at the ignition coil pack/modules (see Chapter 5).

**5** Remove the spark plugs (see Chapter 1) and fit a compression gauge in the number one cylinder **(see illustration)**. Turn the crankshaft clockwise with a socket and breaker bar as described above.

**6** When the piston approaches TDC,

compression will be noted on the compression gauge. Continue turning the crankshaft until the notch in the crankshaft damper is aligned with the TDC mark on the cover **(see illustration)**. At this point number one cylinder is at TDC on the compression stroke. If the marks aligned but there was no compression, the piston was on the exhaust stroke; continue rotating the crankshaft 360-degrees (1-turn) and line-up the marks. **Note:** *If a compression gauge is not available, TDC for the No 1 piston can be obtained by simultaneously aligning the marks on the camshaft (timing belt) sprocket with the marks on the rear timing cover and the marks on the crankshaft damper with the TDC mark on the cover (see illustration 5.9).*

**7** After the number one piston has been positioned at TDC on the compression stroke, TDC for any of the remaining cylinders can be

located by turning the crankshaft 180-degrees and following the firing order (refer to the Specifications). Rotating the engine 180-degrees past TDC No 1 will put the engine at TDC compression for cylinder No 3.

### 4  Valve cover – removal and refitting

#### Removal

**1** Remove the engine cover **(see illustration)**.
**2** On 1.8L engines, remove the secondary air injection valve solenoid, the overrun recirculation valve solenoid, the vacuum reservoir and vacuum hoses from the top of the valve cover **(see illustration)**. Also remove the ignition coils (see Chapter 5) and the breather hose from the top of the valve cover.

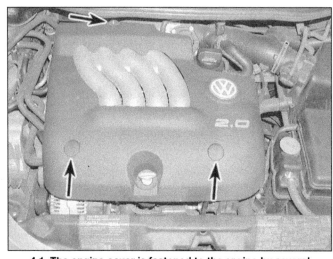

4.1  The engine cover is fastened to the engine by several retaining nuts (arrowed) – pry out the plastic caps, remove the nuts and detach the cover from the engine; on 1.6L engines, the cover simply pulls up and off the engine. It will also be necessary to remove the oil dipstick on 1.6L and 2.0L engines

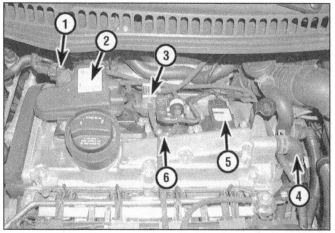

4.2  On 1.8L engines, detach the following components to access the valve cover

1  *Secondary air injection solenoid*
2  *Vacuum reservoir*
3  *Overrun recirculation solenoid*
4  *Crankcase breather hose*
5  *Ignition coil(s)*
6  *Vacuum hoses*

4.3  On 1.6L and 2.0L engines, detach the crankcase breather valve from the valve cover

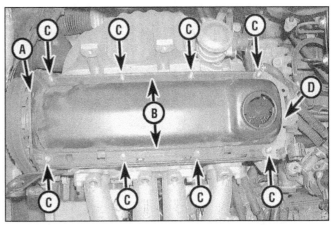

4.6  Valve cover mounting details – 1.6L code AWH and 2.0L engines

A  Upper rear timing belt cover
B  Valve cover reinforcement strips
C  Valve cover mounting bolts
D  Air injection tube bracket

**3** On 1.6L and 2.0L engines, remove the upper intake plenum (see Section 8) and the crankcase breather valve from the top of the valve cover **(see illustration)**
**4** Remove the upper timing belt cover from the engine **(see illustrations 5.5a and 5.5b)**.
**5** On 1.8L engines, remove the earth strap from the valve cover.
**6** Remove the retaining nuts and detach the valve cover from the cylinder head. On 1.6L code AWH and 2.0L engines it will be necessary to detach the upper rear timing belt cover and the valve cover sealing flange reinforcement strips before removing the valve cover **(see illustration)**.
**7** If the cover is stuck to the head, tap the end with a block of wood and a hammer to jar it loose. If that doesn't work, try to slip a flexible

putty knife between the head and cover to break the seal.
*Caution: Don't prise at the cover-to-head joint or damage to the sealing surfaces may occur, leading to oil leaks after the cover is reinstalled.*

### Refitting

**8** The mating surfaces of the housing or cylinder head and cover must be clean when the cover is fitted. Use a gasket scraper to remove all traces of sealant and old gasket material, then clean the mating surfaces with lacquer thinner or acetone. If there's residue or oil on the mating surfaces when the cover is fitted, oil leaks may develop. Also inspect the rubber end plug at the rear of the cylinder head on 1.8L engines for cracks and damage.

Now would be a good time to renew it, if damage has occurred.
**9** On 1.8L engines, apply RTV sealant to the corners of the camshaft No 1 bearing cap and to the camshaft drive chain tensioner where they meet the cylinder head. On 1.6L code AWH and 2.0L engines, apply RTV sealant only to the corners of the camshaft No 1 bearing cap where it meets the cylinder head **(see illustrations)**.
**10** Position a new valve cover gasket over the studs on the cylinder head. On 1.8L engines, refit the spark plug tube grommet gasket over the studs on the cylinder head with the index marks facing the timing belt end of the engine. On 1.6L roller rocker arm engines (codes AYD and BFS) position the rubber gasket on the camshaft bearing frame.
**11** Refit the valve cover and any brackets removed. On 1.6L roller rocker arm engines (codes AYD and BFS) clip the spacer sleeves of the cover retaining bolts into the cover rubber gasket. On all engines refit the retaining bolts/nuts and tighten the retaining nuts to the torque listed in this Chapter's Specifications in several steps.
**12** Refit the remaining parts, run the engine and check for oil leaks.

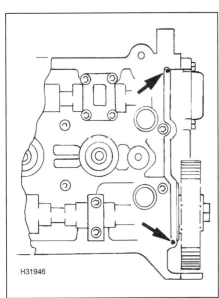

4.9a  On 1.8L engines, apply sealant to the two points at the No 1 camshaft bearing cap . . .

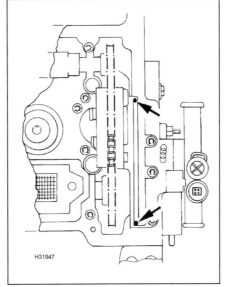

4.9b  . . . and to the corners of the camshaft drive chain tensioner where they meet the cylinder head

4.9c  On 1.6L and 2.0L engines, apply sealant to the corners of the No 1 camshaft bearing cap only

5.5a  The upper timing belt cover is retained by two clips (arrowed)

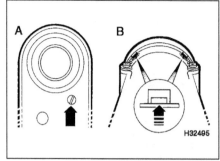

5.5b  On 1.6L codes AYD and BFS engines, turn the twist-lock until the slot on the device head is vertical (A), and pull the two locking tabs upwards (B)

5.11a  The upper two bolts (arrowed) securing the engine mounting support bracket can be accessed from above . . .

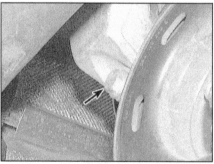

5.11b  . . . and the lower bolt is accessed from below – because of the lack of clearance, it will be necessary to loosen all three bolts and remove the support bracket and the bolts together

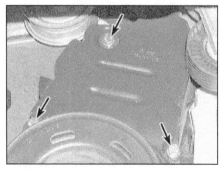

5.12a  Centre timing belt cover retaining bolts (arrowed)

5.12b  Lower timing belt cover retaining bolts (arrowed)

## 5  Timing belt and sprockets – removal, inspection and refitting

⚠️ **Warning: Wait until the engine is completely cool before beginning this procedure.**

**Note:** *Do not rotate the crankshaft or the camshaft separately during this procedure with the timing belt removed as damage to valves may occur. Only rotate the camshaft a few degrees as necessary to align the camshaft sprocket marks with the marks on the rear timing cover.*

### Removal

**1** Relieve the fuel system pressure (see Chapter 4A). Remove the engine cover **(see illustration 4.1)**.

**2** Unbolt the coolant expansion tank and move it to one side without disconnecting the coolant hoses (see Chapter 3).

**3** With reference to Chapter 1, Section 11, remove the auxiliary drivebelt and tensioner.

**4** Remove the spark plugs (see Chapter 1).

**5** Unclip and remove the upper timing belt cover from the engine. On 1.6L roller rocker arm engines (codes AYD and BFS) the upper cover is secured by two locking devices. Turn the twist-lock on the outer face of the cover

5.9  When the engine is positioned at TDC for the No 1 cylinder on the compression stroke, the camshaft sprocket mark (A) will be aligned with the rear cover mark (B)

anti-clockwise until the slot on the device head is vertical, and pull the two locking tabs of the clips upwards on the rear of the upper cover and remove the cover **(see illustrations)**.

**6** Block the rear wheels and set the handbrake. Loosen the wheel nuts on the right front wheel and raise the vehicle. Support the front of the vehicle securely on axle stands and remove the right front wheel.

**7** Remove the engine under cover and the lower wing apron to allow access to the bottom of the engine.

**8** On 1.8L engines, remove the lower hoses and the pipes leading from the intercooler to the turbocharger (see Chapter 4A, if necessary).

**9** Rotate the engine in the normal direction of rotation (clockwise) until the No 1 cylinder is located at TDC (see Section 3). Verify that the camshaft sprocket mark is aligned with the mark on the rear timing belt cover **(see illustration)**.

**10** Use a strap spanner to hold the crankshaft pulley from rotating. Loosen the crankshaft drive sprocket retaining bolt and the crankshaft pulley bolts, then remove the crankshaft pulley (see Section 11). After the bolts are loosened, verify that the crankshaft has not moved from TDC. **Note:** *Loosening the drive sprocket bolt is only required if the crankshaft drive sprocket is expected to be removed. It is not typically necessary to remove the drive sprocket when you're simply renewing a timing belt, but it will need to be removed if you are renewing the crankshaft oil seal or housing. If you do remove the drive sprocket, obtain a new bolt (the manufacturer doesn't recommend re-using it).*

**11** Support the engine from underneath with a jack and a block of wood, then remove the right-hand side engine mount (see Section 17) and the engine mount support bracket from the front of the engine **(see illustrations)**.

**12** Detach the retaining screws from the centre and lower timing belt covers and remove the covers **(see illustrations)**.

**13** If you plan to re-use the timing belt, apply match marks on the sprocket and belt, and an

**5.13 If you intend to re-use the timing belt, apply directional marks on the belt and the rear timing belt cover**

**5.14a On 1.6L and 2.0L engines, loosen the timing belt tensioner retaining nut (arrowed) and let the tensioner rotate to release the tension on the belt**

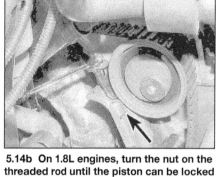

**5.14b On 1.8L engines, turn the nut on the threaded rod until the piston can be locked in position using a metal pin or a twist drill (arrowed) inserted through the hole in the housing**

arrow indicating direction of travel on the belt **(see illustration)**.

**14** Release the timing belt tensioner **(see illustrations)**. **Note:** *On 1.8L engines, it will be necessary to purchase an M5 x 55 stud, nut and washer at your local hardware store to compress the tensioner enough to lock it in place. After compressing the tensioner it can be locked into place using a small drill bit or similar tool.*

**15** Remove the timing belt from the engine, taking care to avoid twisting it excessively.

**16** If you're removing the upper part of the belt only, for camshaft seal renewal or cylinder head removal, it isn't necessary to detach the belt from the crankshaft sprocket. If the sprocket is worn or damaged, or if you need to renew the crankshaft oil seal, remove the drive sprocket retaining bolt which was loosened in Step 10 and detach the crankshaft sprocket from the crankshaft **(see illustration)**.

**17** If the camshaft sprocket is damaged or needs to be removed for other procedures such as cylinder head removal, use a spanner or similar tool to hold the sprocket in place as the sprocket retaining bolt is loosened, then remove the camshaft sprocket from the end of the camshaft **(see illustration)**.

### *Inspection*

*Caution: Do not bend, twist or turn the timing belt inside out. Do not allow it to come in contact with oil, coolant or fuel. Do not turn the crankshaft or camshaft more than a few degrees (if necessary for tooth alignment) while the timing belt is removed.*

**18** Spin the idler pulley(s) and the timing belt tensioner and check the bearings for smooth operation and excessive play. Also inspect the remaining timing belt sprockets for any obvious damage. Renew all worn parts as necessary.

**19** Examine the belt for evidence of contamination by coolant or lubricant. If this is the case, find the source of the contamination before progressing any further. Check the belt for signs of wear or damage, particularly around the leading edges of the belt teeth **(see illustration)**.

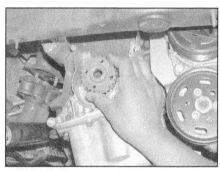

**5.16 With the crankshaft drive sprocket retaining bolt removed, the crankshaft sprocket is easily removed from the engine**

*Caution: If the belt appears to be in good condition and can be re-used, it is essential that it is reinstalled the same way around, otherwise accelerated wear will result, leading to premature failure.*

**20** Renew the belt if its condition is in doubt; the cost of belt renewal is negligible compared with potential cost of the engine repairs, should the belt fail in service. Similarly, if the belt is known to have covered more than 60 000 miles, it is prudent to renew

**5.17 If necessary, the camshaft sprocket bolt can be loosened while holding the sprocket in place with a spanner**

it regardless of condition, as a precautionary measure.

### *Refitting*

**21** Ensure that the crankshaft is still set to TDC on No 1 cylinder, as described in Section 3. If the any of the timing sprockets or idler pulleys were removed for inspection or needed renewal, refit them back onto the engine now. If the timing belt tensioner was removed on a 1.6L or 2.0L engine, be sure the

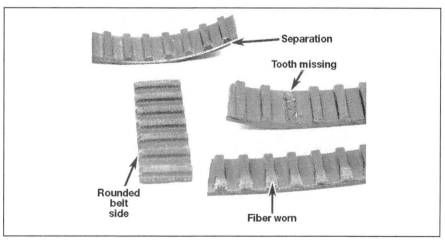

**5.19 Check the timing belt for cracked and missing teeth – wear on one side of the belt indicates sprocket misalignment problems**

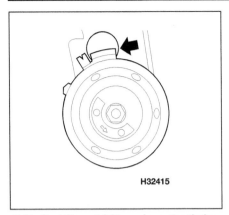

**5.21 On 1.6L and 2.0L engines, the timing belt tensioner is properly seated when the tab on the tensioning roller is engaged in the hole in the rear timing belt cover**

rear tab on the roller is properly positioned in the rear timing belt cover and refit the retaining nut hand-tight **(see illustration)**. If the timing belt tensioner was removed on a 1.8L engine, make sure it is reinstalled with the tensioner locked into place as described in Step 14. **Note:** *A small inspection mirror mounted on a flexible shaft (available at car accessory shops) is helpful in examining the timing marks when the engine is in the vehicle.*
**22** Align the camshaft sprocket mark with the mark on the rear timing belt cover **(see illustration 5.9)**.
**23** Loop the timing belt loosely under the crankshaft sprocket.
*Caution: Observe the direction of rotation markings on the belt.*
**24** Engage the timing belt teeth with the crankshaft sprocket, then manoeuvre it into position over the idler pulley, water pump and the camshaft sprocket. Ensure the belt teeth seat correctly on the sprockets, then refit the belt around the timing belt tensioner. **Note:** *Slight adjustments to the position of the camshaft sprocket may be necessary to achieve this.*
**25** Ensure that the 'front run' of the belt is taut and all the slack is in the section of the belt that passes over the tensioner roller.
**26** On 1.6L and 2.0L engines, tension the belt by turning the eccentrically-mounted tensioner

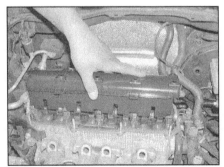

**6.2 The plastic oil deflector(s) are easily removed by simply lifting them off the cylinder head (2.0L engine shown, 1.6L and 1.8L engine similar)**

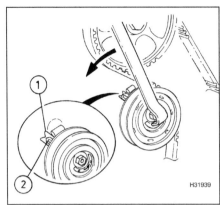

**5.26 Tension the timing belt so that the tension indicator pointer (2) is aligned with the centre of the indicator notch (1) (1.6L and 2.0L engines)**

anti-clockwise until the upper marks align; two holes are provided in the side of the tensioner hub for this purpose – a pair of sturdy right-angled circlip pliers is a suitable substitute for the correct VW tool **(see illustration)**. After the tensioner marks are aligned properly, tighten the tensioner locknut to the specified torque.
**27** On 1.8L engines, remove the tensioner locking pin and loosen the nut on the tensioner compressing tool fabricated earlier. Make sure to take all the slack out of the timing belt while loosening the nut **(see illustration 5.14b)**.
**28** At this point, double check to make sure that the crankshaft is still set to TDC on No 1 cylinder (see Section 3) and the camshaft sprocket mark is aligned with the mark on the rear timing belt cover.
**29** Rotate the crankshaft through two complete revolutions. Reset the engine to TDC on No 1 cylinder, with reference to Section 3 and check the alignment marks again. Also recheck the timing belt tension and adjust it, if necessary.
**30** Refit the lower and centre timing belt covers, then refit the engine mounting support

bracket to the engine. Refit the engine mounting (see Section 17) to secure the engine as the remaining components are fitted onto the vehicle.
**31** The remainder of the refitting is the reverse of removal.

## 6  Camshaft and followers – removal and refitting

**Note 1**: *The camshaft and followers should always be thoroughly inspected before refitting, and camshaft endfloat should always be checked prior to camshaft removal. Although the hydraulic followers are self-adjusting and require no periodic service, there is an in-vehicle procedure for checking excessively noisy hydraulic followers. Refer to Chapter 2D for the camshaft and follower inspection procedures.*
**Note 2**: *1.6L and 2.0L engines have only one camshaft. 1.8L engines have two; the exhaust camshaft is driven by the timing belt, while the inlet camshaft is driven by a chain connected to the rear of the exhaust camshaft.*

### Removal

**1** Remove the engine cover **(see illustration 4.1)**.
**2** Remove the valve cover (see Section 4). Also remove the oil deflector(s) to expose the camshaft(s) **(see illustration)**.
**3** Remove the timing belt and camshaft sprocket (see Section 5).

#### 1.6L roller rocker arm engine (codes AYD and BFS)

**4** Remove the upper rear timing belt cover.
**5** Working from the outside in a diagonal sequence gradually slacken and remove the nuts securing the camshaft bearing frame to the cylinder head.
**6** Lift the camshaft from the cylinder head.
**7** Remove the roller rocker arms complete with the hydraulic clearance compensators **(see illustration)**.

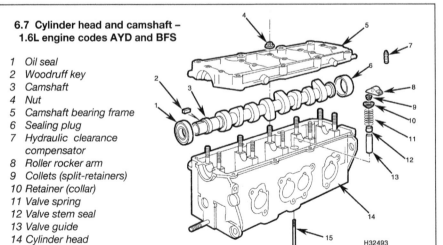

**6.7 Cylinder head and camshaft – 1.6L engine codes AYD and BFS**

1 Oil seal
2 Woodruff key
3 Camshaft
4 Nut
5 Camshaft bearing frame
6 Sealing plug
7 Hydraulic clearance compensator
8 Roller rocker arm
9 Collets (split-retainers)
10 Retainer (collar)
11 Valve spring
12 Valve stem seal
13 Valve guide
14 Cylinder head
15 Valve

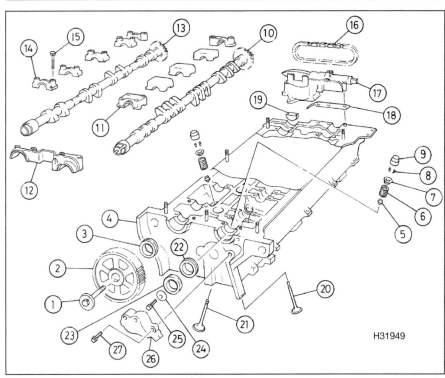

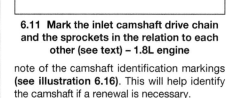

6.11 Mark the inlet camshaft drive chain and the sprockets in the relation to each other (see text) – 1.8L engine

6.10 Exploded view of the camshafts and related components – 1.8L engine

| | | |
|---|---|---|
| 1 Camshaft sprocket bolt | 11 Intake camshaft bearing cap | 19 Grommet |
| 2 Camshaft sprocket | 12 No 1 bearing cap | 20 Exhaust valve |
| 3 Oil seal | 13 Exhaust camshaft | 21 Intake valve |
| 4 Cylinder head | 14 Exhaust camshaft bearing cap | 22 Seal |
| 5 Valve stem oil seal | 15 Bolt | 23 Camshaft position sensor rotor |
| 6 Valve spring | 16 Drive chain | 24 Tapered washer |
| 7 Valve spring retainer | 17 Camshaft drive chain tensioner | 25 Bolt |
| 8 Collets (split-retainers) | 18 Seal | 26 Camshaft position sensor |
| 9 Hydraulic follower | | 27 Bolt |
| 10 Intake camshaft | | |

**Caution: Keep the rocker arms and compensators in order. They must go back in the same location they were removed from.**

### 1.6L engine code AWH

8 Mark the camshaft bearing caps from 1 to 5, starting with the No 1 cap at the timing belt

end. Also mark arrows indicating the timing belt end of the engine (see illustration 6.15). Loosen the No 1, 3 and 5 camshaft bearing caps in two or three steps. Then loosen the No 2 and 4 bearing caps. Be sure to loosen the nuts alternately and evenly.

9 Remove the bearing caps and camshaft. After the camshaft has been removed, make a

note of the camshaft identification markings (see illustration 6.16). This will help identify the camshaft if a renewal is necessary.
*Caution: Keep the caps in order. They must go back in the same location they were removed from.*

### 1.8L engine

10 Remove the camshaft position sensor (see Chapter 6A. Remove the camshaft sensor reluctor ring from the end of the intake camshaft (see illustration).

11 Mark the position of the camshaft drive chain in relationship to the sprockets and the marks on the bearing cap (see illustration). This will ensure that the drive chain is fitted in exactly the same direction and position from which it was removed.

12 Using a special tool, compress the camshaft drive chain tensioner/valve timing adjuster (see illustrations).
*Warning: Compressing the chain tensioner too far can result in damage to the camshaft adjuster mechanism.*

13 Mark the location of the camshaft bearing caps from 1 to 6, starting with the double bearing cap at the timing belt end. Also mark arrows indicating the timing belt end of the engine (see illustration). Loosen the bearing caps nuts alternately in the following order:
1) Loosen and remove the No 2 and 4 bearing caps from the intake and exhaust camshafts.
2) Loosen and remove the No 1 bearing cap.

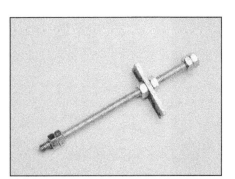

6.12a Home-made tool for locking camshaft adjuster, or chain tensioner, in position – 1.8L engine

6.12b Home-made tool in position, locking camshaft adjuster in its compressed condition (shown with the camshaft adjuster removed for clarity) – 1.8L engine

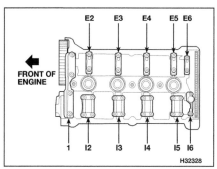

6.13 On 1.8L engines, the camshaft bearing caps should be marked as shown with a number and letter stamp or a marker to ensure correct reinstallation

*3)* *Loosen and remove the No 6 bearing caps from the intake and exhaust camshafts.*

*4)* *Loosen and remove the drive chain tensioner mounting bolts.*

*5)* *Loosen and remove the No 3 and 5 bearing caps from the exhaust camshafts.*

*6)* *Loosen and remove the No 3 and 5 bearing caps from the intake camshafts.*

**14** Remove the camshafts and the drive chain tensioner/adjuster as an assembly from the cylinder head. Separate the tensioner and the drive chain from the camshafts on a workbench. *Caution: Keep the caps in order. They must go back in the same location and direction they were removed from.*

### 2.0L engine

**15** Mark the camshaft bearing caps from 1 to 5, starting with the No 1 cap at the timing belt end. Also mark arrows indicating the timing belt end of the engine **(see illustration)**. Loosen the No 1, 3 and 5 camshaft bearing caps in two or three steps. Then loosen the No 2 and 4 bearing caps. Be sure to loosen the nuts alternately and evenly.
**16** Remove the bearing caps and camshaft. After the camshaft has been removed, make a note of the camshaft identification markings **(see illustration)**. This will help identify the camshaft if a renewal is necessary. *Caution: Keep the caps in order. They must go back in the same location they were removed from.*

### All engines

**17** Where applicable, remove the followers from the cylinder head, keeping them in order with their respective valve and cylinder **(see illustrations)**. *Caution: Keep the followers in order. They must go back in the same location they were removed from.*
**18** Inspect the camshaft and followers as described in Chapter 2D.

### *Refitting*

#### 1.6L roller rocker arm engine (codes AYD and BFS)

**19** Insert the hydraulic clearance compensators

**6.15  On 1.6L and 2.0L engines, simply mark the bearing caps from 1 to 5 starting at the timing belt end of the engine**

into their original locations, and refit the rocker arms to the top of the valve stems and hydraulic compensators. Ensure that the rocker arms engage correctly with the top of the valves, and are clipped onto their respective hydraulic compensators.
**20** Oil the camshaft contact surfaces, and lay the camshaft in position. Note that the camshaft lobes for No 1 cylinder must point upwards.
**21** Apply a thin even beading of suitable sealant into the groove of the camshaft bearing frame, and place the frame over the camshaft bearing studs **(see illustration)**.
**22** Refit the bearing frame retaining nuts, and hand-tighten only at this stage. Ensure that the frame is parallel to the upper surface of the cylinder head.
**23** Working from the centre out in a diagonal sequence, gradually and evenly in several stages, tighten the retaining nuts until the frame contacts the cylinder head. Ensure that the frame remains as parallel as possible to the cylinder head at all times. Tighten the nuts to the specified torque.

#### 1.6L engine code AWH

**24** Apply clean engine oil onto the sides of the hydraulic followers, and refit them into position in their bores in the cylinder head. Push them down until they contact the valves, then lubricate the camshaft lobe contact surfaces.
**25** Lubricate the camshaft and cylinder head

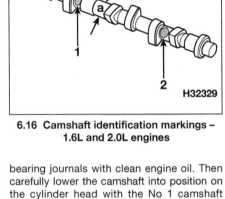

**6.16  Camshaft identification markings – 1.6L and 2.0L engines**

bearing journals with clean engine oil. Then carefully lower the camshaft into position on the cylinder head with the No 1 camshaft lobes facing up. Support the ends of the shaft as it is inserted, to avoid damaging the lobes and journals.
**26** Oil the upper surfaces of the camshaft bearing journals, then refit the No 2 and 4 bearing caps over the camshaft and tighten the retaining nuts alternately and diagonally to the specified torque. **Note:** *The camshaft bearing caps are drilled off centre **(see illustration 6.37)**, make sure they're fitted on the correct journal and with the arrows made in Step 8 facing towards the timing belt end of the engine.*
**27** Apply a small amount of RTV sealant to the mating surface of No 1 bearing cap and refit it, along with cap Nos 3 and 5 over the camshaft **(see illustration 6.38)**. Tighten the nuts to the specified torque starting with the centre cap and working towards the end caps.

#### 1.8L engine

**28** Apply clean engine oil onto the sides of the hydraulic followers, and refit them into position in their bores in the cylinder head. Push them down until they contact the valves, then lubricate the camshaft lobe contact surfaces.
**29** Clean the mating surfaces of the drive chain tensioner and the cylinder head and refit

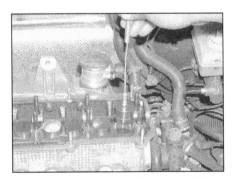

**6.17a  The followers cam be removed from the cylinder head with a magnet . . .**

**6.17b  . . . and stored in individually-marked plastic bags or a divided box as shown – be sure to keep them in order with their respective valves**

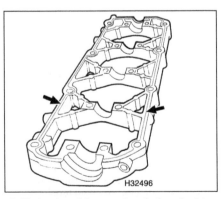

**6.21  Apply a thin even bead of sealant to the groove as shown**

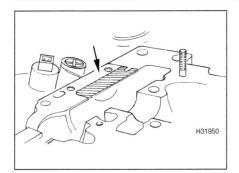

**6.29 Apply sealant to the area of the chain tensioner/camshaft adjuster gasket as shown – 1.8L engine**

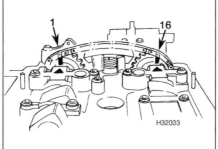

**6.30 On 1.8L engines, install the drive chain over the camshaft drive sprockets with 16 rollers between the notches**

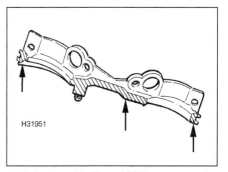

**6.34 Apply a thin film of RTV sealant to the No 1 bearing cap at the shaded areas – 1.8L engine**

a new drive chain tensioner gasket **(see illustration)**.

**30** Align the marks on the drive chain (made previously) with the notches on the camshaft drive gears and refit the chain over the drive gears. If you're refitting a new drive chain, refit the drive chain with exactly 16 rollers between the notches on the drive gears. Note that the exhaust camshaft notch is slightly off-centre. In either case verify that there are 16 rollers between the notches of the intake and exhaust camshaft **(see illustration)**.

**31** Compress the camshaft drive chain tensioner/adjuster with the special tool and insert it between the drive chain and the camshafts.

**32** Lubricate the camshaft and cylinder head bearing journals with clean engine oil. Then carefully lower the camshafts, drive chain and tensioner/adjuster as an assembly into position on the cylinder head with the No 1 camshaft lobes facing up. Support the ends of the shaft as it is inserted, to avoid damaging the lobes and journals.

**33** Refit the drive chain tensioner/adjuster over the dowels on the cylinder head and tighten the bolts to the torque listed in this Chapter's Specifications.

**34** Refit the camshaft bearing caps in the reverse order of removal (see Step 13). Be sure to apply a small amount of RTV sealant to the mating surface of the No 1 bearing cap before refitting it **(see illustration)**. After the

bearing caps have been tightened, remove the drive chain tensioning tool from the tensioner. Reconfirm that there are 16 rollers between the notches of the intake and exhaust camshaft and that the notches align with the arrows on the caps, and that the No 1 camshaft lobes face up.

### 2.0L engine

**35** Apply clean engine oil onto the sides of the hydraulic followers, and refit them into position in their bores in the cylinder head. Push them down until they contact the valves, then lubricate the camshaft lobe contact surfaces.

**36** Lubricate the camshaft and cylinder head bearing journals with clean engine oil. Then carefully lower the camshaft into position on the cylinder head with the No 1 camshaft lobes facing up. Support the ends of the shaft as it is inserted, to avoid damaging the lobes and journals.

**37** Oil the upper surfaces of the camshaft bearing journals, then refit the No 2 and 4 bearing caps over the camshaft and tighten the retaining nuts alternately and diagonally to the specified torque. **Note:** *The camshaft bearing caps are drilled off centre* **(see illustration)**, *make sure they're fitted on the correct journal and with the arrows made in Step 15 facing towards the timing belt end of the engine.*

**38** Apply a small amount of RTV sealant to the mating surface of No 1 bearing cap and refit it, along with cap Nos 3 and 5 over the camshaft **(see illustration)**. Tighten the nuts

to the specified torque starting with the centre cap and working towards the end caps.

### All engines

**39** Clean the oil seal housing bore(s) and lubricate the lip of a new camshaft oil seal with clean engine oil and locate it over the end of the camshaft. Slide the seal along the camshaft until it locates squarely in the housing bore. On 1.6L roller rocker arm engines (codes AYD and BFS) the camshaft transmission end sealing cap must also be renewed.

**40** Using a socket with an outside diameter slightly smaller than the outside diameter of the seal, carefully drive the new seal into place with a hammer **(see illustration)**. Make sure it's fitted squarely and driven in to the same depth as the original. If a socket isn't available, a short section of pipe will also work. **Note:** *On 1.8L engines, make sure to refit both camshaft oil seals, one for the intake camshaft and one for the exhaust camshaft.*

**41** Refit the camshaft sprocket and, on 1.8L engines, the camshaft position sensor reluctor ring, conical washer and retaining bolt. Tighten the bolts to the torque listed in this Chapter's Specifications (where given).

**42** Refit the timing belt (see Section 5). When refitting the timing belt, make sure the crankshaft is at TDC for the No 1 cylinder and the camshaft sprocket mark is aligned with the rear timing cover.

**43** The remainder of refitting is the reverse of removal.

*Caution: If new followers were used, wait*

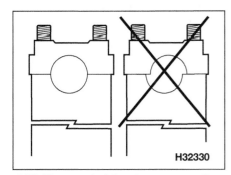

**6.37 The camshaft bearing cap mounting holes are drilled off-centre – be sure they are installed on the correct journal and with the arrows (made earlier) facing towards the timing belt of the engine**

**6.38 Apply a small amount of RTV sealant to the mating surface of the No 1 bearing cap**

**6.40 Gently drive the new seal into place with the spring side facing the engine**

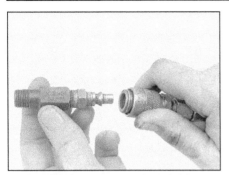

**7.4  This is what the typical air hose adapter that screws into the spark plug hole looks like – available at automotive parts stores**

**7.8  While the valve spring tool is compressing the spring, remove the collets (retainers) with a small magnet or pliers**

**7.10  The old valve stem seals can be removed with a pair of thin-nose pliers**

*at least 30 minutes before starting the vehicle to allow the followers to bleed down. Failure to do so will result in serious engine damage.*

### 7  Valve springs, retainers and seals – renewal

**Note:** *Broken valve springs and defective valve stem seals can be renewed without removing the cylinder heads. Two special tools and a compressed air source are normally required to perform this operation, so read through this Section carefully and rent or buy the tools before beginning the job.*
**1** Remove the valve cover referring to Section 4. Then refer to Section 6 and remove the camshaft and followers.
**2** Remove the spark plug from the cylinder which has the defective component. If all of the valve stem seals are being renewed, all of the spark plugs should be removed.
**3** Turn the crankshaft until the piston in the affected cylinder is at top dead centre (TDC) on the compression stroke (see Section 3 for instructions). If you're renewing all of the valve stem seals, begin with cylinder number one and work on the valves for one cylinder at a time. Move from cylinder-to-cylinder following the firing order sequence (see the Specifications listed at the beginning of this Chapter).

**4** Thread an adapter into the spark plug hole **(see illustration)** and connect an air hose from a compressed air source to it. Most motor factors can supply the air hose adapter. **Note:** *Many cylinder compression gauges utilise a screw-in fitting that may work with your air hose quick-disconnect fitting.*
**5** Apply compressed air to the cylinder. The valves should be held in place by the air pressure.

⚠️ *Warning: If the cylinder isn't exactly at TDC, air pressure may force the piston down, causing the engine to quickly rotate. DO NOT leave a spanner on the crankshaft drive sprocket bolt or you may be injured by the tool.*

**6** Force rags into the cylinder head holes around the valves to prevent parts and tools from falling into the engine.
**7** Using a socket and a hammer gently tap on the top of the each valve spring retainer several times. This will break the bond between the valve collet and the spring retainer and allow the collet to separate from the valve spring retainer as the valve spring is compressed.
**8** Use a valve spring compressor to compress the spring. Remove the collets with small needle-nose pliers or a magnet **(see illustration)**. **Note:** *Several different types of tools are available for compressing the valve springs with the head in place. Be sure to purchase or rent the type that bolts to the top of the cylinder head. This type uses a support*

*bar across the cylinder head for leverage as the valve spring is compressed. The lack of clearance surrounding the valve springs on these engines prohibits typical types of valve spring compressors from being used.*
**9** Remove the valve spring and retainer. **Note:** *If air pressure fails to retain the valve in the closed position during this operation, the valve face or seat may be damaged. If so, the cylinder head will have to be removed for repair.*
**10** Remove the old valve stem seals, noting differences between the intake and exhaust seals **(see illustration)**.
**11** Wrap a rubber band or tape around the top of the valve stem so the valve won't fall into the combustion chamber, then release the air pressure.
**12** Inspect the valve stem for damage. Rotate the valve in the guide and check the end for eccentric movement, which would indicate that the valve is bent.
**13** Move the valve up-and-down in the guide and make sure it doesn't bind. If the valve stem binds, either the valve is bent or the guide is damaged. In either case, the head will have to be removed for repair.
**14** Reapply air pressure to the cylinder to retain the valve in the closed position, then remove the tape or rubber band from the valve stem.
**15** Lubricate the valve stem with engine oil and refit a new seal on the valve guide **(see illustrations)**.

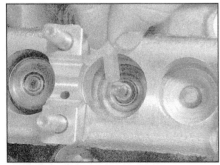

**7.15a  Install the protective plastic sleeve over the valve end face to avoid damage to the valve seal as the seal is installed**

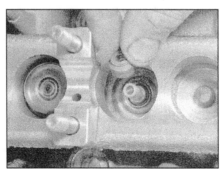

**7.15b  Push a new valve stem seal over the valve and down to the top of the guide, then remove the plastic installation tool**

**7.15c  Gently tap the new seal in place on the guide with a socket**

**16** Refit the valve spring and the spring retainer in position over the valve **(see illustration)**.

**17** Compress the valve spring and carefully position the collets in the groove. Apply a small dab of grease to the inside of each collet to hold it in place **(see illustration)**.

**18** Remove the pressure from the spring tool and make sure the collets are seated.

**19** Disconnect the air hose and remove the adapter from the spark plug hole.

**20** Refit the camshaft, followers, timing belt and the valve cover by referring to the appropriate Sections.

**21** Refit the spark plug(s) and hook up the HT leads(s).

**22** Start and run the engine, then check for oil leaks and unusual sounds coming from the valve cover area.

## 8 Intake manifold – removal and refitting

*Warning: Wait until the engine is completely cool before beginning this procedure.*

**1** Remove the engine cover **(see illustration 4.1)**.

### 1.6L engines

#### Upper intake manifold (plenum)

**2** Clamp-off the coolant hoses that connect to the throttle body **(see illustration 8.39a)**. **Note:** *The coolant hose is easier to clamp-off near the right corner of the upper intake manifold, rather than where it connects to the throttle body.*

**3** Refer to Chapter 4A, Section 9, and remove the air intake duct.

**4** Label and disconnect the hoses and electrical connectors attached to the plenum and throttle body. Be prepared for some coolant leakage at the throttle body. Disconnect the manifold change-over valve vacuum hose.

**5** Remove the bolts at the rear of the upper intake manifold securing it to the support bracket.

**6** Slacken the two bolts securing the upper part to the lower part of the manifold.

**7** Where fitted, disconnect the earth strap from the right-hand side of the throttle valve control assembly.

**8** Pull the centre pin out and remove the two clips either side of the upper manifold securing it to the lower part **(see illustration)**.

**9** Make a final check to ensure all relevant coolant hoses and electrical connections have been released, and push the upper manifold backwards and out of the lower manifold sealing rings.

**10** Examine the lower manifold sealing rings and renew any that are cracked, perished or worn.

**7.16 Install the valve spring and the retainer over the valve**

**11** Ensure that the sealing faces of the upper manifold are clean, and pull the manifold into position, making sure that the sealing rings of the lower manifold engage correctly with the upper manifold.

**12** The remainder of the refitting is the reverse of the removal procedure. Check the coolant level, adding as necessary (see Chapter 1). Run the engine and check for fuel, coolant, and vacuum leaks.

#### Lower intake manifold

**13** Remove the upper intake manifold, as described in Steps 1 to 9.

**14** Refer to Chapter 4A and relieve the fuel pressure. Squeeze the retaining clips and disconnect the fuel supply and return hoses from the fuel injector rail. Be prepared for fluid spillage.

**15** Disconnect the fuel pressure regulator vacuum hose.

**7.17 Apply a small dab of grease to each collet as shown here before installation – it will hold them in place on the valve stem as the spring is released**

**16** Depress the retaining clip and disconnect the wiring plug for the fuel injectors.

**17** Undo the eight bolts securing the lower manifold to the cylinder head and remove the manifold.

**18** Discard the seals between the manifold and cylinder head. New seals must be used.

**19** To refit the lower manifold, ensure that the mating surfaces of the cylinder head and manifold are clean and position the new seals.

**20** Hold the manifold in position and refit the retaining bolts and washers. Tighten the manifold bolts to the specified torque.

**21** The remainder of refitting is the reverse of the removal procedure. Check the coolant level, adding as necessary (see Chapter 1). Run the engine and check for fuel, coolant, and vacuum leaks.

### 1.8L engine

**22** Remove the upper intercooler hose and

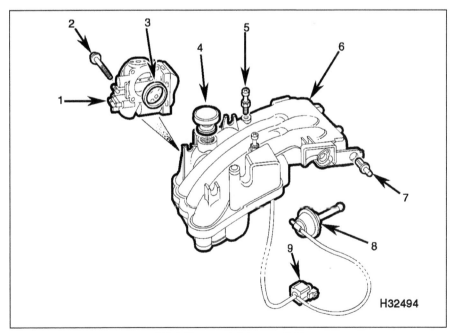

**8.8 1.6L upper intake manifold**

| | | |
|---|---|---|
| 1  Throttle valve control assembly | 4  Pressure relief valve | 8  Manifold change-over diaphragm |
| 2  Bolt | 5  Mounting bolt | 9  Manifold change-over valve |
| 3  Seal ring | 6  Intake manifold | |
| | 7  Clip | |

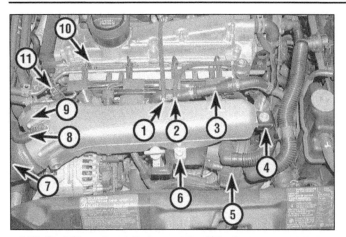

**8.22 On 1.8L engines, disconnect the following components to allow the removal of the intake manifold**

1 Vacuum hose (overrun solenoid)
2 Vacuum hose (fuel pressure regulator)
3 Crankcase ventilation hose
4 Air injection pump mounting bracket
5 Secondary air injection pump motor

6 Air injection pump mounting bracket
7 Upper intercooler hose
8 EVAP hose
9 Throttle control valve
10 Fuel rail and injectors
11 Intake air temperature sensor

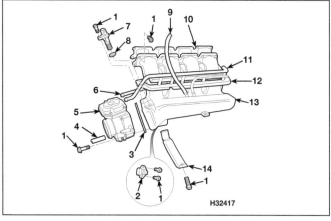

**8.29 Exploded view of the intake manifold and related components – 1.8L engine**

1 Bolt
2 Throttle position sensor
3 Gasket
4 Connecting hose
5 Throttle valve control module
6 Fuel return line/hose
7 Intake air temperature sensor
8 O-ring

9 Vacuum hose
10 Gasket
11 Fuel supply line/hose
12 Fuel rail, fuel injector and fuel pressure regulator
13 Intake manifold
14 Support bracket

the EVAP hose from the throttle body **(see illustration)**.

**23** Disconnect the overrun solenoid and the fuel pressure regulator vacuum hoses from the intake manifold.

**24** Label and detach the electrical connectors from the throttle control valve and the intake air temperature sensor.

**25** Relieve the fuel system pressure and remove the fuel rail and injectors (see Chapter 4A).

**26** Partially drain the engine coolant and remove the upper coolant pipe from the engine (see Chapters 1 and 3).

**27** Remove the secondary air injection pump motor and support brackets (see Chapter 6A).

**28** Remove the intake manifold support brace.

**29** Remove the mounting nuts/bolts **(see illustration)**, then detach the manifold and gasket from the engine.

**30** Use a scraper to remove all traces of old

gasket material and sealant from the manifold and cylinder head, then clean the mating surfaces with lacquer thinner or acetone. If the gasket was leaking, have the manifold checked for warpage at an automotive machine shop and resurfaced if necessary.

**31** Refit a new gasket, then position the manifold on the head and refit the nuts/bolts.

**32** Tighten the nuts/bolts in three or four equal steps to the torque listed in this Chapter's Specifications. Work from the centre out towards the ends to avoid warping the manifold.

**33** Refit the remaining parts in the reverse order of removal.

**34** Before starting the engine, check the throttle linkage for smooth operation.

**35** Check the coolant and add some if necessary, to bring it to the appropriate level. Run the engine and check for coolant and vacuum leaks.

**36** Road test the vehicle and check for proper operation of all accessories, including the cruise control system.

### 2.0L engine

#### Upper intake manifold (plenum)

**37** Clamp-off the coolant hoses that connect to the throttle body **(see illustration 8.39a)**. **Note:** *The coolant hose is easier to clamp-off near the right corner of the upper intake manifold, rather than where it connects to the throttle body.*

**38** Refer to Chapter 4A and remove the air intake duct and the accelerator cable.

**39** Label and disconnect the hoses and electrical connectors attached to the plenum and throttle body **(see illustrations)**. Be prepared for some coolant leakage at the throttle body.

**40** Remove the bolts at the rear of the upper

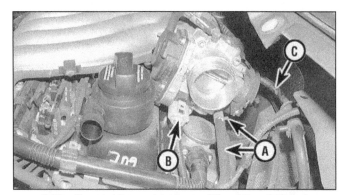

**8.39a Remove the coolant hoses (A) and the electrical connector (B) and the brake servo vacuum hose (C) from the throttle body – 1.6L and 2.0L engines**

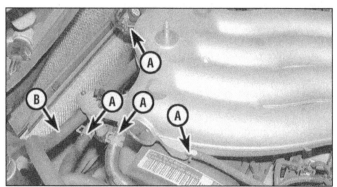

**8.39b Detach the vacuum hoses (A) and the coolant reservoir hose (B) at the rear of the upper intake manifold – 1.6L and 2.0L engines**

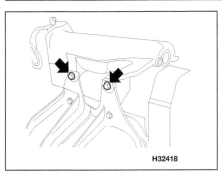

**8.40 Intake manifold-to-warm air deflector plate mounting bolts**

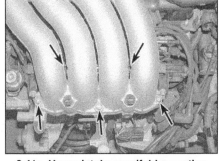

**8.41a Upper intake manifold mounting bolts – 2.0L engine**

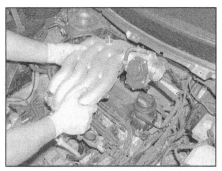

**8.41b Remove the upper intake manifold with the throttle body attached**

intake manifold securing it to the warm air deflector plate **(see illustration)**.
**41** Loosen the upper intake manifold bolts a quarter turn at a time until all bolts are loose. Remove the bolts by hand and remove the plenum with the throttle body attached **(see illustrations)**.
**42** To refit the upper manifold, clean the mounting surfaces of the intake manifold and the upper plenum with lacquer thinner and remove all traces of the old gasket material or sealant.
**43** Refit the new gasket over the intake manifold studs with the marks (if any) facing upward, then refit the plenum onto the lower intake manifold and tighten the bolts in a criss-cross pattern to the torque listed in this Chapter's Specifications. The remainder the refitting is the reverse of removal. Check the coolant level, adding as necessary (see Chapter 1).

**Lower intake manifold**

**44** Remove the upper intake manifold (see Steps 37 through 41).
**45** Label and detach any remaining hoses which would interfere with the removal of the lower intake manifold.
**46** Refer to Chapter 4A and relieve the fuel pressure. Remove the fuel rail and injectors from the lower intake manifold.
**47** Remove the lower intake manifold support bracket and the oil dipstick tube from the

engine **(see illustration)**.
**48** Remove the secondary air injection pump and bracket from the manifold (see Chapter 6A).
**49** Loosen the manifold mounting bolts/nuts in 1/4-turn increments until they can be removed by hand starting at the centre and moving towards the ends **(see illustrations)**.
**50** The manifold will probably be stuck to the cylinder heads and force may be required to break the gasket seal.
*Caution: Don't prise between the manifold and the heads or damage to the gasket sealing surfaces may occur, leading to vacuum leaks.*
**51** Carefully use a scraper to remove all traces of old gasket material and sealant from the manifold and cylinder heads, then clean the mating surfaces with lacquer thinner or acetone.
**52** Refit new gaskets, then position the lower manifold on the engine. Make sure the gaskets and manifolds are aligned over the studs in the cylinder heads and refit the nuts.
**53** Starting at the centre and working towards the ends, tighten the nuts/bolts, in several steps, to the torque listed in this Chapter's Specifications.
**54** The remainder of the refitting is the reverse of the removal procedure. Check the coolant level, adding as necessary (see Chapter 1). Run the engine and check for fuel, coolant vacuum leaks.

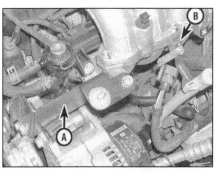

**8.47 Remove the support bracket (A) and the oil dipstick tube (B)**

## 9  Exhaust manifold – removal and refitting

> **Warning: The engine must be completely cool before beginning this procedure.**

### Removal

**1** Remove the engine cover **(see illustration 4.1)**.
**2** Remove the air intake duct (see Chapter 4A).
**3** Remove the scuttle cover (see Chapter 11).
**4** On 1.8L engines, refer to Chapter 4A and remove the turbocharger and all of its related components, then proceed to Step 12.

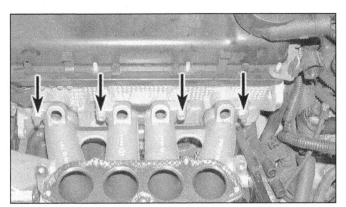

**8.49a Lower intake manifold (upper) mounting bolts/nuts – 2.0L engine**

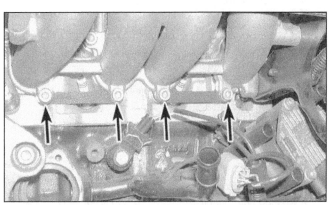

**8.49b Lower intake manifold (lower) mounting bolts – 2.0L engine**

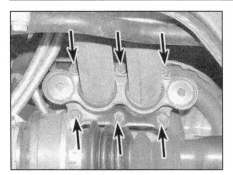

**9.10 Exhaust pipe-to-exhaust manifold mountings nuts (upper arrows – lower arrows shows the location of the exhaust manifold support brace) – 2.0L engine**

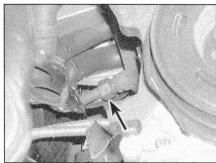

**9.11 Remove the air injection pipe (arrowed) from the exhaust manifold and the air control valve on the warm air deflector plate – 2.0L engine**

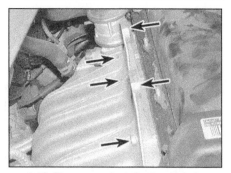

**9.12 The warm air deflector plate is mounted to the cylinder head (right arrows) – 2.0L engine**

**5** On 1.6L and 2.0L engines, remove the upper intake manifold (see Section 8).

**6** Remove the hoses from the secondary air injection control valve (see Chapter 6A).

**7** Raise the front of the vehicle and support it securely on axle stands.

**8** Disconnect the oxygen sensor electrical connectors and detach the wiring harness for the front oxygen sensor from the retaining bracket on the manifold.

**9** Apply penetrating oil to the exhaust manifold mounting nuts/bolts.

**10** Disconnect the exhaust pipe from the exhaust manifold, then remove the front exhaust pipe from the vehicle **(see illustration)**. Remove the exhaust manifold support bracket.

**11** Disconnect the air injection pipe union nuts from the fittings on the exhaust manifold and the secondary air injection control valve **(see illustration)**.

**12** On 1.8L and 2.0L engines, remove the warm air deflector plate from the engine **(see illustration)**.

**13** On 1.6L engines, unscrew the union securing the Exhaust Gas Recirculation (EGR) pipe to the exhaust manifold, the two nuts securing the pipe to the EGR valve, and the two bolts securing the pipe to the throttle valve control part.

**14** Remove the nuts/bolts and detach the manifold and gasket **(see illustrations)**.

---

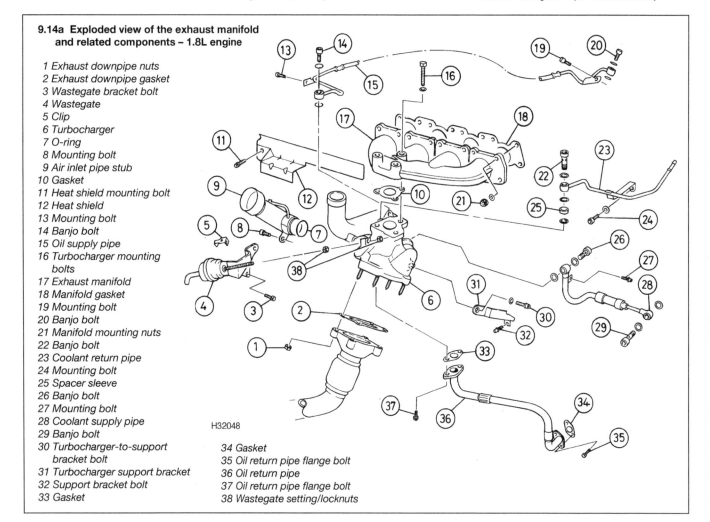

**9.14a Exploded view of the exhaust manifold and related components – 1.8L engine**

1 Exhaust downpipe nuts
2 Exhaust downpipe gasket
3 Wastegate bracket bolt
4 Wastegate
5 Clip
6 Turbocharger
7 O-ring
8 Mounting bolt
9 Air inlet pipe stub
10 Gasket
11 Heat shield mounting bolt
12 Heat shield
13 Mounting bolt
14 Banjo bolt
15 Oil supply pipe
16 Turbocharger mounting bolts
17 Exhaust manifold
18 Manifold gasket
19 Mounting bolt
20 Banjo bolt
21 Manifold mounting nuts
22 Banjo bolt
23 Coolant return pipe
24 Mounting bolt
25 Spacer sleeve
26 Banjo bolt
27 Mounting bolt
28 Coolant supply pipe
29 Banjo bolt
30 Turbocharger-to-support bracket bolt
31 Turbocharger support bracket
32 Support bracket bolt
33 Gasket

H32048

34 Gasket
35 Oil return pipe flange bolt
36 Oil return pipe
37 Oil return pipe flange bolt
38 Wastegate setting/locknuts

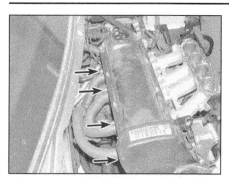

**9.14b Exhaust manifold upper mounting nuts (arrowed – lower nuts not visible in this photo) – 2.0L engine**

**10.9 Remove the coolant outlet flange (arrowed) from the end of the cylinder head**

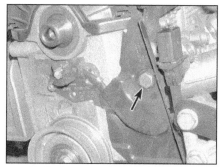

**10.10 On 1.6L code AWH and 2.0L engines, remove the upper bolt (arrowed) from the timing belt rear cover**

### Refitting

**15** Use a scraper to remove all traces of old gasket material and carbon deposits from the manifold and cylinder head mating surfaces. If the gasket was leaking, have the manifold checked for warpage at an automotive machine shop and resurfaced if necessary.

**16** Position a new gasket over the cylinder head studs.

**17** Refit the manifold and thread the mounting nuts/bolts into place. Make sure to use high temperature anti-seize compound on the exhaust manifold fasteners.

**18** Working from the centre out, tighten the nuts/bolts to the torque listed in this Chapter's Specifications in three or four equal steps.

**19** Refit the remaining parts in the reverse order of removal.

**20** Run the engine and check for exhaust leaks.

### 10 Cylinder head – removal and refitting

**Note:** *The cylinder head can be removed with the intake and exhaust manifold attached.*

### Removal

**1** Drain the engine coolant (See Chapter 1).

**2** Refer to Chapter 11 and remove the bonnet and the scuttle cover.

**3** Refer to Section 5 and remove the timing belt. After the timing belt has been removed, refit the right-hand side engine mounting to support the engine during the removal and refitting of the cylinder head.

**4** On 1.8L engines, refer to Chapter 4A and remove the turbocharger and all its related components. On 1.6L and 2.0L engines, disconnect the front exhaust pipe from the exhaust manifold and remove the exhaust manifold support bracket (see Section 9).

**5** Remove the valve cover (see Section 4).

**6** Remove the secondary air injection pump and mounting bracket (see Chapter 6A).

**7** Referring to Chapter 4A, disconnect and remove the fuel supply and return lines from the fuel rail.

**8** Unplug all electrical connectors and vacuum hoses from the cylinder head, labelling each wiring connector or hose to aid the refitting process. On 1.6L engines, although not strictly necessary, we recommend the EGR pipe is removed (see Chapter 4A).

**9** Refer to Chapter 3 and loosen the hose clamps and disconnect the radiator hoses from the ports on the cylinder head. Remove the coolant outlet flange from the end of the cylinder head **(see illustration)**.

**10** On 1.6L code AWH and 2.0L engines, loosen and withdraw the upper retaining screw from the timing belt rear cover **(see illustration)**. Also remove the HT leads. On 1.8L engines, remove the locking pin and the threaded stud, nut and washer (tensioner compressing tool) from the timing belt tensioner. **Note:** *This is the tool that was fabricated in Step 14 of Section 5 during the timing belt removal procedure.*

**11** Working in the reverse of the sequence shown in **illustration 10.26a**, progressively loosen the cylinder head bolts, by half a turn at a time, until all bolts can be unscrewed by hand. Discard the bolts – new ones must be fitted on reassembly.

**12** Check that nothing remains connected to the cylinder head, then lift the head away from the cylinder block; seek assistance if possible, as it is very heavy, especially when being removed with the manifolds. If resistance is felt, carefully prise the cylinder head upward,

beyond the gasket surface, at a casting protrusion **(see illustrations)**.

**13** Remove the gasket from the top of the block. Do not discard the gasket – it will be needed for identification purposes.

**14** If the cylinder head is to be disassembled for service, separate the manifold(s) as described in Sections 8 and 9. Disregard the steps that do not apply since the cylinder head is already removed from the vehicle, then proceed to Chapter 2D for overhaul procedures. Be sure to refit the manifolds back onto the cylinder head before refitting the cylinder head on the vehicle.

### Refitting

**15** The mating faces of the cylinder head and cylinder block must be perfectly clean before refitting the head. Use a hard plastic or wood scraper to remove all traces of gasket and carbon; also clean the piston crowns. Take particular care during the cleaning operations, as aluminium alloy is easily damaged. Also, make sure that the carbon is not allowed to enter the oil and water passages – this is particularly important for the lubrication system, as carbon could block the oil supply to the engine's components. Using adhesive tape and paper, seal the water, oil and bolt holes in the cylinder block.

**16** Check the mating surfaces of the cylinder block and the cylinder head for nicks, deep scratches and other damage. If slight, they

**10.12a Lift the cylinder head off the engine with the manifolds attached**

**10.12b If the cylinder head is stuck, it may be necessary to pry upward on the casting protrusion to dislodge the head from the block**

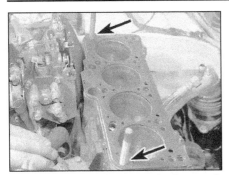

**10.22 Two of the old head bolts (arrowed) can be used as cylinder head alignment dowels**

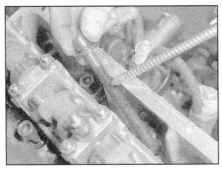

**10.24 Apply oil to the threads of the cylinder head bolts before installing them**

may be removed carefully with abrasive paper.

**17** If warpage of the cylinder head gasket surface is suspected, use a straight-edge to check it for distortion. It may be possible to resurface the cylinder head – refer to Chapter 2D.

**18** Clean out the cylinder head bolt holes using a suitable tap. Be sure they're clean and dry before refitting of the head bolts.

**19** It is possible for the piston crowns to strike and damage the valve heads if the camshaft is rotated with the timing belt removed and the crankshaft set to TDC. For this reason, the crankshaft must be set to a position other than TDC on No 1 cylinder before the cylinder head is reinstalled. Use a spanner and socket on the crankshaft pulley centre bolt to turn the crankshaft anti-clockwise until all four pistons are positioned halfway down their bores – approximately 90-degrees before TDC.

**20** If the cylinder head has been resurfaced, make sure the valve seats have been reworked by the same amount to allow the correct piston-to-valve clearance before refitting the cylinder head. See Chapter 2D for further information.

**21** Cut off the heads from two of the old cylinder head bolts to use as alignment dowels during cylinder head refitting. Also cut a slot in the end of the each bolt, big enough for a screwdriver blade, so that the alignment dowels can be removed after the cylinder head is fitted. A simple hand-held hacksaw can be used to fabricate the alignment dowels.

**22** Refit the alignment dowels in the outer rear holes of the cylinder block and position the new head gasket on the cylinder block, engaging it with the locating dowels **(see illustration)**. Ensure that the manufacturer's TOP and part number markings are face up.

**23** With the help of an assistant, place the cylinder head and manifolds centrally on the cylinder block, ensuring that the locating dowels engage with the recesses in the cylinder head. Check that the head gasket is correctly seated before allowing the full weight of the cylinder head to rest upon it. **Note:** *If the cylinder head had been disassembled for repair, be sure the camshaft(s) are reinstalled on the cylinder head with the No 1 cylinder camshaft lobes pointing upward.*

**24** Oil the threads and the underside of the bolt heads, then carefully enter each bolt into its relevant hole and screw them in hand-tight **(see illustration)**. Be sure to use NEW cylinder head bolts, as the old bolts are stretch type fasteners that will not provide the correct torque readings if re-used.

**25** Unscrew the home-made alignment dowels, using a flat-bladed screwdriver and refit the remaining two bolts hand tight.

**26** Working progressively and in the sequence shown **(see illustration)**, tighten the cylinder head bolts in three steps to the torque and angle of rotation listed in this Chapter's Specifications. **Note:** *It is recommended that an angle-measuring gauge be used during the final stages of the tightening, to ensure accuracy (see*

*illustration). If a gauge is not available, use white paint to make alignment marks between the bolt head and cylinder head prior to tightening; the marks can then be used to check the bolt has been rotated through the correct angle during tightening.*

**27** On 1.6L code AWH and 2.0L engines, refit the timing belt rear cover upper bolt and tighten it securely.

**28** Rotate the crankshaft in the normal direction of rotation (clockwise) 90-degrees to TDC. Be sure the alignment mark on the crankshaft pulley aligns with the mark on the cover. Refer to Section 3, if necessary.

**29** Support the engine from underneath with a jack and a block of wood, then remove the right-hand side engine mount. which was reinstalled to support the engine as the cylinder head was removed.

**30** Refit the timing belt tensioner and the camshaft sprocket on the engine if removed. On 1.6L and 2.0L engines, be sure the tensioner is seated properly. On 1.8L engines, compress the timing belt tensioner and lock it in place (see Section 5).

**31** Refit and adjust the timing belt as described in Section 5.

**32** The remainder of the refitting is the reverse of removal.

**33** Change the engine oil and coolant (see Chapter 1). Run the engine and check for leaks.

## 11 Crankshaft pulley – removal and refitting

**1** With the handbrake applied and the gear selector in Park (automatic) or in gear (manual), loosen the wheel bolts on the right front wheel, then raise the front of the vehicle and support it securely on axle stands.

**2** Remove the right front wheel and the right splash shield from the wheel arch.

**3** Remove the auxiliary drivebelt (see Chapter 1).

**4** Remove the bolts from the crankshaft pulley and detach it from the engine **(see illustration)**.

**5** If you're removing the crankshaft pulley for other procedures in this manual, such as

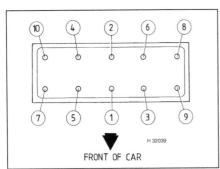

**10.26a Cylinder head bolt TIGHTENING sequence**

FRONT OF CAR

H 32039

**10.26b Using an angle measurement gauge during the final stages of tightening**

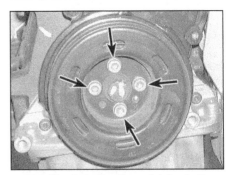

**11.4 Crankshaft pulley retaining bolts (arrowed)**

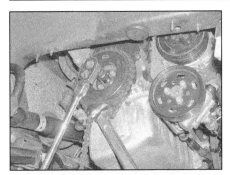

**11.5 If you are removing the crankshaft pulley to access the oil seal or the oil pump drive chain, hold the crankshaft pulley with a chain or strap wrench and loosen the crankshaft drive sprocket retaining bolt first (wrap the pulley with a piece of old drivebelt**

crankshaft oil seal removal or oil pump removal, loosen the drive sprocket retaining bolt first, before removing the crankshaft pulley **(see illustration)**. **Note:** *If you remove this bolt, obtain a new one (the manufacturer doesn't recommend re-using it).* Upon refitting, be sure to tighten the crankshaft drive sprocket bolt to the torque and angle of rotation listed in this Chapter's Specifications.
**6** Position the crankshaft pulley/balancer on the crankshaft drive sprocket and align the mounting holes. Note that the pulley can only go on one way **(see illustration)**.

**12.2a Pry the seal out very carefully with a seal remover tool or screwdriver, being careful not to nick or gouge the seal bore or the crankshaft**

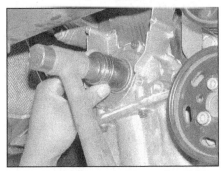

**12.4 Lubricate the lip of the seal and drive the new crankshaft seal into place with a large socket and hammer**

**11.6 Align the crankshaft pulley mounting holes and install the bolts**

**7** Refit the pulley mounting bolts and tighten them to the torque listed in this Chapter's Specifications.
**8** The remaining refitting steps are the reverse of removal.

## 12 Crankshaft timing belt end oil seal and housing – renewal

**1** Remove the timing belt and crankshaft sprocket (see Section 5).
**2** Note how far the seal is recessed in the bore, then carefully prise it out of the cover with a screwdriver or seal removal tool **(see illustration)**. Don't scratch the housing bore or damage the crankshaft in the process (if

**12.5 Oil seal housing bolts (arrowed)**

the crankshaft is damaged, the new seal will end up leaking). **Note:** *If a seal removal tool is unavailable, you can thread two self-tapping screws (180-degrees apart from one another) into the seal to prise the seal out* **(see illustration)**.
**3** Clean the bore in the housing and coat the inner edge of the new seal with engine oil. **Note:** *On 1.6L engines VW have gradually introduced the use of PTFE oil seals. These are identified by the lack of annular spring, and the sealing ring of these seals must not be lubricated.*
**4** Using a socket with an outside diameter slightly smaller than the outside diameter of the seal, carefully drive the new seal into place with a hammer **(see illustration)**. Make sure it's fitted squarely and driven in to the same depth as the original. If a socket isn't available, a short section of large diameter pipe will also work. Check the seal after refitting to make sure the spring didn't pop out of place.
**5** If the oil seal housing needs to be removed for access to other components such as to the oil pump drive chain, simply loosen the housing mounting bolts and remove the housing from the engine **(see illustration)**. In some instances the oil seal removal and refitting is easier with the housing removed, since the seal can be placed on a workbench and driven straight in and out of the bore with no special tools or adapters.
**6** Before refitting the cover, make sure the mating surfaces of the cover, the cylinder block and the sump rail are perfectly clean. Use a hard plastic or wood scraper to remove all traces of gasket material. Take particular care when cleaning the cover, as aluminium alloy is easily damaged.
**7** Apply a 5 mm bead of RTV sealant to the cover rear sealing flange **(see illustration)**. Also apply a 5 mm bead of RTV sealant to the sump flange and refit the cover onto the engine. **Note:** *Be sure to lubricate the oil seal lip before refitting the cover onto the engine (see Step 3 of this section). This will aid the refitting process and prevent dry start-ups, which may damage the seal and lead to future oil leaks.*
**8** Tighten the oil seal housing bolts in several

**12.2b If a seal removal tool is unavailable, the seal can also be removed with self-tapping screws to pry out the seal**

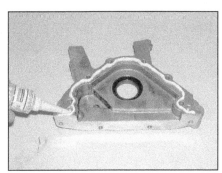

**12.7 Apply a 5 mm bead of RTV sealant to the rear of the oil seal housing as shown**

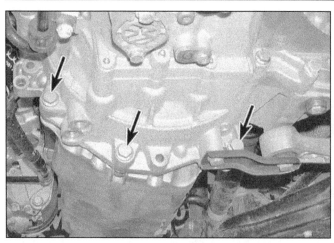

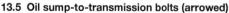

13.5  Oil sump-to-transmission bolts (arrowed)

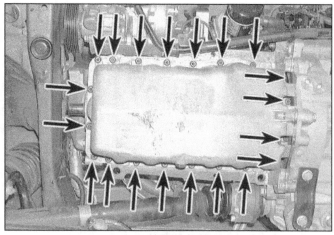

13.6  Oil sump retaining bolts (arrowed)

steps to the torque listed in this Chapter's Specifications.

**9** Refit the crankshaft sprocket and timing belt (see Section 5).

**10** Run the engine and check for oil leaks at the seal.

### 13  Sump – removal and refitting

#### Removal

**1** Set the handbrake and block the rear wheels.

**2** Raise the front of the vehicle and support it securely on axle stands.

**3** Remove the splash shields under the engine, if applicable. **Note:** *On later models, there is a protective cover over the sump. Remove the three fasteners and the cover.*

**4** Drain the engine oil (see Chapter 1). Remove the oil dipstick.

**5** Remove the bellhousing-to sump bolts **(see illustration)**. On 1.8L engines, remove the oil return tube from the sump and the turbocharger (see Chapter 4A). On 1.6L and 1.8L engines unplug the wiring connector for the oil temperature sensor on the base of the sump.

**6** Where applicable on 1.6L and 2.0L models, disconnect the connector for the oil level sensor. Remove the bolts and detach the sump **(see illustration)**. If it's stuck, tap it lightly with a rubber mallet. Don't damage the mating surfaces of the pan and block or oil leaks could develop. **Note:** *Some later models have a two-piece sump. On these models, only the bottom half of the sump should be removed unless the engine is being overhauled.*

#### Refitting

**7** Use a wooden scraper to remove all traces of old sealant from the block and sump. Clean the mating surfaces with lacquer thinner or acetone.

**8** Make sure the threaded bolt holes in the block are clean.

**9** Check the sump flange for distortion, particularly around the bolt holes. Remove any nicks or burrs as necessary.

**10** Inspect the oil pump pick-up tube assembly for cracks and a blocked strainer. If the pick-up was removed, clean it thoroughly and refit it now, using a new O-ring or gasket. Tighten the nuts/bolts to the torque listed in this Chapter's Specifications.

**11** Apply a 5 mm bead of suitable sealant (available from your VW dealer) to the sump flange **(see illustration)**. **Note:** *The sump*

*must be fitted within 5 minutes once the sealant has been applied.*

**12** Carefully position the sump on the engine block and refit the sump-to-engine block bolts loosely. Refit the sump-to-bellhousing bolts and tighten them just a little more than finger-tight. This should draw the sump flush with the bellhousing. If the transmission is not fitted in the vehicle use a straight-edge to align the rear surface of the sump with the rear face of the block.

**13** Working from the centre out, tighten the sump-to-engine block bolts to the torque listed in this Chapter's Specifications in three or four steps.

**14** Tighten the sump-to-bellhousing bolts to the torque listed in this Chapter's Specifications. Where applicable, reconnect the oil level indicator electrical connector.

**15** The remainder of refitting is the reverse of removal. Be sure to wait one hour before adding oil to allow the sealant to properly cure.

**16** Run the engine and check for oil pressure and leaks.

### 14  Oil pump – removal, inspection and refitting

#### Removal

**1** Remove the timing belt and the crankshaft drive sprocket (see Section 5).

**2** After the timing belt has been removed, refit the right-hand side engine mount to support the engine during the removal and refitting of the sump and pump.

**3** Remove the sump (see Section 13).

**4** Remove the crankshaft timing belt end oil seal housing (see Section 12).

**5** Remove the oil pump drive chain tensioner **(see illustration)**. **Note:** *On 2000 and later 2.0L engines, the oil pump is mounted in a case carrying the engine's balance shaft assembly, which bolts to the bottom of the*

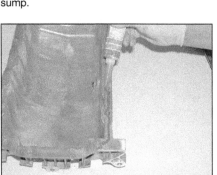

13.11  Apply a 5 mm bead of suitable sealant as shown (see text)

14.5  Remove the oil pump drive chain tensioner

**14.6 Mark the face of the oil pump drive chain and the driven sprocket so the chain can be installed in the same position and direction of travel**

**14.9 Oil pump pick-up tube mounting bolts (arrowed)**

**14.10 Oil pump mounting bolts (arrowed)**

engine block. To remove the oil pump on these models, first remove the centre bolt securing the triangular-shaped chain guide/tensioner assembly to the block, which will provide access to the oil pump sprocket and pump.

**6** Mark the face of the oil pump driven sprocket and chain so they can be fitted the same way **(see illustration)**. **Note:** *Installing the oil pump drive chain in a different direction from which it was originally fitted will accelerate wear and cause premature failure.*

**7** Wedge a screwdriver in one of the holes of the oil pump driven sprocket to hold the sprocket from turning as the driven sprocket retaining bolt is loosened, then remove the oil pump driven sprocket retaining bolt.

**8** Remove the oil pump drive chain and driven sprocket from the engine.

**9** Detach the two retaining bolts and separate the oil pump pick-up tube from the oil pump body. Lift out the pick-up tube and the O-ring **(see illustration)**.

**10** Remove the mounting bolts and separate the oil pump and the sump baffle from the engine **(see illustration)**.

### Inspection

**11** Clean all components with solvent, then inspect them for wear and damage.

**12** If damage or wear is noted, renewal of the entire oil pump assembly is recommended.

### *Refitting*

**13** Use a scraper to remove all traces of sealant and old gasket material from the pump case and engine block, then clean the mating surfaces with lacquer thinner or acetone.

**14** Place the oil pump on the engine block over the dowel pins and refit the two bolts facing the front of the engine block.

**15** Position the sump baffle plate in place and refit the remaining mounting bolt.

**16** Tighten the bolts to the torque listed in this Chapter's Specifications in several steps. Follow a criss-cross pattern to avoid warping the case.

**17** Using a new O-ring, refit the oil pick-up tube assembly **(see illustration)**. Tighten the fasteners to the torque listed in this Chapter's Specifications.

**18** Refit the oil pump drive chain and the driven sprocket in the original direction from which it was removed. Be sure to tighten the driven sprocket bolt to the correct torque Specifications.

**19** Refit the drive chain tensioner and bolt loosely on the engine block.

**20** Engage the tab on the tensioner spring on the inside lip of the engine block **(see illustration)**. Allow the tensioner to apply spring tension to the drive chain and tighten the tensioner retaining bolt.

**21** Refit the remaining parts in the reverse

order of removal. Be sure to refit the crankshaft oil seal housing to the engine block before refitting the sump.

**22** Add oil, start the engine and check for oil pressure and leaks.

**23** Recheck the engine oil level.

### 15 Flywheel/driveplate – removal and refitting

*Caution: The manufacturer recommends renewing the flywheel/driveplate bolts whenever they are removed.*

### *Removal*

**1** Raise the vehicle and support it securely on axle stands, then refer to the relevant part of Chapter 7 and remove the transmission. If it's leaking, now would be a very good time to renew the front pump seal/O-ring (automatic transmission) or input shaft seal (manual transmission).

**2** Remove the clutch pressure plate and driven plate (Chapter 8) (manual transmission-equipped vehicles). Now is a good time to check/renew the clutch components.

**3** Use a centre punch or paint to make alignment marks on the flywheel/driveplate and crankshaft to ensure correct alignment during refitting **(see illustration)**.

**4** Remove the bolts that secure the

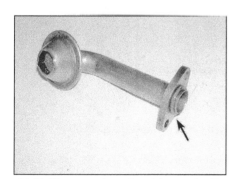

**14.17 Always replace the pick-up tube O-ring (arrowed)**

**14.20 Engage the tab on the chain tensioner spring on the inside lip of the engine block**

**15.3 Mark the flywheel/driveplate and the crankshaft so they can be reassembled in the same relative positions**

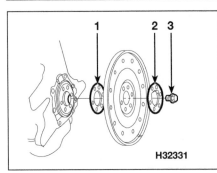

**15.5 On vehicles with automatic transmission, there is a spacer plate on each side of the driveplate – mark each plate as it is removed so it can be installed back in the same position**

*1 Shim     2 Backing plate     3 Bolt*

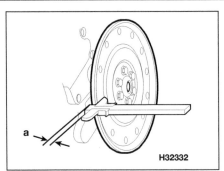

**15.10 The driveplate installed height can be measured with a machinist's rule**

*a = 19.5 to 21.1 mm*

flywheel/driveplate to the crankshaft. If the crankshaft turns, wedge a screwdriver in the ring gear teeth to jam the flywheel.

**5** Remove the flywheel/driveplate from the crankshaft. Since the flywheel is fairly heavy, be sure to support it while removing the last bolt. Automatic transmission-equipped vehicles have spacers on both sides of the driveplate **(see illustration)**. Keep them with the driveplate.

### *Refitting*

**6** Clean the flywheel to remove grease and oil. Inspect the surface for cracks, rivet grooves, burned areas and score marks. Light scoring can be removed with emery cloth. Check for cracked and broken ring gear teeth. Lay the flywheel on a flat surface and use a straight-edge to check for warpage.

**7** Clean and inspect the mating surfaces of the flywheel/driveplate and the crankshaft. If the crankshaft seal is leaking, renew it before reinstalling the flywheel/driveplate.

**8** Position the flywheel/driveplate and spacer (if used) against the crankshaft. Be sure to align the marks made during removal. Note that some engines have an alignment dowel

or staggered bolt holes to ensure correct refitting. Before refitting the new bolts, apply thread locking compound to the threads.

**9** Wedge a screwdriver in the ring gear teeth to keep the flywheel/driveplate from turning and tighten the bolts to the torque listed in this Chapter's Specifications.

**10** On vehicles equipped with automatic transmissions, measure the fitted height at three equal places around the driveplate and take an average **(see illustration)**. If the measurement is incorrect, the driveplate must be removed and shimmed to the proper height.

**11** The remainder of refitting is the reverse of the removal procedure.

### 16 Crankshaft transmission end oil seal – renewal

**1** The transmission must be removed from the vehicle for this procedure (see the relevant part of Chapter 7).

**2** The oil seal and housing are a integral part which must be removed and refitted together as a unit, however the oil seal and housing can be renewed without removing the sump.

**3** Remove the oil seal housing mounting bolts

and remove the housing from the engine **(see illustration)**.

**4** Before refitting a new seal and housing, make sure the mating surfaces of the cover, the cylinder block and the sump are perfectly clean. Use a hard plastic or wood scraper to remove all traces of gasket material. Take particular care when cleaning the cover, as aluminium alloy is easily damaged.

**5** Apply a 5 mm bead of RTV sealant to the rear of the housing flange and to the sump sealing surface **(see illustration)**. Refit the rear seal housing over the dowels onto the engine. **Note:** *Be sure to lubricate the oil seal lip before refitting the housing onto the engine. This will aid the refitting process and prevent dry start-ups, which may damage the seal and to lead to future oil leaks.*

**6** Tighten the oil seal housing bolts in several steps to the torque listed in this Chapter's Specifications. Be sure to wait one hour before starting the engine to allow the sealant to properly cure.

**7** The remaining steps are the reverse of removal.

### 17 Engine mountings – inspection and renewal

**1** Engine mounts seldom require attention, but broken or deteriorated mounts should be renewed immediately or the added strain placed on the power train components may cause damage or wear.

### *Check*

**2** During the check, the engine must be raised slightly to remove the weight from the mounts.

**3** Raise the vehicle and support it securely on axle stands, then position a jack under the engine sump. Place a large block of wood between the jack head and the sump, then carefully raise the engine just enough to take the weight off the mounts. Do not position the wood block under the drain plug.

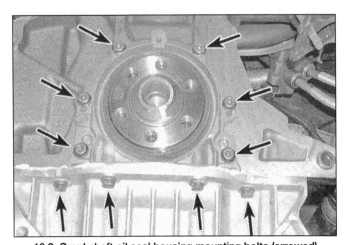

**16.3 Crankshaft oil seal housing mounting bolts (arrowed)**

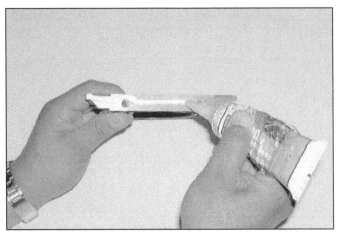

**16.5 Apply a 5 mm bead of RTV sealant to the oil seal housing sealing surfaces**

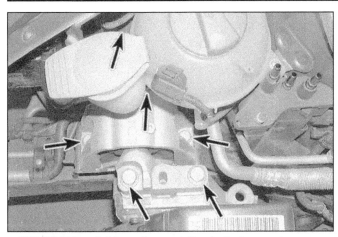

**17.9 Right-hand side engine mounting bolts (arrowed – upper arrow points to the mounting bracket-to-body bolt not visible in this photo)**

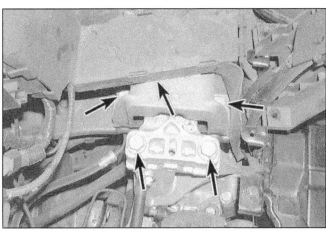

**17.11 Left-hand side engine mounting bolts (arrowed) – upper arrow points to the mounting bracket-to-body bolt not visible in this photo**

*Warning: DO NOT place any part of your body under the engine when it's supported only by a jack.*

**4** Check the mounts to see if the rubber is cracked, hardened or separated from the metal plates. Sometimes the rubber will split right down the centre.

**5** Check for relative movement between the mount plates and the engine or frame (use a large screwdriver or crowbar to attempt to move the mounts). If movement is noted, lower the engine and tighten the mount fasteners.

**6** Rubber preservative should be applied to the mounts to slow deterioration.

### Renewal

**7** Raise the vehicle and support it securely on axle stands (if not already done). Support the engine as described in Step 3.

**8** To remove the right-hand side engine mount, first relieve the fuel system pressure (see Chapter 4A). Disconnect the fuel supply and return hoses. Detach the coolant expansion tank from the inner wing and position it aside without disconnecting the hoses.

**9** Remove the mounting-to-bracket bolts and detach the mount **(see illustration)**.

**10** To remove the left-hand side engine mounting, first remove the air cleaner housing and the air intake duct (see the relevant part of Chapter 4).

**11** Remove the mounting-to-bracket bolts and detach the mount **(see illustration)**.

**12** To remove the lower torque strut, remove the bolt holding the insulator to the transmission bracket, then the two bolts holding the insulator to the chassis **(see illustration)**.

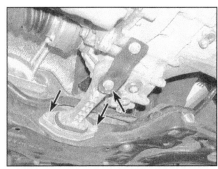

**17.12 Lower torque strut mounting bolts (arrowed)**

**13** Refitting is the reverse of removal. Always refit NEW mounting bolts and be sure to tighten them securely.

# Notes

# Chapter 2 Part C:
# Diesel engine in-car repair procedures

## Contents

## Degrees of difficulty

| | | | | |
|---|---|---|---|---|
| **Easy,** suitable for novice with little experience  | **Fairly easy,** suitable for beginner with some experience  | **Fairly difficult,** suitable for competent DIY mechanic  | **Difficult,** suitable for experienced DIY mechanic | **Very difficult,** suitable for expert DIY or professional |

## Specifications

### General

| | |
|---|---|
| Displacement . . . . . . . . . . . . . . . . . . . . . . . . . . . . . . . . . . . . . . . . . . . | 1896 cc |
| Manufacturer's engine codes* | |
|    Direct injection, turbo . . . . . . . . . . . . . . . . . . . . . . . . . . . . . . . . . | ALH |
|    Direct injection, unit injectors, turbo . . . . . . . . . . . . . . . . . . . . . . | ATD and AXR |
| Maximum power output | |
|    Engine code ALH  . . . . . . . . . . . . . . . . . . . . . . . . . . . . . . . . . . . . . | 66 kW at 3750 rpm |
|    Engine codes ATD and AXR . . . . . . . . . . . . . . . . . . . . . . . . . . . . . | 74 kW at 4000 rpm |
| Maximum torque output | |
|    Engine code ALH  . . . . . . . . . . . . . . . . . . . . . . . . . . . . . . . . . . . . . | 210 Nm at 1900 rpm |
|    Engine codes ATD and AXR . . . . . . . . . . . . . . . . . . . . . . . . . . . . . | 240 Nm at 1800 to 2400 rpm |
| Bore . . . . . . . . . . . . . . . . . . . . . . . . . . . . . . . . . . . . . . . . . . . . . . . . | 79.5 mm |
| Stroke . . . . . . . . . . . . . . . . . . . . . . . . . . . . . . . . . . . . . . . . . . . . . . . | 95.5 mm |
| Compression ratio | |
|    ALH . . . . . . . . . . . . . . . . . . . . . . . . . . . . . . . . . . . . . . . . . . . . . . | 19.5 : 1 |
|    ATD and AXR . . . . . . . . . . . . . . . . . . . . . . . . . . . . . . . . . . . . . . . | 19.0 : 1 |
| Compression pressures | |
|    Minimum compression pressure  . . . . . . . . . . . . . . . . . . . . . . . . . | Approximately 19.0 bar |
|    Maximum difference between cylinders . . . . . . . . . . . . . . . . . . . . | Approximately 5.0 bar |
| Firing order . . . . . . . . . . . . . . . . . . . . . . . . . . . . . . . . . . . . . . . . . . . | 1 – 3 – 4 – 2 |
| No 1 cylinder location . . . . . . . . . . . . . . . . . . . . . . . . . . . . . . . . . . . | Timing belt end |

***Note:** See 'Vehicle identification' at the beginning of this manual for the location of engine code markings.*

### Camshaft

| | |
|---|---|
| Camshaft endfloat (maximum) . . . . . . . . . . . . . . . . . . . . . . . . . . . . . | 0.15 mm |
| Camshaft bearing running clearance (maximum) . . . . . . . . . . . . . . . | 0.11 mm |
| Camshaft run-out (maximum) . . . . . . . . . . . . . . . . . . . . . . . . . . . . . | 0.01 mm |

### Lubrication system

| | |
|---|---|
| Oil pump type . . . . . . . . . . . . . . . . . . . . . . . . . . . . . . . . . . . . . . . . . | Gear type, chain-driven from crankshaft |
| Oil pressure (oil temperature 80°C, at 2000 rpm) . . . . . . . . . . . . . . | 2.0 bar |

## Torque wrench settings

| | Nm | Ft-lbs |
|---|---|---|
| Ancillary (alternator, etc) bracket mounting bolts . . . . . . . . . . . . . . . . . . | 45 | 33 |
| Auxiliary drivebelt tensioner securing bolt . . . . . . . . . . . . . . . . . . . . . . . | 25 | 18 |
| Camshaft bearing cap nuts | | |
|   Engine code ALH . . . . . . . . . . . . . . . . . . . . . . . . . . . . . . . . . . . . . . . | 20 | 15 |
| Camshaft bearing cap bolts* | | |
|   Engine codes ATD and AXR | | |
|     Step 1 . . . . . . . . . . . . . . . . . . . . . . . . . . . . . . . . . . . . . . . . . . . . | 8 | 6 |
|     Step 2 . . . . . . . . . . . . . . . . . . . . . . . . . . . . . . . . . . . . . . . . . . . . | Angle-tighten a further 90° | |
| Camshaft cover nuts/bolts . . . . . . . . . . . . . . . . . . . . . . . . . . . . . . . . . . | 10 | 7 |
| Camshaft sprocket centre bolt | | |
|   Engine code ALH . . . . . . . . . . . . . . . . . . . . . . . . . . . . . . . . . . . . . . . | 45 | 33 |
|   Engine codes ATD and AXR . . . . . . . . . . . . . . . . . . . . . . . . . . . . . . . | 100 | 74 |
| Camshaft sprocket outer bolts | | |
|   Engine codes ATD and AXR . . . . . . . . . . . . . . . . . . . . . . . . . . . . . . . | 25 | 18 |
| Crankshaft oil seal housing bolts . . . . . . . . . . . . . . . . . . . . . . . . . . . . . | 15 | 11 |
| Crankshaft pulley bolts | | |
|   Step 1 . . . . . . . . . . . . . . . . . . . . . . . . . . . . . . . . . . . . . . . . . . . . . . . | 10 | 7 |
|   Step 2 . . . . . . . . . . . . . . . . . . . . . . . . . . . . . . . . . . . . . . . . . . . . . . . | Angle-tighten a further 90° | |
| Crankshaft speed/position sensor wheel-to-crankshaft bolts* | | |
|   Step 1 . . . . . . . . . . . . . . . . . . . . . . . . . . . . . . . . . . . . . . . . . . . . . . . | 10 | 7 |
|   Step 2 . . . . . . . . . . . . . . . . . . . . . . . . . . . . . . . . . . . . . . . . . . . . . . . | Angle-tighten a further 90° | |
| Crankshaft sprocket bolt* | | |
|   Step 1 . . . . . . . . . . . . . . . . . . . . . . . . . . . . . . . . . . . . . . . . . . . . . . . | 120 | 89 |
|   Step 2 . . . . . . . . . . . . . . . . . . . . . . . . . . . . . . . . . . . . . . . . . . . . . . . | Angle-tighten a further 90° | |
| Cylinder head bolts* | | |
|   Step 1 . . . . . . . . . . . . . . . . . . . . . . . . . . . . . . . . . . . . . . . . . . . . . . . | 40 | 30 |
|   Step 2 . . . . . . . . . . . . . . . . . . . . . . . . . . . . . . . . . . . . . . . . . . . . . . . | 60 | 44 |
|   Step 3 . . . . . . . . . . . . . . . . . . . . . . . . . . . . . . . . . . . . . . . . . . . . . . . | Angle-tighten a further 90° | |
|   Step 4 . . . . . . . . . . . . . . . . . . . . . . . . . . . . . . . . . . . . . . . . . . . . . . . | Angle-tighten a further 90° | |
| Engine mountings | | |
|   Left-hand mounting-to-body bolts | | |
|     Large bolts* | | |
|       Step 1 . . . . . . . . . . . . . . . . . . . . . . . . . . . . . . . . . . . . . . . . | 40 | 30 |
|       Step 2 . . . . . . . . . . . . . . . . . . . . . . . . . . . . . . . . . . . . . . . . | Angle-tighten a further 90° | |
|     Small bolts . . . . . . . . . . . . . . . . . . . . . . . . . . . . . . . . . . . . . . . . | 25 | 18 |
|   Left-hand mounting-to-transmission bolts . . . . . . . . . . . . . . . . . . . | 100 | 74 |
|   Right-hand mounting-to-body bolts* | | |
|     Step 1 . . . . . . . . . . . . . . . . . . . . . . . . . . . . . . . . . . . . . . . . . . . | 40 | 30 |
|     Step 2 . . . . . . . . . . . . . . . . . . . . . . . . . . . . . . . . . . . . . . . . . . . | Angle-tighten a further 90° | |
|   Right-hand mounting plate bolts (small bolts) . . . . . . . . . . . . . . . . . | 25 | 18 |
|   Right-hand mounting-to-engine bracket bolts . . . . . . . . . . . . . . . . . | 100 | 74 |
|   Right-hand mounting bracket-to-engine bolts . . . . . . . . . . . . . . . . . | 45 | 33 |
|   Rear engine/transmission mounting | | |
|     Bracket-to-subframe bolts* | | |
|       Step 1 . . . . . . . . . . . . . . . . . . . . . . . . . . . . . . . . . . . . . . . . | 20 | 15 |
|       Step 2 . . . . . . . . . . . . . . . . . . . . . . . . . . . . . . . . . . . . . . . . | Angle-tighten a further 90° | |
|     Bracket-to-transmission bolts* | | |
|       Step 1 . . . . . . . . . . . . . . . . . . . . . . . . . . . . . . . . . . . . . . . . | 40 | 30 |
|       Step 2 . . . . . . . . . . . . . . . . . . . . . . . . . . . . . . . . . . . . . . . . | Angle-tighten a further 90° | |
| Exhaust manifold nuts . . . . . . . . . . . . . . . . . . . . . . . . . . . . . . . . . . . . | 25 | 18 |
| Exhaust pipe-to-manifold/turbocharger nuts . . . . . . . . . . . . . . . . . . . . | 25 | 18 |
| Fuel injector pipe union nuts . . . . . . . . . . . . . . . . . . . . . . . . . . . . . . . | 25 | 18 |
| Glow plugs . . . . . . . . . . . . . . . . . . . . . . . . . . . . . . . . . . . . . . . . . . . . | 15 | 11 |
| Injector rocker arm shafts* | | |
|   Engine codes ATD and AXR | | |
|     Step 1 . . . . . . . . . . . . . . . . . . . . . . . . . . . . . . . . . . . . . . . . . . . | 20 | 15 |
|     Step 2 . . . . . . . . . . . . . . . . . . . . . . . . . . . . . . . . . . . . . . . . . . . | Angle-tighten a further 90° | |
| Injection pump sprocket bolts (see illustration 7.24) | | |
|   Engine code ALH | | |
|     Type 1* | | |
|       Step 1 . . . . . . . . . . . . . . . . . . . . . . . . . . . . . . . . . . . . . . . . | 20 | 15 |
|       Step 2 . . . . . . . . . . . . . . . . . . . . . . . . . . . . . . . . . . . . . . . . | Angle-tighten a further 90° | |
|     Type 2 . . . . . . . . . . . . . . . . . . . . . . . . . . . . . . . . . . . . . . . . . . . | 25 | 18 |
| Oil baffle-to-camshaft cover bolt | | |
|   Engine code ALH . . . . . . . . . . . . . . . . . . . . . . . . . . . . . . . . . . . . . . . | 5 | 4 |
| Oil cooler securing plate . . . . . . . . . . . . . . . . . . . . . . . . . . . . . . . . . . | 25 | 18 |
| Oil drain plug . . . . . . . . . . . . . . . . . . . . . . . . . . . . . . . . . . . . . . . . . . | 30 | 22 |

## Torque wrench settings (continued)

| | Nm | Ft-lbs |
|---|---|---|
| Oil filter housing-to-cylinder block bolts* | | |
| Step 1 | 15 | 11 |
| Step 2 | Angle-tighten a further 90° | |
| Oil filter cover | 25 | 18 |
| Oil level/temperature sensor-to-sump bolts | 10 | 7 |
| Oil pick-up pipe securing bolts | 15 | 11 |
| Oil pressure relief valve plug | 40 | 30 |
| Oil pressure warning light switch | | |
| Engine code ALH | 25 | 18 |
| Engine codes ATD and AXR | 20 | 15 |
| Oil pump chain tensioner bolt | 15 | 11 |
| Oil pump securing bolts | 15 | 11 |
| Oil pump sprocket securing bolt | | |
| Engine code ALH | 20 | 15 |
| Engine codes ATD and AXR | 25 | 18 |
| Sump | | |
| Sump-to-cylinder block bolts | 15 | 11 |
| Sump-to-transmission bolts | 45 | 33 |
| Timing belt idler pulley bolt | | |
| Engine codes ATD and AXR | 20 | 15 |
| Timing belt idler pulleys | | |
| Lower left-hand idler roller nut | | |
| Engine code ALH | 22 | 16 |
| Lower right-hand idler roller (below water pump sprocket) bolt* | | |
| Step 1 | 40 | 30 |
| Step 2 | Angle-tighten a further 90° | |
| Upper idler roller bolt | 20 | 15 |
| Timing belt outer cover bolts | 10 | 7 |
| Timing belt rear cover bolts | | |
| Cover-to-cylinder head bolt | 10 | 7 |
| Cover-to-injection pump bolts | 30 | 22 |
| Timing belt tensioner roller securing nut | | |
| Engine code ALH | 20 | 15 |
| Engine codes ATD and AXR | | |
| Step 1 | 20 | 15 |
| Step 2 | Angle-tighten a further 45° | |
| Turbocharger oil return pipe-to-cylinder block banjo bolt | 40 | 30 |
| Turbocharger oil supply pipe to oil filter housing | | |
| Engine code ALH | 20 | 15 |
| Engine codes ATD and AXR | | |
| Banjo bolt | 25 | 18 |
| Union nut | 22 | 16 |
| Water pump bolts | 15 | 11 |

**\* Note:** *Use new bolts*

## 1  General information

*Caution 1: Avoid disconnecting the battery whenever possible! Disconnecting the battery can cause driveability problems that require a special scan tool to remedy. See Chapter 5, Section 1, for the use of an auxiliary power source before disconnecting the battery.*
*Caution 2: These models are equipped with an anti-theft radio. Before performing a procedure that requires disconnecting the battery, make sure you have the proper activation code.*
**Note:** *The engine cover must removed before performing many of the procedures in this Chapter (see illustration 4.1 in Chapter 2B).*

This Part of Chapter 2 is devoted to in-vehicle repair procedures for the 1.9L turbo diesel in-line four cylinder engine. This engine utilises a cast-iron engine block with an aluminium cylinder head. The aluminium cylinder head is equipped with pressed-in valve guides, hardened valve seats and houses the single overhead camshaft, which is driven from the crankshaft by a timing belt. On the engine with code ALH the timing belt also drives the fuel injection pump. All engines are fitted with a brake servo vacuum pump driven by the camshaft on the transmission end of the cylinder head. On engines with codes ATD and AXR a tandem pump is fitted, incorporating a vacuum pump and a fuel pump, driven by the camshaft. Hydraulic followers are used to actuate the valves. The oil pump is mounted at the timing belt end of the engine and is driven by a chain from the crankshaft.

All information concerning engine removal and refitting and engine block and cylinder head overhaul can be found in Part D of this Chapter.

The following repair procedures are based on the assumption that the engine is fitted in the vehicle. If the engine has been removed from the vehicle and mounted on a stand, many of the steps outlined in this Part of Chapter 2 will not apply:
a) Compression pressure – testing.
b) Camshaft cover – removal and refitting.
c) Crankshaft pulley – removal and refitting.
d) Timing belt covers – removal and refitting.
e) Timing belt – removal, refitting and adjustment.
f) Timing belt tensioner and sprockets – removal and refitting.
g) Camshaft oil seals – renewal.
h) Camshaft and hydraulic tappets – removal, inspection and refitting.

i) Cylinder head – removal and refitting.
j) Cylinder head and pistons –
   decarbonising.
k) Sump – removal and refitting.
l) Oil pump – removal, overhaul and
   refitting.
m) Crankshaft oil seals – renewal.
n) Engine/transmission mountings –
   inspection and renewal.
o) Flywheel/driveplate – removal, inspection
   and refitting.

**Note:** *It is possible to remove the pistons and connecting rods (after removing the cylinder head and sump) without removing the engine. However, this is not recommended. Work of this nature is more easily and thoroughly completed with the engine on the bench, as described in Chapter 2D.*

The Specifications included in this Part of Chapter 2 apply only to the procedures contained in this Part. Part D of Chapter 2 contains the Specifications necessary for cylinder head and engine block rebuilding.

## 2  Compression and leakdown tests – description and interpretation

### Compression test

**Note:** *A compression tester suitable for use with diesel engines will be required for this test.*

**Caution: The following work may insert fault codes in the engine management ECU. These fault codes must be cleared by a VW dealer.**

**1** When engine performance is down, or if misfiring occurs which cannot be attributed to the ignition or fuel systems, a compression test can provide diagnostic clues as to the engine's condition.
**2** If the test is performed regularly, it can give warning of trouble before any other symptoms become apparent.
**3** The engine must be fully warmed-up to normal operating temperature, the battery must be fully-charged and you will require the aid of an assistant.
**4** On engine code ALH, the stop solenoid and fuel metering control wiring must be

disconnected, to prevent the engine from running or fuel from being discharged **(see illustrations)**. **Note:** *As a result of the wiring being disconnected, faults will be stored in the ECU memory. These must be erased after the compression test.*
**5** On engine codes ATD and AXR, disconnect the injector solenoids by disconnecting the connector at the end of the cylinder head **(see illustration)**. **Note:** *As a result of the wiring being disconnected, faults will be stored in the ECU memory. These must be erased after the compression test.*
**6** Remove the glow plugs as described in Chapter 5, then fit a compression tester to the No 1 cylinder glow plug hole. The type of tester which screws into the plug thread is preferred.
**7** Have your assistant, crank the engine for several seconds on the starter motor. After one or two revolutions, the compression pressure should build-up to a maximum figure and then stabilise. Record the highest reading obtained.
**8** Repeat the test on the remaining cylinders, recording the pressure in each.
**9** The cause of poor compression is less easy to establish on a diesel engine than on a petrol engine. The effect of introducing oil into the cylinders (wet testing) is not conclusive, because there is a risk that the oil will sit in the recess on the piston crown, instead of passing to the rings. However, the following can be used as a rough guide to diagnosis.
**10** All cylinders should produce very similar pressures. Any difference greater than that specified indicates the existence of a fault. Note that the compression should build-up quickly in a healthy engine. Low compression on the first stroke, followed by gradually increasing pressure on successive strokes, indicates worn piston rings. A low compression reading on the first stroke, which does not build-up during successive strokes, indicates leaking valves or a blown head gasket (a cracked head could also be the cause).
**11** A low reading from two adjacent cylinders is almost certainly due to the head gasket having blown between them and the presence of coolant in the engine oil will confirm this.
**12** On completion, remove the compression

tester, and refit the glow plugs, with reference to Chapter 5.
**13** Reconnect the fuel quantity adjuster and fuel cut-off solenoid wiring connectors.

### Leakdown test

**14** A leakdown test measures the rate at which compressed air fed into the cylinder is lost. It is an alternative to a compression test, and in many ways it is better, since the escaping air provides easy identification of where pressure loss is occurring (piston rings, valves or head gasket).
**15** The equipment required for leakdown testing is unlikely to be available to the home mechanic. If poor compression is suspected, have the test performed by a suitably-equipped garage.

## 3  Engine assembly and valve timing marks – general information and usage

### General information

**1** TDC is the highest point in the cylinder that each piston reaches as it travels up-and-down when the crankshaft turns. Each piston reaches TDC at the end of the compression stroke and again at the end of the exhaust stroke, but TDC generally refers to piston position on the compression stroke. No 1 piston is at the timing belt end of the engine.
**2** Positioning No 1 piston at TDC is an essential part of many procedures, such as timing belt removal and camshaft removal.
**3** The design of the engines covered in this Chapter is such that piston-to-valve contact may occur if the camshaft or crankshaft is turned with the timing belt removed. For this reason, it is important to ensure that the camshaft and crankshaft do not move in relation to each other once the timing belt has been removed from the engine.

### Setting TDC on No 1 cylinder

#### Engine code ALH

**Note:** *Suitable tools will be required to lock the camshaft and the fuel injection pump sprocket in position during this procedure – see text.*

**2.4a  Fuel cut-off solenoid wiring connector is secured by a nut (arrowed)**

**2.4b  Wiring plug for fuel quantity adjuster is behind oil filter housing**

**2.5  Disconnect the injector solenoids wiring plug connector (arrowed)**

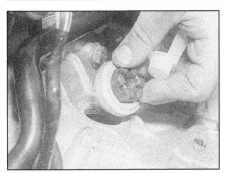

3.7a  Using a large nut to unscrew the inspection plug from the transmission bellhousing

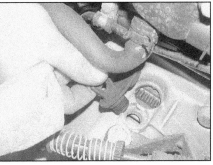

3.7b  Removing the rubber bung from the bellhousing – seen with air cleaner removed

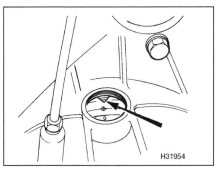

3.7c  Timing mark on the edge of the flywheel (arrowed) lined up with the pointer on the bellhousing casing (manual transmission)

**4**  Remove the camshaft cover as described in Section 4.

**5**  Remove the upper outer timing belt cover as described in Section 6.

**6**  Remove the glow plugs, as described in Chapter 5, to allow the engine to turn more easily.

**7**  Where fitted, remove the inspection plug from the transmission bellhousing, if necessary using a large nut to unscrew it **(see illustrations)**. Access to the inspection plug is greatly improved if the air cleaner is removed first, as described in Chapter 4B.

**8**  Rotate the crankshaft clockwise, using a socket or spanner on the crankshaft sprocket bolt, until the timing mark machined onto the edge of the flywheel/driveplate lines up with the pointer on the transmission casing **and** the timing hole in the fuel injection

sprocket lines up with the hole in the support bracket.

**9**  To lock the engine in the TDC position, the camshaft (not the sprocket) and fuel injection pump sprocket must be locked in position, using special locking tools. Improvised tools may be fabricated, but due to the exact measurements and machining involved, it is strongly recommended that a kit of locking tools is either borrowed or hired from a VW dealer, or purchased from a reputable tool manufacturer **(see illustration)**.

**10**  Engage the edge of the locking bar (VW tool 3418) with the slot in the end of the camshaft **(see illustrations)**.

**11**  With the locking bar still inserted, turn the camshaft slightly (by turning the crankshaft clockwise, as before), so that the locking bar rocks to one side, allowing one end of the bar

to contact the cylinder head surface. At the other side of the locking bar, measure the gap between the end of the bar and the cylinder head using a feeler blade.

**12**  Turn the camshaft back slightly, then pull out the feeler blade. The idea now is to level the locking bar by inserting two feeler blades, each with a thickness equal to *half* the originally measured gap, on either side of the camshaft between each end of the locking bar and the cylinder head. This centres the camshaft, and sets the valve timing in reference condition **(see illustration)**.

**13**  Insert the locking pin (VW tool 3359) through the fuel injection pump sprocket timing hole, so that it passes through the timing hole in the injection pump hub, and into the support bracket behind the hub. This locks the fuel injection pump in the TDC reference position **(see illustration)**.

**14**  The engine is now set to TDC on No 1 cylinder.

### Engine codes ATD and AXR

**Note:** *VAG special tool (T10050) is required to lock the crankshaft sprocket in the TDC position.*

**15**  Remove the auxiliary drivebelt(s) as described in Chapter 1.

**16**  Remove the crankshaft pulley/vibration damper as described in Section 5.

**17**  Remove the timing belt covers as described in Section 6.

**18**  Remove the glow plugs, as described in Chapter 5, to allow the engine to turn more easily.

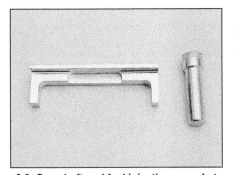

3.9  Camshaft and fuel injection sprocket locking tools

3.10a  Using a straight-edge to assess alignment of the camshaft slot with the head

3.10b  Engage the locking bar with the slot in the camshaft

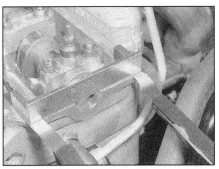

3.12  Camshaft centred and locked using the locking bar and feeler blades

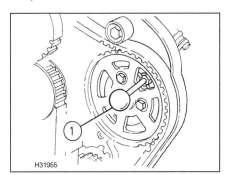

3.13  Injection pump sprocket locked using the locking pin (1)

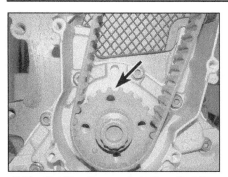

**3.19a Position the crankshaft so that the mark on the sprocket is almost vertical (arrowed) . . .**

**19** Using a spanner or socket on the crankshaft sprocket bolt, turn the crankshaft in the normal direction of rotation (clockwise) until the alignment mark on the face of the sprocket is almost vertical **(see illustrations)**.

**20** The arrow (marked 4Z) on the rear section of the upper timing belt upper cover aligns between the two lugs on the rear of the camshaft hub sender wheel **(see illustration)**.

**21** While in this position it should be possible to insert VAG tool T10050 to lock the crankshaft, and 6 mm diameter rod to lock the camshaft **(see illustration)**. Note: *The mark on the crankshaft sprocket and the mark on the VAG tool T10050 must align, whilst at the same time the shaft of tool T10050 must engage in the drilling in the crankshaft oil seal housing.*

**22** The engine is now set to TDC on No 1 cylinder.

---

**4   Camshaft cover –**
    removal and refitting

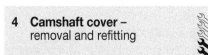

### *Removal*

#### Engine code ALH

**1** Remove the camshaft cover. Removal details vary according to model, but the cover retaining nuts are concealed under circular covers, which are prised out of the main cover. Where plastic screws or turn-fasteners are used, these can be removed using a wide-

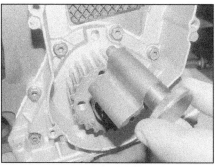

**3.19b . . . then insert the VW tool T10050 . . .**

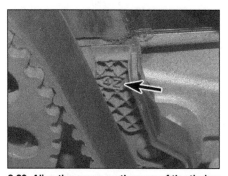

**3.20 Align the arrow on the rear of the timing belt cover (arrowed) between the lugs on the rear of the camshaft hub sender wheel**

bladed screwdriver. Remove the nuts or screws, and lift the cover from the engine **(see illustrations)**.

**2** Where applicable, release any wiring or hoses from the camshaft cover.

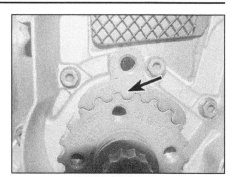

**3.19c . . . and align the marks (arrowed) on the tool and sprocket**

**3.21 Insert a 6 mm drill bit (arrowed) through the camshaft hub into the cylinder head to lock the camshaft**

**3** Disconnect the breather hose from the air inlet duct **(see illustration)**. If wished, the breather valve can be removed from the top of the camshaft cover by carefully pulling upwards, but its removal is not essential.

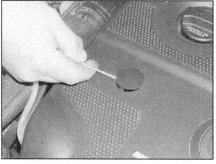

**4.1a Prise out the covers . . .**

**4.1c . . . on this engine, the dipstick has to be removed . . .**

**4.1b . . . remove the nuts beneath . . .**

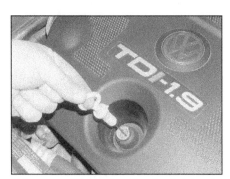

**4.1d . . . before the cover can be lifted off**

**4.3 Disconnecting the pressure-regulating valve breather hose**

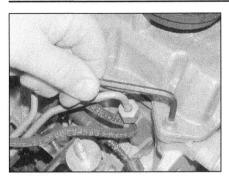

4.4a  Unscrew the retaining bolts . . .

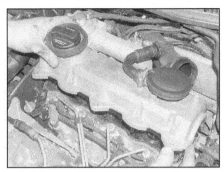

4.4b  . . . and lift off the camshaft cover

4.5  One of the cover locating pegs (arrowed) and also breather pipe (arrowed)

**4** Unscrew the securing nuts/bolts, and lift the camshaft cover from the cylinder head **(see illustrations)**. On most models, the bolts at the rear are very awkward to reach – a selection of Allen keys/bits and a knuckle joint may well be needed. Recover the gasket if it is loose.

### Engine codes ATD and AXR

**5** Remove the dipstick and prise off and remove the camshaft cover, then disconnect the breather hose from the camshaft cover **(see illustration)**.
**6** Unscrew the camshaft cover retaining bolts and lift the cover away. If it sticks, do not attempt to lever it off – instead free it by working around the cover and tapping it lightly with a soft-faced mallet.
**7** Recover the camshaft cover gasket **(see illustration)**. Inspect the gasket carefully,

and renew it if damage or deterioration is evident.
**8** Clean the mating surfaces of the cylinder head and camshaft cover thoroughly, removing all traces of oil and old gasket – take care to avoid damaging the surfaces as you do this.

### *Refitting*

**9** Refit the camshaft cover by following the removal procedure in reverse, noting the following points:
 a) *On engine code ALH, before refitting the camshaft cover, apply a small amount of sealant at the front and rear of the cylinder head, to the two points where the camshaft bearing caps contact the cylinder head **(see illustration)**. Ensure that the gasket is correctly seated on the cylinder head, and take care to avoid*

*displacing it as the camshaft cover is lowered into position.*
 b) *On engine codes ATD and AXR, apply suitable sealant to the points where the camshaft bearing cap contacts the cylinder head **(see illustration)**.*
 c) *Tighten the camshaft cover retaining nuts/bolts progressively to the specified torque. **Note:** On engine codes ATD and AXR, tighten the retaining nuts/bolts in sequence **(see illustration)**.*

## 5  Crankshaft pulley – removal and refitting

### *Removal*

**1** Disconnect the battery negative lead. **Note:** *Refer to 'Battery disconnection' in Chapter 5 first.*
**2** For improved access, raise the front right-hand side of the vehicle, and support securely on axle stands (see *Jacking and towing*). Remove the roadwheel.
**3** Remove the securing screws and withdraw the engine undershield(s) and/or wheel arch liner panels. Unscrew the nut at the rear, and the washer-type fasteners further forward, then release the air hose clip and manipulate out the plastic air duct for the intercooler **(see illustration)**.
**4** Where applicable, prise the cover from the

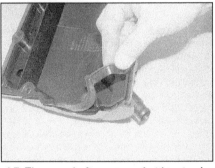

4.7  The camshaft cover gasket locates in a groove in the cover

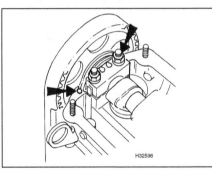
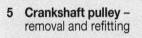

4.9a  Apply sealant to the rear and front (arrowed) bearing cap joints

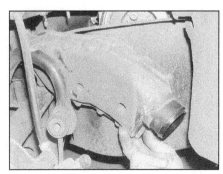

5.3  Removing the intercooler air duct for access to the crankshaft pulley

4.9b  Apply sealant to the points (arrowed) on the cylinder head

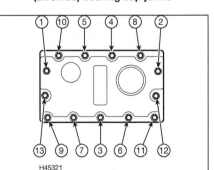

4.9c  Camshaft cover tightening sequence

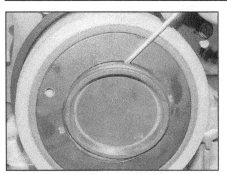

**5.4 Prising out the crankshaft pulley centre cap**

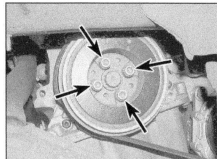

**5.5 Showing the four crankshaft pulley bolts (arrowed)**

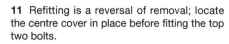

centre of the pulley to expose the securing bolts **(see illustration)**.

**5** Slacken the bolts securing the crankshaft pulley to the sprocket **(see illustration)**. If necessary, the pulley can be prevented from turning by counterholding with a spanner or socket on the crankshaft sprocket bolt.

**6** Remove the auxiliary drivebelt, as described in Chapter 1.

**7** Unscrew the bolts securing the pulley to the sprocket, and remove the pulley.

### Refitting

**8** Refit the pulley over the locating peg on the crankshaft sprocket, then refit the pulley securing bolts.

**9** Refit and tension the auxiliary drivebelt as described in Chapter 1.

**10** Prevent the crankshaft from turning as during removal, then fit the pulley securing bolts, and tighten to the specified torque.

**11** Refit the engine undershield(s), wheel arch liners and the intercooler air duct.

**12** Refit the roadwheel, lower the vehicle to the ground, and reconnect the battery negative lead.

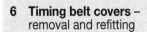

**6  Timing belt covers –** removal and refitting

### Upper outer cover

**1** Where applicable, release the retaining clips and remove the air intake hose from

across the top of the timing belt cover **(see illustration)**.

**2** Release the uppermost part of the timing belt outer cover by prising open the metal spring clips, then withdraw the cover away from the engine **(see illustrations)**.

**3** Refitting is a reversal of removal, noting that the lower edge of the upper cover engages with the centre cover.

### Centre outer cover

**4** Remove the auxiliary drivebelt as described in Chapter 1B.

**5** Remove the crankshaft pulley as described in Section 5. It is assumed that, if the centre cover is being removed, the lower cover will be also – if not, simply remove the components described in Section 5 for access to the crankshaft pulley, and leave the pulley in position.

**6** With the upper cover removed (paragraphs 1 to 3), unscrew and remove the retaining bolts from the centre cover. Withdraw the centre cover from the engine, noting how it fits over the lower cover.

**7** Refitting is a reversal of removal.

### Lower outer cover

**8** Remove the upper and centre covers as described previously.

**9** If not already done, remove the crankshaft pulley as described in Section 5.

**10** Unscrew the remaining bolt(s) securing the lower cover, and lift it out.

**11** Refitting is a reversal of removal; locate the centre cover in place before fitting the top two bolts.

### Rear cover

**12** Remove the upper, centre and lower covers as described previously.

**13** Remove the timing belt, tensioner and sprockets as described in Sections 7 and 8.

**14** Slacken and withdraw the retaining bolts and lift the timing belt inner cover from the studs on the end of the engine, and remove it from the engine compartment.

**15** Refitting is a reversal of removal.

**7  Timing belt** – removal, inspection and refitting

### Removal

**1** The primary function of the toothed timing belt is to drive the camshaft, but it also drives the water pump. On engine code ALH it also drives the fuel injection pump. Should the belt slip or break in service, the valve timing will be disturbed and piston-to-valve contact may occur, resulting in serious engine damage. For this reason, it is important that the timing belt is tensioned correctly, and inspected regularly for signs of wear or deterioration.

**2** Disconnect the battery negative lead. **Note:** *Refer to 'Battery disconnection' in Chapter 5 first.*

**3** Remove the right-hand headlight as described in Chapter 12, and the intake manifold-to-intercooler air trunking.

**4** Apply the handbrake, then jack up the front of the vehicle and support securely on axle stands (see *Jacking and towing*).

**5** Remove the securing screws and withdraw the engine undershield(s), and the right-hand wheel arch liner.

**6** Remove the right-hand engine mounting as described in Section 18, then unbolt and remove the mounting bracket.

**7** Remove the auxiliary drivebelt (see Chapter 1) and drivebelt tensioner, then remove the crankshaft pulley/vibration damper (Section 5 of this Chapter).

**6.1 Removing the air intake hose from across the top of the timing belt cover**

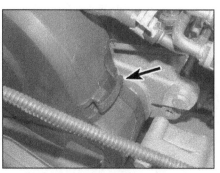

**6.2a Release the retaining clips (one arrowed) . . .**

**6.2b . . . and withdraw the upper cover**

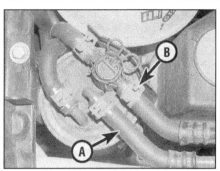

7.8 Fuel supply (A) and return (B) hoses at the fuel filter

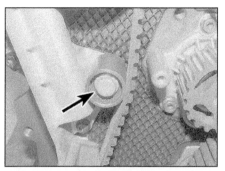

7.18 Undo the retaining bolt (arrowed) and remove the idler roller

7.19a Turn the tensioner arm anti-clockwise until it contacts the stop (A) . . .

**8** Disconnect the fuel supply and return hoses from the fuel filter, referring to Chapter 1 if necessary **(see illustration)**. Label the hoses if necessary, to ensure correct refitting.
**9** If required, to further improve working room, remove the windscreen washer bottle.
**10** Remove the timing belt covers, as described in Section 6.

### Engine code ALH

**11** Remove the camshaft cover as described in Section 4.
**12** Remove the brake servo vacuum pump as described in Chapter 9.
**13** Turn the crankshaft to position No 1 piston at TDC on the firing stroke, and lock the camshaft and the fuel injection sprocket in position, as described in Section 3.
**14** If the original timing belt is to be refitted, mark the running direction of the belt, to ensure correct refitting.
*Caution: If the belt appears to be in good condition and can be re-used, it is essential that it is refitted the same way around, otherwise accelerated wear will result, leading to premature failure.*
**15** Slacken the timing belt tensioner nut, and allow the tensioner to rotate anti-clockwise, relieving the tension on the timing belt.
**16** Slide the belt from the sprockets, taking care not to twist or kink the belt excessively if it is to be re-used.

### Engine codes ATD and AXR

**Note:** *VAG technicians use special tool T10008 to lock the timing belt tensioner in the released position. It is possible to manufacture a home-made alternative – see below.*
**17** Set the engine to TDC on No 1 cylinder as described in Section 3.
**18** Undo the bolt and remove the idler roller **(see illustration)**.
**19** With reference to Section 8, relieve the tension on the timing belt by slackening the tensioner mounting nut slightly, and turning the tensioner anti-clockwise with circlip pliers until it contacts the stop (A). It may take a few moments for the tensioner plunger to fully compress. Lock the plunger by inserting a locking plate (VAG tool No T10008). If this special tool is not available, an alternative can be manufactured by copying the design **(see illustrations)**. Now turn the tensioner

7.19b . . . then insert the locking tool through the slot to lock the tensioner . . .

clockwise onto stop (B) **(see illustration)**.
**20** Examine the timing belt for manufacturer's markings that indicate the direction of rotation. If none are present, make your own using typist's correction fluid or a dab of paint – do not cut or score the belt in any way.
*Caution: If the belt appears to be in good condition and can be re-used, it is essential that it is refitted the same way around, otherwise accelerated wear will result, leading to premature failure.*
**21** Slide the belt off the sprockets, taking care to avoid twisting or kinking it excessively if it is to be re-used.

### Inspection

**22** Examine the belt for evidence of contamination by coolant or lubricant. If this is the case, find the source of the contamination

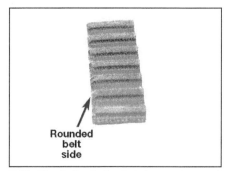

Rounded belt side

7.22 Check the timing belt for cracked and missing teeth – wear on one side of the belt indicates sprocket misalignment problems

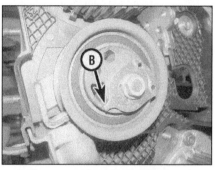

7.19c . . . and turn the tensioner arm clockwise until it contacts the stop (B)

before progressing any further. Check the belt for signs of wear or damage, particularly around the leading edges of the belt teeth **(see illustration)**. Renew the belt if its condition is in doubt; the cost of belt renewal is negligible compared with potential cost of the engine repairs, should the belt fail in service. The belt must be renewed if it has covered the mileage given in Chapter 1, however, if it has covered less, it is prudent to renew it regardless of condition, as a precautionary measure.
**23** If the timing belt is not going to be refitted for some time, it is a wise precaution to hang a warning label on the steering wheel, to remind yourself (and others) not to attempt to start the engine.
**24** On engine code ALH, the bolts securing the injection pump sprocket to the hub may have to be renewed. There are two different

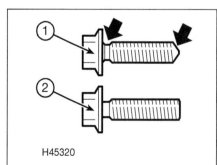

H45320

7.24 Different types of injection pump sprocket retaining bolts – Type 1 bolt is a stretch bolt and must always be renewed

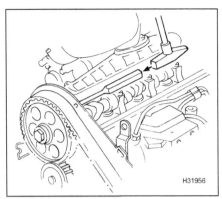

**7.26 Releasing the camshaft sprocket from the taper using soft metal drift**

types of bolts fitted **(see illustration)** the stretch-type of bolt (1), requires angle-tightening and it is for this reason that they cannot be re-used once loosened. VW state that the pump sprocket **must** be reset each time the timing belt is removed – it is not acceptable to simply refit the belt to the sprocket without carrying out the resetting procedure. Where applicable, obtain three new bolts before commencing the refitting procedure.

### *Refitting*

### Engine code ALH

**25** Ensure that the crankshaft and camshaft are still set to TDC on No 1 cylinder, as described in Section 3.

**26** Refer to Section 8, and slacken the camshaft sprocket bolt by half-a-turn. Do not use the timing locking bar to hold the camshaft stationary; it must be removed before loosening the sprocket bolt. Release the sprocket from the camshaft taper mounting by carefully tapping it with a soft metal drift inserted through the hole provided in the timing belt rear cover **(see illustration)**. Refit the timing locking bar (see Section 3) once the sprocket has been released.

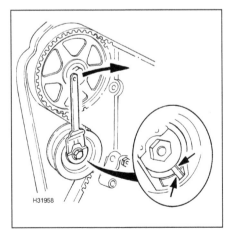

**7.28 The timing belt must locate under the upper idler pulley**

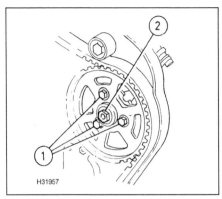

**7.27 Unscrew the three bolts (1) securing the fuel injection pump to the injection pump hub**

***DO NOT** unscrew the central nut (2)*

**27** Unscrew the three bolts securing the fuel injection pump sprocket to the hub on the injection pump **(see illustration)**, and screw the three bolts into position **(see illustration 7.24)** – **do not** tighten the bolts at this stage. Position the injection pump sprocket so that the securing bolts are central in the elongated holes.

 **Warning: Do not loosen the injection pump sprocket central nut, otherwise the basic setting of the injection pump will be lost, and it will require resetting by a VW dealer.**

**28** Fit the timing belt around the crankshaft sprocket, idler pulley, water pump sprocket, injection pump sprocket, camshaft sprocket, and tensioner. Where applicable, ensure that the running direction markings made on the belt during removal are observed. Make sure that the belt teeth seat correctly on the sprockets. The upper belt run must be located beneath the small upper idler pulley (it may be necessary to adjust the position of the camshaft sprocket slightly to achieve this), and the belt run between the tensioner and

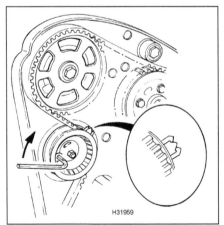

**7.32 Turn the tensioner clockwise until the notch on the hub is aligned with the raised tab on the backplate – engine code ALH**

crankshaft sprocket should be located to the right of the lower small idler pulley (when viewed from the timing belt end of the engine) **(see illustration)**.

**29** Check that the fuel injection pump sprocket is still positioned centrally in the elongated holes.

**30** Ensure that any slack in the belt is in the section which passes over the tensioner.

**31** Check that the tensioner is seated correctly, with the lug on the backplate positioned in the slot in the rear timing belt cover.

**32** On engine code ALH, engage a suitable tool, such as a pair of angled circlip pliers, with the two holes in the belt tensioner hub, then turn the tensioner clockwise until the notch on the hub is aligned with the raised tab on the backplate **(see illustration)**. **Note:** *If the tensioner is turned too far clockwise, it must be completely slackened off before retensioning.* With the tensioner marks aligned, tighten the tensioner nut to the specified torque.

**33** Check that the crankshaft is still set to TDC on No 1 cylinder, as described in Section 3.

**34** Refer to Section 8, and tighten the camshaft sprocket bolt to the specified torque. Do not use the timing locking bar to hold the camshaft stationary; it must be removed before tightening the sprocket bolt.

**35** Refit the timing locking bar (see Section 3) once the sprocket bolt has been tightened.

**36** Tighten the fuel injection pump sprocket bolts to the specified torque. On models with stretch type bolts (see paragraph 24) tighten the bolts to Step 1 torque setting, whilst holding the sprocket stationary. Volkswagen recommend that the bolts are tightened to the final Step 2 setting only after checking the dynamic timing of the injection pump (see Chapter 4B, Section 8) – however, this requires the use of special VW equipment. If the dynamic timing will be checked later, tighten the bolts securely, but not to the full Step 2 angle (the engine *can* be run with the bolts tightened to the Step 1 setting only).

**37** Remove the timing locking bar from the camshaft, and remove the timing pin from the fuel injection pump sprocket.

**38** Turn the engine through two complete turns in the normal direction of rotation, until the timing locking bar and timing pin can be re-inserted to set the engine at TDC on No 1 cylinder (see Section 3).

**39** Check that the timing belt tensioner notch and raised tab are aligned as described in paragraph 32. If the tensioner marks align, proceed to paragraph 41.

**40** If the timing belt tensioner marks are not aligned, repeat the tensioning procedure described in paragraphs 31 to 33, then repeat the checking procedure in paragraphs 38 and 39.

**41** Refit the centre and lower outer timing belt covers, with reference to Section 6.

**42** Refit the crankshaft pulley, with reference to Section 5.

**7.50  Position the camshaft sprocket so that the securing bolts are in the centre part of the elongated holes**

**7.53  Refit the idler roller**

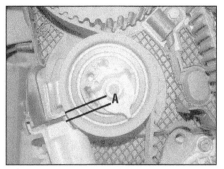

**7.55  The gap between the top edge of the tensioner housing and the tensioner back plate arm (A) must be 4 mm**

**43** Refit the right-hand engine mounting and bracket with reference to Section 18, then disconnect the hoist and lifting tackle from the engine.

**44** If not already done, remove the tools used to lock the camshaft and fuel injection pump sprocket in position with No 1 piston at TDC.

**45** Further refitting is a reversal of the removal procedure. On completion, Volkswagen recommend that the dynamic injection timing is checked using their dedicated test equipment. Once the dynamic timing has been checked, the fuel injection pump sprocket bolts can be tightened fully to their Step 2 torque setting, where applicable, and the upper outer timing belt cover can be refitted.

**46** Refit the splash guard under the engine compartment, then lower the vehicle to the ground. Also refit the camshaft cover.

**47** Reconnect the battery negative (earth) lead (see Chapter 5).

**Engine codes ATD and AXR**

**48** Ensure that the crankshaft and camshaft are still set to TDC on No 1 cylinder, as described in Section 3.

**49** Carefully turn the crankshaft anti-clockwise 90°, to eliminate the possibility of accidental piston-to-valve contact. Refer to Section 5 and slacken the camshaft sprocket bolts by half a turn.

**50** Position the camshaft sprocket so that the securing bolts are in the centre part of the elongated holes **(see illustration)**. Turn the crankshaft clockwise, back to the TDC position.

**51** Loop the timing belt loosely under the crankshaft sprocket. **Note:** *Observe any direction of rotation markings on the belt.*

**52** Engage the timing belt teeth with the camshaft sprocket, then manoeuvre it into position around the tensioning roller, crankshaft sprocket, and finally around the water pump sprocket. Make sure that the belt teeth seat correctly on the sprockets. **Note:** *Slight adjustment to the position of the camshaft sprocket may be necessary to achieve this.* Avoid bending the belt back on itself or twisting it excessively as you do this.

**53** Refit the idler roller and tighten the bolt to the specified torque **(see illustration)**.

**54** Ensure that any slack in the belt is in the

section of belt that passes over the tensioner roller.

**55** Using a suitable tool (eg, circlip pliers) engaged with the two holes in the tensioner hub, turn the tensioner pulley anti-clockwise until the locking plate (T10008) is no longer under tension and can be removed. Turn the tensioner in a clockwise direction until gap of 4 mm exists between the tensioner backplate arm and the top edge of the tensioner housing **(see illustration)**.

**56** With the tensioner held in this position, tighten the locknut to the specified torque.

**57** Tighten the camshaft sprocket bolts to the specified torque, remove the sprocket locking pin and the crankshaft locking tool.

**58** Using a spanner or wrench and socket on the crankshaft pulley centre bolt, rotate the crankshaft through two complete revolutions. Reset the engine to TDC on No 1 cylinder, with reference to Section 3 and check that the camshaft sprocket locking pin (3359 or 6 mm rod) can still be inserted, and that the correct gap still exists between the tensioner backplate arm and top edge of the tensioner housing **(see illustration 7.55)**. If the tensioner gap is incorrect, carry out the tensioning procedure again (paragraphs 55 and 56). If the camshaft sprocket locking pin cannot be inserted, slacken the retaining bolts, turn the **hub** until the pin fits, and tighten the sprocket retaining bolts to the specified torque.

**59** Refit the lower timing belt cover and the auxiliary drivebelt drive pulley. Note that the offset of the pulley mounting holes allows only one fitting position – tighten the bolts to the specified torque.

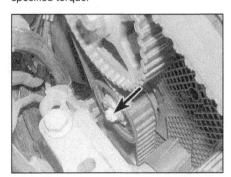

**8.2  Timing belt tensioner nut (arrowed)**

**60** Install the centre timing belt cover, and where applicable, refit the bolts/nuts securing the fuel coolant pipes.

**61** Refit the auxiliary drivebelt tensioner, and the timing belt upper cover.

**62** Refit the crankshaft pulley/vibration damper (Section 5), then refit the auxiliary drivebelt and tensioner (Chapter 1).

**63** Further refitting is a reversal of the removal procedure.

**64** Refit the splash guard under the engine compartment, then lower the vehicle to the ground. Also refit the camshaft cover.

**65** Reconnect the battery negative (earth) lead.

**8  Timing belt tensioner and sprockets** – removal, inspection and refitting

**Timing belt tensioner removal**

**1** Remove the timing belt as described in Section 7.

**Engine code ALH**

**2** Unscrew the timing belt tensioner nut, and remove the tensioner from the engine **(see illustration)**.

**3** When refitting the tensioner to the engine, ensure that the lug on the tensioner backplate engages with the corresponding cut-out in the rear timing belt cover, then refit the tensioner nut **(see illustration)**.

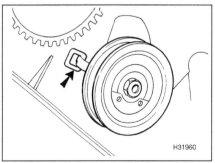

**8.3  Ensure that the lug on the tensioner backplate engages with the cut-out in the rear timing belt cover**

**8.17 Fitting a new crankshaft sprocket securing bolt**

### Engine codes ATD and AXR

**4** Relieve the tension on the timing belt by slackening the tensioner mounting nut slightly, and turning the tensioner anti-clockwise with circlip pliers until it contacts the stop (A). It may take a few moments for the tensioner plunger to fully compress. Lock the plunger by inserting a locking plate (VAG tool No T10008). If this special tool is not available, an alternative can be manufactured by copying the design. Now turn the tensioner clockwise onto stop (B) **(see illustrations 7.19a, 7.19b and 7.19c)**.
**5** Undo the retaining nut fully, and remove the tensioner pulley.
**6** To remove the tensioner plunger and housing assembly, remove the right-hand cover, and the tensioner housing retaining bolts.

### *Timing belt tensioner refitting*

**7** Refit and tension the timing belt as described in Section 7.

### *Idler pulleys*

**Note:** *On engine code ALH, if the lower right-hand idler pulley is removed, a new securing bolt will be required on refitting.*
**8** Remove the timing belt as described in Section 7.
**9** Unscrew the relevant idler pulley securing bolt/nut, then withdraw the pulley.
**10** Refit the pulley and tighten the securing bolt (where applicable, use a new bolt when

**8.28 Using a fabricated tool to counterhold the camshaft hub**

refitting the lower right-hand pulley) or nut to the specified torque.
**11** Refit and tension the timing belt as described in Section 7.

### *Crankshaft sprocket*

**Note:** *A new crankshaft sprocket securing bolt must be used on refitting.*
**12** Remove the timing belt as described in Section 7.
**13** The sprocket securing bolt must now be slackened, and the crankshaft must be prevented from turning as the sprocket bolt is unscrewed. To hold the sprocket, make up a suitable tool, and screw it to the sprocket using a two bolts screwed into two of the crankshaft pulley bolt holes.
**14** Hold the sprocket using the tool, then slacken the sprocket securing bolt. Take care, as the bolt is very tight. **Do not** allow the crankshaft to turn as the bolt is slackened.
**15** Unscrew the bolt, and slide the sprocket from the end of the crankshaft, noting which way round the sprocket's raised boss is fitted.
**16** Commence refitting by positioning the sprocket on the end of the crankshaft, with the raised boss fitted as noted on removal.
**17** Fit a new sprocket securing bolt, then counterhold the sprocket using the method employed on removal, and tighten the bolt to the specified torque in the two steps given in the Specifications **(see illustration)**.
**18** Refit the timing belt as described in Section 7.

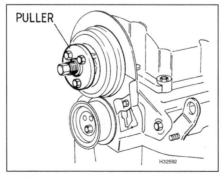

**8.29 Attach a three-legged puller to the hub, and evenly tighten the puller until the hub is free of the camshaft taper**

### *Camshaft sprocket removal*

**19** Remove the timing belt as described in Section 7.
**20** The camshaft sprocket bolt(s) must now be slackened. Do not use the timing locking bar to hold the camshaft stationary; it must be removed before loosening the sprocket bolt. In order to eliminate any possibility of accidental piston-to-valve contact, turn the crankshaft 90° anti-clockwise so that all the pistons are halfway up the cylinder bore.

### Engine code ALH

**21** With the sprocket bolt loosened, release the sprocket from the camshaft taper mounting by carefully tapping it with a soft metal drift inserted through the hole provided in the timing belt rear cover. Refit the timing locking bar (see Section 3) once the sprocket has been released.
**22** Unscrew the sprocket bolt and withdraw it, then withdraw the sprocket from the end of the camshaft, noting which way round it is fitted **(see illustration)**.

### Engine codes ATD and AXR

**23** Unscrew and remove the three retaining bolts and remove the camshaft sprocket from the camshaft hub.

### *Camshaft sprocket refitting*

**24** Refit the sprocket ensuring that it is fitted the correct way round, as noted before removal.
**25** Refit the sprocket bolt(s), and tighten by hand only at this stage.
**26** If the crankshaft has been turned (see paragraph 20) turn the crankshaft clockwise 90° back to TDC. Refit and tension the timing belt as described in Section 7.

### *Camshaft hub*

#### Engine codes ATD and AXR

**Note:** *VAG technicians use special tool T10051 to counterhold the hub, however it is possible to fabricate a suitable alternative – see below.*
**27** Remove the camshaft sprocket as described in this Section.
**28** Engage special tool T10051 with the three locating holes in the face of the hub to prevent the hub from turning. If this tool is not available, fabricate a suitable alternative. Whilst holding the tool, undo the central hub retaining bolt about two turns **(see illustration)**.
**29** Leaving the central hub retaining bolt in place, attach VW tool T10052 (or a similar three-legged puller) to the hub, and evenly tighten the puller until the hub is free of the camshaft taper **(see illustration)**.
**30** Ensure that the camshaft taper and the hub centre is clean and dry, locate the hub on the taper, noting that the built-in key in the

---

**8.22 Removing the camshaft sprocket**

**8.30 The built in key in the hub taper must align with the keyway in the camshaft taper (arrowed)**

hub taper must align with the keyway in the camshaft taper (see illustration).

31 Hold the hub in this position with tool T10051 (or similar home-made tool), and tighten the central bolt to the specified torque.

32 The remainder of refitting is a reversal of removal.

### Fuel injection pump sprocket

#### Engine code ALH

Note: *New fuel injection pump sprocket securing bolts will be required on refitting.*

33 Remove the timing belt as described in Section 7.

34 Unscrew and remove the three bolts securing the fuel injection pump sprocket to the hub on the injection pump. The bolts can be discarded, as new bolts must be used on refitting.

 **Warning: Do not loosen the injection pump sprocket central nut, otherwise the basic setting of the injection pump will be lost, and it will require resetting by a VW dealer.**

35 Temporarily remove the tool used to lock the fuel injection pump sprocket and hub in the TDC position, then slide the sprocket from the hub, noting which way round it is fitted.

Refit the locking tool to the pump hub once the sprocket has been removed.

36 To refit the sprocket, again temporarily remove the locking tool from the hub, then refit the sprocket, ensuring that it is fitted the correct way round, as noted before removal.

37 If necessary turn the sprocket until the locking tool can be inserted through the sprocket and hub to engage with the pump support bracket.

38 Fit the new sprocket securing bolts, then turn the sprocket to that the bolts are positioned centrally in the elongated holes. Tighten the sprocket bolts by hand only at this stage.

39 Refit and tension the timing belt as described in Section 7.

### Water pump sprocket

40 The water pump sprocket is integral with the water pump. Refer to Chapter 3 for details of water pump removal.

### 9 Pump injector rocker shaft assembly – removal and refitting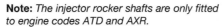

Note: *The injector rocker shafts are only fitted to engine codes ATD and AXR.*

### Removal

1 Remove the camshaft cover as described in Section 4. In order to ensure that the rocker arms are refitted to their original locations, use a marker pen or paint and number the arms 1 to 4, with No 1 nearest the timing belt end of the engine. If the arms are not fitted to their original locations the injector basic clearance setting procedure must be carried out as described in Chapter 4B.

2 Starting with the outer bolts first, carefully and evenly slacken the rocker shaft retaining bolts. Discard the rocker shaft bolts, new ones must be fitted (see illustration).

### Refitting

3 Carefully check the rocker shaft, rocker arms and camshaft bearing cap seating surface for any signs of excessive wear or damage.

4 Ensure that the shaft seating surface is clean and position the rocker shaft assembly in the camshaft bearing caps, making sure that, if reusing the original rocker arms, they are in their original locations.

5 Insert the new rocker shaft retaining bolts, and starting from the inner bolts, gradually and evenly tighten the bolts to the Step 1 torque setting.

6 Again, starting with the inner retaining bolts, tighten the bolts to the Step 2 angle as listed in this Chapter's Specifications.

7 Refit the camshaft cover as described in Section 4.

### 10 Camshaft and hydraulic tappets – removal, inspection and refitting

Note: *A new camshaft oil seal will be required on refitting.*

### Removal

1 Turn the crankshaft to position No 1 piston at TDC on the firing stroke, and lock the camshaft and the fuel injection sprocket in position, as described in Section 3.

2 Remove the timing belt as described in Section 7.

3 Remove the camshaft sprocket as described in Section 8.

4 Remove the brake vacuum pump as described in Chapter 9.

5 On engine codes ATD and AXR remove the injector rocker arms as described in Section 9.

6 Check the camshaft bearing caps for identification markings (see illustration). The bearing caps are normally stamped with their respective cylinder numbers. If no marks are present, make suitable marks using a scriber

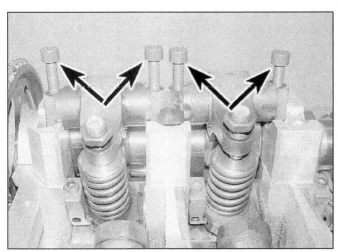

**9.2 Starting with the outer bolts first, carefully and evenly slacken the rocker shaft retaining bolts (arrowed)**

**10.6 Check the camshaft bearing caps (arrowed) for markings**

or punch. The caps should be numbered from 1 to 5, with No 1 at the timing belt end of the engine. Note on which side of the bearing caps the marks are made to ensure that they are refitted the correct way round.

**7** On engine codes ATD and AXR, the camshaft rotates in shell bearings. As the camshaft bearing caps are removed, recover the shell bearing halves from the camshaft. Number the back of the bearings with a felt pen to ensure that, if re-used, the bearings are fitted to their original locations. **Note:** *Fitted into the cylinder head, under each camshaft bearing cap, is a washer for each cylinder head bolt.*

**8** Unscrew the securing nuts, and remove Nos 1, 3 and 5 bearing caps.

**9** Working progressively, in a diagonal sequence, slacken the nuts securing Nos 2 and 4 bearing caps. Note that as the nuts are slackened, the valve springs will push the camshaft up.

**10** Once the nuts securing Nos 2 and 4 bearing caps have been fully slackened, lift off the bearing caps.

**11** Carefully lift the camshaft from the cylinder head, keeping it level and supported at both ends as it is removed so that the journals and lobes are not damaged. Remove the oil seal from the end of the camshaft and discard it – a new one will be required for refitting **(see illustration)**.

**12** Lift the hydraulic tappets from their bores in the cylinder head, and store them with the valve contact surfaces facing downwards, to prevent the oil from draining out. It is recommended that the tappets are kept immersed in oil for the period they are removed from the cylinder head. Make a note of the position of each tappet, as they must be refitted in their original locations on reassembly – accelerated wear leading to early failure will result if the tappets are interchanged.

**13** On engine codes ATD and AXR, recover the lower shell bearing halves from the cylinder head; number the back of the shells with a felt pen to ensure that, if re-used, the bearings are fitted to their original locations.

### Inspection

**14** With the camshaft removed, examine the bearing caps and the bearing locations in the cylinder head for signs of obvious wear or

pitting. If evident, a new cylinder head will probably be required. Also check that the oil supply holes in the cylinder head are free from obstructions.

**15** Visually inspect the camshaft for evidence of wear on the surfaces of the lobes and journals. Normally their surfaces should be smooth and have a dull shine; look for scoring, erosion or pitting and areas that appear highly polished, indicating excessive wear. Accelerated wear will occur once the hardened exterior of the camshaft has been damaged, so always renew worn items. **Note:** *If these symptoms are visible on the tips of the camshaft lobes, check the corresponding tappet, as it will probably be worn as well.*

**16** If the machined surfaces of the camshaft appear discoloured or blued, it is likely that it has been overheated at some point, probably due to inadequate lubrication. This may have distorted the shaft, so check the run-out as follows: place the camshaft between two V-blocks and using a DTI gauge, measure the run-out at the centre journal. If it exceeds the figure quoted in the Specifications at the start of this Chapter, renew the camshaft.

**17** To measure the camshaft endfloat, temporarily refit the camshaft to the cylinder head, then fit Nos 1 and 5 bearing caps and tighten the retaining nuts to the specified torque setting. Anchor a DTI gauge to the timing belt end of the cylinder head **(see illustration)**. Push the camshaft to one end of the cylinder head as far as it will travel, then rest the DTI gauge probe on the end face of the camshaft, and zero the gauge. Push the camshaft as far as it will go to the other end of the cylinder head, and record the gauge reading. Verify the reading by pushing the camshaft back to its original position and checking that the gauge indicates zero again. **Note:** *The hydraulic tappets must not be fitted whilst this measurement is being taken.*

**18** Check that the camshaft endfloat measurement is within the limit listed in the Specifications. If the measurement is outside the specified limit, wear is unlikely to be confined to any one component, so renewal of the camshaft, cylinder head and bearing caps must be considered.

**19** The camshaft bearing running clearance should now be measured. This will be difficult

to achieve without a range of micrometers or internal/external expanding calipers, measure the outside diameters of the camshaft bearing surfaces and the internal diameters formed by the bearing caps (and shell bearings where applicable) and the bearing locations in the cylinder head. The difference between these two measurements is the running clearance.

**20** Compare the camshaft running clearance measurements with the figure given in the Specifications; if any are outside the specified tolerance, the camshaft, cylinder head and bearing caps (and shell bearings where applicable) should be renewed.

**21** Inspect the hydraulic tappets for obvious signs of wear or damage, and renew if necessary. Check that the oil holes in the tappets are free from obstructions.

### Refitting

**22** Smear some clean engine oil onto the sides of the hydraulic tappets, and offer them into position in their original bores in the cylinder head. Push them down until they contact the valves, then lubricate the camshaft lobe contact surfaces.

**23** Lubricate the camshaft and cylinder head bearing journals (and shell bearings where applicable) with clean engine oil.

**24** Carefully lower the camshaft into position in the cylinder head making sure that the cam lobes for No 1 cylinder are pointing upwards.

**25** Refit a new camshaft oil seal on the end of the camshaft. Make sure that the closed end of the seal faces the camshaft sprocket end of the camshaft, and take care not to damage the seal lip. Locate the seal against the seat in the cylinder head.

**26** Oil the upper surfaces of the camshaft bearing journals (and shell bearings where applicable), then fit Nos 2 and 4 bearing caps. Ensure that they are fitted the right way round and in the correct locations (see paragraph 6), then progressively tighten the retaining nuts in a diagonal sequence to the specified torque. Note that as the nuts are tightened, the camshaft will be forced down against the pressure of the valve springs.

**27** Fit bearing caps 1, 3 and 5 over the camshaft and progressively tighten the nuts to the specified torque. Note that it may be necessary to locate No 5 bearing cap by tapping lightly on the end of the camshaft.

**28** Refit the camshaft sprocket as described in Section 8.

**29** Refit and tension the timing belt as described in Section 7.

**30** Refit the brake vacuum pump as described in Chapter 9.

**11 Hydraulic tappets** – testing

**10.11 Remove the camshaft oil seal**

**10.17 Checking camshaft endfloat using a DTI gauge**

⚠ *Warning: After fitting hydraulic tappets, wait a minimum of 30 minutes (or preferably, leave overnight) before starting the engine, to allow the tappets time to settle, otherwise the valve heads will strike the pistons.*

**1** The hydraulic tappets are self-adjusting, and require no attention whilst in service.

**2** If the hydraulic tappets become excessively noisy, their operation can be checked as described below.

**3** Start the engine, and run it until it reaches normal operating temperature, increase the engine speed to approximately 2500 rpm for 2 minutes.

**4** If any hydraulic tappets are heard to be noisy, carry out the following checks.

**5** Remove the camshaft cover as described in Section 4.

**6** Using a socket or spanner on the crankshaft sprocket bolt, turn the crankshaft until the tip of the camshaft lobe above the tappet to be checked is pointing vertically upwards.

**7** Using feeler blades, check the clearance between the top of the tappet, and the cam lobe. If the play is in excess of 0.1 mm, renew the relevant tappet. If the play is less than 0.1 mm, or there is no play, proceed as follows.

**8** Press down on the tappet using a wooden or plastic instrument **(see illustration)**. If free play in excess of 1.0 mm is present before the tappet contacts the valve stem, renew the relevant tappet.

**9** On completion, refit the camshaft cover as described in Section 4.

---

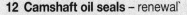

## 12 Camshaft oil seals – renewal

### Right-hand oil seal

**1** Remove the timing belt as described in Section 7.

**2** Remove the camshaft sprocket and hub, as described in Section 8.

**3** Drill two small holes into the existing oil seal, diagonally opposite each other. Take great care to avoid drilling through into the seal housing or camshaft sealing surface. Thread two self-tapping screws into the holes, and using a pair of pliers, pull on the heads of the screws to extract the oil seal.

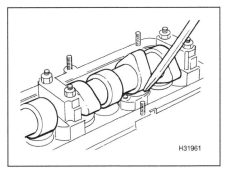

**11.8 Press down on the tappet using a wooden or plastic instrument**

**4** Clean out the seal housing and the sealing surface of the camshaft by wiping it with a lint-free cloth. Remove any swarf or burrs that may cause the seal to leak.

**5** Do **not** lubricate the lip and outer edge of the new oil seal, push it over the camshaft until it is positioned in place above its housing. To prevent damage to the sealing lips, wrap some adhesive tape around the end of the camshaft.

**6** Using a hammer and a socket of suitable diameter, drive the seal squarely into its housing. **Note:** *Select a socket that bears only on the hard outer surface of the seal, not the inner lip which can easily be damaged.*

**7** Refit the camshaft sprocket and its hub, as described in Section 8.

**8** Refit and tension the timing belt as described in Section 7.

### Left-hand oil seal

**9** The left-hand camshaft oil seal is formed by the brake vacuum pump seal. Refer to Chapter 9 for details of brake vacuum pump removal and refitting.

---

## 13 Cylinder head – removal, inspection and refitting

**Note:** *The cylinder head must be removed with the engine cold. New cylinder head bolts and a new cylinder head gasket will be required on refitting, and suitable studs will be required to guide the cylinder head into position – see text.*

### Removal

**1** Disconnect the battery negative lead and remove the camshaft cover. **Note:** *Refer to 'Battery disconnection' in Chapter 5 first.*

**2** Drain the cooling system and engine oil as described in Chapter 1.

**3** Remove the camshaft cover as described in Section 4.

**4** Remove the timing belt as described in Section 7.

**5** Remove the camshaft sprocket and timing belt tensioner as described in Section 8.

**6** Where applicable, unscrew the bolt(s) securing the rear timing belt cover to the cylinder head **(see illustrations)**.

**7** Using two suitable nuts locked together, unscrew the timing belt tensioner mounting stud from the cylinder head **(see illustration)**.

**8** If the engine is currently supported using a hoist and lifting tackle attached to the engine lifting brackets on the cylinder head, it is now necessary to attach a suitable bracket to the cylinder block, so that the engine can still be supported as the cylinder head is removed. Alternatively, the engine can be supported using a trolley jack and a block of wood positioned under the engine sump.

### Engine code ALH

**9** Slacken the clip and disconnect the radiator top hose from the front of the coolant housing on the left-hand side of the cylinder head. Similarly, disconnect the heater hose from the rear of the housing, and the smaller oil cooler hose from the bottom of the housing. Move the hoses to one side.

**10** Slacken the clip, and disconnect the coolant purge hose from the rear left-hand side of the cylinder head.

**11** Disconnect the exhaust front section from the exhaust manifold or the turbocharger, as applicable.

**12** On turbo models, proceed as follows:

a) *Disconnect the vacuum hose from the turbocharger wastegate actuator.*

b) *Where applicable, disconnect the boost pressure solenoid valve hose from the turbocharger.*

c) *Slacken the hose clips, and disconnect the air inlet trunking from the turbocharger.*

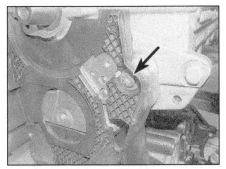

**13.6a Where applicable, undo the bolt (arrowed) from the inner cover . . .**

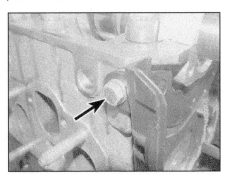

**13.6b . . . and the one (arrowed) on the side of the cover**

**13.7 Using two nuts locked together to unscrew the tensioner mounting stud**

d) Slacken the hose clips, and remove the turbocharger-to-intercooler air trunking.

e) Where applicable, unbolt and remove the turbocharger support bracket.

f) Unscrew the union bolt, and disconnect the turbocharger oil return pipe from the cylinder block. Recover the sealing rings.

g) Slacken the union nut and disconnect the oil supply pipe from the turbocharger. Release the pipe from any brackets on the exhaust manifold and cylinder head.

**13** Disconnect the wiring from the following components, noting the routing of the wiring:

a) Fuel injection pump fuel cut-off solenoid (on top of injection pump – loosen securing nut).

b) Fuel injection pump start-of-injection valve **(see illustration)**.

c) Intake manifold flap adjuster valve – at rear of intake manifold.

d) Coolant temperature sensor/temperature gauge sender (left-hand end of cylinder head).

e) Fuel injector needle lift sensor (behind oil filter housing).

f) Main glow plug feed wiring.

**14** Disconnect the main fuel leak-off hose from the fuel injectors.

**15** Slacken the union nuts, whilst counterholding the unions with a second spanner, and remove the fuel injector pipes as an assembly.

**16** Disconnect the vacuum hoses from the brake vacuum pump and EGR valve **(see illustrations)**.

**13.16b EGR valve and vacuum hose (arrowed)**

**13.13 Disconnect the injection system wiring plug (arrowed) behind the oil filter housing**

**17** On models fitted with an intake manifold flap vacuum damper, either remove the damper reservoir from the bracket on the cylinder head, or remove the reservoir *with* its bracket.

**18** Make a final check to ensure that all relevant pipes, hoses and wires have been disconnected and moved clear of the working area to enable removal of the cylinder head.

**19** Progressively slacken the cylinder head bolts, by one turn at a time, in order **(see illustration)**. Remove the cylinder head bolts.

**20** With all the bolts removed, lift the cylinder head from the block, together with the

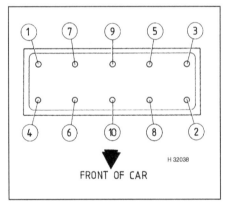

**13.19 Cylinder head bolt slackening sequence**

manifolds and turbocharger. If the cylinder head is stuck, tap it with a soft-faced mallet to break the joint. **Do not** insert a lever into the gasket joint.

**21** Lift the cylinder head gasket from the block. Do not discard the gasket at this stage, as it will be required when determining the thickness of the new gasket required.

**22** If desired, the manifolds can be removed from the cylinder head with reference to Sections 22 (intake manifold) or 24 (exhaust manifold).

### Engine codes ATD and AXR

**Note:** *It is necessary to unplug the central connector for the unit injectors – this may cause a fault code to be logged by the engine management ECU. This code can only be erased by a VW dealer or suitably-equipped specialist.*

**23** Remove the bolt securing the camshaft position sensor to the cylinder head. There is no need to disconnect the wiring at this stage **(see illustration)**.

**24** Disconnect the charge air pipe from the intake manifold to the intercooler and place to one side.

**25** Disconnect the central connector for the unit injectors **(see illustration)**.

**26** Undo the two bolts securing the coolant junction to the end of the cylinder head **(see illustration)**. There is no need to disconnect the pipes or wiring plugs at this stage.

**27** Unscrew the four retaining bolts and pull

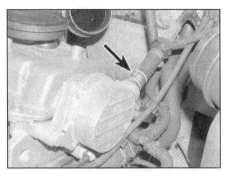

**13.16a Disconnect the vacuum hose (arrowed) from the brake vacuum pump**

**13.23 Unscrew the bolt and remove the camshaft position sensor**

**13.25 Disconnect the central connector for the injectors**

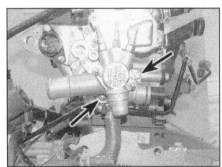

**13.26 Undo the two bolts (arrowed) and remove the coolant outlet from the end of the cylinder head**

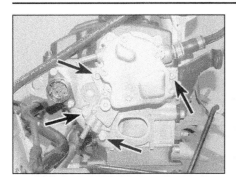

**13.27 Undo the four tandem pump retaining bolts (arrowed)**

**13.28 Disconnect the coolant hose from the end of the cylinder head**

**13.32 Disconnect the vacuum pipes (arrowed)**

the tandem pump away from the cylinder head without disconnecting the fuel or vacuum hoses **(see illustration)**.

**28** Disconnect and remove the hose connecting the upper coolant pipe to the pipe at the end of the cylinder head **(see illustration)**.

**29** Remove the turbocharger as described in Chapter 4B.

**30** Slacken and remove the bolt securing the upper metal coolant pipe to the cylinder head.

**31** Disconnect the wiring connectors from the glow plugs – if necessary, refer to Chapter 5.

**32** Disconnect vacuum pipes to the EGR valve and the manifold flap actuator **(see illustration)**.

**33** Using a multi-splined tool, undo the cylinder head bolts, working from the outside-in, evenly and gradually. Check that nothing remains connected, and lift the cylinder head from the engine block. Seek assistance if possible, as it is a heavy assembly, especially as it is being removed complete with the manifolds.

**34** Remove the gasket from the top of the block, noting the locating dowels. If the dowels are a loose fit, remove them and store them with the head for safe-keeping. Do not discard the gasket yet – it will be needed for identification purposes.

### Inspection

**35** Dismantling and inspection of the cylinder head is covered in Part Chapter 2D.

### *Cylinder head gasket selection*

**Note:** *A dial test indicator (DTI) will be required for this operation.*

**36** Examine the old cylinder head gasket for manufacturer's identification markings **(see illustration)**. These will be in the form of holes or notches, and a part number on the edge of the gasket. Unless new pistons have been fitted, the new cylinder head gasket must be of the same type as the old one. In this case, purchase a new gasket, and proceed to paragraph 43.

**37** If new piston assemblies have been fitted as part of an engine overhaul, or if a new short engine is to be fitted, the projection of the piston crowns above the cylinder head mating face of the cylinder block at TDC must be

measured. This measurement is used to determine the thickness of the new cylinder head gasket required.

**38** Anchor a dial test indicator (DTI) to the top face (cylinder head gasket mating face) of the cylinder block, and zero the gauge on the gasket mating face.

**39** Rest the gauge probe on No 1 piston crown, and turn the crankshaft slowly by hand until the piston reaches TDC. Measure and record the maximum piston projection at TDC **(see illustration)**.

**40** Repeat the measurement for the remaining pistons, and record the results.

**41** If the measurements differ from piston-to-piston, take the highest figure, and use this to determine the thickness of the head gasket required as follows:

| Piston projection | Gasket identification (number of holes/notches) |
|---|---|
| 0.91 to 1.00 mm | 1 |
| 0.01 to 1.10 mm | 2 |
| 1.11 to 1.20 mm | 3 |

**42** Purchase a new gasket according to the results of the measurements.

### *Refitting*

**Note:** *If a VW exchange cylinder head, complete with camshaft, is to be fitted, the manufacturers recommend the following:*
a) *Lubricate the contact surfaces between the tappets and the cam lobes before fitting the camshaft cover.*
b) *Do not remove the plastic protectors from the open valves until immediately before fitting the cylinder head.*

**13.36 The thickness of the cylinder head gasket can be identified by notches or holes**

c) *Additionally, if a new cylinder head is fitted, VW recommend that the coolant is renewed.*

**43** The mating faces of the cylinder head and block must be perfectly clean before refitting the head. Use a scraper to remove all traces of gasket and carbon, also clean the tops of the pistons. Take particular care with the aluminium surfaces, as the soft metal is easily damaged.

**44** Make sure that debris is not allowed to enter the oil and water passages – this is particularly important for the oil circuit, as carbon could block the oil supply to the camshaft and crankshaft bearings. Using adhesive tape and paper, seal the water, oil and bolt holes in the cylinder block.

**45** To prevent carbon entering the gap between the pistons and bores, smear a little grease in the gap. After cleaning a piston, rotate the crankshaft to that the piston moves down the bore, then wipe out the grease and carbon with a cloth rag. Clean the other piston crowns in the same way.

**46** Check the head and block for nicks, deep scratches and other damage. If slight, they may be removed carefully with a file. More serious damage may be repaired by machining, but this is a specialist job.

**47** If warpage of the cylinder head is suspected, use a straight-edge to check it for distortion, as described in Chapter 2D.

**48** Ensure that the cylinder head bolt holes in the crankcase are clean and free of oil. Syringe or soak up any oil left in the bolt holes. This is most important in order that the correct bolt tightening torque can be applied,

**13.39 Measuring the piston projection at TDC using a dial gauge**

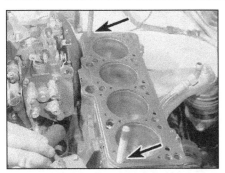

**13.51 Two of the old head bolts (arrowed) can be used as cylinder head alignment guides**

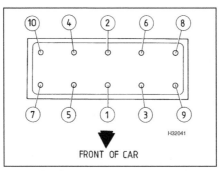

**13.56a Cylinder head bolt tightening sequence**

**13.56b Using a torque wrench to tighten the cylinder head bolts**

and to prevent the possibility of the block being cracked by hydraulic pressure when the bolts are tightened.

**49** Turn the crankshaft anti-clockwise all the pistons at an equal height, approximately halfway down their bores from the TDC position (see Section 3). This will eliminate any risk of piston-to-valve contact as the cylinder head is refitted.

**50** Where applicable, refit the manifolds with reference to Sections 22 and 24.

**51** To guide the cylinder head into position, screw two long studs (or old cylinder head bolts with the heads cut off, and slots cut in the ends to enable the bolts to be unscrewed) into the cylinder block **(see illustration)**.

**52** Ensure that the cylinder head locating dowels are in place in the cylinder block, then fit the new cylinder head gasket over the dowels, ensuring that the part number is uppermost. Where applicable, the OBEN/TOP marking should also be uppermost. Note that VW recommend that the gasket is only removed from its packaging immediately prior to fitting.

**53** Lower the cylinder head into position on the gasket, ensuring that it engages correctly over the guide studs and dowels.

**54** Fit the new cylinder head bolts to the eight remaining bolt locations, and screw them in as far as possible by hand.

**55** Unscrew the two guide studs from the exhaust side of the cylinder block, then screw in the two remaining new cylinder head bolts as far as possible by hand.

**56** Working progressively, in sequence, tighten all the cylinder head bolts to the

specified Step 1 torque **(see illustrations)**.

**57** Again working progressively, in sequence, tighten all the cylinder head bolts to the specified Step 2 torque.

**58** Tighten all the cylinder head bolts, in sequence, through the specified Step 3 angle **(see illustration)**.

**59** Finally, tighten all the cylinder head bolts, in sequence, through the specified Step 4 angle.

**60** After finally tightening the cylinder head bolts, turn the camshaft so that the cam lobes for No 1 cylinder are pointing upwards.

**61** Where applicable, reconnect the lifting tackle to the engine lifting brackets on the cylinder head, then adjust the lifting tackle to support the engine. Once the engine is adequately supported using the cylinder head brackets, disconnect the lifting tackle from the bracket bolted to the cylinder block, and unbolt the improvised engine lifting bracket from the cylinder block. Alternatively, remove the trolley jack and block of wood from under the sump.

**62** The remainder of the refitting procedure is a reversal of the removal procedure, bearing in mind the following points.

a) Refit the camshaft cover with reference to Section 4.

b) Use new sealing rings when reconnecting the turbocharger oil return pipe to the cylinder block.

c) Reconnect the exhaust front section to the exhaust manifold or turbocharger, as applicable, with reference to Chapter 4B.

d) Refit the timing belt tensioner with reference to Section 8.

e) Refit the camshaft sprocket as described in Section 8, and refit the timing belt as described in Section 7.

f) Refill the cooling system and engine oil as described in Chapter 1.

## 14 Sump – removal and refitting

Proceed as described in Chapter 2A, Section 13.

## 15 Oil pump and drive chain – removal, inspection and refitting

Proceed as described in Chapter 2A, Section 14.

## 16 Flywheel/driveplate/clutch pressure plate – removal, inspection and refitting

Proceed as described in Chapter 2A, Section 15.

## 17 Crankshaft oil seals – renewal

**Note 1:** The oil seals are a PTFE (Teflon) type and are fitted dry, without using any grease or oil. These have a wider sealing lip and have been introduced instead of the coil spring type oil seal.
**Note 2:** If the oil seal housing is removed, suitable sealant (VW D 176 404 A2, or equivalent) will be required to seal the housing on refitting.

### Right-hand oil seal

**1** Remove the timing belt as described in Section 7, and the crankshaft sprocket with reference to Section 8.

**2** To remove the seal without removing the housing, drill two small holes diagonally opposite each other, insert self-tapping screws, and pull on the heads of the screws with pliers **(see illustration)**.

**13.58 Angle-tighten the cylinder head bolts**

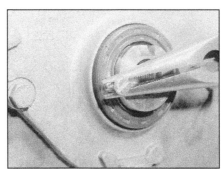

**17.2 Removing the crankshaft oil seal using self-tapping screws**

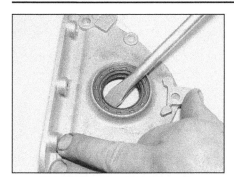

**17.3 Prising the oil seal from the crankshaft oil seal housing**

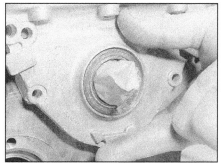

**17.9 Slide the oil seal housing over the end of the crankshaft**

**17.17 Locate the crankshaft oil seal fitting tool over the end of the crankshaft**

**3** Alternatively, to remove the oil seal complete with its housing, proceed as follows.

*a) Remove the sump as described in Section 14. This is necessary to ensure a satisfactory seal between the sump and oil seal housing on refitting.*

*b) Unbolt and remove the oil seal housing.*

*c) Working on the bench, lever the oil seal from the housing using a suitable screwdriver. Take care not to damage the seal seating in the housing **(see illustration)**.*

**4** Thoroughly clean the oil seal seating in the housing.

**5** Wind a length of tape around the end of the crankshaft to protect the oil seal lips as the seal (and housing, where applicable) is fitted.

**6** Fit a new oil seal to the housing, pressing or driving it into position using a socket or tube of suitable diameter. Ensure that the socket or tube bears only on the hard outer ring of the seal, and take care not to damage the seal lips. Press or drive the seal into position until it is seated on the shoulder in the housing. Make sure that the closed end of the seal is facing outwards.

**7** If the oil seal housing has been removed, proceed as follows, otherwise proceed to paragraph 11.

**8** Clean all traces of old sealant from the crankshaft oil seal housing and the cylinder block, then coat the cylinder block mating faces of the oil seal housing with a 2.0 to 3.0 mm thick bead of sealant (VW D 176 404 A2, or equivalent). Note that the seal housing must be refitted within 5 minutes of applying the sealant.

*Caution: DO NOT put excessive amounts of sealant onto the housing as it may get into the sump and block the oil pick-up pipe.*

**9** Refit the oil seal housing, and tighten the bolts progressively to the specified torque **(see illustration)**.

**10** Refit the sump as described in Section 14.

**11** Refit the crankshaft sprocket with reference to Section 8, and the timing belt as described in Section 7.

### Left-hand oil seal

**12** Remove the flywheel/driveplate as described in Section 16.

**13** Remove the sump as described in Section 14. This is necessary to ensure a satisfactory seal between the sump and oil seal housing on refitting.

**14** Unbolt and remove the oil seal housing, complete with the oil seal.

**15** The new oil seal will be supplied ready-fitted to a new oil seal housing.

**16** Thoroughly clean the oil seal housing mating face on the cylinder block.

**17** New oil seal/housing assemblies are supplied with a fitting tool to prevent damage to the oil seal as it is being fitted. Locate the tool over the end of the crankshaft **(see illustration)**.

**18** If the original oil seal housing was fitted using sealant, apply a thin bead of suitable sealant (VW D 176 404 A2, or equivalent) to the cylinder block mating face of the oil seal housing. Note that the seal housing must be refitted within 5 minutes of applying the sealant.

*Caution: DO NOT put excessive amounts of sealant onto the housing as it may get into the sump and block the oil pick-up pipe.*

**19** Carefully fit the oil seal/housing assembly over the end of the crankshaft, then refit the securing bolts and tighten the bolts progressively, in a diagonal sequence, to the specified torque **(see illustrations)**.

**20** Remove the oil seal protector tool from the end of the crankshaft.

**21** Refit the sump as described in Section 14.

**22** Refit the flywheel/driveplate as described in Section 16.

**17.19a Fit the oil seal/housing assembly over the end of the crankshaft . . .**

**17.19b . . . then tighten the securing bolts to the specified torque**

## 18 Engine/transmission mountings – inspection and renewal

Refer to Section 17 in Chapter 2A, but disregard the reference to the charcoal canister and to the top cover air filter. Note that the right-hand engine mounting is significantly different to that on the petrol engine.

## 19 Engine oil cooler – removal and refitting

**Note:** *New sealing rings will be required on refitting.*

### Removal

1 The oil cooler is mounted under the oil filter housing on the front of the cylinder block **(see illustration)**.
2 Position a container beneath the oil filter to catch escaping oil and coolant.
3 Clamp the oil cooler coolant hoses to minimise oil spillage, then remove the clips, and disconnect the hoses from the oil cooler. Be prepared for coolant spillage.
4 Unscrew the oil cooler securing plate from the bottom of the oil filter housing, then slide off the oil cooler. Recover the O-rings from the top and bottom of the oil cooler.

### Refitting

5 Refitting is a reversal of removal, bearing in mind the following points:

a) *Use new oil cooler O-rings.*
b) *Tighten the oil cooler securing plate to the specified torque.*
c) *On completion, check and if necessary top-up the oil and coolant levels.*

## 20 Oil pressure relief valve – removal, inspection and refitting

**Note:** *On engine codes ATD and AXR, the pressure relief valve is part of the oil filter housing and cannot be removed, DO NOT loosen the sealing plug on these models.*

### Removal

1 The oil pressure relief valve is fitted to the right-hand side of the oil filter housing **(see illustration 19.1)**. Remove the camshaft cover to gain access to the switch (see Section 4).
2 Wipe clean the area around the relief valve plug then slacken and remove the plug and sealing ring from the filter housing. Withdraw the valve spring and piston, noting their correct fitted positions. If the valve is to be left removed from the engine for any length of time, plug the oil filter housing aperture.

### Inspection

3 Examine the relief valve piston and spring for signs of wear or damage. At the time of writing it appears that the relief valve components were not available separately; check with your VW dealer for the latest parts availability. If wear or damage is present it will be necessary to renew the complete oil filter housing assembly.

### Refitting

4 Fit the piston to the inner end of the spring then insert the assembly into the oil filter housing. Ensure the sealing ring is correctly fitted to the valve plug then fit the plug to the housing tightening it to the specified torque.
5 On completion, check and, if necessary, top-up the engine oil, and refit the camshaft cover.

## 21 Oil pressure warning light switch – removal and refitting

### Removal

1 The oil pressure warning light switch is fitted to the right-hand side of the oil filter housing **(see illustration 19.1)**. Remove the camshaft cover to gain access to the switch (see Section 4).
2 Disconnect the wiring connector and wipe clean the area around the switch.
3 Unscrew the switch from the filter housing and remove it, along with its sealing washer. If the switch is to be left removed from the engine for any length of time, plug the oil filter housing aperture.

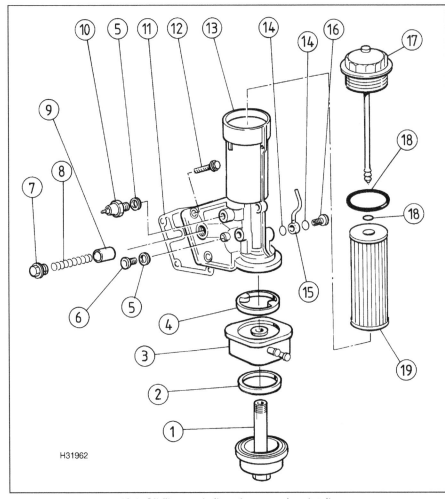

H31962

**19.1 Oil filter and oil cooler mounting details**

1 Oil cooler securing plate
2 O-ring
3 Oil cooler
4 O-ring
5 Washer
6 Sealing plug
7 Sealing plug
8 Oil pressure relief valve spring (engine code ALH)
9 Oil pressure relief valve piston (engine code ALH)
10 Oil pressure warning light switch
11 Gasket
12 Mounting bolt
13 Oil filter housing
14 Seal
15 Oil supply pipe to turbo
16 Banjo bolt
17 Oil filter cover
18 O-ring
19 Oil filter

## Refitting

**4** Examine the sealing washer for signs of damage or deterioration and if necessary renew.

**5** Refit the switch, complete with washer, and tighten it to the specified torque.

**6** Securely reconnect the wiring connector then check and, if necessary, top-up the engine oil. On completion, refit the camshaft cover.

## 22 Intake manifold – removal and refitting

### Engine code ALH

#### Removal

**1** Remove the camshaft cover. Removal details vary according to model, but the cover retaining nuts are concealed under circular covers, which are prised out of the main cover. Remove the nuts, and lift the cover from the engine, releasing any wiring or hoses attached.

**2** Remove the intake manifold flap housing from the intake manifold. If preferred, however, the manifold can be removed with the flap housing – in this case, all services must be disconnected from the housing as described in Section 4, but the housing retaining bolts can be left in place.

**3** Disconnect the wiring plug from the vacuum unit solenoid valve, and unclip the wiring from the manifold.

**4** Support the manifold, then unscrew and remove the six retaining bolts **(see illustration)**. Separate the manifold from the cylinder head, and recover the gasket.

#### Refitting

**5** Refitting is a reversal of removal. Ensure that the mating surfaces are clean. Use a new gasket and tighten the manifold bolts securely.

### Engine codes ATD and AXR

#### Removal

**6** Unclip and remove the camshaft cover.

**7** Undo the bolts securing the EGR pipe to the intake manifold flap assembly.

**8** Undo the retaining screws and separate the intake manifold flap assembly from the intake manifold (see Section 24). Recover the O-ring.

**9** Unbolt the EGR pipe from the exhaust manifold. On automatic transmission models, also release the three retaining bolts and manoeuvre the EGR cooler away from the intake manifold.

**10** Remove the heat shield from the manifold, then unscrew the mounting nuts/bolts and remove the intake manifold from the cylinder head. Recover the gaskets from the intake manifold **(see illustration)**.

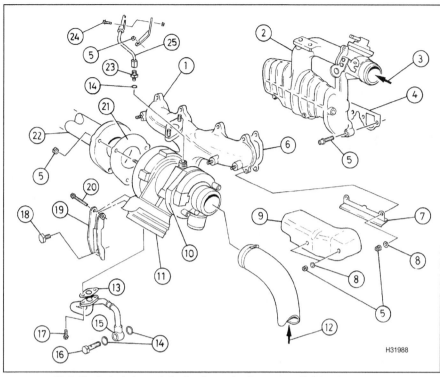

**22.4 Exploded view of the intake and exhaust manifolds components**

| | | |
|---|---|---|
| 1 Exhaust manifold | 10 Turbocharger | 19 Turbocharger support bracket |
| 2 Intake manifold | 11 Wastegate | |
| 3 From intercooler | 12 From air cleaner | 20 Turbocharger support bracket bolt |
| 4 Intake manifold gasket | 13 Gasket | |
| 5 Mounting nut/bolt | 14 Seal | 21 Exhaust pipe gasket |
| 6 Exhaust manifold gasket | 15 Oil return pipe | 22 Exhaust front pipe |
| 7 Heat shield mounting bracket | 16 Banjo bolt | 23 Connection |
| | 17 Flange bolt | 24 Oil supply pipe mounting bolt |
| 8 Washer | 18 Turbocharger support bracket bolt | |
| 9 Heat shield | | 25 Oil supply pipe |

#### Refitting

**11** Refitting is a reversal of removal, using new manifold, EGR pipe and manifold flap assembly gaskets.

## 23 Intake manifold changeover flap and valve – removal and refitting

**Note:** *Engine codes ATD and AXR only.*

### Changeover flap housing and vacuum control element

#### Removal

**1** As diesel engines have a very high compression ratio, when the engine is turned off, the pistons still compress a large quantity of air for a few revolutions and cause the engine unit to shudder. The intake manifold changeover flap is located in the intake flange housing bolted to the intake manifold. When the ignition switch is turned to the 'off' position, the engine management ECU-controlled valve actuates the flap, which shuts off the air supply to the cylinders. This allows the pistons to compress very little air, and the engine runs softly to a halt. The flap must open again approximately 3 seconds after switching off the ignition switch. The EGR (Exhaust Gas Recirculation) valve is also incorporated into the flap housing.

**2** Where fitted, unclip and remove the camshaft cover.

**3** Release the retaining clips, and disconnect the air inlet trucking from the intake manifold flange housing.

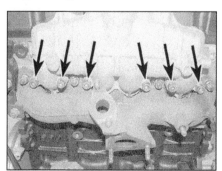

**22.10 Unscrew the intake manifold mounting bolts (arrowed)**

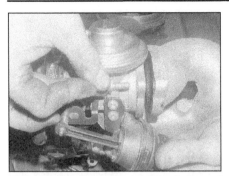

**23.6 Unscrew the three retaining bolts and remove the intake manifold flange housing**

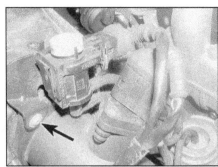

**23.10 Disconnect the vacuum pipes, and unscrew the intake manifold flap control valve mounting screw (arrowed)**

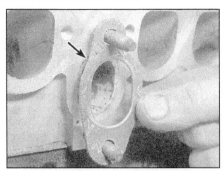

**24.6 The exhaust manifold gaskets must be installed with the 'notched end' (arrowed) facing up**

**4** Undo the two retaining bolts and disconnect the EGR pipe from the underside of the intake flange. Recover the gasket.

**5** Disconnect the vacuum pipe to the actuator. Disconnect the vacuum pipe for the EGR valve.

**6** Unscrew the three retaining bolts and remove the intake manifold flange housing. Discard the sealing O-ring, a new one must be used **(see illustration)**.

**7** Although it is possible to remove the vacuum actuator from the intake flange housing, by unscrewing the two bracket retaining bolts and disengaging the actuating arm from the flap spindle, at the time of writing the intake manifold flange was only available as a unit complete with the vacuum actuator and EGR valve. Consult your VW dealer.

### Refitting

**8** Refitting is a reversal of removal. Tighten the intake manifold flap housing bolts securely.

### Changeover valve

#### Removal

**9** The changeover valve controls the supply of vacuum to the changeover flap. The electrical supply to the valve is controlled by the engine management ECU. When the ignition key is turned to the 'off' position, the ECU signals the valve, which allows vacuum

to pull the flap shut. Approximately three seconds later, the power supply to the valve is cut, the vacuum to the actuator collapses, and the flap opens.

**10** The valve is located on the right-hand side of the engine compartment, on the top of the air filter housing. Note their fitted positions and disconnect the vacuum pipes from the valve **(see illustration)**.

**11** Disconnect the wiring plug from the valve.

**12** Undo the retaining screw and remove the valve.

### Refitting

**13** Refitting is a reversal of removal.

### 24 Exhaust manifold – removal and refitting

⚠️ *Warning: The engine must be completely cool before beginning this procedure.*

### Removal

**1** The exhaust manifold and the turbocharger are integrated and must be renewed as a unit. Follow the procedures outlined in Chapter 4B on turbocharger renewal to remove and disconnect the hoses and related components leading to the turbocharger, then proceed with the following Steps to remove

and refit the exhaust manifold/turbocharger unit.

**2** Apply penetrating oil to the exhaust manifold mounting nuts/bolts.

**3** Remove the mounting nuts/bolts and lower the exhaust manifold/turbocharger from the engine.

**4** Remove the exhaust manifold gaskets from the studs on the cylinder head.

### Refitting

**5** Use a scraper to remove all traces of old gasket material and carbon deposits from the manifold and cylinder head mating surfaces. If the gasket was leaking, have the manifold checked for warpage at an automotive machine shop.

**6** Position the new gaskets over the cylinder head studs. **Note:** *Be sure to position the exhaust manifold gaskets with the 'notched' end facing up, otherwise they will obstruct the intake manifold gasket (see illustration)*.

**7** Refit the exhaust manifold/turbocharger and thread the mounting nuts/bolts into place.

**8** Working from the centre out, tighten the nuts/bolts to the torque listed in this Chapter's Specifications in several equal steps.

**9** Refer to back to Chapter 4B and refit the remaining parts in the reverse order of removal.

**10** Run the engine and check for exhaust leaks.

**11** Check the coolant level, top-up as necessary (see Chapter 1).

# Chapter 2 Part D:
# General engine overhaul procedures

## Contents

## Degrees of difficulty

| | | | | |
|---|---|---|---|---|
| **Easy,** suitable for novice with little experience  | **Fairly easy,** suitable for beginner with some experience  | **Fairly difficult,** suitable for competent DIY mechanic 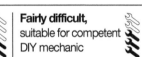 | **Difficult,** suitable for experienced DIY mechanic 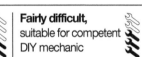 | **Very difficult,** suitable for expert DIY or professional  |

## Specifications

### General

Engine designation
| | |
|---|---|
| 1.4L petrol . . . . . . . . . . . . . . . . . . . . . . . . . . . . . . . . . . . . . . . . . . | BCA |
| 1.6L petrol . . . . . . . . . . . . . . . . . . . . . . . . . . . . . . . . . . . . . . . . . . | AWH |
| 1.6L petrol with roller rocker arms . . . . . . . . . . . . . . . . . . . . . . . | AYD and BFS |
| 1.8L turbo-petrol . . . . . . . . . . . . . . . . . . . . . . . . . . . . . . . . . . . . . | AVC and AWU |
| 1.9L turbo-diesel . . . . . . . . . . . . . . . . . . . . . . . . . . . . . . . . . . . . | ALH, ATD and AXR |
| 2.0L petrol . . . . . . . . . . . . . . . . . . . . . . . . . . . . . . . . . . . . . . . . . | AQY and AZJ |

Displacement
| | |
|---|---|
| BCA . . . . . . . . . . . . . . . . . . . . . . . . . . . . . . . . . . . . . . . . . . . . | 1390 cc |
| AWH, AYD and BFS . . . . . . . . . . . . . . . . . . . . . . . . . . . . . . . . . | 1596 cc |
| AYD . . . . . . . . . . . . . . . . . . . . . . . . . . . . . . . . . . . . . . . . . . . . | 1596 cc |
| AVC and AWU . . . . . . . . . . . . . . . . . . . . . . . . . . . . . . . . . . . . . | 1781 cc |
| ALH, ATD and AXR . . . . . . . . . . . . . . . . . . . . . . . . . . . . . . . . . | 1896 cc |
| AQY and AZJ . . . . . . . . . . . . . . . . . . . . . . . . . . . . . . . . . . . . . | 1984 cc |

Bore and stroke
| | |
|---|---|
| 1.4L . . . . . . . . . . . . . . . . . . . . . . . . . . . . . . . . . . . . . . . . . . . . | 76.5 x 75.6 mm |
| 1.6L . . . . . . . . . . . . . . . . . . . . . . . . . . . . . . . . . . . . . . . . . . . . | 81.01 x 77.40 mm |
| 1.8L . . . . . . . . . . . . . . . . . . . . . . . . . . . . . . . . . . . . . . . . . . . . | 81.01 x 86.38 mm |
| 1.9L . . . . . . . . . . . . . . . . . . . . . . . . . . . . . . . . . . . . . . . . . . . . | 79.9 x 95.5 mm |
| 2.0L . . . . . . . . . . . . . . . . . . . . . . . . . . . . . . . . . . . . . . . . . . . . | 82.51 x 92.78 mm |

## General (continued)

| | |
|---|---|
| Cylinder numbers (timing belt end-to-transmission end) . . . . . . . . . . . | 1-2-3-4 |
| Firing order . . . . . . . . . . . . . . . . . . . . . . . | 1-3-4-2 |

Cylinder compression pressure

Petrol engines

| | |
|---|---|
| Minimum . . . . . . . . . . . . . . . . . . . . . . . . . . . . . . | 7.6 bar |
| Maximum variation between cylinders . . . . . . . . . . . . . . . . . . . | 30-percent from the highest reading |

Diesel engine

| | |
|---|---|
| Minimum . . . . . . . . . . . . . . . . . . . . . . . . . . . . . . | 19.3 bar |
| Maximum variation between cylinders . . . . . . . . . . . . . . . . . . . | 20-percent from the highest reading |

Oil pressure

Petrol engines

| | |
|---|---|
| At idle . . . . . . . . . . . . . . . . . . . . . . . . . . . . . . | 2.0 bar minimum |
| At 2000 rpm . . . . . . . . . . . . . . . . . . . . . . . . . . . . . | 3.0 to 4.6 bar |

Diesel engine

| | |
|---|---|
| At idle . . . . . . . . . . . . . . . . . . . . . . . . . . . . . . | N/A |
| At 2000 rpm . . . . . . . . . . . . . . . . . . . . . . . . . . . . . | 2.0 bar |

Maximum oil pressure

| | |
|---|---|
| All engines . . . . . . . . . . . . . . . . . . . . . . . . . . . . . | 7.1 bar |

## Cylinder head

Warpage limit:

| | |
|---|---|
| 1.4L . . . . . . . . . . . . . . . . . . . . . . . . . . . . . . | 0.05 mm |
| Except 1.4L . . . . . . . . . . . . . . . . . . . . . . . . . . . . | 0.10 mm |

Cylinder head height (minimum)

Petrol engines

| | |
|---|---|
| 1.4L . . . . . . . . . . . . . . . . . . . . . . . . . . . . . . | No reworking permitted |
| 1.6L . . . . . . . . . . . . . . . . . . . . . . . . . . . . . . | 132.6 mm |
| 1.8L . . . . . . . . . . . . . . . . . . . . . . . . . . . . . . | 139.2 mm |
| 2.0L . . . . . . . . . . . . . . . . . . . . . . . . . . . . . . | 132.58 mm |
| Diesel engine . . . . . . . . . . . . . . . . . . . . . . . . . . . | No reworking permitted |

## Valves and related components

| | |
|---|---|
| Valve face angle . . . . . . . . . . . . . . . . . . . . . . . . . . | 45-degrees |
| Valve seat angle . . . . . . . . . . . . . . . . . . . . . . . . . . | 45-degrees |
| Valve margin width . . . . . . . . . . . . . . . . . . . . . . . . . | N/A |

Valve stem diameter:

Intake valves

| | |
|---|---|
| 1.4L . . . . . . . . . . . . . . . . . . . . . . . . . . . . . . | 5.973 mm |
| 1.6L (code AWH) . . . . . . . . . . . . . . . . . . . . . . . . . | 6.92 mm |
| 1.6L (codes AYD and BFS) . . . . . . . . . . . . . . . . . . . . | 5.98 mm |
| 1.8L . . . . . . . . . . . . . . . . . . . . . . . . . . . . . . | 5.963 mm |
| 1.9L . . . . . . . . . . . . . . . . . . . . . . . . . . . . . . | 6.963 mm |
| 2.0L . . . . . . . . . . . . . . . . . . . . . . . . . . . . . . | 6.92 mm |

Exhaust valves

| | |
|---|---|
| 1.4L . . . . . . . . . . . . . . . . . . . . . . . . . . . . . . | 5.953 mm |
| 1.6L (code AWH) . . . . . . . . . . . . . . . . . . . . . . . . . | 6.92 mm |
| 1.6L (code AYD and BFS) . . . . . . . . . . . . . . . . . . . . | 5.96 mm |
| 1.8L . . . . . . . . . . . . . . . . . . . . . . . . . . . . . . | 5.943 mm |
| 1.9L . . . . . . . . . . . . . . . . . . . . . . . . . . . . . . | 6.943 mm |
| 2.0L . . . . . . . . . . . . . . . . . . . . . . . . . . . . . . | 6.92 mm |

Valve stem-to-guide clearance (maximum deflection)

Intake valves

| | |
|---|---|
| 1.4L . . . . . . . . . . . . . . . . . . . . . . . . . . . . . . | N/A |
| 1.6L . . . . . . . . . . . . . . . . . . . . . . . . . . . . . . | 1.0 mm |
| 1.8L . . . . . . . . . . . . . . . . . . . . . . . . . . . . . . | 0.8 mm |
| 1.9L . . . . . . . . . . . . . . . . . . . . . . . . . . . . . . | 1.3 mm |
| 2.0L . . . . . . . . . . . . . . . . . . . . . . . . . . . . . . | 1.0 mm |

Exhaust valves

| | |
|---|---|
| 1.4L . . . . . . . . . . . . . . . . . . . . . . . . . . . . . . | N/A |
| 1.6L . . . . . . . . . . . . . . . . . . . . . . . . . . . . . . | 1.3 mm |
| 1.8L . . . . . . . . . . . . . . . . . . . . . . . . . . . . . . | 0.8 mm |
| 1.9L . . . . . . . . . . . . . . . . . . . . . . . . . . . . . . | 1.3 mm |
| 2.0L . . . . . . . . . . . . . . . . . . . . . . . . . . . . . . | 1.3 mm |

Valve spring

| | |
|---|---|
| Free length . . . . . . . . . . . . . . . . . . . . . . . . . . . | N/A |
| Installed height . . . . . . . . . . . . . . . . . . . . . . . . . | N/A |

## Valves and related components (continued)

Valve installed height (minimum dimension)*
    Intake valves
        1.4L . . . . . . . . . . . . . . . . . . . . . . . . . . . . . . . . . . . . . . . . . . . .    7.6 mm
        1.6L . . . . . . . . . . . . . . . . . . . . . . . . . . . . . . . . . . . . . . . . . . . .    33.8 mm
        1.8L
            Outer valves . . . . . . . . . . . . . . . . . . . . . . . . . . . . . . . . . . .    34.0 mm
            Inner valves . . . . . . . . . . . . . . . . . . . . . . . . . . . . . . . . . . .    33.7 mm
        1.9L . . . . . . . . . . . . . . . . . . . . . . . . . . . . . . . . . . . . . . . . . . . .    35.8 mm
        2.0L . . . . . . . . . . . . . . . . . . . . . . . . . . . . . . . . . . . . . . . . . . . .    33.8 mm
    Exhaust valves
        1.4L . . . . . . . . . . . . . . . . . . . . . . . . . . . . . . . . . . . . . . . . . . . .    7.6 mm
        1.6L . . . . . . . . . . . . . . . . . . . . . . . . . . . . . . . . . . . . . . . . . . . .    34.1 mm
        1.8L . . . . . . . . . . . . . . . . . . . . . . . . . . . . . . . . . . . . . . . . . . . .    34.4 mm
        1.9L . . . . . . . . . . . . . . . . . . . . . . . . . . . . . . . . . . . . . . . . . . . .    36.1 mm
        2.0L . . . . . . . . . . . . . . . . . . . . . . . . . . . . . . . . . . . . . . . . . . . .    34.1 mm

*Measured from tip of valve stem to top surface of cylinder head.

## Crankshaft

**Note:** *See Note in Section 1 for 1.4L.*
Endfloat
    Petrol engines
        Standard . . . . . . . . . . . . . . . . . . . . . . . . . . . . . . . . . . . . . . . .    0.07 to 0.23 mm
        Service limit . . . . . . . . . . . . . . . . . . . . . . . . . . . . . . . . . . . . .    0.30 mm
    Diesel engine
        Standard . . . . . . . . . . . . . . . . . . . . . . . . . . . . . . . . . . . . . . . .    0.07 to 0.17 mm
        Service limit . . . . . . . . . . . . . . . . . . . . . . . . . . . . . . . . . . . . .    0.37 mm
Run-out . . . . . . . . . . . . . . . . . . . . . . . . . . . . . . . . . . . . . . . . . . . .    N/A

## Main bearing journal diameters

**Note:** *See Note in Section 1 for 1.4L.*
Standard . . . . . . . . . . . . . . . . . . . . . . . . . . . . . . . . . . . . . . . . . . .    54.0 mm
1st undersize . . . . . . . . . . . . . . . . . . . . . . . . . . . . . . . . . . . . . . . .    53.75 mm
2nd undersize . . . . . . . . . . . . . . . . . . . . . . . . . . . . . . . . . . . . . . .    53.50 mm
3rd undersize . . . . . . . . . . . . . . . . . . . . . . . . . . . . . . . . . . . . . . .    53.25 mm
Tolerance . . . . . . . . . . . . . . . . . . . . . . . . . . . . . . . . . . . . . . . . . . .    −0.017 to −0.037 mm
Out-of-round limit . . . . . . . . . . . . . . . . . . . . . . . . . . . . . . . . . . . .    0.005 mm
Taper limit . . . . . . . . . . . . . . . . . . . . . . . . . . . . . . . . . . . . . . . . . .    0.007 mm
Main bearing oil clearance
    Petrol engines
        Standard . . . . . . . . . . . . . . . . . . . . . . . . . . . . . . . . . . . . . . . .    0.01 to 0.04 mm
        Service limit . . . . . . . . . . . . . . . . . . . . . . . . . . . . . . . . . . . . .    0.15 mm
    Diesel engine
        Standard . . . . . . . . . . . . . . . . . . . . . . . . . . . . . . . . . . . . . . . .    0.03 to 0.08 mm
        Service limit . . . . . . . . . . . . . . . . . . . . . . . . . . . . . . . . . . . . .    0.17 mm

## Connecting rod bearing journal diameters

**Note:** *See Note in Section 1 for 1.4L.*
Standard . . . . . . . . . . . . . . . . . . . . . . . . . . . . . . . . . . . . . . . . . . .    47.80 mm
1st undersize . . . . . . . . . . . . . . . . . . . . . . . . . . . . . . . . . . . . . . . .    47.55 mm
2nd undersize . . . . . . . . . . . . . . . . . . . . . . . . . . . . . . . . . . . . . . .    47.30 mm
3rd undersize . . . . . . . . . . . . . . . . . . . . . . . . . . . . . . . . . . . . . . .    47.05 mm
Tolerance . . . . . . . . . . . . . . . . . . . . . . . . . . . . . . . . . . . . . . . . . . .    −0.022 to −0.042 mm
Out-of-round limit . . . . . . . . . . . . . . . . . . . . . . . . . . . . . . . . . . . .    0.005 mm
Taper limit . . . . . . . . . . . . . . . . . . . . . . . . . . . . . . . . . . . . . . . . . .    0.007 mm
Connecting rod bearing oil clearance
    Petrol engines
        Standard . . . . . . . . . . . . . . . . . . . . . . . . . . . . . . . . . . . . . . . .    0.01 to 0.06 mm
        Service limit . . . . . . . . . . . . . . . . . . . . . . . . . . . . . . . . . . . . .    0.12 mm
    Diesel engine
        Standard . . . . . . . . . . . . . . . . . . . . . . . . . . . . . . . . . . . . . . . .    0.01 to 0.05 mm
        Service limit . . . . . . . . . . . . . . . . . . . . . . . . . . . . . . . . . . . . .    0.08 mm
Connecting rod side clearance (endfloat) . . . . . . . . . . . . . . . . . . . . .    0.05 to 0.31 mm

## Engine block

Cylinder bore diameter
  1.4L
    Standard . . . . . . . . . . . . . . . . . . . . . . . . . . . . . . . . . . . . . . . . . . . 76.51 mm
    1st oversize . . . . . . . . . . . . . . . . . . . . . . . . . . . . . . . . . . . . . . . . 76.76 mm
  1.6L
    Standard . . . . . . . . . . . . . . . . . . . . . . . . . . . . . . . . . . . . . . . . . . . 81.01 mm
    1st oversize . . . . . . . . . . . . . . . . . . . . . . . . . . . . . . . . . . . . . . . . 81.51 mm
  1.8L
    Standard . . . . . . . . . . . . . . . . . . . . . . . . . . . . . . . . . . . . . . . . . . . 81.01 mm
    1st oversize . . . . . . . . . . . . . . . . . . . . . . . . . . . . . . . . . . . . . . . . 81.51 mm
  1.9L
    Standard . . . . . . . . . . . . . . . . . . . . . . . . . . . . . . . . . . . . . . . . . . . 79.51 mm
    1st oversize . . . . . . . . . . . . . . . . . . . . . . . . . . . . . . . . . . . . . . . . 79.76 mm
    2nd oversize . . . . . . . . . . . . . . . . . . . . . . . . . . . . . . . . . . . . . . . 80.01 mm
  2.0L
    Standard . . . . . . . . . . . . . . . . . . . . . . . . . . . . . . . . . . . . . . . . . . . 82.51 mm
    1st oversize . . . . . . . . . . . . . . . . . . . . . . . . . . . . . . . . . . . . . . . . 83.01 mm
Out-of-round limit
**Note:** *See Note in Section 1 for 1.4L.*
  1.6L   . . . . . . . . . . . . . . . . . . . . . . . . . . . . . . . . . . . . . . . . . . . . . . . . 0.08 mm
  1.8L   . . . . . . . . . . . . . . . . . . . . . . . . . . . . . . . . . . . . . . . . . . . . . . . . 0.04 mm
  1.9L   . . . . . . . . . . . . . . . . . . . . . . . . . . . . . . . . . . . . . . . . . . . . . . . . 0.10 mm
  2.0L   . . . . . . . . . . . . . . . . . . . . . . . . . . . . . . . . . . . . . . . . . . . . . . . . 0.08 mm
Taper limit
**Note:** *See Note in Section 1 for 1.4L.*
  1.6L   . . . . . . . . . . . . . . . . . . . . . . . . . . . . . . . . . . . . . . . . . . . . . . . . 0.08 mm
  1.8L   . . . . . . . . . . . . . . . . . . . . . . . . . . . . . . . . . . . . . . . . . . . . . . . . 0.04 mm
  1.9L   . . . . . . . . . . . . . . . . . . . . . . . . . . . . . . . . . . . . . . . . . . . . . . . . 0.10 mm
  2.0L   . . . . . . . . . . . . . . . . . . . . . . . . . . . . . . . . . . . . . . . . . . . . . . . . 0.08 mm
Block deck warpage limit . . . . . . . . . . . . . . . . . . . . . . . . . . . . . . . 0.10 mm

## Pistons and rings

Piston diameter
  1.4L
    Standard . . . . . . . . . . . . . . . . . . . . . . . . . . . . . . . . . . . . . . . . . . . 76.470 mm
    1st oversize . . . . . . . . . . . . . . . . . . . . . . . . . . . . . . . . . . . . . . . . 76.720 mm
  1.6L
    Standard* . . . . . . . . . . . . . . . . . . . . . . . . . . . . . . . . . . . . . . . . . . 80.965 mm
  1.8L
    Standard* . . . . . . . . . . . . . . . . . . . . . . . . . . . . . . . . . . . . . . . . . . 80.965 mm
    1st oversize* . . . . . . . . . . . . . . . . . . . . . . . . . . . . . . . . . . . . . . . 81.465 mm
  1.9L
    Standard . . . . . . . . . . . . . . . . . . . . . . . . . . . . . . . . . . . . . . . . . . . 79.47 mm
    1st oversize . . . . . . . . . . . . . . . . . . . . . . . . . . . . . . . . . . . . . . . . 79.72 mm
    2nd oversize . . . . . . . . . . . . . . . . . . . . . . . . . . . . . . . . . . . . . . . 79.97 mm
  2.0L
    Standard* . . . . . . . . . . . . . . . . . . . . . . . . . . . . . . . . . . . . . . . . . . 82.465 mm
    1st oversize . . . . . . . . . . . . . . . . . . . . . . . . . . . . . . . . . . . . . . . . 82.965 mm
Piston ring end gap
  1.4L
    Top compression ring . . . . . . . . . . . . . . . . . . . . . . . . . . . . . . . . . 0.20 to 0.50 mm
    Second compression ring . . . . . . . . . . . . . . . . . . . . . . . . . . . . . 0.40 to 0.70 mm
    Oil control ring . . . . . . . . . . . . . . . . . . . . . . . . . . . . . . . . . . . . . . 0.40 to 1.40 mm
  1.6L
    Top compression ring . . . . . . . . . . . . . . . . . . . . . . . . . . . . . . . . . 0.20 to 0.40 mm
    Second compression ring . . . . . . . . . . . . . . . . . . . . . . . . . . . . . 0.20 to 0.40 mm
    Oil control ring . . . . . . . . . . . . . . . . . . . . . . . . . . . . . . . . . . . . . . 0.25 to 0.50 mm
  1.8L
    Top compression ring . . . . . . . . . . . . . . . . . . . . . . . . . . . . . . . . . 0.15 to 0.40 mm
    Second compression ring . . . . . . . . . . . . . . . . . . . . . . . . . . . . . 0.15 to 0.40 mm
    Oil control ring . . . . . . . . . . . . . . . . . . . . . . . . . . . . . . . . . . . . . . 0.25 to 0.50 mm
  1.9L
    Top compression ring . . . . . . . . . . . . . . . . . . . . . . . . . . . . . . . . . 0.20 to 0.40 mm
    Second compression ring . . . . . . . . . . . . . . . . . . . . . . . . . . . . . 0.20 to 0.40 mm
    Oil control ring . . . . . . . . . . . . . . . . . . . . . . . . . . . . . . . . . . . . . . 0.25 to 0.50 mm
  2.0L
    Top compression ring . . . . . . . . . . . . . . . . . . . . . . . . . . . . . . . . . 0.20 to 0.40 mm
    Second compression ring . . . . . . . . . . . . . . . . . . . . . . . . . . . . . 0.20 to 0.40 mm
    Oil control ring . . . . . . . . . . . . . . . . . . . . . . . . . . . . . . . . . . . . . . 0.25 to 0.50 mm

## Pistons and rings (continued)
Piston ring side clearance
  1.4L
    Top compression ring ................................... 0.04 to 0.08 mm
    Second compression ring ............................. 0.04 to 0.08 mm
    Oil control ring ........................................ N/A
  1.6L
    Top compression ring ................................... 0.06 to 0.09 mm
    Second compression ring ............................. 0.06 to 0.09 mm
    Oil control ring ........................................ 0.03 to 0.06 mm
  1.8L
    Top compression ring ................................... 0.02 to 0.07 mm
    Second compression ring ............................. 0.02 to 0.07 mm
    Oil control ring ........................................ 0.02 to 0.06 mm
  1.9L
    Top compression ring ................................... 0.06 to 0.09 mm
    Second compression ring ............................. 0.05 to 0.08 mm
    Oil control ring ........................................ 0.03 to 0.06 mm
  2.0L
    Top compression ring ................................... 0.06 to 0.09 mm
    Second compression ring ............................. 0.06 to 0.09 mm
    Oil control ring ........................................ 0.03 to 0.06 mm
* Dimension without graphite coating (the graphite coating, which is dark grey, will add approximately 0.02 mm to the diameter).

## Torque specifications*

| | Nm | Ft-lbs |
|---|---|---|
| Connecting rod cap nuts (always renew) | | |
|   Step 1 | 30 | 22 |
|   Step 2 | Angle-tighten a further 90-degrees | |
| Engine speed sender wheel-to-crankshaft bolts (always renew) | | |
|   Step 1 | 10 | 7 |
|   Step 2 | Angle-tighten a further 90-degrees | |
| Main bearing cap bolts (always renew) | | |
|   1.6L engine: | | |
|     Step 1 | 40 | 30 |
|     Step 2 | Angle-tighten a further 90-degrees | |
|   1.8L, 1.9L and 2.0L: | | |
|     Step 1 | 65 | 48 |
|     Step 2 | Angle-tighten a further 90-degrees | |
| Oil spray nozzles | 27 | 20 |

* **Note:** Refer to Chapter 2A, 2B or 2C for additional torque specifications. 1.4L crankshaft removal not allowed.

## 1  General information – engine overhaul

**Note:** On the 1.4 litre engine, the crankshaft must not be removed. Just loosening the main bearing cap bolts will cause deformation of the cylinder block. On these engines, if the crankshaft or main bearing surfaces are worn or damaged, the complete crankshaft/cylinder block assembly must be renewed.

Included in this portion of Chapter 2 are the general overhaul procedures for the cylinder head and internal engine components.

The information ranges from advice concerning preparation for an overhaul and the purchase of renewal parts to detailed, step-by-step procedures covering removal and refitting of internal engine components and the inspection of parts.

The following Sections have been written based on the assumption that the engine has been removed from the vehicle. For information concerning in-vehicle engine repair, as well as removal and refitting of the external components necessary for the overhaul, see Chapters 2A and 2B (petrol engines) or Chapter 2C (diesel engines), and Section 8 of this Chapter.

The Specifications included in this Part are only those necessary for the inspection and overhaul procedures which follow. Refer to Chapter 2, Part A, B or C for additional Specifications.

It's not always easy to determine when, or if, an engine should be completely overhauled, as a number of factors must be considered.

High mileage is not necessarily an indication that an overhaul is needed, while low mileage doesn't preclude the need for an overhaul. Frequency of servicing is probably the most important consideration. An engine that's had regular and frequent oil and filter changes, as well as other required maintenance, will most likely give many thousands of miles of reliable service.

Conversely, a neglected engine may require an overhaul very early in its life.

Excessive oil consumption is an indication that piston rings, valve seals and/or valve guides are in need of attention. Make sure that oil leaks aren't responsible before deciding that the rings and/or guides are bad. Perform a cylinder compression check to determine the extent of the work required (see Section 3). Also check the vacuum readings under various conditions (see Section 4).

Loss of power, rough running, knocking or metallic engine noises, excessive valve train noise and high fuel consumption rates may also point to the need for an overhaul, especially if they're all present at the same time. If a complete tune-up doesn't remedy the situation, major mechanical work is the only solution.

An engine overhaul involves restoring the internal parts to the specifications of a new engine. During an overhaul, the piston rings are renewed and the cylinder walls are reconditioned (rebored and/or honed). If a rebore is done by an automotive machine workshop, new oversize pistons will also be fitted. The main bearings and connecting big-end bearings are generally replaced with new ones and, if necessary, the crankshaft may be reground to restore the journals. Generally, the valves are serviced as well, since they're usually in less-than-perfect condition at this point. While the engine is being overhauled, other components, such as the starter and alternator, can be rebuilt as well. The end result should be a like new engine that will give many trouble-free miles. **Note:** *Critical cooling system components such as the hoses, drivebelts, thermostat and water pump should be renewed when an engine is overhauled. The radiator should be checked carefully to ensure that it isn't clogged or leaking (see Chapter 3). If you purchase a rebuilt engine or short block, some rebuilders will not warranty their engines unless the radiator has been professionally flushed. Also, we don't recommend overhauling the oil pump – always refit a new one when an engine is rebuilt.*

Before beginning the engine overhaul, read through the entire procedure to familiarise yourself with the scope and requirements of the job. Overhauling an engine isn't difficult, but it is time-consuming. Plan on the vehicle being tied up for a minimum of two weeks, especially if parts must be taken to an automotive machine workshop for repair or reconditioning. Check on availability of parts and make sure that any necessary special tools and equipment are obtained in advance. Most work can be done with typical hand tools, although a number of precision measuring tools are required for inspecting parts to determine if they must be renewed. Often an automotive machine workshop will handle the inspection of parts and offer advice concerning reconditioning and renewal. **Note:** *Always wait until the engine has been completely disassembled and all components, especially the engine block, have been inspected before deciding what service and repair operations must be performed by an automotive machine workshop.* Since the block's condition will be the major factor to consider when determining whether to overhaul the original engine or buy a rebuilt one, never purchase parts or have machine work done on other components until the block has been thoroughly inspected. As a general rule, time is the primary cost of an overhaul, so it doesn't pay to refit worn or substandard parts.

As a final note, to ensure maximum life and minimum trouble from a rebuilt engine, everything must be assembled with care in a spotlessly-clean environment.

## 2 Oil pressure check

1 Low engine oil pressure can be a sign of an engine in need of rebuilding. A 'low oil pressure' indicator (often called an 'idiot light') is not a test of the lubrication system. Such indicators only come on when the oil pressure is dangerously low. Even a factory oil pressure gauge in the instrument panel is only a relative indication, although much better for driver information than a warning light. A better test is with a mechanical (not electrical) oil pressure gauge. When used in conjunction with an accurate tachometer, an engine's oil pressure performance can be compared to the manufacturers Specifications.
2 Find the oil pressure indicator sender unit **(see illustration)**.
3 Remove the oil pressure sender unit and fit an adapter which will allow you to directly connect your hand-held mechanical oil pressure gauge. Use PTFE tape or sealant on the threads of the adapter and the fitting on the end of your gauge's hose.
4 Connect an accurate tachometer to the engine, according to the tachometer manufacturer's instructions.
5 Check the oil pressure with the engine running (full operating temperature) at the specified engine speed, and compare it to this Chapter's Specifications. If it's extremely low, the bearings and/or oil pump are probably worn out.

## 3 Cylinder compression check

1 A compression check will tell you what mechanical condition the upper end (pistons, rings, valves, head gaskets) of the engine is in. Specifically, it can tell you if the compression is down due to leakage caused by worn piston rings, defective valves and seats or a blown head gasket. **Note:** *The engine must be at normal operating temperature and the battery must be fully-charged for this check.*
2 Begin by cleaning the area around the spark plugs/glow plugs before you remove them. Compressed air should be used, if available, otherwise a small brush will work. The idea is to prevent dirt from getting into the cylinders as the compression check is being done.
3 Remove all of the spark plugs (Chapter 1) or glow plugs (Chapter 5) from the engine.
4 Block the throttle wide open.
5 On petrol engines, disable the fuel and ignition systems by disconnecting the primary electrical connectors at the ignition coil pack/modules (see Chapter 5) and the electrical connectors at the fuel injectors (see Chapter 4A). On diesel engines, disable the fuel injection system by unplugging the electrical connector to the fuel shut-off valve (see Chapter 4B).
6 Install the compression gauge in the number one spark plug/glow plug hole **(see illustration)**.

> ⚠ **Warning: If you are checking the compression on a diesel engine, make sure the gauge is capable of reading pressures up to 34 bar.**

7 Crank the engine over at least seven compression strokes and watch the gauge. The compression should build-up quickly in a healthy engine. Low compression on the first stroke, followed by gradually increasing pressure on successive strokes, indicates worn piston rings. A low compression reading on the first stroke, which doesn't build-up during successive strokes, indicates leaking valves or a blown head gasket (a cracked head could also be the cause). Deposits on the undersides of the valve heads can also cause low compression. Record the highest gauge reading obtained.
8 Repeat the procedure for the remaining cylinders, turning the engine over for the same length of time for each cylinder, and compare the results to this Chapter's Specifications.

### Petrol engines only

> ⚠ **Warning: DO NOT perform this step on a diesel engine. Checking compression on a diesel engine with oil in the**

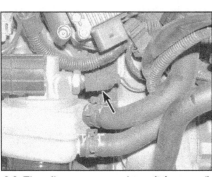

**2.2 The oil pressure sender unit (arrowed) is mounted on the oil filter adapter housing which is located on the (front) side of the engine block (2.0L engine shown, all others similar)**

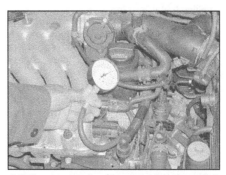

**3.6 A compression gauge with a threaded fitting for the spark plug hole is preferred over the type that requires hand pressure to maintain the seal – be sure to open the throttle valve as far as possible during the compression check**

*cylinder could cause it to fire, which would damage the gauge and possibly the engine, and could cause injury.*

9 If the readings are below normal, add some engine oil (about three squirts from a plunger-type oil can) to each cylinder, through the spark plug hole, and repeat the test.

10 If the compression increases after the oil is added, the piston rings are definitely worn. If the compression doesn't increase significantly, the leakage is occurring at the valves or head gasket. Leakage past the valves may be caused by burned valve seats and/or faces or warped, cracked or bent valves.

### All engines

11 If two adjacent cylinders have equally low compression, there's a strong possibility the head gasket between them is blown. The appearance of coolant in the combustion chambers or the crankcase would verify this condition.

12 If one cylinder is about 20-percent lower than the others, and the engine has a slightly rough idle, a worn exhaust lobe on the camshaft could be the cause.

13 If the compression is unusually high, the combustion chambers are probably coated with carbon deposits. If that's the case, the cylinder heads should be removed and decarbonised.

14 If compression is way down or varies greatly between cylinders, it would be a good idea to have a leakdown test performed by an automotive garage. This test will pinpoint exactly where the leakage is occurring and how severe it is.

15 Refitting of the remaining components is the reverse of removal.

### 4  Vacuum gauge diagnostic checks

**Note:** *This procedure does not apply to diesel engines.*

1 A vacuum gauge provides valuable information about what is going on in the engine at a low cost. You can check for worn rings or cylinder walls, leaking head or intake manifold gaskets, incorrect carburettor adjustments, restricted exhaust, stuck or burned valves, weak valve springs, improper ignition or valve timing and ignition problems.

2 Unfortunately, vacuum gauge readings are easy to misinterpret, so they should be used in conjunction with other tests to confirm the diagnosis.

3 Both the gauge readings and the rate of needle movement are important for accurate interpretation. Most gauges measure vacuum in millimetres of mercury (mm-Hg). As vacuum increases (or atmospheric pressure decreases), the reading will increase. Also, for every 1000-foot increase in elevation above sea level, the gauge readings will decrease about 25.4 mm of mercury.

4 Connect the vacuum gauge directly to intake manifold vacuum, not to ported vacuum **(see illustration)**. Be sure no hoses are left disconnected during the test or false readings will result.

5 Before you begin the test, allow the engine to warm up completely. Block the wheels and set the handbrake. With the transmission in Park (automatic gearbox) or Neutral (manual transmission), start the engine and allow it to run at normal idle speed.

6 Read the vacuum gauge; an average, healthy engine should normally produce about 431 to 558 mm of vacuum with a fairly steady needle. Refer to the following vacuum gauge readings and what they indicate about the engine's condition **(see illustration)**.

7 A low, steady reading usually indicates a leaking gasket between the intake manifold and carburettor or throttle body, a leaky vacuum hose, late ignition timing or incorrect camshaft timing. Eliminate all other possible causes, utilising the tests provided in this Chapter before you remove the timing belt cover to check the timing marks.

8 If the reading is 76 to 200 mm-Hg below normal and it fluctuates at that low reading, suspect an intake manifold gasket leak at an intake port.

9 If the needle has regular drops of about 51 to 102 mm-Hg at a steady rate, the valves are probably leaking. Perform a compression or leakdown test to confirm this.

10 An irregular drop or down-flick of the needle can be caused by a sticking valve or an ignition misfire. Perform a compression or leakdown test and read the spark plugs.

11 A rapid vibration of about 102 mm-Hg at idle combined with exhaust smoke indicates worn valve guides. Perform a leakdown test to confirm this. If the rapid vibration occurs with an increase in engine speed, check for a leaking intake manifold gasket or head gasket, weak valve springs, burned valves or ignition misfire.

**4.4  A simple vacuum gauge can be very handy in diagnosing engine condition and performance**

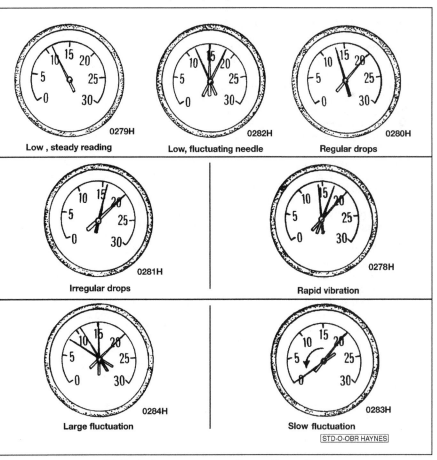

Low , steady reading 0279H
Low, fluctuating needle 0282H
Regular drops 0280H
Irregular drops 0281H
Rapid vibration 0278H
Large fluctuation 0284H
Slow fluctuation 0283H

STD-O-OBR HAYNES

**4.6  Typical vacuum gauge diagnostic readings**

**12** A slight fluctuation, say 25 mm-Hg up and down, may mean ignition problems. Check all the usual tune-up items and, if necessary, run the engine on an ignition analyser.

**13** If there is a large fluctuation, perform a compression or leakdown test to look for a weak or dead cylinder or a blown head gasket.

**14** If the needle moves slowly through a wide range, check for a clogged PCV system, throttle body or intake manifold gasket leaks.

**15** Check for a slow return after revving the engine by quickly snapping the throttle open until the engine reaches about 2500 rpm and let it shut. Normally the reading should drop to near zero, rise above normal idle reading (about 127 mm-Hg over) and then return to the previous idle reading. If the vacuum returns slowly and doesn't peak when the throttle is snapped shut, the rings may be worn. If there is a long delay, look for a restricted exhaust system (often the silencer or catalytic converter). An easy way to check this is to temporarily disconnect the exhaust ahead of the suspected part and retest.

## 5  Engine rebuilding alternatives

The home mechanic is faced with a number of options when performing an engine overhaul. The decision to renew the engine block, piston/connecting rod assemblies and crankshaft depends on a number of factors, with the number one consideration being the condition of the block. Other considerations are cost, access to machine workshop facilities, parts availability, time required to complete the project and the extent of prior mechanical experience.

Give careful thought to which alternative is best for you and discuss the situation with local automotive machine workshops, auto parts dealers and experienced rebuilders before ordering or purchasing renewal parts. Some of the rebuilding alternatives include:

### Individual parts

If the inspection procedures reveal the engine block and most engine components are in re-usable condition, purchasing individual parts may be the most economical alternative. The block, crankshaft and piston/connecting rod assemblies should all be inspected carefully. Even if the block shows little wear, the cylinder bores should be surface-honed.

### Short-block

A short-block consists of an engine block with a crankshaft and piston/connecting rod assemblies already fitted. All new bearings are incorporated and all clearances will be correct. The existing camshaft, valve train components, cylinder head and external parts

can be bolted to the short block with little or no machine workshop work necessary.

### Long-block

A long-block consists of a short block plus an oil pump, sump, cylinder head, valve cover, camshaft and valve train components, timing sprockets and a timing belt. All components are fitted with new bearings, seals and gaskets incorporated throughout. The refitting of manifolds and external parts is all that's necessary.

## 6  Engine removal – methods and precautions

If you've decided the engine must be removed for overhaul or major repair work, several preliminary steps should be taken. Locating a suitable place to work is extremely important. Adequate work space, along with storage space for the vehicle, will be needed.

Cleaning the engine compartment and engine before beginning the removal procedure will help keep tools clean and organised. An engine hoist will also be necessary. Safety is of primary importance, considering the potential hazards involved in removing the engine from this vehicle.

If the engine is being removed by a novice, a helper should be available. Advice and aid from someone more experienced would also be helpful. There are many instances when one person cannot simultaneously perform all of the operations required when lifting or lowering the engine out of the vehicle.

Plan the operation ahead of time. Arrange for or obtain all of the tools and equipment you'll need prior to beginning the job. Some of the equipment necessary to perform engine removal and refitting safely and with relative ease (in addition to a hydraulic jack, jack stands and an engine hoist) are a complete set of spanners and sockets as described in the front of this manual, wooden blocks and plenty of rags and cleaning solvent for mopping-up spilled oil, coolant and fuel.

Plan for the vehicle to be out of use for quite a while. A machine workshop will be required to perform some of the work which the do-it-yourselfer can't accomplish without special equipment. These workshops often have a busy schedule, so it would be a good idea to consult them before removing the engine in order to accurately estimate the amount of time required to rebuild or repair components that may need work.

Always be extremely careful when removing and refitting the engine. Serious injury can result from careless actions. Plan ahead, take your time and a job of this nature, although major, can be accomplished successfully. **Note:** *Because it may be some time before you refit the engine, it is very helpful to make sketches or take photos of various accessory mountings and wiring before removing the engine.*

## 7  Engine – removal and refitting

⚠ *Warning 1: The models covered by this manual are equipped with airbags. Always disable the airbag system before working in the vicinity of any airbag system component to avoid the possibility of accidental deployment of the airbag(s), which could cause personal injury (see Chapter 12).*

⚠ *Warning 2: Petrol is extremely flammable (and diesel fuel only slightly less volatile), so take extra precautions when you work on any part of the fuel system. Don't smoke or allow naked flames or bare light bulbs near the work area, and don't work in a garage where a gas-type appliance (such as a water heater or a clothes dryer) is present. Since petrol and diesel fuel is carcinogenic, wear latex gloves when there's a possibility of being exposed to fuel, and, if you spill any fuel on your skin, rinse it off immediately with soap and water. Mop-up any spills immediately and do not store fuel-soaked rags where they could ignite. The fuel system on petrol engines is under constant pressure, so, if any fuel lines are to be disconnected, the fuel pressure in the system must be relieved first (see Chapter 4A). When you perform any kind of work on the fuel system, wear safety glasses and have a Class B type fire extinguisher on hand.*

⚠ *Warning 3: The air conditioning system is under high pressure – have a dealer service department or service station evacuate the system and recover the refrigerant before disconnecting any of the hoses or fittings.*

*Caution: When disassembling the air intake system on turbocharged vehicles, ensure that no foreign material can get into the turbo air intake port. Cover the opening with a sheet of plastic and a rubber band. The turbocharger compressor blades could be severely damaged if debris is allowed to enter.*

**Note:** *Read through the entire Section before beginning this procedure. The engine and transmission are removed as a unit and then separated outside the vehicle.*

### Removal

**1** Disconnect the cable from the negative terminal of the battery, then disconnect the positive terminal.

*Caution: On models equipped with an anti-theft audio system, be sure to have the correct activation code before performing any procedure which requires disconnecting the battery (see the front of this manual).*

**2** If you're removing a petrol engine, relieve the fuel system pressure (see Chapter 4A).

**3** Place protective covers on the wings and scuttle and remove the bonnet (see Chapter 11).

**4** Remove the air cleaner assembly (see Chapter 4A). Remove the battery and its mounting bracket (see Chapter 5). On turbocharged models, also disconnect the intercooler hoses (see Chapter 4A or 4B).

**5** Raise the vehicle and support it securely on axle stands. Drain the cooling system, transmission and engine oil and remove the auxiliary drivebelts (see Chapter 1 and the relevant part of Chapter 7).

**6** Clearly label, then disconnect all vacuum lines, coolant and emissions hoses, wiring harness connectors, earth straps and fuel lines. Masking tape and/or a touch up paint applicator work well for marking items **(see illustration)**. Take instant photos or sketch the locations of components and brackets.

**7** Remove the cooling fans, and disconnect the radiator hoses and heater hoses (see Chapter 3).

**8** Disconnect the fuel lines from the fuel rail or the injection pump (see Chapter 4A or 4B). Plug or cap all open fittings.

**9** Refer to Chapter 3 and unbolt and set aside the air conditioning compressor, without disconnecting the refrigerant lines.

**10** Disconnect the throttle cable (if applicable) from the engine (see Chapter 4A).

**11** Unbolt the power steering pump. Tie the pump aside without disconnecting the hoses (see Chapter 10). Remove the alternator (see Chapter 5).

**12** Remove the secondary air injection pump and hoses from the engine if applicable (see Chapter 6A).

**13** Label and disconnect the main engine electrical harnesses from the starter and the engine.

**14** On 1.6L and 2.0L engines, it may be helpful to remove the upper intake manifold to make engine removal easier (see Chapter 2B). Be sure to label and disconnect all hoses, connectors, and any earth straps.

**15** Remove the front section of the exhaust system (see Chapter 4A).

**16** Remove the driveshafts and the driveshaft boot protective cover if applicable (see Chapter 8). Disconnect the electrical connectors and the gearchange linkage from the transmission (see Chapter 7A or 7B).

**17** Attach a lifting sling or chain to the lifting eye (if applicable) on the engine **(see illustration)**. If two lifting eyes are not provided, attach the lifting sling or chain to a safe place such as the side of the cylinder head **(see illustration)**. Position a hoist and connect the sling to it. Take up the slack until there is slight tension on the hoist.

**18** Recheck to be sure nothing except the mountings are still connecting the engine/transmission to the vehicle. Disconnect anything still remaining.

**19** Support the transmission with a floor jack. Place a block of wood on the jack head to prevent damage to the transmission. Raise the engine enough to remove the engine mounting bolts **(see illustration)**.

 **Warning: Do not place any part of your body under the engine/transmission when it's supported only by a hoist or other lifting device.**

**20** Except for the 1.4L engine, slowly lower the engine/transmission out of the vehicle. Once the engine/transmission is on the floor, disconnect the engine lifting hoist and have an assistant help you carefully rock the engine/transmission back until it is laying flat on the floor so it can be slid out from under the vehicle. **Note:** *A sheet of old hardboard or panelling between the engine and floor makes moving the assembly easier. A helper will be needed to move the engine/transmission.*

**21** On the 1.4L engine, raise the engine/transmission and withdraw it forwards.

**22** Separate the engine from the transmission (see Chapter 7A or 7B).

**23** Place the engine on the floor or remove the flywheel/driveplate and mount the engine on an engine stand.

## Refitting

**24** Check the engine/transmission mountings. If they're worn or damaged, renew them.

**25** On automatic transmission-equipped models, inspect the torque converter seal and bush, and apply a dab of grease to the nose of the converter and to the seal lips. If the vehicle is equipped with a manual transmission, inspect the clutch components (see Chapter 8).

**26** Carefully guide the transmission into place, following the procedure outlined in Chapter 7A or 7B.

*Caution: Do not use the bolts to force the engine and transmission into alignment. It may crack or damage major components.*

**27** Refit the engine-to-transmission bolts and tighten them securely.

**28** On 1.4L models, raise the engine/transmission and slowly lower it into the engine compartment and refit the engine mounting at the transmission end.

**29** On 1.6L, 1.8L, 1.9L and 2.0L models, slide the engine/transmission over a sheet of hardboard or panelling until it is in the approximate position under the vehicle, then tilt it upright. Roll the engine hoist into position, attach the sling or chain in a position that will allow a good balance, and slowly raise the assembly until the mountings at the transmission end can be attached.

**30** Support the assembly with a floor jack for extra security, then refit the right-side engine mountings. Follow the procedure in the relevant part of Chapter 2A for the final tightening of all engine mounting bolts.

**31** Refit the remaining components and fasteners in the reverse order of removal.

**32** Add coolant, oil, power steering and transmission fluids as needed.

**33** Run the engine and check for proper operation and leaks. Shut off the engine and recheck the fluid levels.

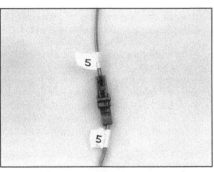

**7.6 Label each wire before unplugging the connector**

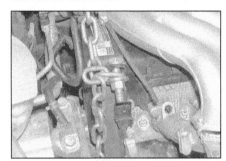

**7.17a Attach the chain or sling to the lifting eyes – all engines are equipped with at least one**

**7.17b On some engines, it will be necessary to attach the sling or chain to the casting protrusion on the cylinder head**

**7.19 Raise the engine enough to remove the engine mountings, then remove the jack supporting the transmission**

## 8 Engine overhaul – disassembly sequence

**Caution: On the 1.4 litre engine, the crankshaft must not be removed. Just loosening the main bearing cap bolts will cause deformation of the cylinder block. On these engines, if the crankshaft or main bearing surfaces are worn or damaged, the complete crankshaft/cylinder block assembly must be renewed.**

1 It's much easier to dismantle and work on the engine if it's mounted on a portable engine stand. A stand can often be rented quite cheaply from an equipment rental shop. Before it's mounted on a stand, the flywheel/driveplate should be removed from the engine.

2 If a stand isn't available, it's possible to dismantle the engine with it blocked up on the floor. Be extra careful not to tip or drop the engine when working without a stand.

3 If you're going to obtain a rebuilt engine, all external components must come off first, to be transferred to the new engine, just as they will if you're doing a complete engine overhaul yourself. These include:

Alternator mounting brackets.
Emissions control components.
Ignition coil/module assembly, spark plug leads and spark plugs (petrol engines).
Glow plug/preheating system components (diesel engines).
Valve/camshaft cover.
Timing belt covers and timing belt.
Water pump.
Thermostat and housing cover and coolant supply hoses.
Fuel system components.
Turbocharger (if equipped).
Intake/exhaust manifolds.
Camshaft and crankshaft position sensors.
Oil filter and adapter housing.
Oil dipstick and tube.
Flywheel/driveplate.

**Note:** When removing the external components from the engine, pay close attention to details that may be helpful or important during refitting. Note the fitted position of gaskets, seals, spacers, pins, brackets, washers, bolts and other small items.

4 If you're obtaining a short-block, then the cylinder heads, sump and oil pump will have to be removed as well. See Engine rebuilding alternatives for additional information regarding the different possibilities to be considered.

5 If you're planning a complete overhaul, the engine must be disassembled and the internal components removed in the following general order:

Camshaft and followers.
Cylinder head.
Oil sump.
Timing belt end oil seal housing.

Oil pump and pick-up tube.
Piston/connecting rod assemblies.
Transmission end oil seal housing.
Crankshaft and main bearings.

6 Before beginning the dismantling and overhaul procedures, make sure the following items are available. Also, refer to Engine overhaul – reassembly sequence for a list of tools and materials needed for engine reassembly.

Common hand tools.
Small cardboard boxes or plastic bags for storing parts.
Gasket scraper.
Ridge reamer.
Engine balancer puller.
Micrometers.
Telescoping gauges.
DTI gauge.
Valve spring compressor.
Cylinder surfacing hone.
Piston ring groove-cleaning tool.
Electric drill motor.
Tap and die set.
Wire brushes.
Oil gallery brushes.
Cleaning solvent.

## 9 Cylinder head – disassembly

**Note:** New and rebuilt cylinder heads are commonly available for most engines at dealerships and motor factors. Due to the fact that some specialised tools are necessary for the dismantling and inspection procedures, and parts aren't always readily available, it may be more practical and economical for the home mechanic to purchase an exchange head rather than taking the time to dismantle, inspect and recondition the original.

1 Cylinder head dismantling involves removal of the intake and exhaust valves and related components. It is already assumed that the camshaft(s) and followers are removed from the cylinder head. If they're not already removed, label the parts and store them separately so they can be reinstalled in their original locations. On the 1.4L engine, unscrew the securing bolt and remove the secondary timing belt tensioner from the timing belt end of the cylinder head.

2 Before the valves are removed, arrange to label and store them, along with their related components, so they can be kept separate and reinstalled in their original locations **(see illustration)**.

3 Compress the springs on the first valve with a spring compressor and remove the collets **(see illustration)**. Carefully release the valve spring compressor and remove the collar (retainer), the spring and the spring seat (if used).

4 Pull the valve out of the head, then remove the oil seal from the guide. If the valve binds in the guide (won't pull through), push it back into the head and de-burr the area around the collet groove with a fine file or whetstone.

5 Repeat the procedure for the remaining valves. Remember to keep all the parts for each valve together so they can be reinstalled in the same locations.

6 Once the valves and related components have been removed and stored in an organised manner, the heads should be thoroughly cleaned and inspected. If a complete engine overhaul is being done, finish the engine dismantling procedures before beginning the cylinder head cleaning and inspection process.

## 10 Cylinder head – cleaning and inspection

1 Thorough cleaning of the cylinder head and related valve train components, followed by a detailed inspection, will enable you to decide how much valve service work must be done during the engine overhaul. **Note:** If the engine was severely overheated, the cylinder head is probably warped (see Step 12).

### Cleaning

2 Scrape all traces of old gasket material and sealant off the head gasket, intake manifold and exhaust manifold mating surfaces. Be

**9.2 A small plastic bag with an appropriate label, can be used to store the valve train components so they can be kept together and reinstalled in the original positions**

**9.3 You'll need a valve spring compressor with a special adapter to compress the spring and allow removal of the collets from the valve stem**

General engine overhaul procedures 2D•11

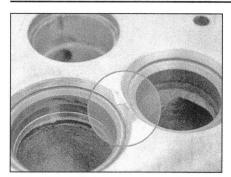

**10.11 Check for cracks between the valve seats**

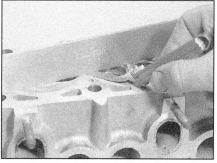

**10.12a Check the cylinder head gasket surface for warpage by trying to slip a feeler gauge under the straight-edge (see this Chapter's Specifications for the maximum warpage allowed and use a feeler gauge of that thickness)**

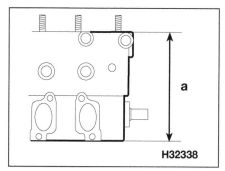

H32338

**10.12b The cylinder head minimum height dimension (a) is measured from the valve cover rail to the gasket surface**

very careful not to gouge the cylinder head. Special gasket-removal solvents that soften gaskets and make removal much easier are available at motor factors.

3 Remove all built-up scale from the coolant passages.

4 Run a stiff wire brush through the various holes to remove deposits that may have formed in them.

5 Run an appropriate-size tap into each of the threaded holes to remove corrosion and thread sealant that may be present. If compressed air is available, use it to clear the holes of debris produced by this operation.

 **Warning: Wear eye protection when using compressed air.**

6 Clean the exhaust manifold and intake manifold stud threads with a wire brush.

7 Clean the cylinder head with solvent and dry it thoroughly.

8 Compressed air will speed the drying process and ensure that all holes and oil passages are clean. **Note:** *Decarbonising chemicals are available and may prove very useful when cleaning cylinder heads and valve train components. They're very caustic and should be used with caution. Be sure to follow the instructions on the container.*

9 Clean all the valve springs, collets and collars (retainers) with solvent and dry them thoroughly. Do the components from one valve at a time to avoid mixing up the parts.

10 Scrape off any heavy deposits that may

have formed on the valves, then use a motorised wire brush to remove deposits from the valve heads and stems. Again, make sure the valves don't get mixed up.

### Inspection

**Note:** *Be sure to perform all of the following inspection procedures before concluding machine workshop work is required. Make a list of the items that need attention.*

#### Cylinder head

11 Inspect the head very carefully for cracks, evidence of coolant leakage and other damage. If cracks are found, check with an automotive machine workshop concerning repair. If repair isn't possible, a new cylinder head must be obtained **(see illustration)**.

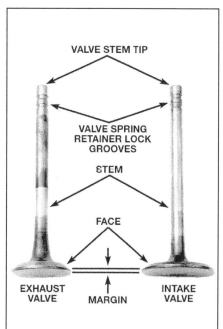

**10.15 Check for valve wear at the points shown here**

12 Using a straight-edge and feeler gauge, check the head gasket mating surface for warpage, then compare the measurement against this Chapter's Specifications **(see illustration)**. If the warpage exceeds the limit on petrol engines, it can be resurfaced at an automotive machine workshop as long as the cylinder head is within the specified minimum height listed in this Chapter's Specifications **(see illustration)**. **Note:** *If the head is resurfaced on petrol engines, it will be necessary to rework the valve seats the same amount which was removed from the cylinder head or piston-to-valve clearance will be compromised, which may lead to severe engine damage. If the cylinder head warpage exceeds the limit on diesel engines, it must be renewed.*

13 Examine the valve seats in each of the combustion chambers. If they're pitted, cracked or burned, the head will require valve service that's beyond the scope of the home mechanic.

14 Check the valve stem-to-guide clearance by measuring the lateral movement of the valve stem with a dial indicator attached securely to the head **(see illustration)**. Refit the valve into the guide until the stem is flush with the top of the guide. The total valve stem movement indicated by the gauge needle must be compared to the specifications in this Chapter. After this is done, if there's still some doubt regarding the condition of the valve guides, they should be checked by an automotive machine workshop (the cost should be minimal).

### Valves

15 Carefully inspect each valve face for uneven wear, deformation, cracks, pits and burned areas. Check the valve stem for scuffing and galling and the neck for cracks. Rotate the valve and check for any obvious indication that it's bent. Look for pits and excessive wear on the end of the stem **(see illustration)**. The presence of any of these conditions indicates the need to consult an automotive machine workshop. **Note:** *The manufacturer recommends the valves be renewed, if refacing is necessary.*

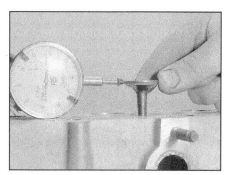

**10.14 A dial indicator (DTI) can be used to determine the valve stem-to-guide clearance – measure the maximum deflection of the valve in its guide**

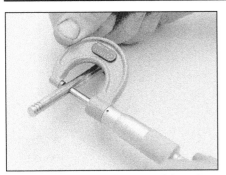

**10.16 Measure the diameter of the valve stems at several points**

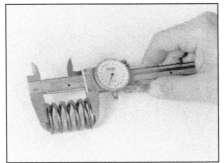

**10.17 Measure the free length of each valve spring with a dial or vernier caliper**

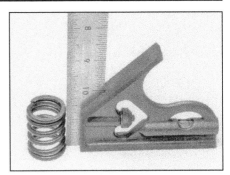

**10.18 Check each valve spring for squareness**

**16** Also measure the stem diameter at several points along their lengths **(see illustration)**. Taper should not be excessive.

### Valve components

**17** Check each valve spring for wear (on the ends) and pits. Measure the free length of each intake valve spring and compare them with one another **(see illustration)**. Any springs that are shorter have sagged and shouldn't be re-used. Now repeat this check on the exhaust valve springs. If, in either check, any of the springs measures shorter than another (intake-to-intake, exhaust-to-exhaust) renew all of the springs as a set. The tension of all springs should be checked with a special fixture before deciding they're suitable for use in a rebuilt engine (take the springs to an automotive machine workshop for this check). **Note:** *If the engine has accumulated many miles, it's a good idea to renew all of the springs as a matter of course.*
**18** Stand each spring on a flat surface and check it for squareness **(see illustration)**. If any of the springs are distorted or sagged, renew all of them.
**19** Check the spring retainers, spring seats and the collets for obvious wear and cracks. Any questionable parts should be replaced with new ones, as extensive damage will occur if they fail during engine operation.

### Camshaft(s) and followers

**20** Refer to Section 21 of this Chapter for the camshaft and follower inspection procedures. Be sure to inspect the camshaft bearing journals on the cylinder head before the head

is sent to a machine workshop to have the valves serviced. If the journals are gouged or scored the cylinder head will have to be renewed regardless of the condition of the valves and related components.

## 11 Valves – servicing

**1** Because of the complex nature of the job and the special tools and equipment needed, servicing of the valve seats and the valve guides, commonly known as a valve job, should be done by a professional (the valves themselves aren't serviceable).
**2** The home mechanic can remove and dismantle the head, do the initial cleaning and inspection, then reassemble and deliver it to an automotive machine workshop for the actual service work. Doing the inspection will enable you to see what condition the head and valve-train components are in and will ensure that you know what work and new parts are required when dealing with an automotive machine workshop. **Note:** *Be aware that Volkswagen cylinder heads have a maximum valve seat refacing dimension. This is the maximum amount of material that can be removed from the valve seats before cylinder head renewal is required. This measurement will be taken by the automotive machine workshop.*
**3** The automotive machine workshop, will remove the valves and springs, recondition the seats, recondition the valve guides, check

and renew the valves, valve springs, spring retainers and collets (as necessary), renew the valve seals with new ones, reassemble the valve components and make sure the valve stem height is correct. If warped, the cylinder head gasket surface will also be resurfaced as long as the cylinder head is within the specified minimum height listed in this Chapter's Specifications (petrol engines only).
**4** After the valve job has been performed by a professional, the head will be in like new condition. When the head is returned, be sure to clean it again before refitting on the engine to remove any metal particles and abrasive grit that may still be present from the valve service or head resurfacing operations. Use compressed air, if available, to blow out all the oil holes and passages.

## 12 Cylinder head – reassembly

**1** Regardless of whether or not the head was sent to an automotive garage for valve servicing, make sure it's clean before beginning reassembly.
**2** If the head was sent out for valve servicing, the valves and related components will already be in place. Begin the reassembly procedure with Step 8. If the head was not sent out for service, the valves, at the very least, should be lapped before reassembly of the cylinder head. Apply a small amount of fine grinding paste on the sealing surface (valve face) of each valve and refit them into their appropriate guide in the cylinder head. Attach a valve lapping tool to the valve head. Using a back-and-forth rotating motion grind the valve head into its seat. Periodically lift the valve and rotate it to redistribute the grinding paste **(see illustration)**. After the lapping process has been completed for each valve it will be necessary to clean the valves and seats of all lapping compound. Be sure to mark the valves before they're removed so they can be fitted back into the same valve guide on reassembly.
**3** Beginning at one end of the head, lubricate and refit the first valve. Apply clean engine oil to the valve stem **(see illustration)**.

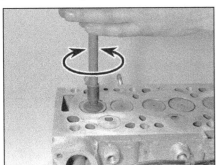

**12.2 Lapping in the valves**

**12.3 Lubricate the valve stem with clean engine oil before installing it into the guide**

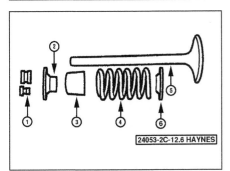

**12.6 Typical valve components**

1 Collets          4 Spring
2 Collar (retainer) 5 Valve
3 Oil seal         6 Valve spring seat

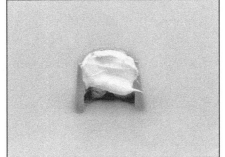

**12.7 Apply a small dab of grease to each collet as shown here before installation – it will hold them in place on the valve stem as the spring is released**

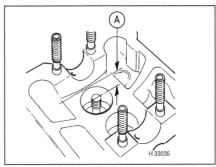

**12.9 Measure the distance (A) between the top face of the valve stem and the top surface of the cylinder head**

4 Refit the spring seat and shims, if originally fitted, before the valve seals.

5 Fit new seals on each of the valve guides. Gently tap each seal into place until it's completely seated on the guide. Many seal sets come with a plastic installer, but use hand pressure. Do not hammer on the seals or they could be driven down too far and subsequently leak. Don't twist or cock the seals during refitting or they won't seal properly on the valve stems.

6 The valve components **(see illustration)** may be fitted in the following order:

*Valves.*
*Valve spring seat.*
*Valve stem seals.*
*Valve spring shims (if any).*
*Valve springs.*
*Collars (retainers).*
*Collets.*

7 Compress the springs with a valve spring compressor and carefully refit the collets in the groove, then slowly release the compressor and make sure the collets seat properly. Apply a small dab of grease to each collet to hold it in place if necessary **(see illustration)**. Tap the valve stem tips with a plastic hammer to seat the collets, if necessary.

8 Repeat the procedure for the remaining valves. Be sure to return the components to their original locations – don't mix them up!

9 Check the fitted valve height with a straight-edge and a dial or vernier caliper. If the head was sent out for service work, the fitted height should be correct (but don't automatically assume it is). The measurement is taken from cylinder head top edge to the top of each valve stem **(see illustration)**. If the height is less than specified in this Chapter, the valve seats have been reworked past their limits and will not allow proper operation of the hydraulic tappets. Valve seats that have been reworked past their limits must be replaced with new ones or a new cylinder head is required.

10 On the 1.4L engine, refit the secondary timing belt tensioner, then refit the securing bolt.

## 13 Pistons and connecting rods – removal

**Note:** *Prior to removing the piston/connecting rod assemblies, remove the cylinder head, the sump, the oil pump drive chain, the oil pump and baffle by referring to the appropriate Sections in Chapter 2A, 2B or 2C.*

1 Use your fingernail to feel if a ridge has formed at the upper limit of ring travel (about 7 mm down from the top of each cylinder). If

carbon deposits or cylinder wear have produced ridges, they must be completely removed with a special tool **(see illustration)**. Follow the manufacturer's instructions provided with the tool. Failure to remove the ridges before attempting to remove the piston/connecting rod assemblies may result in piston ring breakage.

2 After the cylinder ridges have been removed, turn the engine upside-down so the crankshaft is facing up.

3 Before the connecting rods are removed, check the endfloat (side clearance) with feeler gauges. Slide them between the first connecting rod and the crankshaft until the play is removed **(see illustration)**. The endfloat is equal to the thickness of the feeler gauge(s). If the endfloat exceeds the service limit, new connecting rods will be required. If new rods (or a new crankshaft) are fitted, the endfloat may fall under the minimum specified in this Chapter (if it does, the rods will have to be machined to restore it – consult an automotive machine workshop for advice if necessary). Repeat the procedure for the remaining connecting rods. It will be necessary to remove the oil spray jets from the engine block before removing the piston and connecting rod assemblies **(see illustration)**

4 Check the connecting rods and caps for identification marks. If they aren't plainly marked,

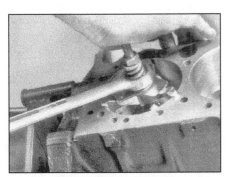

**13.1 A ridge reamer is required to remove the ridge from the top of each cylinder – do this before removing the pistons**

**13.3a Check the connecting rod side clearance with a feeler gauge as shown**

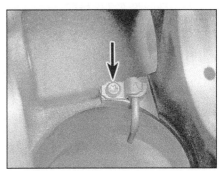

**13.3b The oil spray nozzles must be removed from the block before removing the piston and connecting rod assembly**

use a small centre-punch (see illustration) to make the appropriate number of indentations on each rod and cap (1, 2, 3, etc, depending on the cylinder they're associated with).

5 Loosen each of the connecting rod cap nuts 1/2-turn at a time until they can be removed by hand. Remove the number one connecting rod cap and bearing insert. Don't drop the bearing insert out of the cap.

6 Slip a short length of plastic or rubber hose over each connecting rod cap bolt to protect the crankshaft journal and cylinder wall as the piston is removed (see illustration).

7 Remove the bearing insert and push the connecting rod/piston assembly out through the top of the engine. Use a wooden or plastic hammer handle to push on the upper bearing surface in the connecting rod. If resistance is felt, double-check to make sure all of the ridge was removed from the cylinder.

8 Repeat the procedure for the remaining cylinders.

9 After removal, reassemble the connecting rod caps and bearing inserts in their respective connecting rods and refit the cap nuts finger-tight. Leaving the old bearing inserts in place until reassembly will help prevent the connecting big-end bearing surfaces from being accidentally nicked or gouged.

10 Don't separate the pistons from the connecting rods.

## 14 Crankshaft – removal

**Caution: On the 1.4 litre engine, the crankshaft must not be removed. Just loosening the main bearing cap bolts will cause deformation of the cylinder block. On these engines, if the crankshaft or main bearing surfaces are worn or damaged, the complete crankshaft/cylinder block assembly must be renewed. The following procedure applies to all other engines.**

Note: *On 1.6, 1.8, 1.9 and 2.0L engines, the crankshaft can be removed only after the engine has been removed from the vehicle. It's assumed the flywheel/driveplate, timing belt, sump, oil pump, the oil seal housings and the piston/connecting rod assemblies have already been removed.*

**13.4 Mark the rod bearing caps in order from the front of the engine to the rear (one mark for the front cap, two for the second one, and so on)**

1 Before the crankshaft is removed, check the endfloat. Mount a dial indicator (DTI) with the stem in line with the crankshaft and touching the snout of the crank (see illustration).

2 Push the crankshaft all the way to the rear and zero the dial indicator. Next, prise the crankshaft to the front as far as possible and check the reading on the dial indicator. The distance it moves is the endfloat. If it's greater than listed in this Chapter's Specifications, check the crankshaft thrust surfaces for wear. If no wear is evident, new main bearings should correct the endfloat.

3 If a dial indicator isn't available, feeler gauges can be used. Gently prise or push the crankshaft all the way to the front of the engine. Slip feeler gauges between the crankshaft and the front face of the thrust main bearing to determine the clearance (see illustration). **Note:** *The thrust bearing is located at the number three main bearing cap on all engines.*

4 Check the main bearing caps to see if they're marked to indicate their locations. They should be numbered consecutively from the front of the engine to the rear (see illustration). If they aren't, mark them with number stamping dies or a centre-punch. Main bearing caps generally have a cast-in arrow, which points to the front of the engine. Loosen the main bearing cap bolts 1/4-turn at a time each, until they can be removed by hand. Note if any stud bolts are used and make sure they're returned to their original locations when the crankshaft is reinstalled.

5 Gently tap the caps with a soft-face hammer, then separate them from the engine block. If necessary, use the bolts as levers to

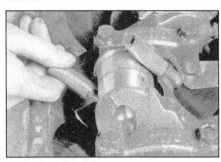

**13.6 To prevent damage to the crankshaft journals and cylinder walls, slip sections of rubber or plastic hose over the rod bolts before removing the pistons/rods**

remove the caps. Try not to drop the bearing inserts if they come out with the caps.

6 Carefully lift the crankshaft straight out of the engine. It may be a good idea to have an assistant available, since the crankshaft is quite heavy. Be careful not to damage the reluctor ring for the crankshaft position sensor. With the bearing inserts in place in the engine block and main bearing caps, return the caps to their respective locations on the engine block and tighten the bolts finger tight.

## 15 Engine block – cleaning

1 Remove the main bearing caps and separate the bearing inserts from the caps and the engine block. Tag the bearings, indicating which cylinder they were removed from and whether they were in the cap or the block, then set them aside.

2 Using a gasket scraper, remove all traces of gasket material from the engine block. Be very careful not to nick or gouge the gasket sealing surfaces.

3 Remove all of the covers and threaded oil gallery plugs from the block. The plugs are usually very tight – they may have to be drilled out and the holes retapped. Use new plugs when the engine is reassembled.

4 Remove the oil filter adapter from the engine. Dismantle the components from the adapter housing and inspect them for wear and damage. Look for nicks and scoring especially on the pressure relief valve piston (see illustrations).

**14.1 Measuring crankshaft endfloat using a dial indicator**

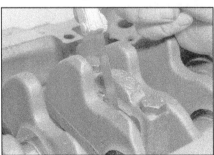

**14.3 Checking crankshaft endfloat with a feeler gauge**

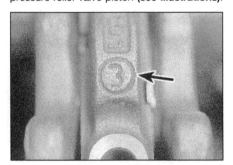

**14.4 Main bearing cap**

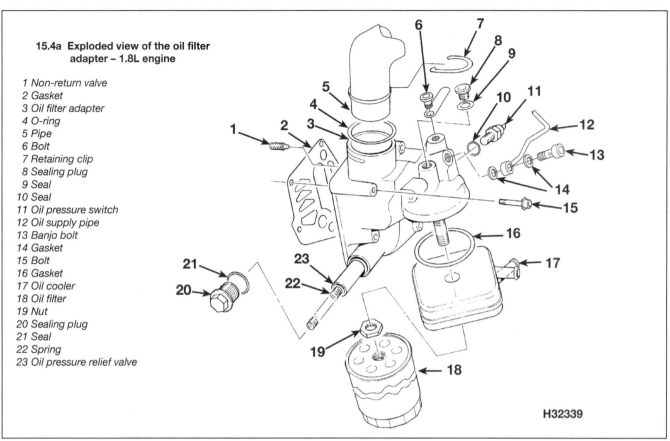

**15.4a  Exploded view of the oil filter adapter – 1.8L engine**

1 Non-return valve
2 Gasket
3 Oil filter adapter
4 O-ring
5 Pipe
6 Bolt
7 Retaining clip
8 Sealing plug
9 Seal
10 Seal
11 Oil pressure switch
12 Oil supply pipe
13 Banjo bolt
14 Gasket
15 Bolt
16 Gasket
17 Oil cooler
18 Oil filter
19 Nut
20 Sealing plug
21 Seal
22 Spring
23 Oil pressure relief valve

H32339

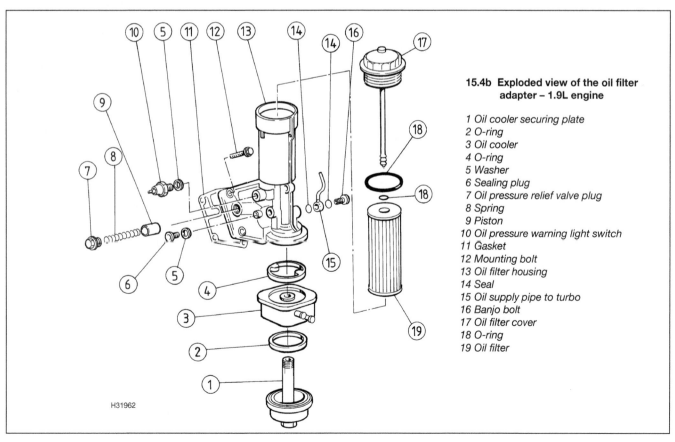

**15.4b  Exploded view of the oil filter adapter – 1.9L engine**

1 Oil cooler securing plate
2 O-ring
3 Oil cooler
4 O-ring
5 Washer
6 Sealing plug
7 Oil pressure relief valve plug
8 Spring
9 Piston
10 Oil pressure warning light switch
11 Gasket
12 Mounting bolt
13 Oil filter housing
14 Seal
15 Oil supply pipe to turbo
16 Banjo bolt
17 Oil filter cover
18 O-ring
19 Oil filter

H31962

2D•16 General engine overhaul procedures

Clean the components and the oil passages in the housing thoroughly with solvent, then dry them with compressed air. If in doubt about the condition of the adapter housing and its components, renew it.

**5** If the engine is extremely dirty, it should be taken to an automotive machine workshop to be cleaned.

**6** After the block is returned, clean all oil holes and oil galleries one more time. Brushes specifically designed for this purpose are available at most auto parts stores. Flush the passages with warm water until the water runs

clear, dry the block thoroughly and wipe all machined surfaces with a light, rust preventive oil. If you have access to compressed air, use it to speed the drying process and blow out all the oil holes and galleries.

⚠️ *Warning: Wear eye protection when using compressed air.*

**7** If the block isn't extremely dirty or sludged up, you can do an adequate cleaning job with hot soapy water and a stiff brush. Take plenty of time and do a thorough job. Regardless of

the cleaning method used, be sure to clean all oil holes and galleries very thoroughly, dry the block completely and coat all machined surfaces with light oil.

**8** The threaded holes in the block must be clean to ensure accurate torque readings during reassembly. Run the proper size tap into each of the holes to remove rust, corrosion, thread sealant or sludge and restore damaged threads **(see illustration)**. If possible, use compressed air to clear the holes of debris produced by this operation. Now is a good time to clean the threads on the head bolts and the main bearing cap bolts as well.

**9** Refit the main bearing caps and tighten the bolts finger-tight.

**10** Apply non-hardening sealant to the new oil gallery plugs and thread them into the holes in the block. Make sure they're tightened securely.

**11** If the engine isn't going to be reassembled right away, cover it with a large plastic bag to keep it clean.

## 16 Engine block – inspection

*Note: The manufacturer recommends checking the block deck for warpage and the main bearing bore for concentricity and alignment. Since special measuring tools are needed, the checks should be done by an automotive machine workshop.*

**1** Before the block is inspected, it should be cleaned as described in Section 15.

**2** Visually check the block for cracks, rust and corrosion. Look for stripped threads in the threaded holes. It's also a good idea to have the block checked for hidden cracks by an automotive machine workshop that has the special equipment to do this type of work. If defects are found, have the block repaired, if possible, or renewed.

**3** Check the cylinder bores for scuffing and scoring.

**4** Check the cylinders for taper and out-of-

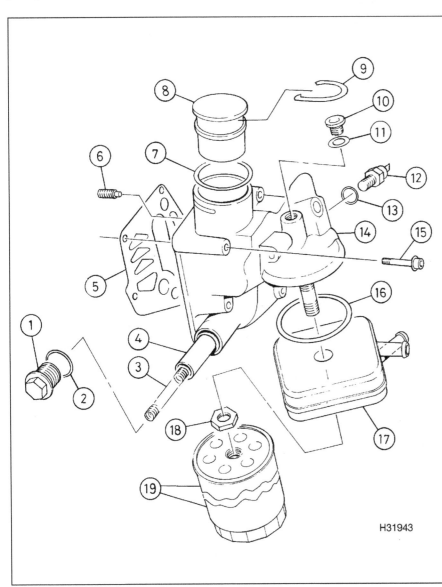

H31943

**15.4c Exploded view of the oil filter adapter – 1.6L and 2.0L engines**

| | | |
|---|---|---|
| 1 Oil pressure relief valve plug | 7 Seal | 13 Seal |
| 2 Sealing ring | 8 Sealing cap | 14 Oil filter housing |
| 3 Spring | 9 Retaining clip | 15 Bolt |
| 4 Piston | 10 Sealing plug | 16 Seal |
| 5 Gasket | 11 Seal | 17 Oil cooler |
| 6 Non-return valve | 12 Oil pressure warning switch | 18 Nut |
| | | 19 Oil filter |

**15.8 All bolt holes in the block – particularly the main bearing cap and head bolt holes – should be cleaned and restored with a tap (be sure to remove debris from the holes after this is done)**

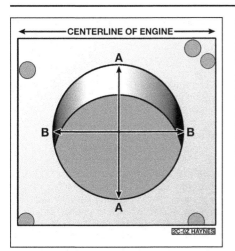

16.4a Measure the diameter of each cylinder at a right angle to the engine centreline (A), and parallel to the engine centreline (B) – out-of-round is the difference between A and B; taper is the difference between the diameter at the top of the cylinder and the diameter at the bottom of the cylinder

round conditions as follows **(see illustrations)**. **Note:** *The following checks should not be made with the engine block mounted on a stand – the cylinders will be distorted and the measurements will be inaccurate.*

**5** Measure the diameter of each cylinder at the top (just under the ridge area), centre and bottom of the cylinder bore, parallel to the crankshaft axis.

**6** Next, measure each cylinder's diameter at the same three locations perpendicular to the crankshaft axis.

**7** The taper of each cylinder is the difference between the bore diameter at the top of the cylinder and the diameter at the bottom. The out-of-round specification of the cylinder bore is the difference between the parallel and perpendicular readings. Compare your results to this Chapter's Specifications.

**8** If the cylinder walls are badly scuffed or scored, or if they're out-of-round or tapered beyond the limits given in this Chapter's Specifications, have the engine block rebored and honed at an automotive machine workshop.

**9** If a rebore is done, oversize pistons and rings will be required.

**10** Using a precision straight-edge and feeler gauge, check the block deck (the surface the cylinder heads mate with) for distortion as you did with the cylinder head (see Section 10). If it's distorted beyond the specified limit, the block decks can be resurfaced by an automotive machine workshop, but is not recommended on these engines.

**11** If the cylinders are in reasonably good condition, and not worn to the outside of the limits, they don't have to be rebored. Honing is all that's necessary (see Section 17).

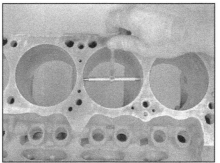

16.4b The ability to 'feel' when the telescoping gauge is at the correct point will be developed over time, so work slowly and repeat the check until you are satisfied the bore measurement is accurate

## 17 Cylinder honing

**1** Prior to engine reassembly, the cylinder bores must be honed so the new piston rings will seat correctly and provide the best possible combustion chamber seal. **Note:** *If you don't have the tools or don't want to tackle the honing operation, most automotive machine workshops will do it for a reasonable fee.*

**2** Before honing the cylinders, refit the main bearing caps and tighten the bolts (use the old bolts) to the torque listed in this Chapter's Specifications.

**3** Two types of cylinder hones are commonly available – the flex hone or 'bottle brush' type and the more traditional surfacing hone with spring-loaded stones. Both will do the job, but for the less-experienced mechanic the 'bottle brush' hone will probably be easier to use. You'll also need some honing oil (paraffin will work if honing oil isn't available), rags and an electric drill motor. Proceed as follows:

a) Mount the hone in the drill motor, compress the stones and slip it into the first cylinder **(see illustration)**. Be sure to wear safety goggles or a face shield.

b) Lubricate the cylinder with plenty of honing oil, turn on the drill and move the

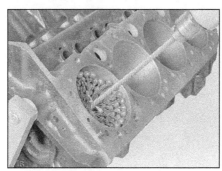

17.3a A 'bottle brush' hone will produce a better crosshatch pattern when using a drill motor to hone the cylinders

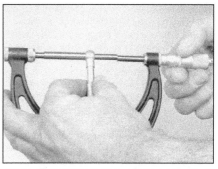

16.4c The gauge is then measured with a micrometer to determine the bore size

hone up-and-down in the cylinder at a pace that will produce a fine crosshatch pattern on the cylinder walls, and with the drill square and centred with the bore. Ideally, the crosshatch lines should intersect at approximately a 45 to 60-degree angle **(see illustration)**. Be sure to use plenty of lubricant and don't take off any more material than is absolutely necessary to produce the desired finish. **Note:** Piston ring manufacturers may specify a different crosshatch angle – read and follow any instructions included with the new rings.

c) Don't withdraw the hone from the cylinder while it's running. Instead, shut off the drill and continue moving the hone up-and-down in the cylinder until it comes to a complete stop, then compress the stones and withdraw the hone. If you're using a 'bottle brush' type hone, stop the drill motor, then turn the chuck in the normal direction of rotation while withdrawing the hone from the cylinder.

d) Wipe the oil out of the cylinder and repeat the procedure for the remaining cylinders.

**4** After the honing job is complete, chamfer the top edges of the cylinder bores with a small file so the rings won't catch when the

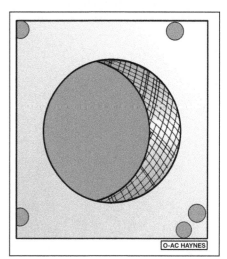

17.3b The cylinder hone should leave a smooth, crosshatch pattern with the lines intersecting at approximately a 60° angle

pistons are fitted. Be very careful not to nick the cylinder walls with the end of the file.

**5** The entire engine block must be washed again very thoroughly with warm, soapy water to remove all traces of the abrasive grit produced during the honing operation. **Note:** *The bores can be considered clean when a lint-free white cloth – dampened with clean engine oil – used to wipe them out doesn't pick up any more honing residue, which will show up as grey areas on the cloth. Be sure to run a brush through all oil holes and galleries and flush them with running water.*

**6** After rinsing, dry the block and apply a coat of light rust preventive oil to all machined surfaces. Wrap the block in a plastic bag to keep it clean and set it aside until reassembly.

## 18 Pistons and connecting rods – inspection

**1** Before the inspection process can be carried out, the piston/connecting rod assemblies must be cleaned and the original piston rings removed from the pistons. **Note:** *Always use new piston rings when the engine is reassembled.*

**2** Using a piston ring refitting tool, carefully remove the rings from the pistons. Be careful

**18.4a The piston ring grooves can be cleaned with a special tool, as shown here ...**

not to nick or gouge the pistons in the process.

**3** Scrape all traces of carbon from the top of the piston. A hand-held wire brush or a piece of fine emery cloth can be used once the majority of the deposits have been scraped away. Do not, under any circumstances, use a wire brush mounted in a drill motor to remove deposits from the pistons. The piston material is soft and may be eroded away by the wire brush.

**4** Use a piston ring groove-cleaning tool to remove carbon deposits from the ring grooves. If a tool isn't available, a piece broken off the old ring will do the job. Be very careful to remove only the carbon deposits – don't remove any metal and do not nick or scratch the sides of the ring grooves **(see illustrations)**.

**5** Once the deposits have been removed, clean the piston/rod assemblies with solvent and dry them with compressed air (if available). Make sure the oil return holes in the back sides of the ring grooves are clear.

⚠️ *Warning: Wear eye protection.*

**6** If the pistons and cylinder walls aren't damaged or worn excessively, and if the engine block isn't rebored, new pistons won't be necessary. Normal piston wear appears as

**18.4b ... or a section of broken ring**

even vertical wear on the piston thrust surfaces and slight looseness of the top ring in its groove. New piston rings, however, should always be used when an engine is rebuilt.

**7** Carefully inspect each piston for cracks around the skirt, at the pin bosses and at the ring lands.

**8** Look for scoring and scuffing on the thrust faces of the skirt, holes in the piston crown and burned areas at the edge of the crown. If the skirt is scored or scuffed, the engine may have been suffering from overheating and/or abnormal combustion, which caused excessively high operating temperatures. The cooling and lubrication systems should be checked thoroughly. A hole in the piston crown is an indication that abnormal combustion (pre-ignition) was occurring. Burned areas at the edge of the piston crown are usually evidence of spark knock (detonation). If any of the above problems exist, the causes must be corrected or the damage will occur again. The causes may include intake air leaks, incorrect fuel/air mixture, low octane fuel, ignition timing and EGR system malfunctions.

**9** Corrosion of the piston, in the form of small pits, indicates coolant is leaking into the combustion chamber and/or the crankcase. Again, the cause must be corrected or the problem may persist in the rebuilt engine.

**10** Measure the piston ring side clearance by laying a new piston ring in each ring groove and slipping a feeler gauge in beside it **(see illustration)**. Check the clearance at three or four locations around each groove. Be sure to use the correct ring for each groove – they are different. If the side clearance is greater than specified in this Chapter, new pistons will have to be used.

**11** Check the piston diameter. Measure the piston across the skirt, at a 90-degree angle to the gudgeon pin **(see illustration)**. The measurement must be taken at a specific

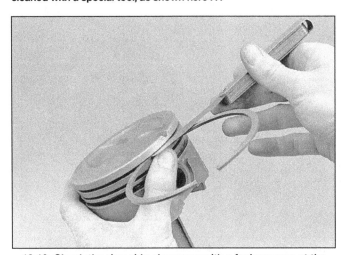

**18.10 Check the ring side clearance with a feeler gauge at the several points around the groove**

**18.11 Measure the piston diameter at a 90° angle to the piston pin and at the specified distance from the bottom of the piston skirt**

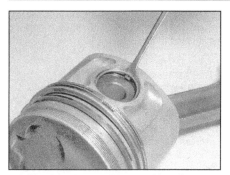

**18.12a Insert a small screwdriver into the slot and pry out the piston pin retaining circlips**

**18.12b The piston pin should require a slight push to remove and install it – any excessive movement or looseness will require renewal of the rod and/or the piston and pin assembly**

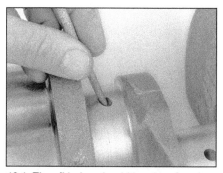

**19.1 The oil holes should be chamfered so sharp edges don't gouge or scratch the new bearings**

point to be accurate: the pistons are measured 6 mm from the bottom of the skirt, at right angles to the gudgeon pin.

**12** Check the gudgeon pin to the rod and piston clearances by twisting the piston and rod in opposite directions. Any noticeable play indicates excessive wear, which must be corrected **(see illustrations)**. The piston/connecting rod assemblies should be taken to an automotive machine workshop to have the pistons and rods resized and new pins fitted.

**13** If the pistons must be removed from the connecting rods for any reason, they should be taken to an automotive machine workshop to also have the connecting rods checked for bend and twist, since automotive machine workshops have special equipment for this purpose. **Note:** *Unless new pistons and/or connecting rods are being fitted it is not necessary to completely dismantle the pistons from the connecting rods.*

**14** Check the connecting rods for cracks and other damage. Temporarily remove the rod caps, lift out the old bearing inserts, wipe the rod and cap bearing surfaces clean and inspect them for nicks, gouges and scratches. After checking the rods, renew the old bearings, slip the caps into place and tighten the nuts finger tight. **Note:** *If the engine is being rebuilt because of a connecting rod knock, be sure to refit new or remanufactured connecting rods.*

## 19 Crankshaft – inspection

**1** Remove all burrs from the crankshaft oil holes with a stone, file or scraper **(see illustration)**.
**2** Clean the crankshaft with solvent and dry it with compressed air (if available). Be sure to clean the oil holes with a stiff brush **(see illustration)** and flush them with solvent.

 **Warning: Wear eye protection when using compressed air.**

**3** Check the main and connecting big-end bearing journals for uneven wear, scoring, pits and cracks.
**4** Check the rest of the crankshaft for cracks and other damage. It should be crack-tested to reveal hidden cracks – an automotive machine workshop will handle the procedure.
**5** Using a micrometer, measure the diameter of the main and connecting rod journals and compare the results to this Chapter's Specifications **(see illustration)**. By measuring the diameter at a number of points around each journal's circumference, you'll be able to determine whether or not the journal is out-of-round. Take the measurement at each end of the journal, near the crank throws, to determine if the journal is tapered.

**6** If the crankshaft journals are damaged, tapered, out-of-round or worn beyond the limits given in the Specifications, have the crankshaft reground by an automotive machine workshop. Be sure to use the correct-size bearing inserts if the crankshaft is reconditioned.
**7** Check the oil seal journals at each end of the crankshaft for wear and damage. If the seal has worn a groove in the journal, or if it's nicked or scratched **(see illustration)**, the new seal may leak when the engine is reassembled. In some cases, an automotive machine workshop may be able to repair the journal by pressing on a thin sleeve. If repair isn't feasible, a new or different crankshaft should be fitted.
**8** Examine the main and big-end bearing inserts (see Section 20). Also inspect the crankshaft reluctor ring at the rear of the crankshaft for nicks and damage. Damage to this component may result in severe driveability problems.

## 20 Main and connecting rod bearings – inspection and selection

**1** Even though the main and connecting big-end bearings should be replaced with new ones during the engine overhaul, the old bearings should be retained for close

**19.2 Use a wire or stiff plastic bristle brush to clean the oil passages in the crankshaft**

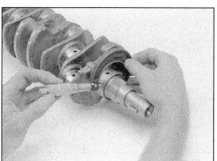

**19.5 Measure the diameter of each crankshaft journal at several points to detect taper and ovality conditions**

**19.7 If the seals have worn grooves in the crankshaft journals, or if the seal contact surfaces are nicked or scratched, the new seals will leak**

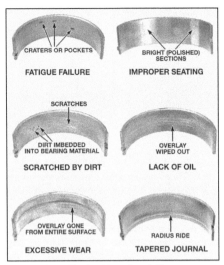

**20.1 Typical bearing failures**

examination, as they may reveal valuable information about the condition of the engine (see illustration).

2 Bearing failure occurs because of lack of lubrication, the presence of dirt or other foreign particles, overloading the engine and corrosion. Regardless of the cause of bearing failure, it must be corrected before the engine is reassembled to prevent it from happening again.

3 When examining the bearings, remove them from the engine block, the main bearing caps, the connecting rods and the rod caps and lay them out on a clean surface in the same general position as their location in the engine. This will enable you to match any bearing problems with the corresponding crankshaft journal.

4 Dirt and other foreign particles get into the engine in a variety of ways. It may be left in the engine during assembly, or it may pass through filters or the PCV system. It may get into the oil, and from there into the bearings. Metal chips from machining operations and normal engine wear are often present. Abrasives are sometimes left in engine

components after reconditioning, especially when parts aren't thoroughly cleaned using the proper cleaning methods. Whatever the source, these foreign objects often end up embedded in the soft bearing material and are easily recognised. Large particles won't embed in the bearing and will score or gouge the bearing and journal. The best prevention for this cause of bearing failure is to clean all parts thoroughly and keep everything spotlessly clean during engine assembly. Frequent and regular engine oil and filter changes are also recommended.

5 Lack of lubrication (or lubrication breakdown) has a number of interrelated causes. Excessive heat (which thins the oil), overloading (which squeezes the oil from the bearing face) and oil leakage or throw off (from excessive bearing clearances, worn oil pump or high engine speeds) all contribute to lubrication breakdown. Blocked oil passages, which usually are the result of misaligned oil holes in a bearing shell, will also oil starve a bearing and destroy it. When lack of lubrication is the cause of bearing failure, the bearing material is wiped or extruded from the steel backing of the bearing. Temperatures may increase to the point where the steel backing turns blue from overheating.

6 Driving habits can have a definite effect on bearing life. Low speed operation in too high a gear (lugging the engine) puts very high loads on bearings, which tends to squeeze out the oil film. These loads cause the bearings to flex, which produces fine cracks in the bearing face (fatigue failure). Eventually the bearing material will loosen in pieces and tear away from the steel backing. Short trip driving leads to corrosion of bearings because insufficient engine heat is produced to drive off the condensed water and corrosive gases. These products collect in the engine oil, forming acid and sludge. As the oil is carried to the engine bearings, the acid attacks and corrodes the bearing material.

7 Incorrect bearing refitting during engine assembly will lead to bearing failure as well. Tight-fitting bearings leave insufficient oil clearance and will result in oil starvation. Dirt

or foreign particles trapped behind a bearing insert result in high spots on the bearing which lead to failure.

## 21 Camshaft, followers and bearings – inspection

1 Visually check the camshaft bearing surfaces for pitting, score marks, galling and abnormal wear. If the bearing surfaces are damaged, the cylinder head will have to be renewed (see illustration).

2 Measure the outside diameter of each camshaft bearing journal and record your measurements (see illustration), then measure the inside diameter of each corresponding camshaft bearing and record the measurements. Subtract each cam journal outside diameter from its respective cam bearing bore inside diameter to determine the oil clearance for each bearing. Compare the results to the specified journal-to-bearing clearance (given in Chapters 2A, 2B or 2C). If any of the measurements fall outside the standard specified wear limits, either the camshaft or the cylinder head, or both, must be renewed.

3 Check camshaft run-out by placing the camshaft back into the cylinder head and set up a dial indicator on the centre journal. Zero the dial indicator. Turn the camshaft slowly and note the dial indicator readings. Record your readings and compare them with the specified run-out in Chapter 2A, 2B or 2C. If the measured run-out exceeds the run-out specified, renew the camshaft.

4 Check the camshaft endfloat by placing a dial indicator with the stem in line with the camshaft and touching the snout (see illustration). Push the camshaft all the way to the rear and zero the dial indicator. Next, prise the camshaft to the front as far as possible and check the reading on the dial indicator. The distance it moves is the endfloat. If it's greater than the Specifications listed in Chapter 2A, 2B or 2C, check the bearing caps for wear. If the bearing caps are worn the cylinder head must be renewed.

**21.1 Inspect the camshaft bearing surfaces in the cylinder head for pits, score marks and abnormal wear – if damage is noted, the cylinder head must be renewed**

**21.2 Measure the outside diameter of each camshaft journal and the inside diameter of each bearing surface on the cylinder head to determine the oil clearance measurement**

**21.4 Checking camshaft endfloat with a dial indicator (DTI)**

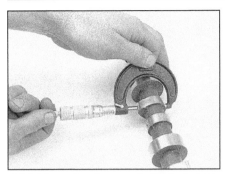

**21.5 Measuring the camshaft lobe height with a micrometer – make sure you move the micrometer to get the highest reading (top of cam lobe)**

**5** Compare the camshaft lobe height by measuring each lobe with a micrometer **(see illustration)**. Measure of each of the intake lobes and write the measurements and relative positions down on a piece of paper. Then measure of each of the exhaust lobes and record the measurements and relative positions also. This will let you compare all of intake lobes to one another and all of the exhaust lobes to one another. If the difference between the lobes exceeds 0.12 mm the camshaft should be renewed. Do not compare intake lobe heights to exhaust lobe heights as lobe lift may be different. Only compare intake lobes-to-intake lobes and exhaust lobes-to exhaust lobes for this comparison.

**6** Inspect the contact and sliding surfaces of each follower/rocker arm for wear and scratches **(see illustrations)**. **Note:** *If the follower/rocker arm pad is worn, it's a good idea to check the corresponding camshaft. Do not lay the followers/compensators on their side or upside down, or air can become trapped inside and the follower/compensator will have to be bled. The followers/compensators can be laid on their side only if they are submerged in a pan of clean engine oil until reassembly.*

**7** Check that each follower moves up and down freely in its bore on the cylinder head. If it doesn't the valve may stick open and cause internal engine damage.

**8** In any case make sure all the parts, new or old, have been thoroughly inspected before reassembly.

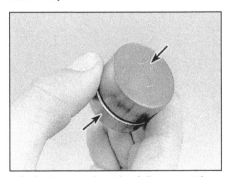

**21.6a Inspect the valve followers at the area shown (arrowed)**

## *Hydraulic followers – in-vehicle check*

**9** Noisy followers can be checked for wear without disassembling the engine by following the procedure outlined below:
   a) *Run the engine until it reaches normal operating temperature.*
   b) *Remove the valve/camshaft cover (see Chapter 2A, 2B or 2C).*
   c) *Rotate the engine by hand until the No 1 piston is located at TDC (see Chapter 2A, 2B or 2C).*
   d) *Insert a feeler gauge between the camshaft lobe and the follower/rocker arm to measure the clearance. If the clearance exceeds 0.2 mm (petrol engine) or 0.1 mm (diesel engine) the follower/rocker arm and/or the camshaft lobe has worn beyond it limits.*
   e) *If no clearance exists, depress the follower/compensator to let it bleed down and check the clearance again* **(see illustration).**
   f) *Follower/rocker arm clearance on the remaining cylinders can be checked by following the firing order sequence and positioning each of the remaining pistons at TDC.* **Note:** *Follower/rocker arm clearance can also be checked on any follower/rocker arm whose cam lobe is pointing upward.*
   g) *If the clearance is beyond the maximum allowed, inspect the camshaft as described in Step 5.*
   h) *If the camshaft is OK, the followers/compensators are faulty and must be renewed.*

## 22 Engine overhaul – reassembly sequence

**1** Before beginning engine reassembly, make sure you have all the necessary new parts, gaskets and seals as well as the following items on hand:
*Common hand tools.*
*Torque spanner (1/2-inch drive) with angle-torque gauge.*
*Piston ring refitting tool.*

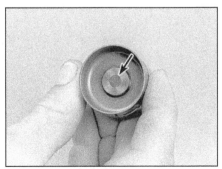

**21.6b Also check the valve stem contact area of the follower**

*Piston ring compressor.*
*Crankshaft balancer refitting tool.*
*Short lengths of rubber or plastic hose to fit over connecting rod bolts.*
*Plastigauge.*
*Feeler gauges.*
*Fine-tooth file.*
*New engine oil.*
*Engine assembly grease or moly-base grease.*
*Gasket sealant.*
*Thread locking compound.*

**2** In order to save time and avoid problems, engine reassembly must be done in the following general order:
*Crankshaft and main bearings.*
*Piston/connecting rod assemblies.*
*Oil spray nozzles.*
*Oil pump, baffle and oil pump pick-up tube.*
*Oil pump drive chain and tensioner.*
*Oil filter adapter housing.*
*Crankshaft oil seal housings.*
*Cylinder head with followers/rocker arms and camshaft(s).*
*Fuel injection pump (non-PD diesel engine).*
*Timing belt.*
*Sump.*
*Valve cover.*
*Flywheel/driveplate.*
*Intake and exhaust manifolds.*
*Vacuum pump (diesel engines only).*

## 23 Piston rings – refitting

**1** Before refitting the new piston rings, the ring end gaps must be checked. It's assumed the piston ring side clearance has been checked and verified correct (see Section 18).
**2** Lay out the piston/connecting rod assemblies and the new ring sets so the ring sets will be matched with the same piston and cylinder during the end gap measurement and engine assembly.
**3** Insert the top (number one) ring into the first cylinder and square it up with the cylinder walls by pushing it in with the top of the piston

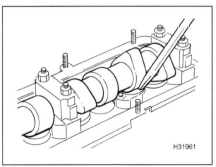

**21.9 When checking noisy followers with the engine in the vehicle, it may be necessary to bleed the follower down by depressing it with a wooden or plastic tool**

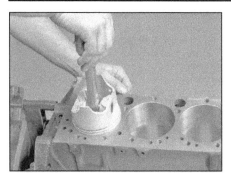

**23.3 When checking the piston ring end gap, the ring must be square in the cylinder bore (this is done by pushing the ring down with the top of a piston as shown)**

**23.4 With the ring square in the cylinder, measure the end gap with a feeler gauge**

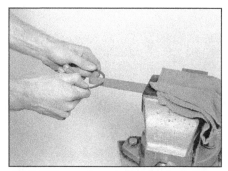

**23.5 Of the end gap is too small, clamp a file in a vice and file the ring ends (from the outside in only) to enlarge the gap slightly**

(see illustration). The ring should be near the bottom of the cylinder, at the lower limit of ring travel.

4 To measure the end gap, slip feeler gauges between the ends of the ring until a gauge equal to the gap width is found (see illustration). The feeler gauge should slide between the ring ends with a slight amount of drag. Compare the measurement to this Chapter's Specifications. If the gap is larger or smaller than specified, double-check to make sure you have the correct rings before proceeding.

5 If the gap is too small, it must be enlarged or the ring ends may come in contact with each other during engine operation, which can cause serious engine damage. The end gap can be increased by filing the ring ends very carefully with a fine file. Mount the file in a vice equipped with soft jaws, slip the ring over the file with the ends contacting the file teeth and slowly move the ring to remove material from the ends. When performing this operation, file only from the outside in (see illustration). Note: When you have the end gap correct, remove any burrs from the filed ends of the rings with a whetstone.

6 Excess end gap isn't critical unless it's greater than 1.0 mm. Again, double-check to make sure you have the correct rings for the engine. If the engine block has been bored oversize, necessitating oversize pistons, matching oversize rings are required.

7 Repeat the procedure for each ring that will

be fitted in the first cylinder and for each ring in the remaining cylinders. Remember to keep rings, pistons and cylinders matched up.

8 Once the ring end gaps have been checked/corrected, the rings can be fitted on the pistons.

9 The oil control ring (lowest one on the piston) is usually fitted first. Some piston ring manufacturers supply one-piece oil rings – others may supply three-piece oil rings. One-piece rings can be fitted as shown in illustration 23.12. If you're refitting three-piece oil rings, slip the spacer/expander into the groove (see illustration). If an anti-rotation tang is used, make sure it's inserted into the drilled hole in the ring groove. Next, refit the lower side rail. Don't use a piston ring refitting tool on the oil ring side rails, as they may be damaged. Instead, place one end of the side rail into the groove between the spacer/expander and the ring land, hold it firmly in place and slide a finger around the piston while pushing the rail into the groove (see illustration). Next, refit the upper side rail in the same manner. Note: Some engines may have a two-piece oil ring. If so, follow the refitting instructions that come with the piston rings if they differ from the instructions outlined here.

10 After the three oil ring components have been fitted, check to make sure both the upper and lower side rails can be turned smoothly in the ring groove.

11 The number two (middle) ring is fitted

next. It's usually stamped with a mark, which must face up, toward the top of the piston. Note: Always follow the instructions printed on the ring package or box – different manufacturers may require different approaches. Don't mix up the top and middle rings, as they have different cross-sections.

12 Use a piston ring refitting tool and make sure the identification mark is facing the top of the piston, then slip the ring into the middle groove on the piston (see illustration). Don't expand the ring any more than necessary to slide it over the piston.

13 Refit the number one (top) ring in the same manner. Make sure the mark is facing up. Be careful not to confuse the number one and number two rings.

14 Repeat the procedure for the remaining pistons and rings.

**24 Crankshaft** – refitting and main bearing oil clearance check

1 Crankshaft refitting is the first step in engine reassembly. It's assumed at this point that the engine block and crankshaft have been cleaned, inspected and repaired or reconditioned.

2 Position the engine with the bottom facing up.

3 Remove the main bearing cap bolts and lift out the caps. Lay them out in the proper order to ensure correct refitting.

**23.9a Installing the spacer/expander in the oil control ring groove**

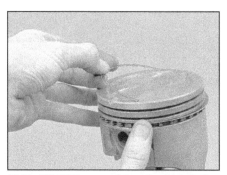

**23.9b DO NOT use a piston ring installation tool when installing the oil ring side rails**

**23.12 Installing the compression rings with a ring expander – the TOP mark (arrowed) must face up**

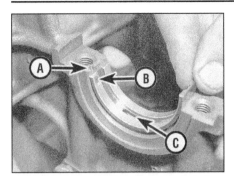

**24.5 Bearing shell correctly installed**

A  *Recess in bearing saddle*
B  *Lug on bearing shell*
C  *Oil hole*

**4** If they're still in place, remove the original bearing inserts from the block and the main bearing caps. Wipe the bearing surfaces of the block and caps with a clean, lint-free cloth. They must be kept spotlessly clean.

### Main bearing oil clearance check

**Note:** *Don't touch the faces of the new bearing inserts with your fingers. Oil and acids from your skin can etch the bearings.*
**5** Clean the back sides of the new main bearing inserts and lay one in each main bearing saddle in the block. If one of the bearing inserts from each set has a large groove in it, make sure the grooved insert is installed in the block **(see illustration)**. Lay the other bearing from each set in the corresponding main bearing cap. Make sure the tab on the bearing insert fits into the recess in the block or cap, neither higher than the cap's edge nor lower. Do not hammer the bearing into place and don't nick or gouge the bearing faces. No lubrication should be used at this time.
**Caution: The oil holes in the block must line up with the oil holes in the bearing inserts.**
**6** The thrustwashers must be fitted on each side of the number three main journal and/or the main bearing cap **(see illustration)**. On 1.6L roller rocker arm engines (codes AYD

**24.15 Measuring the width of the crushed Plastigauge to determine the main bearing oil clearance (be sure to use the correct scale – imperial and metric ones are included)**

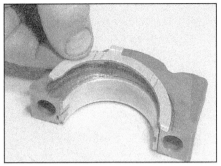

**24.6 Installing the thrustwashers on the No 3 main bearing cap**

and BFS) two thrustwashers are fitted into the corresponding recesses in the cylinder block, whilst on all other petrol engines, the two thrustwashers are fitted either side of the main bearing cap. On diesel engines four thrustwashers are fitted, two into the cylinder block and two into the main bearing cap.
**7** Clean the faces of the bearings in the block and the crankshaft main bearing journals with a clean, lint-free cloth.
**8** Check or clean the oil holes in the crankshaft, as any dirt here can go only one way – straight through the new bearings.
**9** Once you're certain the crankshaft is clean, carefully lay it in position in the main bearings.
**10** Before the crankshaft can be permanently fitted, the main bearing oil clearance must be checked.
**11** Cut several pieces of the appropriate size Plastigauge (they should be slightly shorter than the width of the main bearings) and place one piece on each crankshaft main bearing journal, parallel with the journal axis **(see illustration)**.
**12** Clean the faces of the bearings in the caps and refit the caps in their original locations (don't mix them up) with the arrows pointing toward the front of the engine. Don't disturb the Plastigauge.
**13** Starting with the centre main and working out toward the ends, tighten the main bearing cap bolts to 65 Nm (48 Ft-lbs) in three steps. Don't tighten the bolts any further. Don't rotate the crankshaft at any time during this operation, and do not tighten one cap completely – tighten all caps equally. Before tightening, the main caps should be seated using light taps with a brass or plastic mallet.
**14** Remove the bolts/studs and carefully lift off the main bearing caps. Keep them in order. Don't disturb the Plastigauge or rotate the crankshaft. If any of the main bearing caps are difficult to remove, tap them gently from side-to-side with a soft-face hammer to loosen them.
**15** Compare the width of the crushed Plastigauge on each journal to the scale printed on the Plastigauge envelope to obtain the main bearing oil clearance **(see illustration)**. Check the Specifications to make sure it's correct.

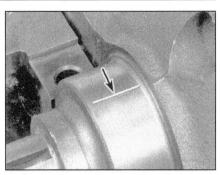

**24.11 Lay the Plastigauge strips (arrowed) on the main bearing journals, parallel to the crankshaft centreline**

**16** If the clearance is not as specified, the bearing inserts may be the wrong size (which means different ones will be required). Before deciding different inserts are needed, make sure no dirt or oil was between the bearing inserts and the caps or block when the clearance was measured. If the Plastigauge was wider at one end than the other, the journal may be tapered (see Section 19).
**17** Carefully scrape all traces of the Plastigauge material off the main bearing journals and/or the bearing faces. Use your fingernail or the edge of a credit card – don't nick or scratch the bearing faces.

### Final crankshaft refitting

**18** Carefully lift the crankshaft out of the engine.
**19** Clean the bearing faces in the block, then apply a thin, uniform layer of moly-base grease or engine assembly grease to each of the bearing surfaces. Be sure to coat the thrust faces as well as the journal face of the thrust bearings.
**20** Make sure the crankshaft journals are clean, then lay the crankshaft back in place in the block.
**21** Clean the faces of the bearings in the caps, then apply lubricant to them.
**22** Refit the caps in their original locations with the arrows (made earlier) pointing toward the front of the engine.
**23** With all caps in place and bolts just started, tap the ends of the crankshaft forward and backward with a lead or brass hammer to line up the main bearing and crankshaft thrust surfaces.
**24** Following the procedures outlined in Step 13, retighten all main bearing cap bolts to the torque listed in this Chapter's Specifications, starting with the centre main and working out toward the ends.
**25** Rotate the crankshaft a number of times by hand to check for any obvious binding.
**26** The final step is to check the crankshaft endfloat with feeler gauges or a dial indicator as described in Section 14. The endfloat should be correct if the crankshaft thrust faces aren't worn or damaged and new bearings have been fitted.

## 25 Crankshaft transmission end oil seal – renewal

All models are equipped with a one-piece oil seal and housing. The crankshaft must be fitted first and the main bearing caps bolted in place before the seal and housing can be fitted on the engine block. Refer to Chapter 2A, 2B or 2C for the seal renewal procedure. Disregard the Steps that do not apply since the engine is out of the vehicle and the sump is not fitted.

## 26 Pistons and connecting rods – refitting and rod bearing oil clearance check

1 Before refitting the piston/connecting rod assemblies, the cylinder walls must be perfectly clean, the top edge of each cylinder must be chamfered, and the crankshaft must be in place.
2 Remove the cap from the end of the number one connecting rod (check the marks made during removal). Remove the original bearing inserts and wipe the bearing surfaces of the connecting rod and cap with a clean, lint-free cloth. They must be kept spotlessly clean.

### Piston refitting and rod bearing oil clearance check

3 Clean the back side of the new upper bearing insert, then lay it in place in the connecting rod. Make sure the tab on the bearing fits into the recess in the rod. Don't hammer the bearing insert into place and be very careful not to nick or gouge the bearing face. Don't lubricate the bearing at this time.
4 Clean the back side of the other bearing insert and refit it in the rod cap. Again, make sure the tab on the bearing fits into the recess in the cap, and don't apply any lubricant. It's critically important that the mating surfaces of the bearing and connecting rod are perfectly clean and oil free when they're assembled.
5 Stagger the piston ring gaps around the piston (see illustrations).

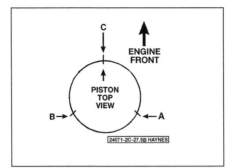

**26.5a Ring end gap positions**

A  Top compression ring gap
B  Second compression ring gap
C  Oil ring gap

6 Slip a section of plastic or rubber hose over each connecting rod cap bolt.
7 Lubricate the piston and rings with clean engine oil and attach a piston ring compressor to the piston. Leave the skirt protruding about 6 mm to guide the piston into the cylinder. The rings must be compressed until they're flush with the piston.
8 Rotate the crankshaft until the number one connecting rod journal is at BDC (bottom dead centre) and apply a coat of engine oil to the cylinder walls.
9 With the mark or notch on top of the piston facing the front of the engine, gently insert the piston/connecting rod assembly into the number one cylinder bore and rest the bottom edge of the ring compressor on the engine block.
10 Tap the top edge of the ring compressor to make sure it's contacting the block around its entire circumference.
11 Gently tap on the top of the piston with the end of a wooden or plastic hammer handle (see illustration) while guiding the end of the connecting rod into place on the crankshaft journal. The piston rings may try to pop out of the ring compressor just before entering the cylinder bore, so keep some pressure down on the ring compressor. Work slowly, and if any resistance is felt as the piston enters the cylinder, stop immediately. Find out what's hanging up and fix it before proceeding. Do not, for any reason, force the

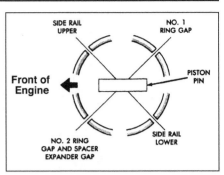

**26.5b Ring end gap positions (with three-piece oil rings)**

piston into the cylinder – you might break a ring and/or the piston.
12 Once the piston/connecting rod assembly is fitted, the connecting big-end bearing oil clearance must be checked before the rod cap is permanently bolted in place.
13 Cut a piece of the appropriate size Plastigauge slightly shorter than the width of the connecting big-end bearing and lay it in place on the number one connecting rod journal, parallel with the journal axis (see illustration).
14 Clean the connecting rod cap bearing face, remove the protective hoses from the connecting rod bolts and refit the rod cap. Make sure the mating mark on the cap is on the same side as the mark on the connecting rod.
15 Refit the nuts/bolts and tighten them to 30 Nm (22 Ft-lbs). Work up to it in three steps. **Note:** *Use a thin-wall socket to avoid erroneous torque readings that can result if the socket is wedged between the rod cap and nut. If the socket tends to wedge itself between the nut and the cap, lift up on it slightly until it no longer contacts the cap. Do not rotate the crankshaft at any time during this operation.*
16 Remove the nuts/bolts and detach the rod cap, being very careful not to disturb the Plastigauge.
17 Compare the width of the crushed Plastigauge to the scale printed on the Plastigauge envelope to obtain the oil clearance (see illustration). Compare it to

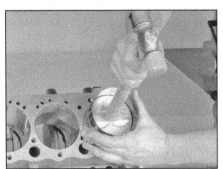

**26.11 Drive the piston into the cylinder bore with the end of a wooden or plastic hammer handle**

**26.13 Lay the Plastigauge strips on each connecting rod bearing journal, parallel to the crankshaft centreline**

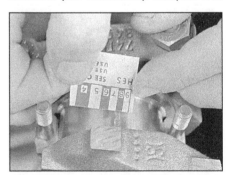

**26.17 Measuring the width of the crushed Plastigauge to determine the rod bearing oil clearance (be sure to use the correct scale – imperial and metric ones are included)**

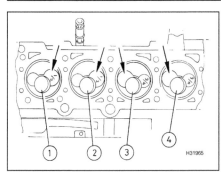

**26.22 On diesel engines, the intake valve reliefs (arrowed) should point towards the transmission on the No 1 and 2 cylinders, and point towards the timing belt on the No 3 and 4 cylinders**

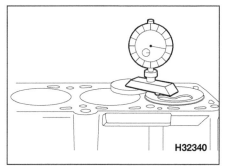

**26.27a Measuring piston projection with a dial indicator (DTI)**

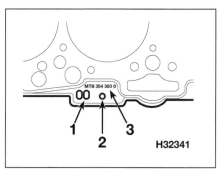

**26.27b Head gasket identification marks – diesel engine**

1  Production control code
2  Identification holes
3  Part number

this Chapter's Specifications to make sure the clearance is correct.
**18** If the clearance is not as specified, the bearing inserts may be the wrong size (which means different ones will be required). Before deciding different inserts are needed, make sure no dirt or oil was between the bearing inserts and the connecting rod or cap when the clearance was measured. Also, recheck the journal diameter. If the Plastigauge was wider at one end than the other, the journal may be tapered (see Section 19).

*Final connecting rod refitting*

**19** Carefully scrape all traces of the Plastigauge material off the rod journal and/or bearing face. Be very careful not to scratch the bearing – use your fingernail or the edge of a credit card.
**20** Make sure the bearing faces are perfectly clean, then apply a uniform layer of clean moly-base grease or engine assembly grease to both of them. You'll have to push the piston into the cylinder to expose the face of the bearing insert in the connecting rod – be sure to slip the protective hoses over the rod bolts first.
**21** Slide the connecting rod back into place on the journal, remove the protective hoses from the rod cap bolts, refit the rod cap and tighten the nuts/bolts to the torque listed in this Chapter's Specifications.
**22** Repeat the entire procedure for the remaining pistons/connecting rods. On diesel engines it will be necessary to double-check the orientation of the valve relief pockets to make sure the pistons are fitted correctly **(see illustration)**.
**23** The important points to remember are:
a) *Keep the back sides of the bearing inserts and the insides of the connecting rods and caps perfectly clean when assembling them.*
b) *Make sure you have the correct piston/rod assembly for each cylinder.*
c) *The arrow or mark on the piston must face the front of the engine.*
d) *Lubricate the cylinder walls with clean oil.*
e) *Lubricate the bearing faces when*

installing the rod caps after the oil clearance has been checked.
**24** After all the piston/connecting rod assemblies have been properly fitted, rotate the crankshaft a number of times by hand to check for any obvious binding.
**25** As a final step, the connecting rod endfloat must be checked (see Section 13).
**26** Compare the measured endfloat to this Chapter's Specifications to make sure it's correct. If it was correct before dismantling and the original crankshaft and rods were reinstalled, it should still be right. If new rods or a new crankshaft were fitted, the endfloat may be inadequate. If so, the rods will have to be removed and taken to an automotive machine workshop for resizing.
**27** On diesel engines, it will be necessary to check the piston projection to help determine the correct thickness of head gasket to be used. Rotate the engine so that the No 1 piston is located at TDC. Using a dial indicator or a depth micrometer measure the distance that the piston protrudes past the gasket surface of the block **(see illustration)**. Repeat the measuring process on the remaining three cylinders and record the highest reading. Three different thickness head gaskets are available for diesel engines depending on the amount the piston protrudes above the gasket surface. Compare the highest reading to the gasket selection chart below to select the proper head gasket thickness **(see illustration)**.

| Piston projection | Gasket holes | Gasket thickness |
|---|---|---|
| 0.89 to 1.00 mm | 1 | 1.45 mm |
| 1.01 to 1.10 mm | 2 | 1.53 mm |
| 1.11 to 1.21 mm | 3 | 1.61 mm |

## 27 Initial start-up after overhaul and reassembly

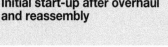

**1** Once the engine has been fitted in the vehicle, double-check the oil and coolant levels. Remove all of the spark plugs (see Chapter 1) or glow plugs (see Chapter 5) from the engine.
**2** On petrol engines, disable the fuel and ignition systems by disconnecting the primary

electrical connectors at the ignition coil pack/modules (see Chapter 5) and the electrical connectors at the fuel injectors (see Chapter 4A). On diesel engines, disable the fuel injection system by unplugging the electrical connector to the fuel shut-off valve (see Chapter 4B).
**3** Turn the engine over using the starter motor until the oil light goes out.
**4** Refit the spark plugs or glow plugs, refit the HT leads or electrical connectors for the glow plugs. Restore the fuel and ignition system functions.
**5** Start the engine. It may take a few moments for the fuel system to build up pressure, but the engine should start without a great deal of effort. **Note:** *If the engine keeps backfiring, recheck the valve timing (and spark plug lead routing on petrol engines).*
**6** After the engine starts, it should be allowed to warm up to normal operating temperature. While the engine is warming-up, make a thorough check for fuel, oil and coolant leaks. **Note:** *On non-PD diesel engines, it may be necessary to reset the injection pump timing with a scan tool before the engine will start (see Chapter 4B).*
**7** Shut the engine off and recheck the engine oil and coolant levels.
**8** Drive the vehicle to an area with no traffic, accelerate from 30 to 50 mph, then allow the vehicle to slow to 30 mph with the throttle closed. Repeat the procedure 10 or 12 times. This will load the piston rings and cause them to seat properly against the cylinder walls. Check again for oil and coolant leaks.
**9** Drive the vehicle gently for the first 500 miles (no sustained high speeds) and keep a constant check on the oil level. It isn't unusual for an engine to use oil during the break-in period.
**10** At approximately 500 to 600 miles, change the oil and filter.
**11** For the next few hundred miles, drive the vehicle normally. Don't pamper it or abuse it.
**12** After 2000 miles, change the oil and filter again and consider the engine broken in.

# Chapter 3
# Cooling, heating and air conditioning systems

## Contents

## Degrees of difficulty

| Easy, suitable for novice with little experience |  | Fairly easy, suitable for beginner with some experience |  | Fairly difficult, suitable for competent DIY mechanic |  | Difficult, suitable for experienced DIY mechanic |  | Very difficult, suitable for expert DIY or professional |

## Specifications

### General

| | |
|---|---|
| Antifreeze type | G12 |
| Coolant capacity | See Chapter 1 |
| Expansion tank pressure cap rating | 1.02 bar |
| Thermostat opening temperature | 85°C |
| Refrigerant type | R-134a |
| Refrigerant capacity | 700 grams |

### Torque specifications

| | Nm | Ft-lbs |
|---|---|---|
| Coolant outlet pipe-to-cylinder head | 10 | 7 |
| Thermostat housing nuts/bolts | | |
| Models to 2004 | 10 | 7 |
| 2005-on models | 15 | 11 |
| Water pump attaching bolts | 15 | 11 |

## 1 General information

All vehicles covered by this manual employ a pressurised engine cooling system with thermostatically controlled coolant circulation. Coolant is drawn from the radiator by an impeller-type water pump mounted at the end of the block. The coolant is then circulated through the engine block and the cylinder head before it's redirected back into the radiator.

A wax pellet type thermostat is located in the thermostat housing on the engine. During warm up, the closed thermostat prevents coolant from circulating through the radiator. When the engine reaches normal operating temperature, the thermostat opens and allows hot coolant to travel through the radiator, where it is cooled before returning to the engine.

The cooling system is pressurised by a spring-loaded expansion tank cap, which, by maintaining pressure, increases the boiling point of the coolant. If the coolant temperature goes above this increased boiling point, the extra pressure in the system forces the reservoir cap valve off its seat and allows the coolant to escape through the overflow tube into the expansion tank. When the system cools, the excess coolant is automatically drawn from the reservoir tank back into the radiator.

The expansion tank serves as both the point at which fresh coolant is added to the cooling system to maintain the proper fluid level and as a holding tank for overheated coolant.

The heating system works by directing air through the heater matrix mounted in the dash and then to the interior of the vehicle by a system of ducts. Temperature is controlled by mixing heated air with fresh air, using a system of doors in the ducts, and a blower motor.

Air conditioning is an optional accessory, consisting of an evaporator matrix located under the dash, a condenser in front of the radiator, a receiver/drier in the engine

compartment and a belt-driven compressor mounted at the end of the engine.

Diesel engines are equipped with an EGR cooler that is mounted at the rear of the engine between the intake manifold and the exhaust manifold/turbocharger, refer to Chapter 6B for more information on this component.

## 2 Antifreeze – general information

 **Warning: Do not allow antifreeze to come in contact with your skin or painted surfaces of the vehicle. Rinse off spills immediately with plenty of water. Antifreeze is highly toxic if ingested. Never leave antifreeze lying around in an open container or in puddles on the floor; children and pets are attracted by it's sweet smell and may drink it. Check with local authorities about disposing of used antifreeze. Many communities have collection centres which will see that antifreeze is disposed of safely. Never dump used antifreeze on the ground or pour it into drains.**
**Caution: The manufacturer recommends using only phosphate-free coolant (G12) for these systems. Phosphate-free antifreeze is red in colour. Never mix green-coloured ethylene glycol antifreeze and red-coloured phosphate-free antifreeze because doing so will destroy the efficiency of the antifreeze.**

The cooling system should be filled with the proper antifreeze solution which will prevent freezing down to at least –30 °C (even lower in cold climates). It also provides protection against corrosion and increases the coolant boiling point.

The cooling system should be drained, flushed and refilled at least every other year (see Chapter 1). The use of antifreeze solutions for periods of longer than two years is likely to cause damage and encourage the formation of rust and scale in the system. However, these

models are filled with a new, long-life phosphate-free coolant which the manufacturer claims is good for the lifetime of the vehicle.

Before adding antifreeze to the system, check all hose connections. Antifreeze can leak through very minute openings.

The exact mixture of antifreeze to water which you should use depends on the relative weather conditions. The mixture should contain at least 40-percent antifreeze, but should never contain more than 60-percent antifreeze. Consult the mixture ratio chart on the antifreeze container before adding coolant. Hydrometers are available at most motor factors to test the coolant **(see illustration)**. Always use antifreeze which meets the vehicle manufacturer's specifications.

## 3 Thermostat – testing and renewal

 **Warning: The engine must be completely cool when this procedure is performed.**
**Caution: Don't drive the vehicle without a thermostat! The engine management ECM may stay in open loop mode and emissions and fuel economy will suffer.**

### Check

1 Before assuming the thermostat is to blame for a cooling system problem, check the coolant level, auxiliary drivebelt tension (see Chapter 1) and temperature gauge (or light) operation.
2 If the engine seems to be taking a long time to warm up (based on heater output or temperature gauge operation), the thermostat is probably stuck open. Renew the thermostat.
3 If the engine runs hot, use your hand to check the temperature of the upper radiator hose. If the hose isn't hot, but the engine is, the thermostat is probably stuck closed, preventing the coolant inside the engine from escaping to the radiator. Renew the thermostat.
4 If the upper radiator hose is hot, it means the coolant is flowing and the thermostat is open. Consult the *Troubleshooting* Section at the front of this manual for cooling system diagnosis.

### Renewal

5 Drain the coolant from the radiator (see Chapter 1). If the coolant is relatively new or in good condition, save it and re-use it. If it is to be renewed, see Section 2 for cautions about proper handling of used antifreeze.
6 Follow the lower radiator hose to the engine to locate the thermostat housing cover. On the 1.4L petrol engine, it is located in a housing at the left-hand end of the cylinder head. On 1.6L, 1.8L and 2.0L petrol models and all diesel models, it located on the side of the engine facing the radiator.
7 Squeeze the tabs on the hose clamp and pull the hose clamp back over the hose.

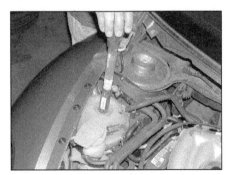

**2.4 An inexpensive hydrometer can be used to test the condition of your coolant**

**3.8 Lower radiator hose clamp at the thermostat housing cover (2.0L engine shown)**

A  *Radiator hose clamp*
B  *Thermostat housing cover bolts*

3.10a  Undo the screws . . .

3.10b  . . . remove the thermostat cover . . .

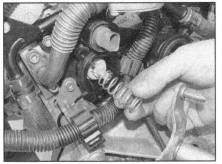

3.10c  . . . followed by the spring . . .

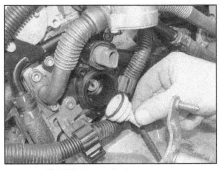

3.10d  . . . and plunger . . .

3.10e  . . . for access to the thermostat
(1.4L engine)

**8** Detach the hose from the thermostat housing cover **(see illustration)**. If the hose sticks, grasp it near the end with a pair of adjustable pliers and twist it to break the seal, then pull it off. If the hose is old or deteriorated, cut it off and refit a new one.
**9** If the outer surface of the cover fitting that mates with the hose is deteriorated (corroded, pitted, etc) it may be damaged further by hose removal. If it is, the thermostat housing cover will have to be renewed.
**10** Remove the bolts/nuts and detach the thermostat cover. If the cover is stuck, tap it

with a soft-face hammer to jar it loose. Be prepared for some coolant to spill as the gasket seal is broken. On 1.4L models, remove the spring and plunger for access to the thermostat **(see illustrations)**.
**11** Note how it's fitted (which end is facing up), then remove the thermostat and the cover O-ring **(see illustration)**.
**12** Clean the mating surfaces of the engine block and the thermostat housing cover.
**13** Refit the thermostat and make sure the correct end faces out – the spring is directed toward the engine. On diesel engines refit the

thermostat and rotate it 1/4 turn clockwise (the brace of the thermostat must be almost vertical). On 1.4L models, refit the spring and plunger.
**14** Refit a new O-ring over the thermostat and reattach the thermostat housing cover to the engine block **(see illustration)**. Tighten the bolts to the torque listed in this Chapter's Specifications. Now may be a good time to check and renew the hoses and clamps (see Chapter 1).
**15** The remaining steps are the reverse of the removal procedure.
**16** Refer to Chapter 1 and refill the system,

3.11  Remove the thermostat, noting which end faces out

3.14  Correct installation of the thermostat and the cover O-ring

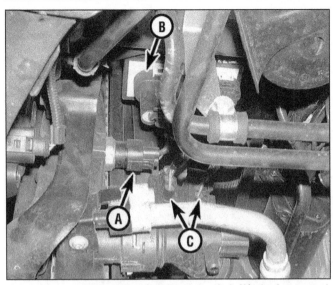

4.1 Location of the cooling fan thermal switch (A), the fan control module (B) and the cooling fan electrical connectors (C)

4.10 Cooling fan-to-shroud mounting bolts (A), the fan motor mounting bolts (B) and the wiring harness retaining clip (C)

then run the engine and check carefully for leaks.

17 Repeat steps 1 through 4 to be sure the repairs corrected the previous problem(s).

### 4  Engine cooling fan(s) and circuit – testing and component renewal

> **Warning: Keep hands, tools and clothing away from the fan. To avoid injury or damage DO NOT operate the engine with a damaged fan. Do not attempt to repair fan blades – renew a damaged fan.**

#### Check

1 To test a fan motor, unplug the electrical connector at the motor and use fused jumper wires to connect battery power and earth directly to the fan (see illustration). If the fan doesn't operate, renew the motor.

2 If the motor tests OK, check the cooling fan thermal switch, located at the bottom of the radiator on the left-hand side.

3 Remove the electrical connector from the cooling fan thermal switch and apply a fused jumper wire between the red wire and the red/white wire with the ignition switch in the On position. Both fans should run at low speed.

4 Next, apply the fused jumper wire between the red wire and the red/yellow wire with the ignition switch in the On position. Both fans should run at high speed.

5 If the fans run as described in Steps 3 and 4, it indicates that the cooling fans and circuit are operating properly and the thermal switch is faulty.

6 If the fans do not operate with the thermal switch bypassed, check for voltage at the red wire of the thermal switch electrical connector. There should be battery voltage.

7 If voltage is not present, check the No 3 and the No 8 fuses in the engine compartment fuse holder and the No 16 fuse in the passenger compartment fuse box. If the fuses are OK, the problem lies in the wiring harness, the fan control module or the coolant temperature sensor. Refer to Chapter 6A to test the coolant temperature sensor.

8 Refer to the wiring schematics at the end of Chapter 12 and check the wiring for open or short circuits. The fan control module can only be diagnosed as faulty through process of elimination.

#### Renewal

9 Raise the vehicle and support it securely on axle stands. Remove the lower engine cover and disconnect the electrical connector(s) from the cooling fan(s).

10 Detach the wiring harness clips and remove the cooling fan-to-shroud mounting bolts (see illustration). Pull the fan assembly outward slightly to dislodge it from the fan shroud, then guide the fan assembly out of engine compartment from the bottom, making sure that all wiring clips are disconnected. Be careful not to contact the radiator cooling fins.

11 If the fan blades or the fan motor are damaged, they can be renewed by removing the fan blade from the fan motor, then removing the fan motor from the fan housing (see illustration 4.10).

12 Refitting is the reverse of removal.

### 5  Radiator and expansion tank – removal and refitting

> **Warning 1: The air conditioning system is under high pressure. DO NOT loosen any fittings or remove any components until**

*after the system has been discharged. Air conditioning refrigerant should be properly discharged into an approved container at a dealership service department or an automotive air conditioning repair facility.*

> **Warning 2: The engine must be completely cool when this procedure is performed.**

#### Radiator

1 Drain the cooling system as described in Chapter 1. Refer to the coolant **Warning** in Section 2.

2 Remove the front wings and bumper cover assembly (see Chapter 11).

3 Disconnect the upper coolant hoses from the radiator (see illustration).

4 Raise the vehicle and support it securely on axle stands.

5 Disconnect the lower coolant hoses and the electrical connector from the fan thermal switch. Also disconnect the cooling fan electrical connectors (see illustration).

6 Remove the auxiliary drivebelt tensioner, if necessary.

5.3 Removing the upper radiator hose

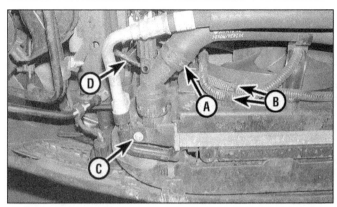

**5.5 Remove the following components from the bottom of the radiator**

A   *Lower radiator hose*
B   *Cooling fan electrical connectors*
C   *Air conditioning pipe retaining clamp*
D   *Cooling fan thermal switch electrical connector*

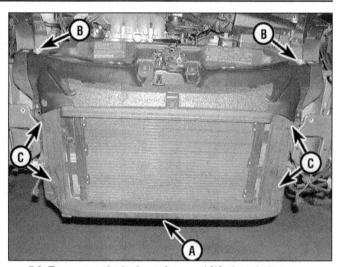

**5.8 To remove the lock carrier panel (A), detach the upper bolts (B) and the radiator mounting bolts (C)**

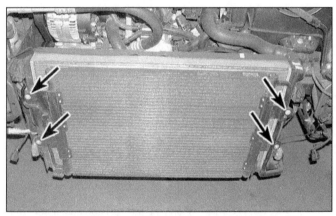

**5.9 Condenser-to-radiator mounting bolts (arrowed)**

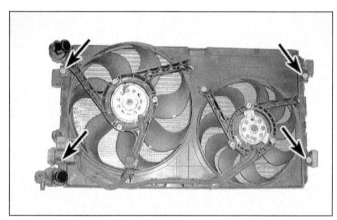

**5.11 Cooling fan shroud mounting bolts (arrowed)**

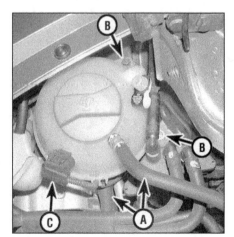

**5.17 Detach the coolant hoses (A), the mounting bolts (B) and the electrical connector (C)**

7 Disconnect the retaining clamps for the air conditioning pipes.
8 Detach the lock carrier panel and the radiator mounting bolts **(see illustration)**.

9 Remove the condenser mounting bolts (if applicable) and separate the condenser from the radiator without disconnecting the air conditioning pipes **(see illustration)**.
10 Remove the radiator and cooling fans as an assembly from the vehicle.
11 Remove the cooling fans and shroud from the radiator **(see illustration)**.
12 Prior to refitting of the radiator, renew any damaged hose clamps and/or radiator hoses. If leaks have been noticed or there have been cooling problems, have the radiator cleaned and tested at a radiator shop.
13 Radiator refitting is the reverse of removal.
14 After refitting, fill the system with the proper mixture of antifreeze, bleed the air from the cooling system as described in Chapter 1.

*Expansion tank*

15 Drain the cooling system as described in Chapter 1 until the expansion tank is empty. Refer to the coolant **Warning** in Section 2.
16 Remove the coolant hoses from the expansion tank.
17 Detach the reservoir mounting bolts, then

lift the expansion tank from the notch on the inner wing and disconnect the coolant level sensor connector **(see illustration)**.
18 Remove the expansion tank from the engine compartment.
19 Prior to refitting make sure the reservoir is clean and free of debris which could be drawn into the radiator (wash it with soapy water and a brush if necessary, then rinse thoroughly).
20 Refitting is the reverse of removal.

**6   Water pump –**
    removal and refitting

 *Warning: Wait until the engine is completely cool before starting this procedure.*

1 Raise the vehicle and support it securely on axle stands.
2 Drain the coolant (see Chapter 1).
3 Remove the auxiliary drivebelt (see Chapter 1).
4 Remove the timing belt (see Chapter 2A or 2B).

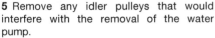

6.6 Water pump retaining bolts (arrowed)

6.8 Seat the water pump O-ring (arrowed) firmly in its groove

**5** Remove any idler pulleys that would interfere with the removal of the water pump.

**6** Remove the water pump mounting bolts from the engine block and the water pump **(see illustration)**. On 1.6L (code AWH) and 2.0L engines, this will include removing the rear timing belt cover as well.

**7** Clean the mating surfaces of the water pump and the engine block. Wipe the mating surfaces with a rag saturated with lacquer thinner or acetone.

**8** First, refit the water pump O-ring to the water pump on the bench, then refit the water pump onto the engine block **(see illustration)**. Apply a small amount of coolant to the O-ring to ease refitting into the block.

**9** Refit the water pump-to-engine block bolts and tighten them to the torque listed in this Chapter's Specifications.

**10** The remainder of the refitting procedure is the reverse of removal. Be sure to properly refit the timing belt. Add coolant to the specified level (see Chapter 1). Start the engine and check for the proper coolant level and the water pump and hoses for leaks.

Bleed the cooling system of air as described in Chapter 1.

## 7 Coolant temperature gauge sending unit – testing and renewal

### Check

**1** The coolant temperature indicator system is composed of a temperature gauge or warning light mounted in the dash and a coolant temperature sensor mounted on the engine. The coolant sensor is fitted to the coolant distribution pipe at the gearbox end of the cylinder head. This coolant temperature sensor doubles as an information sensor for the fuel and emissions systems (see Chapter 6A or 6B) and as a sending unit for the temperature gauge.

**2** If overheating occurs, check the coolant level in the system and then make sure the wiring between the gauge and the sending unit is secure and all fuses are intact.

**3** Check the operation of the coolant temperature sensor (see Chapter 6A or 6B). If the sensor is defective, renew it with a new part of the same specification.

**4** If the coolant temperature sensor is good, have the temperature gauge checked by a dealer service department. This test will require a scan tool to access the information as it is processed by the Engine Control Module.

### Renewal

**5** Refer to the relevant part of Chapter 6 for the engine coolant temperature sensor renewal procedure.

## 8 Blower motor and circuit – testing

**Warning: These models have airbags. Always disconnect the negative battery cable and wait two minutes before working in the vicinity of the impact sensors, steering column or instrument panel to avoid the possibility of accidental deployment of the airbag, which could cause personal injury (see Chapter 12).**

**1** Check the fuses and all connections in the circuit for looseness and corrosion. Make sure the battery is fully charged.

**2** Place the transmission in Park (automatic) or Neutral (manual) and set the handbrake securely. Turn the ignition switch to the Run position, it isn't necessary to start the vehicle.

**3** Remove the cover (below the glovebox) for access to the blower motor. It will be necessary to disconnect the resistor connector, then remove the cover and reconnect the resistor connector for this test **(see illustration)**.

**4** Backprobe the blower motor electrical connector and connect a voltmeter to the two terminals in the blower motor connector **(see illustration)**. **Note:** Refer to Chapter 12 for

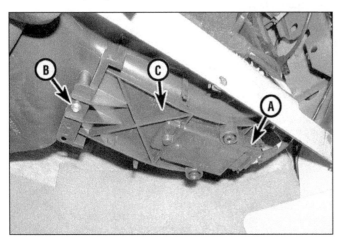

8.3 Disconnect the resistor electrical connector (A), then remove the cover mounting screws (B) and remove the cover (C)

8.4 Connect a voltmeter to the heater blower motor connector by backprobing the connector, operate the blower motor, and check the running voltage at each blower switch position

9.3 Position the lower section of the instrument panel aside and lower the blower motor from the housing

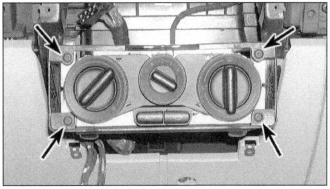

10.2 Rremove the screws (arrowed) retaining the heater/air conditioning control assembly to the instrument panel

additional information on backprobing a connector.

5 Move the blower switch through each of its positions and note the voltage readings. Changes in voltage indicate that the motor speeds will also vary as the switch is moved to the different positions.

6 If there is voltage present, but the blower motor does not operate, the blower motor is probably faulty. Disconnect the blower motor connector, then connect one side of the blower motor terminals to a chassis earth and the other to a fused source of battery voltage. If the blower doesn't operate, it is faulty.

7 If there was no voltage present at the blower motor at one or more speeds, and the motor itself tested OK, check the blower motor resistor.

8 Disconnect the electrical connector from the blower motor resistor **(see illustration 8.3)**. With the ignition On, check for voltage at each of the terminals in the connector as the blower speed switch is moved to the different positions. If the voltmeter does not respond correctly to the switch and the blower is known to be good then the resistor is probably faulty. If there is no voltage present from the switch, then the switch, control panel or related wiring is probably faulty.

9 Follow the blower motor earth wire from the motor to the chassis and check the earth terminal for continuity to earth against the chassis metal.

## 9  Blower motor – removal and refitting

⚠ *Warning: These models have airbags. Always disconnect the negative battery cable and wait two minutes before working in the vicinity of the impact sensors, steering column or instrument panel to avoid the possibility of accidental deployment of the airbag, which could cause personal injury (see Chapter 12).*

1 Remove the glovebox and the glovebox support brace (see Chapter 11, Section 24).

2 Remove the lower cover and disconnect the electrical connector from the blower motor **(see illustration 8.4)**.

3 Pull the lower section of the instrument panel outward and unclip the blower motor from the blower housing **(see illustration)**.

4 Pull the blower motor and fan straight down to remove it from the vehicle.

5 Refitting is the reverse of removal.

## 10  Heater and air conditioning control assembly – removal and refitting

*Warning: These models have airbags.*

⚠ *Always disconnect the negative battery cable and wait two minutes before working in the vicinity of the impact sensors, steering column or instrument panel to avoid the possibility of accidental deployment of the airbag, which could cause personal injury (see Chapter 12).*

### Removal

1 Remove the centre instrument panel bezel to allow access to the heater/air conditioning control mounting screws (see Chapter 11).

2 Remove the control assembly retaining screws and pull the unit from the dash **(see illustration)**.

3 Disconnect the electrical connections from the rear of the control head.

4 Use a small screwdriver to release the clips and detach the cables from the actuating arms **(see illustration)**. Noting the colour and location of the cables as the cables are removed.

### Refitting

5 To refit the control assembly, attach the cables to the actuating arms first, then snap the cable retaining clip in place. **Note:** *When reconnecting cables to the control assembly, be sure to attach the correct colour cable with the correct actuating arm **(see illustration)**.*

6 The remainder of the refitting is the reverse the removal.

10.4 Pull the control assembly outwards and disconnect the electrical connectors, then detach the cable retaining clamps

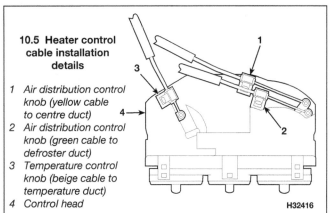

10.5 Heater control cable installation details

1 Air distribution control knob (yellow cable to centre duct)
2 Air distribution control knob (green cable to defroster duct)
3 Temperature control knob (beige cable to temperature duct)
4 Control head

H32416

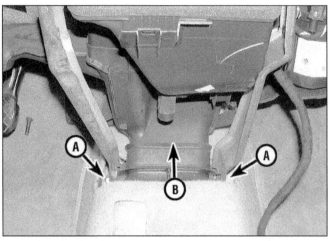

**11.4  Crossbeam support brackets (A) and the lower air duct (B)**

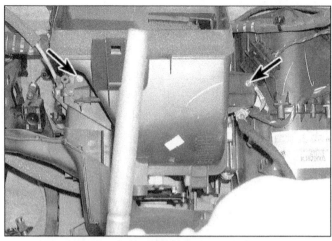

**11.5a  Detach the centre air duct from the heater/air conditioning unit**

## 11 Heater matrix –
removed and refitting

*Warning 1: These models have airbags. Always disconnect the negative battery cable and wait two minutes before working in the vicinity of the impact sensors, steering column or instrument panel to avoid the possibility of accidental deployment of the airbag, which could cause personal injury (see Chapter 12).*

*Warning 2: The air conditioning system is under high pressure. DO NOT loosen any fittings or remove any components until after the system has been discharged. Air conditioning refrigerant should be properly discharged into an approved container at a dealership service department or an automotive air conditioning facility.*

### Removal

**1** Have the air conditioning system discharged by a dealership service department or an automotive air conditioning facility.
**2** Drain the cooling system (see Chapter 1).
**3** Remove the instrument panel and crossbeam from the passenger compartment. Refer to Chapter 11 and read through the entire instrument panel removal procedure before attempting to remove it; the instrument panel removal procedure is quite lengthy and can be particularly difficult for a beginner.
**4** Once the instrument panel crossbeam is removed from the vehicle, detach the crossbeam support braces and the lower air duct **(see illustration)**.
**5** Remove the upper air ducts from the centre of the heater/air conditioning unit **(see illustrations)**.
**6** Disconnect all electrical connectors from the heater/air conditioning unit and position the wiring harness aside **(see illustration)**. Refer to Section 9 to disconnect the wires from the blower motor.
**7** Working in the engine compartment, remove the air intake duct (see Chapter 4A), the engine cover (see Chapter 2A or 2B) and the scuttle cover (see Chapter 11).
**8** Disconnect the heater hoses at the heater

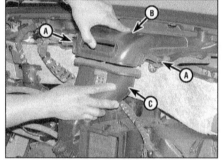

**11.5b  Remove the retaining screws (A), then lift the upper duct (B) to remove the middle duct (C)**

matrix inlet and outlet on the engine side of the bulkhead **(see illustration)** and plug the open fittings. If the hoses are stuck to the pipes, cut them off and renew them upon refitting.
**9** Remove the air conditioning pipes from the evaporator matrix fittings at the bulkhead. Also remove the mounting nuts securing the heater/air conditioning unit to the passenger side of the bulkhead **(see illustration)**.
**10** Remove the mounting nuts securing the

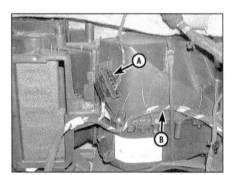

**11.6  disconnect the wiring harness connectors (A) and position the main wiring harness (B) aside**

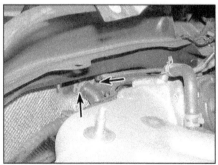

**11.8  Disconnect the heater core hoses (arrowed) at the engine compartment bulkhead**

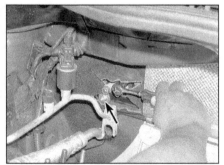

**11.9  Disconnect the air conditioning pipes at the bulkhead (if equipped), then remove the two mounting nuts on the passenger side of the engine compartment**

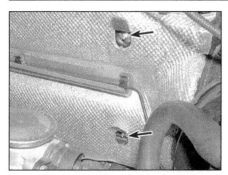

**11.10  Heater/air conditioning unit mounting nuts – driver's side**

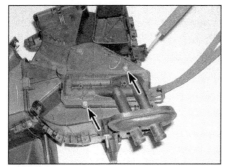

**11.11a  Detach the heater core retaining screws (arrowed) . . .**

**11.11b  . . . and remove the heater core from the housing**

heater/air conditioning unit to the driver's side of the bulkhead **(see illustration)**. Once the heating/air conditioning unit is unbolted from the bulkhead it can be removed from the vehicle and set on a workbench.

**11** Remove the heater matrix retaining screws and carefully remove the heater matrix from the heating/air conditioning unit **(see illustrations)**. **Note:** *The seal around the heater matrix pipes where they pass through the bulkhead has a 'fitting mark' on one end. This mark must align with the corresponding mark on the pipe reinforcing plate.*

### Refitting

**12** Refitting is the reverse of removal. **Note:** *When reinstalling the heater matrix, make sure any original insulating/sealing materials are in place around the heater matrix pipes and around the matrix.*
**13** Refill the cooling system (see Chapter 1).
**14** Start the engine and check for proper operation.

 **12  Air conditioning and heating system** – inspection and maintenance

### Air conditioning system

⚠ *Warning: The air conditioning system is under high pressure. Do not loosen any hose fittings or remove any components until after the system has been discharged. Air conditioning refrigerant should be properly discharged into an approved recovery/recycling unit at a dealer service department or an automotive air conditioning repair facility.*
*Caution 1: All models covered by this manual use environmentally friendly R-134a. This refrigerant (and its appropriate refrigerant oils) are not compatible with R-12 refrigerant system components and must never be mixed or the components will be damaged.*
*Caution 2: When renewing entire components, additional refrigerant oil should be added equal to the amount that is removed with the component being*

*renewed. Be sure to read the can before adding any oil to the system, to make sure it is compatible with the R-134a system.*
**1** The following maintenance checks should be performed on a regular basis to ensure that the air conditioning continues to operate at peak efficiency.
a) *Inspect the condition of the compressor drivebelt. If it is worn or deteriorated, renew it (see Chapter 1).*
b) *Check the auxiliary drivebelt tension and, if necessary, adjust it (see Chapter 1).*
c) *Inspect the system hoses. Look for cracks, bubbles, hardening and deterioration. Inspect the hoses and all fittings for oil bubbles or seepage. If there is any evidence of wear, damage or leakage, renew the hose(s).*
d) *Inspect the condenser fins for leaves, insects and any other foreign material that may have embedded itself in the fins. Use a 'fin comb' or compressed air to remove debris from the condenser.*
e) *Make sure the system has the correct refrigerant charge.*
f) *If you hear water sloshing around in the dash area or have water dripping on the carpet, check the evaporator housing drain tube **(see illustration)** and insert a piece of wire into the opening to check for blockage.*

**12.1  Remove the plug from the bulkhead heat shield and check that the evaporator housing drain flap (arrowed) is clear of any blockage – the view here is from below the engine looking up**

**2** It's a good idea to operate the system for about ten minutes at least once a month. This is particularly important during the winter months because long term non-use can cause hardening, and subsequent failure, of the seals. Note that using the Defrost function operates the compressor.
**3** If the air conditioning system is not working properly, proceed to Step 6 and perform the general checks outlined below.
**4** Because of the complexity of the air conditioning system and the special equipment necessary to service it, in-depth troubleshooting and repairs beyond checking the refrigerant charge and the compressor clutch operation are not included in this manual. However, simple checks and component renewal procedures are provided in this Chapter.
**5** The most common cause of poor cooling is simply a low system refrigerant charge. If a noticeable drop in system cooling ability occurs, one of the following quick checks will help you determine whether the refrigerant level is low. Should the system lose its cooling ability, the following procedure will help you pinpoint the cause.

### Inspection

**6** Warm the engine up to normal operating temperature.
**7** Place the air conditioning temperature selector at the coldest setting and put the blower at the highest setting. Open the doors (to make sure the air conditioning system doesn't cycle off as soon as it cools the passenger compartment).
**8** After the system reaches operating temperature, feel the two pipes connected to the evaporator at the bulkhead.
**9** The pipe (thinner tubing) leading from the condenser outlet to the evaporator should be cold, and the evaporator outlet pipe (the thicker tubing that leads back to the compressor) should be slightly colder (1.5 to 5.0°C colder). If the evaporator outlet is considerably warmer than the inlet, the system needs a charge. Insert a thermometer in the centre air distribution duct **(see illustration)**

**12.9 Insert a thermometer in the centre duct while operating the air conditioning system – the output air should be 20 to 22°C below the ambient temperature, depending on humidity (but not lower than 4°C)**

while operating the air conditioning system at its maximum setting – the temperature of the output air should be 20 to 22°C below the ambient air temperature (down to approximately 4°C). If the ambient (outside) air temperature is very high, for example 40°C, the duct air temperature may be as high as 16°C, but generally the air conditioning is 20 to 22°C cooler than the ambient air.

10  If the air isn't as cold as it used to be, the system probably needs a charge.

11  If the air is warm and the system doesn't seem to be operating properly check the operation of the compressor clutch.

12  Have an assistant switch the air conditioning On while you observe the front of the compressor. The clutch will make an audible click and the centre of the clutch should rotate.

13  If the clutch does not operate, check the appropriate fuses. Inspect the fuses in the interior fuse panel.

14  If the clutch doesn't respond, disconnect the clutch connector at the compressor and check for battery voltage at the compressor clutch connector. There should be battery voltage with the air conditioning switched On.

15  Check for continuity to earth on the black wire terminal of the compressor clutch connector.

16  If power and earth are available and the clutch doesn't operate when connected, the compressor clutch is defective.

17  Further inspection or testing of the system is beyond the scope of the home mechanic and should be left to a professional.

### Heating systems

18  If the carpet under the heater matrix is damp, or if antifreeze vapour or steam is coming through the vents, the heater matrix is leaking. Remove it (see Section 11) and fit a new unit (most radiator workshops will not repair a leaking heater matrix).

19  If the air coming out of the heater vents isn't hot, the problem could stem from any of the following causes:

  a) *The thermostat is stuck open, preventing the engine coolant from warming up enough to carry heat to the heater matrix. Renew the thermostat (see Section 3).*

  b) *There is a blockage in the system, preventing the flow of coolant through the heater matrix. Feel both heater hoses at the bulkhead. They should be hot. If one of them is cold, there is an obstruction in one of the hoses or in the heater matrix, or the heater control valve is shut. Detach the hoses and back flush the heater matrix with a water hose. If the heater matrix is clear but circulation is impeded, remove the two hoses and flush them out with a water hose.*

  c) *If flushing fails to remove the blockage from the heater matrix, the matrix must be renewed (see Section 11).*

### Eliminating air conditioning odours

20  Unpleasant odours that often develop in air conditioning systems are caused by the growth of a fungus, usually on the surface of the evaporator matrix. The warm, humid environment there is a perfect breeding earth for mildew to develop.

21  The evaporator matrix on most vehicles is difficult to access, and factory dealerships have a lengthy, expensive process for eliminating the fungus by opening up the evaporator case and using a powerful disinfectant and rinse on the matrix until the fungus is gone. You can service your own system at home, but it takes something much stronger than basic household germ-killers or deodorisers.

22  Aerosol disinfectants for automotive air conditioning systems are available in most

motor factors, but remember when shopping for them that the most effective treatments are also the most expensive. The basic procedure for using these sprays is to start by running the system in the RECIRC mode for ten minutes with the blower on its highest speed. Use the highest heat mode to dry out the system and keep the compressor from engaging by disconnecting the wiring connector at the compressor (see Section 14).

23  The disinfectant can usually comes with a long spray hose. Remove the blower motor resistor (see Section 8), point the nozzle inside the hole and to the driver's side towards the evaporator matrix, and spray according to the manufacturer's recommendations **(see illustration)**. Try to cover the whole surface of the evaporator matrix, by aiming the spray up, down and sideways. Follow the manufacturer's recommendations for the length of spray and waiting time between applications.

24  Once the evaporator has been cleaned, the best way to prevent the mildew from coming back again is to make sure your evaporator housing drain tube is clear **(see illustration 12.1)**.

### 13  Air conditioning receiver/drier – removal and refitting

#### Removal

⚠️ *Warning: The air conditioning system is under high pressure. DO NOT loosen any fittings or remove any components until after the system has been discharged. Air conditioning refrigerant should be properly discharged into an approved container at a dealership service department or an automotive air conditioning specialist.*

1  Have the air conditioning system discharged (see **Warning** above).

2  Raise the vehicle and support it securely on axle stands.

3  Disconnect the refrigerant outlet pipe from the bottom of the receiver/drier **(see illustration)**. Cap or plug the open pipe immediately to prevent the entry of dirt or moisture.

4  Disconnect the refrigerant inlet pipe from the top of the receiver/drier **(see illustration)**,

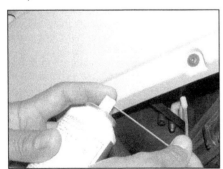

**12.23  With the blower motor removed, spray the disinfectant at the evaporator core**

**13.3  Disconnect the outlet pipe – view here is from below at the front of the vehicle**

**13.4  remove the inlet pipe (A) and the mounting bracket bolt (B) – view here is from above in the engine compartment**

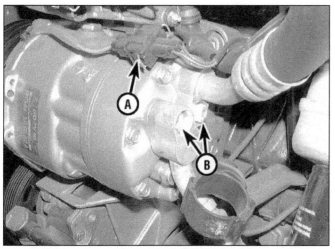

14.7 Disconnect the electrical connector (A) and the retaining bolts (B) securing the refrigerant pipes to the back of the compressor

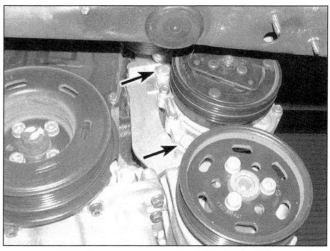

14.8 Compressor mounting bolts (arrowed)

using an Allen key. Cap or plug the open pipe immediately to prevent the entry of dirt or moisture.

5 Loosen the clamp bolt **(see illustration 13.4)** on the mounting bracket and slide the receiver/drier assembly up and out of the engine compartment.

### Refitting

6 If you are replacing the receiver/drier with a new one, 13.5 cc of fresh refrigerant oil to the new unit (oil must be R-134a compatible).

7 Place the new receiver/drier into position in the bracket.

8 Refit the inlet and outlet pipes, using clean refrigerant oil on the new O-rings. Tighten the mounting bolts securely.

9 Have the system evacuated, recharged and leak tested by a dealership service department or an automotive air conditioning repair facility.

### 14 Air conditioning compressor – removal and refitting

**Warning: The air conditioning system is under high pressure. DO NOT loosen any fittings or remove any components until after the system has been discharged. Air conditioning refrigerant should be properly discharged into an approved container at a dealership service department or an automotive air conditioning specialist.**
**Note:** Whenever the compressor is renewed because of internal damage, the expansion valve should also be renewed (see Section 16).
**Note:** The receiver/drier (see Section 13) should be renewed whenever the compressor is renewed.

1 Have the air conditioning system discharged (see **Warning** above).

2 Raise the vehicle and support it securely on axle stands.

3 Remove the splash shield from below the engine (if applicable).

4 Clean the compressor thoroughly around the refrigerant pipe fittings.

5 Remove the auxiliary drivebelt (see Chapter 1).

6 Disconnect the electrical connector from the air conditioning compressor.

7 Disconnect the suction and discharge pipes from the compressor. Both pipes are mounted to the back of the compressor by one bolt for each pipe. Plug the open fittings to prevent the entry of dirt and moisture, and discard the seals between the plate and compressor **(see illustration)**.

8 Remove the compressor mounting bolts **(see illustration)**. Detach the compressor from the mounting bracket and remove the compressor from the engine compartment.

9 If a new compressor is being fitted, pour the oil from the old compressor into a graduated container and add that exact amount of new refrigerant oil to the new

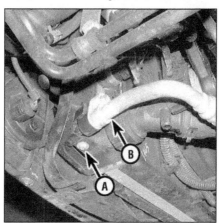

15.5 Condenser inlet pipe retaining bracket (A) and fitting (B)

compressor. Also follow any directions included with the new compressor. **Note:** Some new compressors come with refrigerant oil in them. Follow the directions with the compressor regarding the draining of excess oil prior to refitting.
**Caution: The oil used must be labelled as compatible with R-134a refrigerant systems.**

10 Refitting is the reverse of the dismantling. When refitting the pipe fitting bolt to the compressor, use new seals lubricated with clean refrigerant oil, and tighten the bolt securely.

11 Have the system evacuated, recharged and leak tested by a dealership service department or an automotive air conditioning repair facility.

### 15 Air conditioning condenser – removal and refitting

**Warning: The air conditioning system is under high pressure. DO NOT loosen any fittings or remove any components until after the system has been discharged. Air conditioning refrigerant should be properly discharged into an approved container at a dealership service department or an automotive air conditioning specialist.**

1 Have the air conditioning system discharged (see **Warning** above).

2 Raise the vehicle and support it securely on axle stands.

3 Remove the splash shield from below the engine (if applicable).

4 Remove the front wings and bumper cover assembly (see Chapter 11).

5 Disconnect the condenser inlet and outlet pipes **(see illustration)**. The condenser outlet pipe fastens to the top of the receiver/drier **(see illustration 13.4)**.

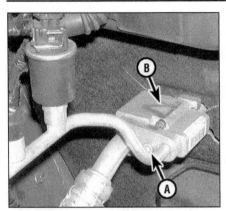

**16.3 Working in the engine compartment, disconnect the refrigerant pipes (A) and the expansion valve (B) – LHD shown**

6 Detach the lock carrier panel **(see illustration 5.8)**.

7 Remove the condenser mounting bolts **(see illustration 5.9)** a separate the condenser from the radiator.

8 Refitting is the reverse of removal. Always use new O-rings on air conditioning system fittings. If you are replacing the condenser with a new one, add 13.5 cc of fresh refrigerant oil to the new unit (oil must be R-134a compatible).

9 Have the system evacuated, recharged and leak tested by a dealership service department or an automotive air conditioning specialist.

## 16  Air conditioning expansion valve – removal and refitting

 *Warning: The air conditioning system is under high pressure. DO NOT loosen any fittings or remove any components until after the system has been discharged. Air conditioning refrigerant should be properly discharged into an approved container at a dealership service department or an automotive air conditioning repair facility.*

1 Have the air conditioning system discharged and the refrigerant recovered (see **Warning** above).

2 Remove the engine cover.

3 Disconnect the evaporator pipe fitting at the bulkhead **(see illustration)**. Cap or plug the open pipes immediately to prevent the entry of dirt or moisture.

4 Detach the expansion valve retaining bolt. Remove the expansion valve and O-rings. Cap or plug the open pipes immediately to prevent the entry of dirt or moisture into the evaporator matrix.

5 Refitting is the reverse of removal. Always use new O-rings when refitting the expansion valve.

6 Retighten the refrigerant pipes, then have the system evacuated, recharged and leak tested by a dealership service department or an automotive air conditioning repair facility.

# Chapter 4 Part A
# Fuel and exhaust systems: petrol engines

## Contents

## Degrees of difficulty

| **Easy,** suitable for novice with little experience |  | **Fairly easy,** suitable for beginner with some experience |  | **Fairly difficult,** suitable for competent DIY mechanic | | **Difficult,** suitable for experienced DIY mechanic | | **Very difficult,** suitable for expert DIY or professional |  |
|---|---|---|---|---|---|---|---|---|---|

## Specifications

### General

| | |
|---|---|
| Fuel pressure | |
|    Key On, engine Off . . . . . . . . . . . . . . . . . . . . . . . . . . . . . . . . . . . . . | 3.0 bar (44 psi) |
|    Engine running . . . . . . . . . . . . . . . . . . . . . . . . . . . . . . . . . . . . . . . . | 2.7 bar (39 psi) |
| Fuel injector resistance . . . . . . . . . . . . . . . . . . . . . . . . . . . . . . . . . . . | 12.0 to 17.0 ohms |

### Torque specifications

| | Nm | Ft-lbs |
|---|---|---|
| Fuel rail mounting bolts . . . . . . . . . . . . . . . . . . . . . . . . . . . . . . . . . . | 10 | 7 |
| Fuel tank mounting strap bolts . . . . . . . . . . . . . . . . . . . . . . . . . . . . | 25 | 18 |
| Throttle control module mounting bolts . . . . . . . . . . . . . . . . . . . . . | 10 | 7 |
| Turbocharger support bracket bolt . . . . . . . . . . . . . . . . . . . . . . . . | 30 | 22 |
| Turbocharger-to-exhaust manifold bolts . . . . . . . . . . . . . . . . . . . . | 30 | 22 |
| Turbocharger-to-exhaust pipe nuts . . . . . . . . . . . . . . . . . . . . . . . . | 40 | 30 |

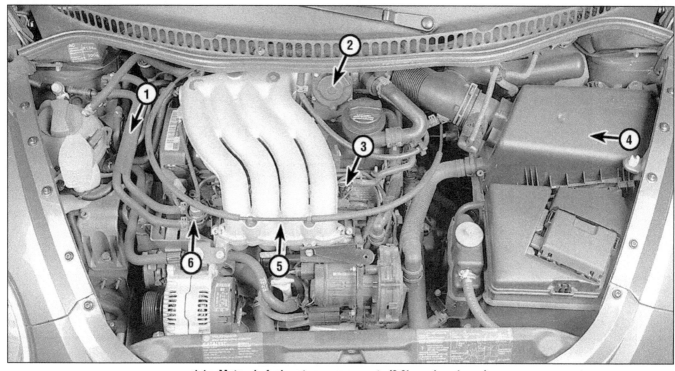

**1.1a  Motronic fuel system components (2.0L engine shown)**

| | | |
|---|---|---|
| 1 *Fuel feed and return pipes* | 3 *Fuel rail and injectors* | 5 *Accelerator cable* |
| 2 *Throttle body/throttle control module* | 4 *Air filter housing* | 6 *Fuel pressure regulator* |

1 *EVAP canister solenoid valve*
2 *Return pipe*
3 *Supply pipe*
4 *Camshaft position sensor*
5 *Variable manifold change-over valve*
6 *Variable manifold change-over diaphragm*
7 *Intake manifold  - upper section*
8 *Intake manifold – lower section*
9 *Throttle control assembly*
10 *EGR valve (hidden)*
11 *Secondary air injection inlet valve (hidden)*
12 *Relays protective housing (hidden)*
13 *Connector*
14 *Engine control module (ECM)*
15 *Connector*
16 *Air mass meter (with integral intake air temperature sensor)*
17 *Air filter*
18 *Secondary air injection system combi-valve*
19 *Coolant temperature sensor*
20 *Ignition coils*
21 *Engine speed sensor*
22 *Fuel injectors*
23 *Secondary air injection pump motor*
24 *Knock sensor*
25 *Fuel pressure regulator*
26 *Connector*
27 *Oxygen sensor (pre-catalyst)*
28 *Connector*
29 *Oxygen sensor (post-catalyst)*

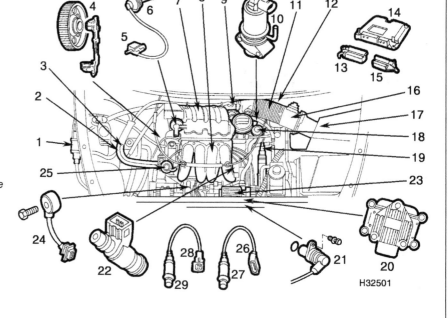

**1.1b  Simos fuel injection system components (1.6L engine)**

## 1 General information

⚠️ *Warning: Petrol is extremely flammable, so take extra precautions when you work on any part of the fuel system. Don't smoke or allow naked flames or bare light bulbs near the work area, and don't work in a garage where a gas-type appliance (such as a water heater or a clothes dryer) is present. Since petrol is carcinogenic, wear latex gloves when there's a possibility of being exposed to petrol, and, if you spill any petrol on your skin, rinse it off immediately with soap and water. Mop up any spills immediately and do not store fuel-soaked rags where they could ignite. The fuel system is under constant pressure, so, if any fuel pipes are to be disconnected, the fuel pressure in the system must be relieved first. When you perform any kind of work on the fuel system, wear safety glasses and have a Class B type fire extinguisher on hand.*

The 1.4L, 1.8L and 2.0L models covered by this manual are equipped with a Bosch Motronic fuel injection system, whilst the 1.6L models are equipped with a Simos fuel injection system (see illustrations). These systems are extremely similar, and use timed impulses to sequentially inject the fuel directly into the intake ports of each cylinder. The injectors are controlled by the Engine Control Module (ECM). The ECM monitors various engine parameters and delivers the exact amount of fuel, in the correct sequence, into the intake ports. This Chapter's information pertains to the air and fuel delivery components of the system only. Refer to Section 12 for additional general information regarding the fuel injection system. Refer to Chapter 6A for information regarding the electronic control system. Simos-equipped models have a variable geometry inlet manifold, where the length of the inlet track is varied to emphasise the torque or power characteristics of the engine dependant on engine speed and load, etc. The inlet path is controlled by a vacuum-operated valve which can operate in one of two positions. At low engine speed/high torque the valve position forces the incoming air through a long inlet track, thus increasing the torque output and low speed driveability. At high engine speed/high power the valve position forces the incoming air through a short inlet track, thus increasing the power output and throttle response. The vacuum supply to the valve is controlled by the engine management ECM.

All models are equipped with an electric fuel pump, mounted in the fuel tank. Access to the fuel pump is provided through an access hole under the rear seat cushion. The fuel level sending unit is an integral component of the fuel pump module and it must be removed from the fuel tank in the same manner.

The exhaust system consists of an exhaust manifold, a catalytic converter, an exhaust pipe and a silencer. Each of these components is renewable. For further information regarding the catalytic converter, refer to Chapter 6A.

1.8L models are equipped with a turbocharger and intercooler. The turbocharger increases power by using an exhaust gas driven turbine to pressurise the intake charge before it enters the combustion chambers. The amount of intake manifold pressure (boost) is regulated by an exhaust by-pass valve (wastegate). The wastegate is controlled by the ECM. The heated compressed air is routed through an air-to-air radiator (intercooler). The intercooler removes excess heat from the compressed air, increasing its density and allowing for more boost pressure.

## 2 Fuel pressure relief procedure

⚠️ *Warning: See the Warning in Section 1.*

Note: *After the fuel pressure has been relieved, it's a good idea to lay a rag over any fuel connection to be disassembled, to absorb* the residual fuel that may leak out when servicing the fuel system.

1 Before servicing any fuel system component, you must relieve the fuel pressure to minimise the risk of fire or personal injury.
2 Remove the fuel filler cap – this will relieve any pressure built up in the tank.
3 Remove the fuel pump fuse (No 28) from the fusebox (see illustration).
4 Attempt to start the engine. The engine should immediately stall. Continue to crank the engine for approximately three seconds.
5 Turn the ignition Off and remove the key.
6 After completing the service or repair, refit the fuel pump fuse.

## 3 Fuel pump/fuel pressure – testing

⚠️ *Warning: See the Warning in Section 1.*

### Preliminary check

1 If you suspect insufficient fuel delivery check the following items first:
 a) *Check the battery and make sure it's fully charged (see Chapter 5).*
 b) *Check the fuel pump fuse (No 28).*
 c) *Check the fuel filter for restriction.*
 d) *Inspect all fuel pipes to ensure that the problem is not simply a leak in a pipe.*
2 Place the transmission in Park (automatic) or neutral (manual) and apply the handbrake. Have an assistant cycle the ignition key On and Off several times (or attempt to start the engine, if the engine does not start) while you listen for the sound of the fuel pump operating inside the fuel tank. Remove the rear seat cushion and the fuel pump access cover and listen at, or feel the top of, the fuel pump module, if necessary. You should hear a 'whirring' sound indicating the fuel pump is operating. If the fuel pump is operating, proceed to the pressure check.
3 If there is no sound, remove the fuel pump access cover and disconnect the fuel pump electrical connector. Connect a test light or voltmeter to terminals 1 and 4 of the fuel pump harness connector (see illustration). Cycle the ignition key On and Off several times (or attempt to start the engine, if the engine does not start) – battery voltage should be indicated. If battery voltage is not indicated, check the fuel pump circuit, referring to Chapter 12 and the wiring diagrams. Check the related fuses, the fuel pump relay and the related wiring to ensure power is reaching the fuel pump connector. Check the earth circuit for continuity.
4 If the power and earth circuits are good and the fuel pump does not operate, remove the fuel pump and check for open circuits in the fuel pump module wiring and connectors. If the wiring and connectors are good, renew the fuel pump (see Section 7).

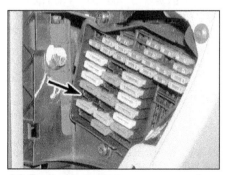

2.3 To disable the fuel pump. remove fuse No 28 (arrowed) from the fusebox

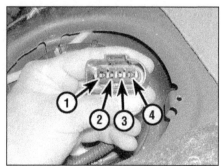

3.3 Check for battery power across terminals 1 and 4 of the fuel pump connector with the ignition key On

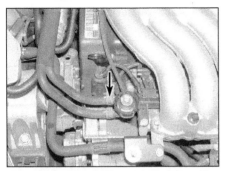

**3.6a  To test the fuel pressure, remove the fuel supply pipe from the fuel rail . . .**

### Pressure testing

**Note:** *In order to perform the fuel pressure test, you will need a fuel pressure gauge capable of measuring high fuel pressure. The fuel gauge must be equipped with the proper fittings or adapters required to attach it to the fuel pipe and fuel rail.*

**5**  Relieve the fuel pressure (see Section 2). Remove the engine cover.

**6**  Disconnect the fuel supply pipe from the fuel rail. Connect the pressure gauge with a T-fitting and adapter hose to the fuel pipe and fuel rail **(see illustrations)**.

**7**  Cycle the ignition key On and Off several times (or attempt to start the engine, if the engine does not start). Note the pressure indicated on the gauge and compare your reading with the pressure listed in this Chapter's Specifications.

**8**  If the fuel pressure is lower than specified, pinch-off the fuel return pipe.

*Caution: Use special pliers designed specifically for pinching a rubber fuel pipe (available at most motor factors). Use of any other type pliers may damage the fuel pipe. Cycle the ignition key On and Off several times and note the fuel pressure.*

*Caution: Do not allow the fuel pressure to rise above 4.5 bar (65 psi) or damage to the fuel pressure regulator may occur.*

**9**  If the fuel pressure is now above the specified pressure, renew the fuel pressure regulator (see Section 15). If the fuel pressure is still lower than

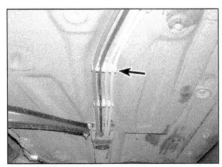

**4.2  The fuel pipes are secured to the underbody with plastic retainers – the fuel pipes are colour-coded; the white pipes are EVAP system vapour pipes, the black pipe is the fuel supply pipe and the blue pipe is the fuel return pipe**

**3.6b  . . . and attach a fuel pressure gauge between the fuel pipe and the fuel rail with a T-fitting**

specified, check the fuel pipes and the fuel filter for restrictions. If no restriction is found, remove the fuel pump module (see Section 7) and check the fuel strainer for restrictions, check the fuel pipe for leaks and check the fuel pump wiring for high resistance. If no problems are found, renew the fuel pump.

**10**  If the fuel pressure recorded in Step 7 is higher than specified, check the fuel return pipe for restrictions. If no restrictions are found, renew the fuel pressure regulator (see Section 15).

**11**  If the fuel pressure is within specifications, start the engine.

> ⚠ *Warning: Make sure the fuel pressure gauge hose is positioned away from the engine drivebelt before starting the engine.*

**12**  With the engine running, the fuel pressure should be 0.2 to 0.7 bar (3 to 10 psi) below the pressure recorded in Step 7. If it isn't, remove the vacuum hose from the fuel pressure regulator and verify there is 305 to 356 mm-Hg of vacuum present at the hose. If vacuum is not present at the hose, check the hose for a restriction or a break. If vacuum is present, reconnect the hose to the fuel pressure regulator. If the fuel pressure regulator does not decrease the fuel pressure with vacuum applied, renew the fuel pressure regulator.

**13**  Now check the fuel system hold pressure. Turn the engine off and monitor the fuel pressure for ten minutes; the fuel pressure should not drop more than 0.7 bar (10 psi) within ten minutes. If it does, there is a leak in the fuel pipe, a fuel injector is leaking, the fuel pump check

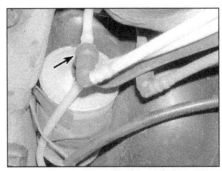

**4.9  To disconnect a quick-release fitting, press the tab in (arrowed) and pull the pipes apart**

valve is defective or the fuel pressure regulator is defective. To determine the source of the leak, cycle the ignition key On and Off several times to obtain the highest fuel pressure reading, then immediately pinch-off the fuel supply hose between the fuel gauge T-fitting and the fuel rail. If the pressure drops below 0.7 bar (10 psi) within ten minutes, the main fuel pipe is leaking or the fuel pump is defective. If the pressure holds, remove the clamp from the supply pipe, pressurise the system and clamp off the return pipe. If the pressure drops below 0.7 bar (10 psi) within ten minutes, an injector is probably leaking (or the fuel rail is leaking, but such a leak should be very apparent). If the pressure holds, remove the clamp from the return pipe. If the pressure now drops, the fuel pressure regulator is defective.

### 4  Fuel pipes and fittings – repair and renewal

> ⚠ *Warning: See the Warning in Section 1.*

**1**  Always relieve the fuel pressure before servicing fuel pipes or fittings (see Section 2).

**2**  Special flexible fuel supply, return and vapour pipes extend from the fuel tank to the engine compartment. The pipes are colour-coded and secured to the underbody with a plastic retainer **(see illustration)**. Rubber hose completes the connection from the engine compartment junction block to the fuel rail. All fuel pipes must be occasionally inspected for leaks or damage.

**3**  If evidence of contamination is found in the system or fuel filter during dismantling, the pipe should be disconnected and blown out. Check the fuel strainer on the fuel pump for damage and deterioration.

**4**  Don't route fuel pipe or hose within 100 mm of any part of the exhaust system or within 250 mm of the catalytic converter. Fuel pipe must never be allowed to chafe against the engine, body or frame. A minimum of 6 mm clearance must be maintained around a fuel pipe.

**5**  Because fuel pipes used on fuel-injected vehicles are under high pressure, they require special consideration.

**6**  In the event of fuel pipe damage, it is necessary to renew the damaged flexible pipes with factory renewal parts. Others may fail from the high pressures of this system.

**7**  When replacing a fuel pipe, remove all fasteners attaching the fuel pipe to the vehicle body and route the new pipe exactly as originally fitted.

**8**  When replacing rubber hose, always use hose specifically designated as fuel hose and renew the hose clamp with a new one.

**9**  If the fuel pipe is equipped with a quick-connect fitting, clean any debris from around the fitting and twist the fitting back-and-forth to loosen the seal. Press in on the tab to disconnect the fitting and carefully remove the fuel pipe from the vehicle **(see illustration)**.

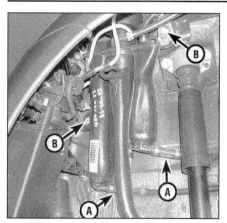

**5.10 Loosen the hose clamps and disconnect the vent hoses (A) from the filler neck – remove the filler neck mounting bolts (B)**

*Caution: The quick-connect fittings are not serviced separately. Do not attempt to repair these types of fuel pipes in the event the fitting or pipe becomes damaged. Renew the entire fuel pipe as an assembly.*

**10** Refitting is the reverse of removal with the following additions:

  a) *Clean the quick-connect fittings with a lint-free cloth and apply clean engine oil to the fittings.*
  b) *After connecting a quick-connect fitting, check the integrity of the connection by attempting to pull the pipes apart.*
  c) *Cycle the ignition key On and Off several times and check for leaks at the fitting, before starting the engine.*

## 5  Fuel tank – removal and refitting

⚠️ **Warning: See the Warning in Section 1.**

**1** Remove the fuel tank filler cap to relieve fuel tank pressure.

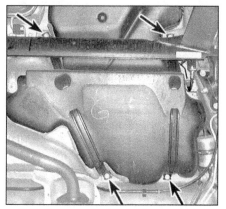
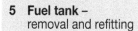

**5.13 Remove the fuel tank strap bolts (arrowed) and remove the straps**

**2** Relieve the fuel system pressure (see Section 2).

**3** Using a siphoning kit (available at most motor factors), siphon the fuel into an approved fuel container.

⚠️ **Warning: Do not start the siphoning action by mouth!**

**4** Remove the rear seat cushion (see Chapter 11).

**5** Remove the fuel pump access cover and disconnect the fuel pump electrical connector (see Section 3).

**6** Loosen the rear wheel bolts, then raise the vehicle and support it securely on axle stands.

**7** Remove the rear axle (see Chapter 10).

**8** Remove the right rear wheelarch liner (see Chapter 11, Section 13, Step 3).

**9** Remove the fuel tank heat shield and cover, if applicable.

**10** Loosen the hose clamps and disconnect the vent hoses from the fuel tank filler neck **(see illustration)**. Remove the fuel filler neck mounting bolts. Detach the overflow valve from the bracket on the inner wing.

**11** Disconnect the fuel supply pipe from the fuel filter **(see illustration)**. Disconnect the return pipe from the fuel pipe at the body (see Section 4).

**12** Disconnect the EVAP hose from the canister **(see illustration)**. Remove the screw from the wing brace and position the EVAP

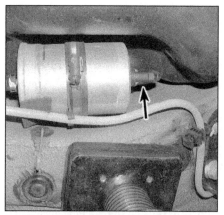

**5.11 Disconnect the fuel supply pipe quick-release fitting from the fuel filter**

**7.2 Remove the screws (arrowed) and the fuel pump access cover**

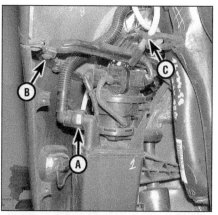

**5.12 Squeeze the tabs and disconnect the EVAP hose (A) from the canister, remove the wing brace screw (B) and move the EVAP hose outside the brace – detach the vapour pipe from the clip (C) at the filler neck**

hose outside the brace. Detach the vapour pipe from the clip on the filler neck.

**13** Position a transmission jack under the fuel tank and support the tank. Remove the fuel tank strap bolts and remove the straps **(see illustration).**

**14** Lower the jack and remove the tank from the vehicle.

**15** Refitting is the reverse of removal.

## 6  Fuel tank cleaning and repair – general information

**1** The fuel tanks fitted in the vehicles covered by this manual are not repairable. If the fuel tank becomes damaged, it must be renewed.

**2** Cleaning the fuel tank (due to fuel contamination) should be performed by a professional with the proper training to carry out this critical and potentially dangerous work. Even after cleaning and flushing, explosive fumes may remain inside the fuel tank.

**3** If the fuel tank is removed from the vehicle, it should not be placed in an area where sparks or naked flames could ignite the fumes coming out of the tank. Be especially careful inside a garage where a natural gas-type appliance is located.

## 7  Fuel pump – removal and refitting

⚠️ **Warning: See the Warning in Section 1.**

**1** Relieve the fuel system pressure (see Section 2).

**2** Remove the rear seat cushion (see Chapter 11). Remove the fuel pump access cover **(see illustration)**.

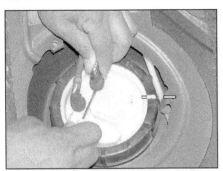

**7.3 Press the tab in and disconnect the fuel supply pipe and fuel return pipe from the fuel pump module – note the alignment marks on the fuel pump flange, retaining ring and body panel**

**7.5 Using an appropriate tool, loosen the fuel pump module retaining ring**

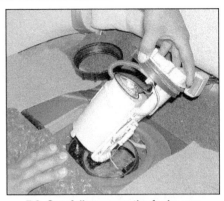

**7.6 Carefully remove the fuel pump module from the tank and drain the fuel from the reservoir**

3 Disconnect the fuel pump electrical connector. Referring to Section 4, disconnect the fuel supply and return pipes from the fuel pump module (see illustration). Note: *The fuel supply pipe is identified with a black mark. The fuel return pipe is identified with a blue mark.*

4 Apply alignment marks on the body and fuel pump module flange so the fuel pump module can be fitted in the original position.

5 Loosen the fuel pump module retaining ring (see illustration).

6 Remove the fuel pump module from the tank (see illustration). Angle the assembly slightly to avoid damaging the fuel level sending unit float. Have several absorbent towels ready and a drain pan nearby to place the module in.

 **Warning: Some fuel may remain the module reservoir and spill as the module is removed.**

7 The electric fuel pump is not serviced separately. In the event of failure, the complete assembly must be replaced. Transfer the fuel level sending unit to the new fuel pump module assembly, if necessary (see Section 8).

8 Clean the fuel tank sealing surface and refit a new seal on the fuel pump module.

9 Refit the fuel pump module aligning the marks made in Step 4.

10 Press the fuel pump module down until seated and tighten the retaining ring.

11 The remainder of refitting is the reverse of removal.

## 8 Fuel level sending unit – testing and renewal

 **Warning: See the Warning in Section 1.**

### Testing

1 Remove the fuel pump module (see Section 7).

2 Connect the probes of an ohmmeter to the two fuel level sensor terminals (2 and 3) of the fuel pump module electrical connector (see illustration).

3 Position the float in the down (empty) position and note the reading on the ohmmeter.

4 Move the float up to the full position while watching the meter.

5 If the fuel level sending unit resistance does not change smoothly as the float travels from empty to full, renew the fuel level sending unit assembly.

### Renewal

6 Remove the fuel pump module (see Section 7).

7 Disconnect the two fuel level sending unit wire terminals from the module connector terminals under the flange (see illustration). Detach the wires from the retaining clips, noting the routing of the wiring for refitting.

8 Using a small screwdriver, prise the retaining tabs up and slide the fuel level sending unit off the module (see illustration).

9 Refit the fuel level sending unit onto the fuel pump module. Slide the unit up until the retaining tabs snap into place. Connect the two wire terminals to the module connector. Route the wires as originally fitted and secure them to the retaining clips.

10 The remainder of refitting is the reverse of removal.

**8.2 Check the resistance of the fuel level sending unit across terminals 2 and 3**

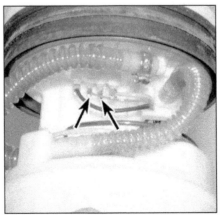

**8.7 Disconnect the two fuel level sending unit wire terminals from the fuel pump module**

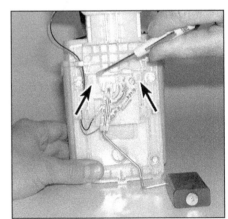

**8.8 Pry the retaining tabs up and slide the fuel level sending unit off the module**

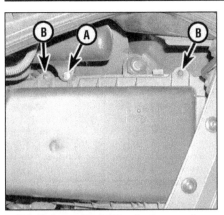

9.1 Remove the intake duct resonator screw (A) and the air filter cover screws (B) – screw locations vary with model year

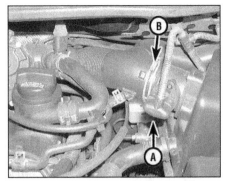

9.3 Disconnect the electrical connector from the mass airflow sensor (A), squeeze the tabs on the hose clamp together (B) and separate the mass airflow sensor from the air intake duct

9.5 Remove the air filter housing mounting screws (arrowed)

## 9 Air filter housing – removal and refitting

**Note:** *On the 1.4L engine, the air filter housing is incorporated in the engine top cover. See Chapter 1 for more details.*

1 Remove intake duct resonator screw and the air filter cover screws **(see illustration)**.
2 Lift the back of the cover up and detach the cover from the retainers along the front edge.
3 Disconnect the electrical connector from the Mass Airflow sensor. Loosen the hose clamp and detach the mass airflow sensor from the air intake duct **(see illustration)**. On 1.6L models, disconnect the EGR ventilation pipe from the air filter cover. Remove the cover with the mass airflow sensor attached.
4 Remove air filter element.
5 Disconnect the secondary air injection pump hose from the air filter housing. Remove the mounting bolts, pull the housing up and detach the duct from the inner wing **(see illustration)**. Remove the assembly from the engine compartment.
6 If necessary, detach the breather hoses and separate the air intake duct from the throttle module.
7 Refitting is the reverse of removal.

## 10 Accelerator cable (2.0L engine) – renewal

**Note:** *Some 2000 and later models have Electronic Power Control, in which the throttle control is operated by an electric motor on the throttle body. There is no mechanical cable in the system (see Section 11).*

1 Remove the engine cover.
2 Rotate the throttle quadrant and separate the accelerator cable end from the throttle quadrant **(see illustration)**.
3 Detach the cable grommet from the bracket **(see illustration)**. Detach the cable from the cable retainers on the intake manifold.
4 Remove the trim panel from under the dash and detach the cable from the accelerator pedal **(see illustration)**.
5 Push the cable and the bulkhead grommet through the bulkhead and into the engine compartment.
6 Remove the cable from the engine compartment.
7 Refitting is the reverse of removal, but before refitting the cable grommet on the bracket, adjust the cable as follows:
 a) *Have an assistant fully depress the accelerator pedal.*
 b) *Remove the retaining clip.*
 c) *Adjust the cable by rotating the grommet on the cable housing until the slot on the grommet is aligned with the bracket and throttle plate is at wide open throttle.*
 d) *Refit the cable grommet onto the bracket.*
 e) *Refit the retaining clip.*
 f) *Have your assistant release and depress the accelerator pedal several times. Check the throttle lever and make sure it contacts both the closed throttle and wide open throttle stops, if it doesn't, readjust the cable.*

## 11 Electronic accelerator pedal module (1.4L, 1.6L & 1.8L engines) – renewal

1 1.4L, 1.6L and 1.8L models are equipped with an electronically-controlled accelerator, called Electronic Power Control (EPC) system. The system consists of the accelerator pedal module, the throttle control module and the ECM. The system does not use the traditional accelerator cable. The ECM controls the throttle position based on the voltage signal received from the accelerator pedal module. Refer to Chapter 6A for more information on the electronic accelerator system.
2 Remove the insulation panel in the driver's footwell.

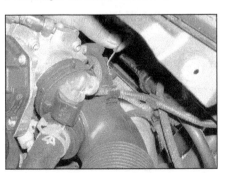

10.2 Rotate the throttle quadrant and pass the cable through the slot in the quadrant

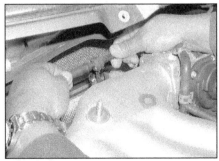

10.3 Remove the cable grommet from the bracket

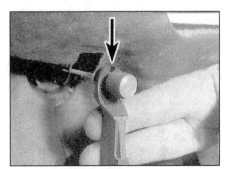

10.4 Pull the accelerator cable retainer out of the pedal and slide the cable through the slot (arrowed)

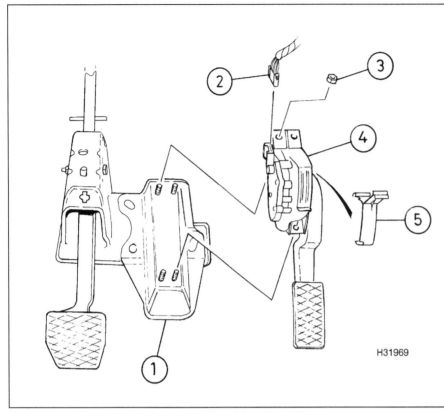

**11.4 Accelerator pedal and throttle position sensor**

1  Bracket
2  Position sensor wiring connector
3  Mounting nuts

4  Position sensor
5  Retainer for footwell cover

**3** Disconnect the electrical connector from the pedal module.
**4** Remove the mounting nuts and remove the module from the footwell **(see illustration)**.
**5** Refitting is the reverse of removal.

## 12 Fuel injection system –
general information

The fuel injection systems consist of three sub-systems: air intake, engine control and fuel delivery. The systems use an Engine Control Module (ECM) along with the sensors (coolant temperature sensor, throttle position sensor, mass airflow sensor, oxygen sensor, etc) to determine the proper air/fuel ratio under all operating conditions.

The fuel injection systems and the engine control system are closely linked in function and design. For additional information, refer to Chapter 6A.

### Air intake system

The air intake system consists of the air filter, the air intake ducts, the throttle body, the air intake plenum and the intake manifold.

When the engine is idling, the air/fuel ratio is controlled by the idle control system, which consists of the Engine Control Module (ECM)

and the throttle position actuator. The throttle position actuator is an electric motor contained within the throttle control module and controlled by the ECM. The ECM commands the throttle position actuator to open or close the throttle plate depending upon the running conditions of the engine (air conditioning system, power steering, cold and warm running, etc). The ECM receives information from the sensors (vehicle speed, coolant temperature, air conditioning, power steering mode, etc) and adjusts the idle according to the demands of the engine and driver. Refer to Chapter 6A for information on the throttle control module.

### Emissions and engine control system

The emissions and engine control system is described in detail in Chapter 6A.

### Fuel delivery system

The fuel delivery system consists of these components: the fuel pump, the fuel pressure regulator, the fuel rail, the fuel injectors, and the associated hoses and pipes.

The fuel pump is an electric type located in the fuel tank. Fuel is drawn through an inlet screen into the pump, flows through the one-way valve, passes through the fuel filter and is delivered to the fuel rail and injectors. The

pressure regulator maintains a constant fuel pressure to the injectors. Excess fuel is routed back to the fuel tank through the fuel pressure regulator.

The injectors are solenoid-actuated pintle type consisting of a solenoid, plunger, needle valve and housing. When current is applied to the solenoid coil, the needle valve raises and pressurised fuel sprays out the nozzle. The injection quantity is determined by the length of time the valve is open (the length of time during which current is supplied to the solenoid coils).

The fuel pump relay is located in the relay panel at the driver's side end of the instrument panel. The fuel pump relay connects battery voltage to the fuel pump. The ECM controls the fuel pump relay. If the ECM senses there is NO signal from the engine speed sensor (as with the engine not running or cranking), the ECM will de-energise the relay.

## 13 Fuel injection system –
testing

**Note:** *The following procedure is based on the assumption that the fuel pressure is adequate (see Section 3).*

**1** Check all electrical connectors that are related to the system. Check the earth wire connections for tightness. The main engine earth point is located on the transmission case. Other earth points in the engine compartment are located on the left side of the engine compartment under the battery tray and on the left side of the engine compartment behind the headlight. Loose connectors and poor earths can cause many problems that resemble more serious malfunctions.
**2** Check to see that the battery is fully charged, as the control unit and sensors depend on an accurate supply voltage in order to properly meter the fuel. In order for the systems to function correctly, battery voltage must be at least 11.5V.
**3** Check the air filter element – a dirty or partially blocked filter will severely impede performance and economy (see Chapter 1).
**4** Check the related fuses. If a blown fuse is found, renew it and see if it blows again. If it does, search for a wire shorted to earth in the harness.
**5** Check the air intake duct to the intake manifold for leaks, which will result in an excessively lean mixture. Also check the condition of all vacuum hoses connected to the intake manifold and/or throttle body.
**6** Remove the air intake duct from the throttle body and check for dirt, carbon or other residue build-up. If it's dirty, clean it with carburettor cleaner spray, a toothbrush and a cloth.
**7** With the engine running, place an automotive stethoscope against each injector,

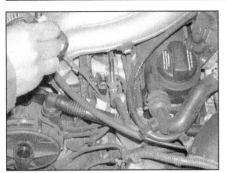

**13.7 Use a stethoscope to determine if the injectors are working properly – they should make a steady clicking sound that rises and falls with the engine speed changes**

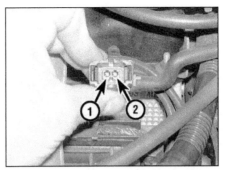

**13.8 Fuel injector harness connector terminal identification**

*1 12 volt supply    2 Injector control*

**13.9 Install the LED light into each injector electrical connector and confirm that it blinks when the engine is cranking (see text)**

one at a time, and listen for a clicking sound, indicating operation **(see illustration)**. If you don't have a stethoscope, place the tip of a screwdriver against the injector and listen through the handle. If you hear the injectors operating, the electrical circuits are functioning, but the injectors may be dirty or fouled from carbon deposits – commercial cleaning products may help or they may require renewal. If one or more injectors are not operating, proceed with the injector check.

**8** Turn the engine Off. Disconnect any one of the injector connectors and check for battery voltage at terminal No 1 of the injector harness connector with the ignition key On **(see illustration)**. If battery voltage is not present, check the fuse, fuel pump relay and related wiring (see Chapter 12).

**9** Connect a test light (LED) into the disconnected injector electrical connector **(see illustration)**. Crank the engine over. Confirm that the light flashes. This tests the ECM control of the injectors. If the light does not flash, have the ECM checked at a dealer service department or other properly-equipped repair facility. Test each injector connector, if necessary.

**10** Disconnect the injector electrical connectors and measure the resistance of

each injector **(see illustration)**. Compare the measurements with the resistance value listed in this Chapter's Specifications. Renew any injector whose resistance value does not fall within specifications.

**11** The remainder of the engine control system checks can be found in Chapter 6A.

**14 Throttle control module –**
**removal and refitting**

**Note:** *In order for a new throttle control module to function correctly, it must be matched to the engine management ECM using a dealer scan tool.*

**1** Remove the engine cover.

**2** Remove the air intake duct and air filter cover (see Section 9).

**3** Disconnect the electrical connector from the throttle control module.

**4** Detach the hoses from the throttle control module.

**5** On 2.0L models, detach the accelerator cable from the throttle control module (see Section 10).

**6** Remove the mounting bolts/nuts and remove the throttle control module and gasket **(see illustration)**.

**7** Remove all traces of old gasket material from the throttle control module and intake manifold and refit a new gasket.

*Caution: Do not use solvent or a sharp tool to clean the throttle control module gasket surface or damage to the throttle control module may occur.*

**8** Refit the throttle control module and tighten the bolts to the torque listed in this Chapter's Specifications.

**9** The remainder of refitting is the reverse of removal.

**15 Fuel pressure regulator –**
**renewal**

⚠ *Warning: See the Warning in Section 1.*

**1** Relieve the fuel system pressure (see Section 2).

**2** Remove the engine cover.

**3** Disconnect the vacuum hose from the port on the regulator.

**4** Remove the fuel pressure regulator retaining clip and withdraw the fuel pressure regulator from the fuel rail **(see illustration)**.

**5** Be sure to renew the O-ring seals,

**13.10 Measure the resistance of each injector across the two terminals of the injector**

**14.6 Throttle control module mounting bolts (arrowed)**

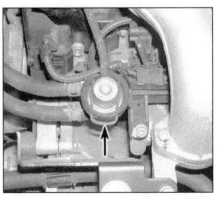

**15.4 Remove the fuel pressure regulator retaining clip (arrowed) and withdraw the regulator from the fuel rail**

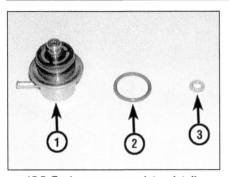

**15.5 Fuel pressure regulator details**

1 Fuel pressure regulator
3 Large O-ring
4 Small O-ring

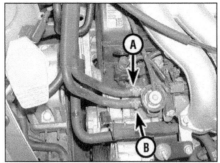

**16.5 Disconnect the fuel supply pipe (A) and the return pipe (B) from the fuel rail**

**16.6 Disconnect the electrical connectors from the fuel injectors, detach the wiring harness retainers and position the wiring harness aside**

lubricating them with a light film of engine oil **(see illustration)**. **Note:** *The small O-ring may remain in the fuel rail; recover and renew it.*

**6** Press the fuel pressure regulator into the fuel rail until fully seated and refit the retaining clip.

**7** The remainder of refitting is the reverse of removal.

## 16 Fuel rail and injectors – removal and refitting

> **Warning: See the Warning in Section 1.**

**Note:** *On 1.6L models, in order for new injectors to function correctly, they must be matched to the engine management ECM using a dealer scan tool.*

### Removal

**1** Relieve the fuel pressure (see Section 2).
**2** Remove the engine cover.
**3** On 1.6L and 2.0L models, remove the upper intake manifold (see Chapter 2A). Cover the lower intake manifold ports to prevent any foreign objects from entering the engine.
**4** Disconnect the vacuum hose from the fuel pressure regulator. Clearly label and remove any other vacuum hoses or electrical wiring that will interfere with the fuel rail removal.
**5** Disconnect the fuel inlet and return pipes from the fuel rail **(see illustration)**.

**6** Disconnect the fuel injector electrical connectors. Detach the wiring harness retainers from the fuel rail and position the harness aside **(see illustration)**. **Note:** *Apply a numbered tag to each connector with the corresponding cylinder number.*
**7** Clean any debris from around the injectors. Remove the fuel rail mounting bolts **(see illustration)**. Gently rock the fuel rail and injectors to loosen the injectors. Remove the fuel rail and fuel injectors as an assembly.
**8** Remove the retaining clip and remove the injector(s) from the fuel rail assembly **(see illustrations)**. Remove and discard the O-rings and seals. **Note:** *Whether you're renewing an injector or a leaking O-ring, it's a good idea to remove all the injectors from the fuel rail and renew all the O-rings.*

### Refitting

**9** Coat the new O-rings with clean engine oil and refit them on the injector(s), then insert each injector into its corresponding bore in the fuel rail. Refit the injector retaining clip.
**10** Refit the injector and fuel rail assembly on the intake manifold. Fully seat the injectors, then tighten the fuel rail mounting nuts to the torque listed in this Chapter's Specifications.
**11** Connect the fuel pipes and make sure they're securely fitted.
**12** Connect the electrical connectors to each injector, referring to the numbered tags.
**13** The remainder of refitting is the reverse of removal.

**14** After the injector/fuel rail assembly refitting is complete, turn the ignition switch to On, but don't operate the starter (this activates the fuel pump for about two seconds, which builds up fuel pressure in the fuel pipes and the fuel rail). Repeat this about two or three times, then check the fuel pipes, fuel rail and injectors for fuel leakage.

## 17 Intake manifold changeover valve – renewal

**1** 1.6L models are equipped with a variable length intake manifold as described in Section 1. Removal of the changeover valve and diaphragm is described below – further dismantling is not possible. In the event of apparent failure of the system, check the vacuum hoses for damage, and ensure that the operating rod is free to move – lubricate if necessary. In-depth testing of the system must be left to a VW dealer.

### Removal

**2** The changeover valve and vacuum diaphragm are located on the right-hand side of the intake manifold **(see illustration 1.1b)**. Remove the engine cover.
**3** Disconnect the vacuum hose from the valve or diaphragm unit, as applicable.
**4** The diaphragm unit operating rod has a ball-end fitting which is clipped into the operating rod on the manifold. Prise the end

**16.7 Remove the bolts (arrowed) securing the fuel rail to the intake manifold**

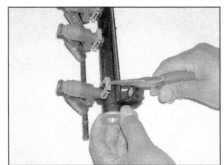

**16.8a Remove the injector retaining clip and pull the injector off the fuel rail**

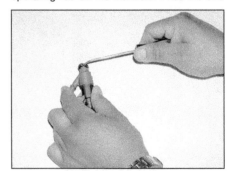

**16.8b Carefully remove the O-rings from the injector**

fitting out of the operating rod, and unclip the unit from its location.

**5** To remove the changeover valve, first disconnect the wiring plug from it.

**6** Unclip the valve from the underside of the intake manifold, and disconnect the vacuum hose as the valve is removed.

### Refitting

**7** Refitting is the reversal of removal.

---

## 18 Turbocharger and intercooler (1.8L turbo engine) – testing and renewal

### Testing

**1** The turbocharger is a precision component which can be severely damaged by a lack of lubrication or from foreign material entering the air intake duct. Turbocharger failure may be indicated by poor engine performance, blue/grey exhaust smoke or unusual noises

from the turbocharger. If a turbocharger failure is suspected, check the following areas:

   a) *Check the intake air duct for looseness or damage. Make sure there are no restrictions in the air intake system, dirty air filter element or damaged intercooler.*

   b) *Check the system vacuum hoses for restrictions or damage.*

   c) *Check the system wiring for damage and electrical connectors for looseness or corrosion.*

   d) *Make sure the wastegate actuator linkage is not binding.*

   e) *Check the exhaust system for damage or restrictions.*

   f) *Check the lubricating oil supply and return pipes for damage or restrictions.*

   g) *Check the coolant supply and return pipes for damage and restrictions.*

   h) *If the turbocharger requires renewal due to failure, be sure to change the engine oil and filter (see Chapter 1).*

**2** Complete diagnosis of the turbocharger and control system require special techniques and equipment. If the previous checks fail to identify the problem, take the vehicle to a dealership service department or other properly equipped repair facility for diagnosis.

### Renewal

#### Turbocharger

> ⚠ *Warning: Wait until the engine is completely cool before beginning this procedure.*

**3** Drain the cooling system (see Chapter 1).

**4** Remove the engine cover.

**5** Remove the scuttle panel (see Chapter 11).

**6** Raise the vehicle and support it securely on axle stands.

**7** Remove the engine compartment undercover.

**8** Remove the nuts securing the exhaust pipe to the turbocharger **(see illustration)**. Remove the exhaust support bolts, as necessary and lower the exhaust pipe.

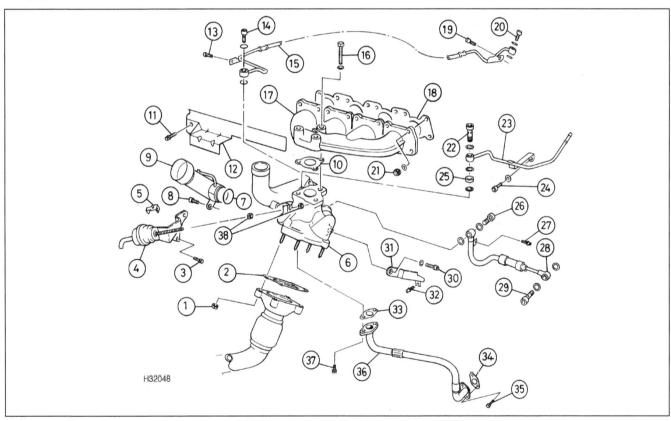

H32048

**18.8 Turbocharger and related components**

| | | | |
|---|---|---|---|
| *1 Exhaust downpipe nuts* | *11 Heat shield mounting bolt* | *20 Banjo bolt* | *30 Turbocharger-to-support* |
| *2 Exhaust downpipe gasket* | *12 Heat shield* | *21 Mounting bolts* | *bracket bolt* |
| *3 Wastegate bracket bolt* | *13 Mounting bolt* | *22 Banjo bolt* | *31 Turbocharger support bracket* |
| *4 Wastegate* | *14 Banjo bolt* | *23 Coolant return pipe* | *32 Support bracket bolt* |
| *5 Clip* | *15 Oil supply pipe* | *24 Mounting bolt* | *33 Gasket* |
| *6 Turbocharger* | *16 Turbocharger mounting* | *25 Spacer sleeve* | *34 Gasket* |
| *7 O-ring* | *bolts* | *26 Banjo bolt* | *35 Oil return pipe flange bolt* |
| *8 Mounting bolt* | *17 Exhaust manifold* | *27 Mounting bolt* | *36 Oil return pipe* |
| *9 Air inlet pipe stub* | *18 Manifold gasket* | *28 Coolant supply pipe* | *37 Oil return pipe flange bolt* |
| *10 Gasket* | *19 Mounting bolt* | *29 Banjo bolt* | *38 Wastegate setting/locknuts* |

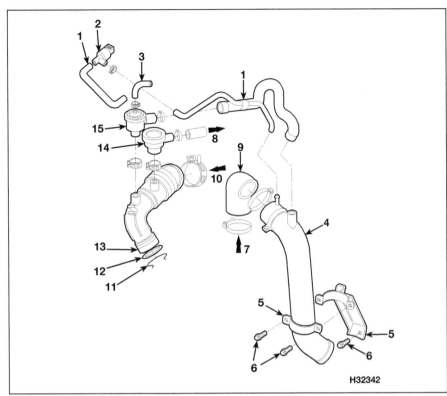

**18.12 Turbocharger connecting pipes**

1 Hose
2 Wastegate regulator valve
3 Vacuum hose
4 Turbocharger outlet pipe
5 Support bracket
6 Bolt

7 Airflow from turbocharger
8 Airflow from crankcase
   ventilation housing
9 Elbow
10 Airflow from air filter
11 Retaining ring

12 O-ring
13 Intake hose
14 Crankcase pressure
   regulating valve
15 Overrun recirculation
   valve

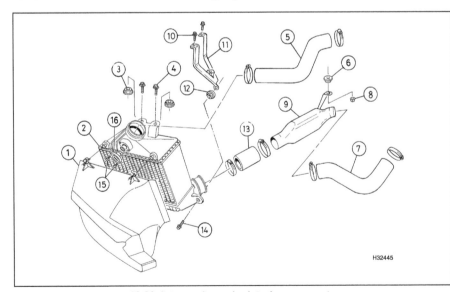

**18.20 Intercooler and related components**

1 Air deflector
2 Intercooler
3 Grommet
4 Bolt
5 Intercooler-to-intake
   manifold pipe

6 Grommet
7 Hose
8 Nut
9 Turbocharger-to-
   intercooler pipe
10 Bolt

11 Support bracket
12 Grommet
13 Hose
14 Bolt
15 Bolt
16 Boost pressure sensor

**9** Disconnect the vacuum hose from the wastegate actuator.

**10** Remove the turbocharger support bracket.

**11** Remove the bolts and disconnect the oil return pipe from the turbocharger.

**12** Disconnect the hoses from the recirculation valve and crankcase breather valve on the air intake duct. Loosen the intake duct clamp at the air filter and separate the duct from the air filter assembly. Remove the retaining clip, disconnect the air intake duct from the turbocharger intake and remove the duct **(see illustration)**.

**13** Loosen the clamps, remove the bracket bolts and remove the turbocharger outlet pipe and elbow.

**14** Loosen the coolant return pipe union bolt at the turbocharger. Remove the bracket bolt and disconnect the coolant return pipe from the turbocharger. Be sure to recover the sealing washers and spacer.

**15** Loosen the oil supply union bolt from the turbocharger. Remove the bracket bolt from the heat shield and disconnect the oil supply pipe from the turbocharger.

**16** Remove the heat shield.

**17** Remove the turbocharger-to-exhaust manifold bolts. Lower the turbocharger, tilt it to the side, loosen the coolant supply pipe union bolt and disconnect the coolant supply pipe from the turbocharger.

**18** Remove the turbocharger from the engine compartment. **Note:** *The manufacturer recommends renewing the turbocharger/ exhaust manifold as a unit only.*

**19** Refitting is the reverse of removal with the following additions:

  a) *Renew all gaskets, seals, union bolt washers and self-locking nuts.*

  b) *Tighten the turbocharger mounting bolts to the torque listed in this Chapter's Specifications.*

  c) *Change the oil and filter (see Chapter 1).*

  d) *Before starting the engine, remove the fuel pump fuse from the fusebox and crank the engine over until oil pressure builds.*

### Intercooler

**20** The intercooler is located in the lower section of the right front wing ahead of the front wheel **(see illustration)**.

**21** Loosen the right front wheel bolts, then raise the vehicle and support it securely on axle stands.

**22** Remove the right front wheel.

**23** Remove the retainers and remove the right front wheelarch liner (see Chapter 11, Section 13, Step 3).

**24** Remove the right direction indicator lamp housing (see Chapter 12). Working through the direction indicator opening, disconnect the boost pressure sensor electrical connector, loosen the hose clamp and disconnect the outlet air duct from the intercooler **(see illustration)**.

**25** Loosen the hose clamps and disconnect the air inlet duct from the intercooler.

**26** Remove the mounting bolts and remove

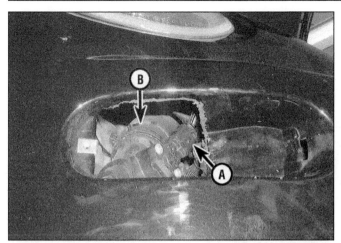

**18.24 Working through the direction indicator lamp opening, disconnect the boost pressure sensor electrical connector (A) and the outlet duct hose clamp (B)**

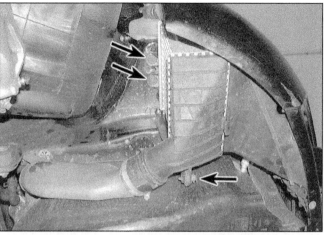

**18.26 Remove the mounting colts (arrowed) and remove the intercooler and air deflector from the wheelarch**

the intercooler and air deflector from the wheelarch **(see illustration)**. Detach the air deflector from the intercooler.
**27** Refitting is the reverse of removal.

## 19 Exhaust system servicing – general information

⚠️ *Warning: Inspection and repair of exhaust system components should be done only after enough time has elapsed after driving the vehicle to allow the system components to cool completely. Also, when working under the vehicle, make sure it is securely supported on axle stands.*

**1** The exhaust system consists of the exhaust manifold, catalytic converter, silencer, resonators, the tailpipe, and all connecting pipes, brackets and clamps. The exhaust system is attached to the body with mounting brackets and rubber mountings. If any of the parts are improperly fitted, excessive noise and vibration will be transmitted to the body.

### Silencer and pipes

**2** Conduct regular inspections of the exhaust system to keep it safe and quiet. Look for any damaged or bent parts, open seams, holes, loose connections, excessive corrosion or other defects which could allow exhaust fumes to enter the vehicle **(see illustrations)**. Also check the catalytic converter when you inspect the exhaust system (see below). Deteriorated exhaust system components should not be repaired; they should be renewed.
**3** If the exhaust system components are extremely corroded or rusted together, welding equipment will probably be required to remove them. The convenient way to accomplish this is to have a garage remove the corroded sections with a cutting torch. If,

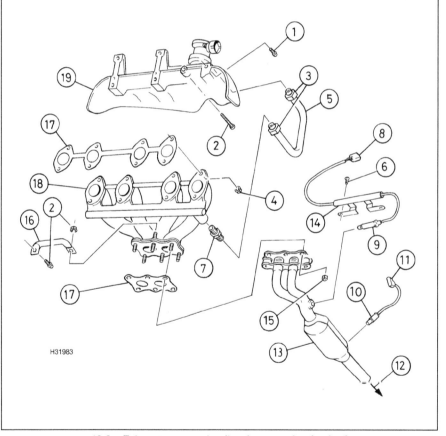

**19.2a Exhaust system details – front section (typical)**

1 Heat shield bolt
2 Mounting nut/bolt
3 Union nut
4 Exhaust manifold mounting nut
5 Secondary air injection pipe
6 Wiring mounting bracket bolt
7 Secondary air injection pipe union
8 Oxygen sensor wiring plug
9 Oxygen sensor (pre-catalyst)
10 Oxygen sensor wiring plug
11 Oxygen sensor (post-catalyst)
12 To centre silencer
13 Catalyst
14 Wiring guide tube
15 Manifold-to-downpipe nut
16 Manifold support bracket
17 Gasket
18 Exhaust manifold
19 Heat shield

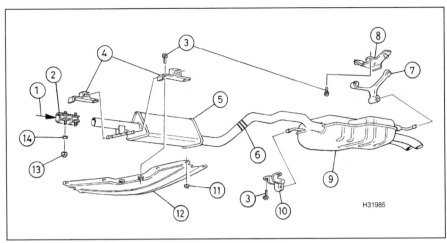

**19.2b Exhaust system details – rear section**

1 From front section
2 Exhaust clamp
3 Mounting bolts
4 Front mounting-to-cradle
5 Centre silencer

6 Centre marking for cutting point
7 Rear silencer rear mounting
8 Bracket
9 Rear silencer

10 Rear silencer front mounting
11 Cradle-to-floor nut
12 Cradle
13 Clamp nut
14 Washer

however, you want to save money by doing it yourself (and you don't have a welding outfit with a cutting torch), simply cut the exhaust pipes with a hacksaw at the separation point. If you do decide to tackle the job at home, be sure to wear safety goggles to protect your eyes from metal chips and work gloves to protect your hands.

4 Here are some simple guidelines to follow when repairing the exhaust system:

a) Work from the back to the front when removing exhaust system components.
b) Apply penetrating oil to the exhaust system component fasteners to make them easier to remove.
c) Use new gaskets, mounting rubbers and clamps when refitting exhaust system components.
d) Apply high-temperature anti-seize compound to the threads of all exhaust system fasteners during reassembly.
e) Be sure to allow sufficient clearance between newly fitted parts and all points on the underbody to avoid overheating the floor pan and possibly damaging the interior carpet and insulation. Pay particularly close attention to the catalytic converter and heat shield.

## Catalytic converter

 **Warning: The converter gets very hot during operation. Make sure it has cooled down before you touch it.**

**Note:** See Chapter 6A for additional information on the catalytic converter.

5 Periodically inspect the heat shield for cracks, dents and loose or missing fasteners.
6 Inspect the converter for cracks or other damage.
7 If the catalytic converter requires renewal, refer to Chapter 6A.

# Chapter 4 Part B:
# Fuel and exhaust systems: Diesel engine

## Contents

## Degrees of difficulty

| Easy, suitable for novice with little experience  | Fairly easy, suitable for beginner with some experience  | Fairly difficult, suitable for competent DIY mechanic 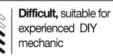 | Difficult, suitable for experienced DIY mechanic 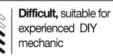 | Very difficult, suitable for expert DIY or professional 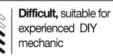 |
|---|---|---|---|---|

## Specifications

### General

| | |
|---|---|
| Engine code by type* | |
|    Electronic direct injection, turbocharged . . . . . . . . . . . . . . . . . . . | ALH |
|    Electronic direct injection, unit injectors, turbocharged . . . . . . . . . | ATD and AXR |
| Firing order . . . . . . . . . . . . . . . . . . . . . . . . . . . . . . . . . . . . . . . . . . . . . | 1-3-4-2 |
| Maximum engine speed . . . . . . . . . . . . . . . . . . . . . . . . . . . . . . . . . . . . | N/A (ECM controlled) |
| Engine idle speed (ECM controlled) | |
|    Code ALH . . . . . . . . . . . . . . . . . . . . . . . . . . . . . . . . . . . . . . . . . . . . | 900 ± 30 rpm |
|    Code ATD and AXR | |
|       Manual transmission . . . . . . . . . . . . . . . . . . . . . . . . . . . . . . . | 860 to 940 rpm |
|       Automatic transmission . . . . . . . . . . . . . . . . . . . . . . . . . . . . | 790 to 870 rpm |
| Engine fast idle speed (ECM controlled) . . . . . . . . . . . . . . . . . . . . . . | N/A |

*\* Note: See 'Vehicle identification' for the location of the code marking on the engine.*

### Fuel injectors

| | |
|---|---|
| Injection pressure | |
|    Engine code ALH . . . . . . . . . . . . . . . . . . . . . . . . . . . . . . . . . . . . . . | 200 bar minimum |
|    Engine codes ATD and AXR . . . . . . . . . . . . . . . . . . . . . . . . . . . . . | 180 to 2050 bar |

### Tandem pump

| | |
|---|---|
| Fuel pressure at 1500 rpm . . . . . . . . . . . . . . . . . . . . . . . . . . . . . . . . . | 3.5 bar |

### Turbocharger

| | |
|---|---|
| Type . . . . . . . . . . . . . . . . . . . . . . . . . . . . . . . . . . . . . . . . . . . . . . . . . . | Garrett or KKK |

## Torque specifications

| | Nm | Ft-lbs |
|---|---|---|
| EGR pipe flange bolts | 25 | 18 |
| EGR valve mounting bolts | | |
|     Engine code ALH | 25 | 18 |
|     Engine codes ATD and AXR | 10 | 7 |
| Fuel cut-off solenoid valve | 40 | 30 |
| Fuel pump return pipe cap nut | 25 | 18 |
| Injection pump head fuel union stubs (engine code ALH) | 45 | 33 |
| Injection pump sprocket (engine code ALH) | | |
|     Step 1 | 20 | 15 |
|     Step 2 | Angle-tighten a further 90° | |
| Injection pump-to-support bracket bolts (engine code ALH) | 25 | 18 |
| Injector clamp bolt | | |
|     Engine code ALH | 20 | 15 |
|     Engine codes ATD and AXR* | | |
|         Step 1 | 12 | 9 |
|         Step 2 | Angle-tighten a further 270° | |
| Injector pipe union nut (engine code ALH) | 25 | 18 |
| Inlet manifold flap housing to manifold | 10 | 7 |
| Inlet manifold to cylinder head | 25 | 18 |
| Pump injector rocker shaft bolts (engine codes ATD and AXR)* | | |
|     Step 1 | 20 | 15 |
|     Step 2 | Angle-tighten a further 90° | |
| Tandem pump bolts | | |
|     Upper | 20 | 15 |
|     Lower | 10 | 7 |
| Turbocharger oil return pipe to cylinder block | | |
|     Engine code ALH | 30 | 22 |
|     Engine codes ATD and AXR | 40 | 30 |
| Turbocharger to catalytic converter | 25 | 18 |
| Turbocharger to exhaust manifold* | 25 | 18 |

*Use new fasteners*

---

## 1  General information

 **Warning 1: Diesel fuel isn't as volatile as petrol, but it is flammable, so take extra precautions when you work on any part of the fuel system. Don't smoke or allow naked flames or bare light bulbs near the work area. Don't work in a garage or other enclosed space where there is a gas-type appliance (such as a water heater or clothes dryer). Avoid direct skin contact with diesel fuel – wear protective clothing, safety glasses and gloves when handling fuel system components and have a Class B fire extinguisher on hand. Ensure that the work area is well ventilated to prevent the build-up of diesel fuel vapour.**

 **Warning 2: Fuel injectors operate at extremely high pressures and the jet of fuel produced at the nozzle is capable of piercing skin, with potentially fatal results. When working with pressurised injectors, take great to avoid exposing any part of the body to the fuel spray. It is recommended that any pressure testing of the fuel system**

**components should be carried out by a diesel fuel systems specialist.**
**Caution: Under no circumstances should diesel fuel be allowed to come into contact with coolant hoses, wiring or rubber components – wipe off accidental spillage immediately. Hoses that have been contaminated with fuel for an extended period should be renewed. Diesel fuel systems are particularly sensitive to contamination from dirt, air and water. Pay particular attention to cleanliness when working on any part of the fuel system, to prevent the entry of dirt. Thoroughly clean the area around fuel unions before disconnecting them. Store dismantled components in sealed containers to prevent contamination and the formation of condensation. Only use lint-free cloths and clean fuel for component cleansing. Avoid using compressed air when cleaning components in place.**

### General information

Two different diesel fuel injection systems are fitted to the range of engines covered by this manual. Whilst both are direct injection systems, the difference lies in how the fuel is delivered to the injectors. Both systems consist of a fuel tank, an engine-bay mounted fuel filter with an integral water separator, fuel supply and return lines and four fuel injectors.

On engine code ALH, the fuel is pressurised by an injection pump, and commencement of injection is controlled by the engine control module (ECM) and a solenoid valve on the injection pump. The pump is driven at half crankshaft speed by the camshaft timing belt. Fuel is drawn from the fuel tank and through the filter by the injection pump, which then distributes the fuel under very high pressure to the injectors through separate delivery pipes. On engine codes ATD and AXR, the fuel is delivered by a camshaft driven 'tandem pump' at low pressure to the injectors (known as 'Unit injectors'). A 'roller rocker' assembly, mounted above the camshaft bearing caps, uses an extra set of camshaft lobes to compress the top of each injector once per firing cycle. This arrangement creates far higher injection pressures. The precise timing of the pre-injection and main injection is controlled by the engine management ECM and a solenoid on each injector. The resultant effect of this system is improved engine torque and power output, greater combustion efficiency, and lower exhaust emissions. All engines are fitted with a turbocharger.

The direct-injection fuelling system is controlled electronically by a diesel engine management system, consists of an Electronic Control Module (ECM) and its associated sensors, actuators and wiring.

1.6a  Vacuum reservoir for inlet manifold flap valve

1.6b  Vacuum capsule on inlet manifold below EGR valve

Refer to Chapter 6B for information regarding the electronic engine control system.

On engine code ALH, basic injection timing is set mechanically by the position of the pump on its mounting bracket. Dynamic timing and injection duration are controlled by the ECM and are dependent on engine speed, throttle position and rate of opening, inlet air flow, inlet air temperature, coolant temperature, fuel temperature, ambient pressure (altitude) and manifold depression information, received from sensors mounted on and around the engine. Closed loop control of the injection timing is achieved by means of an injector needle lift sensor. Note that injector No 3 is fitted with the needle lift sensor. Two-stage injectors are used, which improve the engine's combustion characteristics, leading to quieter running and better exhaust emissions.

In addition, the ECM manages the operation of the Exhaust Gas Recirculation (EGR) emission control and turbocharger boost pressure control systems (Chapter 6B), and the glow plug control system (Chapter 5).

A flap valve fitted to the inlet manifold is closed by the ECM for 3 seconds as the engine is switched off, to minimise the air intake as the engine shuts down. This minimises the vibration felt as the pistons come up against the volume of highly-compressed air present in the combustion chambers. A vacuum reservoir mounted on the front of the engine provides the vacuum supply to a vacuum capsule which operates the flap **(see illustrations)**.

The exhaust system consists of an exhaust manifold, a catalytic converter, an exhaust pipe and a silencer. Each of these components is renewable. For further information regarding the catalytic converter, refer to Chapter 6A.

It should be noted that fault diagnosis of the diesel engine management system is only possible with dedicated electronic test equipment. Problems with the system's operation should therefore be referred to a VW dealer or suitably-equipped specialist for assessment. Once the fault has been identified, the removal/refitting sequences detailed in the following Sections will then allow the appropriate component(s) to be renewed as required.

## 2  Electronic accelerator system – general information

All diesel models are equipped with an electronically-controlled accelerator system. The system consists of the throttle position sensor (located at the throttle pedal), the fuel injection pump (engine code ALH only) and the ECM. On later models, the throttle position sensor and accelerator pedal are combined into a single module. The system does not use the traditional accelerator cable.

The engine speed of a diesel engine is governed by the amount of fuel injected into each cylinder, the more fuel injected, the faster the engine runs.

On non-PD models (engine code ALH), the fuel injection pump contains an electronic component known as the fuel quantity adjuster. The fuel quantity adjuster varies the amount of fuel delivered to the fuel injectors. The ECM controls the fuel quantity adjuster based on the voltage signal received from the throttle position sensor. Refer to Chapter 6B for more information on the throttle position sensor and the fuel quantity adjuster.

On PD models (engine codes ATD and AXR), the quantity of fuel is controlled electronically by the ECM.

## 3  Fuel shut-off valve – testing and renewal

**Note:** Engine code ALH only.

⚠ **Warning: Observe the precautions in Section 1 before working on any component of the fuel system.**

## Testing

1 The fuel shut-off valve shuts fuel off from the fuel injection pump when the ignition key is turned Off, stopping the engine from running. The ECM controls the fuel shut-off valve, supplying battery power to the valve when the ignition key is operated. A faulty fuel shut-off valve would not allow the engine to start, or conversely, not allow the engine to shut down when the ignition key is switched off. The fuel shut-off valve is located on the fuel injection pump **(see illustration 8.3)**.

2 To check the fuel shut-off valve, connect a 12 volt test light or voltmeter to the electrical terminal on the valve. Have an assistant turn the ignition key On – voltage should be indicated on the light or meter and you should hear the valve click.

3 If voltage is not indicated, check the wiring from the valve to the ECM. If the wiring is good, have the ECM checked at a dealer service department or other properly-equipped repair facility.

4 If voltage is indicated but the valve did not click, the valve is probably defective. Remove the valve, spring and plunger and check the plunger for freedom of movement in the valve. If the plunger binds in the valve, renew the valve. Also, check the bore in the injection pump for foreign material that may cause the valve to bind in the injection pump.

## Renewal

5 Clean the area around the fuel shut-off valve and place a cloth towel around the valve to absorb the fuel.

6 Disconnect the electrical terminal from the valve.

7 Remove the valve from the fuel injection pump.

8 Refit the valve with a new O-ring. Tighten the valve to the torque listed in this Chapter's Specifications and clean up the fuel.

9 Connect the electrical terminal to the valve.

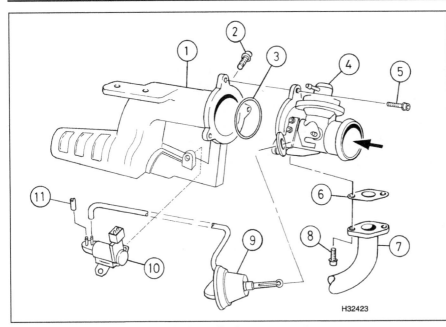

**4.1 Air shut-off valve components**

1 Intake manifold
2 Bolt
3 O-ring
4 Intake manifold inlet flange (with EGR valve and air shut-off valve flap)
5 Bolt
6 Gasket
7 EGR pipe
8 Bolt
9 Air shut-off valve actuator
10 Air shut-off valve vacuum valve/solenoid
11 Vacuum hose

## 4 Air shut-off valve – testing and renewal

### Testing

1 The air shut-off valve closes off the intake air passage when the engine is shut down. Cutting off the air reduces the shock associated with shutting down a diesel engine. The air shut-off valve is comprised of three components; the valve flap in the intake manifold flange, the valve actuator and the vacuum valve/solenoid **(see illustration)**. The ECM controls the vacuum valve/solenoid. When the ignition key is turned off, the ECM energises the vacuum valve/solenoid and

vacuum is applied to the valve actuator, opening the flap in the intake manifold flange. After approximately three seconds from shutting the engine down, the ECM de-energises the vacuum valve/solenoid, vacuum is vented and the air valve opens.

2 If a problem is suspected with the air shut-off valve, check the vacuum supply to the vacuum valve/solenoid. Vacuum should be present with the engine running. Check the actuator and linkage for binding. Disconnect the vacuum hose from the actuator and apply vacuum to the actuator with a hand-held vacuum pump. Make sure the actuator opens and closes the valve flap.

3 Disconnect the electrical connector from the vacuum valve/solenoid. Using an ohmmeter, measure the resistance across the

two terminals of the valve/solenoid **(see illustration)**. The valve/solenoid resistance should be 25 to 45 ohms; if it isn't, renew the vacuum valve/solenoid.

### Renewal

#### Air valve flap

**Note:** *The air valve flap is incorporated into the intake manifold flange along with the EGR valve. If the air valve flap is defective, the entire flange must be renewed.*

4 Disconnect the vacuum hose from the EGR valve.
5 Disconnect the linkage from the air valve actuator.
6 Remove the intake hose from the flange.
7 Remove the bolts and disconnect the EGR pipe from the flange.
8 Remove the flange mounting bolts and remove the flange.
9 Refitting is the reverse of removal, using a new O-ring seal and EGR pipe gasket.

#### Air valve actuator

10 Disconnect the vacuum hose from the actuator.
11 Disconnect the actuator linkage from the air valve flap.
12 Remove the actuator from the flange.
13 Refitting is the reverse of removal.

#### Vacuum valve/solenoid

14 Disconnect the electrical connector from the vacuum valve/solenoid.
15 Disconnect the vacuum hoses from the vacuum valve/solenoid.
16 Remove the mounting bolts and remove the vacuum valve/solenoid from the intake manifold.
17 Refitting is the reverse of removal.

## 5 Cold start valve – testing and renewal

**Note:** *Engine code ALH only.*

⚠ **Warning: Observe the precautions in Section 1 before working on any component of the fuel system.**

### Testing

1 The cold start valve advances the fuel injection timing during cold starts. The cold start valve is located on the fuel injection pump **(see illustration 8.3)**. A problem with the valve or circuit may cause unstable engine idle (timing advanced) or loss of power (timing retarded).
2 Disconnect the fuel injection pump electrical connector. Using an ohmmeter, measure the resistance across terminals 9 and 10 at the connector on the fuel injection pump side **(see illustration)**. The cold start valve resistance should be 12 to 20 ohms, renew the valve if it isn't.

### Renewal

3 Clean the area around the cold start valve

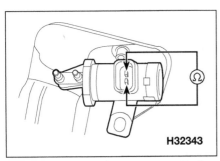

**4.3 Measure the resistance across the two terminals of the air shut-off valve vacuum valve/solenoid**

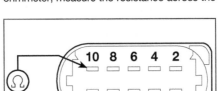

**5.2 To check the cold start valve, measure the resistance across terminals No 9 and 10 of the fuel injection pump electrical connector**

and place a cloth towel around the valve to absorb the fuel.

**4** Remove the mounting screws and remove the valve from the fuel injection pump.

**5** Refit the valve with new O-rings and clean-up the fuel.

## 6 Fuel injection system – general information

The fuel injection system consists of three sub-systems: air intake, engine control and fuel delivery. The system uses an Engine Control Module (ECM) along with the sensors (coolant temperature sensor, throttle position sensor, mass airflow sensor, engine speed sensor, etc) to determine the proper fuel delivery rate under all operating conditions.

The fuel injection system and the engine control system are closely linked in function and design. For additional information, refer to Chapter 6B.

### Air intake system

The air intake system consists of the air filter, the air intake ducts, the air shut-off valve, the turbocharger, the intercooler and the intake manifold.

There is no restriction device, such as a throttle plate, used in a diesel engine. Each cylinder draws in the maximum amount of air. In a turbocharged diesel engine, such as this one, the intake manifold is pressurised by an exhaust-driven turbocharger, forcing the air into each cylinder.

The air shut-off valve is a flap in the intake manifold inlet that closes when the engine is shut down. Cutting-off the air prior to shutting-off the fuel reduces the shock associated with diesel engine shut down.

### Emissions and engine control system

The emissions and engine control system is described in detail in Chapter 6B.

### Fuel delivery system

Fuel is drawn from the fuel tank and through the fuel filter by the fuel injection pump (engine code ALH) or tandem fuel pump (engine codes ATD and AXR) – no other fuel pump is used. Refer to Section 1 for more information.

## 7 Fuel delivery system – testing

> ⚠ **Warning: Observe the precautions in Section 1 before working on any component of the fuel system.**

**1** If the engine is hard to start or unable to start and you suspect a fuel delivery problem, perform the following test to verify fuel is reaching the fuel injectors.

**2** Check for fuel leaks at the injection pump/tandem fuel pump, fuel pipes, fittings and injectors. If a leak is detected it must be repaired before proceeding.

**3** The following check is only possible on engine code ALH (non-PD engine). Clean the area around the number one fuel injector pipe fitting. Using a flare-nut spanner, loosen the fitting approximately one-half turn. Wrap a cloth towel around the fitting to absorb the fuel and crank the engine with the starter. If a steady stream of fuel is discharged from the injector fitting, the fuel delivery system is functioning properly.

**4** If necessary, check the following items:

a) *Check for fuel in the tank.*
b) *Check the fuel shut-off valve (see Section 3).*
c) *Check the fuel pipes from the fuel tank to the fuel injection pump for an air leak or restriction.*
d) *Check the fuel filter for a restriction.*
e) *Check for an engine mechanical problem, such as a broken timing belt.*

**5** If all the items listed are good, have the fuel injection system checked at a dealer service department or other properly-equipped repair facility.

**6** Where applicable, tighten the fuel injector pipe fitting and clean-up the fuel.

## 8 Fuel injection pump – removal and refitting

**Note 1:** *This Section only applies to engine code ALH.*

> ⚠ **Warning: Observe the precautions in Section 1 before working on any component of the fuel system.**

**Note 2:** *Special tools are required to perform this procedure. Obtain the tools before beginning work.*

**Note 3:** *After pump refitting, final fuel injection pump timing must be checked with the engine running using the manufacturer's scan tool (or equivalent) and adjusted, if necessary. If the proper scan tool is not available, complete the procedure and drive the vehicle to a dealer service department or other properly-equipped repair facility for the final injection pump timing procedure.*

### Removal

**1** Disconnect the fuel injection pump electrical connector and remove the wire terminal from the fuel shut-off valve.

**2** Remove the fuel supply hose from the fuel injection pump. Cap the fitting of the pump and plug the hose.

**3** Loosen the fuel pipe fittings at the fuel injectors and fuel injection pump **(see illustration)**. Remove the fuel pipes as an

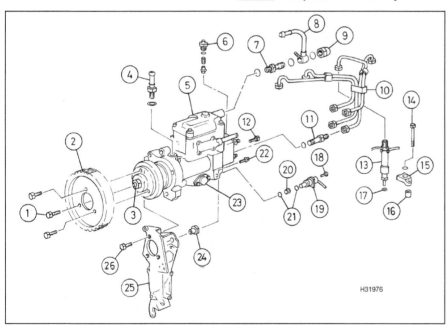

H31976

**8.3 Fuel injection pump and fuel injector components**

| | | |
|---|---|---|
| 1 Sprocket bolts | 10 Injector pipe assembly | 18 Mounting bolt |
| 2 Injection pump sprocket | 11 Injector pipe connection | 19 Cold start valve |
| 3 Hub nut (do not loosen) | 12 Injection pump bracket bolt | 20 Strainer |
| 4 Fuel supply connection | 13 No 3 injector (with needle | 21 O-ring |
| 5 Injection pump | lift sensor) | 22 Injection pump bracket bolt |
| 6 Fuel shut-off solenoid valve | 14 Injector retaining bolt | 23 Timing control cover |
| 7 Fuel return connection | 15 Retainer plate | 24 Sleeve nut |
| 8 Fuel return pipe | 16 Mounting sleeve | 25 Mounting bracket |
| 9 Union nut | 17 Heat shield | 26 Mounting bolt |

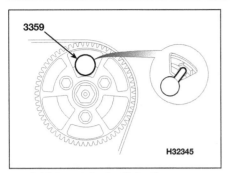

8.10 Insert the fuel injection pump sprocket alignment pin through the slot in the sprocket hub

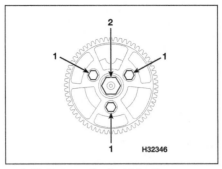

8.13 Remove the fuel injection pump sprocket bolts (1) – DO NOT loosen the centre hub nut (2)

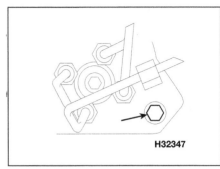

8.14 Remove the fuel injection pump support bracket bolt

assembly. Be very careful not to bend a high-pressure fuel pipe.

4 Cap the fittings on the fuel injection pump and cap all the injectors to prevent contamination.

5 Remove the intercooler-to-intake manifold air duct (see Section 10).

6 Remove the valve cover and the timing belt upper cover (see Chapter 2C).

7 Remove the vacuum pump (see Chapter 9).

8 Position the engine with number one cylinder at TDC (see Chapter 2C).

9 Lock the camshaft in position with a special setting bar (see Chapter 2C).

10 Lock the fuel injection pump sprocket in position with the special alignment pin (see illustration).

11 Loosen the camshaft sprocket bolt one-half turn. Using a brass drift inserted through the hole in the rear timing belt cover, tap the sprocket until the sprocket is loose on the camshaft taper.

12 Loosen the timing belt tension (see Chapter 2C) and slip the timing belt off the fuel injection pump sprocket.

13 If the original pump is to be reinstalled, scribe a mark on the sprocket around each fuel injection pump sprocket bolt head. Remove the fuel injection pump sprocket bolts (see illustration). Remove the alignment pin and remove the sprocket.

Caution: Do not loosen the centre hub nut on the fuel injection pump. If the centre hub nut is inadvertently loosened and the

hub moved, the fuel injection pump must be sent to a qualified fuel injection repair facility for recalibration.

14 Remove the fuel injection pump support bracket bolt (see illustration).

15 Remove the fuel injection pump mounting bolts and remove the pump (see illustration). Note: If the original pump is to be reinstalled, cap all fuel pipe fittings and store the pump so the fuel will not drain out.

## Refitting

16 Refit the pump onto the engine and tighten the pump mounting bolts hand-tight. Tighten the support bracket bolt first, then tighten the pump mounting bolts to the torque listed in this Chapter's Specifications.

17 Refit the pump sprocket onto the pump hub. Fit new sprocket bolts and tighten them hand-tight. Refit the pump alignment pin (see illustration 8.10). If refitting the original pump align the pump bolts with the marks made in Step 13. If refitting a new pump, centre the bolt heads in the sprocket slots. Tighten the bolts to the torque listed in this Chapter's Specifications. Note: If a scan tool is available for the final fuel injection pump timing check, tighten the bolts to the first step (20 Nm/15 Ft-lbs) at this time. Tighten the bolts to the final torque after adjusting the fuel injection pump timing.

18 Make sure the engine is positioned with number one cylinder at TDC, the camshaft is locked in position and the camshaft sprocket

is loose on the shaft. Refit and tension the timing belt (see Chapter 2C).

19 Tighten the camshaft sprocket bolt to the torque listed in the Chapter 2C Specifications.

20 Remove the fuel injection pump sprocket alignment pin and the camshaft setting bar. Using a breaker bar and socket on the crankshaft pulley bolt, rotate the engine two complete revolutions and recheck the timing belt tension.

21 Refit the fuel injection pipes and the fuel supply pipe. Connect the electrical connectors to the pump.

22 Refit the valve cover and the vacuum pump. Refit the timing belt upper cover (unless a scan tool is available to check the injection pump timing).

23 Refit the intake air duct.

24 If installing a new fuel injection pump, remove the fuel return pipe port fitting and connect a hand-held vacuum pump to the fuel injection pump using clear section of hose and the appropriate adapter (see illustration). Using the vacuum pump, draw fuel into the fuel injection pump until fuel is visible exiting the fuel injection pump. Do not draw fuel into a plastic vacuum pump or the pump may be damaged.

Caution: Do not attempt to start the engine without priming a dry pump first or damage to the fuel injection pump will occur.

25 Remove the vacuum pump and adapter and refit the fuel return pipe.

26 Start the engine and check for fuel leaks at the fuel pipes.

27 If a scan tool is available, connect the scan tool, start the engine and check and adjust the fuel injection pump timing following the instructions provided with the scan tool. After completing the timing procedure, refit the timing belt upper cover.

28 If a scan tool is not available, drive the vehicle to a dealer service department or other properly-equipped repair facility and have the fuel injection pump timing checked and adjusted. Note: It will be necessary for the repair facility to renew the fuel injection pump sprocket bolts if timing adjustment is required.

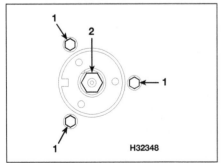

8.15 Remove the fuel injection pump mounting bolts (1) – DO NOT loosen the centre hub nut (2)

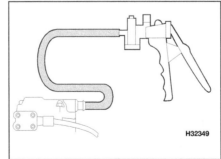

8.24 If the fuel injection pump is dry, connect a hand-held vacuum pump to the return pipe fitting and draw fuel into the fuel injection pump

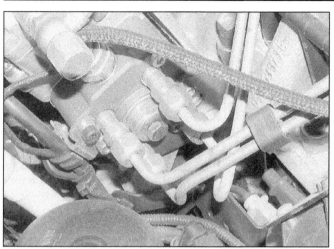

9.7 View of injector pipe union nuts at injection pump

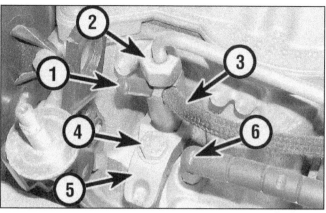

9.10 View of No 1 injector

1 End cap
2 Union nut
3 Leak-off pipe

4 Retaining bolt
5 Retaining plate

6 Glow plug wiring
   connector

## 9 Fuel injectors –
removal and refitting

> **Warning: Exercise extreme caution when working on the fuel injectors. Never expose the hands or any part of the body to injector spray, as the high working pressure can cause the fuel to penetrate the skin, with possibly fatal results. You are strongly advised to have any work which involves testing the injectors under pressure carried out by a dealer or fuel injection specialist. Refer to the precautions given in Section 1 of this Chapter before proceeding.**

### General information

1 Injectors deteriorate with prolonged use, and it is reasonable to expect them to need reconditioning or renewal after 60 000 miles or so. Accurate testing, overhaul and calibration of the injectors must be left to a specialist.
2 A defective injector which is causing knocking or smoking can be located without dismantling as follows.
3 Run the engine at a fast idle. Slacken each

injector union in turn, placing rag around the union to catch spilt fuel and being careful not to expose the skin to any spray. When the union on the defective injector is slackened, the knocking or smoking will stop. **Note:** *This test is not possible on engines fitted with unit injectors (engine codes ATD and AXR).*

### Removal

**Note:** *Take care not to allow dirt into the injectors or fuel pipes during this procedure. Do not drop the injectors or allow the needles at their tips to become damaged. The injectors are precision-made to fine limits, and must not be handled roughly.*

#### Engine code ALH

4 Cover the alternator with a clean cloth or plastic bag, to protect it from any fuel being spilt onto it.
5 Carefully clean around the injectors and pipe union nuts.
6 Disconnect the return pipe from the injector.
7 Wipe clean the pipe unions, then slacken the union nut securing the relevant injector pipes to each injector and the relevant union nuts securing the pipes to the rear of the injection pump (the pipes are removed as one assembly); as each pump union nut is

slackened, retain the adapter with a suitable open-ended spanner to prevent it being unscrewed from the pump **(see illustration)**.
8 With the union nuts undone, remove the injector pipes from the engine. Cover the injector and pipe unions to prevent the entry of dirt into the system.

> **HAYNES HiNT** *Cut the fingertips from an old rubber glove and secure them over the open unions with elastic bands to prevent dirt ingress.*

9 Disconnect the wiring for the needle lift sender from injector No 3.
10 Unscrew and remove the retaining nut or bolt, and recover the washer, retaining plate and mounting collar **(see illustration)**. Note the fitted position of all components, for use when refitting. Withdraw the injector from the cylinder head, and recover the heat shield washer – new washers must be obtained for refitting.

#### Engine codes ATD and AXR

11 With reference to Chapter 2C, remove the upper timing belt cover and camshaft cover.
12 Using a spanner or socket, turn the crankshaft pulley until the rocker arm for the injector which is to be removed is at its highest, ie, the injector plunger spring is under the least amount of tension.
13 Slacken the locknut of the adjustment screw on the end of the rocker arm above the injector, and undo the adjustment screw until the rocker arm lies against the plunger pin of the injector **(see illustration)**.
14 Starting at the outside and working in, gradually and evenly slacken and remove the rocker shaft retaining bolts. Lift off the rocker shaft. Check the contact face of each adjustment screw, and renew any that show signs of wear.
15 Undo the clamping block securing bolt and remove the block from the side of the injector **(see illustration)**.

9.13 Undo the adjustment screw until the rocker arm lies against the plunger pin of the injector

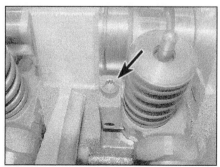

9.15 Remove the clamping block securing bolt (arrowed)

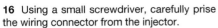

**9.17a Unit injector removal tool**

a  5 mm
b  15 mm
c  25 mm
d  Weld/braze the rod to the angle-iron
e  Threaded rod
f  Cylindrical weight
g  Locknut

H32626

**9.17b Seat the slide hammer/tool in the slot on the side on the injector, and pull the injector out**

**16** Using a small screwdriver, carefully prise the wiring connector from the injector.
**17** VW technicians use a slide hammer (tool No T10055) to pull the injector from the cylinder head. This is a slide hammer which engages in the side of the injector. If this tool is not available, it is possible to fabricate an equivalent using a short section of angle-iron, a length of threaded rod, a cylindrical weight, and two locknuts. Weld/braze the rod to the angle-iron, slide the weight over the rod, and lock the two nuts together at the end of the rod to provide the stop for the weight **(see illustration)**. Seat the slide hammer/tool in the slot on the side on the injector, and pull the

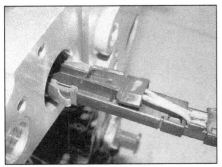

**9.18a Undo the two nuts at the back of the head and slide the injector loom/rail out**

injector out using a few gently taps. Recover circlip, the heat shield and O-rings and discard. New ones must be used for refitting **(see illustration)**.
**18** If required, the injector wiring loom/rail can be removed from the cylinder head by undoing the two retaining nuts/bolts at the back of the head. To prevent the wiring connectors fouling the cylinder head casting as the assembly is withdrawn, insert the connectors into the storage slots in the plastic wiring rail. Carefully push the assembly to the rear, and out of the casting **(see illustrations)**.

### Refitting

#### Engine code ALH

**19** Insert the injector into position, using a new heat shield washer. Make sure that the injector with the needle lift sender is located in No 3 position (No 1 is at the timing belt end of the engine).
**20** Fit the mounting collar and retaining plate then refit the retaining nut or bolt (as applicable) and tighten it to the specified torque.
**21** Reconnect the wiring for the needle lift sender on injector No 3.
**22** Refit the injector pipes and tighten the union nuts to the specified torque setting. Position any clips attached to the pipes as noted before removal.

**23** Reconnect the return pipe to the injector.
**24** Reconnect the battery negative (earth) lead.
**25** Start the engine and check that it runs correctly.

### Engine codes ATD and AXR

**26** Prior to refitting the injectors, the three O-rings, heat insulation washer and clip must be renewed. Due to the high injection pressures, it is essential that the O-rings are fitted without being twisted. VW recommend the use of three special assembly sleeves to install the O-rings squarely. It may be prudent to entrust O-ring renewal to a VW dealer or suitably-equipped injection specialist, rather than risk subsequent leaks **(see illustration)**.
**27** After renewing the O-rings, fit the heat shield and secure it in place with the circlip **(see illustration)**.
**28** Smear clean engine oil onto the O-rings, and push the injector evenly down into the cylinder head onto its stop.
**29** Fit the clamping block alongside the injector, but only hand-tighten the new retaining bolt at this stage.
**30** It is essential that the injectors are fitted at right-angles to the clamping block. In order to

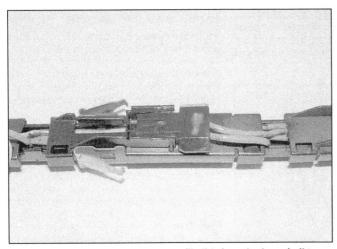

**9.18b The injector connectors will slide into the loom/rail to prevent them from being damaged as the assembly is withdrawn/inserted into the cylinder head**

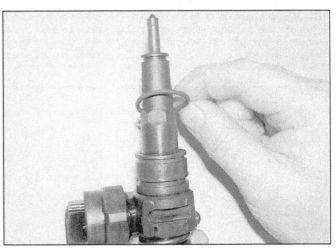

**9.26 Care must be used to ensure that the injector O-rings are fitted without being twisted**

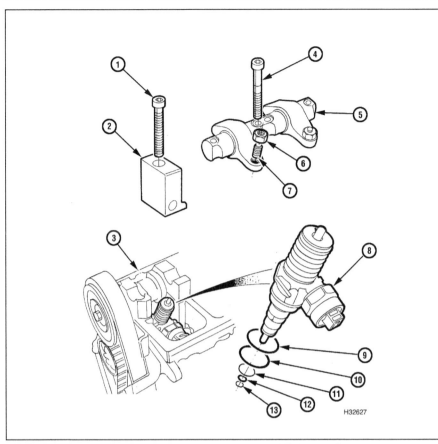

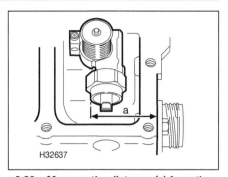

**9.30a Measure the distance (a) from the rear of the cylinder head to the rounded section of the injector (see text)**

**9.30b Use a set square against the edge of the injector . . .**

**9.27 Unit injector – engine codes ATD and AXR**

| | | |
|---|---|---|
| 1 Bolt | 6 Nut | 10 O-ring |
| 2 Clamping block | 7 Adjuster | 11 O-ring |
| 3 Cylinder head | 8 Unit injector | 12 Heat shield |
| 4 Bolt | 9 O-ring | 13 Circlip |
| 5 Rocker arm | | |

achieve this, measure the distance from the rear face of the cylinder head to the rounded section of the injector **(see illustrations)**. The dimensions (a) are as follows:

    Cylinder 1 = 332.2 ± 0.08 mm
    Cylinder 2 = 244.2 ± 0.08 mm
    Cylinder 3 = 152.8 ± 0.08 mm
    Cylinder 4 = 64.8 ± 0.08 mm

**31** Once the injector(s) are aligned correctly, tighten the clamping bolt to the specified Step one torque setting, and the Step two angle tightening setting. **Note:** *If an injector has been renewed, it is essential that the adjustment screw, locknut of the corresponding rocker and ball-pin are renewed at the same time. The ball-pins simply pull out of the injector spring cap. There is an O-ring in each spring cap to stop the ball-pins from falling out.*

**32** Smear some grease (VW No G000 100) onto the contact face of each rocker arm adjustment screw, and refit the rocker shaft assembly to the camshaft bearing caps, tightening the retaining bolts as follows. Starting from the inside out, hand-tighten the bolts. Again, from the inside out, tighten the

bolts to the Step one torque setting. Finally, from the inside out, tighten the bolts to the Step two angle tightening setting.

**33** The following procedure is only necessary if an injector has been removed and refitted/renewed. Attach a DTI (Dial Test Indicator) gauge to the cylinder head upper surface, and position the DTI probe against the top of the adjustment screw **(see illustration)**. Turn the crankshaft until the rocker arm roller is on the highest point of its corresponding camshaft lobe, and the adjustment screw is at its lowest. Once this position has been established, remove the DTI gauge, screw the adjustment screw in until firm resistance is felt, and the injector spring cannot be compressed further. Turn the adjustment screw **anti-clockwise** 225°, and tighten the locknut to the specified torque. Repeat this procedure for any other injectors that have been refitted.

**34** Reconnect the wiring plug to the injector.

**35** Refit the camshaft cover and upper timing belt cover, as described in Chapter 2C.

**36** Start the engine and check that it runs correctly.

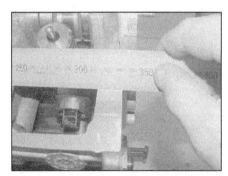

**9.30c . . . and measure the distance to the rear of the cylinder head**

**9.33 Attach a DTI (Dial Test Indicator) gauge to the cylinder head upper surface, and position the DTI probe against the top of the adjustment screw**

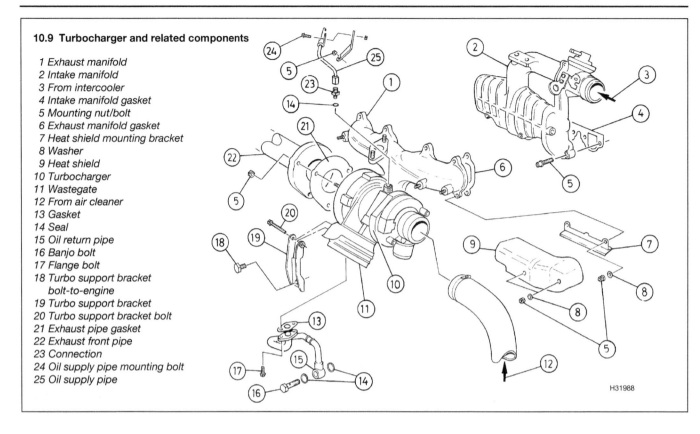

**10.9 Turbocharger and related components**

1 Exhaust manifold
2 Intake manifold
3 From intercooler
4 Intake manifold gasket
5 Mounting nut/bolt
6 Exhaust manifold gasket
7 Heat shield mounting bracket
8 Washer
9 Heat shield
10 Turbocharger
11 Wastegate
12 From air cleaner
13 Gasket
14 Seal
15 Oil return pipe
16 Banjo bolt
17 Flange bolt
18 Turbo support bracket
   bolt-to-engine
19 Turbo support bracket
20 Turbo support bracket bolt
21 Exhaust pipe gasket
22 Exhaust front pipe
23 Connection
24 Oil supply pipe mounting bolt
25 Oil supply pipe

H31988

## 10 Turbocharger and intercooler – testing and renewal

### Testing

1 The turbocharger is a precision component which can be severely damaged by a lack of lubrication or from foreign material entering the air intake duct. Turbocharger failure may be indicated by poor engine performance, blue/grey exhaust smoke or unusual noises from the turbocharger. If a turbocharger failure is suspected, check the following areas:

a) Check the intake air duct for looseness or damage. Make sure there are no restrictions in the air intake system, dirty air filter element or damaged intercooler.
b) Check the system vacuum hoses for restrictions or damage.
c) Check the system wiring for damage and electrical connectors for looseness or corrosion.
d) Make sure the wastegate actuator linkage is not binding.
e) Check the exhaust system for damage or restrictions.
f) Check the lubricating oil supply and return pipes for damage or restrictions.
g) If the turbocharger requires renewal due to failure, be sure to change the engine oil and filter (see Chapter 1).

2 Complete diagnosis of the turbocharger

and control system require special techniques and equipment. If the previous checks fail to identify the problem, take the vehicle to a dealership service department or other properly-equipped repair facility for diagnosis.

### Renewal

#### Turbocharger

⚠️ **Warning: Wait until the engine is completely cool before beginning this procedure.**

**Note:** The turbocharger and exhaust manifold are integrated and renewed as a unit.

3 Remove the engine cover. Remove the scuttle panel (see Chapter 11).
4 Raise the vehicle and support it securely on axle stands.
5 Remove the engine compartment undercover. Drain the cooling system (see Chapter 1).
6 Remove the right-hand side driveshaft (see Chapter 8).
7 Remove the nuts securing the exhaust pipe to the turbocharger. Remove the front section of the exhaust pipe.
8 Disconnect the vacuum hose from the wastegate actuator.
9 Remove the turbocharger support bracket **(see illustration)**.
10 Remove the bolts and disconnect the oil return pipe from the turbocharger.
11 Loosen the intake duct clamp at the air filter and separate the duct from the air filter assembly. Remove the retaining clip,

disconnect the air intake duct from the turbocharger intake and remove the duct.
12 Loosen the oil supply union bolt from the turbocharger. Remove the bracket bolt from the heat shield and disconnect the oil supply pipe from the turbocharger.
13 Remove the heat shield. Remove the EGR cooler (see Chapter 6B).
14 Remove the exhaust manifold bolts (see Chapter 2C) and remove the turbocharger and exhaust manifold from the engine.
15 Refitting is the reverse of removal with the following additions:
a) Renew all gaskets, seals, union bolt washers and self-locking nuts.
b) Tighten the exhaust manifold nuts/bolts to the torque listed in Chapter 2C Specifications.
c) Change the engine oil and filter (see Chapter 1).
d) Refill the cooling system (see Chapter 1).
e) Before starting the engine, disconnect the electrical lead from the fuel shut-off valve and crank the engine over until oil pressure builds.

#### Intercooler

16 The intercooler is located in the lower section of the right front wing, ahead of the front wheel **(see illustrations)**.
17 Raise the vehicle and support it securely on axle stands.
18 Remove the engine compartment undercover.
19 Remove the right front wheel.

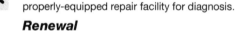

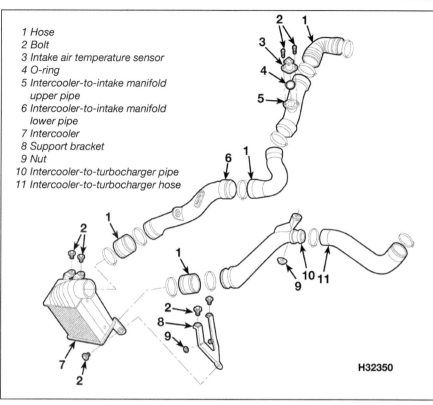

1 Hose
2 Bolt
3 Intake air temperature sensor
4 O-ring
5 Intercooler-to-intake manifold
   upper pipe
6 Intercooler-to-intake manifold
   lower pipe
7 Intercooler
8 Support bracket
9 Nut
10 Intercooler-to-turbocharger pipe
11 Intercooler-to-turbocharger hose

H32350

**10.16a Intercooler and related components**

**10.16b View of the intercooler from beneath the front bumper**

**11.2 Disconnect the injector connectors**

**20** Remove the retainers and remove the right front wheel arch liner (see Chapter 11, Section 13, Step 3).

**21** Loosen the hose clamps and disconnect the inlet and outlet ducts from the intercooler.

**22** Remove the mounting bolts and remove the intercooler and air deflector from the wheel arch. Detach the air deflector from the intercooler.

**23** Refitting is the reverse of removal.

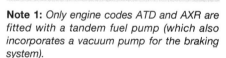

**11 Tandem fuel pump –** removal and refitting

**Note 1:** *Only engine codes ATD and AXR are fitted with a tandem fuel pump (which also incorporates a vacuum pump for the braking system).*
**Note 2:** *Disconnecting the central connector for the unit injectors may cause a fault code to be logged by the engine management ECU. This code can only be erased by a VW dealer or suitably-equipped specialist.*

### Removal

**1** Unclip and remove the engine top cover.
**2** Disconnect the charge air pipe, and place it to one side. Disconnect the central connector for the unit injectors **(see illustration)**.
**3** Release the retaining clip (where fitted) and disconnect the brake servo pipe from the tandem pump **(see illustration)**.

**4** Disconnect the fuel supply hose (marked white) from the tandem pump. Be prepared for fuel spillage.
**5** Unscrew the four retaining bolts and move the tandem pump away from the cylinder head. As the pump is lifted up, disconnect the fuel return hose (marked blue). Be prepared for fuel spillage. There are no serviceable parts within the tandem pump. If the pump is faulty, it must be renewed.

### Refitting

**6** Reconnect the fuel return hose to the pump and refit the pump to the cylinder head, using new rubber seals, and ensuring that the pump pinion engages correctly with the drive slot in the camshaft **(see illustration)**.

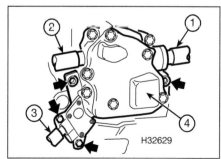

**11.3 Fuel tandem pump securing bolts (arrowed)**

1  Brake servo hose
2  Fuel supply hose
3  Fuel return hose
4  Tandem pump

**7** Refit the pump retaining bolts, and tighten them to the specified torque.
**8** Re-attach the fuel supply hose and brake servo hose to the pump.
**9** Reconnect the central connector for the unit injectors.
**10** Refit the charge air pipe.
**11** Disconnect the fuel filter return hose (marked blue), and connect the hose to a hand vacuum pump. Operate the vacuum pump until fuel comes out of the return hose. This primes the tandem pump. Take care not to suck any fuel into the vacuum pump. Reconnect the return hose to the fuel filter.
**12** Refit the engine top cover.
**13** Have the engine management ECU's fault memory interrogated and erased by a VW dealer or suitably-equipped specialist.

**11.6 Ensure that the tandem pump pinion engages correctly with the drive slot in the camshaft**

**Notes**

# Chapter 5
# Engine electrical systems

## Contents

## Degrees of difficulty

| Easy, suitable for novice with little experience  | Fairly easy, suitable for beginner with some experience  | Fairly difficult, suitable for competent DIY mechanic  | Difficult, suitable for experienced DIY mechanic  | Very difficult, suitable for expert DIY or professional |

## Specifications

### General
| | |
|---|---|
| Alternator brush wear limit | 5.0 mm |
| Battery voltage | |
| Engine off | 12.0 to 12.5 volts |
| Engine running | 13.5 to 14.5 volts |
| Ignition coil secondary resistance (1.6L and 2.0L code AQY engines) | 4000 to 6000 ohms |
| Spark plug HT lead resistance (1.6L and 2.0L code AQY engines) | 4000 to 6000 ohms |
| Spark plug boot resistance (1.4L, 1.8L and 2.0L code AZJ engines) | 2000 ohms |

### Torque specifications
| | Nm | Ft-lbs |
|---|---|---|
| Alternator mounting bolts | 25 to 30 | 18 to 22 |
| Battery hold-down clamp bolt | 22 | 16 |
| Glow plugs (diesel engine) | 15 | 11 |
| Starter mounting bolts | 60 | 44 |

**1.1 Typical engine electrical system components**

1  Spark plug HT leads
2  Battery cable

3  Engine compartment fuse box
4  Battery (inside housing)

5  Ignition coils
6  Alternator

## 1  General information, precautions and battery disconnection

### General information

The engine electrical systems include all ignition, charging and starting components **(see Illustration)**. Because of their engine-related functions, these components are discussed separately from body electrical devices such as the lights, the instruments, etc (which are included in Chapter 12).

### Precautions

Always observe the following precautions when working on the electrical system:

a) *Be extremely careful when servicing engine electrical components. They are easily damaged if checked, connected or handled improperly.*
b) *Never leave the ignition switched on for long periods of time when the engine is not running.*
c) *Never disconnect the battery cables while the engine is running.*
d) *Maintain correct polarity when connecting battery cables from another vehicle during jump starting – see the 'Jump starting' section at the front of this manual.*
e) *Always disconnect the negative battery cable from the battery before working on*

the electrical system, but read the following battery disconnection procedure first.

It's also a good idea to review the safety-related information regarding the engine electrical systems located in the 'Safety first!' section at the front of this manual, before beginning any operation included in this Chapter.

### Battery disconnection

Several systems on the vehicle require battery power to be available at all times, either to ensure their continued operation (such as the radio, alarm system, power door locks, windows, etc) or to maintain control unit memories (such as that in the engine management system's Engine Control Module [ECM]) which would be lost if the battery were to be disconnected. Therefore, whenever the battery is to be disconnected, first note the following to ensure that there are no unforeseen consequences of this action:

a) *These models are equipped with an anti-theft radio. Before performing a procedure that requires disconnecting the battery, make sure you have the proper activation code.*
b) *The engine management system's ECM will lose the information stored in its memory when the battery is disconnected. This includes idling and operating values, any fault codes*

detected and system monitors required for emissions testing. Whenever the battery is disconnected, the information relating to idle speed control and other operating values will have to be re-programmed into the unit's memory using a scan tool (see Chapter 6A).
c) *On any vehicle with central locking, it is a wise precaution to remove the key from the ignition and to keep it with you, so that it does not get locked inside if the central locking should engage accidentally when the battery is reconnected!*

Devices known as 'memory-savers' can be used to avoid some of the above problems. Precise details vary according to the device used. Typically, it is plugged into the cigarette lighter and is connected by its own wires to a spare battery; the vehicle's own battery is then disconnected from the electrical system, leaving the 'memory-saver' to pass sufficient current to maintain audio unit security codes and ECM memory values, and also to run permanently live circuits such as the clock and radio memory, all the while isolating the battery in the event of a short-circuit occurring while work is carried out.

⚠ *Warning 1: Some of these devices allow a considerable amount of current to pass, which can mean that many of the vehicle's systems are still operational when the main battery is disconnected. If* a 'memory-saver' is used, ensure that the circuit concerned is actually 'dead' before carrying out any work on it!

 *Warning 2: If work is to be performed around any of the airbag system components, the battery must be disconnected. If a memory-saver device is used, power will be supplied to the airbag and personal injury may result if the airbag is accidentally deployed.*

The battery on these vehicles is located under a cover at the left front corner of the engine compartment. To disconnect the battery for service procedures requiring power to be cut from the vehicle, lift the battery cover lid, peel back the insulator, loosen the negative cable clamp nut and detach the negative cable from the negative battery post (see Section 3). Isolate the cable end to prevent it from accidentally coming into contact with the battery post.

## 2 Battery – emergency jump starting

Refer to the *Jump starting* procedure at the front of this manual.

## 3 Battery – testing and renewal

 *Warning: Hydrogen gas is produced by the battery, so keep naked flames and lighted cigarettes away from it at all times. Always wear eye protection when working around a battery. Rinse off spilled electrolyte immediately with large amounts of water.*
*Caution 1: These models are equipped with an anti-theft radio. Before performing a procedure that requires disconnecting*

the battery, make sure you have the activation code.
*Caution 2: Disconnecting the battery can cause driveability problems that require a scan tool to remedy. See Section 1 for the use of an auxiliary voltage input device ('memory-saver') before disconnecting the battery.*

### Check

**1** A battery cannot be accurately tested unless it is at or near a fully charged state. Disconnect the negative battery cable from the battery and perform the following tests:

#### Battery state of charge test

Visually inspect the indicator eye (if equipped) on the top of the battery. If the indicator eye is dark in colour, charge the battery as described in Chapter 1. If the battery is equipped with removable caps, check the battery electrolyte. The electrolyte level should be above the upper edge of the plates. If the level is low, add distilled water. DO NOT OVERFILL. The excess electrolyte may spill over during periods of heavy charging. Test the specific gravity of the electrolyte using a hydrometer **(see illustration)**. Remove the caps and extract a sample of the electrolyte and observe the float inside the barrel of the hydrometer. Follow the instructions from the tool manufacturer and determine the specific gravity of the electrolyte for each cell. A fully-charged battery will indicate approximately 1.270 (green zone) at 20°C. If the specific gravity of the electrolyte is low (red zone), charge the battery as described in Chapter 1.

#### Open circuit voltage test

Using a digital voltmeter, perform an open circuit voltage test **(see illustration)**. Connect the negative probe of the voltmeter to the negative battery post and the positive probe to the positive battery post. The battery voltage should be greater than 12.5 volts. If the battery is less than the specified voltage,

charge the battery before proceeding to the next test. Do not proceed with the battery load test until the battery is fully charged.

#### Battery load test

An accurate check of the battery condition can only be performed with a load tester (available at most auto parts stores). This test evaluates the ability of the battery to operate the starter and other accessories during periods of heavy amperage draw (load). Fit a special battery load testing tool onto the battery terminals **(see illustration)**. Load test the battery according to the tool manufacturer's instructions. This tool utilises a carbon pile to increase the load demand (amperage draw) on the battery. Maintain the load on the battery for 15 seconds and observe that the battery voltage does not drop below 9.6 volts. If the battery condition is weak or defective, the tool will indicate this condition immediately. **Note:** *Cold temperatures will cause the minimum voltage requirements to drop slightly. Follow the chart given in the tool manufacturer's instructions to compensate for cold climates. Minimum load voltage for freezing temperatures (0°C) should be approximately 9.1 volts.*

#### Battery drain test

This test will indicate whether there's a constant drain on the vehicle's electrical system that can cause the battery to discharge. Make sure all accessories are turned Off. If the vehicle has an engine compartment light, verify it's working properly, then disconnect it. Connect one lead of a digital ammeter to the disconnected negative battery cable clamp and the other lead to the negative battery post. A drain of approximately 100 milliamps or less is considered normal (due to the engine control computer, digital clocks, digital radios and other components which normally cause a key-off battery drain). An excessive drain (approximately 500 milliamps or more) will cause the battery to discharge. The problem

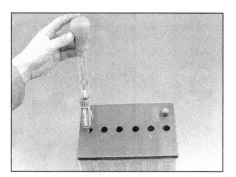

**3.1a Use a battery hydrometer to draw electrolyte from the battery cell – this hydrometer is equipped with a thermometer to make temperature corrections**

**3.1b To test the open circuit voltage of the battery, connect the black probe of the voltmeter to the negative terminal and the red probe to the positive terminal of the battery – a fully-charged battery should indicate approximately 12.5 volts depending on the outside air temperature**

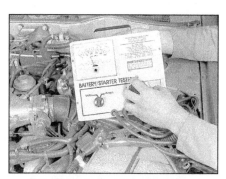

**3.1c Some battery load testers are equipped with an ammeter which enables the battery load to be precisely dialled in, as shown – less expensive testers have a load switch and a voltmeter only**

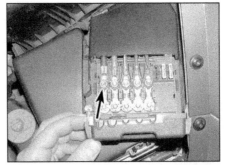

3.2 Squeeze the latch and lift the battery cover lid

3.4 Open the fusebox cover and disconnect the positive cable from the fusebox

3.6 Remove the power steering reservoir bolt (A) and the battery cover bolt (B)

circuit or component can be located by removing the fuses, one at a time, until the excessive drain stops and normal drain is indicated on the meter.

### Renewal

**Caution: Always disconnect the negative cable first and reconnect it last or the battery may be shorted by the tool being used to loosen the cable clamps.**
2 Squeeze the latch and lift the battery cover lid **(see illustration)**. Peel back the top insulator.
3 Loosen the cable clamp nut and remove the negative battery cable from the negative battery post. Isolate the cable end to prevent it from accidentally coming into contact with the battery post.
4 Open the fusebox cover, remove the nut and disconnect the positive cable from the fusebox **(see illustration)**. Carefully remove the fusebox cover and wiring harness protector. Position the fusebox and the battery cover lid aside.
5 Loosen the cable clamp nut and remove the positive battery cable from the positive battery post.
6 Remove the power steering reservoir mounting bolt and the battery cover bolt **(see illustration)**. Position the reservoir aside (without disconnecting the hoses). Detach the battery cover from the locating tabs and remove the battery cover.
7 Remove the battery clamp **(see illustration)**.
8 Remove the battery insulator and lift out the

battery. Be careful – it's heavy. **Note:** *Battery straps and handlers are available at most motor factors for a reasonable price. They make it easier to remove and carry the battery.*
9 While the battery is out, inspect the battery tray for corrosion. If corrosion exists, clean the deposits with a mixture of baking soda and water to prevent further corrosion. Flush the area with plenty of clean water and dry thoroughly.
10 If you are renewing the battery, make sure you renew it with a battery with the identical dimensions, amperage rating, cold cranking rating, etc.
11 When refitting the battery, make sure the centre notch in the battery foot is aligned with the clamp hole in the battery tray. Refit the clamp and tighten the bolt to the torque listed in this Chapter's Specifications. Do not over-tighten the bolt.
12 The remainder of refitting is the reverse of removal.

### 4 Battery cables – renewal

**Caution 1: These models are equipped with an anti-theft radio. Before performing a procedure that requires disconnecting the battery, make sure you have the activation code.**
**Caution 2: Disconnecting the battery can cause driveability problems that require a scan tool to remedy. See Section 1 for the**

**use of an auxiliary voltage input device ('memory-saver') before disconnecting the battery.**
1 Periodically inspect the entire length of each battery cable for damage, cracked or burned insulation and corrosion. Poor battery cable connections can cause starting problems and decreased engine performance.
2 Check the cable-to-terminal connections at the ends of the cables for cracks, loose wire strands and corrosion. The presence of white, fluffy deposits under the insulation at the cable terminal connection is a sign that the cable is corroded and should be renewed. Check the terminals for distortion, missing mounting bolts and corrosion.
3 When removing the cables, always disconnect the negative cable from the negative battery post first and reconnect it last, or the battery may be shorted by the tool used to loosen the cable clamps. Even if only the positive cable is being renewed, be sure to disconnect the negative cable from the negative battery post first (see Chapter 1 for further information regarding battery cable maintenance).
4 Disconnect the old cables from the battery, then disconnect them from the opposite end. Detach the cables from the starter solenoid, engine compartment fusebox and earth terminals, as necessary **(see illustrations)**. Note the routing of each cable to ensure correct refitting.
5 If you are renewing either or both of the battery cables, take them with you when buying new cables. It is vitally important that

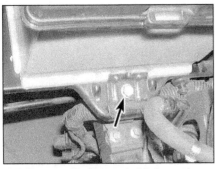

3.7 Remove the battery hold-down clamp bolt (arrowed)

4.4a The positive cable is connected to the starter

4.4b The negative battery cable is connected to a transmission bolt stud

you renew the cables with identical parts. Cables have characteristics that make them easy to identify: Positive cables are usually red and larger in cross-section; earth cables are usually black and smaller in cross-section.
**6** Clean the threads of the starter solenoid or earth connection with a wire brush to remove rust and corrosion. Apply a light coat of battery terminal corrosion inhibitor or petroleum jelly to the threads to prevent future corrosion.
**7** Attach the cable to the terminal and tighten the mounting nut/bolt securely.
**8** Before connecting a new cable to the battery, make sure that it reaches the battery post without having to be stretched.
**9** After refitting the cables, connect the negative cable to the negative battery post.

## 5  Ignition system – general information

All petrol engine models are equipped with a distributorless ignition system. The ignition system consists of the battery, ignition coils, spark plugs, camshaft position sensor, engine speed sensor and the Engine Control Module (ECM). The ECM controls the ignition timing and spark advance characteristics for the engine. The ignition timing is not adjustable.

The engine speed sensor and camshaft position sensor generate pulses that are input to the Engine Control Module. The ECM determines piston position and engine speed from these two sensors. The ECM calculates injector sequence and ignition timing from the piston position. Refer to Chapter 6A for testing and renewal procedures for the engine speed sensor and camshaft position sensor.

The 1.6L and 2.0L code AQY engines utilise a coil pack consisting of two ignition coils and a power unit. This type of ignition system uses a 'waste spark' method of spark distribution. Each cylinder is paired with its opposing cylinder in the firing order (1-4, 2-3) so one cylinder under compression fires simultaneously with its opposing cylinder, where the piston is on the exhaust stroke. Since the cylinder on the exhaust stroke requires very little of the available voltage to fire its plug, most of the voltage is used to fire the plug of the cylinder on the compression stroke. In a conventional ignition system, one end of the ignition coil secondary winding is connected to engine earth. In a waste spark system, neither end of the secondary winding is earthed – instead, one end of the coil secondary winding is directly attached to the spark plug and the other end is attached to the spark plug of the companion cylinder.

1.4L, 1.8L and 2.0L code AZJ models utilise an individual ignition coil/power unit for each cylinder. The unit is positioned directly over each spark plug. The ECM fires each coil sequentially in the firing order sequence.

The ECM controls the ignition system by opening and closing the primary ignition coil control circuit. The computerised ignition system provides complete control of the ignition timing by determining the optimum timing in response to engine speed, coolant temperature, throttle position and engine load. These parameters are relayed to the ECM by the camshaft position sensor, engine speed sensor, throttle position sensor, coolant temperature sensor and mass airflow sensor. Refer to Chapter 6A for additional information on the various sensors.

The ignition system is also integrated with a knock sensor system. The system uses two knock sensors in conjunction with the ECM to control spark timing. The knock sensor system allows the engine to use maximum spark advance without spark knock, which improves driveability and fuel economy.

## 6  Ignition system – testing

> ⚠ **Warning: Because of the high voltage generated by the ignition system, extreme care should be taken whenever an operation is performed involving ignition components. This not only includes the ignition coil, but related components and test equipment.**

**1** If a malfunction occurs and the vehicle won't start, do not immediately assume that the ignition system is causing the problem. First, check the following items:
a) *Make sure the battery cable clamps, where they connect to the battery, are clean and tight.*
b) *Test the condition of the battery (see Section 3). If it does not pass all the tests, renew it.*

**6.2  To use a calibrated ignition tester, disconnect an HT lead from a spark plug, connect the tester to the spark plug boot, clip the tester to a convenient ground and crank the engine over – if there's enough power to fire the plug, bright blue sparks will be visible between the electrode tip and the tester body (weak sparks or intermittent sparks are the same as no sparks)**

c) *Check the external ignition coil wiring and connections.*
d) *Check the related fuses inside the fusebox (see Chapter 12). If they're blown, determine the cause and repair the circuit.*

**2** If the engine turns over but won't start, make sure there is sufficient secondary ignition voltage to fire the spark plug. On 1.6L and 2.0L code AQY models, disconnect a spark plug HT lead from one of the spark plugs and attach a calibrated ignition system tester (available at most motor factors) to the spark plug boot. Connect the clip on the tester to a bolt or metal bracket on the engine **(see illustration)**. On 1.4L, 1.8L and 2.0L code AZJ models, remove an ignition coil (see Section 7) and attach the calibrated ignition system tester to the spark plug boot. Reconnect the electrical connector to the coil and clip the tester to a good earth. Crank the engine and watch the end of the tester to see if a bright blue, well-defined spark occurs (weak spark or intermittent spark is the same as no spark).
**3** If spark occurs, sufficient voltage is reaching the plug to fire it (repeat the test at the remaining HT leads or ignition coils to verify that the HT leads, connectors and ignition coils are good). If the ignition system is operating properly the problem lies elsewhere; i.e. a mechanical or fuel system problem. However, the plugs themselves may be fouled, so remove and check them as described in Chapter 1.
**4** If no spark occurs, remove the spark plug HT lead or boot from the suspected ignition coil and check the terminals for damage. Using an ohmmeter, check the lead or boot for an open or high resistance (compare your measurement with the values listed in this Chapter's Specifications). On 1.6L and 2.0L code AQY models, disconnect the HT leads from all the ignition coil towers and test the ignition coil secondary resistance across each pair of coil towers **(see illustration)**. Compare your measurement with the values listed in this Chapter's Specifications. Renew the ignition coil assembly if either coil is not within specifications.
**5** Check for battery voltage to the ignition coil with the ignition key On (engine not running).

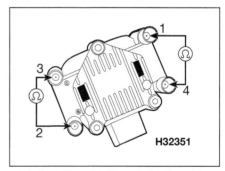

**6.4  On 1.6L and 2.0L code AQY models, measure the ignition coil secondary resistance across each pair of coil towers**

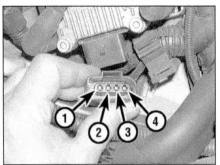

6.5 Ignition coil electrical connector terminal identification

7.3 Ignition coil pack mounting screws – 1.6L and 2.0L code AQY models

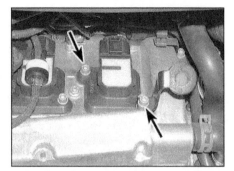

7.4 On 1.8L turbo models, remove the ignition coil mounting screws (arrowed) and pull the coil straight up

Disconnect the coil electrical connector and check for power at the indicated terminals of the coil connector (see illustration):

a) On 1.6L and 2.0L code AQY models connect a voltmeter to terminals 2 and 4.
b) On 1.4L, 1.8L and 2.0L code AZJ models, connect a voltmeter to terminals 1 and 2; then 1 and 4.

6 Battery voltage should be available with the ignition key On. If there is no battery voltage present, check the wiring and/or circuit between the fusebox and ignition coil (don't forget to check the fuses). Also test the earth circuit for continuity. Note: Refer to the wiring diagrams at the end of Chapter 12 for wire colour identification for testing and additional information on the circuits.

7 If battery voltage is available to the ignition coil, test the ignition coil control circuits as follows (see illustration 6.5):

Caution: Use only an LED test light to avoid damaging the ECM.

a) Remove fuse No 32 from the fusebox (this disables the fuel injectors so the engine will not start or flood).
b) On 1.6L and 2.0L code AQY models, connect an LED test light to terminals 1 and 4 of the coil harness connector. Perform the remainder of the test, then connect the LED test light to terminals 3 and 4 and perform the test.
c) On 1.4L, 1.8L and 2.0L code AZJ, connect an LED test light to terminals 2 and 3 of the coil harness connector.
d) Crank the engine with the starter and confirm that the LED test light flashes as the engine rotates. A flashing LED test light indicates the ECM, camshaft position sensor and engine speed sensor are functioning properly.

8 If a control signal is not present at the ignition coil, refer to Chapter 6A and check the camshaft position sensor and the engine speed sensor. If the sensors are good and there is no control signal, have the ECM checked by a dealer service department or other qualified garage.

9 If battery voltage and a control signal exist at the ignition coil and there is no spark, renew the ignition coil.

## 7 Ignition coil(s) – renewal

1 Remove the engine cover.
2 On 1.6L and 2.0L code AQY models, remove the secondary air injection pump (see Chapter 6A).
3 On 1.6L and 2.0L code AQY models, disconnect the electrical connector from the ignition coil. Label and detach the HT leads. Remove the mounting bolts and remove the coil assembly (see illustration).
4 On 1.4L, 1.8L and 2.0L code AZJ models, disconnect the electrical connector from the ignition coil. Remove the ignition coil mounting screws and pull the coil straight up and out of the cylinder head (see Illustration).
5 Refitting is the reverse of removal.

## 8 Charging system – general information and precautions

The charging system includes the alternator, a charge indicator light, the battery and the wiring between all the components. The battery supplies electrical power for the vehicle electrical system. The charging system maintains the battery in a fully-charged condition. The alternator generates DC voltage to charge the battery and is driven by an auxiliary drivebelt at the end of the engine.

The alternator voltage regulator regulates the alternator voltage output. The voltage regulator limits the charging voltage to a maximum pre-set value. This prevents overcharging the battery. The voltage regulator and brush assembly may be renewed in the event of failure.

The charging system doesn't ordinarily require periodic maintenance. However, the drivebelt, battery, battery cables, wiring and connections should be inspected at the intervals outlined in Chapter 1.

The dashboard warning light should come On when the ignition key is turned to On, but it should go off immediately after the engine is started. If it remains on, there is a malfunction

in the charging system. Some vehicles are also equipped with a voltmeter. If the voltmeter indicates abnormally high or low voltage, examine the charging system (see Section 9).

Be very careful when making electrical circuit connections to a vehicle equipped with an alternator and note the following:

a) When reconnecting wires to the alternator from the battery, be sure to note the polarity.
b) Before using arc welding equipment to repair any part of the vehicle, disconnect the wires from the alternator and the battery terminals.
c) Never start the engine with a battery charger connected.
d) Always disconnect both battery cables before using a battery charger.
e) The alternator is turned by an engine drivebelt which could cause serious injury if your hands, hair or clothes become entangled in it with the engine running.
f) Because the alternator is connected directly to the battery, it could arc or cause a fire if overloaded or shorted out.
g) Wrap a plastic bag over the alternator and secure it with rubber bands before steam-cleaning the engine.

## 9 Charging system – testing

1 If a malfunction occurs in the charging circuit, do not immediately assume that the alternator is causing the problem. First check the following items:

a) The battery cables where they connect to the battery. Make sure the connections are clean and tight.
b) Check the battery as described in Section 3. If the battery is defective, renew the battery.
c) Check the external alternator wiring and connections.
d) Check the auxiliary drivebelt condition and tension (see Chapter 1).
e) Check the alternator mounting bolts for tightness.
f) Run the engine and check the alternator for abnormal noise.

9.6  To measure battery voltage, attach the voltmeter leads to the remote battery terminals (engine Off) – to measure charging voltage, start the engine

10.4  Disconnect the alternator electrical connections (arrowed)

10.5  Remove the alternator mounting bolts (arrowed)

**2** The charging system warning light on the instrument cluster should illuminate when the ignition key is switched On and go off when the engine is running.

**3** If the warning light does not illuminate when the ignition key is switched On, switch the ignition off and disconnect the wiring connector from the alternator (do not disconnect the large output wire). Connect the black wire terminal in the harness connector to a good engine earth point using a jumper wire and switch the ignition on. The warning light should illuminate – if it doesn't, there is an open circuit in the black wire between the alternator and the instrument cluster, or the instrument cluster is defective.

**4** If the warning light illuminates with the connector earthed but not when connected to the alternator, remove the voltage regulator brush assembly and check the brushes (see Section 11). Measure the brush length and compare it with the value listed in this Chapter's Specifications. Check the brush holder and springs for damage. If the brushes are worn or defective, renew the voltage regulator/brush assembly. If the brushes are good, renew the alternator.

**5** If the warning light is illuminated with the engine running, switch the engine off and disconnect the wiring connector from the alternator (do not disconnect the large output wire). Switch the ignition on and observe the warning light. If the warning light is still on, the black wire from the alternator to the instrument cluster is earthed or the instrument cluster is defective. If the warning light went out, switch the ignition off, reconnect the connector and proceed with the charging system testing.

**6** Lift up the battery cover lid and connect a voltmeter to the positive and negative battery terminals **(see illustration)**. Check the battery voltage with the engine off. It should be approximately 12.4 to 12.6 volts if the battery is fully-charged.

**7** Start the engine and check the battery voltage again. It should now be greater than the voltage recorded in Step 6, but not more than 14.5 volts. Turn on all the vehicle

accessories (air conditioning, rear window demister, blower motor, etc) and increase the engine speed to 2000 rpm – the voltage should not drop below the voltage recorded in Step 6.

**8** If the indicated voltage is greater than the specified charging voltage, renew the voltage regulator (see Section 11).

**9** If the indicated voltage reading is less than the specified charging voltage, the alternator is probably defective. Have the charging system checked at a dealer service department or other properly-equipped repair facility. **Note:** *Many motor factors will bench test an alternator off the vehicle. Refer to your local auto parts store regarding their policy, many will perform this service free of charge.*

## 10  Alternator – removal and refitting

*Caution 1: These models are equipped with an anti-theft radio. Before performing a procedure that requires disconnecting the battery, make sure you have the activation code.*
*Caution 2: Disconnecting the battery can cause driveability problems that require a scan tool to remedy. See Section 1 for the use of an auxiliary voltage input device ('memory-saver') before disconnecting the battery.*

**1** Disconnect the negative battery cable from the battery.

**2** Remove the engine cover.

**3** Remove the alternator auxiliary drivebelt (see Chapter 1).

**4** Disconnect the output wire and the electrical connector from the alternator **(see illustration)**. Where fitted, undo the wiring loom cable clamp from the rear of the alternator.

**5** Remove the mounting bolts and remove the alternator from the engine **(see illustration)**.

**6** If you are renewing the alternator, take the old one with you when purchasing a renewal unit. Make sure the new/rebuilt unit looks

identical to the old alternator. Look at the terminals – they should be the same in number, size and location as the terminals on the old alternator. Finally, look at the identification numbers – they will be stamped into the housing or printed on a tag attached to the housing. Make sure the numbers are the same on both alternators.

**7** Many new/rebuilt alternators do not have a pulley fitted, so you may have to switch the pulley from the old unit to the new/rebuilt one. When buying an alternator, find out the shop's policy regarding pulleys; some shops will perform this service free of charge.

**8** Refitting is the reverse of removal. Tighten the mounting bolts to the torque listed in this Chapter's Specifications.

**9** Refit the drivebelt (see Chapter 1).

**10** Check the charging voltage to verify proper operation of the alternator (see Section 9).

## 11  Voltage regulator and brushes – renewal

**1** Remove the alternator (see Section 10).

**2** Place the alternator on a clean work surface, with the pulley facing down.

**3** Remove the retaining screws, prise open the clips and remove the plastic cover from the rear of the alternator **(see illustrations)**.

11.3a  Remove the retaining screws (arrowed) . . .

**11.3b ... then pry open the clips ...**

**11.3c ... and remove the plastic cover from the rear of the alternator**

**11.4a Unscrew the voltage regulator/brush assembly screws ...**

**4** Remove the voltage regulator/brush assembly screws and remove the unit from the alternator **(see illustrations)**.

**5** Measure the brush contact free length and compare your measurement with the value listed in this Chapter's specifications **(see illustration)**. Renew the unit if the brushes are worn below the minimum value.

**6** Inspect the brush contact surface of the slip rings **(see illustration)**. Minor imperfections may be cleaned with crocus cloth. If they are excessively worn, burnt or pitted, renew the alternator.

**7** Refitting is the reverse of removal.

**8** Refit the alternator and check the charging voltage as described in Section 9.

## 12 Starting system – general information and precautions

The sole function of the starting system is to turn over the engine quickly enough to allow it to start. The starting system consists of the battery, starter circuit, starter motor assembly and the wiring connecting the components.

The starter motor assembly is bolted to the front of the transmission bellhousing.

When the ignition key is turned to the Start position, the starter solenoid is actuated through the starter control circuit which includes a starter relay located in the relay panel. The starter solenoid then connects the battery to the starter motor. The battery supplies the electrical energy to the starter

motor, which does the actual work of cranking the engine.

Always observe the following precautions when working on the starting system:

a) Excessive cranking of the starter motor can overheat it and cause serious damage. Never operate the starter motor for more than 15 seconds at a time without pausing to allow it to cool for at least two minutes.

b) The starter is connected directly to the battery and could arc or cause a fire if mishandled, overloaded or shorted.

c) Always detach the cable from the negative terminal of the battery before working on the starting system (see Section 1).

## 13 Starter motor and circuit – testing

**1** If a malfunction occurs in the starting circuit, do not immediately assume that the starter is causing the problem. First, check the following items:

a) Make sure the battery cable clamps, where they connect to the battery, are clean and tight.

b) Check the condition of the battery cables (see Section 4). Renew any defective battery cables.

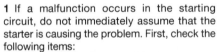
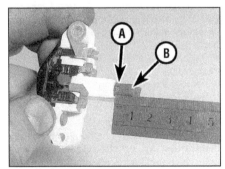

**11.5 Measure the free length of the brush contacts – take the measurement from the manufacturers emblem (A) etched in the side of the brush contact, to the shallowest part of the curved end face of the brush (B)**

c) Test the condition of the battery (see Section 3). If it does not pass all the tests, renew it.

d) Check the starter motor wiring and connections.

e) Check the starter motor mounting bolts for tightness.

f) Check the related fuses in the fusebox (see Chapter 12). If they're blown, determine the cause and repair the circuit.

g) Check the ignition switch circuit for correct operation (see Chapter 12).

h) Check the starter relay (see Chapter 12).

i) Check the operation of the Park/Neutral position switch (see Chapter 7B, Section 5) or the clutch start switch (see Chapter 8). These systems must operate correctly to provide battery voltage to the starter solenoid.

**2** If the starter does not activate when the ignition switch is turned to the Start position, check for battery voltage to the starter solenoid. This will determine if the solenoid is receiving the correct voltage from the ignition switch. Connect a 12 volt test light or a voltmeter to the starter solenoid terminal. While an assistant turns the ignition switch to the start position, observe the test light or voltmeter. The test light should shine brightly or battery voltage should be indicated on the voltmeter. If voltage is not available to the starter solenoid, refer to the wiring diagrams in Chapter 12 and check the fuses, switches and starter relay in series with the starting system. If voltage is available but there is no movement from the starter motor, remove the

**11.4b ... and remove the assembly from the alternator**

**11.6 Inspect the surfaces of the slip rings (arrowed), at the end of the alternator shaft**

starter from the engine (see Section 14) and bench test the starter (see Step 4).

**3** If the starter turns over slowly, check the starter cranking voltage and the current draw from the battery. This test must be performed with the starter assembly on the engine. Crank the engine over (for 10 seconds or less) and observe the battery voltage. It should not drop below 8.5 volts. Also, observe the current draw using an ammeter. Typically a starter amperage draw should not exceed 200 amps. If the starter motor amperage draw is excessive, have it tested by a dealer service department or other qualified garage. There are several conditions that may affect the starter cranking potential. The battery must be in good condition and the battery cold-cranking rating must not be underrated for the particular application. Be sure to check the battery specifications carefully. The battery terminals and cables must be clean and not corroded. Also, in cases of extreme cold temperatures, make sure the battery and/or engine block is warmed before performing the tests.

**4** If the starter is receiving voltage but does not activate, remove and check the starter motor assembly on the bench. Most likely the starter motor or solenoid is defective. In some rare cases the engine may be seized, so be sure to try and rotate the crankshaft pulley (see Chapter 2A or 2B) before proceeding. With the starter assembly mounted in a vice on the bench, refit one jump lead from the positive terminal of a test battery to the B+ terminal on the starter. Refit another jump lead from the negative terminal of the battery to the body of the starter. Connect a starter switch and apply battery voltage to the solenoid S terminal (for 10 seconds or less) and observe the solenoid plunger, gearchange lever and overrunning clutch extend and rotate the pinion drive. If the pinion drive extends but does not rotate, the solenoid is operating but the starter motor is defective. If there is no movement but the solenoid clicks, the solenoid and/or the starter motor is defective. If the solenoid plunger extends and rotates the pinion drive, the starter assembly is operating properly.

## 14 Starter motor – removal and refitting

*Caution 1: These models are equipped with an anti-theft radio. before performing a procedure that requires disconnecting the battery, make sure you have the activation code.*

*Caution 2: Disconnecting the battery can cause driveability problems that require a scan tool to remedy. See Section 1 for the use of an auxiliary voltage input device ('memory-saver') before disconnecting the battery.*

**1** Disconnect the negative battery cable from the battery.

**2** Raise the vehicle and support it securely on axle stands.

**3** Remove the splash pan from under the engine. **Note:** *On some models, the starter is accessible from above if the battery and battery tray are removed (see Section 3). Unbolt the clamp securing the power steering fluid line and position the line to one side for starter access.*

**4** Disconnect the wires from the terminals on the starter motor solenoid.

**5** Remove the starter mounting bolts.

**6** Withdraw the starter from the transmission bellhousing.

**7** Refitting is the reverse of removal.

## 15 Glow plug system (diesel engine) – general information

To assist cold starting, diesel engine models are equipped with a pre-heating system, which comprises four glow plugs, a glow plug relay, a dash-mounted warning lamp, the Engine Control Module (ECM) and the associated electrical wiring.

The glow plugs are miniature electric heating elements, encapsulated in a metal case with a probe at one end and electrical connection at the other. Each combustion chamber has a glow plug threaded into it. When the glow plug is energised, the air in the combustion chamber is heated, allowing optimum combustion temperature to be achieved more readily before fuel is injected into the cylinder.

The duration of the pre-heating period is governed by the Engine Control Module, which monitors the temperature of the engine via the coolant temperature sensor and alters the pre-heating time to suit the conditions.

A dash-mounted warning lamp informs the driver that pre-heating is taking place. The lamp extinguishes when sufficient pre-heating has taken place to allow the engine to be started, but power will still be supplied to the glow plugs for a further period until the engine is started. If no attempt is made to start the engine, the power supply to the glow plugs is switched off to prevent battery drain and glow plug burn-out.

After the engine has been started, the glow plugs continue to operate for a further period of time. This helps to improve fuel combustion while the engine is warming up, resulting in quieter, smoother running and reduced exhaust emissions.

The Check Engine warning lamp will illuminate during normal driving if a pre-heating system malfunction occurs and a diagnostic trouble code will be stored in the ECM memory. Refer to Chapter 6B for additional information on the On-Board Diagnostic system.

## 16 Glow plugs – testing and renewal

### Check

**1** Remove the engine cover.

**2** Disconnect the electrical connector from the engine coolant temperature sensor (see Chapter 6B). **Note:** *This will allow the glow plugs to be energised, regardless of engine temperature.*

**3** Carefully disconnect the electrical connector for each glow plug and position the strip connector so the electrical terminals will not contact any engine component.

**4** Connect a 12 volt test light or voltmeter to one of the glow plug terminals and switch the ignition key On. Battery voltage should be indicated on the meter for approximately 20 seconds. If no voltage is indicated, check the glow plug fuses and glow plug relay (see Chapter 12). **Note:** *The glow plug fuses are located in the fusebox on the battery cover. The glow plug relay is located in the relay panel under the right-hand side of the instrument panel.* Test each glow plug terminal, then switch the ignition key Off.

**5** Connect the clip of a 12 volt test light to the *positive* battery terminal. Touch the electrical terminal on the glow plug with the test light tip. If the glow plug is good, the test light will illuminate.

**6** Renew any defective glow plugs. Refit the strip connector and connect the engine coolant temperature sensor.

### Renewal

**7** Remove the engine cover,

**8** Carefully disconnect the electrical terminal for each glow plug and position the strip connector aside.

**9** Using a deep socket, remove the glow plugs from the cylinder head.

**10** Refitting is the reverse of removal. Tighten the glow plugs to torque listed in this Chapter's Specifications.

# Chapter 6 Part A
# Emissions and engine control systems – petrol engines

## Contents

## Degrees of difficulty

| Easy, suitable for novice with little experience |  | Fairly easy, suitable for beginner with some experience |  | Fairly difficult, suitable for competent DIY mechanic |  | Difficult, suitable for experienced DIY mechanic |  | Very difficult, suitable for expert DIY or professional |
|---|---|---|---|---|---|---|---|---|

## Specifications

| Torque wrench setting | Nm | Ft-lbs |
|---|---|---|
| Knock sensor . . . . . . . . . . . . . . . . . . . . . . . . . . . . . . . . . . . . . . . . . . . | 20 | 15 |

**1.1a Typical emission and engine control system components – 2.0L models**

1 Crankcase ventilation hose
2 Secondary air injection solenoid valve
3 Mass airflow sensor/intake air temperature sensor
4 Engine coolant temperature sensor
5 Secondary air injection pump
6 Knock sensor
7 Camshaft position sensor

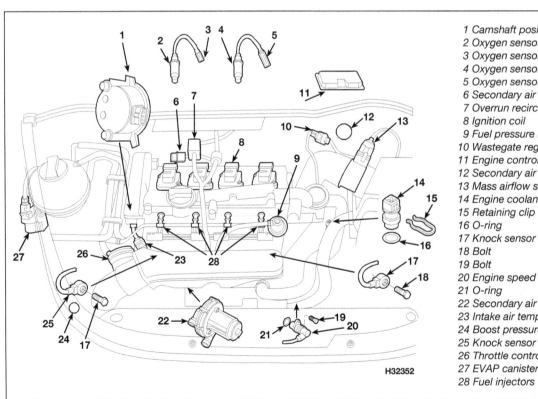

1 Camshaft position sensor
2 Oxygen sensor – pre catalyst
3 Oxygen sensor connector – pre catalyst
4 Oxygen sensor – post catalyst
5 Oxygen sensor connector – post catalyst
6 Secondary air injection solenoid valve
7 Overrun recirculation valve
8 Ignition coil
9 Fuel pressure regulator
10 Wastegate regulator valve
11 Engine control module (ECM)
12 Secondary air injection pump relay
13 Mass airflow sensor
14 Engine coolant temperature sensor
15 Retaining clip
16 O-ring
17 Knock sensor
18 Bolt
19 Bolt
20 Engine speed sensor
21 O-ring
22 Secondary air injection pump
23 Intake air temperature sensor
24 Boost pressure sensor
25 Knock sensor
26 Throttle control module
27 EVAP canister purge valve
28 Fuel injectors

H32352

**1.1b Typical emission and engine control system components – 1.8L turbo models**

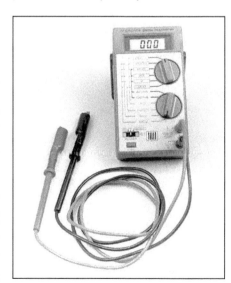

**1.1c  Typical emission and engine control system components – 1.6L models**

1  Secondary air injection 'combi' valve
2  Secondary air pump
3  Fuel pressure regulator
4  Mass airflow sensor
5  Secondary air injection hose
6  Camshaft position sensor
7  Knock sensor
8  EVAP valve
9  Inlet manifold change-over valve
10 Engine coolant temperature sensor

## 1  General information

To prevent pollution of the atmosphere from incompletely burned and evaporating gases, and to maintain good driveability and fuel economy, a number of emission control systems are incorporated **(see illustrations)**. They include:

*Electronic engine control system*
*Crankcase ventilation system*
*Evaporative emissions control system*
*Exhaust gas recirculation (EGR) system*
   *(1.4L-pre 2006 and 1.6L engines only)*
*Secondary air injection system*
*Catalytic converter*

All of these systems are linked, directly or indirectly, to the emission control system. The Sections in this Chapter include general descriptions, checking procedures within the scope of the home mechanic (when possible) and component renewal procedures for each of the systems listed above.

Before assuming that an emissions control system is malfunctioning, check the fuel and ignition systems carefully. The diagnosis of some emission control devices requires specialised tools, equipment and training. If checking and servicing become too difficult or if a procedure is beyond your ability, consult a dealer service department or other properly-equipped repair facility. Remember, the most frequent cause of emissions problems is simply a loose or broken vacuum hose or wire, so always check the hose and wiring connections first.

This doesn't mean, however, that emission control systems are particularly difficult to maintain and repair. You can quickly and easily perform many checks and service procedures at home with common test equipment and hand tools.

Pay close attention to any special precautions outlined in this Chapter. It should be noted that the illustrations of the various systems may not exactly match the system fitted on the vehicle you're working on because of changes made by the manufacturer during production or from year-to-year.

**2.1  Digital multimeters can be used for testing all types of circuits; because of the high impedance, they are much more accurate than analogue meters for measuring low-voltage computer circuits**

## 2  On-Board Diagnostic (OBD) system and trouble codes

### *Diagnostic tool information*

**1** A digital multimeter is necessary for checking fuel injection and emission related components **(see illustration)**. A digital volt-ohmmeter is preferred over the older style analogue multimeter for several reasons. The analogue multimeter cannot display the volts-ohms or amps measurement in hundredths and thousandths increments. When working with electronic circuits which are often very low voltage, this accurate reading is most important. Another good reason for the digital multimeter is the high impedance circuit. The digital multimeter is equipped with a high resistance internal circuitry (10 million ohms). Because a voltmeter is hooked up in parallel with the circuit when testing, it is vital that none of the voltage being measured should be allowed to travel the parallel path set up by the meter itself. This dilemma does not show itself when measuring larger amounts of voltage (9 to 12 volt circuits) but if you are measuring a low voltage circuit such as the oxygen sensor signal voltage, a fraction of a volt may be a significant amount when diagnosing a problem. However, there are several exceptions where using an analogue voltmeter may be necessary to test certain sensors.

**2** Hand-held scanners are the most powerful and versatile tools for analysing engine management systems used on later model vehicles. Each brand scan tool must be examined carefully to match the year, make and model of the vehicle you are working on. Often interchangeable cartridges are available to access the particular manufacturer (Ford, GM, Chrysler, etc). Some manufacturers will specify by continent (Asia, Europe, USA, etc).

**3** The On-Board Diagnostic (OBD) facility built into the vehicles' electronic systems, can only be accessed by a dedicated scan tool. Although hand-held scan tools are now becoming generally available, your local VW dealer or specialist will have the necessary equipment to interrogate the OBD system.

### *On-Board Diagnostic system general description*

**4** All models described in this manual are equipped with the second generation On-Board Diagnostic system. The system consists of an on-board computer, known as the Engine Control Module (ECM), information sensors and output actuators.

**5** The information sensors monitor various functions of the engine and send data to the ECM. Based on the data and the information programmed into the computer's memory, the ECM generates output signals to control various engine functions via control relays, solenoids and other output actuators. The

ECM is specifically calibrated to optimise the emissions, fuel economy and driveability of the vehicle.

6 It isn't a good idea to attempt diagnosis or renewal of the ECM at home while the vehicle is under warranty. Take the vehicle to a dealer service department if the ECM or a system component malfunctions.

### Information sensors

#### Camshaft position sensor

The camshaft position sensor provides information on camshaft position. The ECM uses this information, along with the engine speed sensor information, to control the ignition timing and fuel injection synchronisation.

#### Engine speed sensor

The engine speed sensor senses crankshaft position (TDC) and speed during each engine revolution. The ECM uses this information to control the ignition system.

#### Engine coolant temperature sensor

The engine coolant temperature sensor senses engine coolant temperature. The ECM uses this information to control fuel injection duration and ignition timing.

#### Intake air temperature sensor

The intake air temperature sensor senses the temperature of the air entering the intake manifold. The ECM uses this information to control fuel injection duration.

#### Knock sensor(s)

The knock sensor is a piezoelectric element that detects the sound of engine detonation, or 'pinking.' The ECM uses the input signal from the knock sensor to recognise detonation and retard spark advance to avoid engine damage.

#### Mass airflow sensor

Note: *1.4L models are not fitted with a mass airflow sensor*

The mass airflow sensor measures the amount of air passing through the sensor body and ultimately entering the engine. The ECM uses this information to control fuel delivery.

#### Oxygen sensor

The oxygen sensors generate a voltage signal that varies with the difference between the oxygen content of the exhaust and the oxygen in the surrounding air. The ECM uses this information to determine if the fuel system is running rich or lean.

#### Throttle position sensor

The throttle position sensor senses throttle movement and position. This signal enables the ECM to determine when the throttle is closed, in a cruise position, or wide open. The ECM uses this information to control fuel delivery and ignition timing. The throttle position sensor is a component of the throttle control module.

#### Closed throttle position switch

The closed throttle position switch signals the ECM when the throttle is in the fully closed position. The ECM uses this information to control the engine idle speed. The closed throttle position switch is a component of the throttle control module.

#### Vehicle speed sensor

The vehicle speed sensor provides information to the ECM to indicate vehicle speed.

#### Miscellaneous ECM inputs

In addition to the various sensors, the ECM monitors various switches and circuits to determine vehicle operating conditions. The switches and circuits include:

a) Accelerator pedal position (1.4L, 1.6L and 1.8L engines)
b) Air conditioning system
c) Antilock brake system
d) Barometric pressure sensor (inside ECM)
e) Battery voltage
f) Brake switch
g) Clutch pedal switch
h) Cruise control system
i) EVAP system
j) Park/neutral position switch
k) Power steering pressure switch
l) Turbocharger boost pressure (1.8L turbo engine)
m) Sensor signal and earth circuits
n) Transmission control module

### Output actuators

#### Check Engine light

The ECM will illuminate the Check Engine light if a malfunction in the electronic engine control system occurs.

#### EVAP canister purge valve solenoid

The evaporative emission canister purge valve solenoid is operated by the ECM to purge the fuel vapour canister and route fuel vapour to the intake manifold for combustion.

#### Secondary air injection pump and vacuum valve/solenoid

The ECM operates the secondary air injection pump and opens the vacuum valve to inject fresh air into the exhaust stream, lowering emission levels under certain operating conditions.

#### Fuel injectors

The ECM opens the fuel injectors individually in firing order sequence. The ECM also controls the time the injector is held open (pulse width). The pulse width of the injector (measured in milliseconds) determines the amount of fuel delivered. For more information on the fuel delivery system and the fuel injectors, including injector renewal, refer to Chapter 4A.

#### Fuel pump relay

The fuel pump relay is activated by the ECM with the ignition switch in the Start or Run position. When the ignition switch is turned on, the relay is activated to supply initial line pressure to the system. For more information on fuel pump check and renewal, refer to Chapter 4A.

#### Throttle valve actuator (2.0L engine)

The throttle valve actuator controls the throttle plate at idle position. The more the throttle plate is opened, the higher the idle speed. The throttle plate opening and the resulting idle speed is controlled by the ECM. The throttle valve actuator is a component of the throttle control module.

#### Throttle valve actuator (1.4L, 1.6L & 1.8L engines)

The throttle valve actuator controls the throttle plate at all engine speeds. The more the throttle plate is opened, the higher the engine speed. The throttle plate opening and the resulting engine speed is controlled by the ECM. The throttle valve actuator is a component of the throttle control module.

#### Ignition coils

The ECM controls spark delivery and ignition timing depending on engine operation conditions. Refer to Chapter 5 for more information on the ignition system.

#### Oxygen sensor heaters

Each oxygen sensor is equipped with a heating element. Heating the oxygen sensor allows it to reach operating temperature quickly. The ECM controls the oxygen sensor heaters.

#### Turbocharger boost control (1.8L turbo engine)

The ECM monitors intake manifold pressure and controls the turbocharger wastegate with the boost pressure control valve. The engine control system calculates the engine torque needed depending on driver demand and engine operating conditions, the ECM will then adjust the boost pressure to meet the demands.

### Obtaining diagnostic trouble codes

Note: *The diagnostic trouble codes on all models can only be extracted from the Engine Control Module (ECM) using a specialised scan tool. Have the vehicle diagnosed by a dealer service department or other qualified automotive repair facility if the proper scan tool is not available.*

7 The ECM will illuminate the CHECK ENGINE light (also known as the Malfunction Indicator Lamp) on the dash if it recognises a fault in the system. The light will remain illuminated until the problem is repaired and the code is cleared or the ECM does not detect any malfunction for several consecutive drive cycles.

8 The diagnostic codes for the On-Board Diagnostic (OBD) system can only be extracted from the ECM using a scan tool. The scan tool is programmed to interface with the OBD system by plugging into the diagnostic connector located under the dashboard on the driver's side **(see**

**2.8 The 16-pin diagnostic connector is typically located under the instrument panel**

illustration). When used, the scan tool has the ability to diagnose in-depth driveability problems. If the tool is not available and intermittent driveability problems exist, have the vehicle checked at a dealer service department or other qualified garage.

### Clearing diagnostic trouble codes

**9** After the system has been repaired, the codes must be cleared from the ECM memory using a scan tool. Do not attempt to clear the codes by disconnecting battery power. If battery power is disconnected from the ECM, the ECM will lose the current engine operating parameters and driveability will suffer until the ECM is programmed with a scan tool.

**10** Always clear the codes from the ECM before starting the engine after a new electronic emission control component is fitted onto the engine. The ECM stores the operating parameters of each sensor. The ECM may set a trouble code if a new sensor is allowed to operate before the parameters from the old sensor have been erased.

### Diagnostic trouble code identification

**11** The accompanying list of diagnostic trouble codes is a compilation of all the codes that may be encountered using a generic scan tool. Additional trouble codes may be available with the use of the manufacturer specific scan tool. Not all codes pertain to all models and not all codes will illuminate the Check Engine light when set. All models require a scan tool to access the diagnostic trouble codes.

## Trouble codes

| Code | Code Identification |
|---|---|
| P0011-P0013 | Intake cam position sensor |
| P0016 | Crankshaft sensor circuit, correlations fault |
| P0030-P0032 | Oxygen sensor heater circuit |
| P0036-P0038 | Oxygen sensor circuit, sensor 2 |
| P0042-P0044 | Oxygen sensor circuit, sensor 3 |
| P0068 | MAP/MAF, TPS circuit |
| P0097 | IAT circuit, low |
| P0098 | IAT circuit, high |
| P0101 | MAF circuit, range |
| P0102 | Mass air flow sensor circuit, low input |
| P0103 | Mass air flow sensor circuit, high input |
| P0106 | Barometric pressure sensor, range or performance problem |
| P0107-P0108 | MAP circuit, voltage |
| P0112 | Intake air temperature circuit, low input |
| P0113 | Intake air temperature circuit, high input |
| P0116 | Engine coolant temperature circuit, range or performance problem |
| P0117 | Engine coolant temperature circuit, low input |
| P0118 | Engine coolant temperature circuit, high input |
| P0120 | Throttle position sensor circuit, malfunction |
| P0121 | Throttle position sensor circuit, range or performance problem |
| P0122 | Throttle position sensor circuit, low input |
| P0123 | Throttle position sensor circuit, high input |
| P0125 | Insufficient coolant temperature for closed loop fuel control |
| P0130 | Oxygen sensor circuit malfunction (pre-converter sensor) |
| P0131 | Oxygen sensor circuit, low voltage (pre-converter sensor) |
| P0132 | Oxygen sensor circuit, high voltage (pre-converter sensor) |
| P0133 | Oxygen sensor circuit, slow response (pre-converter sensor) |
| P0134 | Oxygen sensor circuit – no activity detected (pre-converter sensor) |
| P0135 | Oxygen sensor heater circuit malfunction (pre-converter sensor) |
| P0136 | Oxygen sensor circuit malfunction (post-converter sensor) |
| P0137 | Oxygen sensor circuit, low voltage (post-converter sensor) |
| P0138 | Oxygen sensor circuit, high voltage (post-converter sensor) |
| P0139 | Oxygen sensor circuit, slow response (post-converter sensor) |
| P0140 | Oxygen sensor circuit – no activity detected (post-converter sensor) |

| Code | Code Identification |
|---|---|
| P0141 | Oxygen sensor heater circuit malfunction (post-converter sensor) |
| P0142 | Oxygen sensor circuit, sensor 2, slow response |
| P0143 | Oxygen sensor circuit, sensor 3, low voltage |
| P0144 | Oxygen sensor circuit, sensor 3, high voltage |
| P0145 | Oxygen sensor circuit, sensor 3, slow response |
| P0146 | Oxygen sensor circuit, sensor 3, no response |
| P0147 | Oxygen sensor circuit, sensor 3, heater circuit |
| P0170 | Fuel trim malfunction |
| P0171 | System too lean |
| P0172 | System too rich |
| P0201 | Injector circuit, cylinder 1, open |
| P0202 | Injector circuit, cylinder 2, open |
| P0203 | Injector circuit, cylinder 3, open |
| P0204 | Injector circuit, cylinder 4, open |
| P0219 | Engine overspeed |
| P0221-P0230 | Throttle pedal position sensor |
| P0234 | Turbocharger overboost condition |
| P0235-P0246 | Turbocharger boost sensor circuit, range or performance problem |
| P0237 | Turbocharger boost sensor circuit, low input |
| P0238 | Turbocharger boost sensor circuit, high input |
| P0261 | Injector circuit, cylinder 1, current low |
| P0262 | Injector circuit, cylinder 1, current high |
| P0264 | Injector circuit, cylinder 2, current low |
| P0265 | Injector circuit, cylinder 2, current high |
| P0267 | Injector circuit, cylinder 3, current low |
| P0268 | Injector circuit, cylinder 3, current high |
| P0270 | Injector circuit, cylinder 4, current low |
| P0271 | Injector circuit, cylinder 4, current low |
| P0299 | Turbocharger, low boost |
| P0300 | Random/multiple cylinder misfire detected |
| P0301 | Cylinder No 1 misfire detected |
| P0302 | Cylinder No 2 misfire detected |
| P0303 | Cylinder No 3 misfire detected |
| P0304 | Cylinder No 4 misfire detected |
| P0318 | Rough road sensor, circuit A |
| P0321 | Engine speed sensor, range or performance problem |
| P0322 | Engine speed sensor, no input |
| P0324 | Knock sensor, system error |
| P0327 | Knock sensor No 1 circuit, low input |
| P0328 | Knock sensor No 1 circuit, high input |
| P0332 | Knock sensor No 2 circuit, low input |
| P0333 | Knock sensor No 2 circuit, high input |
| P0340 | Camshaft position sensor, A circuit |

| Code | Code Identification | Code | Code Identification |
|---|---|---|---|
| P0341 | Camshaft position sensor circuit, range or performance problem | P1102-P1103 | Oxygen sensor heater circuit, short to B+ (pre-converter sensor) |
| P0342 | Camshaft position sensor circuit, low input | P1105 | Oxygen sensor heater circuit, short to B+ (post-converter sensor) |
| P0343 | Camshaft position sensor circuit, high input | | |
| P0351 | Ignition coil, A circuit | P1111 | Oxygen sensor control, lean |
| P0352 | Ignition coil, B circuit | P1112 | Oxygen sensor control, rich |
| P0353 | Ignition coil, C circuit | P1113-P1114 | Oxygen sensor circuit, incorrect resistance (pre-converter sensor) |
| P0354 | Ignition coil, D circuit | | |
| P0411 | Secondary air injection system, incorrect flow | P1115 | Oxygen sensor heater circuit, short to ground (pre-converter sensor) |
| P0412-P0418 | Secondary air injection system, switching valve circuit | | |
| P0420 | Catalyst system efficiency below threshold | P1116 | Oxygen sensor heater circuit, open (pre-converter sensor) |
| P0422 | Catalyst system efficiency below threshold | P1117 | Oxygen sensor heater circuit, short to ground (post-converter sensor) |
| P0440 | Evaporative emission control system malfunction | | |
| P0441 | Evaporative emission control system, incorrect purge flow | P1118 | Oxygen sensor heater circuit, open (post-converter sensor) |
| P0442 | Evaporative emission control system, small leak detected | | |
| P0445 | Evaporative emission control system, large leak detected | P1127 | Long term fuel trim too rich |
| P0458-P0459 | Evaporative emission control system, purge valve circuit | P1128 | Long term fuel trim too lean |
| P0501 | Vehicle speed sensor circuit, range or performance problem | P1136 | Fuel trim too rich at idle |
| | | P1137 | Fuel trim too lean at idle |
| P0506 | Idle control system, rpm lower than expected | P1142-P1143 | Load detection, value out of range |
| P0507 | Idle control system, rpm higher than expected | P1149 | Oxygen sensor control, value out of range |
| P0510 | Closed throttle position switch malfunction | P1151 | Long-term fuel trim, lean |
| P0532 | Air conditioning refrigerant pressure sensor circuit, low input | P1152-P1166 | Long-term fuel trim, rich |
| | | P1171 | Throttle actuator position sensor range or performance problem |
| P0533 | Air conditioning refrigerant pressure sensor circuit, high input | | |
| | | P1172 | Throttle actuator position sensor, signal low |
| P0560 | System voltage malfunction | P1173 | Throttle actuator position sensor, signal high |
| P0562 | System voltage low | P1176 | Oxygen sensor, correction limit attained |
| P0563 | System voltage high | P1196 | Oxygen sensor heater electrical malfunction (pre-converter sensor) |
| P0571 | Brake switch malfunction | | |
| P0600 | Engine Control Module, communications error | P1198 | Oxygen sensor heater electrical malfunction (post-converter sensor) |
| P0601-P0602 | Engine Control Module, programming error | | |
| P0604 | Engine Control Module, memory error (RAM) | P1201 | Fuel injector circuit, cylinder 1, open |
| P0605 | Engine Control Module, memory error (ROM) | P1202 | Fuel injector circuit, cylinder 2, open |
| P0606 and | Transmission Control Module, programming error | P1203 | Fuel injector circuit, cylinder 3, open |
| P0614 | ECM/TCM, incompatibility | P1204 | Fuel injector circuit, cylinder 4, open |
| P0627-P0629 | Fuel pump, circuit A | P1213 | Fuel injector circuit, short to B+ (cylinder No 1) |
| P0638 | Throttle control actuator, range | P1214 | Fuel injector circuit, short to B+ (cylinder No 2) |
| P0686-P0688 | Engine Control Module, power relay control circuit | P1215 | Fuel injector circuit, short to B+ (cylinder No 3) |
| P0700 | Transmission control system, module | P1216 | Fuel injector circuit, short to B+ (cylinder No 4) |
| P0702 | Transmission control system, electrical | P1225 | Fuel injector circuit, short to ground (cylinder No 1) |
| P0704 | Transmission clutch circuit, input | P1226 | Fuel injector circuit, short to ground (cylinder No 2) |
| P0705 | Transmission range sensor, circuit | P1227 | Fuel injector circuit, short to ground (cylinder No 3) |
| P0706 | Transmission range sensor, performance | P1228 | Fuel injector circuit, short to ground (cylinder No 4) |
| P0710-P0714 | Transmission fluid temp sensor, performance or circuit | P1237 | Fuel injector circuit, open (cylinder No 1) |
| P0715-P0717 | Transmission turbine speed sensor, performance or circuit | P1238 | Fuel injector circuit, open (cylinder No 2) |
| P0720-P0722 | Transmission output speed sensor, performance or circuit | P1239 | Fuel injector circuit, open (cylinder No 3) |
| P0725-P0727 | Engine speed input, circuit or performance | P1240 | Fuel injector circuit, open (cylinder No 4) |
| P0729-P0735 | Automatic transmission, incorrect gear ratio | P1255-P1256 | ECT circuit, open or short |
| P0740 | Torque converter clutch circuit, open | P1287 | Turbocharger bypass valve, open |
| P0743 | Torque converter clutch circuit, electrical | P1288 | Turbocharger bypass valve, short to B+ |
| P0746-P0749 | Transmission pressure control solenoid | P1289 | Turbocharger bypass valve, Short to ground |
| P0751-P0753 | Transmission shift solenoid A | P1295 | Turbocharger bypass, faulty input |
| P0756-P0758 | Transmission shift solenoid B | P1296 | Turbocharger cooling system, malfunction |
| P0761-P0763 | Transmission shift solenoid C | P1297 | Turbocharger throttle valve, loose hose, pressure drop |
| P0766-P0768 | Transmission shift solenoid D | P1300 | Misfire detected, fuel problem |
| P0771-P0773 | Transmission shift solenoid E | P1325 | Knock sensor limit attained (cylinder No 1) |
| P0776-P0778 | Transmission pressure control solenoid B | P1326 | Knock sensor limit attained (cylinder No 2) |
| P0785 | Transmission shift timing solenoid | P1327 | Knock sensor limit attained (cylinder No 3) |
| P0796-P0798 | Transmission pressure control solenoid C | P1328 | Knock sensor limit attained (cylinder No 4) |
| P0811 | Excessive clutch slippage | P1335 | Engine torque control adaptation at limit |
| P0840-P0844 | Transmission fluid pressure sensor, circuit B | P1336 | Engine torque control adaptation at limit |
| P0845-P0849 | Transmission fluid pressure sensor, circuit A | P1338 | Camshaft position sensor, open or short |
| P0863-P0865 | Transmission control module, circuit | P1340 | Camshaft position sensor out of sequence |
| P0884-P0892 | Transmission Control module, power relay | P1355 | Ignition control circuit, open (cylinder No 1) |

| Code | Code Identification | Code | Code Identification |
|---|---|---|---|
| P1356 | Ignition control circuit, short to B+ (cylinder No 1) | P1556 | Turbocharger boost pressure control valve, positive deviation |
| P1357 | Ignition control circuit, short to ground (cylinder No 1) | P1557 | Turbocharger boost pressure control valve, negative deviation |
| P1358 | Ignition control circuit, open (cylinder No 2) | P1558 | Throttle valve actuator, electrical malfunction |
| P1359 | Ignition control circuit, short to B+ (cylinder No 2) | P1559 | Throttle control module to Engine Control Module adaptation error |
| P1360 | Ignition control circuit, short to ground (cylinder No 2) | P1560 | Engine overspeed condition |
| P1361 | Ignition control circuit, open (cylinder No 3) | P1564 | Throttle control valve, voltage low |
| P1362 | Ignition control circuit, short to B+ (cylinder No 3) | P1565 | Throttle valve actuator, lower limit not attained |
| P1363 | Ignition control circuit, short to ground (cylinder No 3) | P1568 | Throttle valve actuator, mechanical malfunction |
| P1364 | Ignition control circuit, open (cylinder No 4) | P1569 | Cruise control switch signal |
| P1365 | Ignition control circuit, short to B+ (cylinder No 4) | P1580 | Throttle control valve, drive malfunction |
| P1366 | Ignition control circuit, short to ground (cylinder No 4) | P1582 | Idle adaptation at limit |
| P1386 | Engine Control Module malfunction | P1592 | Charge air pressure sensor |
| P1387 | Engine Control Module malfunction | P1602 | Engine Control Module, power supply low voltage |
| P1388 | Engine Control Module malfunction | P1603 | Engine Control Module, failed self-check |
| P1409 | EVAP system, purge control valve circuit | P1604 | Engine Control Module malfunction |
| P1410 | Fuel tank vent valve, short to B+ | P1606 | ABS control unit, road surface information fault |
| P1420 | Secondary air injection valve circuit, malfunction | P1609 | ABS control unit, crash shut-off triggered |
| P1421 | Secondary air injection valve circuit, short to ground | P1610 | ABS control unit, memory error |
| P1422 | Secondary air injection valve circuit, Short to B+ | P1612 | Engine Control Module, incorrect programming |
| P1424 | Secondary air injection system, leak detected | P1624 | ABS control unit, fault lamp active |
| P1425 | Fuel tank vent valve circuit, short to ground | P1626 | Engine Control Module, no manual transaxle data |
| P1426 | Fuel tank vent valve circuit, open | P1630 | Accelerator pedal position sensor No 1, signal low |
| P1432 | Secondary air injection valve open | P1631 | Accelerator pedal position sensor No 1, signal high |
| P1433 | Secondary air injection system, pump relay circuit open | P1633 | Accelerator pedal position sensor No 2, signal low |
| P1434 | Secondary air injection system, pump relay circuit short to B+ | P1634 | Accelerator pedal position sensor No 2, signal high |
| P1435 | Secondary air injection system, pump relay circuit short to ground | P1635 | Data bus, no drivetrain message |
| P1436 | Secondary air injection system, pump relay circuit, electrical fault | P1639 | Accelerator pedal position sensor, range or performance problem |
| P1450 | Secondary air injection system, pump relay circuit short to B+ | P1640 | Engine Control Module, ROM error |
| P1451 | Secondary air injection system, pump relay circuit short to ground | P1648 | Engine Control Module, no powertrain data |
| P1452 | Secondary air injection system, pump relay circuit open | P1649 | Engine Control Module, no ABS data |
| P1470 | Leak detection pump, electrical fault | P1650 | Engine Control Module, no instrument cluster data |
| P1471 | EVAP system leak detection pump circuit, short to B+ | P1676 | Electronic accelerator pedal warning light circuit malfunction |
| P1472 | EVAP system leak detection pump circuit, short to ground | P1677 | Electronic accelerator pedal warning light circuit, short to B+ |
| P1473 | EVAP system leak detection pump circuit, open | P1678 | Electronic accelerator pedal warning light circuit, short to ground |
| P1475 | EVAP system leak detection pump vent system malfunction | P1679 | Electronic accelerator pedal warning light circuit, open |
| P1476 | EVAP system leak detection pump, pressure low | P1681 | Engine Control Module, programming not finished |
| P1477 | EVAP system leak detection pump vent system malfunction | P1690 | MIL circuit, electrical fault |
| P1478 | EVAP system leak detection pump, breather blocked | P1691 | Check Engine light circuit, open |
| P1500 | Fuel pump relay circuit malfunction | P1692 | Check Engine light circuit, short to ground |
| P1501 | Fuel pump relay circuit, short to ground | P1693 | Check Engine light circuit, short to B+ |
| P1502 | Fuel pump relay circuit, short to B+ | P1778 | Automatic transmission, valve 7, electrical fault |
| P1517 | ECM, main relay voltage supply | P1780 | Automatic transmission, valve 7, torque retraction fault |
| P1539 | Clutch pedal switch signal | P1823 | Automatic transmission, valve 3, pressure control |
| P1541 | Fuel pump relay circuit, open | P1820 | Automatic transmission, valve 4, pressure control |
| P1542 | Throttle actuator sensor, range or performance problem | P1847 | ABS control unit, valve 3, memory fault |
| P1543 | Throttle actuator sensor, signal low | P1851 | Engine Control Module, no ABS data |
| P1544 | Throttle actuator sensor, signal high | P1853 | Engine Control Module, no ABS data |
| P1545 | Throttle valve actuator malfunction | P1854 | Data bus, software fault |
| P1546 | Turbocharger boost pressure control valve circuit, short to B+ | P1855 | Data bus, hardware fault |
| P1547 | Turbocharger boost pressure control valve circuit, short to ground | P1854 | Data bus, software fault |
| P1548 | Turbocharger boost pressure control valve circuit, open | P1857 | ECM, load signal fault |
| P1550 | Turbocharger boost pressure control valve, pressure deviation | P1861 | TPS sensor, fault from ECM |
| P1555 | Turbocharger boost pressure control valve, upper limit exceeded | P1866 | TCM data bus, missing information |

**3.3  To disconnect the electrical connectors from the ECM, pry the locking tab out**

**3.4  Carefully pry off the ECM retaining clips (arrowed)**

### 3  Engine Control Module (ECM) – removal and refitting

*Caution: Avoid static electricity damage to the Engine Control Module (ECM) by grounding yourself to the body of the vehicle before touching the ECM and using a special anti-static pad to store the ECM on, once it is removed.*

**Note 1:** *Anytime the ECM is renewed it must be reprogrammed by a dealership service department with special equipment. The following procedure pertains to removal and refitting of the original ECM only. If the ECM must be renewed, take the vehicle to a dealership service department.*

**Note 2:** *Anytime battery power is disconnected from the ECM, stored operating parameters will be lost from the ECM, which will cause various driveability problems until the ECM can be reset with a scan tool.*

1 Disconnect the cable from the negative battery terminal.

*Caution: These models are equipped with an anti-theft radio. Before performing a procedure that requires disconnecting the battery, make sure you have the activation code.*

2 The ECM is located under the plenum cover, at the base of the windscreen on the left-hand side. Remove the plenum panel on the left-hand side (see Chapter 11). Remove the metal plenum close-out plate under the plenum panel.

3 Disconnect the electrical connectors from the ECM **(see illustration)**.
4 Carefully prise off the ECM retainer clips **(see illustration)**. Remove the ECM from the plenum.
5 Refitting is the reverse of removal.

### 4  Throttle control module – testing and renewal

1 The throttle control module is connected to the end of the throttle shaft on the throttle body. The throttle control module contains four major components of the engine control system; the throttle position sensor, the closed throttle switch, the throttle valve actuator and a feedback sensor for the throttle valve actuator. The ECM uses the throttle position sensor to control fuel delivery based on driver demand. On 2.0L models, the throttle valve actuator controls the idle speed and cruise control functions. 1.4L, 1.6L and 1.8L models are not equipped with a throttle cable, the throttle valve actuator controls the throttle plate under all driving conditions. The throttle control module is calibrated to the throttle body during manufacture, therefore is the throttle control module requires renewal, the complete throttle body assembly must be renewed.

### Testing

**Note:** *Performing the following test will set a*

*diagnostic trouble code and illuminate the Check Engine light. Clear the diagnostic trouble code after performing the tests and making the necessary repairs (see Section 2).*

2 The throttle control module is located on the side of the throttle body **(see illustration)**. Check the terminals in the connector and the wires leading to the sensor for looseness and breaks. Repair as required.

3 A scan tool is required for complete diagnosis of the throttle control module (see Section 2), but the following checks may identify a definite failure with the throttle control module or circuit.

4 Disconnect the electrical connector from the throttle control module and check the voltage supply and earth circuits **(see illustration)**. On 2.0L models, connect a voltmeter to terminals 2 and 5 (4 and 7 for vehicles without cruise control) – a minimum of 4.5 volts should be present. Connect a voltmeter to terminals 2 and 6 – a minimum of 9.0 volts should be present.

5 On 1.4L, 1.6L and 1.8L models to 2003, connect a voltmeter to terminals 2 and 6 (3 and 7 for vehicles without cruise control) – a minimum of 4.5 volts should be present **(see illustration)**. On 2004-on models, check between 2 and 4 (vehicles with cruise control) or between 4 and 7 (without cruise control).

6 If the specified voltage is not present, check the power and earth circuits. **Note:** *Refer to the wiring diagrams at the end of Chapter 12 for additional information of the circuits.*

7 Using an ohmmeter, measure the resistance between terminals 7 and 8 (2.0L) or terminals 3 and 5 (1.4L, 1.6L & 1.8L) on the throttle control module. On 1.4L, 1.6L & 2.0L models the resistance should be 3.0 to 200 ohms. On 1.8L turbo models the resistance should be 1.0 to 5.0 ohms. If the resistance is not as specified, renew the throttle control module.

### Renewal

*Caution: If the throttle control module is renewed, the ECM must be programmed with a scan tool to accept the new throttle control module.*

8 The throttle control module is calibrated to

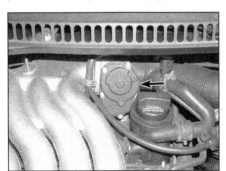

**4.2  The throttle control module (arrowed) is located on the side of the throttle body**

**4.4  Disconnect the electrical connector from the throttle control module and check the voltage supply and ground circuits at the harness connector**

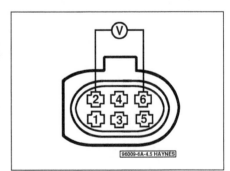

**4.5  Throttle control module electrical connector terminal identification (harness-side) – 1.4L, 1.6L and 1.8L engines**

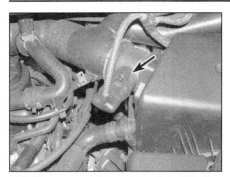

5.2 The mass airflow sensor is located in the air intake duct attached to the air filter housing

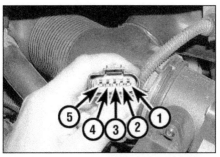

5.3 Disconnect the electrical connector from the mass airflow sensor and check the voltage supply and ground circuits at the harness connector

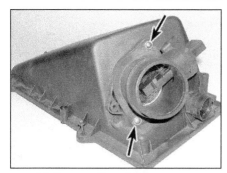

5.6 Remove the retaining screws (arrowed) and remove the mass airflow sensor

the throttle body during manufacture, therefore if the throttle control module requires renewal, renew the throttle body assembly (see Chapter 4A).

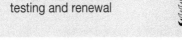

## 5   Mass airflow sensor – testing and renewal

**Note:** *1.4L models are not fitted with a mass airflow sensor*

1 The mass airflow sensor measures the amount of air passing through the sensor body and ultimately entering the engine through the throttle body. The ECM uses this information to control fuel delivery – the more air entering the engine (acceleration), the more fuel required.

### Testing

**Note:** *Performing the following test will set a diagnostic trouble code and illuminate the Check Engine light. Clear the diagnostic trouble code after performing the tests and making the necessary repairs (see Section 2).*

2 The mass airflow sensor is located in the air intake duct attached to the air filter housing cover **(see illustration)**. A scan tool is necessary to check the output of the mass airflow sensor (see Section 2). The scan tool displays the sensor output in g/s. With the

engine idling at normal operating temperature, the display should read approximately 2.8 to 5.6 g/s (2.0L), 2.0 to 4.5 g/s (1.6L) or 1.0 to 10.0 g/s (1.8L). When the engine is accelerated the values should rise quickly and remain steady at a steady engine speed.

3 Before checking the mass airflow sensor operation, check the voltage supply circuit. Disconnect the electrical connector from the mass airflow sensor and connect the positive lead of a voltmeter to terminal No 2 and the negative lead to a good engine earth point **(see illustration)**. Turn the ignition key On – the voltage should read approximately 12.0 volts. If the voltage is incorrect, check the circuit from the mass airflow sensor to the fusebox (don't forget to check the fuses first). If the power circuit is good, check the mass airflow sensor operation with a scan tool. If the mass airflow sensor does not respond as described in Step 2, renew the mass airflow sensor. **Note:** *Before condemning the mass airflow sensor, check the air intake duct for leaks between the sensor and the intake manifold. A reading below the specified value may be caused by an air leak.*

### Renewal

4 Disconnect the electrical connector from the mass airflow sensor.

5 Remove the air filter housing cover (see Chapter 4A).

6 Remove the screws retaining the mass

airflow sensor to the air filter cover and remove the sensor **(see illustration)**. *Caution: Handle the mass airflow sensor with care. Damage to this sensor will affect the operation of the entire fuel injection system.*

7 Refitting is the reverse of removal.

## 6   Intake air temperature sensor – testing and renewal

1 The intake air temperature sensor is a thermistor (a resistor which varies the value of its resistance in accordance with temperature changes). The change in the resistance values will directly affect the voltage signal from the sensor to the ECM. As the sensor temperature INCREASES, the resistance values will DECREASE. As the sensor temperature DECREASES, the resistance values will INCREASE.

### Testing

2 On 1.4L models, the inlet air temperature/ pressure sender is located on the right-hand side of the inlet manifold. Note that access is limited. On 1.6L and 2.0L models, the intake air temperature sensor is incorporated into the mass airflow sensor. On 1.8L turbo models, the intake air temperature sensor is located on the intake manifold near the throttle body **(see illustration)**. Check the terminals in the connector and the wires leading to the sensor for looseness and breaks. Repair as required.

3 With the ignition switch Off, disconnect the electrical connector from the mass airflow sensor (1.6L and 2.0L) or intake air temperature sensor (1.4L and 1.8L) **(see illustration)**. Using an ohmmeter, measure the resistance between the two intake air temperature sensor terminals on the sensor while it is completely cold – at 30°C the resistance should be 1.5 to 2.0 kohms. Reconnect the electrical connector to the sensor, start the engine and warm it up until it reaches operating temperature. Disconnect the connector and check the resistance again – at 80°C the resistance should be 275 to 375 ohms. Compare your measurements to

6.2 Intake air temperature sensor location – 1.8L turbo models

6.3a On 1.6L and 2.0L models, disconnect the electrical connector from the mass airflow sensor and measure the intake sensor resistance across terminals 1 and 3

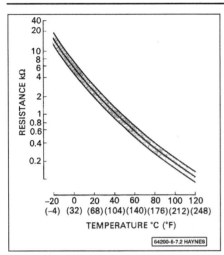

6.3b Intake air temperature sensor and engine coolant temperature sensor approximate temperature vs. resistance values

the resistance chart **(see illustration)**. If the sensor resistance test results are incorrect, renew the intake air temperature sensor.

4 On 1.4L models, disconnect the wiring, then undo the two screws and remove the sensor from the inlet manifold. Recover the seal and discard, as a new one must be used on refitting.

### Renewal

5 On 1.6L and 2.0L models, renew the mass airflow sensor (see Section 5).

6 On 1.8L turbo models, disconnect the electrical connector from the sensor, remove the mounting bolt and withdraw the sensor from the intake manifold.

7 Refitting is the reverse of removal.

### 7 Engine coolant temperature sensor – testing and renewal

1 The engine coolant temperature sensor is a thermistor (a resistor which varies the value of its resistance in accordance with temperature changes). The change in the resistance values will directly affect the voltage signal from the sensor to the ECM. As the sensor

7.2a Engine coolant temperature sensor location – 1.6L and 2.0L models

temperature INCREASES, the resistance values will DECREASE. As the sensor temperature DECREASES, the resistance values will INCREASE.

### Testing

2 The engine coolant temperature sensor is located in the coolant pipe near the coolant outlet **(see illustrations)**. Check the terminals in the connector and the wires leading to the sensor for looseness and breaks. Repair as required.

3 With the ignition switch Off, disconnect the electrical connector from the engine coolant temperature sensor. Using an ohmmeter, measure the resistance between terminals 1 and 3 on the sensor while it is completely cold **(see illustration)** – at 30°C the resistance should be 1.5 to 2.0 kohms. Reconnect the electrical connector to the sensor, start the engine and warm it up until it reaches operating 80°C) the resistance should be 275 to 375 ohms. Compare your measurements to the resistance chart **(see illustration 6.3b)**. If the sensor resistance test results are incorrect, renew the engine coolant temperature sensor. **Note:** *A more accurate check may be performed by removing the sensor and suspending the tip of the sensor in a container of water. Heat the water on the stove while you monitor the resistance of the sensor.*

### Renewal

 *Warning: Wait until the engine is completely cool before beginning this procedure.*

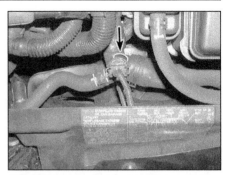

7.2b Engine coolant temperature sensor – 1.8L turbo models

4 Partially drain the cooling system (see Chapter 1).

5 Disconnect the electrical connector from the sensor.

6 Carefully prise the retaining clip out and withdraw the sensor from the coolant pipe.

7 Before refitting the new sensor, renew the O-ring.

8 Refitting is the reverse of removal.

### 8 Engine speed sensor – testing and renewal

1 The engine sensor provides the ECM with a crankshaft position signal. The ECM uses the signal to determine a crankshaft reference point (Top Dead Centre) and calculate engine speed (RPM). The signal is also used by the On-board Diagnostic system for misfire detection. The ignition system will not operate if the ECM does not receive an engine speed sensor input.

### Testing

2 The engine speed sensor is located on the side of the engine block near the oil filter. The sensor is equipped with a pigtail lead and a remote connector **(see illustration)**. Check the terminals in the connector and the wires leading to the sensor for looseness and breaks. Repair as required.

3 Disconnect the electrical connector from the engine speed sensor. Using an ohmmeter, measure the resistance of the sensor across terminals 2 and 3 **(see illustration)**. The

7.3 Measure the resistance of the engine coolant air temperature sensor across terminals 1 and 3

8.2 Engine speed sensor electrical connector location (arrowed)

8.3 Measure the resistance of the engine speed sensor across terminals 2 and 3

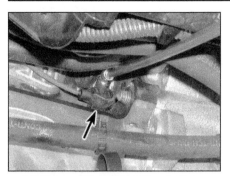

**8.7 Remove the engine speed sensor mounting bolt**

**9.2a Camshaft position sensor electrical connector location – 1.6L and 2.0L models**

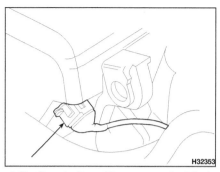

**9.2b Camshaft position sensor electrical connector location – 1.8L turbo models**

resistance should be 480 to 1000 ohms (2.0L) or 730 to 1000 ohms (1.6L and 1.8L).

**4** Check for continuity between terminals 1 and 2, then 1 and 3. No continuity (infinity) should be indicated.

**5** If the engine speed sensor fails either test, renew the sensor.

### Renewal

**6** Disconnect the engine speed sensor electrical connector.

**7** Remove the engine speed sensor mounting bolt and withdraw the sensor from the engine block **(see illustration)**.

**8** Renew the O-ring and lightly lubricate it with clean engine oil.

**9** Refitting is the reverse of removal.

## 9  Camshaft position sensor – testing and renewal

**1** The camshaft position sensor, in conjunction with the crankshaft position sensor (engine speed sensor), determines the ignition timing and fuel injection synchronisation on each cylinder. The sensor is a magnetic pick-up device triggered from a reluctor wheel on the camshaft sprocket (1.6L and 2.0L) or camshaft (1.4L and 1.8L).

### Testing

**Note:** *Performing the following test will set a diagnostic trouble code and illuminate the*

*Check Engine light. Clear the diagnostic trouble code after performing the tests and making the necessary repairs (see Section 2).*

**2** On 1.4L models, the camshaft position sensor is located on the top, left-hand rear of the camshaft housing. On 1.6L and 2.0L models, the camshaft position sensor is located behind the camshaft sprocket and is equipped with a pigtail lead and a remote connector **(see illustration)**. On 1.8L turbo models, the camshaft position sensor is located at the front of the intake camshaft **(see illustration)**. Check the terminals in the connector and the wires leading to the sensor for looseness and breaks. Repair as required.

**3** Before checking the camshaft position sensor, check the voltage supply and earth circuits from the ECM. Disconnect the electrical connector from the camshaft position sensor and connect a voltmeter to terminals 1 and 3 at the harness connector **(see illustration)**. Turn the ignition key On – the voltage should read approximately 5.0 volts. If the voltage is incorrect, check the wiring from the camshaft position sensor to the ECM. If the circuits are good, have the ECM checked at a dealer service department or other properly-equipped repair facility.

**4** To check the camshaft position sensor operation, reconnect the connector to the camshaft position sensor and using a suitable probe, backprobe terminal No 2 of the camshaft position sensor connector **(see illustration)** (see Chapter 12 for additional information on how to backprobe a

connector). Connect the positive lead of a voltmeter to the probe and the negative lead to a good engine earth point. Turn the ignition key On. Rotate the engine slowly with a breaker bar and socket attached to the crankshaft pulley centre bolt while watching the meter. The voltage should fluctuate between zero volts and 10.0 volts as the vanes in the reluctor wheel pass the sensor. If the test results are incorrect, renew the camshaft position sensor. **Note:** *Rotate the engine slowly through at least two complete revolutions. Removing the spark plugs from the engine will make the crankshaft much easier to turn.*

⚠ **Warning: Unplug the primary (low voltage) electrical connector(s) from the ignition coil(s) to disable the ignition system.**

### Renewal

#### 1.4L models

**5** First, remove the engine top cover.

**6** Disconnect the camshaft position sensor electrical connector **(see illustration)**.

**7** Undo the screw and remove the sensor. Recover the O-ring seal.

**8** Refitting is the reverse of removal, but fit a new O-ring seal.

#### 1.6L and 2.0L models

**9** Remove the timing belt and the camshaft sprocket (see Chapter 2B).

**10** Remove the timing belt rear cover.

**9.3 Disconnect the electrical connector from the camshaft position sensor and check the voltage supply and ground circuits at the harness connector**

**9.4 To check the camshaft position sensor, backprobe terminal No 2 of the sensor connector with a voltmeter**

**9.6 On 1.4L models, disconnect the camshaft position sensor wiring**

**9.11 On 1.6L and 2.0L models, remove the timing belt rear cover bolts (A) and the camshaft position sensor mounting bolt (B)**

Disconnect the camshaft position sensor electrical connector and detach the electrical connector from the bracket.

**11** Remove the camshaft position sensor mounting bolt and remove the sensor from the cylinder head **(see illustration)**.

**12** Refitting is the reverse of removal.

### 1.8L turbo models

**13** Disconnect the camshaft position sensor electrical connector.

**14** Remove the timing belt upper cover (see Chapter 2B).

**15** Remove the camshaft position sensor mounting bolts and remove the sensor from the cylinder head.

**16** Refitting is the reverse of removal.

## 10 Oxygen sensor – testing and renewal

**Note:** *All models are equipped with two oxygen sensors; one pre-catalytic converter oxygen sensor and one post-converter oxygen sensor.*

**1** The oxygen in the exhaust reacts with the elements inside the oxygen sensor to produce a voltage output that varies from 0.1 volt (high oxygen, lean mixture) to 0.9 volt (low oxygen, rich mixture). The pre-converter oxygen sensor (mounted in the exhaust system before the catalytic converter) provides a feedback signal to the ECM that indicates the amount of oxygen remaining in the exhaust gas after combustion. The ECM monitors this variable voltage continuously to determine the required fuel injector pulse width and to control the engine air/fuel ratio. A mixture ratio of 14.7 parts air to 1 part fuel is the ideal ratio for minimum exhaust emissions, as well as the best combination of fuel economy and engine performance. Based on oxygen sensor signals, the ECM tries to maintain this air/fuel ratio of 14.7:1 at all times.

**2** The post-converter oxygen sensor (mounted in the exhaust system after the catalytic converter) has no effect on ECM control of the air/fuel ratio. However, the post-converter sensor is identical to the pre-converter sensor and operates in the same way. The ECM uses the post-converter signal to monitor the efficiency of the catalytic converter. A post-converter oxygen sensor will produce a slower fluctuating voltage signal that reflects the lower oxygen content in the post-catalyst exhaust.

**3** An oxygen sensor produces no voltage when it is below its normal operating temperature of about 320°C. During this warm-up period, the ECM operates in an open-loop fuel control mode. It does not use the oxygen sensor signal as a feedback indication of residual oxygen in the exhaust. Instead, the ECM controls fuel metering based on the inputs of other sensors and its own programs.

**4** Proper operation of an oxygen sensor depends on four conditions:

a) *Electrical – The low voltages generated by the sensor require good, clean connections which should be checked whenever a sensor problem is suspected or indicated.*

b) *Outside air supply – The sensor needs air circulation to the internal portion of the sensor. Whenever the sensor is fitted, make sure the air passages are not restricted.*

c) *Proper operating temperature – The ECM will not react to the sensor signal until the sensor reaches approximately 320°C. This factor must be considered when evaluating the performance of the sensor.*

d) *Unleaded fuel – Unleaded fuel is essential for proper operation of the sensor.*

**5** The ECM can detect several different oxygen sensor problems and set diagnostic trouble codes to indicate the specific fault (see Section 2). When an oxygen sensor fault occurs, the ECM will disregard the oxygen sensor signal voltage and revert to open-loop fuel control as described previously.

### Testing

***Caution:*** *The oxygen sensor is very sensitive to excessive circuit loads and circuit damage of any kind. For safest testing, disconnect the oxygen sensor connector, refit jumper wires between the two connectors and connect your voltmeter to the jumper wires. If jumper wires aren't available, carefully backprobe the wires in the connector shell with suitable probes (such as T-pins). Do not puncture the oxygen sensor wires or try to backprobe the sensor itself. Use only a digital voltmeter to test an oxygen sensor.*

**Note:** *Performing the following test will set a diagnostic trouble code and illuminate the Check Engine light. Clear the diagnostic trouble code after performing the tests and making the necessary repairs (see Section 2).*

**6** The oxygen sensor connectors are located under a cover on the vehicle underbody **(see illustrations)**. Connect a voltmeter to the black wire and the brown wire at the oxygen sensor connector. Turn the ignition On but do not start the engine. The meter should read approximately 400 to 450 millivolts (0.40 to 0.45 volt). If it doesn't, trace and repair the circuit from the sensor to the ECM. **Note:** *Refer to the wiring diagrams at the end of Chapter for additional information on the oxygen sensor circuits.*

**7** Start the engine and let it warm up to normal operating temperature; again check the oxygen sensor signal voltage.

a) *Voltage from a pre-converter sensor should range from 100 to 900 millivolts (0.1 to 0.9 volt) and switch actively between high and low readings.*

b) *Voltage from a post-converter sensor should also read between 100 to 900 millivolts (0.1 to 0.9 volt) but it should not switch actively. The post-converter*

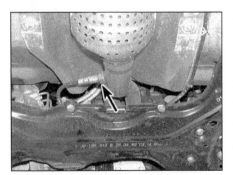

**10.6a The pre-catalyst oxygen sensor is located in the exhaust pipe before the catalytic converter**

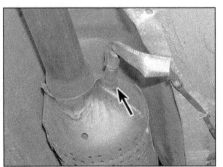

**10.6b The post-catalyst oxygen sensor is located in the exhaust pipe after the catalytic converter**

**10.6c The electrical connector for the oxygen sensors are located under a cover**

*oxygen sensor voltage may stay toward the centre of its range (about 400 millivolts) or stay for relatively longer periods of time at the upper or lower limits of the range.*

8 Check the battery voltage supply and earth circuits to the oxygen sensor heater. Disconnect the electrical connector and connect a voltmeter to terminals 1 and 2 of the sensor harness connector **(see illustration)**. Turn the ignition On, the meter should read approximately 12 volts. If battery voltage is not present, check the power and earth circuits to the sensor (don't forget to check the fuses first).

9 Allow the oxygen sensor to cool and check the oxygen sensor heater for an open circuit. With the connector disconnected. Connect an ohmmeter to the two oxygen sensor heater terminals of the connector (oxygen sensor side). The oxygen sensor pigtail is generally not colour-coded, but the heater wires are usually the white wires. If an open circuit or excessive resistance is indicated, renew the oxygen sensor. **Note:** *If the tests indicate that a sensor is good, and not the cause of a driveability problem or diagnostic trouble code, check the wiring harness and connectors between the sensor and the ECM for an open or short circuit. If no problems are found, have the vehicle checked by a dealer service department or other qualified garage.*

### Renewal

10 The exhaust pipe contracts when cool, and the oxygen sensor may be hard to loosen when the engine is cold. To make sensor removal easier, start and run the engine for a minute or two; then shut it off. Be careful not to burn yourself during the following procedure. Also observe these guidelines when renewing an oxygen sensor.

a) *The sensor has a permanently attached pigtail and electrical connector which should not be removed from the sensor. Damage or removal of the pigtail or electrical connector can harm operation of the sensor.*

b) *Keep grease, dirt and other contaminants away from the electrical connector and the louvered end of the sensor.*

c) *Do not use cleaning solvents of any kind on the oxygen sensor.*

d) *Do not drop or roughly handle the sensor.*

11 Raise the vehicle and place it securely on axle stands.

12 Remove the cover and disconnect the electrical connector from the sensor.

13 Using a suitable spanner or specialised oxygen sensor socket, unscrew the sensor from the exhaust manifold **(see illustration)**.

14 High temperature anti-seize compound must be used on the threads of the sensor to aid future removal. The threads of most new sensors will be coated with this compound. If not, be sure to apply anti-seize compound before refitting the sensor.

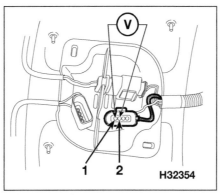

10.8 **Check the battery voltage supply and ground circuits to the oxygen sensor heater**

15 Refit the sensor and tighten it securely.
16 Reconnect the electrical connector to the sensor, refit the cover and lower the vehicle.

## 11 Knock sensor – testing and renewal

1 The knock sensor detects abnormal vibration (spark knock or pinking) in the engine. The knock control system is designed to reduce spark knock during periods of heavy detonation. This allows the engine to use maximum spark advance to improve driveability. Knock sensors produce AC output voltage which increases with the severity of the knock. The signal is fed into the ECM and the timing is retarded to compensate for the severe detonation.

### Testing

2 1.6L models are equipped with one knock sensor, whilst 1.4L, 1.8L and 2.0L models are equipped with two knock sensors. They are located on the side of the engine block below the intake manifold **(see illustration)**.
3 A scan tool is required to thoroughly check the knock sensor system, but the following check can be performed to identify a definite knock sensor failure.
4 Disconnect the electrical connector from the knock sensor. Using an ohmmeter, check for continuity across the two terminals of the knock sensor. No continuity (infinity) should

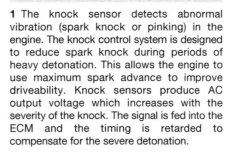

11.2  **Knock sensor location**

10.13 **A special slotted socket, allowing clearance for the wiring harness, may be required for oxygen sensor removal (the tool is available at most automotive tool stores)**

be indicated on the meter, if continuity is indicated, renew the knock sensor.

### Renewal

5 Disconnect the electrical connector from the knock sensor.
6 Remove the sensor from the engine block **(see illustration 11.2)**.
7 Refitting is the reverse of removal. Tighten the knock sensor bolt to the specified torque.

## 12 Vehicle speed sensor – testing and renewal

1 The Vehicle Speed Sensor (VSS) is mounted on the transmission. The sensor is triggered by a toothed rotor on the transmission output shaft. As the output shaft rotates, the sensor produces a fluctuating voltage, the frequency of which is proportional to vehicle speed. The ECM uses the sensor input signal for several different engine and transmission control functions. The VSS signal also drives the speedometer on the instrument panel. A defective VSS can cause various driveability and transmission problems.

### Testing

2 Raise the vehicle and support it securely on axle stands. Locate the vehicle speed sensor **(see illustration)**. Check the terminals in the connector and the wires leading to the sensor for looseness and breaks. Repair as required.

12.2  **Vehicle speed sensor location**

**3** To check the VSS operation with a voltmeter, backprobe the white/blue wire terminal of the VSS connector using a suitable probe (see Chapter 12 for additional information on how to backprobe a connector). Connect the other lead of the voltmeter to a good earth and turn the ignition key On. Hold the right front tyre steady and rotate the left front tyre by hand while watching the voltmeter. The sensor should produce a fluctuating voltage from zero to approximately 5.0 volts.

### Renewal

**4** Raise the vehicle and support it securely on axle stands.
**5** Disconnect the electrical connector from the VSS.
**6** Remove mounting bolt and withdraw the VSS from the transmission case.
**7** Renew the sensor O-ring.
**8** Refitting is the reverse of removal.

## 13 Accelerator control system (1.6L and 1.8L engines)

Models equipped with 1.4L, 1.6L or 1.8L engines utilise an electronic accelerator control system. The system does not use an accelerator cable, the throttle valve is operated by the throttle valve actuator contained within the throttle control module. The throttle valve actuator is controlled by the ECM. The accelerator pedal module contains a pedal position sensor. The pedal position signal is fed to the ECM and the ECM commands the throttle valve actuator to open the throttle accordingly.

With the engine off and the ignition key On, the ECM opens the throttle valve in direct relationship to the accelerator pedal input. But when the engine is running, under load, the ECM operates the throttle valve independently of the accelerator pedal. The throttle valve may be opened significantly farther than the driver may be demanding. This allows the ECM to maintain the engine at peak operating efficiency.

The system operation is monitored by the On-Board Diagnosis system, but uses a separate warning light. The Electronic Power Control (EPC) warning light is located near the top of the speedometer. The EPC light will illuminate with the ignition key On and should go out when the engine is started. If the EPC warning light remains on, or comes on with the engine running, a problem with the system has been identified and a Diagnostic Trouble Code is retained in the ECM memory. If there is a complete failure with the system the ECM will limit the engine speed to approximately 1200 rpm.

A quick check of the system can be performed by removing the air intake duct and observing the throttle valve as an assistant depresses the accelerator pedal. When the accelerator pedal is depressed half-way, the throttle valve should open to half throttle. When the accelerator pedal is depressed fully, the throttle valve should open to full throttle. The manufacturer's scan tool is required to properly diagnose the system. If a fault is suspected with the system or if the EPC warning light is on, take the vehicle to a dealership service department as soon as possible. For additional information, refer to Chapter 4A for information on the electronic accelerator pedal module and Section 4 of this Chapter for information on the throttle control module.

## 14 Turbocharger boost control system

The turbocharger boost control system consists of the boost pressure sensor, the boost pressure (wastegate) control valve, the recirculation air valve and solenoid, the ECM and the connecting hoses and wiring (see illustration).

The ECM monitors boost pressure sensor signal and controls the vacuum supplied to the turbocharger wastegate actuator with the boost pressure control valve. The engine control system calculates the engine torque needed depending on driver demand and engine operating conditions, the ECM will then adjust the boost pressure to meet the demands. The recirculation air valve returns air to the intake duct when the throttle is closed minimising turbo lag. The ECM controls the recirculation air valve with a vacuum valve/solenoid.

If a problem is suspected with the system, check the wiring, connectors, vacuum hoses and connecting pipes. Using a hand-held vacuum pump, apply vacuum to the wastegate actuator (with the engine not running) and check the actuator arm and lever

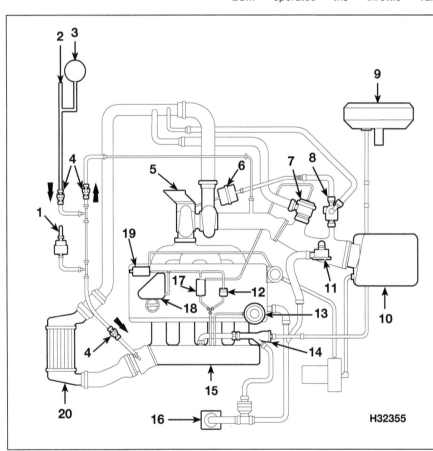

**14.1 Turbocharger Boost pressure control system**

| | | |
|---|---|---|
| *1 EVAP purge valve* | *9 Brake servo* | *16 Crankcase ventilation* |
| *2 Hose* | *10 Air filter assembly* | *housing* |
| *3 Vacuum reservoir* | *11 Crankcase pressure* | *17 Recirculation valve* |
| *4 Check valve* | *regulator valve* | *solenoid* |
| *5 Turbocharger* | *12 Check valve* | *18 Vacuum reservoir* |
| *6 Wastegate actuator* | *13 Fuel pressure regulator* | *19 Secondary air injection* |
| *7 Recirculation air valve* | *14 Vacuum amplifier* | *valve* |
| *8 Boost pressure control* | *15 Intake manifold* | *20 Intercooler* |
| *valve* | | |

H32355

for freedom of movement. Disconnect the electrical connector from the boost pressure control valve and using an ohmmeter, check the solenoid windings for an open circuit. The boost pressure control valve should measure approximately 25 to 35 ohms, if an open circuit or excessive resistance is indicated, renew the control valve.

A scan tool is required for complete diagnosis of the system control circuits. If a scan tool is not available, have the system checked at a dealer service department or other properly-equipped repair facility.

## 15 Crankcase ventilation system

1 When the engine is running, a certain amount of the gases produced during combustion escapes past the piston rings into the crankcase as blow-by gases. The crankcase ventilation system is designed to reduce the resulting hydrocarbon emissions (HC) by routing the gases and vapours from the crankcase into the intake manifold and combustion chambers, where they are consumed during engine operation.

2 Crankcase vapours pass through a hose connected from the valve cover to the air intake duct (see illustration). The oil/air separator at the valve cover separates the oil suspended in the blow-by gases and allows the oil to drain back into the crankcase. The crankcase vapours are drawn from the oil/air separator through a hose connected to the air intake duct where they mix with the incoming air and are burned during the normal combustion process. A heating element is incorporated into the air intake duct to prevent icing in extremely cold weather. On 1.8L turbo models, a pressure regulating valve is fitted in the breather hose (see illustration).

3 A blocked breather, valve or hose will cause excessive crankcase pressures resulting in oil leaks and sludge build-up in the crankcase.

Check the components for restrictions and clean or renew the components as necessary. Be sure to check the basic mechanical condition of the engine before condemning the crankcase ventilation system (see Chapter 2C).

## 16 Evaporative emissions control system

1 The fuel evaporative emissions control (EVAP) system absorbs fuel vapours from the fuel tank and, during engine operation, releases them into the engine intake system where they mix with the incoming air/fuel mixture. The main components of the evaporative emissions system are the canister (filled with activated charcoal to absorb fuel vapours), the purge control valve, the fuel tank and the vapour and purge lines.

2 After passing through a check valve, fuel tank vapour is carried through the vapour hose to the charcoal canister. The activated charcoal in the canister absorbs and stores the vapours. When a programmed set of conditions are met (engine running, warmed to a pre-set temperature, etc), the ECM opens the purge valve. Fuel vapours from the canister are then drawn through the purge hose by intake manifold vacuum into the intake manifold and combustion chamber where they are consumed during normal engine operation.

3 The ECM regulates the rate of vapour flow from the canister to the intake manifold by controlling the duty cycle of the EVAP purge control valve solenoid. During cold running conditions and hot start time delay, the ECM does not energise the solenoid. After the engine has warmed up to the correct operating temperature, the ECM purges the vapours into the intake manifold according to the running conditions of the engine. The ECM will cycle (ON then OFF) the purge control valve solenoid about 5 to 10 times per

second. The flow rate will be controlled by the pulse width, or length of time, the solenoid is allowed to be energised.

4 On US 1.8L and 2.0L models, the EVAP system is equipped with a leak detection monitor system. The system is a self-diagnostic system designed to detect a leak in the EVAP system. Each time the engine is started cold, the PCM energises the leak detection pump. The pump pressurises the EVAP system then shuts off. The PCM is able to detect a leak if the pump continues to run, unable to pressurise the system. If a leak is detected, the PCM will trigger a diagnostic trouble code (see Section 2).

### Testing

5 Always check the hoses first. A disconnected, damaged or missing hose is the most likely cause of a malfunctioning EVAP system. Determine whether the hoses are correctly routed and attached. Repair any damaged hoses or renew any missing hoses as necessary.

6 Check the related fuses and wiring to the purge valve. Refer to the wiring diagrams at the end of Chapter 12, if necessary. The purge valve is normally closed – no vapours will pass through the ports. When the ECM energises the solenoid (by completing the circuit to earth), the valve opens and vapours flow through.

7 A scan tool is required to thoroughly check the system. If the above checks fail to identify the problem area, have the system diagnosed by a dealer service department or other qualified garage.

### Component renewal

**EVAP canister and leak detection pump**

8 The EVAP canister and leak detection pump are attached to a bracket in the right rear wheelarch (see illustration).

9 Loosen the right rear wheel bolts, then raise the vehicle and support it securely on axle stands. Remove the right rear wheel.

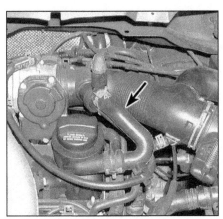

**15.2a  The crankcase ventilation system hose (arrowed) runs from the valve cover to the intake duct**

**15.2b  1.8L turbo models are equipped with a crankcase ventilation pressure regulator valve (arrowed)**

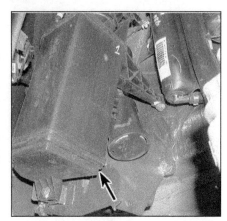

**16.8  The EVAP canister and leak detection pump are mounted in the right rear wheelarch**

**16.10 To disconnect an EVAP system quick-release fitting, squeeze the tabs together**

10 Label and remove the hoses from the canister. Many of the EVAP system hoses are equipped with quick-release fittings (see illustration). Disconnect the fitting as follows:
   a) Clean the area around the fitting.
   b) Twist the fitting back-and-forth several times to loosen the seal.
   c) Depress the locking tabs and pull the fitting straight off the nipple.
11 Remove the mounting bolts and remove the canister. Remove the leak detection pump from the canister, if necessary.
12 Refitting is the reverse of removal.

### Purge control valve

13 The purge control valve is mounted on a

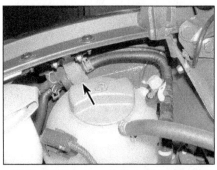

**16.13 EVAP purge control valve location (arrowed)**

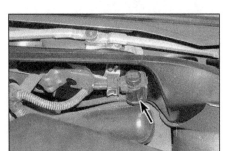

**17.11 Secondary air injection vacuum valve location (arrowed)**

bracket above the right front wheelarch (see illustration).
14 Disconnect the electrical connector. Label and remove the hoses from the purge control valve.
15 Remove the mounting bolts and remove the purge control valve from the bracket.
16 Refitting is the reverse of removal.

## 17 Secondary air injection system

1 The secondary air injection system is used to reduce tailpipe emissions on initial engine start-up. The system uses an electric motor/pump assembly, vacuum valve/ solenoid, combination air shut-off/check valve and tubing to inject fresh air directly into the exhaust manifold. The fresh air (oxygen) reacts with the exhaust gas in the catalytic converter to reduce HC and CO levels. The air pump and solenoid are controlled by the ECM. During initial start-up, when the coolant temperature is between 15 and 35°C, the ECM will energise the vacuum valve/solenoid, opening the check valve and operate the air pump for approximate one minute. During normal operation, the check valve is closed to prevent exhaust backflow into the system.

### Testing

2 Check the air pump hoses and the vacuum

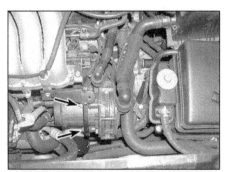

**17.7 Remove the secondary air injection pump mounting bolts (arrowed) (two of three shown)**

**17.15 Secondary air injection check valve location (arrowed)**

hoses. Repair any damaged hoses or renew any missing hoses as necessary. Check the vacuum source to the vacuum valve. Intake manifold vacuum should be present with the engine running.
3 Check the related fuses and wiring to the air pump and vacuum valve/solenoid. Refer to the wiring diagrams at the end of Chapter 12, if necessary. The vacuum valve is normally closed – no vacuum is applied to the check valve. When the ECM energises the solenoid (by completing the circuit to earth), the valve opens, vacuum is applied to the check valve, the check valve opens and air flows through the tube into the exhaust pipe.
4 A scan tool is required to thoroughly check the system. If the above checks fail to identify the problem area, have the system diagnosed by a dealer service department or other qualified garage.

### Component renewal

#### Air pump

5 Remove the engine cover.
6 Disconnect the electrical connector and remove the hoses from the air pump.
7 Remove the mounting bolts and remove the air pump assembly (see illustration).
8 Refitting is the reverse of removal.

#### Vacuum valve

9 Disconnect the electrical connector from the vacuum valve.
10 Label and disconnect the vacuum hoses from the valve.
11 Remove the mounting nut and remove the vacuum valve (see illustration).
12 Refitting is the reverse of removal.

#### Check valve (combination valve)

13 Remove the air intake duct.
14 Remove the vacuum hose and the air hose from the check valve.
15 Remove the mounting bolts and remove the check valve (see illustration).
16 Refitting is the reverse of removal.

## 18 Catalytic converter

1 The catalytic converter is an emission control device added to the exhaust system to reduce pollutants from the exhaust gas stream. A three-way (reduction) catalyst design is used. The catalytic coating on the three-way catalyst contains platinum and rhodium, which lowers the levels of oxides of nitrogen (NOx) as well as hydrocarbons (HC) and carbon monoxide (CO).
2 The test equipment for a catalytic converter is expensive and highly sophisticated. If you suspect that the converter on your vehicle is malfunctioning, take it to a dealer or emissions specialist for diagnosis and repair.

## Testing

**3** Whenever the vehicle is raised for servicing of underbody components, check the converter for leaks, corrosion, dents and other damage. Check the welds/flange bolts that attach the front and rear ends of the converter to the exhaust system. If damage is discovered, the converter should be renewed.

**4** A catalytic converter may become blocked. The easiest way to check for a restricted converter is to use a vacuum gauge to diagnose the effect of a blocked exhaust on intake vacuum.

a) *Connect a vacuum gauge to an intake manifold vacuum source.*

b) *Warm the engine to operating temperature, place the transmission in Neutral (manual transmission) or Park (automatic transmission) and apply the handbrake.*

c) *Note and record the vacuum reading at idle.*

d) *Open the throttle until the engine speed is about 2000 rpm.*

e) *Release the throttle quickly and record the vacuum reading.*

f) *Perform the test three more times, recording the reading after each test.*

g) *If the reading after the fourth test is more than 25.4 mm-Hg lower than the reading recorded at idle, the catalytic converter, silencer or exhaust pipes may be blocked or restricted.*

## Renewal

**Note:** *Refer to the exhaust system servicing section in Chapter 4A for additional information.*

**5** Raise the vehicle and support it securely on axle stands.

**6** Disconnect the electrical connectors from the oxygen sensors **(see illustration)**.

**7** Remove the exhaust pipe-to-exhaust manifold flange bolts and separate the exhaust pipe from the exhaust manifold (see Chapter 2A). Support the exhaust pipe.

**8** Loosen the clamp bolts and detach the catalytic converter and exhaust manifold pipe from the exhaust system **(see illustration)**.

**9** Clean the carbon deposits from the mounting flanges and refit new gaskets.

**10** Refitting is the reverse of removal.

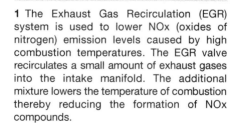

## 19 Exhaust Gas Recirculation (EGR) system – testing and renewal

**1** The Exhaust Gas Recirculation (EGR) system is used to lower NOx (oxides of nitrogen) emission levels caused by high combustion temperatures. The EGR valve recirculates a small amount of exhaust gases into the intake manifold. The additional mixture lowers the temperature of combustion thereby reducing the formation of NOx compounds.

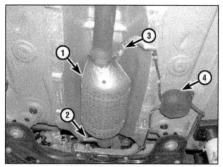

**18.6 Catalytic converter and related components**

1  *Catalytic converter*
2  *Per-catalyst oxygen sensor*
3  *Post-catalyst oxygen sensor*
4  *Oxygen sensor electrical connectors (under cover)*

**2** The EGR system consists of the EGR valve, the EGR vacuum regulator valve, the ECM and a series of connecting pipes and vacuum

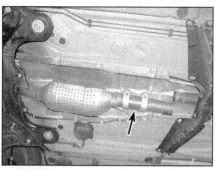

**18.8 Loosen the clamp bolts, slide the clamp forward (arrowed) and separate the catalytic converter pipe from the exhaust system**

hoses. The EGR valve is located behind the secondary air injection combi-valve at the left-hand end of the cylinder head. The EGR gases flow from the exhaust manifold, through the EGR valve, and into the throttle body **(see illustration)**.

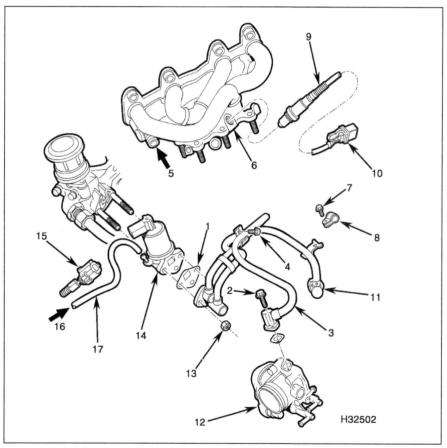

**19.2 EGR system components – 1.4L-pre 2006 and 1.6L models only**

| | | |
|---|---|---|
| 1  *Gasket* | 6  *Exhaust manifold* | 12 *Throttle body* |
| 2  *Bolt* | 7  *Bolt* | 13 *Nut* |
| 3  *Pipe to throttle body* | 8  *Clamp* | 14 *EGR valve* |
| 4  *Bolt* | 9  *Oxygen sensor* | 15 *Connector* |
| 5  *From secondary air injection system combi-valve* | 10 *Connector* | 16 *From air filter* |
| | 11 *Connection to exhaust manifold* | 17 *Vacuum hose* |

**3** The ECM controls the EGR flow rate by energising the EGR vacuum regulator valve solenoid coil. When the vacuum regulator valve is energised vacuum is applied the EGR valve, opening the EGR passage.

## Testing

### EGR system

**4** The manufacturer's scan tool is required to test the EGR components. However, basic checks can be performed by the DIY mechanic. Check the relevant system components for leaks, split/perished vacuum hoses, dirty/loose electrical connectors and blocked pipes.

**5** If these checks fail to identify a fault, have the system inspected by a VW dealer or specialist.

## Renewal

### EGR valve

**6** Disconnect the EGR pipe assembly from the exhaust manifold and throttle body.

**7** Release bolt securing the pipe assembly support bracket **(see illustration 19.2)**.

**8** Undo the two nuts securing the pipe assembly to the EGR valve.

**9** Disconnect the vacuum hose from the EGR valve.

**10** Depress the retaining clip and disconnect the wiring plug from the valve

**11** Slide the EGR valve from the two studs and recover the gaskets.

**12** Refitting is the reverse of removal, using a new gaskets.

# Chapter 6 Part B
# Emissions and engine control systems –
# diesel engine

## Contents

## Degrees of difficulty

| | | | | |
|---|---|---|---|---|
| **Easy,** suitable for novice with little experience  | **Fairly easy,** suitable for beginner with some experience  | **Fairly difficult,** suitable for competent DIY mechanic  | **Difficult,** suitable for experienced DIY mechanic | **Very difficult,** suitable for expert DIY or professional |

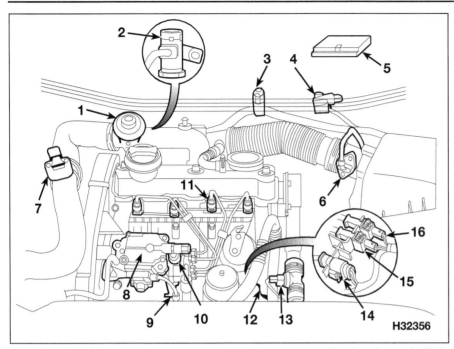

**1.1 Typical emission and engine control system components – diesel engine code ALH**

1 EGR valve
2 Air shut-off valve vacuum valve
3 EGR vacuum regulator valve
4 Wastegate regulator valve
5 Engine control module (ECM)
6 Mass airflow sensor
7 Manifold absolute pressure/intake air
   temperature sensor
8 Fuel injection pump quantity adjuster

9 Cold start valve
10 Fuel shut-off valve
11 Fuel injector needle lift sensor
12 Engine speed sensor
13 Engine coolant temperature sensor
14 Fuel injection pump electrical connector
15 Engine speed sensor electrical connector
16 Fuel injector needle lift sensor electrical
   connector

## 1  General information

To prevent pollution of the atmosphere from incompletely burned fuel and to maintain good driveability and fuel economy, a number of emission control systems are incorporated **(see illustration)**. They include the:

*Electronic engine control system*
*Crankcase ventilation system*
*Exhaust Gas Recirculation system*
*Catalytic converter*

All of these systems are linked, directly or indirectly, to the emission control system.

The Sections in this Chapter include general descriptions, checking procedures within the scope of the home mechanic (when possible) and component renewal procedures for each of the systems listed above.

Before assuming that an emissions control system is malfunctioning, check the fuel system carefully. The diagnosis of some emission control devices requires specialised tools, equipment and training. If checking and servicing become too difficult or if a procedure is beyond your ability, consult a dealer service department or other properly-equipped repair facility. Remember, the most frequent cause of emissions problems is simply a loose or broken vacuum hose or wire, so always check the hose and wiring connections first.

This doesn't mean, however, that emission control systems are particularly difficult to maintain and repair. You can quickly and easily perform many checks and do most of the regular maintenance at home with common hand tools. Pay close attention to any special precautions outlined in this Chapter. It should be noted that the illustrations of the various systems may not exactly match the system fitted on the vehicle you're working on because of changes made by the manufacturer during production or from year-to-year.

## 2  On-Board Diagnostic (OBD) system and trouble codes

### Diagnostic tool information

1 A digital multimeter is necessary for checking fuel injection and emission related components **(see illustration)**. A digital volt-ohmmeter is preferred over the older style analog multimeter for several reasons. The

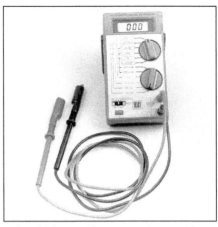

**2.1 Digital multimeter can be used for testing all types of circuits. Because of their high impedance, they are much more accurate than analogue meters for measuring low-voltage computer circuits**

analog multimeter cannot display the volts-ohms or amps measurement in hundredths and thousandths increments. When working with electronic circuits which are often very low voltage, this accurate reading is most important.

2 Another good reason for the digital multimeter is the high impedance circuit. The digital multimeter is equipped with a high resistance internal circuitry (10 million ohms). Because a voltmeter is hooked up in parallel with the circuit when testing, it is vital that none of the voltage being measured should be allowed to travel the parallel path set up by the meter itself. This dilemma does not show itself when measuring larger amounts of voltage (9 to 12 volt circuits) but if you are measuring a low voltage circuit such as sensor signal voltage, a fraction of a volt may be a significant amount when diagnosing a problem. However, there are several exceptions where using an analog voltmeter may be necessary to test certain sensors.

3 Several tool manufacturers have released OBD scan tools for the home mechanic. Hand-held scanners are the most powerful and versatile tools for analyzing engine management systems used on later model vehicles. Alternatively, your local VW dealer or specialist will have the necessary equipment to interrogate the OBD system.

### On-Board Diagnostic system general description

4 All models described in this manual are equipped with the second generation On-Board Diagnostic system. The system consists of an on-board computer, known as the Engine Control Module (ECM), information sensors and output actuators.

5 The information sensors monitor various functions of the engine and send data to the ECM. Based on the data and the information programmed into the computer's memory, the

ECM generates output signals to control various engine functions via control relays, solenoids and other output actuators. The ECM is specifically calibrated to optimise the emissions, fuel economy and driveability of the vehicle. It isn't a good idea to attempt diagnosis or renewal of the ECM at home while the vehicle is under warranty. Take the vehicle to a dealer service department if the ECM or a system component malfunctions.

## Information sensors

### Engine speed sensor

The engine speed sensor senses crankshaft position (TDC) and speed during each engine revolution. The ECM uses this information to control fuel injection quantity and timing.

### Engine coolant temperature sensor

The engine coolant temperature sensor senses engine coolant temperature. The ECM uses this information to control fuel injection quantity and timing.

### Fuel injector needle lift sensor

*Note: Engine code ALH only*

The ECM monitors the fuel injection timing with the signal from the fuel injection needle lift sensor. The sensor is located in fuel injector number three.

### Fuel temperature sensor

The fuel temperature sensor senses the temperature of the fuel being delivered to the fuel injectors. The ECM uses this information to control fuel injection quantity and timing.

### Intake air temperature sensor

The intake air temperature sensor senses the temperature of the air entering the intake manifold. The ECM uses this information to control fuel injection quantity and timing.

### Manifold absolute pressure sensor

The ECM monitors the turbocharger boost pressure with the signal from the manifold absolute pressure sensor. The ECM uses this information to control the turbocharger wastegate regulator valve.

### Mass airflow sensor

The mass airflow sensor measures the amount of air passing through the sensor body and ultimately entering the engine. The ECM uses this information to control fuel injection quantity and turbocharger boost pressure.

### Modulating piston displacement sensor

*Note: Engine code ALH only*

The ECM monitors the fuel injection quantity with the modulating piston displacement sensor.

### Throttle position sensor

The throttle position sensor senses throttle movement and position. The ECM uses this

information to control fuel delivery and engine speed according to driver demand.

### Vehicle speed sensor

The vehicle speed sensor provides information to the ECM to indicate vehicle speed.

### Miscellaneous ECM inputs

In addition to the various sensors, the ECM monitors various switches and circuits to determine vehicle operating conditions. The switches and circuits include:

a) *Air conditioning system*
b) *Antilock brake system*
c) *Barometric pressure sensor (inside ECM)*
d) *Battery voltage*
e) *Brake switch*
f) *Clutch pedal switch*
g) *Cruise control system*
h) *Park/neutral position switch*
i) *Power steering pressure switch*
j) *Sensor signal and ground circuits*
k) *Transmission control module*

## Output actuators

### Air shut-off valve

The ECM closes the air shut-off valve when the ignition key is turned off. Cutting off the air supply softens the shock of shutting-down a diesel engine.

### Check Engine light

The ECM will illuminate the Check Engine light if a malfunction in the electronic engine control system occurs.

### Cold start valve

*Note: Engine code ALH only*

The ECM energises the cold start valve when the engine is started cold. The cold start valve advances the fuel injection timing to aid in cold starting. See Chapter 4B for more information regarding the cold start valve.

### EGR regulator valve

The ECM controls the operation of the EGR valve by regulating the vacuum supply to the valve.

### Fuel shut-off valve

*Note: Engine code ALH only*

The ECM controls the operation of the fuel shut-off valve. The fuel shut-off valve interrupts fuel flow to the fuel injection pump and is used to start and stop the engine from running.

### Fuel quantity adjuster

*Note: Engine code ALH only*

The ECM precisely controls the fuel injection quantity (and resulting engine speed) based on signals received from the various engine sensors.

### Glow plugs

The ECM controls the operation of the glow plug system. The glow plugs allow the engine to start easily in cold conditions.

### Turbocharger wastegate regulator valve

The ECM monitors intake manifold pressure and controls the turbocharger wastegate with the wastegate regulator valve. The engine control system calculates the engine torque needed depending on driver demand and engine operating conditions, the ECM will then adjust the boost pressure to meet the demands.

## Obtaining diagnostic trouble codes

**Note:** *The diagnostic trouble codes on all models can only be extracted from the Engine Control Module (ECM) using a specialised scan tool. Have the vehicle diagnosed by a dealer service department or other qualified automotive repair facility if the proper scan tool is not available.*

6 The ECM will illuminate the CHECK ENGINE light (also known as the Malfunction Indicator Lamp) on the dash if it recognises a fault in the system. The light will remain illuminated until the problem is repaired and the code is cleared or the ECM does not detect any malfunction for several consecutive drive cycles.

7 The diagnostic codes for the On-Board Diagnostic (OBD) system can only be extracted from the ECM using a scan tool. The scan tool is programmed to interface with the OBD system by plugging into the diagnostic connector **(see illustration)**. When used, the scan tool has the ability to diagnose in-depth driveability problems. If the tool is not available and intermittent driveability problems exist, have the vehicle checked at a dealer service department or other qualified garage.

## Clearing diagnostic trouble codes

8 After the system has been repaired, the codes must be cleared from the ECM memory using a scan tool. Do not attempt to clear the codes by disconnecting battery power. If battery power is disconnected from the ECM, the ECM will lose the current engine operating parameters and driveability will suffer until the ECM is programmed with a scan tool.

9 Always clear the codes from the ECM before starting the engine after a new

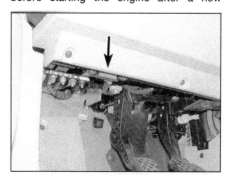

**2.7 The diagnostic connector is typically located under the instrument panel**

electronic emission control component is fitted onto the engine. The ECM stores the operating parameters of each sensor. The ECM may set a trouble code if a new sensor is allowed to operate before the parameters from the old sensor have been erased.

### Diagnostic trouble code identification

10 The accompanying list of diagnostic trouble codes is a compilation of all the codes that may be encountered using a generic scan tool. Additional trouble codes may be available with the use of the manufacturer specific scan tool. Not all codes pertain to all models and not all codes will illuminate the Check Engine light when set. All models require a scan tool to access the diagnostic trouble codes.

### Trouble codes

| Code | Code Identification |
|---|---|
| P0030 | HO$_2$S, heater control circuit |
| P0100-P0103 | Mass air flow sensor, faulty signal |
| P0105-P0108 | MAP sensor, circuit or performance |
| P0112-P0113 | IAT, circuit |
| P0116 | Engine coolant temperature sensor, faulty signal |
| P0117-P0118 | ECT, circuit |
| P0121 | Throttle position sensor, faulty signal |
| P0123 | Throttle position sensor circuit, short to B+ |
| P0128 | Coolant thermostat |
| P0135 | O$_2$ sensor, heater circuit |
| P0181-P0183 | Fuel temperature sensor |
| P0200 | Injector circuit, cylinder 1, open |
| P0201 | Injector circuit, cylinder 2, open |
| P0202 | Injector circuit, cylinder 3, open |
| P0203 | Injector circuit, cylinder 4, open |
| P0216 | Injector timing control circuit |
| P0225-P0228 | Accelerator pedal position switch |
| P0230-P0232 | Fuel pump circuit |
| P0234 | Turbocharger overboost condition |
| P0237-P0238 | Turbocharger boost solenoid, A circuit |
| P0243-P0246 | Turbocharger wastegate solenoid |
| P0251-P0252 | Injection pump metering control |
| P0263 | Contribution or balance, cylinder 1 |
| P0266 | Contribution or balance, cylinder 2 |
| P0269 | Contribution or balance, cylinder 3 |
| P0272 | Contribution or balance, cylinder 4 |
| P0299 | Turbocharger underboost condition |
| P0300 | Random/multiple cylinder misfire detected |
| P0301 | Cylinder No 1 misfire detected |
| P0302 | Cylinder No 2 misfire detected |
| P0303 | Cylinder No 3 misfire detected |
| P0304 | Cylinder No 4 misfire detected |
| P0321 | Engine speed sensor, faulty signal |
| P0322 | Engine speed sensor, no signal output |
| P0380-P0381 | Glow plug monitor circuit |
| P0401 | EGR, insufficient flow |
| P0402 | EGR, excess flow |
| P0403 | EGR, control circuit |
| P0404 | EGR, range, performance |
| P0501 | Vehicle speed sensor circuit, faulty signal |
| P0560 | System voltage malfunction |
| P0600 | Serial communication, memory error |
| P0602 | Control module, program error |
| P0604 | Engine Control module, internal RAM error |
| P0605 | Engine Control Module, internal ROM error |
| P0606 | ECM/PCM, communication |
| P0607 | Control module, performance |
| P0613 | TCM, processor |
| P0614 | ECM/TCM, incompatibility |
| P0642-P0645 | Sensor reference, voltage A |
| P0652-P0653 | Sensor reference, voltage B |
| P0670 | Glow plug circuit |
| P0671 | Glow plug circuit, cylinder 1 |
| P0672 | Glow plug circuit, cylinder 2 |
| P0673 | Glow plug circuit, cylinder 3 |

| Code | Code Identification |
|---|---|
| P0674 | Glow plug circuit, cylinder 4 |
| P0684 | Glow plug control module, communication to ECM |
| P0700 | Automatic transmission control system, MIL request |
| P0701 | Automatic transmission control system, range |
| P0702 | Automatic transmission control system, MIL electrical |
| P0705 | Automatic transmission control system, range sensor |
| P0710-P0713 | Transmission fluid temperature sensor, A circuit |
| P0715-P0717 | Input turbine speed sensor |
| P0720-P0722 | Output turbine speed sensor |
| P0725-P0727 | Engine speed input |
| P0730-P0734 | Automatic transmission, incorrect gear ratio |
| P0740-P0743 | Torque converter clutch, circuit |
| P0746-P0749 | Automatic transmission, pressure control solenoid A |
| P0751-P0753 | Automatic transmission, shift solenoid A |
| P0756-P0758 | Automatic transmission, shift solenoid B |
| P0761-P0763 | Automatic transmission, shift solenoid C |
| P0766-P0768 | Automatic transmission, shift solenoid D |
| P0771-P0773 | Automatic transmission, shift solenoid E |
| P0776-P0778 | Automatic transmission, pressure control solenoid B |
| P0781 | Automatic transmission, first-to-second shift |
| P0782 | Automatic transmission, second-to-third shift |
| P0783 | Automatic transmission, third-to-fourth shift |
| P0784 | Automatic transmission, fourth-to-fifth shift |
| P0785 | Automatic transmission, shift timing solenoid |
| P0791 | Automatic transmission, intermediate shaft speed sensor |
| P0796-P0798 | Automatic transmission, pressure control solenoid |
| P0811 | Automatic transmission, clutch slippage |
| P0829 | Automatic transmission, fifth-to-sixth shift |
| P0840-P0841 | Automatic transmission, fluid pressure sensor switch A |
| P0845-P0846 | Automatic transmission, fluid pressure sensor switch B |
| P0863-P0865 | TCM, communication circuit |
| P0889-P0892 | TCM, power relay circuit |
| P0914 | Automatic transmission, gear shift position circuit |
| P0919 | Automatic transmission, gear shift position error |
| P0929-P0931 | Automatic transmission, gear shift lock control solenoid |
| P1144 | Mass airflow sensor, short to ground or open circuit |
| P1145 | Mass airflow sensor, short to B+ |
| P1146 | Mass airflow sensor, voltage supply circuit open or shorted |
| P1155 | Manifold absolute pressure sensor, short to B+ |
| P1156 | Manifold absolute pressure sensor, short to ground or open circuit |
| P1157 | Manifold absolute pressure sensor, voltage supply circuit shorted or open |
| P1160 | Intake air temperature sensor, short to ground |
| P1161 | Intake air temperature sensor, short to B+ or open circuit |
| P1162 | Fuel temperature sensor, short to ground |
| P1163 | Fuel temperature sensor, short to B+ or open circuit |
| P1245 | Fuel injector needle lift sensor, short to ground |
| P1246 | Fuel injector needle lift sensor, faulty signal |
| P1247 | Fuel injector needle lift sensor, short to B+ or open circuit |
| P1248 | Fuel injection control malfunction |
| P1251 | Cold start valve circuit, short to B+ |
| P1252 | Cold start valve circuit, short to ground or open circuit |
| P1255 | Engine coolant temperature sensor, short to ground |
| P1256 | Engine coolant temperature sensor, short to B+ or open circuit |

Emissions and engine control systems – diesel engine  6B•5

| Code | Code Identification | Code | Code Identification |
|------|---------------------|------|---------------------|
| P1354 | Modulating piston displacement sensor circuit, open or shorted | P1612 | Engine Control Module, incorrect programming |
| | | P1616 | Glow plug indicator light, short to B+ |
| P1402 | EGR regulator valve circuit, short to B+ | P1617 | Glow plug indicator light, short to ground or open circuit |
| P1403 | EGR system control malfunction | P1618 | Glow plug relay circuit, short to B+ |
| P1441 | EGR regulator valve circuit, short to ground or open circuit | P1619 | Glow plug relay circuit, short to ground or open circuit |
| P1537 | Fuel shut-off valve malfunction | P1626 | Engine Control Module, no communication with transaxle |
| P1538 | Fuel shut-off valve circuit, short to ground or open circuit | | control module |
| P1540 | Vehicle speed sensor, signal high | P1632 | Throttle position sensor circuit, voltage supply open or shorted |
| P1546 | Turbocharger wastegate regulator valve circuit, short to B+ | | |
| P1549 | Turbocharger wastegate regulator valve circuit, short to ground or open circuit | P1693 | Check Engine light circuit, short to B+ |
| | | P1694 | Check Engine light circuit, short to ground or open circuit |
| P1550 | Turbocharger boost pressure control | P1851 | Engine Control Module, no communication with ABS |
| P1561 | Fuel quantity adjuster control malfunction | | module |
| P1562 | Fuel quantity adjuster reaches upper limit | P1854 | Engine Control Module, data bus failure |
| P1563 | Fuel quantity adjuster reaches lower limit | | |

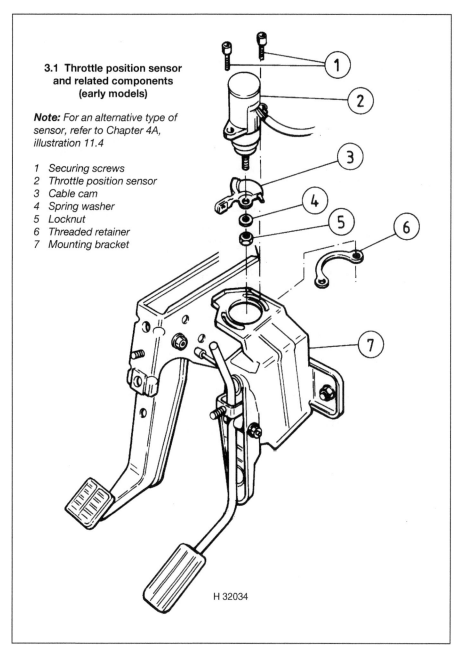

**3.1 Throttle position sensor and related components (early models)**

*Note: For an alternative type of sensor, refer to Chapter 4A, illustration 11.4*

1 Securing screws
2 Throttle position sensor
3 Cable cam
4 Spring washer
5 Locknut
6 Threaded retainer
7 Mounting bracket

H 32034

## 3 Throttle position sensor – testing and renewal

1 The throttle position sensor is connected to the accelerator pedal. The throttle position sensor sends a varying voltage signal to the ECM as the accelerator is depressed. The ECM uses the throttle position sensor signal to control fuel delivery based on driver demand. No models are equipped with a throttle cable; the ECM controls the fuel quantity supplied by the injectors depending on the position of the throttle pedal. Depending on the transmission fitted, a separate sensor may be fitted above the pedal bracket, secured by two screws **(see illustration)**.

### *Testing*

2 Check the terminals in the connector and the wires leading to the sensor for looseness and breaks. Repair as required.
3 A scan tool is required for complete diagnosis of the throttle control system (see Section 2), but the following checks may identify a definite failure with the throttle position sensor.
4 Disconnect the electrical connector from the throttle position sensor. Using an ohmmeter, measure the resistance between

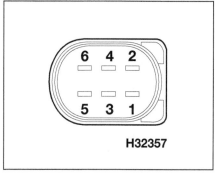

H32357

**3.4 Throttle position sensor terminal identification on early models**

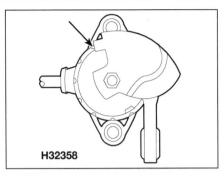

3.10 When installing the cable disc to the throttle position sensor on early models, align the cable cam with the notch as shown

terminals 1 and 3, then 2 and 3 on the sensor (see illustration). With the throttle closed, the resistance should be 800 to 1400 ohms at each pair of terminals.
5 Measure the resistance between terminals 4 and 6. With the throttle closed, the resistance should be 800 to 1200 ohms. Depress the throttle fully, an open circuit (infinity) should now be indicated on the meter. On models equipped with an automatic transmission, repeat this step on terminals 5 and 6, the same results should be indicated.
6 If the resistance is not as specified, renew the throttle position sensor.

### Renewal

7 Remove the insulation panel from the driver's footwell.
8 Disconnect the electrical connector from the throttle position sensor.
9 Remove the mounting screws, detach the cable cam from the accelerator pedal and remove the sensor.
10 Remove the nut and transfer the cable disc to the new sensor. Align the cable cam with the indicated notch on the sensor (see illustration).
11 Refit the sensor, leaving the mounting screws loose.
12 Depress the accelerator pedal against the pedal stop. If the pedal stop cannot be reached, rotate the throttle position sensor in the bracket slots.
13 Tighten the throttle position sensor

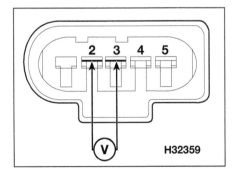

4.3 Mass airflow sensor electrical connector terminal identification (harness side)

mounting screws and connect the electrical connector.
14 Refit the insulation panel.

### Late models

15 Unscrew the mounting nuts and remove the pedal/sensor module.
16 Refitting is the reverse of removal, but tighten the nuts securely.

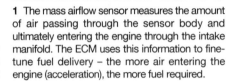

## 4  Mass airflow sensor – testing and renewal

1 The mass airflow sensor measures the amount of air passing through the sensor body and ultimately entering the engine through the intake manifold. The ECM uses this information to fine-tune fuel delivery – the more air entering the engine (acceleration), the more fuel required.

### Testing

2 The mass airflow sensor is located on the air filter housing (see illustration 1.1). A scan tool is necessary to check the output of the mass airflow sensor (see Section 2). The scan tool displays the sensor output in mg/H. With the engine idling at normal operating temperature, the display should read approximately 200 to 450 mg/H. When engine is accelerated to 3000 rpm the values should rise above 800 mg/H.
3 Before checking the mass airflow sensor operation, check the voltage supply circuits. Disconnect the electrical connector from the mass airflow sensor and connect a voltmeter to terminals 2 and 3 (harness side) (see illustration). Turn the ignition key On – the voltage should read approximately 12.0 volts. If the voltage is incorrect, check the circuit from the mass airflow sensor to the fusebox (don't forget to check the fuses first). Connect the voltmeter to terminals 3 and 4 – the voltage should read approximately 5.0 volts. If the voltage is incorrect, check the circuit from the mass airflow sensor to the ECM. If the power circuits are good, check the mass airflow sensor operation with a scan tool. If the mass airflow sensor does not respond as described in Step 2, renew the mass airflow sensor. Note: Before condemning the mass airflow sensor, check the air intake duct for

leaks between the sensor and the intake manifold. A reading below the specified value may be caused by an air leak.

### Renewal

4 Disconnect the electrical connector from the mass airflow sensor.
5 Remove the retaining screws and remove the sensor from the air intake duct.
Caution: Handle the mass airflow sensor with care. Damage to this sensor will affect the operation of the engine control system.
6 Refitting is the reverse of removal.

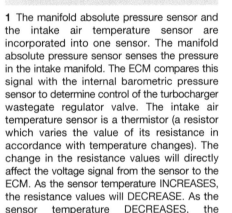

## 5  Manifold absolute pressure/ intake air temperature sensor – testing and renewal

1 The manifold absolute pressure sensor and the intake air temperature sensor are incorporated into one sensor. The manifold absolute pressure sensor senses the pressure in the intake manifold. The ECM compares this signal with the internal barometric pressure sensor to determine control of the turbocharger wastegate regulator valve. The intake air temperature sensor is a thermistor (a resistor which varies the value of its resistance in accordance with temperature changes). The change in the resistance values will directly affect the voltage signal from the sensor to the ECM. As the sensor temperature INCREASES, the resistance values will DECREASE. As the sensor temperature DECREASES, the resistance values will INCREASE.

### Testing

2 The manifold absolute pressure/intake air temperature sensor is located in the intake duct ahead of the intake manifold on models up to 1999 (see illustration 1.1). On later models, it is located on the top of the intercooler beneath the right-hand end of the front bumper. Check the terminals in the connector and the wires leading to the sensor for looseness and breaks. Repair as required.
3 Because much of the manifold absolute pressure sensor circuitry is located inside the ECM, a scan tool is required for diagnosis (see Section 2), but the intake air temperature sensor can be checked as follows.
4 With the ignition switch Off, disconnect the electrical connector from the manifold absolute pressure/intake air temperature sensor. Using an ohmmeter, measure the resistance between terminals 1 and 2 on the sensor (see illustration). With the engine cool, the resistance should be 1.5 to 2.0 kohms at 30°C. Reconnect the electrical connector to the sensor, start the engine and warm it up until it reaches operating temperature, disconnect the connector and check the resistance again. At 80°C the resistance should be 275 to 375 ohms. If the sensor resistance test results are incorrect, renew the intake air temperature sensor.

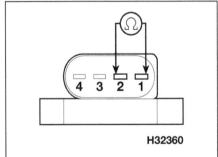

5.4 Manifold absolute pressure/intake air temperature sensor terminal identification

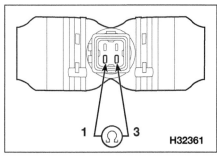

6.3 Measure the resistance of the engine coolant temperature sensor across terminals 1 and 3

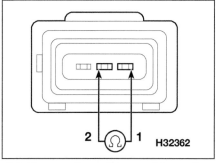

7.3 Measure the resistance of the engine speed sensor across terminals 1 and 2

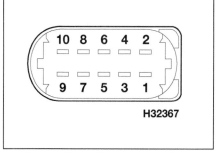

8.3 Fuel injection pump electrical connector terminal identification

### Renewal

5 Disconnect the electrical connector from the sensor, remove the mounting screws and withdraw the sensor from the intake duct.
6 Refitting is the reverse of removal.

## 6  Engine coolant temperature sensor – testing and renewal

1 The engine coolant temperature sensor is a thermistor (a resistor which varies the value of its resistance in accordance with temperature changes). The change in the resistance values will directly affect the voltage signal from the sensor to the ECM. As the sensor temperature INCREASES, the resistance values will DECREASE. As the sensor temperature DECREASES, the resistance values will INCREASE.

### Testing

2 The engine coolant temperature sensor threads into a coolant pipe near the coolant outlet **(see illustration 1.1)**. Check the terminals in the connector and the wires leading to the sensor for looseness and breaks. Repair as required.
3 With the ignition switch Off, disconnect the electrical connector from the engine coolant temperature sensor. Using an ohmmeter, measure the resistance between terminals 1 and 3 on the sensor **(see illustration)**. With the engine cool (30 °C), the resistance should be 1.5 to 2.0 kohms. Reconnect the electrical connector to the sensor, start the engine and warm it up until it reaches operating temperature. Disconnect the connector and check the resistance again. At 80°C the resistance should be 275 to 375 ohms. If the sensor resistance test results are incorrect, renew the engine coolant temperature sensor.

### Renewal

 **Warning: Wait until the engine is completely cool before beginning this procedure.**

4 Partially drain the cooling system (see Chapter 1).

5 Disconnect the electrical connector from the sensor and carefully unscrew the sensor.
6 Before refitting the new sensor, wrap the threads with Teflon sealing tape to prevent leakage and thread corrosion.
7 Refitting is the reverse of removal. Refill the cooling system (see Chapter 1).

## 7  Engine speed sensor – testing and renewal

1 The engine sensor provides the ECM with a crankshaft position signal. The ECM uses the signal to determine a crankshaft reference point (Top Dead Centre) and calculate engine speed (RPM). The signal is also used by the On-Board Diagnostic system for misfire detection. The fuel system will not operate if the ECM does not receive an engine speed sensor input.

### Testing

2 The engine speed sensor is located on the side of the engine block near the oil filter. The sensor is equipped with a pigtail lead and a remote connector **(see illustration 1.1)**. Check the terminals in the connector and the wires leading to the sensor for looseness and breaks. Repair as required.
3 Disconnect the electrical connector from the engine speed sensor. Using an ohmmeter, measure the resistance of the sensor across terminals 1 and 2 of the connector (sensor side) **(see illustration)**. The resistance should be approximately 1000 to 1600 ohms.
4 If the engine speed sensor resistance is not as specified, renew the sensor.

### Renewal

5 Disconnect the engine speed sensor electrical connector and remove the connector from the bracket.
6 Remove the engine speed sensor mounting bolt and withdraw the sensor from the engine block.
7 Renew the O-ring and lightly lubricate it with clean engine oil.
8 Refitting is the reverse of removal.

## 8  Fuel temperature sensor – testing and renewal

1 The fuel temperature sensor is a thermistor (a resistor which varies the value of its resistance in accordance with temperature changes). The change in the resistance values will directly affect the voltage signal from the sensor to the ECM. As the sensor temperature INCREASES, the resistance values will DECREASE. As the sensor temperature DECREASES, the resistance values will INCREASE.

### Testing

2 On non-PD models (engine code ALH), the fuel temperature sensor is located in the fuel injection pump. On PD models (engine codes ATD and AXR), the sensor is located in the fuel return line to the fuel filter in the engine compartment. Check the wires leading to the sensor for looseness and breaks. Repair as required.
3 With the ignition switch Off, disconnect the electrical connector from the sensor. Using an ohmmeter, measure the resistance between terminals 4 and 7 of the connector **(see illustration)**. With the engine cool (30°C), the resistance should be 1.5 to 2.0 kohms. Reconnect the electrical connector, then start the engine and warm it up until it reaches operating temperature. Disconnect the connector and check the resistance again. At 80°C the resistance should be 275 to 375 ohms. If the sensor resistance test results are incorrect, renew the fuel injection pump (engine code ALH) or sensor (engine codes ATD and AXR).

### Renewal

4 On engine code ALH, the fuel temperature sensor is an integral component of the fuel injection pump. If the fuel temperature sensor is defective, renew the fuel injection pump (see Chapter 4B).
5 On engine codes ATD and AXR, remove the securing clip, then extract the sensor from the fuel line housing and recover the O-ring seal. Fit the new sensor using a reversal of removal, but fit a new O-ring seal.

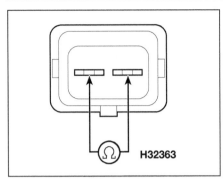

**9.3 Measure the resistance of the fuel injector needle lift sensor across the two terminals of the sensor**

### 9 Fuel injector needle lift sensor – testing and renewal

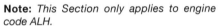

**Note:** *This Section only applies to engine code ALH.*

1 The fuel injector needle lift sensor provides the ECM with a fuel injector needle position signal. The ECM uses the signal to determine fuel injection timing.

#### *Testing*

2 The fuel injector needle lift sensor is incorporated into the cylinder No 3 fuel injector. The sensor is equipped with a pigtail lead and a remote connector **(see illustration 1.1)**. Check the terminals in the connector and the wires leading to the sensor for looseness and breaks. Repair as required.
3 Disconnect the electrical connector from the fuel injector needle lift sensor. Using an ohmmeter, measure the resistance across the two terminals of the sensor connector (sensor side) **(see illustration)**. The resistance should be 80 to 120 ohms.
4 If the fuel injector needle lift sensor is not as specified, renew the sensor.

#### *Renewal*

5 The fuel injector needle lift sensor is incorporated into the cylinder No 3 fuel injector. If the fuel injector needle lift sensor is defective, renew the cylinder No 3 fuel injector (see Chapter 4B).

### 10 Fuel injection quantity adjuster – testing and renewal

**Note:** *This Section only applies to engine code ALH.*
1 The quantity of fuel delivered to the fuel injectors control the engine speed in a diesel engine. The fuel injection quantity adjuster is an electromagnetic positioner connected to the modulating piston in the fuel injection pump. The fuel injection quantity adjuster and resulting engine speed, is controlled by the

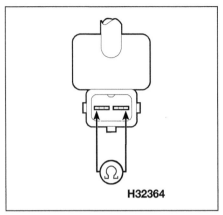

**11.3 Measure the resistance of the wastegate regulator valve across the two terminals of the valve**

ECM. The modulating piston is equipped with a feedback sensor, used by the ECM to fine-tune the fuel injection quantity adjuster.

#### *Testing*

2 The fuel injection quantity adjuster is located in the fuel injection pump. The fuel injection pump is equipped with a pigtail lead and a remote connector **(see illustration 1.1)**. Check the terminals in the connector and the wires leading to the sensor for looseness and breaks. Repair as required.
3 Disconnect the electrical connector from the fuel injection pump. Using an ohmmeter, measure the resistance across the following terminals of the fuel injection pump connector (fuel injection pump side) **(see illustration 8.3)**.
 a) Terminals 1 and 3 – 4.9 to 7.5 ohms
 b) Terminals 2 and 3 – 4.9 to 7.5 ohms
 c) Terminals 5 and 6 – 0.5 to 2.5 ohms
4 If the resistance is not as specified, renew the fuel injection pump.

#### *Renewal*

5 The fuel injection quantity adjuster is an integral component of the fuel injection pump. If the fuel injection quantity adjuster is defective, renew the fuel injection pump (see Chapter 4B).

### 11 Turbocharger wastegate regulator valve – testing and renewal

1 The ECM monitors the manifold absolute pressure sensor signal and controls the vacuum supplied to the turbocharger wastegate actuator with the wastegate regulator valve.

#### *Testing*

2 The wastegate regulator valve is located at the driver's side of the engine compartment, under the scuttle **(see illustration 1.1)**. Check the terminals in the connector and the wires leading to the valve for looseness and breaks. Repair as required.

3 Disconnect the electrical connector from the wastegate regulator valve. Using an ohmmeter, measure the resistance of the valve across the two terminals **(see illustration)**. The resistance should be approximately 25 to 45 ohms.
4 If the wastegate regulator valve resistance is not as specified, renew the valve.

#### *Renewal*

5 Disconnect the electrical connector and vacuum hoses from the valve.
6 Remove the mounting screw and remove the valve.
7 Refitting is the reverse of removal.

### 12 Crankcase ventilation system

1 When the engine is running, a certain amount of the gases produced during combustion escapes past the piston rings into the crankcase as blow-by gases. The crankcase ventilation system is designed to reduce the resulting hydrocarbon emissions (HC) by routing the gases and vapours from the crankcase into the intake manifold and combustion chambers, where they are consumed during engine operation.
2 Crankcase vapours pass through a hose connected from the valve cover to the air intake duct. The oil/air separator at the valve cover separates the oil suspended in the blow-by gases and allows the oil to drain back into the crankcase. The crankcase vapours are drawn from the oil/air separator through a hose connected to the air intake duct where they mix with the incoming air and are burned during the normal combustion process. A heating element is incorporated into the air intake duct to prevent icing in extremely cold weather.
3 A blocked breather, valve or hose will cause excessive crankcase pressures resulting in oil leaks and sludge build-up in the crankcase. Check the components for restrictions and clean or renew the components as necessary. Be sure to check the basic mechanical condition of the engine before condemning the crankcase ventilation system (see Chapter 2C).

### 13 Exhaust Gas Recirculation (EGR) system – testing and renewal

1 The Exhaust Gas Recirculation (EGR) system is used to lower NOx (oxides of nitrogen) emission levels caused by high combustion temperatures. The EGR valve recirculates a small amount of exhaust gases into the intake manifold. The additional mixture lowers the temperature of combustion thereby reducing the formation of NOx compounds.
2 The EGR system consists of the EGR valve,

an EGR gas cooler, the EGR vacuum regulator valve, the ECM and a series of connecting pipes and vacuum hoses. The EGR valve is incorporated into the intake manifold inlet flange. The EGR gas cooler is connected to the exhaust manifold and the EGR valve by a semi-flexible pipe. The EGR vacuum valve regulator valve is mounted under the cowl.

**3** The ECM controls the EGR flow rate by energising the EGR vacuum regulator valve solenoid coil. When the vacuum regulator valve is energised vacuum is applied the EGR valve, opening the EGR passage.

**4** Exhaust gas from the exhaust manifold is cooled by the EGR gas cooler as the gas flows through the cooler. Cooling the exhaust gas further improves the efficiency of the EGR system.

## Testing

### EGR valve

**5** Remove the air intake duct from the intake manifold flange.

**6** Disconnect the vacuum hose from the EGR valve and connect a hand-held vacuum pump to the vacuum port on the EGR valve.

**7** Apply vacuum to the EGR valve while watching the diaphragm rod through the intake flange opening **(see illustration)**. The EGR valve diaphragm should pull the rod up when vacuum is applied. Release the vacuum and the rod should move down to its original position.

**8** If the EGR valve does not operate as described, renew the EGR valve/intake manifold flange.

### EGR vacuum regulator valve

**9** The EGR vacuum regulator valve is located in the engine compartment, under the scuttle **(see illustration 1.1)**. Check the terminals in the connector and the wires leading to the sensor for looseness and breaks. Check the vacuum hoses for damage or restrictions and make sure vacuum is present at the hose from the vacuum pump with the engine running. Repair as required.

**10** Disconnect the electrical connector from the EGR vacuum regulator valve. Using an ohmmeter, measure the resistance of the sensor across the two terminals of the valve **(see illustration)**. The resistance should be 14 to 20 ohms.

**11** If the EGR vacuum regulator valve resistance is not as specified, renew the valve.

## Renewal

### EGR valve

**Note:** *The EGR valve is incorporated into the intake manifold flange along with the air valve flap. If the EGR valve is defective, the entire flange must be renewed.*

**12** Disconnect the vacuum hose from the EGR valve.

**13** Disconnect the air valve actuator linkage

from the air valve flap and remove the actuator.

**14** Remove the intake hose from the flange.

**15** Remove the bolts and disconnect the EGR pipe from the flange **(see illustration)**.

**16** Remove the flange mounting bolts and remove the flange.

**17** Refitting is the reverse of removal, using a new O-ring seal and EGR pipe gasket.

### EGR vacuum regulator valve

**18** Disconnect the electrical connector from the vacuum regulator valve.

**19** Label and remove the vacuum hoses from the valve ports. Make a *careful* note of their orientation to aid refitting later.

**20** Remove the retaining screws and remove the valve.

**21** Refitting is a reversal of removal.

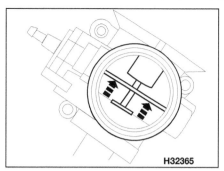

**13.7 Apply vacuum to the EGR valve while watching the diaphragm rod through the intake flange opening – the EGR valve diaphragm should pull the rod up when vacuum is applied**

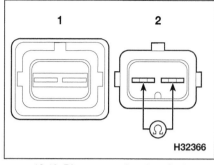

**13.10 Disconnect the electrical connector (1) and measure the resistance of the EGR vacuum regulator valve across the two terminals of the valve (2)**

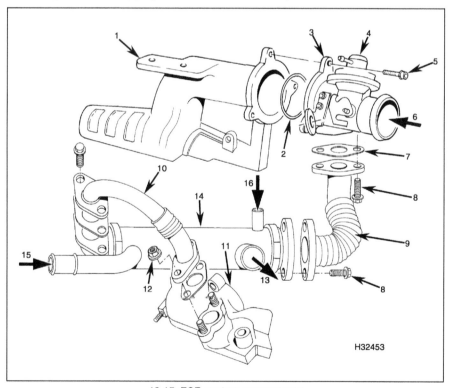

**13.15 EGR system components**

| | | |
|---|---|---|
| 1  Intake manifold | 8  Bolt | 12  Nut |
| 2  O-ring | 9  EGR cooler-to-EGR valve | 13  Coolant flow to radiator |
| 3  Intake manifold inlet flange |     pipe | 14  EGR gas cooler |
| 4  EGR valve | 10  Exhaust manifold-to-EGR | 15  Coolant flow from heater |
| 5  Bolt |     cooler pipe | 16  Coolant flow from |
| 6  Intake air from air filter | 11  Exhaust manifold |     expansion tank |
| 7  Gasket | | |

# Notes

# Chapter 7 Part A
# Manual transmission

## Contents

## Degrees of difficulty

| **Easy,** suitable for novice with little experience  | **Fairly easy,** suitable for beginner with some experience  | **Fairly difficult,** suitable for competent DIY mechanic  | **Difficult,** suitable for experienced DIY mechanic  | **Very difficult,** suitable for expert DIY or professional |
|---|---|---|---|---|

## Specifications

| Torque specifications | Nm | Ft-lbs |
|---|---|---|
| Balance weight to selector lever . . . . . . . . . . . . . . . . . . . . . . . . . . . . . . | 25 | 18 |
| Drive shaft flange retaining bolt . . . . . . . . . . . . . . . . . . . . . . . . . . . . | 25 | 18 |
| Gearchange cable bolt to transmission selector lever . . . . . . . . . . . . . | 25 | 18 |
| Gearchange cable bracket to transmission . . . . . . . . . . . . . . . . . . . . | 25 | 18 |
| Gearchange lever housing-to-body fasteners . . . . . . . . . . . . . . . . . . | 25 | 18 |
| Engine-to-transmission bolts **(see illustration 5.24a)** | | |
| Bolts No 1 (M12 x 55) . . . . . . . . . . . . . . . . . . . . . . . . . . . . . . . . . | 80 | 59 |
| Bolts No 2 (M12 x 150) . . . . . . . . . . . . . . . . . . . . . . . . . . . . . . . . | 80 | 59 |
| Bolts No 3 (M12 x 50) . . . . . . . . . . . . . . . . . . . . . . . . . . . . . . . . . | 45 | 33 |
| Bolts No 4 (M7 x 12) . . . . . . . . . . . . . . . . . . . . . . . . . . . . . . . . . . | 10 | 7 |
| Bolt No 5 (M7 x 12) . . . . . . . . . . . . . . . . . . . . . . . . . . . . . . . . . . . | 10 | 7 |
| Transmission-to-engine bolts – 02M transmission **(see illustration 5.24b)** | | |
| Bolts No 1 (M12 x 55) . . . . . . . . . . . . . . . . . . . . . . . . . . . . . . . . . | 80 | 59 |
| Bolts No 2 (M10 x 105) . . . . . . . . . . . . . . . . . . . . . . . . . . . . . . . . | 80 | 59 |
| Bolts No 3 (M10 x 50) . . . . . . . . . . . . . . . . . . . . . . . . . . . . . . . . . | 40 | 30 |
| Transmission mounting bracket-to-transmission bolts | | |
| Step 1 . . . . . . . . . . . . . . . . . . . . . . . . . . . . . . . . . . . . . . . . . . . . . | 40 | 30 |
| Step 2 . . . . . . . . . . . . . . . . . . . . . . . . . . . . . . . . . . . . . . . . . . . . . | Tighten an additional 90-degrees | |
| Transmission mount-to-body bolts **(see illustration 5.19a)** | | |
| Bolts A . . . . . . . . . . . . . . . . . . . . . . . . . . . . . . . . . . . . . . . . . . . . . | 25 | 18 |
| Bolts B | | |
| Step 1 . . . . . . . . . . . . . . . . . . . . . . . . . . . . . . . . . . . . . . . . . . . . . | 60 | 44 |
| Step 2 . . . . . . . . . . . . . . . . . . . . . . . . . . . . . . . . . . . . . . . . . . . . . | Tighten an additional 90-degrees | |

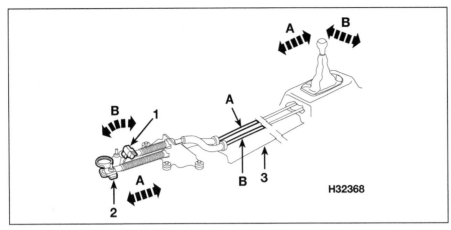

**2.2a Operation details of the gearchange cables**

| 1 | Relay lever/actuating arm | 3 | Heat shield | A | Gear selector cable |
|---|---|---|---|---|---|
| 2 | Gear selector lever | | | B | Gear selector cable |

## 1 General information

The vehicles covered by this manual have either a 5-speed or 6-speed manual transmission, or a 4-speed (01M), 6-speed (09G) or 6-speed direct shift (02E) automatic transmission. Information on the manual transmission is included in this Part of Chapter 7. Service procedures for the automatic transmission are contained in Chapter 7B.

The manual transmission is a compact, lightweight aluminium alloy housing containing both the transmission and differential assemblies.

Because of the complexity of the transmission and the special tools needed to work on it, internal repair procedures for the manual transmission are beyond the scope of this manual. The information in this Chapter is devoted to removal and refitting procedures.

## 2 Gearchange cables and lever – removal, refitting and adjustment

### Vehicles up to May 1999

#### Cables

**1** Remove the air filter housing (see Chapter 4A).

**2** Remove the clips retaining the cables to the bracket on the transmission **(see illustrations)**.

**3** Detach the cables from the levers on the transmission. The gate selector cable can be detached from its lever by pulling up on the plastic tab and sliding the cable eye off the pin **(see illustrations)**; the gear selector cable is attached to its lever by a bolt.

**4** Apply the handbrake. Raise the front of the vehicle and support it securely on axle stands.

**5** Unbolt the exhaust pipe from the exhaust manifold (see Chapter 2A or 2B), then separate the front half of the exhaust system

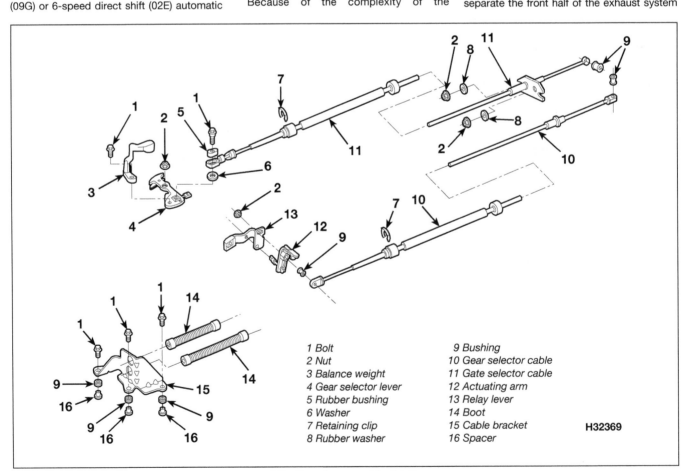

| 1 | Bolt | 9 | Bushing |
|---|---|---|---|
| 2 | Nut | 10 | Gear selector cable |
| 3 | Balance weight | 11 | Gate selector cable |
| 4 | Gear selector lever | 12 | Actuating arm |
| 5 | Rubber bushing | 13 | Relay lever |
| 6 | Washer | 14 | Boot |
| 7 | Retaining clip | 15 | Cable bracket |
| 8 | Rubber washer | 16 | Spacer |

**2.2b Gearchange cable details**

**2.2c Remove the clips that retain the cables to the bracket**

**2.3a Pull up on this plastic tab and slide the gate selector cable off the post on the lever**

**2.3b Remove this bolt (arrowed) to detach the gear selector cable from its lever**

from the rear half at the clamp (see Chapter 6A, *Catalytic converter*).

**6** Remove the crossmember that supports

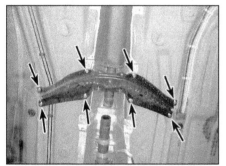

**2.6 Unbolt the exhaust system crossmember and allow it to hang down**

the rear portion of the exhaust system **(see illustration)**.

**7** Prise the retainers off their posts and remove the heat shields for access to the cables **(see illustration)**.

**8** Unscrew the bolts and, using a long prybar and a hammer, drive the cover plate off the bottom of the gearchange housing **(see illustrations)**.

*Caution: Make sure the prybar only contacts the cover plate, not the gearchange housing.*

**9** Remove the spring clips and detach the cables from their pins on the gate selector and gear lever **(see illustration)**.

**10** Unscrew the nuts securing the cable bracket, then pull the cables out of the gearchange housing **(see illustration)**.

**11** Guide the cables down between the

engine and the bulkhead and remove them.

**12** Refitting is the reverse of removal, with the following points:

a) Lubricate the pins on the gearchange levers with multi-purpose grease.

b) Renew the gaskets on the gearchange cover plate and the cable bracket if they are damaged.

c) Tighten the cable bracket nuts and the gearchange housing (cover plate) bolts to the torque values listed in this Chapter's Specifications.

d) Adjust the cables as described below.

**Gearchange lever**

**13** Perform Steps 4 to 10.

**14** Working inside the vehicle, pull the gearchange lever boot and the sealing boot from the centre console **(see illustration)**.

**2.7 Remove the retainers (arrowed) and guide the heat shields out towards the rear for access to the shift cables**

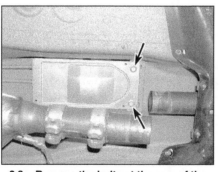

**2.8a Remove the bolts at the rear of the cover plate . . .**

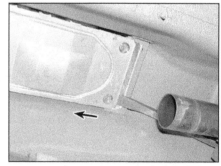

**2.8b . . . then knock the cover forward and off the gearchange housing**

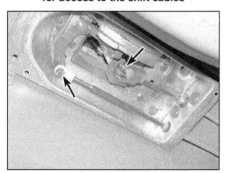

**2.9 Pull out the spring clips and detach the cable ends from the levers . . .**

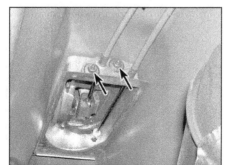

**2.10 . . . then remove the nuts securing the cable bracket**

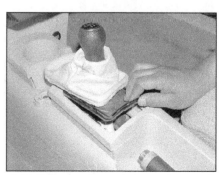

**2.14 Pull up on the gearchange boot and the sealing boot to detach them (this can usually be done without the use of tools)**

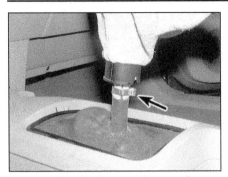

**2.15 Cut off this clamp (arrowed) to remove the shift knob**

**2.16 Remove the gearchange housing retaining nuts (arrowed)**

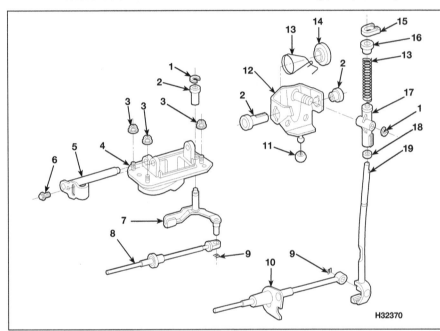

H32370

**2.18 Exploded view of the gearchange lever assembly**

| | | |
|---|---|---|
| 1 Lock washer | 8 Gate selector cable | 14 Guide bushing |
| 2 Bushing | 9 Spring clip | 15 Circlip |
| 3 Nut | 10 Gear selector cable | 16 Spacer sleeve |
| 4 Mounting plate | 11 Cap | 17 Gear lever guide |
| 5 Fulcrum pin | 12 Gate selector housing | 18 Damping washer |
| 6 Bolt | 13 Spring | 19 Gearchange lever |
| 7 Gate selector bracket | | |

**2.21a To adjust the gate selector cable, loosed this bolt at the gearchange lever mechanism (arrowed) . . .**

**2.21b . . . and this nut at the transmission – with the transmission and gearchange lever in Neutral, move the gearchange lever into the 3rd/4th gear plane and tighten the bolt**

**15** Cut off the clamp and remove the gearchange knob and boot **(see illustration)**.
**16** Remove the nuts securing the gearchange housing to the floor pan **(see illustration)**.
**17** Lower the gearchange housing and lever through the floor pan.
**18** The gearchange lever assembly can be disassembled and inspected **(see illustration)**, but if any components are worn or broken you'll have to check on the availability of renewal parts – you may have to renew the entire mechanism.
**19** Refitting is the reverse of removal, with the following points:
a) Lubricate all contact surfaces with multi-purpose grease.
b) Renew any torn gaskets.
c) Tighten the gearchange housing fasteners and the cable bracket fasteners to the torque listed in this Chapter's Specifications.
d) Adjust the gearchange cables if gearchange operation isn't smooth.

### Adjustment

**Note:** While the manufacturer calls for a couple of special tools to adjust the gearchange cables/shifter mechanism, satisfactory results can usually be obtained with a little thought, patience and the help of an assistant.
**20** Remove the air filter housing (see Chapter 4A).
**21** With the cables attached and the transmission gearchange lever in the Neutral position (the car will be able to roll if it's in Neutral), check the position of the gearchange lever inside the vehicle – it should be resting right in the middle, in the 3rd/4th gear plane. If it isn't, lift up on the gearchange lever boot and the sealing boot and loosen the nut that holds the fulcrum pin to the mounting plate **(see illustration)** and, in the engine compartment, the nut holding the relay lever to the actuating arm **(see illustration)**. Verify that the transmission is in Neutral, have an assistant move the gearchange lever to the 3rd/4th gear plane, then tighten the bolt and the nut. This will adjust the gate selector cable.
**22** Move the gearchange lever back-and-forth several times between 3rd and 4th gears with the clutch pedal depressed – you should be able to feel an equal amount of movement in each direction. If the detent, or engagement, into one gear is more positive than the other, place the lever back into Neutral and have an assistant hold it there. Working in the engine compartment, loosen the bolt holding the gear selector cable to the gear selector lever **(see illustration 2.3b)**. Make sure the transmission is in Neutral, have your assistant hold the gearchange lever in Neutral, then tighten the bolt and check the operation of the lever.
**23** Repeat Steps 21 and 22 if necessary, then refit the air filter housing and road test the vehicle.

### *Vehicles from June 1999*
#### Cables

**24** Remove the air filter housing (see Chapter 4A).

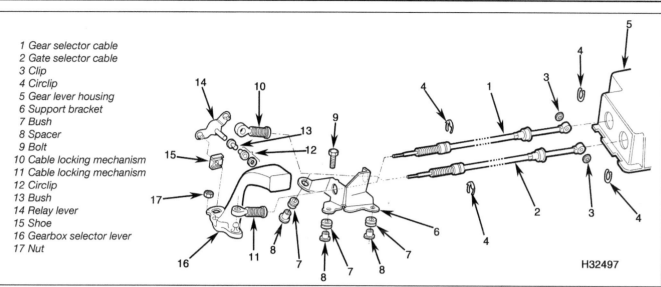

1 Gear selector cable
2 Gate selector cable
3 Clip
4 Circlip
5 Gear lever housing
6 Support bracket
7 Bush
8 Spacer
9 Bolt
10 Cable locking mechanism
11 Cable locking mechanism
12 Circlip
13 Bush
14 Relay lever
15 Shoe
16 Gearbox selector lever
17 Nut

H32497

**2.25 Selector cable assembly – June 1999-on**

**25** Lever the gate selector cable and gear selector cable from selector levers using a 13 mm open-ended spanner **(see illustration)**.
**26** Remove the circlips securing the cables to the support bracket on the gearbox.
**27** Apply the handbrake. Raise the front of the vehicle and support it securely on axle stands.
**28** Unbolt the exhaust pipe from the exhaust manifold (see Chapter 2A or 2B), then separate the front half of the exhaust system from the rear half at the clamp (see Chapter 6A, Catalytic converter).
**29** Remove the crossmember that supports the rear portion of the exhaust system **(see illustration 2.6)**.
**30** Prise the retainers off their posts and remove the heat shields for access to the cables.
**31** Bend back the retaining tabs and remove the base plate from the lever housing.
**32** Prise off the circlips and pull the inner cables from their levers inside the housing.
**33** Remove the circlips securing the outer cables to the lever housing and withdraw the cables.
**34** Refitting is the reverse of removal, with the following points:
  a) Lubricate the pins on the gearchange levers with multi-purpose grease.
  b) Renew the gear lever housing baseplate.
  c) Adjust the cables as described below.

### Gearchange lever

**35** Perform steps 27 to 33.
**36** Working inside the vehicle, pull the gearchange lever boot and the sealing boot from the centre console.
**37** Cut off the clamp and remove the gearchange knob and boot **(see illustration 2.15)**.
**38** Remove the nuts securing the gearchange housing to the floor pan.
**39** Lower the gearchange housing and lever through the floor pan.
**40** The gearchange lever assembly can be disassembled and inspected **(see illustration)**, but if any components are worn

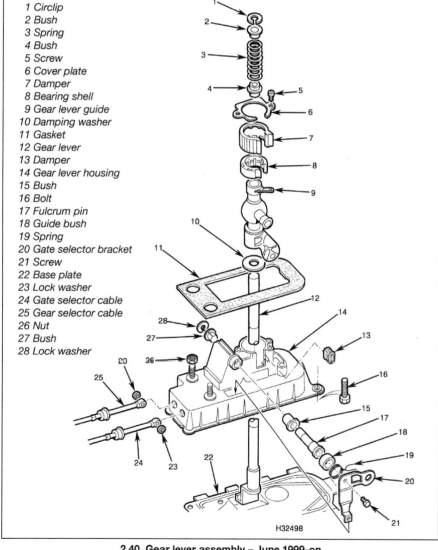

1 Circlip
2 Bush
3 Spring
4 Bush
5 Screw
6 Cover plate
7 Damper
8 Bearing shell
9 Gear lever guide
10 Damping washer
11 Gasket
12 Gear lever
13 Damper
14 Gear lever housing
15 Bush
16 Bolt
17 Fulcrum pin
18 Guide bush
19 Spring
20 Gate selector bracket
21 Screw
22 Base plate
23 Lock washer
24 Gate selector cable
25 Gear selector cable
26 Nut
27 Bush
28 Lock washer

H32498

**2.40 Gear lever assembly – June 1999-on**

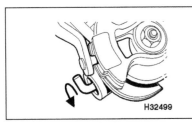

**2.44 Turn the right-angle locking pin clockwise to lock and anti-clockwise to unlock**

or broken you'll have to check on the availability of renewal parts – you may have to renew the entire mechanism.

**41** Refitting is the reverse of removal, with the following points:

a) Lubricate all contact surfaces with multi-purpose grease.

b) Renew any torn gaskets.

c) Tighten the gearchange housing fasteners and the cable bracket fasteners to the torque listed in this Chapter's Specifications.

d) Adjust the gearchange cables if gearchange operation isn't smooth.

### Adjustment

**Note:** While the manufacturer calls for a couple of special tools to adjust the gearchange cables/shifter mechanism, satisfactory results can usually be obtained with a little thought, patience and the help of an assistant.

**42** Remove the air filter housing (see Chapter 4A).

**43** With the cables attached and the transmission gearchange lever in the Neutral position (the car will be able to roll if it's in Neutral), check the position of the gearchange lever inside the vehicle – it should be resting right in the middle, in the 3rd/4th gear plane. If it isn't, working in the engine compartment, release the inner cable locking mechanisms by pulling the spring-loaded locking collars towards the end of the cables and then twisting them anti-clockwise (viewed from the end of the cables).

**44** Press the selector shaft on the gearbox down and turn the right-angle locking pin clockwise **(see illustration)**.

**45** Pull the gearchange lever boot and the

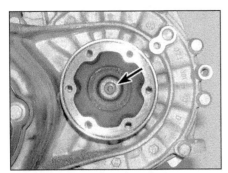

**3.4 The driveshaft flange is retained by a single bolt (arrowed)**

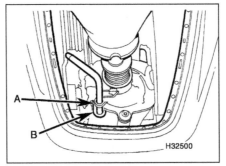

**2.46 Insert a rod or drill bit through 'A' and into 'B'**

sealing boot from the centre console.

**46** Set the lever in the correct position by inserting a drill bit of the same diameter as the aligning holes of the lever and housing **(see illustration)**.

**47** With the selector shaft and gear lever positioned as described, set the inner cable locking mechanisms by turning the spring-loaded locking collars clockwise (viewed from the end of the cables) and releasing them.

**48** Turn the right-angled locking pin anti-clockwise to release the selector shaft.

**49** Remove the drill from the gearchange lever and housing, and check for correct operation of the selector mechanism. If satisfactory, refit the gearchange lever gaiters, and the air filter housing.

### 3  Driveshaft flange oil seal – renewal

**1** The driveshaft flange oil seals are located on the sides of the transmission, where the driveshaft flange enter the transmission. Renewal of these seals is relatively easy, since the repairs can be performed without removing the transmission from the vehicle.

**2** If you suspect that one of these seals is leaking, raise the vehicle and support it securely on axle stands. If the seal is leaking, you'll see lubricant on the side of the transmission, below the seal.

**3** Unbolt the inner end of the driveshaft, then

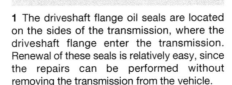

**3.5 Carefully pry out the oil seal with a seal removal tool or a screwdriver; make sure you don't damage the seal bore or the new seal may leak**

support it out of the way with a piece of wire (see Chapter 8). Don't let the driveshaft hang by the outer CV joint. If you're renewing the right-side seal, remove the CV joint protector bolted to the engine.

**4** Remove the bolt securing the driveshaft flange, then pull the flange shaft out of the transmission **(see illustration)**.

**5** Using a seal removal tool, screwdriver or lever, carefully prise the seal out of the transmission bore **(see illustration)**. If the seal is stubborn and won't come out, a slide hammer and VW removal attachment may be necessary.

**6** Using a seal refitting tool or a large socket as a drift, refit the new oil seal. Drive it into the bore squarely and make sure it's fully seated **(see illustration)**.

**7** Lubricate the lip of the new seal with multi-purpose grease. Also pack the space between the seal lips with the some grease.

**8** Refit the driveshaft flange, tightening the bolt to the torque listed in this Chapter's Specifications.

**9** If you removed the right side driveshaft, refit the CV joint protector.

**10** Reconnect the driveshaft to the flange and tighten the bolts to the torque listed in the Chapter 8 Specifications.

### 4  Reversing light switch – testing and renewal

### Testing

**1** Turn the ignition key to the On position and move the gearchange lever to the Reverse position. The switch should close the reversing light circuit and turn on the reversing lights.

**2** If it doesn't, check the reversing light fuse (see Chapter 12).

**3** If the fuse is okay, verify that there's voltage available on the battery side of the switch (with the ignition turned to On) (see illustration 4.7 for the location of the switch).

**4** If there's no voltage on the battery side of the switch, check the wire between the fuse and the switch (refer to the wiring diagrams at the back of this manual for the proper wire to

**3.6 Installing the driveshaft flange oil seal with a seal installation tool**

**4.7 The reversing light switch is located on the top of the transmission, just forward of the selector levers – it's secured by two bolts (arrowed) (transmission removed for clarity)**

check); if there is voltage, put the gearchange lever in Reverse and see if there's voltage on the other terminal of the switch.

5 If there's no voltage available, renew the switch; if there is voltage, check to see if the wire between the switch and the bulbs has a break somewhere.

6 Keep in mind that it is possible that both bulbs could be burned out, but not very likely.

### Renewal

*Caution 1: These models are equipped with an anti-theft radio. Before performing a procedure that requires disconnecting the battery, make sure you have the activation code.*
*Caution 2: Disconnecting the battery can cause driveability problems that require a scan tool to remedy. If the vehicle exhibits driveability problems after the battery is reconnected, it may be necessary to take it to a dealer service department or other qualified garage to reprogram the ECM. See Chapter 5, Section 1, for information on the use of an auxiliary voltage input device ('memory-saver') before disconnecting the battery.*

7 The reversing light switch is located on the top of the transmission, forward of the gearchange levers **(see illustration)**.
8 Remove the air filter housing (see Chapter 4A).

9 Remove the battery (see Chapter 5).
10 Unplug the electrical connector from the switch.
11 Unscrew the mounting bolts and detach the switch from the transmission.
12 Refitting is the reverse of removal. Tighten the switch bolts securely.

### 5 Manual transmission – removal and refitting

*Warning: The manufacturer recommends renewing the transmission mounting bracket-to-transmission bolts and the transmission mount-to-body bolts whenever they are removed.*
*Caution 1: These models are equipped with an anti-theft radio. Before performing a procedure that requires disconnecting the battery, make sure you have the activation code.*
*Caution 2: Disconnecting the battery can cause driveability problems that require a scan tool to remedy. If the vehicle exhibits driveability problems after the battery is reconnected, it may be necessary to take it to a dealer service department or other qualified garage to reprogram the ECM. See Chapter 5, Section 1, for information on the use of an auxiliary voltage input device ('memory-saver') before disconnecting the battery.*

### Removal

1 Select a solid, level surface to park the vehicle upon. Give yourself enough space to move around it easily. Apply the handbrake and block the rear wheels.
2 Refer to Chapter 11 and remove the bonnet from its hinges.
3 Remove the battery (see Chapter 5).
4 Remove the air filter housing (see Chapter 4A).
5 Remove the windscreen wiper arms (see Chapter 12), the scuttle cover and plenum close-out panel (see Chapter 11).
6 Detach the gearchange cables from their levers on the transmission (see Section 2),

then unbolt the cable bracket from the top of the transmission. Secure the cables and bracket out of the way.
7 Unplug the electrical connectors from the Vehicle Speed Sensor (see Chapter 6A) and the reversing light switch.
8 Unbolt the clutch release cylinder from the transmission and tie it out of the way (see Chapter 8). Don't disconnect the hose.
*Caution: Don't depress the clutch pedal while the release cylinder is removed.*
9 Unbolt the balance weight from the gear selector lever.
10 Support the engine from above with an engine support fixture, using the engine lifting points (see Chapter 2C; these are the same points that are used when attaching an engine hoist for engine removal). You can obtain one of these at most equipment rental shops.
11 Raise the front of the vehicle and support it securely on axle stands.
12 Remove the under-vehicle splash shield and the left-side inner wing panel.
13 Turn the steering wheel all the way to the left. Unbolt the inner ends of the driveshafts from the driveshaft flanges (see Chapter 8). Support the driveshafts with pieces of wire, as high up as possible.
14 Remove the right-hand side driveshaft flange (see Section 3).
15 Remove the starter motor (see Chapter 5).
16 Support the transmission with a jack (preferably a special jack made for this purpose; these can be obtained at most equipment rental shops). Safety chains will help steady the transmission on the jack.
17 Remove the engine support strut (see Chapter 2A, Section 17).
18 Remove the transmission mounting bolts that are accessible from underneath **(see illustrations)**. Lay them out in order or mark them so they can be returned to their original locations.
19 Working from above, remove the left-hand side transmission mounting bolts **(see illustrations)**. Also unbolt the support strut between the mounting bracket and transmission.
20 Lower the engine support bracket and the jack supporting the transmission

**5.18a Remove the engine-to-transmission bolt (lower arrow) and the flywheel cover plate bolt (upper arrow) from the right-hand side . . .**

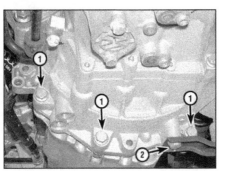

**5.18b . . . and the transmission-to-engine bolts from the left-hand side (1); the support strut bolt (2) will already have been removed**

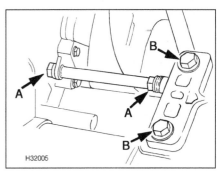

**5.19a Working in the engine compartment, remove the support strut bolts (A) and transmission mounting bolts (B) . . .**

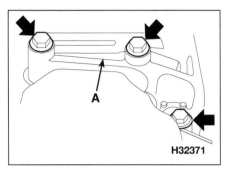

5.19b . . . then lower the engine/
transmission assembly and unbolt the
transmission mounting bracket (A) and
remove it

simultaneously, then unbolt the transmission
mounting bracket from the left side of the
transmission. Also unbolt the clips that secure
the power steering pipe to the end of the
transmission and reposition the pipe.
**21** Remove the transmission mounting bolts
that are accessible from above **(see
illustration)**. Lay them out in order or mark
them so they can be returned to their original
locations.
**22** Check that nothing remains connected to
the transmission. Carefully pull the
transmission away from the engine, lowering
the jack and engine support fixture, as
necessary, to allow the transmission to clear
the left side of the vehicle.
*Caution: Don't allow the transmission to
hang by the input shaft.*
**23** Lower the transmission and remove it
from under the vehicle.

### Refitting

**24** Refitting of the transmission is essentially
a reversal of the removal procedure, but note
the following points:
 a) *Lubricate the splines of the input shaft
 with a thin film of high-temperature
 grease.*
 b) *Tighten the transmission mounting
 fasteners to the torque values listed in this
 Chapter's Specifications* **(see
 illustrations)**.
 c) *Refer to Chapter 2A and tighten the
 engine mounting bolts to the correct
 torque.*
 d) *Refer to Chapter 8 and reconnect the
 driveshafts.*
 e) *On completion, refer to Chapter 1 and
 check the transmission lubricant level.*

### 6 Manual transmission overhaul – general information

**1** Overhauling a manual transmission is a
difficult job for the do-it-yourselfer. It involves
the dismantling and reassembly of many small
parts. Numerous clearances must be precisely
measured and, if necessary, changed with
select fit spacers and circlips. As a result, if

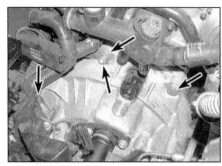

5.21 Transmission upper mounting
fasteners

transmission problems arise, it can be
removed and fitted by a competent do-it-
yourselfer, but overhaul should be left to a
transmission garage. Rebuilt transmissions
may be available, check with your dealer parts
department and motor factors. At any rate, the
time and money involved in an overhaul is
almost sure to exceed the cost of a rebuilt unit.
**2** Nevertheless, it's not impossible for an
inexperienced mechanic to rebuild a
transmission if the special tools are available
and the job is done in a deliberate step-by-
step manner so nothing is overlooked.
**3** The tools necessary for an overhaul include
internal and external circlip pliers, a bearing
puller, a slide hammer, a set of pin punches, a
dial indicator and possibly a hydraulic press.
In addition, a large, sturdy workbench and a
vice or transmission stand will be required.
**4** During dismantling of the transmission,
make careful notes of how each piece comes
off, where it fits in relation to other pieces and
what holds it in place. If you note how each
part is fitted before removing it, getting the
transmission back together again will be
much easier.
**5** Before taking the transmission apart for
repair, it will help if you have some idea what
area of the transmission is malfunctioning.
Certain problems can be closely tied to
specific areas in the transmission, which can
make component examination and renewal
easier. Refer to the *Troubleshooting* section at
the front of this manual for information
regarding possible sources of trouble.

### 7 Manual transmission lubricant – renewal

**1** This procedure should be performed after
the vehicle has been driven so the lubricant
will be warm and therefore will flow out of the
transmission more easily. Raise the vehicle
and support it securely on axle stands.
**2** Move a drain pan, rags, newspapers and
spanners under the transmission.
**3** Remove the transmission drain plug at the
differential portion of the case and allow the
lubricant to drain into the pan **(see illustration)**.
**4** After the lubricant has drained completely,
reinstall the plug and tighten it securely.

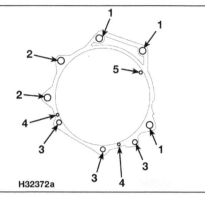

5.24a Several different lengths and sizes of
bolts are used to secure the transmission
and engine together – they must be returned
to their proper positions (02J transmission)

| | |
|---|---|
| 1 M12 x 55 | 4 M7 x 12 |
| 2 M12 x 150 | 5 M7 x 12 |
| 3 M12 x 50 | |

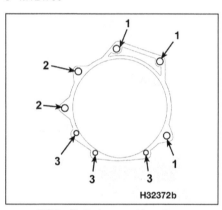

5.24b Bolt sizes and lengths –
02M transmission

*1 M12 x 55    2 M10 x 105    3 M10 x 50*

**5** Remove the filler plug from the side of the
transmission case. Using a hand pump,
syringe or squeeze bottle, fill the transmission
with the specified lubricant until it just reaches
the bottom edge of the hole (see Chapter 1).
Reinstall the filler plug and tighten it securely.
**6** Lower the vehicle.
**7** Drive the vehicle for a short distance, then
check the drain and filler plugs for leakage.

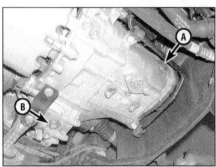

7.3 The manual transmission check/filler
plug (A) is located at the front side of the
transmission – (B) is the drain plug

# Chapter 7 Part B
# Automatic transmission

---

## Contents

## Degrees of difficulty

| Easy, suitable for novice with little experience  | Fairly easy, suitable for beginner with some experience  | Fairly difficult, suitable for competent DIY mechanic  | Difficult, suitable for experienced DIY mechanic  | Very difficult, suitable for expert DIY or professional |
|---|---|---|---|---|

## Specifications

| Torque specifications | Nm | Ft-lbs |
|---|---|---|
| Gearchange cable adjusting bolt | 5 | 4 |
| Torque converter-to-driveplate nuts | 60 | 44 |
| Transmission fluid cooler banjo bolts | 35 | 26 |
| Transmission mounting support to transmission | | |
|   Step 1 | 60 | 44 |
|   Step 2 | Tighten an additional 90-degrees | |
| Transmission-to-engine bolts | | |
|   M10 | 45 | 33 |
|   M12 | 80 | 59 |
| Transmission mounting to transmission support | | |
|   Step 1 | 60 | 44 |
|   Step 2 | Tighten an additional 90-degrees | |

## 1 General information

The vehicles covered by this manual have either a 5-speed or 6-speed manual transmission, or a 4-speed (01M), 6-speed (09G) or 6-speed direct shift (02E) automatic transmission. All information on the automatic transmission is included in this Part of Chapter 7. Information for the manual transmission can be found in Part A of this Chapter.

The overall operation of the transmission is managed by a Transmission Control Module (TCM) and as a result there are no manual adjustments (aside from gearchange cable adjustment). Comprehensive fault diagnosis can therefore only be carried out using dedicated electronic test equipment.

If the transmission requires major repair work, it should be taken to a dealer service department or an automotive transmission specialist.

## 2 Automatic transmission troubleshooting – general

Automatic transmission malfunctions may be caused by five general conditions:
a) Poor engine performance
b) Improper adjustments
c) Hydraulic malfunctions
d) Mechanical malfunctions
e) Malfunctions in the computer or its signal network

Diagnosis of these problems should always begin with a check of the easily repaired items: fluid level and condition (see Chapter 1) and gearchange cable adjustment. Next, perform a road test to determine if the problem has been corrected or if more diagnosis is necessary. If the problem persists after the preliminary tests and corrections are completed, additional diagnosis should be done by a dealer service department or transmission garage. Refer to the *Troubleshooting* Section at the front of this manual for information on symptoms of transmission problems.

### Preliminary checks

1 Drive the vehicle to warm the transmission to normal operating temperature.
2 Check the fluid level as described in Chapter 1.
a) If the fluid level is unusually low, add enough fluid to bring the level up, then check for external leaks (see below).
b) If the fluid level is abnormally high, drain off the excess, then check the drained fluid for contamination by coolant. The presence of engine coolant in the automatic transmission fluid indicates that a failure has occurred in the transmission fluid cooler (see Section 8).

c) If the fluid is foaming, drain it and refill the transmission, then check for coolant in the fluid, or a high fluid level.
3 Check the engine idle speed. **Note:** *If the engine is malfunctioning, do not proceed with the preliminary checks until it has been repaired and runs normally.*
4 Inspect the gearchange cable (see Section 3). Make sure that it's properly adjusted and that it operates smoothly.

### Fluid leak diagnosis

5 Most fluid leaks are easy to locate visually. Repair usually consists of renewing a seal or gasket. If a leak is difficult to find, the following procedure may help.
6 Identify the fluid. Make sure it's transmission fluid and not engine oil or brake fluid (automatic transmission fluid is a deep red colour).
7 Try to pinpoint the source of the leak. Drive the vehicle several miles, then park it over a large sheet of cardboard. After a minute or two, you should be able to locate the leak by determining the source of the fluid dripping onto the cardboard.
8 Make a careful visual inspection of the suspected component and the area immediately around it. Pay particular attention to gasket mating surfaces. A mirror is often helpful for finding leaks in areas that are hard to see.
9 If the leak still cannot be found, clean the suspected area thoroughly with a degreaser or solvent, then dry it.
10 Drive the vehicle for several miles at normal operating temperature and varying speeds. After driving the vehicle, visually inspect the suspected component again.
11 Once the leak has been located, the cause must be determined before it can be properly repaired. If a gasket is renewed but the sealing flange is bent, the new gasket will not stop the leak. The bent flange must be straightened.
12 Before attempting to repair a leak, check to make sure that the following conditions are corrected or they may cause another leak. **Note:** *Some of the following conditions cannot be fixed without highly specialised tools and expertise. Such problems must be referred to a transmission shop or a dealer service department.*

### Gasket leaks

13 Check the pan periodically. Make sure the bolts are tight, no bolts are missing, the gasket is in good condition and the pan is flat (dents in the pan may indicate damage to the valve body inside).
14 If the pan gasket is leaking, the fluid level may be too high, the vent may be blocked, the pan bolts may be too tight, the pan sealing flange may be warped, the sealing surface of the transmission housing may be damaged, the gasket may be damaged or the transmission casting may be cracked or porous. If sealant instead of gasket material

has been used to form a seal between the pan and the transmission housing, it may be the wrong sealant.

### Seal leaks

15 If a transmission seal is leaking, the fluid level may be too high, the vent may be blocked, the seal bore may be damaged, the seal itself may be damaged or improperly fitted, the surface of the shaft protruding through the seal may be damaged or a loose bearing may be causing excessive shaft movement.
16 Make sure the filler tube seal is in good condition and the tube is properly seated. If transmission fluid is evident, check the O-ring for damage.

### Casing leaks

17 If the casing itself appears to be leaking, the casting is porous and will have to be repaired or renewed.
18 Make sure the oil cooler hose fittings are tight and in good condition.

### Fluid comes out vent pipe or fill tube

19 If this condition occurs, the transmission is overfilled, the transmission is overheated, there is coolant in the fluid, the case is porous, the vent is blocked or the drain-back holes are blocked.

## 3 Gearchange cable – removal, refitting and adjustment

### Removal and refitting

1 Move the gearchange lever to the 'P' position. Remove the air filter housing (see Chapter 4A).
2 At the transmission end of the cable, prise the cable end off the selector lever, then remove the clip holding the cable to its bracket **(see illustration)**.

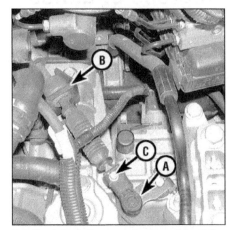

**3.2 To detach the gearchange cable at the transmission, pry the cable end off the selector lever (A), then remove the clip (B) and detach the cable from the bracket – (C) is the adjustment bolt**

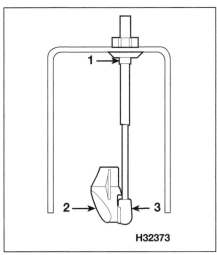

**3.6 To detach the gearchange cable at the gearchange lever housing, pry the cable end (3) off the bottom of the selector lever (2), then remove the clip (1) and pass the cable through the housing**

3 Raise the vehicle and support it securely on axle stands. Apply the handbrake.
4 Refer to Chapter 7A, Section 2, and perform Steps 5 through 7.
5 Remove the cover from the bottom of the gearchange lever housing.
6 Prise the gearchange cable end off the gearchange lever pin, then remove the clip and pass the cable and casing through the housing **(see illustration)**.
7 Guide the cable down between the engine and the bulkhead and remove it.
8 Refitting is the reverse of removal, with the following points:
  a) Lubricate the pins on the gearchange levers with multi-purpose grease.
  b) When connecting the cable end to the selector lever at the transmission, squeeze it on with a pair of pliers – don't try to press it on just by pushing down on it, as the selector lever might get bent.
  c) Renew the gasket on the shifter cover plate if it is damaged.
  d) Adjust the cables as described below.

## Adjustment

9 Move the selector lever to the 'P' position.
10 At the transmission end of the cable, loosen the bolt at the ball socket of the cable end **(see illustration 3.2)**. Push the selector shaft up against its end stop, corresponding to the 'P' position; try to turn the front wheels by hand – they should be locked. Now tighten the bolt to the torque listed in this Chapter's Specifications.
11 Verify the operation of the gearchange lever by shifting through all gear positions and checking that every gear can be selected smoothly and without delay.

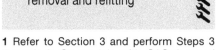

**4   Selector lever assembly –** removal and refitting

1 Refer to Section 3 and perform Steps 3 through 6. On models with O9G 6-speed transmission, position the shift lever in Reverse.
2 Working inside the vehicle, push down on the sleeve of the gearchange handle, then push in on the knob and pull the handle up and off the lever. The button can be retained in the 'In' position by inserting a pin or drill bit in the hole at the left-forward side of the button, while the button is depressed.
3 Prise the covers off the left and right rear of the gearchange housing.
4 Refer to Chapter 11 and remove the centre console.
5 Detach the gearchange interlock cable from the locking lever (see Section 5).
6 Detach all wire harness clips from the gearchange housing. Disconnect the electrical connectors from the gearchange lock solenoid and the gear position indicator **(see illustration)**.
7 Prise the frame off at each corner, being careful not to crack it.
8 Place the gearchange lever in position 1 and unscrew the two retaining bracket nuts, then remove the bracket.
9 Remove the two bolts that retain the gearchange lock solenoid **(see illustration 4.6)**.
10 Remove the two nuts that secure the front of the housing.
11 Carefully lower the assembly down through the floor.
12 The gearchange lever assembly can be disassembled and inspected **(see illustration overleaf)**, but if any components are worn or broken you'll have to check on the availability of renewal parts – you may have to renew the entire mechanism.
13 Refitting is the reverse of removal, with the following points:
  a) Adjust the gearchange cable (see Section 3).
  b) Adjust the gearchange interlock cable (see Section 5).
  c) Tighten the gearchange lever housing bolts securely.

**5   Gearchange interlock system** – description, testing and component renewal

⚠ *Warning: These models are equipped with airbags. Always disable the airbag system before working in the vicinity of any airbag system component to avoid the possibility of accidental deployment of the airbag(s), which could cause personal injury (see Chapter 12).*
*Caution 1: These models are equipped with an anti-theft radio. Before performing a procedure that requires disconnecting the battery, make sure you have the activation code.*
*Caution 2: Disconnecting the battery can cause driveability problems that require a scan tool to remedy. If the vehicle exhibits driveability problems after the battery is reconnected, it may be necessary to take it to a dealer service department or other qualified garage to reprogram the ECM. Warning: Do not use a memory-saving device to preserve the ECM's memory when working on or near airbag system components.*

### Description

1 The gearchange lock system prevents the gearchange lever from being shifted out of Park or Neutral until the brake pedal is applied and the button on the lever is pushed in. It also prevents the ignition key from being turned to the Lock position until the gearchange lever has been placed in the Park position.

### Solenoid check

2 Remove the centre console (see Chapter 11).
3 Follow the wiring harness from the gearchange lock solenoid back to the electrical connector, then unplug the

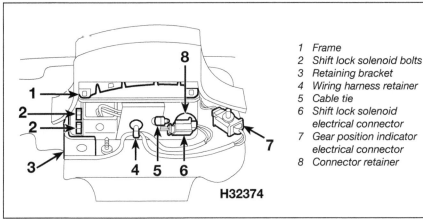

1 Frame
2 Shift lock solenoid bolts
3 Retaining bracket
4 Wiring harness retainer
5 Cable tie
6 Shift lock solenoid electrical connector
7 Gear position indicator electrical connector
8 Connector retainer

**4.6  Selector lever details**

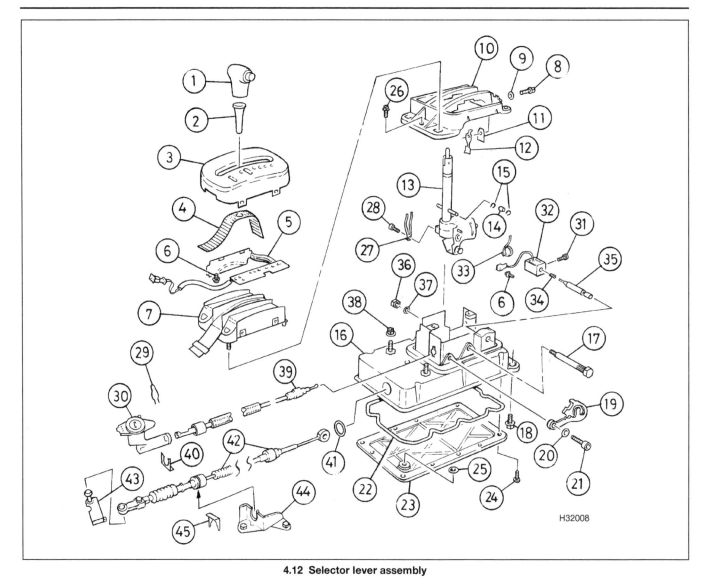

**4.12 Selector lever assembly**

| | | | | |
|---|---|---|---|---|
| 1 Selector lever handle | 11 Plate | 19 Locking lever | 28 Bolt | 37 Washer |
| 2 Sleeve | 12 Locating spring with | 20 Washer | 29 Clip | 38 Nut |
| 3 Cover | roller | 21 Bolt | 30 Steering lock | 39 Locking cable |
| 4 Cover strip | 13 Selector lever | 22 Gasket | 31 Bolt | 40 Circlip |
| 5 Lever position display | 14 Roller | 23 Cover | 32 Lock solenoid | 41 Gasket |
| 6 Retaining clip | 15 Circlip | 24 Bolt | 33 Cable tie | 42 Selector cable |
| 7 Frame | 16 Lever housing | 25 O-ring | 34 Spring | 43 Lever |
| 8 Bolt | 17 Pivot pin | 26 Bolt | 35 Locking pin | 44 Support bracket |
| 9 Shim | 18 Bolt | 27 Contact spring | 36 Nut | 45 Circlip |
| 10 Locking segment | | | | |

connector **(see illustration 4.6)**. Using a pair of jumper wires, momentarily apply battery voltage and earth to the solenoid terminals and verify that there's an audible 'click.'
**Caution: Don't apply battery voltage any longer than necessary to perform this check.**
**4** If the gearchange lock solenoid doesn't click when energised, renew it.

### Gearchange lock solenoid renewal

**5** Refer to Section 4 and remove the gearchange lever assembly. Remove the console (see Chapter 11).
**6** Place the selector lever in position 1, then wiggle the lever back and forth and work the solenoid and locking pin/spring out from the housing. On models with the O9G transmission, disconnect the electrical connector at the printed circuit board on the left side of the selector lever, then disconnect the solenoid connector. Access the solenoid by removing the cover on the underside of the floorpan.
**7** Refitting is the reverse of removal.

### Key interlock cable

**8** Disconnect the cable from the negative terminal of the battery.
**9** Remove the steering wheel (see Chapter 10).
**10** Remove the steering column cover (see Chapter 11).
**11** Remove the centre console (see Chapter 11).
**12** Turn the ignition key to the On position and place the gearchange lever in the Park position.

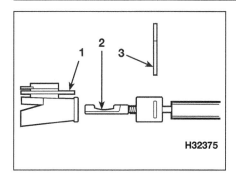

**5.14  The key interlock cable (2) is retained to the key lock cylinder housing (1) with a spring clip (3)**

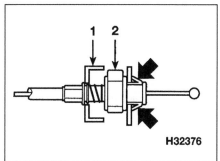

**5.15  To detach the interlock cable from the gearchange housing, depress the tabs (arrowed)**

*1  Sliding sleeve     2  Adjustment clip*

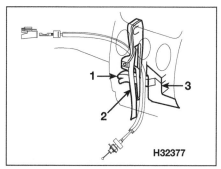

**5.16  Key interlock cable routing details**

*1  Footwell vent*
*2  Instrument panel support*
*3  Heater unit*

**13** Remove the gearchange lever handle (see Section 4, Step 2).
**14** Pull out the clip that retains the cable to the key lock cylinder housing, then detach the cable from the housing **(see illustration)**.
**15** Detach the interlock cable from the locking lever at the lever housing **(see illustration 4.12)**, then push in on the tabs and detach the cable casing from the lever housing **(see illustration)**.
**16** Remove the cable from the instrument panel, noting how it's routed **(see illustration)**. To ease refitting of the new cable, it's a good idea to attach a length of wire to the end of the old cable; as you remove the old cable, the length of wire will occupy its place. Then attach the wire to the new cable and use it to help you pull the new cable into place.
**17** To refit the cable, reverse the removal procedure, then adjust the cable as described below.

**Adjustment**

**18** Remove the centre console, if not already done (see Chapter 11).
**19** Place the selector lever in the Park position, then turn the ignition key to Lock and remove it from the lock cylinder.
**20** Move the sliding sleeve on the cable housing forward, then push up on the

adjustment clip **(see illustration 5.15)**.
**21** Remove the bracket from the gearchange housing **(see illustration 4.12)**.
**22** Insert a 0.8 mm feeler gauge between the selector lever roller and the locking lever **(see illustration)**, then pull lightly on the cable casing, away from the lever housing. Now push the adjustment clip down and slide the sleeve over the clip. **Note:** *On models with the O9G transmission, a factory adjustment pin is required to align the interlock cable.*

## 6  Driveshaft flange oil seal – renewal

**1** The driveshaft flange oil seals are located at the sides of the transmission, where the driveshafts are attached. If leakage at the seal is suspected, raise the vehicle and support it securely on axle stands. If a seal is leaking, lubricant will be found on the sides of the transmission.
**2** Refer to Chapter 8 and unbolt the driveshaft from the driveshaft flange. Position the driveshaft out of the way and support it with a piece of wire. **Note:** *It may be necessary to unbolt the engine support strut and prise the engine/transmission forward to provide clearance for driveshaft repositioning.*

**3** Place a drain pan under the transmission. Prise the cap from the centre of the flange, then remove the circlip. Remove the drive flange, using a puller, if necessary **(see illustration)**.
**4** Prise the oil seal out of the transmission bore with a seal removal tool or a large screwdriver.
**5** Pack the open side of the new seal with multi-purpose grease, then drive it into its bore using a seal refitting tool or a large socket with an outside diameter slightly smaller than that of the seal. Make sure the seal enters the bore squarely, and is driven in until it is completely seated.
**6** If a groove is worn in the driveshaft flange where it contacts the seal, the driveshaft flange must be renewed.
**7** Lubricate the seal contact area of the flange with multi-purpose grease. Refit the driveshaft flange and use a new circlip. If the driveshaft flange will not go on by hand, slight tapping with a hammer may seat it. If not, it will have to be pressed on using a threaded rod, a piece of metal fabricated to contact the flange surface, and a nut **(see illustration)**.

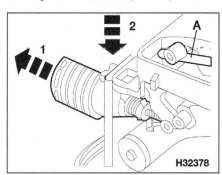

**5.22  Place a 0.8 mm feeler gauge (A) between the selector lever roller and the locking lever, then pull the cable casing in the direction of arrow (1) to remove any slack; finally, depress the adjustment clip (2)**

**6.3  If the drive flange won't come off by hand, remove it with a puller**

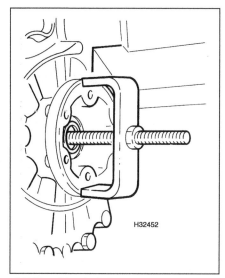

**6.7  The driveshaft flange may have to be pressed on using a setup like this**

**7.3 On early models, the Transmission Range (TR) switch is located on the rear side of the transmission – it is retained by a clamp and a bolt (arrowed)**

8 Reconnect the driveshaft to the driveshaft flange, tightening the bolts to the torque listed in the Chapter 8 Specifications.

9 Check the differential lubricant, adding as necessary to bring it to the appropriate level (see Chapter 1).

## 7 Multi-function Transmission Range (TR) switch – testing and renewal

### Testing

1 The Transmission Range (TR) switch is a solid state electronic device that works in conjunction with the Transmission Control Module (TCM). Diagnosis must be performed with a special factory scan tool. For this reason, if the reversing lights don't work or the vehicle starts in any gear position other than Park or Neutral, have the problem diagnosed by a technician equipped with the proper tool.

### Renewal

2 Remove the air filter housing (see Chapter 4A).

3 Disconnect the electrical connector from the switch (see illustration).

4 On early models, remove the bolt from the

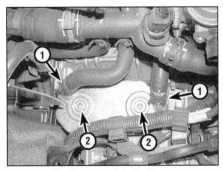

**8.3a Pinch off the coolant hoses to prevent excessive coolant loss, then squeeze the clamps (1) and slide them back on the hoses, detach the hoses, then unscrew the banjo bolts (2) – typical, later models have a round cooler with one mounting bolt**

hold-down clamp, then pull the switch out of the case.

5 On later models, the range switch is serviced by removing the nut and washer securing the shift arm, then removing the two mounting bolts.

6 Refitting is the reverse of the removal procedure. On early models, be sure to fit a new O-ring on the switch and lubricate it with clean automatic transmission fluid before fitting. Tighten the hold-down bolt(s) securely.

## 8 Automatic transmission fluid cooler – removal and refitting

**Warning: Wait until the engine is completely cool before beginning this procedure.**
**Caution 1: These models are equipped with an anti-theft radio. Before performing a procedure that requires disconnecting the battery, make sure you have the activation code.**
**Caution 2: Disconnecting the battery can cause driveability problems that require a scan tool to remedy. If the vehicle exhibits driveability problems after the battery is reconnected, it may be necessary to take it to a dealer service department or other qualified garage to reprogram the ECM. See Chapter 5, Section 1, for information on the use of an auxiliary voltage input device ('memory-saver') before disconnecting the battery.**

1 Remove the air filter housing (see Chapter 4A).

2 Remove the battery and battery tray (see Chapter 5).

3 Pinch off the coolant lines using locking pliers, then detach the lines from the cooler (see illustrations). Be prepared for coolant spillage.

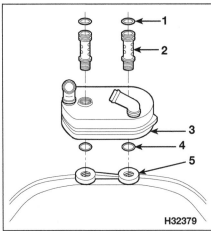

**8.3b Transmission fluid cooler details (typical)**

| | |
|---|---|
| 1  O-ring | 4  O-ring |
| 2  Banjo bolt | 5  Transmission |
| 3  Cooler | |

4 Unscrew the banjo bolts securing the cooler, then lift the cooler from the transmission. Be careful not to drip coolant or transmission fluid on the vehicle's paint.

5 Refitting is the reverse of removal. Be sure to renew the O-rings with new ones, and tighten the banjo bolts to the torque listed in this Chapter's Specifications.

6 After refitting the cooler, check the coolant and automatic transmission fluid, adding as necessary to bring them to the appropriate levels (see Chapter 1).

## 9 Automatic transmission – removal and refitting

**Warning 1: Wait until the engine is completely cool before beginning this procedure.**
**Warning 2: The manufacturer recommends renewing the transmission mount bolts and mount support bolts whenever they are removed.**
**Caution 1: These models are equipped with an anti-theft radio. Before performing a procedure that requires disconnecting the battery, make sure you have the activation code.**
**Caution 2: Disconnecting the battery can cause driveability problems that require a scan tool to remedy. If the vehicle exhibits driveability problems after the battery is reconnected, it may be necessary to take it to a dealer service department or other qualified garage to reprogram the ECM. See Chapter 5, Section 1, for information on the use of an auxiliary voltage input device ('memory-saver') before disconnecting the battery.**

### Removal

1 Select a solid, level surface to park the vehicle upon. Give yourself enough space to move around it easily. Apply the handbrake and chock the rear wheels.

2 Refer to Chapter 11 and remove the bonnet from its hinges.

3 Remove the air filter housing and air intake duct (see Chapter 4A).

4 Remove the battery and battery tray (see Chapter 5).

5 Remove the windscreen wiper arms (see Chapter 12), the scuttle cover and plenum close-out panel (see Chapter 11).

6 Refer to Section 3 and disconnect the gearchange cable from the transmission selector shaft. Also remove the clip and detach the cable from its bracket.

7 Unbolt the earth strap from the transmission.

8 Clamp off the coolant hoses leading to and from the transmission fluid cooler unit, then loosen the hose clamps and pull off the hoses (see Section 8). Absorb any coolant that escapes with old rags.

9 Disconnect the wiring harness from the

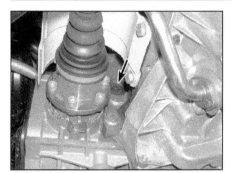

9.17a Pry out this access plug (arrowed) . . .

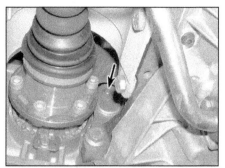

9.17b . . . turn the crankshaft to bring one of the torque converter nuts in line with the hole . . .

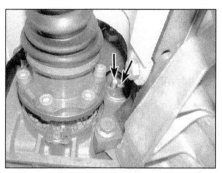

9.17c . . . then unscrew the nut and mark the relationship of the stud to the driveplate

transmission at the multi-way connectors, labelling each one to aid refitting later.

**10** Support the engine from above with an engine support fixture, using the engine lifting points (see Chapter 2C; these are the same points that are used when attaching an engine hoist for engine removal). You can obtain one of these at most equipment rental shops.

**11** If the vehicle is equipped with a 2.0L engine, remove the Vehicle Speed Sensor (see Chapter 6A). Also, remove the exhaust manifold heat shield (see Chapter 2A).

**12** Raise the front of the vehicle and support it securely on axle stands. Apply the handbrake.

**13** Remove the under-vehicle splash shield and both lower inner wing panels.

**14** Unbolt the protective plate from the underside of the transmission sump.

**15** Refer to Chapter 5 and remove the starter motor.

**16** If the vehicle is equipped with a diesel engine, remove the duct between the turbocharger and intercooler (see Chapter 4B).

**17** Remove the access plug, then unscrew each torque converter-to-driveplate nut in turn **(see illustrations)**. As each nut is removed, rotate the crankshaft using a spanner and socket on the crankshaft pulley bolt to expose the next nut. There are three nuts, spaced 120-degrees apart.

**18** Remove the engine support strut (see Chapter 2A, Section 17).

**19** Support the transmission with a jack

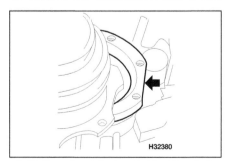

9.20 Turn the right-hand side driveshaft flange so its flat is vertical – this will allow it to clear the engine block as the transmission is removed

(preferably a special jack made for this purpose; these can be obtained at most equipment rental shops). Safety chains will help steady the transmission on the jack.

**20** Refer to Chapter 8 and unbolt the driveshafts from the transmission driveshaft flanges. Remove the CV joint shield above the right driveshaft. Turn the right-side driveshaft flange so the flat portion of the flange is vertical **(see illustration)**.

**21** Refer to Chapter 10 and separate the balljoint from the left control arm. Detach the anti-roll bar link from the left control arm. Pass the left hand driveshaft over the suspension arm and swing it towards the rear of the vehicle, out of the way.

**22** Suspend the right hand driveshaft as high as possible using cable-ties or wire. Turn the steering to full left lock.

**23** Remove the transmission mounting bolts, then unbolt the mounting support from the transmission **(see illustrations)**.

**24** Remove the transmission mounting bolts that are accessible from underneath.

**25** Check that nothing remains connected to the transmission before attempting to separate it from the engine.

**26** Remove the bolts from the top of the bellhousing and pull the transmission away from the engine.

**27** When all the locating dowels are clear of their mounting holes, slowly lower the transmission, turning it as necessary to manoeuvre it out from between the engine and the left side of the chassis. Strap a restraining bar across the front of the bellhousing to keep the torque converter in position.

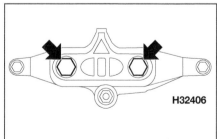

9.23a Unscrew the two transmission mounting bolts (arrowed) . . .

**Caution: Take care to prevent the torque converter from falling out as the transmission is removed.**

### Refitting

**28** Refitting of the transmission is essentially a reversal of the removal procedure, but note the following points:

a) *As the torque converter is fitted, ensure that the drive pins at the centre of the torque converter hub engage with the recesses in the automatic transmission fluid pump inner wheel.*

b) *When refitting the transmission, be sure to align the marked torque converter stud with its marked hole.*

c) *Tighten the bellhousing bolts and torque converter-to-driveplate bolts to the specified torque.*

d) *Refer to Chapter 2A and tighten the engine support strut bolts to the specified torque.*

e) *Tighten the transmission mounting bolts and the mounting support bolts to the torque listed in this Chapter's Specifications.*

f) *Tighten the driveshaft-to-driveshaft flange bolts to the torque listed in the Chapter 8 Specifications.*

g) *Refer to Section 3 and check the gearchange cable adjustment.*

h) *Add the recommended type and amount of automatic transmission fluid (see Chapter 1).*

i) *Check the coolant level, adding as necessary (see Chapter 1)*

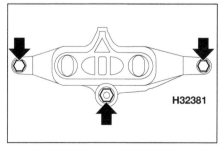

9.23b . . . then unbolt the mounting support from the transmission

## 10 Automatic transmission fluid and filter – renewal

1 Since the fluid will remain hot long after driving, perform this procedure only after the engine has cooled down completely.

2 Before beginning work, purchase the specified transmission fluid (see Chapter 1) and a new filter and pan gasket.

3 Other tools necessary for this job include a floor jack, axle stands to support the vehicle in a raised position, a drain pan capable of holding at least eight litres, newspapers and clean rags.

4 Raise the vehicle and support it securely on axle stands.

5 Place the drain pan underneath the transmission pan.

6 Remove the transmission pan mounting bolts, then carefully pry the transmission pan loose with a screwdriver, leaving one end loosely attached so that the fluids flows out at one end of the pan.

 **Warning: The transmission fluid may be hot.**

7 Remove the pan completely and carefully clean the gasket surface of the transmission to remove all traces of the old gasket and sealant.

8 Clean the pan with solvent and wipe it dry. **Note:** *Some models are equipped with magnets in the transmission pan to catch metal debris. Clean the magnet thoroughly. A small amount of metal material is normal at the magnet. If there is considerable debris, consult a dealer or transmission specialist.*

9 Remove the filter from the valve body inside the transmission. **Note:** *Be very careful not to gouge the delicate aluminum gasket surface on the valve body.*

10 Install a new seal and filter. On many renewal filters, the gasket is attached to the filter to simplify installation.

11 Make sure the gasket surface on the transmission pan is clean, then install a new gasket on the pan. Put the pan in place against the transmission and, working around the pan, securely tighten each bolt a little at a time.

12 Reinstall the components removed for access to the pan bolts.

13 Lower the vehicle and add approximately 2.5 litres of the specified type of automatic transmission fluid through the filler (see Chapter 1).

14 With the transmission in Park and the parking brake set, run the engine at a fast idle, but don't race it.

15 Move the gear selector through each range and back to Park, then let the engine idle for a few minutes. Check the fluid level. It will probably be low. Add enough fluid to bring the level up until it just drips out of the level-check hole. **Note:** *The fluid level must be checked at a certain temperature* (see Chapter 1).

16 Check under the vehicle for leaks during the first few trips.

# Chapter 8
# Clutch and driveshafts

## Contents

## Degrees of difficulty

| Easy, suitable for novice with little experience | Fairly easy, suitable for beginner with some experience | Fairly difficult, suitable for competent DIY mechanic | Difficult, suitable for experienced DIY mechanic | Very difficult, suitable for expert DIY or professional |
|---|---|---|---|---|

## Specifications

| Torque specifications | Nm | Ft-lbs |
|---|---|---|
| Clutch master cylinder retaining nuts | 25 | 18 |
| Clutch pedal support bracket nuts* | 25 | 18 |
| Clutch pressure plate bolts | | |
| One-piece flywheel | 20 | 15 |
| Two-piece flywheel | 13 | 10 |
| Clutch release cylinder retaining bolts | 25 | 18 |
| Driveshaft/hub nut* | | |
| Step 1 | 300 | 221 |
| Step 2 | Loosen one turn | |
| Step 3 | 50 | 37 |
| Step 4 | Tighten an additional 30-degrees | |
| Flywheel bolts | See Chapter 2A | |
| Inner CV joint-to-drive flange bolts | 40 | 30 |

*Renew with new nut(s)

## 1 General information

The information in this Chapter deals with the components from the engine to the front wheels, except for the transmission, which is dealt with in Chapter 7A and 7B. For the purposes of this Chapter, these components are grouped into two categories: Clutch and driveshafts. Separate Sections within this Chapter offer general descriptions and checking procedures for both groups.

Since nearly all the procedures covered in this Chapter involve working under the vehicle, make sure it's securely supported on sturdy axle stands or a hoist where the vehicle can be easily raised and lowered.

## 2 Clutch –
description and testing

1 All models with a manual transmission use a single dry plate, diaphragm spring type clutch **(see illustration)**. The driven plate has a splined hub which allows it to slide along the splines of the transmission input shaft. The clutch and pressure plate are held in contact by spring pressure exerted by the diaphragm in the pressure plate.

2 The clutch release system is hydraulically-operated. The release system consists of the clutch pedal, the clutch master cylinder, the clutch release cylinder, the hydraulic pipe between the master cylinder and release cylinder, the clutch release bearing and the clutch release lever.

3 When pressure is applied to the clutch pedal to release the clutch, the clutch master cylinder transmits this movement to the clutch release cylinder, which moves the clutch

release lever. As the lever pivots, the release bearing pushes against the fingers of the diaphragm spring of the pressure plate assembly, which in turn releases the clutch plate.

4 Terminology can be a problem regarding the clutch components because common names have in some cases changed from that used by the manufacturer. For example, the clutch release cylinder is sometimes referred to as a slave cylinder, the driven plate is also called the clutch plate or disc, the pressure plate assembly is also known as the clutch cover, and the clutch release bearing is sometimes called a thrust bearing.

5 Other than renewing components that have obvious damage, some preliminary checks should be performed to diagnose a clutch system failure.

a) *To check clutch 'spin down' time, run the engine at normal idle speed with the transmission in Neutral (clutch pedal up, engaged). Disengage the clutch (pedal down), wait several seconds and shift the transmission into Reverse. No grinding noise should be heard. A grinding noise would most likely indicate a problem in the pressure plate or the driven plate.*

b) *To check for complete clutch release, run the engine (with the handbrake applied to prevent movement) and hold the clutch pedal approximately 12 mm from the floor. Shift the transmission between 1st gear and Reverse several times. If the shift is not smooth, component failure is indicated.*

c) *Visually inspect the clutch pedal bushing at the top of the clutch pedal to make sure there is no sticking or excessive wear.*

d) *Make sure that the hydraulic pipes aren't leaking at either the master cylinder or the release cylinder (see Sections 3 and 4). Bleed the system if necessary (see Section 5).*

## 3 Clutch master cylinder –
removal and refitting

⚠ **Warning: These models are equipped with airbags. Always disable the airbag system before working in the vicinity of any airbag system component to avoid the possibility of accidental deployment of the airbag(s), which could cause personal injury (see Chapter 12).**
**Caution 1: These models are equipped with an anti-theft radio. Before performing a procedure that requires disconnecting the battery, make sure you have the activation code.**
**Caution 2: Disconnecting the battery can cause driveability problems that require a scan tool to remedy. If the vehicle exhibits driveability problems after the battery is reconnected, it may be necessary to take it to a dealer service department or other qualified garage to reprogram the ECM.**

⚠ **Warning: Do not use a memory-saving device to preserve the ECM's memory when working on or near airbag system components.**

### Removal

1 Disconnect the cable from the negative terminal of the battery.

2 Remove the air filter housing and the air intake duct (see Chapter 4A). On 2.0L models, remove the protective housing for relays from the cable channel.

3 Detach the fluid supply hose from the brake master cylinder reservoir. Have a plug ready and immediately plug the port on the reservoir.

4 Remove the clip securing the pressure pipe to the clutch master cylinder, then separate the pipe from the cylinder **(see illustration)**.

5 Working inside the vehicle, remove the driver's side under-dash panel.

6 Remove the clutch start switch (see Section 8).

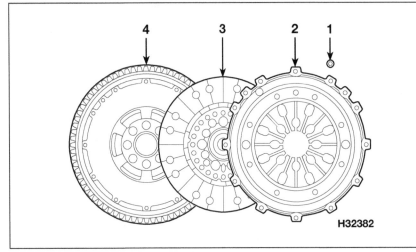

**2.1 Clutch components**

| 1 Bolt | 2 Pressure plate | 3 Driven plate | 4 Flywheel |

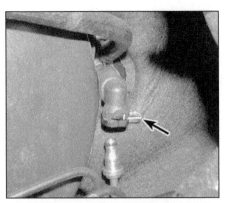

**3.4 Pull out the clip retaining the clutch fluid pressure pipe to the clutch master cylinder, then pull the pipe out of the fitting**

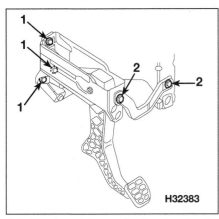

**3.7 Clutch pedal mounting bracket details**

1  *Clutch pedal mounting bracket nuts*
2  *Reinforcement plate nuts*

**7** Remove the reinforcement plate connecting the clutch pedal bracket and the brake pedal bracket, then unbolt the clutch pedal bracket from the bulkhead **(see illustration)**. Remove the clutch pedal, bracket and master cylinder as an assembly.

**8** Disconnect the pushrod from the clutch pedal. To do this you'll have to prise the pushrod retaining tabs inward, then pull the pushrod and retainer out of the clutch pedal **(see illustration)**.

**9** Twist the clutch pedal stop anti-clockwise and remove it from the pedal bracket **(see illustration)**.

**10** Push the clutch master cylinder down and away from the pedal over-centre spring, then separate it from the bracket **(see illustration)**.

### Refitting

**Note:** *The manufacturer recommends renewing the clutch pedal mounting bracket nuts and the reinforcement plate nuts whenever they are removed.*

**11** Refitting is the reverse of removal, with the following points:
 a) *Tighten all fasteners to the torque values listed in this Chapter's Specifications.*
 b) *Check the O-ring on the pressure pipe, renewing it if necessary. Lubricate the O-ring with clean brake fluid before installing or reconnecting the pipe.*

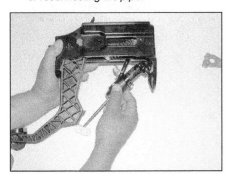

**3.10  Push the master cylinder away from the over-centre spring, angle it down and detach it from the pedal bracket**

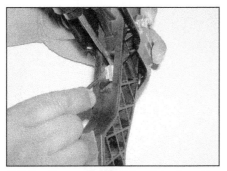

**3.8** Pry the pushrod retainer tabs from the holes on either side of the clutch pedal, then pull the pushrod and retainer out of the pedal slot

 c) *Bleed the clutch hydraulic system (see Section 5).*
 d) *Check the brake fluid level in the brake fluid reservoir, adding as necessary to bring it to the appropriate level (see Chapter 1).*
 e) *Wash off any spilled brake fluid with water.*

### 4  Clutch release cylinder – removal and refitting

*Caution 1: These models are equipped with an anti-theft radio. Before performing a procedure that requires disconnecting the battery, make sure you have the activation code.*

*Caution 2: Disconnecting the battery can cause driveability problems that require a scan tool to remedy. If the vehicle exhibits driveability problems after the battery is reconnected, it may be necessary to take it to a dealer service department or other qualified garage to reprogram the ECM. See Chapter 5, Section 1, for information on the use of an auxiliary voltage input device ('memory-saver') before disconnecting the battery.*

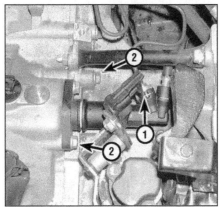

**4.4  Clutch release cylinder mounting details**

1  *Pressure pipe retaining clip*
2  *Mounting bolts*

**3.9** Turn the clutch pedal stop anti-clockwise to detach it from the bracket

### Removal

**1** Disconnect the cable from the negative terminal of the battery.
**2** Remove the air filter housing (see Chapter 4A).
**3** Detach the gearchange cables from the levers at the transmission (see Chapter 7A).
**4** Remove the clip retaining the pressure pipe to the release cylinder, then detach the pipe **(see illustration)**. Have some rags handy, as some fluid will be spilled when the pipe is disconnected.
**5** Remove the release cylinder mounting bolts and detach the cylinder from the transmission. **Note:** *On some models there is a brace from the clutch pedal bracket to the brake pedal bracket – remove the brace.*

### Refitting

**6** Lubricate the end of the pushrod with a little moly-base grease, then refit the release cylinder on the transmission. Make sure the pushrod is seated in the release lever pocket. Refit the mounting bolts and tighten them to the torque listed in this Chapter's Specifications.
**7** Check the O-ring on the pressure pipe, renewing it if necessary. Lubricate the O-ring with clean brake fluid before refitting or reconnecting the pipe. Connect the pipe to the release cylinder and refit the retaining clip.
**8** Bleed the system (see Section 5).
**9** Check the brake fluid level in the brake fluid reservoir, adding as necessary to bring it to the appropriate level (see Chapter 1).
**10** Wash off any spilled brake fluid with water.
**11** Refit the air filter housing and reconnect the battery.

### 5  Clutch hydraulic system – bleeding

**1** The hydraulic system should be bled of all air whenever any part of the system has been removed or if the fluid level has been allowed to fall so low that air has been drawn into the

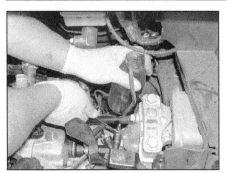

**5.3 Push one end of a clear hose over the bleed screw on the release cylinder and submerge the other end of the hose in a container of clear brake fluid – open the bleed screw when the pedal is depressed, then close it before the pedal is released**

**6.5 Mark the relationship of the pressure plate to the flywheel (in case you are going to re-use the same pressure plate)**

**6.7 When removing the pressure plate, be careful not to let the driven plate fall out**

master cylinder. The procedure is similar to bleeding a brake system.

**2** Fill the brake master cylinder with new brake fluid conforming to DOT 4 specifications.

> *Warning: Do not re-use any of the fluid coming from the system during the bleeding operation or use fluid which has been inside an open container for an extended period of time.*

**3** Remove the air filter housing (see Chapter 4A). Locate the bleed screw on the clutch release cylinder. Remove the dust cap from the bleed screw and push a length of snug-fitting (preferably clear) hose over the valve. Place the other end of the hose into a clear container with about two inches of brake fluid in it. The hose end must be submerged in the fluid **(see illustration)**.

**4** Have an assistant depress the clutch pedal and hold it. Open the bleed screw on the release cylinder, allowing fluid to flow through the hose. Close the bleed screw when fluid stops flowing from the hose. Once closed, have your assistant release the pedal.

**5** Continue this process until all air is evacuated from the system, indicated by a full, solid stream of fluid being ejected from the bleed screw each time and no air bubbles in the hose or container. Keep a close watch on the fluid level inside the brake master cylinder reservoir; if the level drops too low, air will be sucked back into the system and the process will have to be started over again.

**6** Refit the dust cap on the bleed screw. Check carefully for proper operation before placing the vehicle in normal service.

**7** Recheck the brake fluid level.

**8** Refit the air filter housing.

---

**6 Clutch components –**
removal, inspection and refitting

> *Warning: Dust produced by clutch wear and deposited on clutch components is hazardous*

*to your health. DO NOT blow it out with compressed air and DO NOT inhale it. DO NOT use petrol or petroleum-based solvents to remove the dust. Brake system cleaner should be used to flush the dust into a drain pan. After the clutch components are wiped clean with a rag, dispose of the contaminated rags and cleaner in a labelled, covered container.*

### Removal

**1** Access to the clutch components is normally accomplished by removing the transmission, leaving the engine in the vehicle. If, of course, the engine is being removed for major overhaul, then the opportunity should always be taken to check the clutch for wear and renew worn components as necessary. However, the relatively low cost of the clutch components compared to the time and labour involved in gaining access to them warrants their renewal any time the engine or transmission is removed, unless they are new or in near-perfect condition. The following procedures assume that the engine will stay in place.

**2** Remove the transmission from the vehicle (see Chapter 7A). Support the engine while the transmission is out. Preferably, an engine hoist or support fixture should be used to support it from above. However, if a jack is used underneath the engine, make sure a piece of wood is used between the jack and sump to spread the load.

**3** The release lever and release bearing can remain attached to the transmission; however, you should inspect them (see Section 7) while the transmission is removed.

**4** To support the driven plate during removal, refit a clutch alignment tool through the plate hub.

**5** Carefully inspect the flywheel and pressure plate for indexing marks. The marks are usually an X, an O or a white letter. If they cannot be found, scribe marks yourself so the pressure plate and the flywheel will be in the same alignment during refitting **(see illustration)**. Of course, this won't be necessary if you're planning on renewing the pressure plate.

**6** Slowly loosen the pressure plate-to-flywheel bolts. Work in a criss-cross pattern

and loosen each bolt a little at a time until all spring pressure is relieved.

**7** Hold the pressure plate securely and completely remove the bolts, followed by the pressure plate and driven plate **(see illustration)**. On later models with O2M transmissions, there are several small square plates behind the clutch cover perimeter that lock to the flywheel. The plates must be held with an open-end spanner in order to remove the pressure plate bolts.

### Inspection

**8** Ordinarily, when a problem occurs in the clutch, it can be attributed to wear of the clutch driven plate assembly. However, all components should be inspected at this time.

**9** Inspect the flywheel for cracks, heat checking, score marks and other damage. If the imperfections are slight, an engineering shop can resurface it to make it flat and smooth. Refer to Chapter 2A for the flywheel removal procedure.

**10** Inspect the lining on the driven plate. There should be at least 1.5 mm of lining above the rivet heads. Check for loose rivets, distortion, cracks, broken springs and other obvious damage **(see illustration)**. As mentioned above, ordinarily the driven plate is renewed as a matter of course, so if in doubt about the condition, renew it.

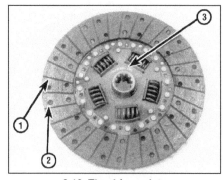

**6.10 The driven plate**

1 *Lining – this will wear down in use*
2 *Rivets – these secure the lining and will damage the flywheel or pressure plate if allowed to contact the surfaces*
3 *Hub – Be sure this is installed facing the proper direction (see the text)*

 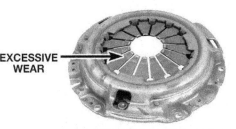 

NORMAL FINGER WEAR     EXCESSIVE WEAR     EXCESSIVE FINGER WEAR     BROKEN OR BENT FINGERS

6.12 Renew the pressure plate if excessive wear is noted

**11** The release bearing should be renewed along with the driven plate (see Section 7).
**12** Check the machined surface and the diaphragm spring fingers of the pressure plate **(see illustration)**. If the surface is grooved or otherwise damaged, renew the pressure plate assembly. Also check for obvious damage, distortion, cracking, etc. Light glazing can be removed with emery cloth or sandpaper. If a new pressure plate is indicated, new or factory rebuilt units are available.

### Refitting

**13** Position the driven plate and pressure plate with the clutch held in place with an alignment tool. Make sure the plate is fitted properly. If your vehicle is equipped with a one-piece flywheel, the spring cage must face the pressure plate. If the vehicle is equipped with a two-piece flywheel, the shorter hub end must face the pressure plate.
**14** Tighten the pressure plate-to-flywheel bolts only finger tight, working around the pressure plate.
**15** Centre the driven plate by ensuring the alignment tool is through the splined hub and into the recess in the crankshaft **(see illustration)**. Wiggle the tool up, down or side-to-side as needed to bottom the tool. Tighten the pressure plate-to-flywheel bolts a little at a time, working in a criss-cross pattern to prevent distortion of the cover. After all of the bolts are snug, tighten them to the torque

listed in this Chapter's Specifications. Remove the alignment tool.
**16** Using moly-base grease, lubricate the inner surface of the release bearing (see Section 7), and to the face of the bearing where it contacts the fingers of the pressure plate diaphragm. Also place grease on the release lever contact areas and the transmission input shaft.
*Caution: Don't use too much grease.*
**17** Refit the clutch release bearing (see Section 7).
**18** Refit the transmission and all components removed previously, tightening all fasteners to the proper torque specifications.

### 7 Clutch release bearing and lever – removal, inspection and refitting

⚠ *Warning: Dust produced by clutch wear and deposited on clutch components is hazardous to your health. DO NOT blow it out with compressed air and DO NOT inhale it. DO NOT use petrol or petroleum-based solvents to remove the dust. Brake system cleaner should be used to flush it into a drain pan. After the clutch components are wiped clean with a rag, dispose of the contaminated rags and cleaner in a labelled, covered container.*
*Caution 1: These models are equipped with an anti-theft radio. Before performing a procedure that requires disconnecting the battery, make sure you have the activation code.*

*Caution 2: Disconnecting the battery can cause driveability problems that require a scan tool to remedy. If the vehicle exhibits driveability problems after the battery is reconnected, it may be necessary to take it to a dealer service department or other qualified garage to reprogram the ECM. See Chapter 5, Section 1, for information on the use of an auxiliary voltage input device ('memory-saver') before disconnecting the battery.*

### Removal

**1** Disconnect the cable from the negative terminal of the battery.
**2** Remove the transmission (see Chapter 7A).
**3** Disengage the clutch release lever from the ball stud, then remove the bearing and lever **(see illustration)**.

### Inspection

**4** Detach the bearing from the lever. Hold the bearing by the outer race and rotate the inner race while applying pressure **(see illustration)**. If the bearing doesn't turn smoothly or if it's noisy, renew the bearing/hub assembly. Wipe the bearing with a clean rag and inspect it for damage, wear and cracks. Don't immerse the bearing in solvent; it's sealed for life and to do so would ruin it. Also check the release lever for cracks and bends.

### Refitting

**5** Lubricate the surface of the guide sleeve with a light film of moly-base grease.

6.15 Centre the driven plate with a clutch alignment tool, then tighten the pressure plate bolts a little at a time, in a criss-cross pattern, to the torque listed in this Chapter's Specifications

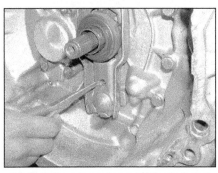

7.3 Pull the release lever off the ball stud

7.4 To check the bearing, hold it be the outer race and rotate the inner race while applying pressure; if the bearing doesn't turn smoothly or if it's noisy, renew it

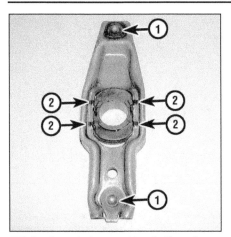

**7.6 Apply moly-base grease to the release lever ball socket and release cylinder ball socket (1). When assembling the release bearing to the lever, make sure the retaining clips engage correctly (2)**

6 Lubricate the release lever ball socket and release cylinder pushrod socket with moly-base grease **(see illustration)**.
7 Attach the retainer spring and the release bearing to the release lever.
8 Slide the release bearing and lever onto the guide sleeve, then push the release lever onto the ball stud until it's firmly seated.
9 Apply a light coat of high-temperature grease to the face of the release bearing where it contacts the pressure plate diaphragm fingers.
10 The remainder of refitting is the reverse of removal.

## 8 Clutch start switch – testing and renewal

### Testing

1 The clutch start switch is located on the clutch pedal bracket **(see illustration)**.
2 Verify that the engine will not start when the clutch pedal is released.
3 Verify that the engine will start when the clutch pedal is depressed all the way.
4 If the clutch start switch doesn't perform as described above, check switch continuity.
5 Remove the driver's side under-dash panel. Unplug the electrical connector from the switch and verify that there is continuity between the two clutch start switch terminals when the pedal is depressed.
6 Verify that no continuity exists between the switch terminals when the pedal is released.
7 If the switch fails either of these continuity tests, renew it.

### Renewal

8 Remove the driver's side under-dash panel.
9 Unplug the electrical connector from the switch.

**8.1 The clutch start switch (1) is mounted on the clutch pedal bracket; the other switch on the pedal bracket (2) is the cruise control cut-off switch**

10 Rotate the switch 90-degrees anti-clockwise and pull it out of the bracket.
11 To refit the new switch, depress the clutch pedal, insert the switch into the bracket (position the switch 1/4-turn from its fitted position), rotate it 90-degrees clockwise and release the pedal.
12 Reconnect the electrical connector and check the operation of the clutch start switch.
13 Refit the under-dash panel.

## 9 Driveshafts – general information and inspection

1 Power is transmitted from the transmission to the wheels through a pair of driveshafts. The inner end of each driveshaft is bolted to a driveshaft flange protruding from the differential; the outer end of each driveshaft has a stub shaft that is splined to the front hub and bearing assembly and locked in place with a large nut.
2 The inner ends of the driveshafts are equipped with sliding constant velocity (CV) joints, which are capable of both angular and axial motion. Each inner CV joint assembly consists of a either a triple rotor-type bearing or a ball-and-cage type bearing and a housing in which the joint is free to slide in-and-out as the driveshaft moves up-and-down with the wheel.
3 The outer ends of the driveshafts are equipped with 'ball-and-cage' type CV joints, which are capable of angular but not axial movement. Each outer CV joint consists of six ball bearings running between an inner race and an outer cage.
4 The boots should be inspected periodically for damage and leaking lubricant. Torn CV joint boots must be renewed immediately or the joints will be damaged. If either boot of a driveshaft is damaged, that driveshaft must

be removed in order to renew the boot (see Section 10).
5 Should a boot be damaged, the CV joint can be disassembled and cleaned, but if any parts are damaged, the entire driveshaft assembly may have to be renewed as a unit – check with your local auto parts store regarding the availability of renewal parts and CV joints (see Section 11).
6 The most common symptom of worn or damaged CV joints, besides lubricant leaks, is a clicking noise in turns, a clunk when accelerating after freewheeling and vibration at highway speeds. To check for wear in the CV joints and driveshaft shafts, grasp each axle (one at a time) and rotate it in both directions while holding the CV joint housings, feeling for play indicating worn splines or sloppy CV joints. Also check the driveshaft shafts for cracks, dents and distortion.

## 10 Driveshaft – removal and refitting

⚠ **Warning: The manufacturer recommends renewing the driveshaft/hub nut whenever it is removed.**

### Removal

1 Remove the wheel trim/hub cap (as applicable) and loosen the driveshaft/hub nut with the vehicle resting on its wheels **(see illustration)**. Also loosen the wheel bolts.
2 Block the rear wheels of the car, firmly apply the handbrake, then raise the front of the vehicle and support it securely on axle stands. Remove the front wheel. On models with a diesel engine, remove the duct between the turbocharger and the intercooler (see Chapter 4B). **Note:** *On models with an automatic transmission, it may be necessary to unbolt the transmission support from the subframe and the transmission, and prise the engine/transmission forward to provide clearance for driveshaft removal.*
3 Unscrew the bolts securing the inner CV joint to the transmission driveshaft flange and remove the retaining plates from underneath

**10.1 Loosen the driveshaft/hub nut while the wheel is still on the ground**

**10.3 Remove the bolts retaining the inner CV joint to the driveshaft flange**

**10.6 Pull the hub out and detach the driveshaft**

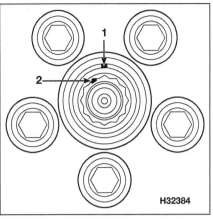

**10.15 The distance between each point of a twelve-point nut is 30° – make a mark on one of the points on the nut (2), then another mark above the next point of the nut to the right (1); during the final tightening step, aligning these marks will give the proper angle of rotation**

the bolts **(see illustration)**. Support the driveshaft by suspending it with wire or string – do not allow it to hang under its weight, or the joint may be damaged.

**4** Using a marking pen, draw around the end of the suspension control arm, marking the correct fitted position of the balljoint. Unscrew the balljoint retaining bolts and remove the retaining plate from the control arm (see Chapter 10).

**5** Remove the driveshaft/hub nut. Also remove the inner wing panel and the under-vehicle splash shield.

**6** Carefully pull the hub assembly outwards and withdraw the driveshaft outer constant velocity joint from the hub assembly **(see illustration)**. If the splines of the outer joint are stuck in the hub, tap the joint out of the hub using a soft-faced mallet. If this fails to free it from the hub, the joint will have to be pressed out using a puller which is bolted to the hub.

**7** Manoeuvre the driveshaft out from underneath the vehicle and recover the gasket from the end of the inner constant velocity joint, if present. Discard the gasket – a new one should be used on refitting.

**8** Don't allow the vehicle to rest on its wheels with one or both driveshaft(s) removed, as damage to the wheel bearing(s) may result. If moving the vehicle is unavoidable, temporarily insert the outer end of the driveshaft(s) in the hub(s) and tighten the driveshaft/hub nut(s); in this case, the inner end(s) of the driveshaft(s) must be supported, for example by suspending with string from the vehicle underbody. Do not allow the driveshaft to hang down under its weight, or the joint may be damaged.

### Refitting

**9** Ensure that the transmission driveshaft flange and inner joint mating surfaces are clean and dry. Refit a new gasket to the joint by peeling off its backing foil and sticking it in position.

**10** Ensure that the outer joint and hub splines and threads are clean, then lubricate the splines with a light coat of multi-purpose grease.

**11** Manoeuvre the driveshaft into position

and engage the outer joint with the hub. Ensure that the threads are clean and use the nut to draw the joint fully into position.

**12** Connect the balljoint to the control arm and refit the retaining bolts, tightening them to the torque listed in the Chapter 10 Specifications, using the marks made on removal to ensure that the balljoint is correctly positioned.

**13** Align the driveshaft inner joint with the transmission flange and refit the retaining bolts and plates. Tighten the bolts to the torque listed in this Chapter's Specifications.

**14** Ensure that the outer joint is drawn fully into position, then refit the wheel and lower the vehicle to the earth.

**15** The remainder of refitting is the reverse of removal, with the following points:

a) Tighten the driveshaft/hub nut to torque and angle of rotation listed in this Chapter's Specifications. If you don't have a torque angle meter, you can mark one point of the twelve-point nut and make another mark on the wheel hub, directly above the next point to the right **(see illustration)**; when tightening the nut in the final Step of the torque sequence, turn the nut until both marks align (the distance between each point of a twelve-point nut is 30-degrees).

b) Once the driveshaft/hub nut is correctly tightened, tighten the wheel bolts to the torque listed in the Chapter 1 Specifications and install the wheel trim/hub cap.

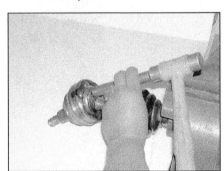

**11.4 Drive the outer CV joint off the shaft with a hammer and a brass punch**

### 11 Driveshaft boot renewal

**1** Remove the driveshaft from the vehicle as described in Section 10.

### Outer CV joint

**2** Secure the driveshaft in a vice equipped with soft jaws, then loosen the two outer joint boot retaining clamps. If necessary, the clamps can be cut off.

**3** Slide the boot down the shaft to expose the constant velocity (CV) joint and wipe off as much grease as possible.

**4** Using a hammer and a brass punch, tap the joint off the end of the driveshaft **(see illustration)**.

*Caution: Place the punch on the inner race of the CV joint only.*

**5** Remove the circlip from the driveshaft groove, then slide off the thrust washer and dished washer, noting which way they are fitted **(see illustration)**.

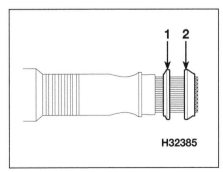

**11.5 Proper positioning of the dished washer (1) and thrust washer (2) for the outer CV joint**

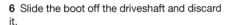

**11.7 Mark the relationship of the bearing cage, inner race and housing**

**11.8 If necessary, pry the balls out with a screwdriver**

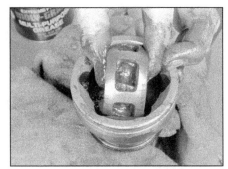

**11.9 Tilt the inner race and cage 90°, then align the windows in the cage with the lands and rotate the inner race up and out of the outer race**

6 Slide the boot off the driveshaft and discard it.

7 Clean the outer CV joint assembly to remove as much grease as possible. Mark the relative position of the bearing cage, inner race and housing **(see illustration)**.

8 Mount the outer CV joint in a vice equipped with soft jaws. Push down on one side of the cage and remove the ball bearing from the opposite side. Repeat this procedure until all of the balls are removed **(see illustration)**. If the joint is tight, tap on the inner race (not the cage) with a hammer and brass punch.

9 Remove the cage and inner race assembly from the housing by tilting it vertically and aligning two opposing cage windows in the area between the ball grooves **(see illustration)**.

10 Turn the inner race 90-degrees to the cage and align one of the spherical lands with a cage window. Raise the land into the window and swivel the inner race out of the cage **(see illustration)**.

11 Clean all of the parts with solvent and dry them off.

12 Inspect the housing, splines, balls and races for damage, corrosion, wear and cracks. Check the inner race for wear and scoring in the races. If any of the components

are not serviceable, the entire CV joint assembly must be renewed. If the joint is in satisfactory condition, obtain a boot renewal kit; kits usually contain a new boot and retaining clamps, a constant velocity joint circlip and the correct type of grease. If grease isn't included in the kit, be sure to obtain some CV joint grease.

13 Coat all of the CV joint components with CV joint grease before beginning reassembly.

14 Refit the inner race in the cage and align the marks made in Step 7.

15 Refit the inner race and cage assembly into the CV joint housing, aligning the marks on the inner race and cage assembly with the mark on the housing.

16 Refit the balls into the holes, one at a time, until they are all in place.

17 Apply CV joint grease through the hole in the inner race, then force a wooden dowel down through the hole **(see illustration)**. This will force the grease into the joint. Continue this procedure until the joint is completely packed. Joints with an outer diameter of 81 mm will require 80 grams of grease; joints with an outer diameter of 90 mm will require 120 grams of grease. Pack the joint with as much grease as you can, then place the remainder of the grease in the boot.

18 Place the driveshaft in the vice. Clean the end of the driveshaft, then slide the new clamp and boot into place. **Note:** *It's a good idea to wrap the driveshaft splines with electrical tape to prevent damage to the boot.* Apply the remainder of the grease from the kit into the CV joint boot.

19 Remove the protective tape from the driveshaft splines. Slide on the dished washer, convex side first, followed by the thrust washer **(see illustration 11.5)**.

20 Refit a new circlip in the groove on the driveshaft, then tap the joint onto the driveshaft until the circlip engages with the groove in the inner race. Make sure the joint is securely retained by the circlip.

21 Ease the boot over the joint, making sure that the boot lips are correctly located on both the driveshaft and CV joint. Lift the outer sealing lip of the boot to equalise air pressure within the boot.

22 Refit the large retaining clamp on the boot. Pull the clamp as tight as possible and locate the hooks on the clamp in their slots. Tighten the clamp by crimping the raised area with a special boot clamp tool **(see illustration 11.38)**. Due to the relatively hard composition of the boots, this type of tool is

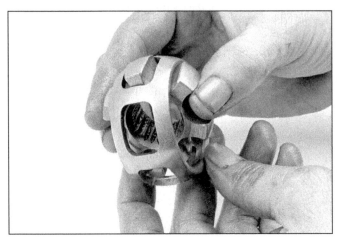

**11.10 Align the inner race with the cage windows and rotate the inner race out of the cage**

**11.17 Apply grease through the splined hole, then insert a wooden dowel into the hole and push down – the dowel will force the grease into the joint**

1  Hub nut
2  Outer joint gaiter
3  Gaiter securing clip
4  Driveshaft
5  Gaiter securing clip
6  Inner joint
7  Driveshaft-to-transmission
   flange bolts
8  Tripod roller
9  Tripod
10 Circlip
11 Seal (original)
12 Seal (repair)
13 Metal cover
14 Gaiter securing clip
15 Inner joint gaiter
16 Gaiter securing clip
17 Dished washer
18 Thrust washer
19 Circlip
20 Outer joint

11.25a  Exploded view of a driveshaft with a triple-rotor inner joint

required to apply adequate crimping force on the clamps. Secure the small retaining clamp using the same procedure.

**23** Make sure the constant velocity joint moves freely in all directions, then refit the driveshaft as described in Section 10.

### Inner CV joint

#### Triple-rotor type joint

**24** Remove the boot clamps and discard them, then pull the boot back on the shaft (or it can be cut off).

**25** Mount the driveshaft in a vice equipped with soft jaws, then prise the cover off the inner end of the joint and remove the O-ring from the groove **(see illustrations)**. Discard

the cover and O-ring – it isn't necessary to refit a new cover or O-ring, as a square-section O-ring will take its place.

**26** Mark the relationship of the housing, triple-rotor spider and the end of the driveshaft **(see illustration)**, then remove the driveshaft from the vice and slide it down the shaft.

**27** Mark the relationship of the rollers to the spider **(see illustration)**.

**28** Remove the circlip from the end of the driveshaft with a pair of circlip pliers, then slide the spider off the shaft **(see illustration)**. **Note:** If the spider won't slide off or tap off easily, it will be necessary to push it off with a hydraulic press.

**29** Remove the housing from the shaft, then clean all of the components with solvent. Inspect all components for pitting and other signs of wear (shiny, polished spots are

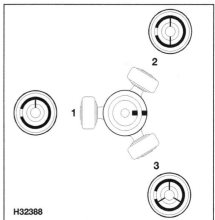

11.27  Use a felt-tip pen to mark the position of each roller to its post on the spider

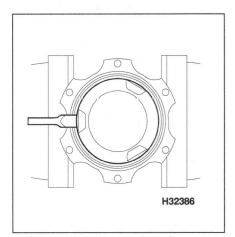

11.25b  If this is the first time the inner boot is being renewed, you'll have to pry off this cover and remove the O-ring from the groove underneath

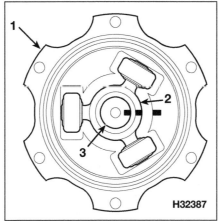

11.26  Mark the relationship of the inner joint housing, spider and driveshaft

1  Inner joint housing     3  Driveshaft
2  Triple-rotor spider

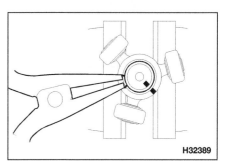

11.28  Remove the circlip from the end of the driveshaft, then remove the spider

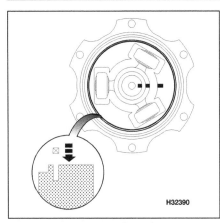

11.36 When installing the square-section O-ring in the groove in the housing, make sure it seats properly and doesn't get twisted

11.38 Clamp crimping pliers like these are available from most auto parts stores

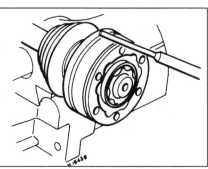

11.41 Use a hammer and punch to dislodge the inner joint cap

normal and won't affect operation). If any signs of wear are found, renew the entire joint.
30  Slide the joint housing onto the shaft, then place the shaft back in the vice.
31  Refit the small clamp and the boot onto

the shaft. It's a good idea to wrap the splines of the shaft with electrical tape to prevent damage to the boot.
32  Refit the spider on the shaft, aligning the marks made in Step 26. **Note:** *The chamfered side of the spider splines face the opposite side of the shaft.* If necessary, use a deep socket or a piece of pipe to drive the spider onto the shaft until it contacts its stop. Refit a new circlip, making sure it seats completely in its groove.
33  Lubricate the posts of the spider with CV joint grease, then refit the rollers onto their respective posts. Now coat the outside of the rollers with CV joint grease.
34  Release the shaft from the vice, then slide the housing up onto the triple-rotor spider, aligning the marks made in Step 26.
35  Clamp the housing in the vice, allowing the shaft to hang straight down.
36  Refit the square-section O-ring (included in the kit) into the groove in the housing **(see illustration)**.
37  Fill the joint with approximately 90 grams of CV joint grease from the top, then remove the housing from the vice and place the same amount of grease into the back side of the joint.
38  Refit the boot onto the housing, making sure it isn't stretched or twisted, then place the clamps in position and tighten them with a pair of clamp crimping pliers **(see illustration)**.
39  Make sure the constant velocity joint moves freely in all directions, then install the driveshaft as described in Section 10.
*Caution: When handling the driveshaft, be careful not to allow the housing to become pushed back onto the shaft – if this happens, the triple rotor spider and rollers may protrude from the housing and fall apart. Also, some of the grease will be forced from the housing.*

**Ball-and-cage type joint**

40  Remove the boot clamp and discard it.
41  Mount the driveshaft in a vice equipped with soft jaws. Using a hammer and a punch, knock the boot cap off the inner CV joint **(see illustration)**.
42  Using a pair of circlip pliers, remove the circlip from its groove in the end of the driveshaft **(see illustration)**.

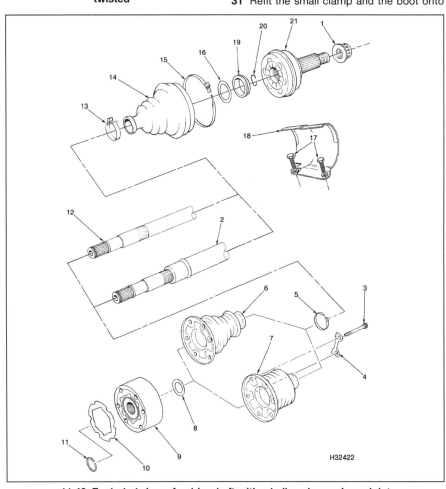

11.42 Exploded view of a driveshaft with a ball-and-cage inner joint

1  Nut
2  Driveshaft (right side)
3  Bolt
4  Retaining plate
5  Clamp
6  Inner CV joint boot (left side)
7  Inner CV joint boot (right side)
8  Dished washer
9  Inner CV joint
10  Gasket
11  Circlip
12  Driveshaft (left-side)
13  Clamp
14  Outer CV joint boot
15  Clamp
16  Dished washer
17  Bolts
18  Heat shield
19  Thrust washer
20  Circlip
21  Outer CV joint

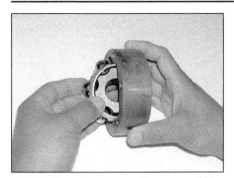

11.45 Turn the cage and inner race 90° and rotate it out of the housing

11.47 Line up one of the inner race grooves with the edge of the cage, then lift the race out

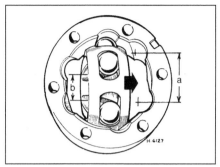

11.50 The wide (a) and narrow (b) grooves must line up to allow installation

43 Pull the inner joint off the end of the driveshaft. If it is stuck, use a hammer and a brass punch to drive it off the shaft; apply force to the inner race of the joint only. If it still won't come off, it'll be necessary to push it off with a hydraulic press. Remove the dished washer from the shaft, then pull off the boot.

44 Wipe the grease off the joint and mark the relationship of the inner race, cage and housing.

45 Rotate the cage and inner race 90-degrees and remove it from the housing (see illustration).

46 Remove each ball bearing from the cage, keeping track of their positions so they can be reinstalled in the same spot.

47 Turn the inner race 90-degrees in the cage, align one of the grooves with the edge of the cage and rotate the inner race out (see illustration).

48 Clean all of the components and inspect for worn or damaged splines, race grooves, ball bearings and cage. Shiny spots are normal and won't affect operation. Renew the

joint with a new one if any of the components show signs of wear.

49 Coat the components of the joint with CV joint grease, then assemble the inner race and cage, aligning the marks made in Step 44.

50 Press the ball bearings into their openings, then insert the inner race, cage and balls into the housing. The chamfered side of the splines must face the larger diameter side of the housing. When the components are rotated into place, the wide-spaced grooves of the inner race must be lined up with the wide-spaced grooves in the housing (see illustration).

51 Refit the new boot and clamp on the driveshaft. It's a good idea to wrap the splines of the driveshaft with electrical tape to prevent damage to the boot. Remove the tape.

52 Refit the dished washer on the driveshaft with the concave side facing the end of the shaft (see illustration).

53 If you're renewing the boot on the left-side driveshaft, adjust the inner end of the boot so that it is 17 mm past the innermost groove on

the driveshaft (see illustration). If you're renewing the boot on the right-side driveshaft, seat the inner end of the boot on the larger diameter portion of the driveshaft (see illustration).

54 Place the inner joint assembly on the driveshaft and refit a new circlip. Make sure the circlip seats in its groove completely.

55 Pack the CV joint with CV joint grease. Models with 94 mm diameter joints require 90-grams of grease; models with 100 mm joints require 120-grams. Place 1/3 of the grease in the joint and the other 2/3 on the inner side of the joint and in the boot.

56 Seat the cap of the boot on the joint housing, aligning the bolt holes. Make sure the boot is not twisted or deformed in any way.

57 Clean the surface of the joint housing, then stick a new gasket onto the housing.

58 Make sure the constant velocity joint moves freely in all directions, then refit the driveshaft as described in Section 10.

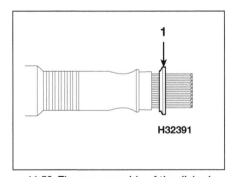

11.52 The concave side of the dished washer (1) must face the end of the driveshaft (ball–and–cage inner CV joint)

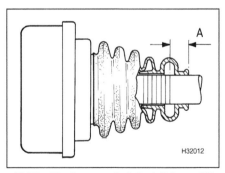

11.53a The inner end of the left inner CV joint boot must be positioned 17 mm past the inner groove on the driveshaft (dimension 'A')

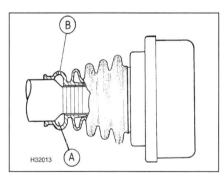

11.53b Installation position of the inner joint gaiter on right-hand driveshaft

A   Vent chamber in gaiter
B   Vent hole

**Notes**

# Chapter 9
# Brakes

## Contents

## Degrees of difficulty

| Easy, suitable for novice with little experience | 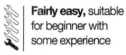 | Fairly easy, suitable for beginner with some experience | | Fairly difficult, suitable for competent DIY mechanic | 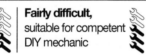 | Difficult, suitable for experienced DIY mechanic | | Very difficult, suitable for expert DIY or professional | |

## Specifications

### General

| | |
|---|---|
| Brake fluid type ...................................... | See Chapter 1 |
| Minimum pad thickness ............................... | See Chapter 1 |
| Brake disc minimum thickness ........................ | Cast into disc |
| Maximum disc runout (front and rear) ................. | 0.1 mm |
| Maximum disc thickness variation (parallelism) | |
| Front ............................................. | 0.01 mm |
| Rear .............................................. | 0.02 mm |

### Torque specifications

| | Nm | Ft-lbs |
|---|---|---|
| Brake caliper | | |
| Caliper guide pins (front) ................................ | 28 | 21 |
| Caliper mounting bolts (rear) ........................... | 35 | 26 |
| Caliper mounting bracket bolts | | |
| Front (FN 3 caliper only) ............................. | 125 | 92 |
| Rear ................................................ | 65 | 48 |
| Brake hose-to-caliper inlet fitting bolt | | |
| Front | | |
| FS III caliper ..................................... | 35 | 26 |
| FN 3 ............................................. | 15 | 11 |
| Rear ................................................ | 35 | 26 |
| Brake servo mounting nuts* ............................ | 20 | 15 |
| Master cylinder-to-brake servo retaining nuts* .......... | 20 | 15 |
| Wheel speed sensor bolt | | |
| Front | | |
| FS III caliper ..................................... | 8 | 6 |
| FN 3 caliper ...................................... | 10 | 7 |
| Rear ................................................ | 8 | 6 |

* Use new nuts

## 1 General information

The vehicles covered by this manual are equipped with hydraulically-operated front and rear brake systems. Both front and rear brakes are disc type. Both the front and rear brakes are self-adjusting. The disc brakes automatically compensate for pad wear.

### Hydraulic system

The hydraulic system consists of two separate circuits. The master cylinder has separate reservoirs for the two circuits, and, in the event of a leak or failure in one hydraulic circuit, the other circuit will remain operative. A pressure regulator valve on non-ABS models provides brake balance between the front and rear brakes.

### Brake servo

The brake servo, utilising engine manifold vacuum and atmospheric pressure (or a vacuum pump on diesel models) to provide assistance to the hydraulically-operated brakes, is mounted on the bulkhead in the engine compartment.

### Handbrake

The handbrake operates the rear brakes only, through cable actuation. It's activated by a lever mounted in the centre console.

### Service

After completing any operation involving dismantling of any part of the brake system, always test drive the vehicle to check for proper braking performance before resuming normal driving. When testing the brakes, perform the tests on a clean, dry, flat surface. Conditions other than these can lead to inaccurate test results.

Test the brakes at various speeds with both light and heavy pedal pressure. The vehicle should stop evenly without pulling to one side or the other. Avoid locking the brakes, because this slides the tyres and diminishes braking efficiency and control of the vehicle.

Tyres, vehicle load and wheel alignment are factors which also affect braking performance.

## 2 Anti-lock Brake System (ABS) – general information and component removal and refitting

### General information

**Note:** *On models equipped with traction control, the ABS unit is a dual function unit, controlling both the anti-lock braking system (ABS) and the electronic differential locking (EDL) system functions.*

ABS is available as an option on the models covered in this manual. The system comprises a hydraulic unit (which contains the hydraulic solenoid valves and accumulators) **(see illustration)**, and four wheel sensors (one fitted on each wheel), the ABS control module and the brake light switch. The purpose of the system is to prevent the wheel(s) locking during heavy braking. This is achieved by automatic release of the brake on the relevant wheel, followed by re-application of the brake.

The solenoids are controlled by the control unit, which itself receives signals from the four wheel sensors (one fitted on each hub), which monitor the speed of rotation of each wheel. By comparing these signals, the ECU can determine the speed at which the vehicle is travelling. It can then use this speed to determine when a wheel is decelerating at an abnormal rate, compared to the speed of the vehicle, and therefore predicts when a wheel is about to lock. During normal operation, the system functions in the same way as a non-ABS braking system.

If the control unit senses that a wheel is about to lock, it operates the relevant solenoid valve in the modulator block, which then isolates the brake caliper on the wheel which is about to lock from the master cylinder, effectively sealing-in the hydraulic pressure.

If the speed of rotation of the wheel continues to decrease at an abnormal rate, the control unit switches on the electrically driven return pump, which pumps the brake fluid back into the master cylinder, releasing pressure on the brake caliper so that the brake is released. Once the speed of rotation of the wheel returns to an acceptable rate, the pump stops; the solenoid valve opens, allowing the master cylinder hydraulic pressure to return to the caliper, which then re-applies the brake. This cycle can be carried out at 10 times a second.

The action of the solenoid valves and return pump creates pulses in the hydraulic circuit. When the ABS system is functioning, these pulses can be felt through the brake pedal.

The operation of the ABS system is entirely dependent on electrical signals. To prevent the system responding to any inaccurate signals, a built-in safety circuit monitors all signals received by the control unit. If an inaccurate signal or low battery voltage is detected, the ABS system is automatically shut down, and the warning light on the instrument panel is illuminated, to inform the driver that the ABS system is not operational. Normal braking would still be available, however.

If a fault does develop in the ABS system,

**2.1 ABS control unit**

the vehicle must be taken to a VW dealer service department or other qualified garage for fault diagnosis and repair.

### Component removal and refitting

#### Hydraulic unit

**1** Removal and refitting of the hydraulic unit should be entrusted to a VW dealer. Great care has to be taken not to allow any fluid to escape from the unit as the pipes are disconnected. If the fluid is allowed to escape, air can enter the unit, causing air locks which cause the hydraulic unit to malfunction.

#### Control module

**2** The ABS control module is mounted to the underside of the hydraulic unit and can only be removed after the hydraulic unit has been removed. New control modules are not coded, but must be coded prior to vehicle operation. This requires a VW scan tool, and even with the proper scan tool the control unit can only be coded after a 'dealership code' has been entered into the tool. For this reason, any work involving the ABS control module must be left to a dealer service department or other properly-equipped repair facility.

#### Wheel speed sensor

**3** Loosen the wheel bolts. Chock the rear wheels, then firmly apply the handbrake, raise the front of the vehicle and support it securely on axle stands. Remove the appropriate front wheel.
**4** Disconnect the electrical connector from the wheel speed sensor **(see illustration)**.
**5** Remove the bolt securing the sensor to the steering knuckle, and remove the sensor from the knuckle.
**6** Prior to refitting, apply a thin coat of multi-purpose grease to the sensor tip.
**7** Ensure that the sensor and steering knuckle sealing faces are clean, then refit the sensor

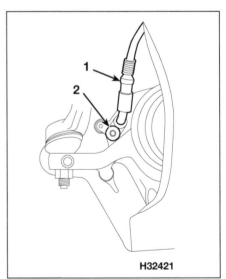

H32421

**2.4 Wheel speed sensor mounting details (front shown, rear similar)**

*1 Electrical connector    2 Mounting bolt*

on the knuckle. Refit the retaining bolt and tighten it to the torque listed in this Chapter's Specifications.

**8** Plug in the electrical connector.

**9** Refit the wheel, then lower the vehicle to the earth and tighten the wheel bolts to the torque listed in the Chapter 1 Specifications.

### Reluctor rings

**10** The reluctor rings are an integral part of the wheel hubs. Examine the rings for damage such as chipped or missing teeth. If renewal is necessary, the complete hub assembly must be disassembled and the bearings renewed as described in Chapter 10.

### 3 Disc brake pads – renewal

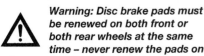

⚠ *Warning: Disc brake pads must be renewed on both front or both rear wheels at the same time – never renew the pads on only one wheel. Also, the dust created by the brake system is harmful to your health. Never blow it out with compressed air and don't inhale any of it. An approved filtering mask should be worn when working on the brakes. Do not, under any circumstances, use petroleum-based solvents to clean brake parts. Use brake system cleaner only!*

*Caution: Don't depress the brake pedal with the caliper removed.*

**1** Remove the cap from the brake fluid reservoir. Remove about two-thirds of the fluid from the reservoir, then reinstall the cap.

⚠ *Warning: Brake fluid is poisonous – never siphon it by mouth. Use a suction gun or old poultry baster. If a baster is used, never again use it for the preparation of food.*
*Caution: Brake fluid will damage paint. If any fluid is spilled, wash it off immediately with plenty of clean, cold water.*

**2** Loosen the front or rear wheel bolts, raise the front or rear of the vehicle and support it securely on axle stands. Block the wheels at the opposite end.

**3** Remove the wheels. Work on one brake assembly at a time, using the assembled brake for reference if necessary.

**4** Inspect the brake disc carefully as outlined in Section 5. If machining is necessary, follow the information in that Section to remove the disc, at which time the pads can be removed as well.

**5** If you are renewing the front brake pads, follow the first photo sequence **(see illustrations 3.5a to 3.5n)**. Be sure to stay in

3.5a Before disassembling the brake, wash it thoroughly with brake system cleaner and allow it to dry – position a drain pan under the brake to catch the residue – **DO NOT** use compressed air to blow off the brake dust

3.5b To make room for the new pads, use a G-clamp to depress the piston(s) into the caliper before removing the caliper and pads – do this a little at a time, keeping a eye on the fluid level in the master cylinder to make sure it doesn't overflow

3.5c If you're working on a model with a FN 3 caliper, pry out the ends of the retaining spring out of the holes in the caliper then remove the spring

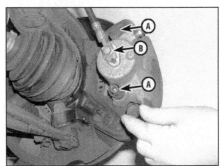

3.5d Remove the caps from the caliper guide pins (A), then unscrew the guide pins. Don't remove the brake hose inlet fitting bolt (B) unless the caliper or hose is being renewed

3.5e If the inner pad is equipped with a wear sensor, unplug this electrical connector (arrowed)

3.5f Remove the inner brake pad (FS III caliper shown) . . .

3.5g . . . then remove the outer pad from the caliper frame (FS III caliper shown)

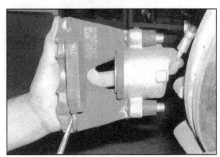

3.5h On a FN 3 caliper the brake pad is stuck to the caliper frame with an adhesive backing – it will probably be necessary to prise it off. On later models, first prise off the large spring clip securing the pad

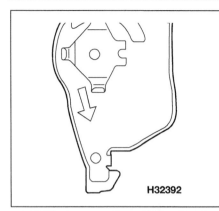

3.5i The inner pad in an FN 3 caliper is directional – when installed, the arrow must point downward

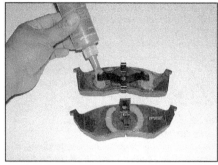

3.5j If the new pads are adhesive-backed, peel the foil from the backing plates before installing them. If they are not adhesive-backed, apply a film of anti-squeal compound to the backing plates (follow the instructions on the product)

3.5k Install the inner pad . . .

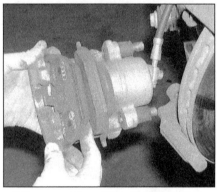

3.5l . . . and the outer pad (FS III caliper shown)

3.5m On models with FN 3 calipers, remove the foil from the backing plate and install the outer brake pad in the caliper mounting bracket

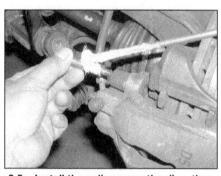

3.5n Install the caliper over the disc, then clean, lubricate (use high-temperature grease) and install the guide pins, tightening them to the specified torque. On FN 3 calipers, install the retaining spring. If equipped with wear sensors, plug in the electrical connector

order and read the caption under each illustration. **Note:** *There are two different types of front brake calipers which may be encountered: FS III and FN 3. The FS III caliper mounts directly to the steering knuckle by two guide pins, and the brake pads are retained to the caliper by clips. The FN 3 caliper has two guide pins that attach the caliper to a mounting bracket which is bolted to the steering knuckle. It also has a* *retaining spring on the front side of the caliper.*

6 If you're renewing the rear brake pads, follow the second photo sequence (**see illustrations 3.6a to 3.6i**). Be sure to stay in order and read the caption under each illustration. On later model rear disc brakes, the handbrake cable operates a lever on the caliper. Release the cable end from the bracket before removing the caliper (**see illustration 14.6**).

7 When reinstalling the caliper, be sure to tighten the mounting bolts to the torque listed in this Chapter's Specifications.

8 After the job has been completed, firmly depress the brake pedal a few times to bring the pads into contact with the disc. Check the level of the brake fluid, adding some if necessary. Check the operation of the brakes carefully before placing the vehicle into normal service.

3.6a Clean the brake with brake system cleaner (see illustration 3.5a), then hold the caliper slide pins with an open-ended spanner and unscrew the mounting bolts with another spanner . . .

3.6b . . . then hang the caliper with the length of wire (don't let it hang by the hose)

3.6c Remove the inner brake pad from the caliper mounting bracket . . .

3.6d . . . then remove the outer pad

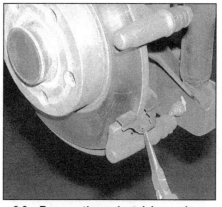

3.6e Remove the pad retaining springs from the caliper mounting bracket and renew them

3.6f Of the new pads are adhesive-backed, peel off the foil from the backing plates before installation. If not, apply anti-squeal compound to the backing plates (follow the instructions on the product), then install the inner pad . . .

3.6g . . . and the outer pad

3.6h To provide room for the new pads, the piston must be retracted – to do this, rotate the piston clockwise while pushing in on it. Piston rotating tools, like the one shown here, are available at most auto parts stores

3.6i Clean the caliper slide pins and lubricate them with high-temperature grease, then install them in the caliper mounting bracket, making sure the boots seat properly. Install the caliper and tighten the mounting bolts to the specified torque

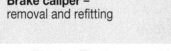

## 4 Brake caliper –
removal and refitting

*Warning: The dust created by the brake system is harmful to your health. Never blow it out with compressed air and don't inhale any of it. An approved filtering mask should be worn when working on the brakes. Do not, under any circumstances, use petroleum-based solvents to clean brake parts. Use brake system cleaner only!*

### Removal

**1** Loosen the front or rear wheel bolts, raise the front or rear of the vehicle and place it securely on axle stands. Block the wheels at the opposite end. Remove the front or rear wheel.

**2** To disconnect the handbrake cable from the rear caliper, unbolt the cable bracket from the caliper and disengage the cable from the toggle lever.

**3** Remove the inlet hose fitting bolt and

discard the old sealing washers **(see illustration 3.5d)**. Disconnect the brake hose from the caliper. Plug the brake hose to keep contaminants out of the brake system and to prevent losing any more brake fluid than is necessary **(see illustration)**. **Note:** *If you're removing the caliper for access to other components, don't disconnect the hose. Suspend the caliper with a piece of wire to prevent damaging the brake hose.*

**4** Remove the caliper guide pins (or, on the

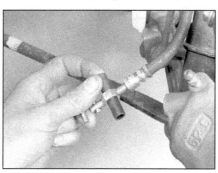

4.3 The brake hose can be plugged using a snug-fitting piece of tubing

rear, the mounting bolts) and detach the caliper **(see illustration 3.5d [front] or 3.6a [rear])**. If the brake pads are equipped with wear sensors, disconnect the electrical connector **(see illustration 3.5e)**.

### Refitting

**5** Refitting is the reverse of removal. Don't forget to use new sealing washers on each side of the brake hose inlet fitting **(see illustration)**.

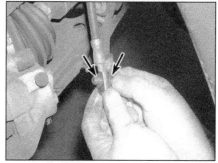

4.5 There is a sealing washer on either side of the brake hoses inlet fitting; be sure to renew these when reconnecting the hose

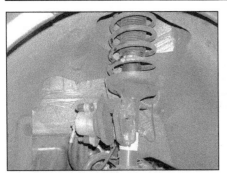

5.2 Hang the caliper with a piece of wire – don't let it hang by the brake hose

5.3 The brake pads on this vehicle were obviously neglected, as they wore down to the rivets and cut deep grooves into the disc – wear this severe means the disc must be renewed

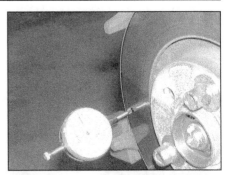

5.4a Use a dial indicator (DTI) to check disc runout – if the reading exceeds the specified allowable runout limit, the disc will have to be machined or renewed

5.4b Using a swirling motion, remove the glaze from the disc surface with sandpaper or emery cloth

6 Bleed the brake system (see Section 11). Make sure there are no leaks from the hose connections. Pump the brake pedal several times before driving the vehicle, and test the brakes carefully before returning the vehicle to normal service.

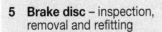

## 5 Brake disc – inspection, removal and refitting

### Inspection

1 Loosen the wheel bolts, raise the vehicle and support it securely on axle stands.

Remove the wheel and refit a couple of bolts to hold the disc in place. **Note:** *If the bolts don't contact the disc when screwed on all the way, refit washers under them.*

2 Remove the brake caliper (see Section 4). It isn't necessary to disconnect the brake hose. After removing the caliper bolts, suspend the caliper out of the way with a piece of wire **(see illustration)**.

3 Visually inspect the disc surface for score marks and other damage. Light scratches and shallow grooves are normal after use and may not always be detrimental to brake operation, but deep scoring requires disc removal and refinishing by an automotive engineering workshop. Be sure to check both sides of the disc **(see illustration)**. If pulsating has been noticed during application of the brakes, suspect disc runout (although the ABS can also cause the pedal to pulsate - see Section 2).

4 To check disc runout, place a dial indicator at a point about 12 mm from the outer edge of the disc. Set the indicator to zero and turn the disc. The indicator reading should not exceed the specified allowable runout limit. If it does, the disc should be refinished by an automotive engineering workshop. **Note:** *When renewing the brake pads, it's a good idea to resurface the discs regardless of the dial indicator reading, as this will impart a smooth finish and ensure a perfectly flat*

*surface, eliminating any brake pedal pulsation or other undesirable symptoms related to questionable discs. At the very least, if you elect not to have the discs resurfaced, remove the glaze from the surface with emery cloth or sandpaper, using a swirling motion* **(see illustrations)**.

5 It's absolutely critical that the disc not be machined to a thickness under the specified minimum allowable thickness. The minimum (or discard) thickness is cast into the disc. The disc thickness can be checked with a micrometer **(see illustrations)**.

### Removal

6 If you're removing a front disc on a model with a FN 3 caliper, or a rear disc on any model, remove the two caliper mounting bracket bolts and detach the mounting bracket **(see illustrations)**.

7 Remove the bolts which you fitted to hold the disc in place. If applicable, remove the disc retaining screw **(see illustration)**, then slide the disc off the hub.

### Refitting

8 Place the disc in position on the hub flange, aligning the bolt holes. Refit the retaining screw and tighten it securely.

9 If applicable, refit the caliper mounting bracket and tighten the bolts to the torque listed in this Chapter's Specifications.

5.5a On the front disc, the minimum thickness is cast into the outside of the disc, between the friction surface and the hub area

5.5b On the rear disc, the minimum thickness is cast into the side of the hub area

5.5c Use a micrometer to measure disc thickness at several points

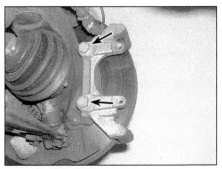

**5.6a Remove the caliper mounting bracket bolts and detach the mounting bracket – this is a front caliper mounting bracket for an FN 3 caliper . . .**

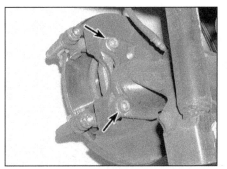

**5.6b . . . and this is a rear caliper mounting bracket**

**5.7 Sometimes disc retaining screws become 'frozen' and are too tight to remove by hand; if so, use an impact screwdriver**

10 Refit the caliper, tightening the guide pins (front) or mounting bolts (rear) to the torque listed in this Chapter's Specifications.

11 Refit the wheel, lower the vehicle and tighten the wheel bolts to the torque listed in the Chapter 1 Specifications. Depress the brake pedal a few times to bring the brake pads into contact with the disc. Bleeding won't be necessary unless the brake hose was disconnected from the caliper. Check the operation of the brakes carefully before driving the vehicle.

## 6 Master cylinder – removal and refitting

*Warning: The manufacturer recommends renewing the master cylinder mounting nuts whenever they are removed.*

### Removal

1 On models up to 2000, remove the windscreen wiper arms (see Chapter 12), the cowl cover and plenum upper panel (see

Chapter 11). On all models, remove the air filter housing (see Chapter 4A).

2 Unplug the electrical connector for the fluid level warning switch **(see illustrations)**. On ABS-equipped models, disconnect the brake pressure switch electrical connector at the underside of the master cylinder. On some models there are two sensors and two connectors.

3 Remove as much fluid as possible from the reservoir with a syringe, suction gun or poultry baster.

*Warning: Brake fluid is poisonous – never siphon it by mouth. If a baster is used, never again use it for the preparation of food.*

4 On LHD 1.8L and 2.0L models, slide the relay box that's adjacent to the master cylinder forward, out of its bracket. On all

models, detach the hose leading to the clutch master cylinder from the brake fluid reservoir.

5 Place rags under the fittings and prepare caps or plastic bags to cover the ends of the pipes once they're disconnected. Cover all body parts and be careful not to spill fluid during this procedure. Loosen the fittings at the ends of the brake pipes where they enter the master cylinder. To prevent rounding off the flats, use a flare-nut wrench, which wraps around the fitting hex.

*Caution: Brake fluid will damage paint. If any fluid is spilled, wash it off immediately with plenty of clean, cold water.*

6 Pull the brake pipes away from the master cylinder and plug the ends to prevent contamination.

7 Remove the nuts attaching the master cylinder to the brake servo **(see illus-**

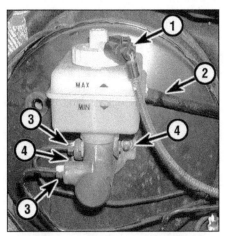

**6.2a Master cylinder mounting details**
1 Fluid level sensor electrical connector
2 Supply hose for clutch master cylinder
3 Fluid line fittings
4 Mounting nuts

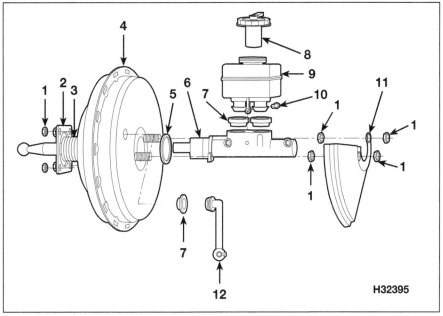

**6.2b Exploded view of the master cylinder, reservoir and servo**

| | | |
|---|---|---|
| 1 Nut | 6 Master cylinder | 10 Reservoir retaining pin |
| 2 Gasket | 7 Grommet | 11 Heat shield (1.8L turbo |
| 3 Boot | 8 Cap/fluid lever sensor | models) |
| 4 Servo | 9 Reservoir | 12 Vacuum hose |
| 5 O-ring | | |

H32395

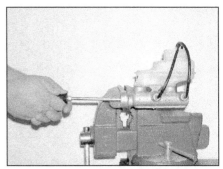

**6.9 The best way to bleed air from the master cylinder before installing it on the vehicle is with a pair of bleeding tubes that direct brake fluid into the reservoir during the bleeding**

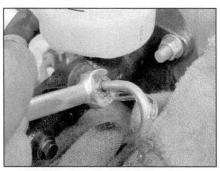

**6.17 Have an assistant depress the brake pedal and hold it down, then loosen the fitting nut, allowing air and fluid to escape; repeat this procedure on both fittings until the fluid is clear of air bubbles**

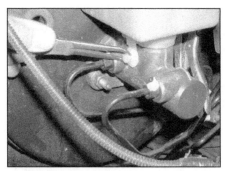

**6.20 Pull the retaining pin out with a pair of pliers, then rock the reservoir back-and-forth while pulling up to remove it**

tration **8.2a)**. Pull the master cylinder off the studs to remove it. Again, be careful not to spill the fluid as this is done. Remove and discard the old O-ring on the master cylinder.

### *Refitting*

**8** Bench bleed the new master cylinder before refitting it. Mount the master cylinder in a vice, with the jaws of the vice clamping on the mounting flange.

**9** Attach a pair of master cylinder bleed tubes to the outlet ports of the master cylinder **(see illustration)**.

**10** Fill the reservoir with brake fluid of the recommended type (see Chapter 1).

**11** Slowly push the pistons into the master cylinder (a large Phillips screwdriver can be used for this) – air will be expelled from the pressure chambers and into the reservoir. Because the tubes are submerged in fluid, air can't be drawn back into the master cylinder when you release the pistons.

**12** Repeat the procedure until nor more air bubbles are present.

**13** Remove the bleed tubes, one at a time, and refit plugs in the open ports to prevent fluid leakage and air from entering. Refit the reservoir cap.

**14** Refit the master cylinder over the studs on the brake servo and tighten the attaching nuts only finger tight at this time. Don't forget to refit a new O-ring.

**15** Thread the brake pipe fittings into the master cylinder. Since the master cylinder is still a bit loose, it can be moved slightly so the fittings thread in easily. Don't strip the threads as the fittings are tightened.

**16** Tighten the mounting nuts to the torque listed in this Chapter's Specifications. Tighten the brake pipe fittings securely.

**17** Fill the master cylinder reservoir with fluid, then bleed the pipes at the master cylinder, followed by bleeding the remainder of the brake system (see Section 9). To bleed the pipes at the master cylinder, have an assistant depress the brake pedal and hold it down. Loosen the fitting to allow air and fluid to escape **(see illustration)**. Tighten the fitting, then allow your assistant to return the pedal to

its rest position. Repeat this procedure on both fittings until the fluid is free of air bubbles, then bleed the rest of the system. Check the operation of the brake system carefully before driving the vehicle.

 *Warning: If you do not have a firm brake pedal at the end of the bleeding procedure, or have any doubts as to the effectiveness of the brake system, DO NOT drive the vehicle. Have it towed to a dealer service department or other qualified repair shop for diagnosis.*

### *Reservoir/grommet renewal*

**Note:** *The brake fluid reservoir can be renewed separately from the master cylinder body if it becomes damaged. If there is leakage between the reservoir and the master cylinder body, the grommets in the master cylinder body can be renewed.*

**18** Remove as much fluid as possible from the reservoir with a suction gun, large syringe or a poultry baster.

 *Warning: If a poultry baster is used, never again use it for the preparation of food.*

**19** Place rags under the master cylinder to absorb any fluid that may spill out once the reservoir is detached from the master cylinder.

*Caution: Brake fluid will damage paint. Cover all body parts and be careful not to spill fluid during this procedure.*

**20** Using a pair of pliers, pull out the retaining pin that retains the reservoir to the master cylinder **(see illustration)**.

**21** Pull the reservoir out of the master cylinder body.

**22** If you are simply renewing the grommets, carefully prise the old grommets out of the master cylinder body an refit new ones.

**23** Lubricate the grommets with clean brake fluid, then press the reservoir into place on the master cylinder body and secure it with the retaining pin.

**24** Refill the reservoir with the recommended brake fluid (see Chapter 1) and check for leaks.

**25** Bleed the master cylinder **(see illustration 6.17)**.

### 7 Brake hoses and pipes – inspection and renewal

### *Inspection*

**1** About every six months, with the vehicle raised and supported securely on axle stands, the rubber hoses which connect the steel brake pipes with the front and rear brake assemblies should be inspected for cracks, chafing of the outer cover, leaks, blisters and other damage. These are important and vulnerable parts of the brake system and inspection should be complete. A light and mirror will be helpful for a thorough check. If a hose exhibits any of the above conditions, renew it.

### *Renewal*

#### Front brake hose

**2** Loosen the wheel bolts, raise the vehicle and support it securely on axle stands. Remove the wheel.

**3** At the bracket, unscrew the brake pipe fitting from the hose **(see illustration)**. Use a flare-nut spanner to prevent rounding off the

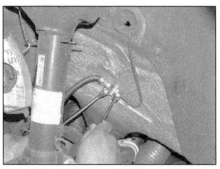

**7.3 Using a brake pipe spanner, unscrew the threaded fitting on the brake pipe, while holding the hose end stationary with an open-ended spanner . . .**

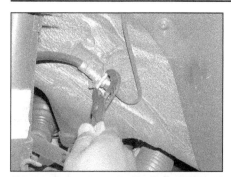

**7.4 ... then remove the U-clip and detach the hose from the bracket**

**7.6 Unclip the hose from the bracket on the suspension strut**

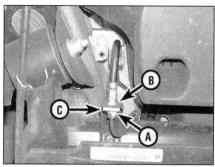

**7.13 At each end of the chassis-to-rear axle brake hose, unscrew the pipe fitting (A) with a brake pipe spanner while holding the end of the brake hose (B) with an open-ended spanner, then remove the U-clip (C)**

corners, and hold the hose fitting with another spanner to prevent the pipe or bracket from twisting.

**4** Remove the U-clip from the female fitting at the bracket with a pair of pliers **(see illustration)**, then pass the hose through the bracket.

**5** At the caliper end of the hose, remove the inlet fitting bolt, then separate the hose from the caliper. Note that there are two sealing washers on either side of the inlet fitting – they should be renewed during refitting **(see illustration 4.5)**.

**6** Detach the hose from the bracket on the strut **(see illustration)**.

**7** To refit the hose, connect the fitting to the caliper with the inlet fitting bolt and new sealing washers.

**8** Route the hose into the frame bracket, making sure it isn't twisted, then connect the brake pipe fitting, starting the threads by hand. Refit the U-clip and tighten the fitting securely.

**9** Push the hose into the bracket on the strut.

**10** Bleed the caliper (see Section 8).

**11** Refit the wheel, lower the vehicle and tighten the wheel bolts to the torque listed in the Chapter 1 Specifications.

### Chassis-to-rear axle hose

**12** Loosen the rear wheel bolts, raise the rear of the vehicle and support it securely on axle stands. Remove the wheel.

**13** There's a flexible brake hose on each side of the rear axle beam, connecting the rigid pipes on the chassis to the rigid pipes leading

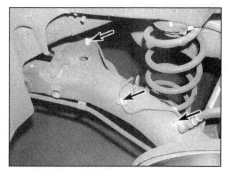

**7.18 The rear brake pipe is secured to the rear axle trailing arm with plastic clips (arrowed)**

to the rear brakes **(see illustration)**. These hoses are renewed using the same technique as described in Steps 3 and 4.

**14** After renewal, bleed the caliper or wheel cylinder served by the hose that was renewed (see Section 9).

### Axle-to-caliper pipe

**15** Loosen the rear wheel bolts, raise the rear of the vehicle and support it securely on axle stands. Remove the wheel.

**16** Disconnect the forward end of the pipe using the technique described in Step 3. There's no need to remove the U-clip or detach the hose from its bracket.

**17** Remove the inlet fitting bolt and detach the hose from the caliper. Discard the sealing washers – new ones should be used on refitting.

**18** Detach the pipe from the plastic clips along the rear axle **(see illustration)** and remove the pipe from the vehicle.

**19** Refitting is the reverse of removal. Be sure to use new sealing washers on either side of the inlet fitting **(see illustration 4.5)**, and tighten the inlet fitting bolt to the torque listed in this Chapter's Specifications.

**20** Bleed the caliper served by the pipe that was renewed (see Section 9). Refit the wheel, lower the vehicle and tighten the wheel bolts to the torque listed in the Chapter 1 Specifications.

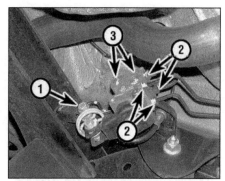

**8.1 Pressure regulator valve mounting details**

*1 Spring-to-axle bolt*
*2 Brake pipe fittings*
*3 Valve mounting bolts*

### Metal brake pipes

**21** When renewing brake pipes, be sure to use the correct parts. Don't use copper tubing for any brake system components. Purchase steel brake pipes from a dealer or auto parts store.

**22** Prefabricated brake pipe, with the tube ends already flared and fittings fitted, is available at motor factors and dealer parts departments. These pipes must be bent to the proper shapes using a tubing bender.

**23** When refitting the new pipe, make sure it's securely supported in the brackets and has plenty of clearance between moving or hot components.

**24** After refitting, check the master cylinder fluid level and add fluid as necessary. Bleed the brake system (see Section 9) and test the brakes carefully before driving the vehicle in traffic.

### 8 Brake pressure regulator valve – testing, removal and refitting

**Note:** *Models equipped with ABS are not equipped with a rear brake pressure regulator valve; the function is automatically controlled by the ABS unit.*

### *Removal*

**1** The valve is mounted next to the rear axle, attached to the axle by a spring **(see illustration)**. As the load being carried by the vehicle is altered, the suspension moves in relation to the vehicle body, altering the tension in the spring. The spring then adjusts the pressure regulator valve lever so that the correct pressure is applied to the rear brakes to suit the load being carried.

**2** Minimise fluid loss by first removing the master cylinder reservoir cap, then tightening it down onto a piece of cellophane to obtain an airtight seal.

**3** Unscrew the nut and bolt securing the valve spring to the axle.

**4** Wipe clean the area around the brake pipe fittings on the valve, and place absorbent rags beneath the pipe fittings to catch any fluid that spills out. Make identification marks on the brake pipes; these marks can then be used on refitting to ensure each pipe is correctly reconnected.

**5** Using a flare-nut spanner, if available, loosen the fitting nuts and disconnect the brake pipes from the valve. Plug or tape over the pipe ends and valve orifices, to minimise the loss of brake fluid and to prevent the entry of dirt into the system. Wash off any spilled fluid immediately with cold water.

**6** Unscrew the bolts and remove the pressure regulator valve and spring.

### Refitting

**7** Refitting is the reverse of the removal procedure, noting the following points:

a) *If a new valve is being installed, set the spring adjustment bolt to the same position as the one on the old valve, and tighten it securely.*

b) *Ensure that the brake pipes are correctly connected to the valve, and that their fitting nuts are securely tightened.*

c) *Coat the ends of the spring with grease prior to installation.*

d) *Remove the cellophane from under the reservoir cap, then reinstall the cap.*

e) *Bleed the complete brake system as described in Section 9.*

f) *On completion, take the vehicle to a dealer service department or other qualified repair shop to have the valve operation (brake balance) checked and, if necessary, adjusted.*

## 9  Brake hydraulic system – bleeding

> ⚠ *Warning: Wear eye protection when bleeding the brake system. If the fluid comes in contact with your eyes, immediately rinse them with water and seek medical attention.*

**Note:** *Bleeding the hydraulic system is necessary to remove any air that manages to find its way into the system when it's been opened during removal and refitting of a hose, pipe, caliper or master cylinder.*

**1** You'll probably have to bleed the system at all four brakes if air has entered it due to low fluid level, or if the brake pipes have been disconnected at the master cylinder.

**2** If a brake pipe was disconnected only at one wheel, then only that caliper must be bled.

**3** If a brake pipe is disconnected at a fitting located between the master cylinder and any of the brakes, that part of the system served by the disconnected pipe must be bled.

**4** Remove any residual vacuum from the brake servo by applying the brake several times with the engine off.

**5** Remove the master cylinder reservoir cap and fill the reservoir with brake fluid. Refit the cap. **Note:** *Check the fluid level often during the bleeding operation and add fluid as necessary to prevent the fluid level from falling low enough to allow air bubbles into the master cylinder.*

**6** Have an assistant on hand, as well as a supply of new brake fluid, a clear plastic container partially filled with clean brake fluid, a length of clear tubing to fit over the bleed valve and a spanner to open and close the bleeder valve.

**7** Beginning at the right rear wheel, loosen the bleed valve slightly, then tighten it to a point where it's snug but can still be loosened quickly and easily.

**8** Place one end of the tubing over the bleed valve and submerge the other end in brake fluid in the container **(see illustration)**.

**9** Have the assistant slowly depress the brake pedal, then hold the pedal down firmly.

**10** While the pedal is held down, open the bleed valve just enough to allow a flow of fluid to leave the valve. Watch for air bubbles to exit the submerged end of the tube. When the fluid flow slows, close the valve and have your assistant release the pedal.

**11** Repeat Steps 9 and 10 until no more air is seen leaving the tube, then tighten the bleed valve and proceed to the left rear wheel, the right front wheel and the left front wheel, in that order, and perform the same procedure. Be sure to check the fluid in the master cylinder reservoir frequently.

**12** Never use old brake fluid. It contains moisture which can cause the fluid to boil, rendering the brake system inoperative.

**13** Refill the master cylinder with fluid at the end of the operation.

**14** Check the operation of the brakes. The pedal should feel solid when depressed, with no sponginess. If necessary, repeat the entire process.

> ⚠ *Warning: Do not operate the vehicle if you're in doubt about the effectiveness of the brake system, or if the ABS light on the instrument panel does not go out.*

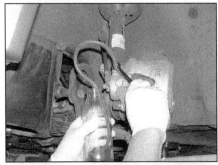

**9.8 When bleeding the brakes, a hose is connected to the bleed screw at the caliper and then submerged in the brake fluid – air will be seen as bubbles in the tube and container (all air must be expelled before moving to the next wheel)**

## 10  Brake servo – testing, removal and refitting

> ⚠ *Warning: The manufacturer recommends renewing the servo mounting nuts whenever they are removed.*

### Testing

#### Operating check

**1** Depress the brake pedal several times with the engine off and make sure there's no change in the pedal reserve distance.

**2** Depress the pedal and start the engine. If the pedal goes down slightly, operation is normal. If the pedal does not go down, check the vacuum hose for a leak. If the hose is good, check the intake manifold vacuum with a vacuum gauge (petrol engines, see Chapter 2C) or the vacuum pump (diesel engines, see Section 11).

#### Airtightness check

**3** Start the engine and turn it off after one or two minutes. Depress the brake pedal slowly several times. If the pedal depresses less each time, the servo is airtight.

**4** Depress the brake pedal while the engine is running, then stop the engine with the pedal depressed. If there's no change in the pedal reserve travel after holding the pedal for 30 seconds, the servo is airtight.

#### Check valve and hose check

**5** Detach the vacuum hose from the booster and blow into the hose; air should flow through.

**6** Attach a hand-held vacuum pump to the hose and apply vacuum; the valve and hose should hold vacuum.

> ⚠ *Warning: It isn't a good idea to perform this check by sucking on the valve with your mouth. If the valve is faulty, you could inhale fuel fumes.*

**7** If the valve (or hose) fails either test, renew the valve and hose as an assembly. **Note:** *When fitted, the arrow on the check valve must point towards the engine.*

### Removal

**Note 1:** *A special tool (VW T 10006, or equivalent) is required to disconnect the brake servo pushrod from the brake pedal. Check on the availability of this tool before proceeding.*

**Note 2:** *On early left-hand drive models equipped with ABS, it is not possible to remove the brake servo without first removing the ABS hydraulic unit (see Section 2). Therefore, servo unit removal and refitting on models with ABS should be left to a VW dealer service department or other qualified garage.*

**8** Remove the master cylinder as described in Section 6.

**9** Remove the heat shield (if applicable) from the front of the servo, then carefully ease the

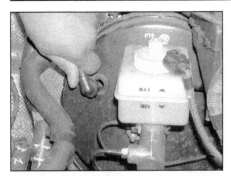

**10.9 Pull the vacuum hose out of the servo grommet**

**10.11a The brake servo is retained by these four nuts (arrowed)**

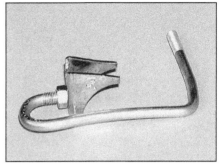

**10.11b Improvised special tool constructed from a modified exhaust clamp, used to release the brake pedal from the servo pushrod**

vacuum hose out from the grommet in the booster **(see illustration)**.

**10** From inside the vehicle, remove the brake light switch as described in Section 14. Where equipped, remove the plastic cover on the inside of the firewall, for access to the booster-retaining nuts.

**11** Unscrew the four nuts securing the servo unit to the pedal mounting bracket. Reach up behind the brake pedal, carefully expand the lugs of the pushrod retaining clips and detach the pushrod ball from the pedal. A special tool will be required to do this **(see illustrations)**.

**12** Return to the engine compartment and manoeuvre the servo unit out of position, noting the gasket which is fitted on the rear of the unit.

### Refitting

**13** Check the servo unit vacuum hose sealing grommet for signs of damage or deterioration and renew it if necessary.

**14** Refit a new gasket on the rear of the servo unit, then reposition the unit in the engine compartment.

**15** From inside the vehicle, ensure that the servo pushrod is correctly engaged with the brake pedal, then clip the pedal onto the pushrod ball. Check that the pedal is securely retained, then refit the servo mounting nuts and tighten them to the torque listed in this Chapter's Specifications.

**10.11c Using the tool to release the brake pedal from the servo pushrod**

**16** Carefully ease the vacuum hose back into position in the servo, taking great care not to displace the sealing grommet. On models so equipped, refit the heat shield to the servo.

**17** Refit the master cylinder as described in Section 6 of this Chapter.

**18** Refit the brake light switch as described in Section 14.

**19** On completion, start the engine and check for a vacuum leak at the vacuum hose-to-servo grommet. Check the operation of the brake system in an isolated area before returning the vehicle to normal service.

## 11 Vacuum pump – testing, removal and refitting

**Note:** *This Section applies to models with diesel engines only.*

### Mechanical pump

**Note:** *Removal and refitting of the tandem pump fitted to engine codes ATD and AXR is described in Chapter 4B. Testing of this pump*

**10.11d Rear view of the brake pedal (pedal removed) showing plastic lugs (arrowed) securing the pedal to the servo pushrod**

*is as described below. This sub-Section applies to engine code ALH.*

### Testing

**1** The operation of the braking system vacuum pump can be checked using a vacuum gauge.

**2** Disconnect the vacuum hose from the pump, and connect the gauge to the pump union using a suitable length of hose.

**3** Start the engine and allow it to idle, then measure the vacuum created by the pump. As a guide, after one minute, a minimum of approximately 500 mm Hg should be recorded. If the vacuum registered is significantly less than this, it is likely that the pump is faulty. However, seek the advice of a VW dealer before condemning the pump.

**4** Reconnect the vacuum hose. Overhaul of the vacuum pump is not possible, since no major components are available separately for it. If faulty, the complete pump assembly must be renewed.

### Removal

**Note:** *A new pump O-ring will be required on refitting.*

**5** Release the retaining clip, and disconnect the vacuum hose from the top of pump. Also, where applicable, disconnect the outlet hose from the pump **(see illustration)**.

**6** Slacken and remove the pump retaining

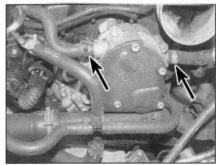

**11.5 Inlet and outlet hoses fitted to the vacuum pump on the diesel engine**

**11.6 Undo the pump retaining nut and bolts**

**11.9 Align the drive gear with the slot in the end of the camshaft**

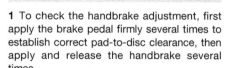

## 12 Handbrake – adjustment

bolt, and the two pump retaining nuts **(see illustration)**.

**7** Withdraw the vacuum pump from the cylinder head, and recover the O-ring seal. Discard the O-ring – a new one should be used on refitting.

### Refitting

**8** Fit the new O-ring to the vacuum pump, and apply a smear of oil to the O-ring to aid installation.

**9** Manoeuvre the vacuum pump into position, making sure that the slot in the pump drive gear aligns with the slot on the pump driveshaft **(see illustration)**.

**10** Refit the pump retaining nuts and bolt, and tighten to the specified torque.

**11** Reconnect the vacuum hose(s) to the pump, and secure in position with the retaining clip(s).

### *Electric pump*

**Note:** *The electric vacuum pump is only fitted to models with ABS, EDL, TCS and ESP.*

### Testing

**12** With the engine stopped, depress the brake pedal several times to exhaust the vacuum in the servo unit. The pedal will become firm.

**13** Start the engine, then slowly depress the brake pedal. An audible 'click' must be heard as the electric vacuum pump is activated, and the pedal will be easier to depress. Confirmation that the pump is running can be made by an assistant touching the pump as the pedal is depressed.

**14** Overhaul of the electric vacuum pump is not possible, therefore, if faulty, the pump must be renewed.

### Removal

**15** The electric brake vacuum pump is located on the left-hand side of the front suspension subframe. Apply the handbrake, then jack up the front of the vehicle and support it on axle stands (see *Jacking and towing*). Remove the left-hand front roadwheel.

**16** Disconnect the wiring from the vacuum pump.

**17** Unscrew the mounting bolts from the hydraulic unit bracket, then disconnect the vacuum hose from the pump.

**18** Unbolt the bracket from the suspension subframe, and withdraw the vacuum pump.

### Refitting

**19** Refitting is a reversal of removal, but tighten the mounting bolts/nut to the specified torque.

**1** To check the handbrake adjustment, first apply the brake pedal firmly several times to establish correct pad-to-disc clearance, then apply and release the handbrake several times.

**2** Applying normal, moderate pressure, pull the handbrake lever to the fully applied position, counting the number of clicks emitted from the handbrake ratchet mechanism. If adjustment is correct, there should be approximately 4 to 7 clicks before the handbrake is fully applied. If this is not the case, adjust as follows.

**3** Remove the rear section of the centre console as described in Chapter 11 to gain access to the handbrake adjusting nut **(see illustration)**.

**4** Block the front wheels, then raise the rear of the vehicle and support it securely on axle stands.

**5** With the handbrake fully released, equally loosen the handbrake adjusting nut until the handbrake levers on both rear calipers are back against their stops.

**6** From this point, tighten the adjusting nut until both handbrake levers just move off the caliper stops. Ensure that the gap between each caliper handbrake lever and its stop is less than 1.5 mm, and ensure both the right- and left-hand gaps are equal **(see illustration)**. Check that both wheels/discs rotate freely, then check the adjustment by applying the handbrake fully, counting the clicks emitted from the handbrake ratchet. If necessary, re-adjust.

**7** Once adjustment is correct, hold the adjusting nuts and securely tighten the locknuts. Refit the centre console section/ashtray (as applicable).

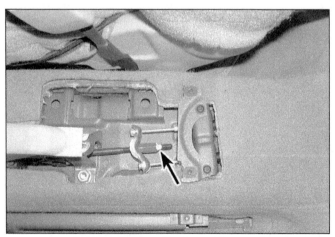

**12.3 Handbrake adjusting nut (arrowed)**

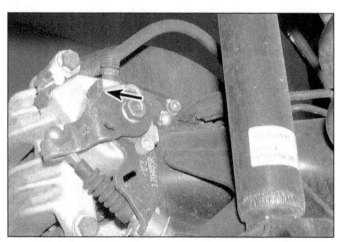

**12.6 Adjust the handbrake so the clearance between the handbrake lever and its stop (arrowed) is as specified**

## 13 Handbrake cables –
removal and refitting

### Removal

**1** Remove the rear section of the centre console as described in Chapter 11 to gain access to the handbrake lever. Each rear brake has its own cable, which is connected to the lever by an equaliser plate.
**2** Loosen the handbrake adjuster nut enough to detach the handbrake cable(s) from the equaliser **(see illustration)**.
**3** Block the front wheels, then raise the rear of the vehicle and support it securely on axle stands.
**4** From the vehicle underbody, free the front end of the outer cable from the body and withdraw the cable from its guide tube.
**5** Work back along the length of the cable, noting its correct routing, and free it from all of the retaining clips **(see illustration)**.
**6** Disengage the inner cable from the caliper handbrake lever **(see illustration)**, then remove the outer cable retaining clip and detach the cable from the caliper.

### Refitting

**7** Refitting is a reversal of the removal procedure. Prior to refitting the centre console, adjust the handbrake as described in Section 12.

## 14 Brake light switch – testing, adjustment and renewal

### Testing

**1** The brake light switch is located on the brake pedal mounting bracket **(see illustration)**. The switch activates the brake lights at the rear of the vehicle when the pedal is depressed. To gain access to the switch, remove the driver's side under-dash panel and the heater/air conditioning duct.
**2** If the brake lights are inoperative, check the fuse first (see Chapter 12).
**3** If the fuse is good, check for voltage to the switch on the feed wire (refer to the wiring diagrams at the end of this manual for the

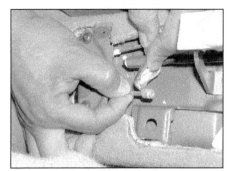

**13.2  Detaching the handbrake cable from the equaliser plate**

proper colour wire to check). If no voltage is present, repair the wire between the switch and the fusebox.
**4** If voltage is present, depress the brake pedal and check for voltage at the output wire terminal (again, refer to the wiring diagrams). If no voltage is present, renew the switch.
**5** If voltage is present, check for power on the brake light wires at the tail light housings (with the brake pedal depressed). If voltage is not present, repair the circuit between the switch and the brake lights.
**6** If voltage is present, check for a bad earth; using a jumper wire connected to a good earth, probe the earth wire terminal at the tail light connector. If the brake lights go on, repair the earth circuit (follow the earth wire from the tail light housing).
**7** Keep in mind that the brake light bulbs *could* be burned out, but the likelihood of all the bulbs being burned out is very slim.

**13.6  Detach the cable from the lever at the caliper, then remove the clip and disconnect the cable casing from the bracket on the caliper**

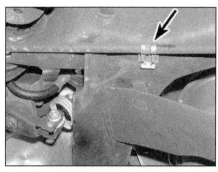

**13.5  Release the handbrake cable from all of the retaining clips**

### Adjustment

**8** The brake light switch on these vehicles is not adjustable. If it doesn't work as described above, renew it.

### Renewal

**9** Remove driver's side under-dash panel.
**10** Unplug the electrical connector from the switch.
**11** Rotate the switch 90-degrees in either direction and pull it out of the bracket.
**12** To refit the new switch, depress the brake pedal, insert the switch into the bracket (position the switch 1/4-turn from its fitted position), rotate it 90-degrees and release the brake pedal.
**13** Reconnect the electrical connector and check the operation of the brake lights.
**14** Refit the under-dash panel.

**14.1  The brake light switch is mounted just behind the brake pedal on the pedal bracket – twist the switch 90° to remove it**

# Chapter 10
# Suspension and steering systems

## Contents

## Degrees of difficulty

| Easy, suitable for novice with little experience  | Fairly easy, suitable for beginner with some experience  | Fairly difficult, suitable for competent DIY mechanic  | Difficult, suitable for experienced DIY mechanic | Very difficult, suitable for expert DIY or professional  |
|---|---|---|---|---|

## Specifications

| Torque specifications | Nm | Ft-lbs |
|---|---|---|
| **Front suspension** | | |
| Anti-roll bar | | |
| Link-to anti-roll bar bolt/nut | 30 | 22 |
| Link-to-control arm bolt | 45 | 33 |
| Clamp bolts | 24 | 18 |
| Balljoint-to-control arm bolts* | | |
| Step 1 | 20 | 15 |
| Step 2 | Turn an additional 90-degrees | |
| Balljoint-to-steering knuckle nut* | 45 | 33 |
| Control arm pivot bolt* | | |
| Step 1 | 71 | 52 |
| Step 2 | Turn an additional 90-degrees | |
| Control arm rear mounting bolt* | | |
| Step 1 | 71 | 52 |
| Step 2 | Turn an additional 90-degrees | |
| Driveshaft/hub nut | See Chapter 8 | |
| Subframe mounting bolts* | | |
| Step 1 | 100 | 74 |
| Step 2 | Turn an additional 90-degrees | |
| Suspension strut damper shaft nut | 60 | 44 |
| Suspension strut-to-steering knuckle bolt/nut* | | |
| Step 1 | 50 | 37 |
| Step 2 | Turn an additional 90-degrees | |
| Suspension strut upper mounting nut* | 60 | 44 |

## Torque specifications (continued)

| | Nm | Ft-lbs |
|---|---|---|
| **Rear suspension** | | |
| Hub/bearing assembly retaining nut* | 175 | 129 |
| Rear axle* | | |
|    Mounting bracket retaining bolts | 75 | 55 |
|    Pivot bolt/nut | 80 | 59 |
| Shock absorber-to-axle bolt/nut* | 60 | 44 |
| Shock absorber-to-body bolts* | | |
|    Step 1 | 30 | 22 |
|    Step 2 | Turn an additional 90-degrees | |
| Shock absorber upper mounting-to-damper shaft nut* | 24 | 18 |
| Stub axle mounting bolts* | 60 | 44 |
| **Steering** | | |
| Power steering pump | | |
|    Mounting bolts | 24 | 18 |
|    Feed pipe banjo fitting bolt | 38 | 28 |
|    Pulley retaining bolts | 24 | 18 |
| Steering column | | |
|    Lower mounting bolt/nut | 10 | 7 |
|    Upper mounting bolts | 24 | 18 |
|    Universal joint pinch bolt/nut* | | |
|      Step 1 | 20 | 15 |
|      Step 2 | Turn an additional 90-degrees | |
| Steering rack | | |
|    Mounting bolts* | | |
|      Step 1 | 20 | 15 |
|      Step 2 | Turn an additional 90-degrees | |
|    Power steering hose banjo fitting bolts | | |
|      Pressure pipe | 45 | 33 |
|      Return pipe | 41 | 30 |
| Steering wheel bolt | | |
|    Models up to 2004 | 50 | 37 |
|    Models from 2005-on | 44 | 32 |
| Track rod end-to-steering knuckle nut* | | |
|    Models up to 2004 | 45 | 33 |
|    Models from 2005-on | 50 | 37 |
| **Wheels** | | |
| Wheel bolts | 120 | 89 |

* Use new fasteners

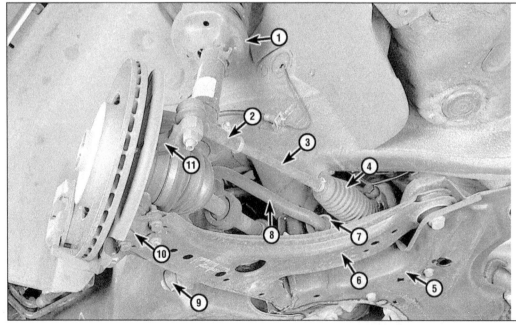

1 Strut/coil spring assembly
2 Track rod end
3 Track rod
4 Steering rack boot
5 Subframe
6 Control arm
7 Anti-roll arm bushing/clamp
8 Anti-roll bar
9 Anti-roll bar link
10 Ball joint
11 Steering knuckle

**1.1 Front suspension and steering components**

## 1  General information

The independent front suspension is of the MacPherson strut type, incorporating coil springs and integral telescopic shock absorbers **(see illustration)**. The MacPherson struts are located by transverse control arms, which use rubber inner mounting bushings, and incorporate a balljoint at the outer ends. The front steering knuckles, which carry the wheel bearings, brake calipers and the hub/disc assemblies, are bolted to the MacPherson struts, and connected to the control arms through the balljoints. An anti-roll bar, connected to the chassis and both control arms, reduces body roll when cornering.

The rear suspension consists of a torsion axle with shock absorbers and coil springs **(see illustration)**. A anti-roll bar is incorporated into the rear axle assembly (it's integral with the axle beam and isn't removable).

The steering column incorporates a universal joint, and is connected to the steering rack by a second individual universal joint.

The steering rack is mounted onto the front subframe, and is connected by two track rods, with balljoints at their outer ends, to the steering arms projecting rearwards from the steering knuckles.

Power-assisted steering is standard equipment. The hydraulic steering system is powered by a belt-driven pump, which is driven off the crankshaft pulley.

All later models are fitted with an Anti-lock Brake System (ABS), and can also be fitted with a Traction Control System (TCS), an Electronic Differential Lock (EDL) system and an Electronic Stability Program (ESP). The ABS may also be referred to as including EBD (Electronic Brake Distribution) which means it adjusts the front and rear braking forces according to the weight being carried, and the TCS may also be referred to as ASR (Anti Slip Regulation).

The TCS system prevents the front wheels from losing traction during acceleration by reducing the engine output. The system is switched on automatically when the engine is started, and it utilises the ABS system sensors to monitor the rotational speeds of the front wheels.

The ESP system extends the ABS, TCS and EDL functions to reduce wheel spin in difficult driving conditions. It does this by using highly-sensitive sensors which monitor the speed of the vehicle, lateral movement of the vehicle, the brake pressure, and the steering angle of the front wheels. If, for example, the vehicle is tending to oversteer, the brake will be applied to the front outer wheel to correct the situation. If the vehicle is tending to understeer, the brake will be applied to the rear inside wheel. The steering angle of the front wheels is monitored by an angle sensor on the top of the steering column.

The TCS/ESP systems should always be switched on, except when driving with snow chains, driving in snow or driving on loose surfaces, when some wheel spin may be advantageous. The ESP switch is located in the centre of the facia.

The EDL system reduces unequal traction from the front wheels. If one front wheel spins 100 rpm or more faster than the other, the faster wheel is slowed down by applying the brake to that wheel. The system is not the same as the traditional differential lock, where the actual differential gears are locked. Because the system applies a front brake, in the event of a brake disc overheating the system will shut down until the disc has cooled. No warning light is displayed if the system shuts down. As is the case with the TCS system, the EDL system uses the ABS sensors to monitor front wheel speeds.

### Precautions

Frequently, when working on the suspension or steering system components, you may come across fasteners which seem impossible to loosen. These fasteners on the underside of the vehicle are continually subjected to water, road grime, mud, etc, and can become rusted or 'seized,' making them extremely difficult to remove. In order to unscrew these stubborn fasteners without damaging them (or other components), be sure to use lots of penetrating oil and allow it to soak in for a while. Using a wire brush to clean exposed threads will also ease removal of the nut or bolt and prevent damage to the threads. Sometimes a sharp blow with a hammer and punch will break the bond between a nut and bolt threads, but care must be taken to prevent the punch from slipping off the fastener and ruining the threads. Heating the stuck fastener and surrounding area with a torch sometimes helps too, but isn't recommended because of the obvious dangers associated with fire. Long breaker bars and extension pipes will increase leverage, but never use an extension pipe on a ratchet – the ratcheting mechanism could be damaged. Sometimes tightening the nut or bolt first will help to break it loose. Fasteners that require drastic measures to remove should always be renewed with new ones.

Since most of the procedures dealt with in this Chapter involve jacking up the vehicle and working underneath it, a good pair of axle stands will be needed. A hydraulic floor jack is the preferred type of jack to lift the vehicle, and it can also be used to support certain components during various operations.

⚠️ *Warning: Never, under any circumstances, rely on a jack to support the vehicle while working on it. Whenever any of the suspension or steering fasteners are loosened or removed they must be inspected and, if necessary, renewed with ones of the same part number or of original equipment quality and design. Torque specifications must be followed for proper reassembly and component retention. Never attempt to heat or straighten any suspension or steering components. Instead, renew any bent or damaged part with a new one.*

**1.2  Rear suspension components**

*1 Shock absorber        2 Coil spring        3 Rear axle*

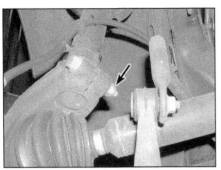

**2.8 Remove the strut-to-steering knuckle pinch bolt/nut . . .**

**2.9 . . . then spread the steering knuckle apart slightly by driving a chisel into the gap**

**2.11 Remove the strut upper mounting nut with a spark plug socket and a wrench, and a long hex bit inserted through the socket and into the damper shaft (to prevent the shaft from turning)**

## 2 Strut/coil spring assembly (front) – removal, inspection and refitting

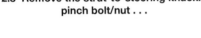

⚠ *Warning: The manufacturer recommends renewing the strut upper mounting nut and the strut-to-steering knuckle pinch bolt whenever they are removed.*

### Removal

**1** Remove the windscreen wiper arms (see Chapter 12, Section 18), the scuttle cover and plenum close-out panel (see Chapter 11).

**2** Loosen the wheel bolts, raise the front of the vehicle and support it securely on axle stands. Remove wheel.

**3** Without detaching the hose from the caliper, remove the brake caliper (see Chapter 9) and suspend it with a piece of wire (don't let it hang by the brake hose). Unclip the hose from the bracket on the strut. If the inner brake pad is equipped with a wear sensor, detach the wiring harness bracket from the strut.

**4** If the vehicle is equipped with an Anti-lock Braking System (ABS), detach the wheel speed sensor harness from the bracket on the strut.

**5** On diesel engine models, remove the splash shield and the air intake duct connecting the turbocharger and the intercooler (see Chapter 4B).

**6** If you're removing the right-side strut, unbolt the inner CV joint from the driveshaft flange (see Chapter 8).

**7** Unbolt the anti-roll bar link from the control arm (see Section 6).

**8** Remove the strut-to-steering knuckle pinch bolt **(see illustration)**.

**9** Insert a chisel into the slot in the steering knuckle and drive it in slightly to spread the joint apart (this will make separating the strut from the knuckle easier) **(see illustration)**.

**10** Pull the steering knuckle down, off the strut. If it sticks, apply some penetrating oil to the area where the strut meets the knuckle.

**11** Remove the strut upper mounting nut and stop plate. This will require holding the strut

rod from turning by using a hex key and turning the nut with a deep socket that has a hex for a spanner, such as a spark plug socket **(see illustration)**. An assistant would be helpful at this point to hold the strut while the nut is loosened.

**12** Remove the strut from the wheelarch.

### Refitting

**13** Refitting is the reverse of removal, with the following points:

a) Refit a new upper mounting nut.

b) Refit a new pinch bolt and nut.

c) Tighten the strut upper mounting nut and the pinch bolt nut to the torque values listed in this Chapter's Specifications.

d) Tighten the brake caliper guide pins to the torque listed in the Chapter 9 Specifications.

e) If the right-side strut was removed, connect the inner CV joint to the drive flange and tighten the bolts to the torque listed in the Chapter 8 Specifications.

f) Tighten the wheel bolts to the torque listed in the Chapter 1 Specifications.

**14** Have the front wheel alignment checked and, if necessary, adjusted.

## 3 Strut or coil spring (front) – renewal

⚠ *Warning: Always renew the struts or coil springs in pairs – never renew just one of them.*

**1** If the struts or coil springs exhibit the telltale signs of wear (leaking fluid, loss of damping capability, chipped, sagging or cracked coil springs) explore all options before beginning any work. The strut/shock absorber assemblies are not serviceable and must be renewed if a problem develops. However, strut assemblies complete with springs may be available on an exchange basis, which eliminates much time and work. Whichever route you choose to take, check on the cost and availability of parts before disassembling your vehicle.

⚠ *Warning: Disassembling a strut is potentially dangerous and utmost attention must be directed to the job, or serious injury may result. Use only a high-quality spring compressor and carefully follow the manufacturer's instructions furnished with the tool. After removing the coil spring from the strut assembly, set it aside in a safe, isolated area.*

**2** Remove the strut and spring assembly following the procedure described in the previous Section. Mount the strut assembly in a vice. Line the vice jaws with wood or rags to prevent damage to the unit and don't tighten the vice excessively.

**3** Following the tool manufacturer's instructions, refit the spring compressor (which can be obtained at most motor factors or equipment yards on a daily rental basis) on the spring and compress it sufficiently to relieve all pressure from the upper spring seat **(see illustration)**. This can be verified by wiggling the spring.

**4** Loosen and remove the damper shaft nut, while retaining the damper shaft with a hex bit, then remove the upper mounting, bearing

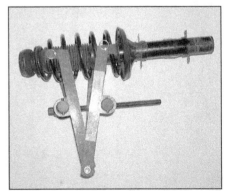

**3.3 Install the spring compressor following the tool manufacturer's instructions and compress the spring until all pressure is removed from the upper spring seat**

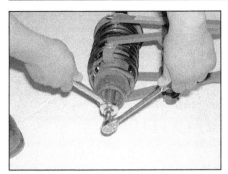

3.4a  Remove the damper shaft nut . . .

3.4b  . . . lift off the upper mounting . . .

3.4c  . . . followed by the bearing . . .

3.4d  . . . and spring seat

and spring seat **(see illustrations)**. Also remove the bush, if applicable.

**5** Remove the coil spring, then slide off the boot and rubber bump stop **(see illustrations)**.

⚠️ **Warning: Keep the ends of the spring away from your body.**

**6** With the strut now completely disassembled, examine all the components for wear, damage or deformation, and check the bearing for smoothness of operation. Renew any of the components as necessary.

**7** Examine the strut for signs of fluid leakage (a slight amount of seepage is normal). Check the strut piston for signs of pitting along its entire length, and check the strut body for signs of damage. While holding it in an upright position, test the operation of the strut by moving the damper shaft through a full stroke, and then through several short strokes. In both

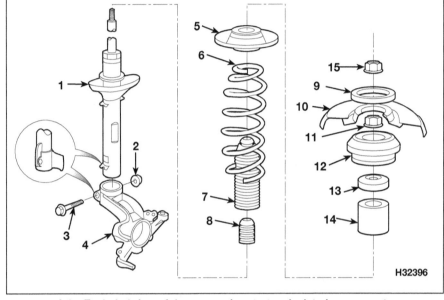

3.4e  Exploded view of the suspension strut and related components

| | | |
|---|---|---|
| 1 Strut body | 6 Spring | 11 Damper shaft nut |
| 2 Nut | 7 Boot | 12 Upper mounting |
| 3 Pinch bolt | 8 Bump stop | 13 Bearing |
| 4 Steering knuckle | 9 Stop | 14 Bushing |
| 5 Spring seat | 10 Strut tower | 15 Upper mounting nut |

cases, the resistance felt should be smooth and continuous. If the resistance is jerky, or uneven, or if there is any visible sign of wear or damage to the strut, renewal is necessary.

**8** If any doubt exists about the condition of the coil spring, carefully remove the spring compressor and check the spring for distortion and signs of cracking. Renew the spring if it is damaged or distorted, or if there is any doubt as to its condition.

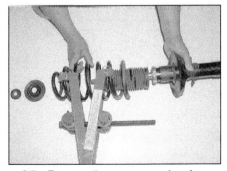

3.5a  Remove the compressed spring, keeping the ends of the spring pointed away from your body

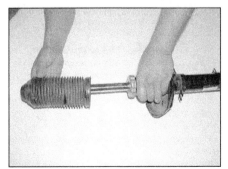

3.5b  Remove the boot . . .

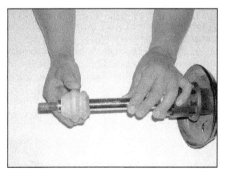

3.5c  . . . and the bump stop

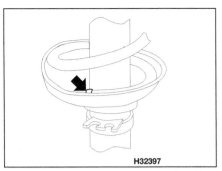

**3.11 Make sure the end of the coil spring is positioned against the stop on the spring seat**

9 Inspect all other components for signs of damage or deterioration, and renew any that are suspect.

10 Slide the bump stop and boot onto the strut piston rod.

11 Refit the coil spring onto the strut, making sure its end is correctly located against the spring seat stop **(see illustration)**.

12 Refit the upper spring seat, bush (if applicable), bearing and upper mounting, and screw on the damper shaft nut. Tighten the retaining nut to the torque listed in this Chapter's Specifications while preventing the piston rod from turning.

### 4 Steering knuckle and hub – removal and refitting

⚠ *Warning: The manufacturer recommends renewing the driveshaft/hub nut, strut-to-steering knuckle pinch bolt and nut, and the track rod end nut whenever they are removed.*

### Removal

1 Remove the wheel cover and loosen the driveshaft retaining nut with the vehicle resting on its wheels. Also loosen the wheel bolts.

2 Chock the rear wheels of the car, firmly apply the handbrake, then raise the front of the car and support it securely on axle stands. Remove the front wheel.

3 Remove the driveshaft retaining nut.

4 On models with ABS, remove the wheel speed sensor as described in Chapter 9.

5 Remove the brake caliper (don't disconnect the hose) and brake disc (see Chapter 9). Using a piece of wire or string, tie the caliper to the coil spring – don't let the caliper hang by the hose.

6 Detach the track rod end from the steering knuckle (see Section 17).

7 Mark the positions of the balljoint bolt heads to the control arm. Unscrew the balljoint retaining bolts and remove the retaining plate from the control arm (see Section 8).

8 Detach the steering knuckle from the strut (see Section 2).

9 Carefully pull the hub assembly outwards while pushing the driveshaft from the hub. If necessary, tap the joint out of the hub using a soft-faced hammer. If this fails to free it from the hub, the joint will have to be pressed out using a puller.

*Caution: Be careful not to overextend the inner CV joint.*

10 If necessary, loosen the balljoint nut a few turns, then break loose the balljoint stud from the steering knuckle with a balljoint removal tool. Remove the nut and separate the balljoint from the knuckle.

### Refitting

11 Lubricate the splines of the driveshaft with multi-purpose grease.

12 If removed, attach the balljoint to the steering knuckle, refit a new nut, then tighten the nut to the torque listed in this Chapter's Specifications.

13 Manoeuvre the hub assembly into position and engage it with the driveshaft stub shaft. Refit a new driveshaft/hub nut, but don't attempt to tighten it yet.

14 Engage the steering knuckle with the strut. Refit a new pinch bolt and nut, then tighten the nut to the torque listed in this Chapter's Specifications.

15 Connect the balljoint to the control arm. Refit the nut plate and the bolts, tightening the bolts to the torque listed in this Chapter's Specifications.

16 Engage the track rod end with the steering knuckle, then refit a new retaining nut and tighten it to the torque listed in this Chapter's Specifications.

17 Refit the brake disc and caliper, tightening the caliper mounting bracket bolts (if applicable) and caliper guide pins to the torque listed in the Chapter 9 Specifications.

18 If applicable, refit the ABS wheel speed sensor as described in Chapter 9.

19 Refit the wheel and lower the vehicle to the earth.

20 Tighten the driveshaft retaining nut to the torque listed in the Chapter 8 Specifications, then tighten the wheel bolts to the torque listed in the Specifications.

### 5 Hub and wheel bearing assembly (front) – removal, bearing renewal and refitting

⚠ *Warning: The manufacturer recommends renewing the driveshaft/hub nut whenever it is removed.*

**Note 1:** *The bearing is a sealed, pre-adjusted and pre-lubricated, double-row roller type, and is intended to last the car's entire service life without maintenance or attention. Never overtighten the driveshaft nut beyond the specified torque spanner setting in an attempt to 'adjust' the bearing.*

**Note 2:** *A press will be required to dismantle and rebuild the assembly; if such a tool is not*

*available, take the steering knuckle and hub assembly to an automotive machine workshop to have the old bearing pressed out and the new one pressed in. The bearing's inner races are an interference fit on the hub; if the inner race remains on the hub when it is pressed out of the hub carrier, a knife-edged bearing puller will be required to remove it.*

1 Remove the steering knuckle assembly as described in Section 4.

2 Support the steering knuckle securely on blocks or in a vice. Using a tubular spacer which bears only on the inner end of the hub flange, press the hub flange out of the bearing. If the bearing's outboard inner race remains on the hub, remove it using a bearing puller (see note 2 above).

3 Extract the bearing retaining circlip from the steering knuckle assembly **(see illustration)**.

4 Securely support the outer face of the steering knuckle. Using a tubular spacer, press the complete bearing assembly out of the steering knuckle.

5 Thoroughly clean the hub and steering knuckle, removing all traces of dirt and grease, and polish away any burrs or raised edges which might hinder reassembly. Check both for cracks or any other signs of wear or damage, and renew them if necessary. Renew the circlip, regardless of its apparent condition.

6 On reassembly, apply a light coating of moly-based grease to the bearing outer race and bearing surface of the steering knuckle.

7 Securely support the steering knuckle, and locate the bearing in the hub. Press the bearing fully into position, ensuring that it enters the hub squarely, using a tubular spacer which bears only on the bearing outer race.

8 Refit the circlip, making sure it seats properly. The opening between the ends of the circlip must be pointing down (towards the balljoint) when the knuckle is in its fitted position.

9 Securely support the outer face of the hub flange, and locate the steering knuckle bearing inner race over the end of the hub flange. Press the bearing onto the hub, using a tubular spacer which bears only on the inner race of the hub bearing, until it seats against the hub shoulder. Check that the hub flange rotates freely, and wipe off any excess grease.

10 Refit the steering knuckle assembly as described in Section 4.

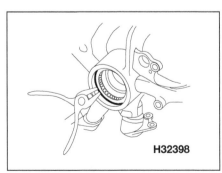

**5.3 The hub bearing is retained by a circlip**

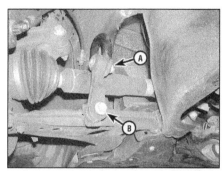

**6.8 Remove the nut and bolt (A) securing the anti-roll bar link to the bar – remove bolt (B) if you're removing the control arm**

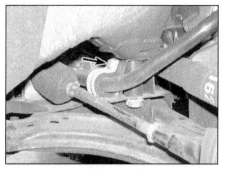

**6.9 The anti-roll bar bushing clamps are each retained by one bolt**

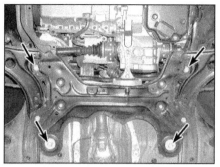

**6.11 Subframe mounting bolts (arrowed)**

## 6 Anti-roll bar and bushings (front) – removal and refitting

**⚠ Warning: The manufacturer recommends renewing the balljoint mounting bolts, steering rack bolts and the subframe mounting bolts whenever they are removed.**

### Removal

**1** Remove the wheel covers and loosen the driveshaft retaining nuts with the vehicle resting on its wheels. Loosen the wheel bolts, raise the front of the vehicle and support it securely on axle stands placed under the body frame rails or sill flanges. Remove the wheels.
**2** Remove the under-vehicle splash shield.
**3** On diesel engine models, remove the splash shield and the air intake duct connecting the turbocharger and the intercooler (see Chapter 4B).
**4** Remove the driveshafts (see Chapter 8).
**5** Unbolt the transmission support from the subframe and the transmission.
**6** Unbolt the steering rack from the subframe (see Section 19).
**7** If the vehicle is equipped with a diesel engine, unbolt the exhaust system from the subframe.
**8** Unbolt the anti-roll bar links from the anti-roll bar **(see illustration)**.

**9** Unbolt the anti-roll bar bush clamps from the subframe **(see illustration)**.
**10** Support the subframe with a jack – preferably a floor jack equipped with a transmission jack head adapter.
**11** Remove the subframe mounting bolts **(see illustration)**. Carefully lower the subframe enough to manoeuvre the anti-roll bar out.
**12** Remove the anti-roll bar. If necessary, unbolt the anti-roll bar links from the control arms.
**13** Inspect the clamp bushings and the link bushings. If they're cracked, hardened or deteriorated in any way, renew them.

### Refitting

**14** Begin by positioning the anti-roll bar on the subframe, making sure it is centred. Refit the clamps and bolts, but don't tighten the bolts yet.
**15** Raise the subframe and connect the steering rack to it, making sure it is positioned properly. Refit new steering rack mounting bolts, but don't tighten them completely yet.
**16** Attach the subframe to the vehicle, using new bolts. Tighten the bolts to the torque listed in this Chapter's Specifications.
**17** Tighten the steering rack mounting bolts to the torque listed in this Chapter's Specifications.
**18** Tighten the anti-roll bar bush clamp bolts to the torque listed in this Chapter's Specifications.
**19** Refit the anti-roll bar links, tightening the

fasteners to the torque listed in this Chapter's Specifications.
**20** The remainder of refitting is the reverse of removal, following the appropriate Sections in this Chapter, Chapter 7A and Chapter 8. Tighten all fasteners to the proper torque Specifications.
**21** Refit the wheels and lower the vehicle, then tighten the wheel bolts to the torque listed in the Chapter 1 Specifications, and the driveshaft/hub nuts to the torque listed in the Chapter 8 Specifications.
**22** Have the front end alignment checked and, if necessary, adjusted.

## 7 Control arm (front) – removal, bush renewal and refitting

**⚠ Warning: The manufacturer recommends renewing the control arm pivot bolt, the rear mounting bolt and the balljoint securing bolts whenever they are removed.**

### Removal

**1** Loosen the wheel bolts. Chock the rear wheels, firmly apply the handbrake, then raise the front of the vehicle and support it securely on axle stands. Remove the wheel.
**2** Unbolt the anti-roll bar link from the control arm **(see illustration 6.8)**.
**3** Mark the position of the balljoint bolt heads to the control arm. Unscrew the balljoint retaining bolts and remove the retaining plate from the top of the control arm (see Section 8).
**4** Loosen and remove the control arm pivot bolt and rear mounting bolt **(see illustrations)**.
**5** Lower the arm out of position, and remove it from underneath the vehicle.

### Bush renewal

**6** Thoroughly clean the control arm and the area around the bushings, removing all traces of dirt and underseal if necessary, then check carefully for cracks, distortion or any other signs of wear or damage, paying particular

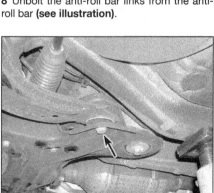

**7.4a Control arm rear mounting bolt (arrowed)**

**7.4b Control arm pivot bolt (arrowed)**

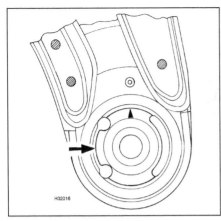

**7.7 The control arm rear bushing must be installed with one of the arrows pointing towards the front pivot bushing, and the kidney-shaped cut-out facing the centre of the vehicle**

attention to the pivot and rear mounting bushings. If either bush requires renewal, the control arm should be taken to an automotive machine workshop. A hydraulic press and suitable spacers are required to press the rear bush out of the arm and refit the new one, and a drawbolt-type bush removal tool is required to renew the front pivot bush.

**7** If you do have access to the necessary equipment, be sure to orient the rear bush properly **(see illustration)**.

### Refitting

**8** Manoeuvre the control arm into position, engaging it with the balljoint.

**9** Refit the new pivot bolt and rear mounting bolt.

**10** Position the retaining plate on the top of the arm, then refit the control arm balljoint retaining bolts. Align the balljoint with the marks made prior to removal, then tighten the retaining bolts to the torque listed in this Chapter's Specifications.

**11** Tighten the control arm rear mounting bolt to the torque listed in this Chapter's Specifications. Tighten the pivot bolt lightly only at this stage.

**12** Using a floor jack, raise the outer end of the control arm to simulate normal ride height, then tighten the control arm front pivot bolt to the torque listed in this Chapter's Specifications.

**8.6a Mark the positions of the balljoint bolt heads on the lower control arm . . .**

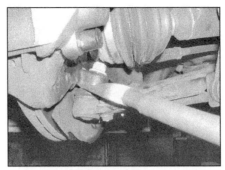

**8.5 Separating the balljoint from the steering knuckle (the use of a balljoint separator will most likely damage the balljoint boot)**

**13** Connect the anti-roll bar link to the control arm, tightening the bolt to the torque listed in this Chapter's Specifications.

**14** Refit the wheel, then lower the vehicle and tighten the wheel bolts to the torque listed in the Chapter 1 Specifications.

**15** Have the front end alignment checked and, if necessary, adjusted.

### 8 Balljoints – examination and renewal

 *Warning: The manufacturer recommends renewing the balljoint-to-control arm bolts and the balljoint-to-steering knuckle nut whenever they are removed.*

**1** Loosen the wheel bolts, raise the front of the vehicle and support it securely on axle stands. Remove the wheel.

### Examination

**2** Grasp the control arm and attempt to move it up-and-down – you shouldn't be able to feel any movement. Now grasp the bottom of the tyre and try to move it in-and-out. If you can feel movement during either of these checks, renew the balljoint. **Note:** *Don't confuse play in the wheel bearings with balljoint wear.*

**3** Inspect the balljoint boot. If it is torn, renew the balljoint.

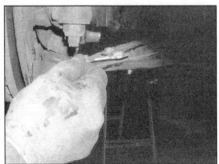

**8.6b . . . then remove the bolts and the nut retaining plate**

### Renewal

**4** Loosen the balljoint-to-steering knuckle nut a few turns, but don't remove it.

**5** Break loose the balljoint stud from the steering knuckle with a balljoint removal tool **(see illustration)**. Remove the nut and separate the balljoint from the knuckle.

**6** Mark the position of the balljoint bolt heads to the control arm. Unscrew the balljoint retaining bolts and remove the retaining plate from the top of the control arm **(see illustrations)**. Detach the balljoint from the control arm.

**7** Refitting is the reverse of removal. Align the balljoint-to-control arm bolt heads with the marks made in Step 6, then tighten the balljoint-to-control arm bolts, and the balljoint-to-steering knuckle nut, to the torque values listed in this Chapter's Specifications.

**8** Refit the wheel, lower the vehicle and tighten the wheel bolts to the torque listed in the Specifications.

### 9 Shock absorber (rear) – removal and refitting

 *Warning 1: Always renew the coil springs in pairs – never renew just one of them.*

 *Warning 2: The manufacturer recommends renewing the shock absorber upper mounting bolts, damper rod nut, and lower mounting bolt/nut whenever they are removed.*

**1** Loosen the rear wheel nuts. Chock the front wheels to keep the vehicle from rolling, then raise the rear of the vehicle and support it securely on axle stands placed underneath the sill flanges. Remove the rear wheels.

**2** Support the rear axle with a floor jack placed under the coil spring pocket.

 *Warning: The jack must remain in this position until the shock absorber is reinstalled.*

**3** Remove the shock absorber lower mounting bolt/nut **(see illustration)**.

**4** Remove the shock absorber upper

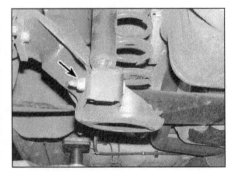

**9.3 Shock absorber lower mounting bolt/nut**

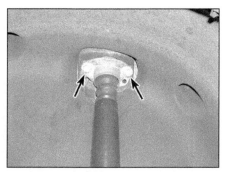

**9.4  Shock absorber upper mounting bolts**

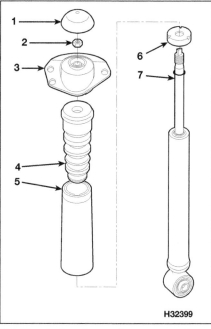

**9.5  Shock absorber and upper mounting – exploded view**

1  Cover
2  Damper rod nut
3  Upper mounting
4  Bump stop
5  Boot
6  Cap
7  Shock absorber

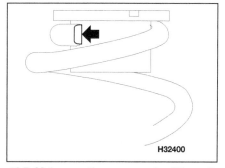

**10.7  Make sure the upper ends of the coil springs are positioned like this, against the stop in the upper seat**

mounting bolts and remove the shock absorber **(see illustration)**.

5  Remove the cover from the top of the shock absorber upper mounting, then unscrew the damper rod nut **(see illustration)**. It'll probably be necessary to hold the damper rod with another spanner to prevent it from turning when loosening the nut.

6  Remove the upper mounting, bump stop, boot and cap from the damper rod.

7  Refit the cap, boot, bump stop and upper mounting on the new shock absorber. Refit a new nut on the damper shaft and tighten it to the torque listed in this Chapter's Specifications. Refit the cover on the upper mounting.

8  Guide the shock absorber into position and refit new upper mounting bolts and a new lower mounting bolt and nut. Don't tighten the lower mounting bolt/nut yet.

9  Tighten the upper mounting bolts to the torque listed in this Chapter's Specifications.

10  Raise the rear axle to simulate normal ride height, then tighten the lower mounting bolt/nut to the torque listed in this Chapter's Specifications.

11  Repeat the procedure to renew the other rear shock absorber.

12  Refit the wheels and lower the vehicle. Tighten the wheel bolts to the torque listed in the Specifications.

## 10  Coil spring (rear) – removal and refitting

**Warning 1: Always renew the coil springs in pairs – never renew just one of them.**
**Warning 2: The manufacturer recommends renewing the shock absorber upper mounting bolts whenever they are removed.**

1  Loosen the wheel bolts. Chock the front wheels to prevent the vehicle from rolling, then raise the rear of the vehicle and support it securely on axle stands placed under the sill flanges. Remove the wheel. **Note:** *It is not absolutely necessary to remove the wheels,*

but doing so greatly improves access to the springs.

2  Support the rear axle with a floor jack placed under one of the spring pockets. Raise the jack slightly to take the spring pressure off the shock absorber upper mounting.

3  Remove the shock absorber upper mounting bolts **(see illustration 9.4)**.

4  Slowly lower the floor jack; at this point the spring will not be fully extended, as the shock absorber on the other side is limiting the downward travel of the axle.

5  Place the floor jack under the other spring seat, remove the shock absorber upper mounting bolts, then slowly lower the jack until the coil springs are fully extended.

6  Remove the spring, upper insulator and lower bush. Check the spring for cracks and chips, renewing the springs as a set if any defects are found. Also check the upper

insulator and the lower zinc bush for damage and deterioration, renewing them as necessary.

7  Refitting is the reverse of the removal procedure, but make sure the coil springs are positioned properly against their upper mountings **(see illustration)**.

8  Tighten the shock absorber upper mounting bolts to the torque listed in this Chapter's Specifications. Tighten the wheel bolts to the torque listed in the Specifications.

## 11  Hub and wheel bearing assembly (rear) – removal and refitting

**Warning: The manufacturer recommends renewing the hub nut whenever it is removed. The dust cap should also be renewed upon reassembly.**

### Removal

1  Loosen the rear wheel bolts, raise the rear of the vehicle, support it securely on axle stands and remove the wheels.

2  Remove the brake caliper (don't detach the hose), mounting bracket and disc (see Chapter 9). Hang the caliper with a piece of wire – don't let it hang by the brake hose.

3  Remove the dust cap **(see illustration)**.

4  Remove the hub nut **(see illustration)**.

5  Using a puller, remove the hub flange and outer bearing from the stub axle **(see**

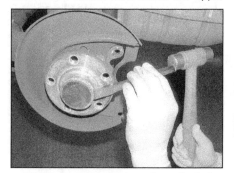

**11.3  Remove the dust cap from the hub flange**

**11.4  Unscrew the hub nut**

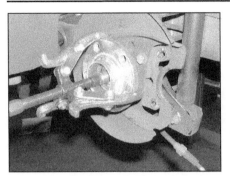

**11.5 Removing the hub flange and outer bearing with a puller**

**11.6a Knock the inner race of the inner bearing away from the shoulder of the stub axle . . .**

**11.6b . . . then remove it the rest of the way with a puller**

illustration). The inner bearing will most likely remain on the stub axle.

6 Using a hammer and chisel, drive the inner race of the inner bearing away from the shoulder of the stub axle, far enough to allow the jaws of a puller to grasp the inner race. Now, using a puller, remove the inner bearing assembly from the stub axle **(see illustrations)**.

### Refitting

7 Before refitting the hub and bearing assembly, clean the stub axle and apply a film of wheel bearing grease to the area on the stub axle where the bearings ride.

8 Push the hub and bearing assembly onto the stub axle as far as possible by hand. Make sure it goes on straight – not cocked to the side.

9 Using a hammer and a large socket that fits inside the hub opening and mates with the inner race of the outer bearing, drive the hub and bearing assembly onto the stub axle far enough to allow you to refit the hub nut **(see illustration)**.

10 Refit the old hub nut onto the stub axle and tighten it to the torque listed in this Chapter's Specifications. This will push the hub and bearing assembly into place.

11 Remove the old hub nut and fit the new one, tightening it to the torque listed in this Chapter's Specifications.

12 Refit a new dust cap.

13 The remainder of refitting is the reverse of removal. Tighten the caliper mounting bracket

bolts and the caliper bolts to the torque listed in the Chapter 9 Specifications.

14 Refit the wheel, lower the vehicle and tighten the wheel bolts to the torque listed in the Specifications.

## 12 Stub axle (rear) – removal and refitting

> ⚠ *Warning: The manufacturer recommends renewing the hub nut and the stub axle mounting bolts whenever they are removed.*

1 Loosen the wheel bolts. Chock the front wheels, then raise the rear of the vehicle and support it securely on axle stands. Remove the rear wheel.

2 Remove the hub and bearing assembly (see Section 11). Be sure to hang the caliper with a piece of wire – don't let it hang by the brake hose.

3 Inspect the stub axle surface for signs of damage such as scoring, and renew if necessary. Do not attempt to straighten the stub axle. Also check the threads; if they are damaged in any way, renew the stub axle. Don't attempt to 'clean up' the threads with a thread file or a die.

4 If the vehicle is equipped with an Anti-lock Braking System (ABS), remove the rear wheel speed sensor (see Chapter 9).

5 Remove the stub axle mounting bolts **(see**

illustration). Remove the stub axle along with the disc splash shield.

6 Refitting is the reverse of removal, with the following points:

  a) *Make sure the stub axle mating surfaces and the mounting bolt holes on the axle beam are clean.*

  b) *Use new stub axle mounting bolts and tighten them to the torque listed in this Chapter's Specifications.*

  c) *Refit a new hub nut and tighten it to the torque listed in this Chapter's Specifications.*

  d) *Tighten the caliper mounting bracket bolts and the caliper bolts to the torque listed in the Chapter 9 Specifications.*

## 13 Anti-roll bar (rear) – removal and refitting

The rear suspension anti-roll bar runs along the length of the axle beam. It is an integral part of the axle assembly, and cannot be removed. If the anti-roll bar is damaged, which is very unlikely, the complete axle assembly must be renewed.

## 14 Rear axle assembly – removal and refitting

> ⚠ *Warning: The manufacturer recommends renewing all suspension fasteners whenever they are removed.*

### Removal

1 Loosen the rear wheel bolts. Chock the front wheels, then raise the rear of the vehicle and support it securely on axle stands. Remove both rear wheels.

2 Referring to Chapter 9, fully loosen the handbrake cable adjuster nut.

3 Detach the handbrake cables from the calipers (see Chapter 9).

4 Remove the brake calipers, mounting brackets and discs (see Chapter 9).

5 On models equipped with an Anti-lock

**11.9 Drive the hub and bearing assembly onto the stub axle with a large socket that contacts the inner race of the bearing**

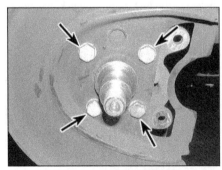

**12.5 Stub axle mounting bolts**

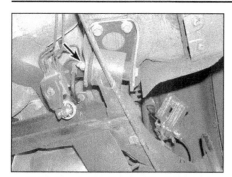

**14.12  Rear axle pivot bolt/nut (the nut should only be tightened with the suspension at normal ride height)**

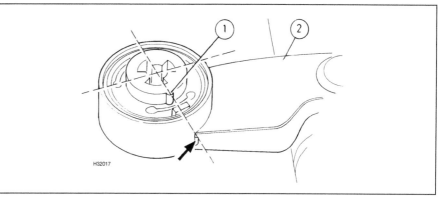

**14.14  The rear axle pivot bushing must be installed with the mark (1) pointing towards the area where the trailing arm portion of the axle (2) connects to the bushing boss (arrowed)**

Braking System (ABS), remove the rear wheel speed sensors.

**6** If the axle is to be renewed, remove the hub and bearing assemblies (see Section 11) and the stub axles (see Section 12).

**7** Detach the handbrake cables from the retaining clips along the axle trailing arms.

**8** Unscrew the brake pipe fittings from the brake hoses on each side of the rear axle (near the pivot bushings). Use a flare-nut spanner, if available, to prevent rounding-off the fittings (see Chapter 9). Plug the hoses to minimise fluid loss and prevent the entry of dirt into the hydraulic system. If the rear axle is to be renewed, detach the brake pipes from the clips on the axle.

**9** On models without ABS, unbolt the brake pressure regulator spring from the left side of the axle beam (see Chapter 9). Also unbolt the valve from its bracket (it isn't necessary to detach the brake pipes from it, but unbolting it from the bracket will help prevent damage to the valve as the axle is lowered).

**10** Remove the coil springs (see Section 10).

**11** Make a final check that all necessary components have been disconnected and positioned so that they will not hinder the removal procedure, then position a floor jack beneath the centre of the rear axle assembly. Raise the jack until it is just supporting the weight of the axle.

**12** Remove the nuts from the axle pivot bolts on each side of the vehicle, then remove the bolts **(see illustration)**. Slowly lower the jack, being careful not to let the axle hit the pressure regulator valve (if fitted).

**13** Inspect the axle pivot bushings for signs of damage or deterioration. If renewal is necessary, they can be removed with a drawbolt-type bush renewal tool (and suitable adapters) or a slide hammer, and fitted with the drawbolt-type bush renewal tool (and suitable adapters). If you don't have access to the necessary tools, take the axle to an automotive machine workshop to have the old bushings removed and the new ones fitted.

**14** If the bushings are in need of renewal, make sure the new ones are fitted properly **(see illustration)**.

**15** Don't unbolt the rear axle mounting brackets from the floor pan unless they are

damaged (bent, cracked, or if the pivot bolt holes are worn). If renewal is necessary, mark the position of the bracket to the floor pan and refit the new bracket in the same position (this will preserve rear wheel alignment).

### Refitting

**16** Refitting of the rear axle is the reverse of the removal procedure, with the following points:

a) Renew all suspension fasteners.
b) Ensure that the brake pipes, handbrake cables and wiring (as applicable) are correctly routed, and retained by all the necessary retaining clips.
c) Don't tighten the rear axle pivot bolts or the shock absorber lower mounting bolts until the weight of the vehicle is on its wheels (or until the rear suspension has been raised to simulate normal ride height). This will prevent the bushings from 'winding-up,' which could eventually damage them.
d) Tighten all fasteners to the proper torque Specifications.
e) Bleed the brake system (see Chapter 9).
f) If either mounting bracket was removed from the floor pan, have the rear wheel alignment checked and, if necessary, adjusted.

### 15 Steering wheel – removal and refitting

**Warning 1: These models are equipped with airbags. Always disable the airbag system before working in the vicinity of any airbag system component to avoid the possibility of accidental deployment of the airbag(s), which could cause personal injury (see Chapter 12).**

**Warning 2: Do not use a memory-saving device to preserve the ECM's memory when working on or near airbag system components.**

*Caution 1: These models are equipped with an anti-theft radio. Before performing a procedure that requires disconnecting the battery, make sure you have the activation code.*

*Caution 2: Disconnecting the battery can cause driveability problems that require a scan tool to remedy. If the vehicle exhibits driveability problems after the battery is reconnected, it may be necessary to take it to a dealer service department or other qualified garage to reprogram the ECM.*

### Removal

**1** Park the vehicle with the wheels pointing straight ahead. Disconnect the cable from the negative terminal of the battery.

**2** Refer to Chapter 12 and disable the airbag system, then remove the instrument cluster (also in Chapter 12).

**3** Turn the steering wheel 90-degrees to gain access to the hole in the back of the steering wheel. Insert a screwdriver into the hole for the spring clip that retains the airbag module and push the spring aside to release the pin **(see illustrations)**. Now turn the steering wheel 180-degrees in the other direction and do the same thing to release the other pin. **Note:** *This step can be very difficult and frustrating. Take your time and be careful not*

**15.3a  Insert a screwdriver into the hole in the steering wheel and pry up, which will release the clip securing one side of the airbag module (repeat this one the other side)**

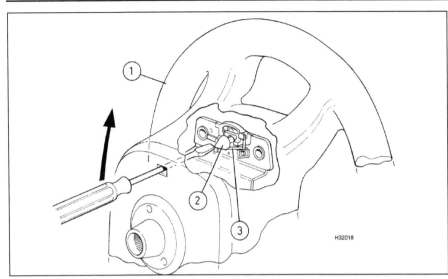

**15.3b  Here's a ghost view showing the screwdriver prying the spring clip away from the airbag module retaining post**

*1 Steering wheel     2 Locking lug     3 Clip*

to tear the rubber steering wheel trim when levering.

**4** Disconnect the electrical connector from the airbag module **(see illustration)**. Set the module aside in a safe, isolated area, with the airbag side of the module facing UP.

⚠️ *Warning: When carrying the airbag module, keep the driver's (trim) side of it away from your*

body and, when you set it down, make sure the driver's side is facing up.

**5** Centre the steering wheel.

**6** Unplug the airbag/horn wiring harness from the clockspring and airbag securing plate **(see illustration)**.

**7** Using a 12 mm 12-point spline-drive bit, remove the steering wheel retaining bolt and mark the position of the steering wheel to the

shaft, if marks don't already exist or don't line up **(see illustrations)**.

**8** Remove the steering wheel from the shaft. If it is tight, tap it up near the centre using the palm of your hand, or twist it from side-to-side while pulling upwards.

*Caution: Don't hammer on the shaft to remove the wheel.*

**9** Lift the steering wheel from the shaft.

⚠️ *Warning: Don't allow the steering shaft to turn with the steering wheel removed. If the shaft turns, the airbag clockspring will become uncentered, which may cause the wire inside to break when the vehicle is returned to service.*

### Refitting

**10** Before refitting the steering wheel, make sure the airbag clockspring is centred **(see illustration)**.

**11** If the airbag system clockspring is not centred, remove the steering column covers (see Chapter 11). Release the locking tabs, unplug the electrical connector and lift the clockspring off the steering column. Unplug the electrical connector.

**12** To centre the clockspring, depress the spring-loaded plunger and turn the hub in either direction until it stops (don't apply too much force). Now, rotate the hub in the other direction, counting the number of turns it takes to reach the opposite stop. Divide that number by two, then turn the hub back that many turns, approximately, until the yellow flag appears in the window **(see illustration 15.10)**. Refit the clockspring, making sure the locking tabs engage securely. Refit the steering column covers.

**13** Refit the wheel on the steering shaft, aligning the marks.

**14** Refit the steering wheel bolt and tighten it to the torque listed in this Chapter's Specifications. **Note:** *This bolt can be used up to five times. Using a centre punch, place a mark on the head of the bolt after you tighten it, to keep track of how many times the bolt has been tightened* **(see illustration)**.

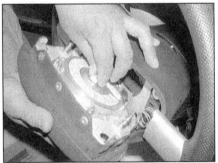

**15.4  Pull the electrical connector straight out of the airbag module**

**15.6  Unplug the wiring harness from the airbag clockspring and securing plate**

**15.7a  Unscrew the steering wheel bolt with a 12mm, 12-point spline-drive bit**

**15.7b  After removing the bolt, check for alignment marks on the steering wheel and steering shaft – if there aren't any, make your own**

**15.10  After centring the clockspring make sure the yellow flag appears in the window**

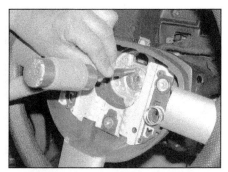

**15.14 Make a punch mark on the steering wheel bolt after installing it (it can be used up to five times)**

**15** Plug in the electrical connector for the airbag and horn into the clockspring. Attach the earth leads to the airbag securing plate.
**16** Connect the airbag connector to the back of the airbag module.
**17** Position the airbag module on the steering wheel and push it in until the pins on the module engage with the spring clips.
**18** Refer to Chapter 12 for the procedure to enable the airbag system.

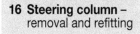

### 16 Steering column – removal and refitting

*Warning 1: These models are equipped with airbags. Always disable the airbag system before working in the vicinity of any airbag system component to avoid the possibility of accidental deployment of the airbag(s), which could cause personal injury (see Chapter 12).*

*Warning 2: Do not use a memory-saving device to preserve the ECM's memory when working on or near airbag system components.*
*Caution 1: These models are equipped with an anti-theft radio. Before performing a procedure that requires disconnecting the battery, make sure you have the activation code.*
*Caution 2: Disconnecting the battery can*

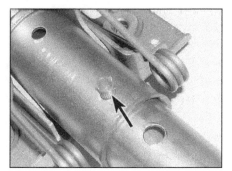

**16.10 Align the holes in the steering shafts, then insert a clip or pin to hold them together**

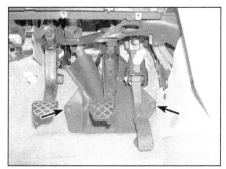

**16.3 Unscrew these fasteners and remove the cover for access to the steering shaft universal joint**

*cause driveability problems that require a scan tool to remedy. If the vehicle exhibits driveability problems after the battery is reconnected, it may be necessary to take it to a dealer service department or other qualified garage to reprogram the ECM.*

### Removal

**1** Park the vehicle with the wheels in the straight-ahead position. Disconnect the cable from the negative terminal of the battery. Disable the airbag system (see Chapter 12).
**2** Remove the steering wheel (see Section 15).
**3** Remove the lower instrument panel trim (under the steering column) (see Chapter 11). Also remove the cover from the bottom of the steering column, below the brake pedal **(see illustration)**.
**4** Remove the steering column covers (see Chapter 11).

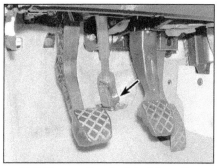

**16.9 Remove the pinch bolt from the steering shaft U-joint**

**5** Remove the airbag system clockspring (see Section 15).
**6** Remove the multi-function switch (see Chapter 12, Section 7).
**7** Remove the plastic cover from over the ignition switch shear-head bolts.
**8** On models equipped with an automatic transmission, detach the gearchange interlock cable from the ignition switch (see Chapter 7B).
**9** Mark the relationship of the steering shaft lower universal joint to the steering rack input shaft, then remove the pinch bolt from the universal joint **(see illustration)**. Separate the universal joint from the steering rack input shaft.
**10** Push or pull the lower steering shaft in-or-out of the upper portion of the shaft until the holes in the shaft are aligned. Insert a pin or clip into the hole to hold the shafts in this relationship **(see illustration)**.
**11** Remove the steering column mounting bolts **(see illustration)**, then guide the column out from the instrument panel.

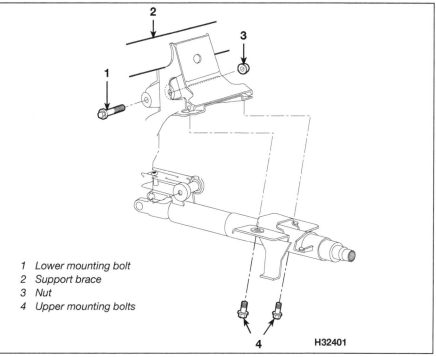

1 Lower mounting bolt
2 Support brace
3 Nut
4 Upper mounting bolts

H32401

**16.11 Steering column mounting details**

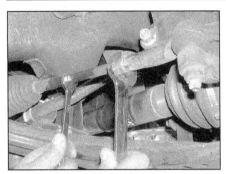

**17.2 Hold the track rod still with a spanner, then undo the lock nut**

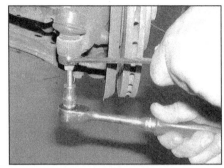

**17.3a If the track rod end turns while attempting to loosen the nut, hold it with an Allen key**

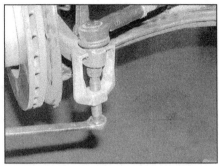

**17.3b Disconnect the track rod end from the steering knuckle arm with a balljoint separator**

## Refitting

12 Guide the column into position, connecting the universal joint with the steering rack input shaft.

13 Refit the mounting bolts. Tighten the lower mounting bolt/nut to the torque listed in this Chapter's Specifications.

14 Tighten the upper mounting bolts to the torque listed in this Chapter's Specifications.

15 Remove the clip fitted in Step 10. If a new steering column was fitted, remove the plastic clip holding the shafts in proper relationship.

16 Tighten the universal joint pinch bolt to the torque listed in this Chapter's Specifications.

17 The remainder of refitting is the reverse of the removal procedure. Be sure the airbag clockspring is centred, and tighten the steering wheel bolt to the torque listed in this Chapter's Specifications.

## 17 Track rod ends – removal and refitting

!  *Warning: The manufacturer recommends renewing the track rod end-to-steering knuckle nuts whenever they are removed.*

## Removal

1 Loosen the wheel bolts, raise the front of the vehicle and support it securely on axle stands. Apply the handbrake and block the rear wheels to keep the vehicle from rolling off the axle stands. Remove the wheel.

2 Break loose the track rod end locking nut **(see illustration)**. Don't back the nut off; once it has just been loosened, it will serve as the point to which the track rod end will be threaded. If you are removing the track rod end to renew the steering rack boot, mark the threads of the track rod on the *inner* side of the nut.

3 Loosen (but don't remove) the nut on the track rod end balljoint, then disconnect the track rod end from the steering knuckle arm with a puller **(see illustrations)**.

4 Unscrew the track rod end from the track rod.

## Refitting

5 If the locking nut was removed, thread it onto the track rod until it meets the mark applied in Step 2. Thread the track rod end onto the track rod until it contacts the locking nut, then connect the track rod end to the steering arm. Refit the balljoint nut and tighten it to the torque listed in this Chapter's Specifications.

6 Tighten the locking nut securely and refit the wheel. Lower the vehicle and tighten the wheel bolts to the torque listed in the Chapter 1 Specifications.

7 Have the front end alignment checked and, if necessary, adjusted.

## 18 Steering rack boots – renewal

!  *Warning: The manufacturer recommends renewing the track rod end-to-steering knuckle nuts whenever they are removed.*

1 Loosen the wheel bolts, raise the front of the vehicle and support it securely on axle stands. Remove the wheels.

2 Remove the track rod end from the track rod (see Section 17).

3 Remove the track rod end locking nut.

4 Remove the inner and outer boot clamps and discard them **(see illustration)**. The

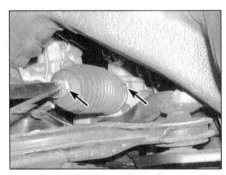

**18.4 Pry open or cut off the steering rack boot clamps**

clamps can be pried apart at the crimped area, or cut off with a pair of cutting pliers.

5 Remove the boot.

6 Refit a new clamp on the inner end of the boot.

7 Slide the boot into place.

8 Make sure the boot isn't twisted, then tighten the inner clamp with a pair of clamp crimping pliers **(see illustration)**.

9 Refit and tighten the outer clamp.

10 Refit the track rod ends (see Section 17).

11 Have the front end alignment checked and, if necessary, adjusted.

## 19 Steering rack – removal and refitting

!  *Warning 1: These models equipped with airbags. Always disable the airbag system before working in the vicinity of the any airbag system component to avoid the possibility of accidental deployment of the airbag, which could cause personal injury (see Chapter 12). Also, don't allow the steering wheel to turn after the steering rack has been removed. To prevent this, pass the seat belt through the steering wheel and plug it into its latch.*

!  *Warning 2: The manufacturer recommends renewing the subframe mounting bolts, track rod end-to-steering knuckle*

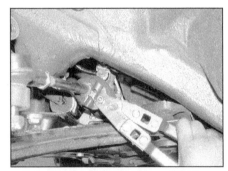

**18.8 Clamp crimping pliers, available at most auto parts stores, are needed to tighten the boot clamps properly**

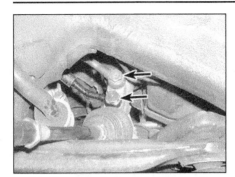

**19.7 Unscrew the banjo bolts from the pressure and return pipe fittings at the steering rack, then plug the fittings to prevent leakage and the entry of contaminants**

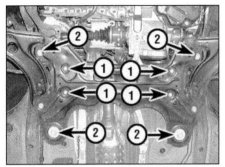

**19.8 The power steering rack is bolted to the subframe**

1 Steering gear mounting bolts
2 Subframe mounting bolts

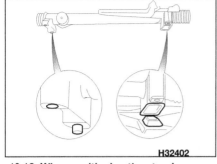

**19.12 When positioning the steering gear on the subframe, the threaded post on the left side mount must engage with the hole in the subframe, and the right side of the steering gear must engage with the raised rectangle**

nuts, steering rack retaining nuts, and steering shaft U-joint pinch bolt whenever they are removed.

### Removal

**1** Loosen the wheel bolts. Chock the rear wheels, firmly apply the handbrake, then raise the front of the vehicle and support it securely on axle stands. Remove both front wheels.
**2** Detach the track rod ends from the steering knuckles (see Section 17).
**3** Remove the cover from the bottom of the steering column, below the brake pedal. Mark the relationship of the steering shaft lower universal joint to the steering rack input shaft, then remove the pinch bolt from the universal joint. Separate the universal joint from the steering rack input shaft (see Section 16).
**4** Remove the under-vehicle splash shield.
**5** Unbolt the transmission support from the subframe and the transmission.
**6** If the vehicle is equipped with a diesel engine, unbolt the exhaust system from the subframe.
**7** Remove the power steering pressure and return pipe banjo bolts **(see illustration)**. Detach the pipes from the steering rack and plug them or wrap them tightly with plastic bags and tape to prevent fluid leakage and contamination. Discard the sealing washers – new ones should be used during refitting.
**8** Loosen the steering rack mounting bolts **(see illustration)**.
**9** Support the subframe with a jack – preferably a floor jack equipped with a transmission jack head adapter.
**10** Remove the subframe mounting bolts **(see illustration 19.8)**. Carefully lower the subframe enough to manoeuvre the steering rack out. If it won't lower far enough to get the steering rack out, unbolt the anti-roll bar link from the control arms (see Section 6).

### Refitting

**11** Make sure the mounting areas on the subframe are clean. Also make sure the steering rack is in the centred position.

Inspect the gasket around the steering rack input shaft, renewing it if necessary.
**12** Guide the rack into position on the subframe, then refit the bolts finger tight. The threaded sleeve at the left front mounting bolt hole of the steering rack must be engaged with the hole in the subframe, and the right side steering rack mounting must be engaged with the rectangular protrusion on the subframe **(see illustration)**.
**13** Raise the subframe into position and refit the mounting bolts, tightening them to the torque listed in this Chapter's Specifications.
**14** Tighten the steering rack mounting bolts to the torque listed in this Chapter's Specifications.
**15** Using new sealing washers, connect the power steering pressure and return pipes to the steering rack. **Note:** The manufacturer recommends lubricating the sealing washers with liquid soap before refitting. Tighten the banjo fitting bolts to the torque listed in this Chapter's Specifications.
**16** The remainder of refitting is the reverse of removal, with the following points:
a) Tighten all fasteners to the recommended torque specifications.
b) Bleed the power steering system (see Section 21).
c) Have the front end alignment checked and, if necessary, adjusted.

**20 Power steering pump – removal and refitting**

**Note:** On some models the power steering pump is mounted to the lower portion of the mounting bracket on the front of the engine. On other models it's mounted to the upper portion of the bracket.
**1** Loosen the right front wheel bolts. Raise the front of the vehicle and support it securely on axle stands. Remove the wheel.
**2** Remove inner wing panel.
**3** Remove the auxiliary drivebelt (see Chapter 1).
**4** Remove the bolts and detach the pulley from the pump **(see illustration)**. To prevent the pulley from rotating, insert a screwdriver through one of the slots in the pulley and brace it against the pump, or hold the pulley by inserting the proper-sized Allen key in the centre bolt.
**5** Clamp the pressure and feed pipes shut, then detach them from the power steering pump **(see illustration)**.

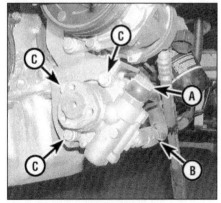

**20.5 Power steering pump mounting details**

A Pressure pipe banjo fitting
B Return hose clamp
C Mounting bolts (3 of 4)

**20.4 The pulley is held to the power steering pump with three bolts**

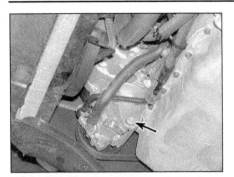

**20.6a There's one more mounting bolt on the back of the pump**

**6** Remove the pump mounting bolts **(see illustrations and illustration 20.5)** and detach the pump from the mounting bracket.

**7** Refitting is the reverse of removal, with the following points:

a) *Use new sealing washers on either side of the pressure pipe banjo fitting. The manufacturer recommends lubricating these washers with liquid soap before refitting.*

b) *Tighten mounting fasteners and the pressure pipe banjo fitting bolt to the torque values listed in this Chapter's Specifications.*

c) *Tighten the wheel bolts to the torque listed in the Specifications.*

d) *Bleed the power steering system (see Section 21).*

## 21 Power steering system – bleeding

**1** Following any operation in which the power steering fluid pipes have been disconnected, the power steering system must be bled to remove all air and obtain proper steering performance.

**2** With the front wheels in the straight ahead position, check the power steering fluid level and, if low, add fluid until it is between the Cold marks on the reservoir.

**3** Raise the front of the vehicle and support it securely on axle stands.

**4** Turn the steering wheel back-and-forth repeatedly, lightly hitting the stops.

**5** Start the engine and allow it to run at fast idle. Recheck the fluid level and add more if necessary to reach the Cold marks.

**6** Bleed the system by turning the wheels from side to side, just barely contacting the stops. This will work the air out of the system. Keep the reservoir full of fluid as this is done.

**7** When the air is worked out of the system and the fluid level stabilises, return the wheels to the straight ahead position and leave the vehicle running for several more minutes before turning it off. Lower the vehicle.

**8** Road test the vehicle to be sure the steering system is functioning normally and noise-free.

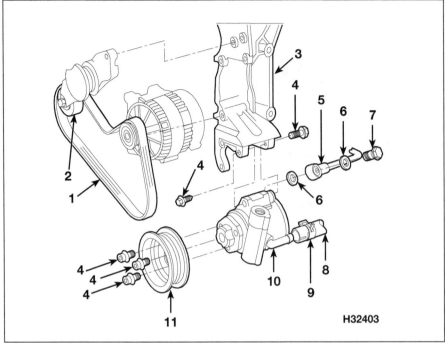

**20.6b Power steering pump mounting details – low-mounted pump**

1 Belt
2 Tensioner
3 Mounting bracket
4 Bolt

5 Pressure pipe
6 Sealing washers
7 Banjo bolt
8 Return hose

9 Hose clamp
10 Power steering pump
11 Pulley

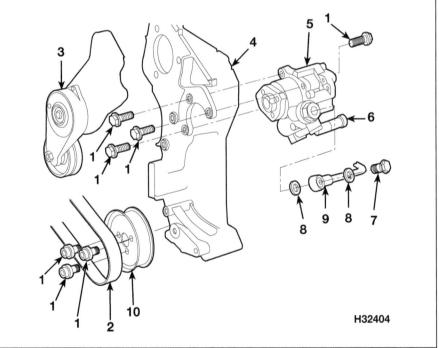

**20.6c Power steering pump mounting details – high-mounted pump**

1 Bolt
2 Belt
3 Tensioner
4 Mounting bracket

5 Power steering pump
6 Return hose fitting
7 Banjo bolt

8 Sealing washer
9 Pressure pipe
10 Pulley

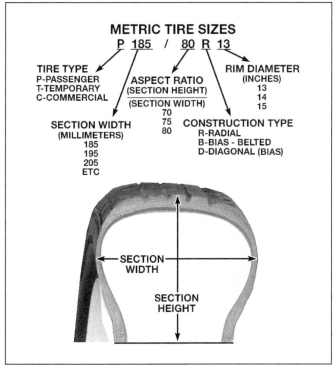

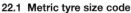

22.1 Metric tyre size code

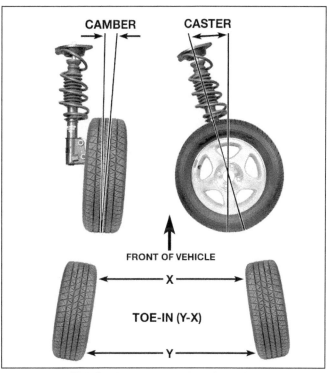

23.1 Camber, caster and toe-in angles

9 Recheck the fluid level to be sure it is between the Hot marks on the reservoir while the engine is at normal operating temperature. Add fluid if necessary (see Chapter 1).

## 22 Wheels and tyres – general information

1 All vehicles covered by this manual are equipped with metric-sized steel belted radial tyres **(see illustration)**. Use of other size or type of tyres may affect the ride and handling of the vehicle. Don't mix different types of tyres, such as radials and bias belted, on the same vehicle as handling may be seriously affected. It's recommended that tyres be renewed in pairs on the same axle, but if only one tyre is being renewed, be sure it's the same size, structure and tread design as the other.

2 Because tyre pressure has a substantial effect on handling and wear, the pressure on all tyres should be checked at least once a month or before any extended trips (see Chapter 1).

3 Wheels must be renewed if they are bent, dented, leak air, have elongated bolt holes, are heavily rusted, out of vertical symmetry or if the wheel bolts won't stay tight. Wheel repairs that use welding or peening are not recommended.

4 Tyre and wheel balance is important in the overall handling, braking and performance of the vehicle. Unbalanced wheels can adversely affect handling and ride characteristics as well as tyre life. Whenever a tyre is fitted on a wheel, the tyre and wheel should be balanced by a shop with the proper equipment.

## 23 Wheel alignment – general information

A wheel alignment refers to the adjustments made to the wheels so they are in proper angular relationship to the suspension and the ground. Wheels that are out of proper alignment not only affect vehicle control, but also increase tyre wear. The front end angles normally measured are camber, caster and toe-in **(see illustration)**. Camber and caster are pre-set at the factory on the vehicle covered by this manual, but are usually checked to see if any suspension components are worn or damaged; front toe-in is the only adjustable angle on these vehicles. The rear toe-in should also be checked to make sure it is equal on each side, but each wheel is not adjustable individually (the entire axle can be shifted if the toe angles are not equal). Camber and caster are usually measured to check for a bent axle.

Getting the proper wheel alignment is a very exacting process, one in which complicated and expensive machines are necessary to perform the job properly. Because of this, you should have a technician with the proper equipment perform these tasks. We will, however, use this space to give you a basic idea of what is involved with a wheel alignment so you can better understand the process and deal intelligently with the workshop that does the work.

Toe-in is the turning in of the wheels. The purpose of a toe specification is to ensure parallel rolling of the wheels. In a vehicle with zero toe-in, the distance between the front edges of the wheels will be the same as the distance between the rear edges of the wheels. The actual amount of toe-in is normally only a millimetre or so. On the front end, toe-in is controlled by the track rod end position on the track rod. Incorrect toe-in will cause the tyres to wear improperly by making them scrub against the road surface.

Camber is the tilting of the wheels from vertical when viewed from one end of the vehicle. When the wheels tilt out at the top, the camber is said to be positive (+). When the wheels tilt in at the top the camber is negative (–). The amount of tilt is measured in degrees from vertical and this measurement is called the camber angle. This angle affects the amount of tyre tread which contacts the road and compensates for changes in the suspension geometry when the vehicle is cornering or travelling over an undulating surface.

Caster is the tilting of the front steering axis from the vertical. A tilt toward the rear is positive caster and a tilt toward the front is negative caster.

# Chapter 11
## Body

---

## Contents

---

## Degrees of difficulty

| Easy, suitable for novice with little experience | Fairly easy, suitable for beginner with some experience | Fairly difficult, suitable for competent DIY mechanic | Difficult, suitable for experienced DIY mechanic | Very difficult, suitable for expert DIY or professional |
|---|---|---|---|---|

## 1  General information

The Volkswagen New Beetle features a 'unibody' layout, using a floor pan with front and rear frame side rails which support the body components, front and rear suspension systems and other mechanical components. Certain components are particularly vulnerable to accident damage and can be unbolted and repaired or renewed. Among these parts are the bumpers, front and rear wings, doors, the bonnet and hatch. Only general body maintenance practices and body panel repair procedures within the scope of the do-it-yourselfer are included in this chapter.

Although all covered models are very similar, some procedures may differ somewhat from one body to another.

*Caution 1: These models are equipped with an anti-theft radio. Before performing a procedure that requires disconnecting the battery, make sure you have the proper activation code.*

*Caution 2: Disconnecting the battery can cause driveability problems that require a scan tool to remedy. See Chapter 5 for the use of an auxiliary voltage input device ('memory-saver') before disconnecting the battery.*

 *Warning: Do not use a memory-saving device to preserve the ECM's memory when working on or near airbag system components.*

## 2  Body – maintenance

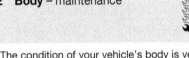

1 The condition of your vehicle's body is very important, because the resale value depends a great deal on it. It's much more difficult to repair a neglected or damaged body than it is to repair mechanical components. The hidden areas of the body, such as the wheel arches, the frame and the engine compartment, are equally important, although they don't require as frequent attention as the rest of the body.

2 Once a year, or every 12 000 miles, it's a good idea to have the underside of the body steam cleaned. All traces of dirt and oil will be removed and the area can then be inspected carefully for rust, damaged brake pipes, frayed electrical wires, damaged cables and other problems. The front suspension components should be greased after completion of this job.

3 At the same time, clean the engine and the engine compartment with a steam cleaner or water-soluble degreaser.

4 The wheel arches should be given close attention, since undercoating can peel away and stones and dirt thrown up by the tyres

can cause the paint to chip and flake, allowing rust to set in. If rust is found, clean down to the bare metal and apply an anti-rust paint.

5 The body should be washed about once a week. Wet the vehicle thoroughly to soften the dirt, then wash it down with a soft sponge and plenty of clean soapy water. If the surplus dirt is not washed off very carefully, it can wear down the paint.

6 Spots of tar or asphalt thrown up from the road should be removed with a cloth soaked in solvent.

7 Once every six months, wax the body and chrome trim. If a chrome cleaner is used to remove rust from any of the vehicle's plated parts, remember that the cleaner also removes part of the chrome, so use it sparingly. After cleaning chrome trim, apply paste wax to preserve it.

## 3  Vinyl trim – maintenance

Don't clean vinyl trim with detergents, caustic soap or petroleum-based cleaners. Plain soap and water works just fine, with a soft brush to clean dirt that may be ingrained. Wash the vinyl as frequently as the rest of the vehicle. After cleaning, application of a high-quality rubber and vinyl protectorant will help prevent oxidation and cracks. The protectorant can also be applied to weather-stripping, vacuum pipes and rubber hoses, which often fail as a result of chemical degradation, and to the tyres.

## 4  Upholstery and carpets – maintenance

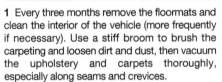

1 Every three months remove the floormats and clean the interior of the vehicle (more frequently if necessary). Use a stiff broom to brush the carpeting and loosen dirt and dust, then vacuum the upholstery and carpets thoroughly, especially along seams and crevices.

2 Dirt and stains can be removed from carpeting with basic household or automotive carpet shampoos available in spray cans. Follow the directions and vacuum again, then use a stiff brush to bring back the 'nap' of the carpet.

3 Most interiors have cloth or vinyl upholstery, either of which can be cleaned and maintained with a number of material-specific cleaners or shampoos available in auto supply stores. Follow the directions on the product for usage, and always spot-test any upholstery cleaner on an inconspicuous area (bottom edge of a backseat cushion) to ensure that it doesn't cause a colour change in the material.

4 After cleaning, vinyl upholstery should be treated with a protectorant. **Note:** *Make sure the protectorant container indicates the*

*product can be used on seats – some products may make a seat too slippery.* *Caution: Do not use protectorant on vinyl-covered steering wheels.*

5 Leather upholstery requires special care. It should be cleaned regularly with saddlesoap or leather cleaner. Never use alcohol, fuel, water, nail polish remover or thinner to clean leather upholstery.

6 After cleaning, regularly treat leather upholstery with a leather conditioner, rubbed in with a soft cotton cloth. Never use car wax on leather upholstery.

7 In areas where the interior of the vehicle is subject to bright sunlight, cover leather seating areas of the seats with a sheet if the vehicle is to be left out for any length of time.

## 5  Body repair – minor damage

### Plastic body panels

The following repair procedures are for minor scratches and gouges. Repair of more serious damage should be left to a dealer service department or qualified auto body workshop. Below is a list of the equipment and materials necessary to perform the following repair procedures on plastic body panels. Although a specific brand of material may be mentioned, it should be noted that equivalent products from other manufacturers may be used instead.

*Wax, grease and silicone removing solvent*
*Cloth-backed body tape*
*Sanding discs*
*Drill motor with three-inch disc holder*
*Hand sanding block*
*Rubber squeegees*
*Sandpaper*
*Non-porous mixing palette*
*Wood paddle or putty knife*
*Curved-tooth body file*
*Flexible parts repair material*

1 Remove the damaged panel, if necessary or desirable. In most cases, repairs can be carried out with the panel fitted.

2 Clean the area(s) to be repaired with a wax, grease and silicone removing solvent applied with a water-dampened cloth.

3 If the damage is structural, that is, if it extends through the panel, clean the backside of the panel area to be repaired as well. Wipe dry.

4 Sand the rear surface about 40 mm beyond the break.

5 Cut two pieces of fibreglass cloth large enough to overlap the break by about 40 mm. Cut only to the required length.

6 Mix the adhesive from the repair kit according to the instructions included with the kit, and apply a layer of the mixture approximately 3 mm thick on the backside of the panel. Overlap the break by at least 40 mm.

**7** Apply one piece of fibreglass cloth to the adhesive and cover the cloth with additional adhesive. Apply a second piece of fibreglass cloth to the adhesive and immediately cover the cloth with additional adhesive in sufficient quantity to fill the weave.

**8** Allow the repair to cure for 20 to 30 minutes at 16°C to 26°C.

**9** If necessary, trim the excess repair material at the edge.

**10** Remove all of the paint film over and around the area(s) to be repaired. The repair material should not overlap the painted surface.

**11** With a drill motor and a sanding disc (or a rotary file), cut a 'V' along the break line approximately 12 mm. Remove all dust and loose particles from the repair area.

**12** Mix and apply the repair material. Apply a light coat first over the damaged area; then continue applying material until it reaches a level slightly higher than the surrounding finish.

**13** Cure the mixture for 20 to 30 minutes at 16°C to 26°C.

**14** Roughly establish the contour of the area being repaired with a body file. If low areas or pits remain, mix and apply additional adhesive.

**15** Block sand the damaged area with sandpaper to establish the actual contour of the surrounding surface.

**16** If desired, the repaired area can be temporarily protected with several light coats of primer. Because of the special paints and techniques required for flexible body panels, it is recommended that the vehicle be taken to a paint workshop for completion of the body repair.

### Steel body panels

#### Repair of minor scratches

**17** If the scratch is superficial and does not penetrate to the metal of the body, repair is very simple. Lightly rub the scratched area with a fine rubbing compound to remove loose paint and built up wax. Rinse the area with clean water.

**18** Apply touch-up paint to the scratch, using a small brush. Continue to apply thin layers of paint until the surface of the paint in the scratch is level with the surrounding paint. Allow the new paint at least two weeks to harden, then blend it into the surrounding paint by rubbing with a very fine rubbing compound. Finally, apply a coat of wax to the scratch area.

**19** If the scratch has penetrated the paint and exposed the metal of the body, causing the metal to rust, a different repair technique is required. Remove all loose rust from the bottom of the scratch with a pocket-knife, then apply rust-inhibiting paint to prevent the formation of rust in the future. Using a rubber or nylon applicator, coat the scratched area with glaze-type filler. If required, the filler can be mixed with thinner to provide a very thin

paste, which is ideal for filling narrow scratches. Before the glaze filler in the scratch hardens, wrap a piece of smooth cotton cloth around the tip of a finger. Dip the cloth in thinner and then quickly wipe it along the surface of the scratch. This will ensure that the surface of the filler is slightly hollow. The scratch can now be painted over as described earlier in this Section.

#### Repair of dents

**20** When repairing dents, the first job is to pull the dent out until the affected area is as close as possible to its original shape. There is no point in trying to restore the original shape completely as the metal in the damaged area will have stretched on impact and cannot be restored to its original contours. It is better to bring the level of the dent up to a point that is about 3 mm below the level of the surrounding metal. In cases where the dent is very shallow, it is not worth trying to pull it out at all.

**21** If the backside of the dent is accessible, it can be hammered out gently from behind using a soft-face hammer. While doing this, hold a block of wood firmly against the opposite side of the metal to absorb the hammer blows and prevent the metal from being stretched.

**22** If the dent is in a section of the body which has double layers, or some other factor makes it inaccessible from behind, a different technique is required. Drill several small holes through the metal inside the damaged area, particularly in the deeper sections. Screw long, self-tapping screws into the holes just enough for them to get a good grip in the metal. Now pulling on the protruding heads of the screws with locking pliers can pull out the dent.

**23** The next stage of repair is the removal of paint from the damaged area and from 25 mm or so of the surrounding metal. This is easily done with a wire brush or sanding disc in a drill motor, although it can be done just as effectively by hand with sandpaper. To complete the preparation for filling, score the surface of the bare metal with a screwdriver or the tang of a file or drill small holes in the affected area. This will provide a good grip for the filler material. To complete the repair, see the Section on filling and painting.

#### Repair of rust holes or gashes

**24** Remove all paint from the affected area and from 25 mm or so of the surrounding metal using a sanding disc or wire brush mounted in a drill motor. If these are not available, a few sheets of sandpaper will do the job just as effectively.

**25** With the paint removed, you will be able to determine the severity of the corrosion and decide whether to renew the whole panel, if possible, or repair the affected area. New body panels are not as expensive as most people think and it is often quicker to refit a new panel than to repair large areas of rust.

**26** Remove all trim pieces from the affected

area except those which will act as a guide to the original shape of the damaged body, such as headlight shells, etc. Using metal snips or a hacksaw blade, remove all loose metal and any other metal that is badly affected by rust. Hammer the edges of the hole in to create a slight depression for the filler material.

**27** Wire-brush the affected area to remove the powdery rust from the surface of the metal. If the back of the rusted area is accessible, treat it with rust inhibiting paint.

**28** Before filling is done, block the hole in some way. This can be done with sheet metal riveted or screwed into place, or by stuffing the hole with wire mesh.

**29** Once the hole is blocked off, the affected area can be filled and painted. See the following subsection on filling and painting.

#### Filling and painting

**30** Many types of body fillers are available, but generally speaking, body repair kits which contain filler paste and a tube of resin hardener are best for this type of repair work. A wide, flexible plastic or nylon applicator will be necessary for imparting a smooth and contoured finish to the surface of the filler material. Mix up a small amount of filler on a clean piece of wood or cardboard (use the hardener sparingly). Follow the manufacturer's instructions on the package, otherwise the filler will set incorrectly.

**31** Using the applicator, apply the filler paste to the prepared area. Draw the applicator across the surface of the filler to achieve the desired contour and to level the filler surface. As soon as a contour that approximates the original one is achieved, stop working the paste. If you continue, the paste will begin to stick to the applicator. Continue to add thin layers of paste at 20-minute intervals until the level of the filler is just above the surrounding metal.

**32** Once the filler has hardened, the excess can be removed with a body file. From then on, progressively finer grades of sandpaper should be used, starting with a 180-grit paper and finishing with 600-grit wet-or-dry paper. Always wrap the sandpaper around a flat rubber or wooden block, otherwise the surface of the filler will not be completely flat. During the sanding of the filler surface, the wet-or-dry paper should be periodically rinsed in water. This will ensure that a very smooth finish is produced in the final stage.

**33** At this point, the repair area should be surrounded by a ring of bare metal, which in turn should be encircled by the finely feathered edge of good paint. Rinse the repair area with clean water until all of the dust produced by the sanding operation is gone.

**34** Spray the entire area with a light coat of primer. This will reveal any imperfections in the surface of the filler. Repair the imperfections with fresh filler paste or glaze filler and once more smooth the surface with sandpaper. Repeat this spray-and-repair procedure until you are satisfied that the surface of the filler and the feathered edge of the paint are perfect. Rinse the area with clean water and allow it to dry completely.

**35** The repair area is now ready for painting. Spray painting must be carried out in a warm, dry, windless and dust-free atmosphere. These conditions can be created if you have access to a large indoor work area, but if you are forced to work in the open, you will have to pick the day very carefully. If you are working indoors, dousing the floor in the work area with water will help settle the dust that would otherwise be in the air. If the repair area is confined to one body panel, mask off the surrounding panels. This will help minimise the effects of a slight mismatch in paint colour. Trim pieces such as chrome strips, door handles, etc, will also need to be masked off or removed. Use masking tape and several thickness of newspaper for the masking operations.

**36** Before spraying, shake the paint can thoroughly, then spray a test area until the spray painting technique is mastered. Cover the repair area with a thick coat of primer. The thickness should be built up using several thin layers of primer rather than one thick one. Using 600-grit wet-or-dry sandpaper, rub down the surface of the primer until it is very smooth. While doing this, the work area should be thoroughly rinsed with water and the wet-or-dry sandpaper periodically rinsed as well. Allow the primer to dry before spraying additional coats.

**37** Spray on the top coat, again building up the thickness by using several thin layers of paint. Begin spraying at the top of the repair area and then, using a side-to-side motion, work down until the whole repair area and about 50 mm inches of the surrounding original paint is covered. Remove all masking material 10 to 15 minutes after spraying on the final coat of paint. Allow the new paint at least two weeks to harden, then use a very fine rubbing compound to blend the edges of the new paint into the existing paint. Finally, apply a coat of wax.

## 6 Body repair – major damage

**1** Major damage must be repaired by an auto body workshop specifically equipped to perform unibody repairs. These shops have the specialised equipment required to do the job properly.
**2** If the damage is extensive, the body must be checked for proper alignment or the vehicle's handling characteristics may be adversely affected and other components may wear at an accelerated rate.
**3** Due to the fact that all of the major body components (bonnet, wings, etc) are separate and reneweable units, any seriously damaged components should be renewed rather than repaired.

## 7 Hinges and locks – maintenance

Once every 3000 miles, or every three months, the hinges and latch assemblies on the doors, bonnet and boot should be given a few drops of light oil or lock lubricant. The door latch strikers should also be lubricated with a thin coat of grease to reduce wear and ensure free movement. Lubricate the door and boot locks with spray-on graphite lubricant.

## 8 Windscreen and fixed glass – renewal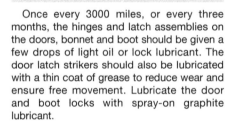

Renewal of the windscreen and fixed glass requires the use of special fast-setting adhesive/caulk materials and some specialised tools and techniques. These operations should be left to a dealer service department or a shop specialising in glass work.

## 9 Radiator grille – removal and refitting

**1** From behind the bumper cover, release the plastic clips and detach the grille **(see illustration)**.
**2** On models with fog lights, disconnect the electrical connectors, and remove the fog light mounting screws before detaching the grille.
**3** To refit, place the grille in position and seat the clips into the holes in the bumper cover.

## 10 Bonnet – removal, refitting and adjustment

**Note:** *The bonnet is heavy and somewhat awkward to remove and refit – at least two people should perform this procedure.*

### Removal and refitting

**1** Use blankets or pads to cover the cowl area of the body and the wings. This will protect the body and paint as the bonnet is lifted off.
**2** Scribe alignment marks around the hinge plate to insure proper alignment during refitting (a permanent-type felt-tip marker also will work for this) **(see illustration)**.
**3** Disconnect the windscreen washer hoses from the jets at the rear of the bonnet, and the underbonnet light, if applicable.
**4** Have an assistant support the weight of the bonnet, and remove the hinge-to-bonnet bolts **(see illustration 10.2)**.
**5** Lift off the bonnet.
**6** Refitting is the reverse of removal.

### Adjustment

**7** Fore-and-aft and side-to-side adjustment of the bonnet is done by moving the bonnet in relation to the hinge plates after loosening the bolts.
**8** Scribe or trace a line around the entire hinge plate so you can judge the amount of movement **(see illustration 10.2)**.

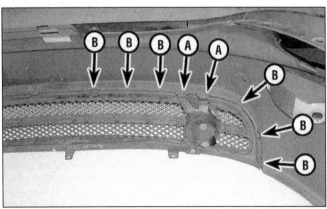

**9.1 Remove the fog light mounting screws (A), then release the tabs (B) from behind the front bumper cover to release the grille (right half shown, left side similar)**

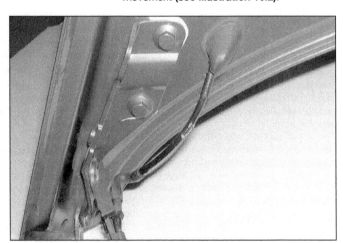

**10.2 Use a marking pen to outline the hinge plate**

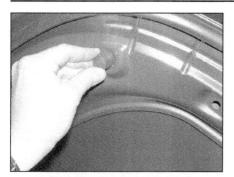

**10.10 Adjust the bonnet height by screwing the bonnet stops in or out**

9 Loosen the bolts and move the bonnet into correct alignment. Move it only a little at a time. Tighten the hinge bolts or nuts and carefully lower the bonnet to check the alignment.

10 Adjust the bonnet stops on the front edge of the bonnet, so the bonnet is flush with the wings when closed **(see illustration)**.

11 The safety lock assembly can also be adjusted up-and-down and side-to-side after loosening the nuts **(see illustration)**.

12 The bonnet lock assembly, as well as the hinges, should be periodically lubricated with white lithium-base grease to prevent sticking and wear.

## 11 Bonnet lock and release cable – removal and refitting

### Lock

1 Open the bonnet. On 2001 and later models, there is an exterior pull handle. To separate the handle from the lock, prise open the tabs on the handle with a screwdriver until the handle separates from the pin on the lock assembly.

2 Remove the nuts and detach the lock assembly **(see illustration 10.11)**.

3 Detach the cable end from the back of the lock assembly, the remove the lock **(see illustration)**.

4 Refitting is the reverse of removal.

### Cable

5 Use a screwdriver to release the cable end, then detach the cable case from the bracket on the back of the lock **(see illustration 11.3)**.

6 In the passenger compartment, remove the left-hand side kick panel, prise out the clip and remove the bonnet release handle **(see illustrations)**.

7 Remove the bonnet release handle mounting screws, pull the handle mount out and release the cable **(see illustration)**.

8 Under the dash, remove the cable grommet from the bulkhead.

9 Release the clips at the inner edge of the left front inner wing until the cable is free of the body.

10 Attach a wire or string to the bonnet end of the old cable and pull the cable through into the vehicle's interior.

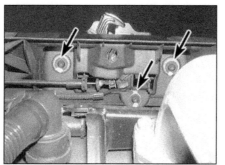

**10.11 Loosen the bolts (arrowed) and move the lock to adjust the bonnet fit in the closed position**

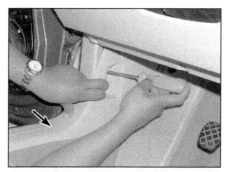

**11.6a Pull back the bonnet release handle to remove the kick panel screw, and pry up at the door sill end (arrowed)**

11 Connect the string or wire to the new cable and pull it through the bulkhead into the engine compartment.

12 The remainder of refitting is the reverse of removal.

## 12 Bumpers – removal and refitting

1 Front and rear bumpers on all models are composed of an exterior cover, and a foam-covered structural beam.

### Front bumper

2 Apply the handbrake, raise the vehicle and support it securely on axle stands. Disconnect the fog lights (if equipped), and remove the

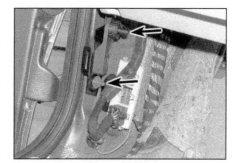

**11.7 Bonnet release handle mounting screws (arrowed)**

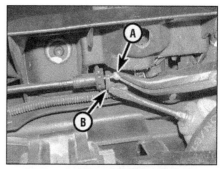

**11.3 Detach the cable end from the lock (A) and the cable body from the bracket (B)**

**11.6b Pull the bonnet release lever back enough to allow using a small screwdriver to pull the clip out, then remove the handle and the kick panel**

radiator grille (see Section 9). Remove the wheel arch liners (see Section 13).

3 The front bumper cover is part of the front body assembly, which consists of the two front wings and the bumper cover. The assembly should be removed as a unit (see Section 13).

4 With the assembly removed, remove the bolts and nuts securing the front bumper beam to the impact dampers at the chassis **(see illustration)**.

5 Refitting is the reverse of the removal procedure.

### Rear bumper

6 The rear bumper cover is part of the rear body assembly, which includes the bumper cover and the rear wings. Like the front assembly, it's very difficult to remove the rear bumper cover while the rear wings remain on the vehicle. See

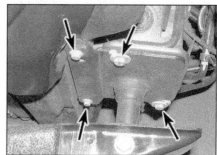

**12.4 Remove the bolts/nuts (arrowed) to remove the bumper beam**

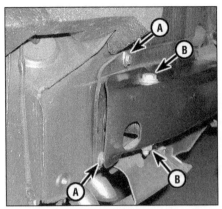

**12.7 Remove the bolts/nuts (arrowed) to remove the rear bumper beam**

A Impact damper mounting bolts
B Bumper beam mounting bolt/nut

Section 13 for removal of the rear assembly (wings and bumper cover together).

**7** If the rear bumper reinforcement beam is to be removed, remove the bolt and nuts **(see illustration)**.

**8** Refitting is the reverse of removal.

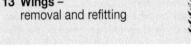

**13 Wings –**
removal and refitting

**Front**

**1** Loosen the front wheel bolts, raise the

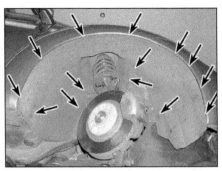

**13.3a Remove these screws (arrowed) and the wheel arch liner**

vehicle, support it securely on axle stands and remove the front wheels. The front bumper cover is part of the front body assembly, which includes the bumper cover and both wings. It's best to remove the assembly as a unit, then separate the wing(s). **Note:** *This is a job for two people.*

**2** Apply wide masking tape along the front edge of the scuttle and doors to prevent scratching the paint during wing removal.

**3** Remove the screws and take out the plastic wheel arch liner **(see illustrations)**.

**4** Remove the wing-to-scuttle mounting bolts **(see illustrations)**.

**5** Remove the headlight housings, disconnect the direction indicator lights, and if applicable, disconnect the electrical connectors at the back of the fog lights. Remove the one body

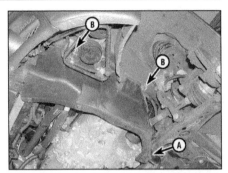

**13.3b To remove the lower splash shield (not required for wing removal), remove the screw (A) and the two fasteners (B)**

bolt inside the headlight housing opening **(see illustration)**.

**6** Remove the screws along the bottom edge of the front bumper cover and the top of the bonnet opening **(see illustrations)**.

**7** Open the bonnet, and remove the screws securing the front assembly to the body **(see illustration)**.

**8** Have an assistant help you remove front body assembly from the vehicle, pulling the back of the wings out slightly while pulling the whole assembly forward. To renew the wing, remove the bolts holding the front of the wing to the bumper cover.

**9** Refitting is the reverse of removal. Make sure that the foam cushion for the top rear of the wing is in place and that the anti-squeak strip along the top of the body is aligned with

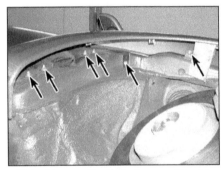

**13.4a Remove the bolts (arrowed) inside the wheel arch**

**13.4b At the front of the wheel arch, remove the wing brace bolts (A) and the brace (B)**

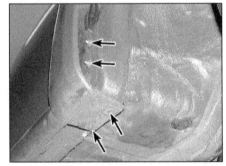

**13.4c At the rear of the wheel arch, remove the brace bolts and the two lower wing to sill bolts (arrowed)**

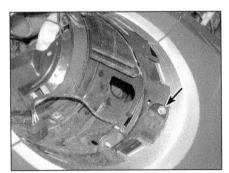

**13.5 Remove this one bolt (arrowed) securing the headlight housing cavity to the front bumper cover**

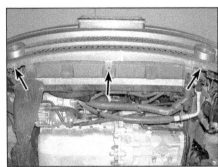

**13.6a Remove the screws (arrowed) along the bottom front of the bumper cover . . .**

**13.6b . . . and the two in the front of the bonnet opening (arrowed)**

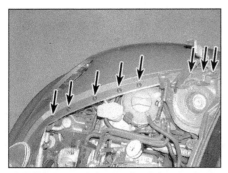

**13.7 Where each front wing joins the body, remove the screws (arrowed)**

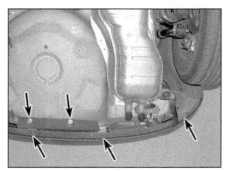

**13.13 Remove the screws (arrowed) securing the rear bumper cover to the bottom of the body**

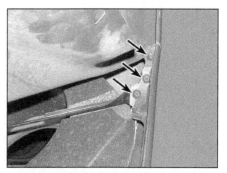

**13.14a Pull back the plastic wheel arch liner to access these screws (arrowed)**

the holes in the body. **Note:** *Most body bolts on the New Beetle pass through two body part flanges; on one side they must be fitted with reinforcement strips or zinc washers, and they thread into a metal strip with nuts welded on. These should all be in place finger-tight until the final wing-to-bumper cover fit is exact before final tightening.*

**10** Tighten all nuts, bolts and screws securely.

### *Rear*

**11** Loosen the rear wheel bolts, raise the vehicle, support it securely on axle stands and remove the rear wheels. As with the front body assembly, the rear wings and bumper cover are best removed as a unit, then separated for individual part renewal.

**12** Apply wide masking tape along the rear quarter panel to prevent scratching the paint during wing removal.

**13** From below, remove the fasteners retaining the bottom edge of the rear bumper cover to the body **(see illustration)**. Disconnect the electrical connectors at the number plate light and reversing lights.

**14** In each rear wheel arch, remove the screws securing the wheel arch liner to the bumper cover ends, and the bolts holding the wing to the body **(see illustrations)**.

**15** Refer to Chapter 12, Section 17, and remove the taillights.

**16** At the right-side wing, disconnect the fuel

door release cable from the fuel door opening by levering out the small retaining clip inside the fuel door opening.

**17** Open the rear hatch and remove the remaining bolts securing the wing and bumper cover to the body **(see illustration)**. With an assistant, spread the front portion of the plastic rear wings apart enough to clear the body and lift off the rear assembly. With the assembly off, there is access to the bolts and reinforcement strips that hold the wings to the rear bumper cover.

**18** Refitting is the reverse of the removal procedure. Make sure the anti-squeak material is in place at the wing/body joint.

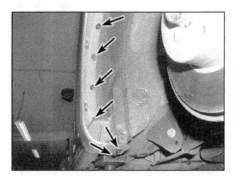

**13.14b At the front of the rear wheel arch, remove these bolts (arrowed) holding the wing to the body . . .**

### 14 Scuttle cover and plenum closeout panel – removal and refitting

**1** Open the bonnet, then refer to Chapter 12, Section 18, and remove the windscreen wiper arms.

**2** Remove the rubber weatherstrip at the front of the scuttle cover **(see illustration)**.

**3** Lift off the plastic scuttle cover.

**4** To remove the plenum closeout panel, first separate the Secondary Air Injection solenoid from its bracket on the plenum closeout panel **(see illustration)**.

**13.14c . . . and these (arrowed) along the top edge**

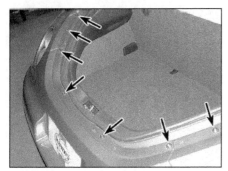

**13.17 Remove the bolts (arrowed) around the rear hatch opening (not all are shown in this view)**

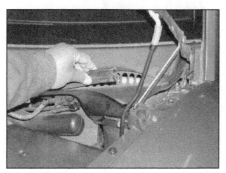

**14.2 With the wiper arms removed, pull off the rubber weatherstrip, then lift off the scuttle cover**

**14.4 Remove the Secondary Air Injection solenoid (arrowed) from the front of the plenum closeout panel**

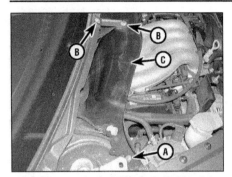

14.5 Remove the bolt (A) at each side of the panel, the two bolts (B) at the centre bracket, then remove the closeout panel (C)

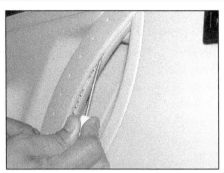

15.2a Pry off the door pull cover . . .

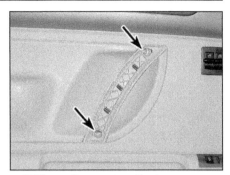

15.2b . . . then remove the two screws (arrowed)

5 Remove the fasteners and lift out the plenum closeout panel **(see illustration)**.
6 Refitting is the reverse of removal.

### 15 Door trim panels – removal and refitting

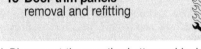

1 Disconnect the negative battery cable, but read the **Cautions** in Section 1.
2 Remove the door pull cover and the two door panel screws behind it **(see illustrations)**.

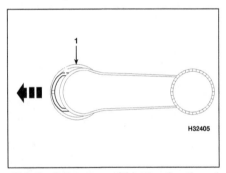

15.3 Push the spacer (1) in the direction of the arrow to disengage the clip behind the manual window handle

3 If applicable with manual windows, slide the spacer (between the handle and the door trim panel) away from the knob end of the handle to release the handle clip **(see illustration)**. Remove the handle.
4 Remove the screws retaining the bottom of the door panel to the door **(see illustration)**.
5 Using a flat-bladed lever, prise along the sides of the door panel to disengage the clips.
6 Grasp the trim panel and pull up sharply to detach it from the door. Disconnect the inner door handle lock rod from the handle and unplug any electrical connectors **(see illustrations)**.

15.4 Remove the screws (arrowed) securing the door panel – then use a flat-bladed lever along the front and rear edges of the panel to release the clips in the back of the panel – later models also have a bolt at the lower rear of the door panel

7 To refit the panel, connect the wire harness connectors and door handle rod, then place the panel in position in the door. Press the trim panel down into place until the clips are seated.
8 Refit the screws and screw covers, where used. Reconnect the negative battery cable.

### 16 Door – removal, refitting and adjustment

1 Remove the door trim panel (see Section 15).
2 If removing the driver's door, refer to Section 11 and remove the bonnet release handle assembly from the kick panel. On either side, pull first at the top, then the bottom to release the kick panel from its clips.
3 At the front door pillar, disconnect the electrical connectors **(see illustration)**. Pull the rubber harness boot out of the body and feed the harness out.
4 Remove the bolt securing the door check strap to the door **(see illustration)**.
5 Place a jack under the door or have an assistant on hand to support it when the hinge bolts are removed. **Note:** *If a jack is used, place a rag between it and the door to protect the door's painted surfaces.*
6 Scribe around the hinge mounting bolts

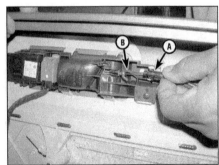

15.6a Pry the door handle cable end (A) from the handle assembly at the back of the door panel, then twist to disengage the hook (B)

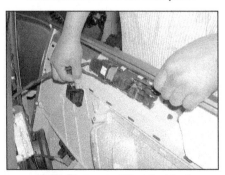

15.6b Disconnect the electrical connectors at the door panel

16.3 Disconnect the electrical connectors (arrowed) in the door jamb and feed the wires out through the body pillar

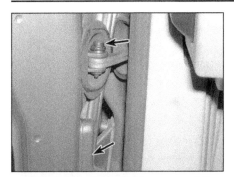

16.4 Remove the bolt (upper arrow) to detach the door check strap from the body – pull the rubber boot out (lower arrow) and feed the door wiring harness out

16.6 Remove the hinge bolts (arrowed) and lift the door off (upper hinge shown, lower hinge similar)

16.8 The striker can be loosened and moved slightly to achieve secure latch engagement

with a marking pen, remove the bolts and carefully lift off the door **(see illustration)**. **Note:** *The lower door hinges are attached with bolts from the inside of the door, requiring that the inner door carrier be removed (see Section 17).*
7 Refitting is the reverse of removal, making sure to align the hinge with the marks made during removal before tightening the bolts.
8 Following refitting of the door, check the alignment and adjust it if necessary as follows:
*a) Up-and-down and in-and-out adjustments are made by loosening the hinge-to-door bolts/nuts and moving the door as necessary.*

17.5 Remove the two Torx bolts (arrowed) securing the latch to the door frame

*b) Forward-and-backward adjustments are made by loosening the hinge-to-body bolts and moving the door as necessary.*
*c) The door lock striker can also be adjusted both up-and-down and sideways to provide positive engagement with the lock mechanism. This is done by loosening the mounting screws and moving the striker as necessary (see illustration).*

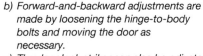

### 17 Door lock, lock cylinder and outside handle – removal and refitting

### Lock

1 Remove the door trim panel (see Section 15). The door latch, radio speaker and window regulator are all attached to a large metal carrier, which must be removed from the door as a unit.
2 Refer to Steps 9 and 10 and remove the lock cylinder.
3 Lower the window glass until the glass track bolts can be loosened (see Section 18). With the glass separated from the regulator, pull the glass up by hand and tape it in the UP position.
4 Refer to Steps 2 and 3 in Section 16 and

disconnect the electrical harness for the door, feeding the wires into the door cavity.
5 Remove the two Torx-head mounting screws from the end of the door (it may be necessary to use an impact-type screwdriver to loosen them) and detach the latch from the door **(see illustration)**.
6 Remove the bolts securing the carrier to the door, then lift it up and out, working towards the hinged end of the door **(see illustration)**. At the rear of the carrier, disconnect the electrical connector at the door lock solenoid.
7 To remove the latch from the carrier, use a punch to drive out the two pins, then flip the latch over and disconnect the cable and the linkage rod **(see illustration)**.
8 Refitting is the reverse of the removal procedure.

### Lock cylinder

9 Remove the plastic plug in the lock end of the door and loosen the setscrew at the lock cylinder **(see illustration)**.
*Caution: Do not turn the setscrew all the way out, or it will fall into the door.*
10 Insert the key in the lock cylinder and pull the cylinder out of the door.
11 Refitting is the reverse of removal.

### Outside handle

12 Refer to Steps 9 and 10 and remove the lock cylinder.

17.6 Plastic carrier mounting bolts (arrowed)

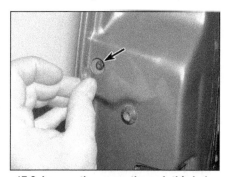

17.7 Tap out these pins (A) with a punch and hammer, then disconnect the cable (B)

17.9 Loosen the screw through this hole (arrowed) after removing the plug

**17.13 Pull this clip (arrowed), then remove the door handle**

13 Remove the clip, swing the key-end of the handle outward from the door, then rearward **(see illustration)**.
14 Refitting is the reverse of removal.

## 18 Door window glass –
removal and refitting

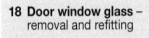

### Removal

1 Remove the door trim panel (see Section 15).
2 Working through the two holes in the carrier, use a socket and extension to loosen the bolts retaining the regulator glass channel

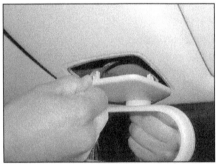

**20.1 Pull down the panel in the overhead console and disconnect the electrical connector to the overhead light**

**20.2 Push inward on the two clips, then slide the mirror base rearward out of the panel**

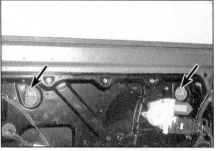

**18.2 Remove the rubber plugs from the carrier, then loosen the glass track bolts (arrowed) – you may have to spread the clips with a screwdriver to renew the glass**

to the glass **(see illustration)**. Separate the clamps to free the glass.
3 Secure the glass in this position with tape, then lower the window regulator all the way down.
4 Tilt the rear end of the glass up and out of the door until the glass clears the door.

### Refitting

5 Raise the regulator until the glass channel bolts align with the holes in the carrier **(see illustration 18.2)**.
6 Lower the glass into the door front end first, then tilt it until the clamps fit around the glass and the bolts can be tightened.
7 The remainder of the refitting is the reverse of the removal procedure.

## 19 Door window glass regulator/motor –
removal and refitting

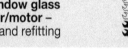

1 Remove the door trim panel (see Section 15).
2 The window regulator and motor is part of the plastic inner door carrier.
3 The regulator is part of the carrier assembly and can't be renewed separately, although the window winder (manual windows) or electric motor (power windows) can be renewed.
4 On manual-window models, remove the carrier from the door (See Section 17), access the fasteners on the back of the window winder and remove the winder from the front.

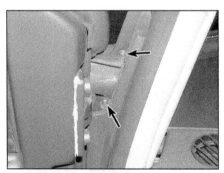

**20.6 Remove the mirror hinge cover mounting screws (arrowed)**

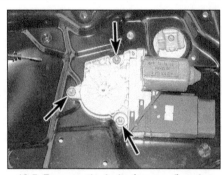

**19.5 Remove the bolts (arrowed) at the front of the carrier assembly to remove the power window motor**

5 On models with power windows, remove the fastener(s) at the front of the carrier and remove the motor **(see illustration)**. The carrier does not have to be removed from the door.
6 Refitting is the reverse of removal.

## 20 Mirrors and associated components – removal and refitting

### Interior mirror

1 Pull down the panel at the front of the overhead console **(see illustration)**.
2 Depress the spring clip where the base of the mirror fits through the overhead panel, and slide the mirror out **(see illustration)**.
3 Refitting is the reverse of removal.

### Exterior mirror assembly

4 Refer to Section 15 and remove the door trim panel.
5 Disconnect the electrical connector for the mirror, inside the door, then apply tape to the connector so that it can be withdrawn through the mirror harness hole in the outside of the door without snagging.
6 With the door open, remove the two screws securing the mirror's hinge cover, then remove the hinge cover **(see illustration)**.
7 Remove the screws and detach the mirror from the door **(see illustration)**. Work the mirror harness through the hole in the door.
8 Refitting is the reverse of removal.

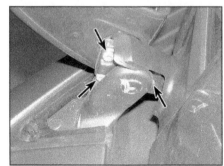

**20.7 Swivel the mirror so that all three of the screws (arrowed) can be removed, then take the mirror off its base**

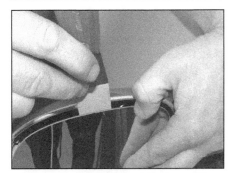

20.9a Carefully lever out the top of the mirror glass . . .

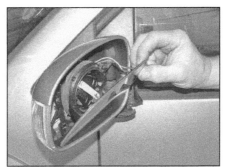

20.9b . . . from the motor . . .

20.10 . . . then disconnect the wiring

## Exterior mirror glass

**Note:** *The mirror glass is clipped into place. Removal of the glass without the VW special forked tool (number 80-200) is likely to result in breakage of the glass. Wear protective gloves and glasses to prevent personal injury.*

9 Press in the bottom of the mirror glass so that the top edge is furthest from the housing. Protect the edge of the housing with masking tape, then insert the special tool and lever the mirror glass from its mounting clips. Take great care when removing the glass; do not use excessive force as the glass is easily broken. If the VW special tool is not available, use a flat-bladed lever with tape around to prevent any damage to the mirror housing **(see illustrations)**.

10 Disconnect the wiring from the mirror heating element **(see illustration)**.
11 Refitting is the reverse of removal. Press firmly at the centre of the mirror glass taking care not to use excessive force, as the glass is easily broken.

## Exterior mirror housing

12 Remove the mirror glass as described in paragraphs 5 and 6.

### Early models

13 Fold the mirror assembly forwards and position the glass vertical to ease the removal of the housing.
14 Remove the small plastic plug in the bottom of the mirror assembly, then insert a screwdriver. Carefully push the screwdriver

forwards to release the securing clip, pulling the cover upwards over the mirror glass to remove **(see illustrations)**.

### Later models

**Note:** *On later models, the mirror housing incorporates the direction indicator side repeater.*

15 Using a screwdriver, carefully release the surround from inside the mirror housing, starting at the upper, inner corner **(see illustrations)**.
16 Disconnect the side repeater wiring from the mirror base unit **(see illustration)**.
17 Using a screwdriver, release the upper clip securing the housing to the rear of the mirror bracket **(see illustration)**.

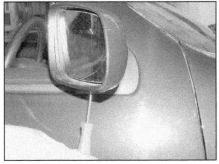

20.14a Push the screwdriver forwards . . .

20.14b . . . then lift the cover upwards over the mirror glass

20.15a Use a screwdriver to release the surround . . .

20.15b . . . then remove it from inside the mirror housing

20.16 Disconnect the wiring . . .

20.17 . . . release the housing upper clip . . .

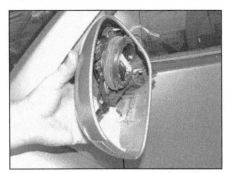

20.18a . . . then withdraw the housing . . .

20.18b . . . noting the location slot on the inner end of the housing

**18** Unhook the bottom of the housing from the base unit, then lift it upwards noting that the inner end of the housing locates on a vertical extension. Withdraw the housing from the base unit **(see illustrations)**.
**19** Refitting is the reverse of removal.

### Exterior mirror switch

**20** Refer to Chapter 12.

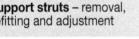

**21 Rear hatch and hatch support struts** – removal, refitting and adjustment

**Note:** *The procedure is virtually the same for the 2003 and later convertible rear lid.*

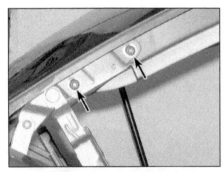

21.3 Draw around the bolt heads (arrowed) with a marking pen so the hatch can be installed in the same position

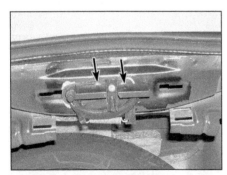

21.8b To adjust the striker, mark around the edges with a pen, then loosen the bolts (arrowed) and move the striker slightly and retighten

**Note:** *The hatch is heavy and somewhat awkward to remove and refit – at least two people should perform this procedure.*

### Hatch

**1** Open the hatch and cover the edges of the boot compartment with pads or cloths to protect the painted surfaces when the lid is removed.
**2** Disconnect the electrical connector at the rear window demister, if applicable.
**3** Use a marking pen to make alignment marks around the hinge bolt heads **(see illustration)**.
**4** Prop the hatch open with a long prop like a broom handle. Refer to Steps 9, 10 and 11 and remove the two support struts.
**5** While an assistant supports its weight,

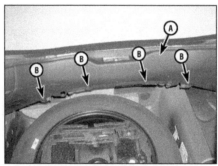

21.8a To access the striker, remove the screws (arrowed) and this lower trim panel in the boot

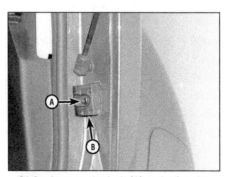

21.8c Loosen the bolt (A) and raise the buffer (B) – close and open the hatch, then check the height of the buffer; raise it 1 or 2 mm and tighten the bolt

remove the hinge bolts from both sides and lift the hatch off.
**6** Refitting is the reverse of removal. **Note:** *When reinstalling the hatch, align the hinge bolt heads with the marks made during removal.*
**7** After refitting, close the hatch and see if it's in proper alignment with the surrounding panels. Fore-and-aft and side-to-side adjustments of the hatch are controlled by the position of the hinge bolts in the holes. To adjust it, loosen the hinge bolts, reposition the hatch and retighten the bolts.
**8** The height of the hatch in relation to the surrounding body panels when closed can be adjusted by loosening the lock striker bolts, repositioning the striker and retightening the bolts **(see illustrations)**. Some adjustment can also be made through positioning the adjustment 'buffer' cushion **(see illustration)**.

### Hatch support struts

**9** The hatch supports are attached to upper and lower studs on the body and the hatch.
**10** To renew hatch supports, open the hatch and support it with a prop.
**11** Prise out the locking caps at the top and bottom of the support struts and pull the struts from their mounting studs **(see illustration)**. **Note:** *Only prise out the clips just enough to release the strut from the ball-stud. If the clip comes completely off, the strut will have to be renewed.* **Note:** *Always renew support struts as a pair, but refit the new one on one side of the vehicle before removing the old one from the other side. Always have one strut in place.*
**12** Refitting is the reverse of the removal procedure.

**22 Rear hatch lock and lock cylinder** – removal and refitting

### Lock

**1** Open the hatch and remove the two screws, then use a flat-bladed lever to

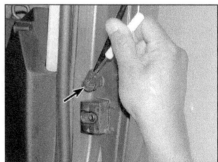

21.11 Pry the hatch support strut locking clips out (arrowed), then pry the ends from their mounting studs (lower end shown, upper end similar)

**22.1 Remove the screws (arrowed), then use a flat-bladed lever to pry around the edges of the hatch trim panel**

prise off the hatch trim panel **(see illustration)**.

2 Scribe a line around the lock assembly for a reference point to aid the refitting procedure.

3 Disconnect the electrical connector (on power models), pop the link from the rod connecting the lock and the lock cylinder, and remove the latch mounting screws **(see illustration)**.

4 Refitting is the reverse of removal.

### Lock cylinder

5 Open the hatch and remove the two screws, then use a trim tool to prise off the

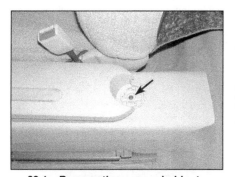

**23.1a Remove the rear cupholder to access this screw (arrowed) . . .**

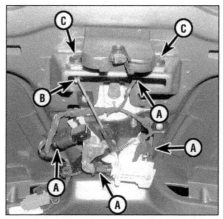

**22.3 Disconnect the electrical connectors (A, only one is on the latch itself), pry off the control rod (B), then remove the mounting screws (C)**

hatch lower trim panel **(see illustration 22.1)**.

6 Disconnect the lock cylinder rod and remove the three screws **(see illustration)**.

7 Lower the lock cylinder and its carrier down from the hatch. **Note:** *The exterior VW emblem will come off as you take down the carrier, since the carrier screws go through the hatch and into the emblem.*

8 Refitting is the reverse of removal.

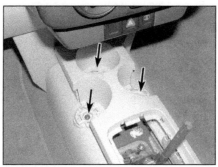

**23.1b . . . and the cupholders at the front of the console to access these screws (arrowed)**

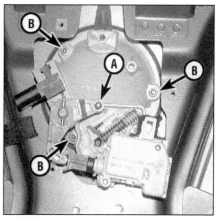

**22.6 Disconnect the lock cylinder rod from the stud (A), then remove the screws (B) – when you pull down the lock cylinder and carrier, the VW emblem on the outside will also come off**

### 23 Centre console – removal and refitting

⚠ *Warning: The models covered by this manual are equipped with Supplemental Restraint Systems (SRS), more commonly known as airbags. Always disable the airbag system before working in the vicinity of any airbag system components to avoid the possibility of accidental deployment of the airbags, which could cause personal injury (see Chapter 12).*

1 Remove the front and rear cupholders to access the screws holding the console cover **(see illustrations)**.

2 Remove the one screw near the handbrake handle and prise up the console cover to release it from the clips. Disconnect the electrical connector to the power outlet **(see illustrations)**.

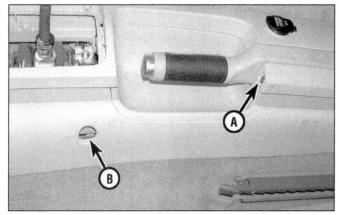

**23.2a Remove this screw (A) at the rear of the handbrake cavity, and remove the plastic caps to access a screw on each side of the console (B)**

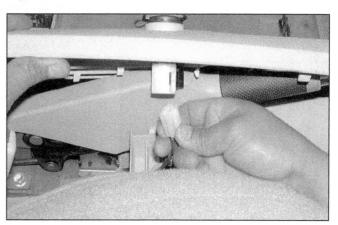

**23.2b Pry up the console cover, then disconnect the electrical connector from the power outlet in the cover**

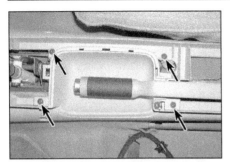

**23.3a Remove the screws (arrowed) around the handbrake handle . . .**

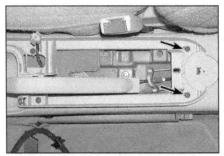

**23.3b . . . then these two (arrowed) at the rear of the console . . .**

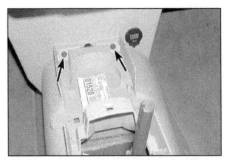

**23.3c . . . and these two (arrowed) at the front of the console**

3 Remove the screws and lift the console out **(see illustrations)**. Note: *The screw locations vary with the year and model, but are visible on all models when the upper panel is removed.*
4 Refitting is the reverse of the removal procedure.

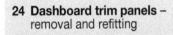

**24 Dashboard trim panels –**
removal and refitting

*Warning: The models covered by this manual are equipped with Supplemental Restraint Systems (SRS), more commonly known as airbags. Always disable the airbag system before working in the vicinity of any airbag system components to avoid the possibility of accidental deployment of*

*the airbags, which could cause personal injury (see Chapter 12).*

### Dashboard end caps

1 The end caps are held in place by clips.
2 Grasp the cover securely and pull sharply to remove it. If necessary, gently prise with a trim tool.
3 Refitting is the reverse of removal.

### Instrument cluster bezel

4 Lower the tilt steering wheel to its lowest position.
5 Pull the instrument cluster bezel straight back to release the three clips **(see illustration)**.
6 Refitting is the reverse of removal.

### Driver's knee bolster

7 Remove the screws retaining the bottom of the bolster to the instrument panel **(see illustration)**. Remove the driver's side dashboard end cap to access two side screws.

8 Pull backward on the top of the bolster to release it from the clips, and disconnect the electrical connectors at the headlight and dimmer switches.
9 If the bolster reinforcement panel needs to be removed to perform a repair procedure, remove the reinforcement panel screws **(see illustration)**.
10 Refitting is the reverse of removal.

### Centre trim panels

11 To access the upper screws for the centre trim panel, push forward on the centre panel's front extension until it comes free of its clips, then lift it up and off **(see illustration)**.
12 Refer to Chapter 12 and remove the radio.
13 Remove the screws at the top of the centre trim panel, then the two that had been hidden by the radio **(see illustrations)**. Lift out the trim panel.
14 Refitting is the reverse of removal.

**24.5 Pull straight back on the instrument cluster bezel to remove it**

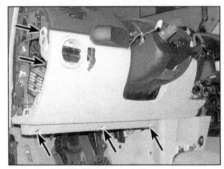

**24.7 The bolster is held by screws (arrowed) at the side, bottom and clips at the top (LHD model shown)**

**24.9 Remove the screws (arrowed) to remove the knee bolster reinforcement panel (LHD model shown)**

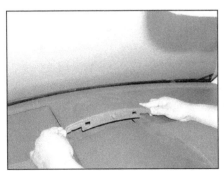

**24.11 Push forward on the centre trim panel forward extension, then lift it up to clear the clips**

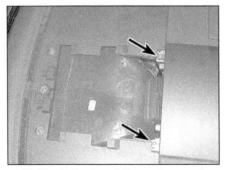

**24.13a At the top of the centre panel, remove the two screws (arrowed) . . .**

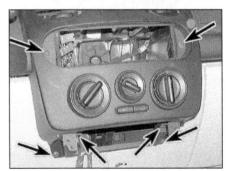

**24.13b . . . then remove the remaining screws (arrowed) and lift off the centre trim panel**

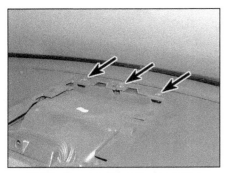

24.16a Remove these three screws (arrowed) . . .

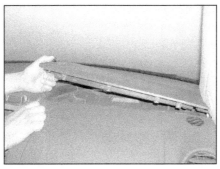

24.16b . . . then remove the left and right covers

24.18 Plenum closeout panel fasteners (arrowed) – right panel shown

## Upper dash covers and plenum closeout panels

**15** Remove the centre trim panel forward extension **(see illustration 24.11)**. On models so equipped, remove the flower vase and prise the vase bracket from its clips.

**16** Remove the Torx screws at the centre of the instrument panel securing the two upper dash covers, then pull the covers up from the centre of the dash, and remove the covers **(see illustrations)**. Note that the covers have location lugs which engage in the left- and right-hand A-pillars. On later models, there is a panel of switches below the HVAC controls. Remove the screws (prise off the caps for access), then lower the panel and disconnect the electrical connectors.

**17** Below the plastic dash covers are left and right plenum closeout panels. These need to

be removed for access to other components (the Engine Control Module is under the left cover, the pollen filter under the right on LHD models, or the left on RHD models).

**18** To remove the plenum closeout panels, remove the Torx screws and angle the panels out **(see illustration)**.

**19** Refitting is the reverse of the removal procedure.

### Glovebox

**20** Snap out the passengers side dashboard end cap and remove the glovebox screws **(see illustration)**.

**21** Remove the mounting screw (under a plastic cap) at the right-hand end of the glovebox assembly and the screws below the glovebox **(see illustrations)**.

**22** For some repair procedures, the frame

behind the glovebox may need to be removed. Remove the screws and the frame **(see illustration)**.

**23** Refitting is the reverse of removal.

## 25 Steering column covers – removal and refitting

**1** Remove the screws from the lower steering column cover, then remove the upper cover **(see illustration)**. On later models, remove the two bolts and the upper cover first, then the three bolts and the lower cover.

**2** To remove the lower cover, the steering wheel must be removed (see Chapter 10). Pull down on the steering column tilt lever, then remove the lower cover.

**3** Refitting is the reverse of removal.

## 26 Instrument panel – removal and refitting

⚠ **Warning: The models covered by this manual are equipped with Supplemental Restraint Systems**

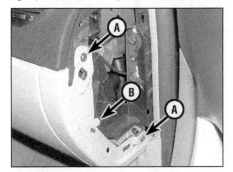

24.20 Remove screws (A) after removing the right dashboard end cap, then release the clip (B) (LHD model shown)

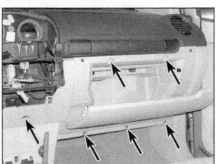

24.21a Remove the screws (arrowed) to take out the glovebox and panel (LHD model shown)

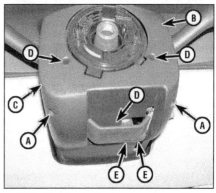

25.1 Steering column cover mounting details

A Upper cover mounting screws
B Upper column cover
C Lower column cover
D Lower cover mounting screws
E Tilt lever handle mounting screws

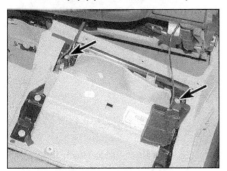

21.21b Disconnect the electrical connectors (arrowed) behind the glovebox (LHD model shown)

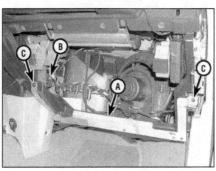

24.22 To remove the glovebox frame (A), remove the screws and the bolt (B and C) (LHD model shown)

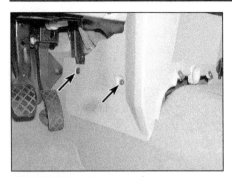

26.7 Remove the screws (arrows, two are on the left side, one on the right) and the panel below the centre of the dash (LHD model shown)

26.10 Centre instrument panel mounting screw (arrowed)

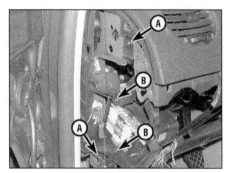

26.11a At the left end of the dash, remove the end cap, the instrument panel mounting screws (A) and the mounting screws for the fuse/relay box (B) (LHD model shown)

*(SRS), more commonly known as airbags. Always disable the airbag system before working in the vicinity of any airbag system components to avoid the possibility of accidental deployment of the airbags, which could cause personal injury (see Chapter 12).*
*Caution: This is a difficult procedure for the home mechanic, involving tedious dismantling and the disconnection/ reconnection of numerous electrical connectors. If you do attempt this procedure, make sure you take good notes and mark all matching connectors (and their mounting points) to aid reassembly.*

**1** Disconnect the negative battery cable (see Chapter 5). Read the **Cautions** in Section 1.
**2** Remove the centre console (see Section 23).
**3** Remove the steering column covers (see Section 25).
**4** Remove the dashboard trim panels (see Section 24).
**5** Remove the audio components, the multi-function switch, the instrument cluster, the centre dash switch panel and the passenger airbag (see Chapter 12).
**6** Remove the two screws and the trim panel below the driver's side of the instrument panel.
**7** Remove the screws and the panel below the centre of the dash **(see illustration)**.
**Note:** *Disconnect the electrical connector at the back of the power outlet.*
**8** At the upper centre of the instrument panel, remove the screws and the left and right upper dash and the plenum closeout panels below them (see Section 24).
**9** Refer to Chapter 3 and remove the heating/air conditioning controls.
**10** At the top centre of the dash, remove the mounting screw **(see illustration)**.
**11** Remove the instrument panel screws at the left and right end of the dash **(see illustrations)**.
**12** Remove all of the fasteners securing the instrument panel, and any electrical connectors still attached to the panel **(see illustrations)**. Have an assistant help you pull the panel back and out of the vehicle.
**13** Refitting is the reverse of removal.

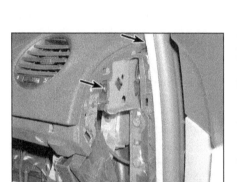

26.11b Remove the mounting screws (arrowed) at the right end of the instrument panel (LHD model shown)

26.12b With the cluster housing removed, one more dash screw (arrowed) is revealed

26.12d Arrows here indicate electrical connectors to be disconnected at the left end of the instrument panel – there are others at the lower centre and right-hand end (LHD model shown)

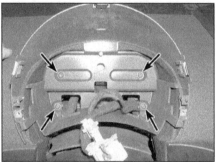

26.12a Behind the instrument cluster, remove the mounting screws (arrowed) and remove the cluster housing

26.12c Pry off the grab bar covering, then remove these two screws (arrowed)

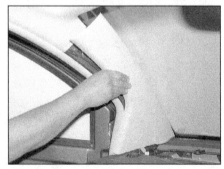

26.12e Use a flat-bladed lever to remove the inner windshield post trim covers

26.12f At each upper corner of the instrument panel, remove the upper mounting bolt and remove the instrument panel

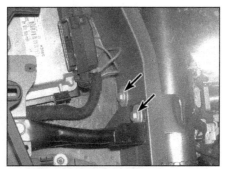

26.16 Remove the beam-to-bulkhead brace bolts (arrowed)

26.17a Remove the left beam-to-floor-bracket bolts (arrowed) (LHD model shown) . . .

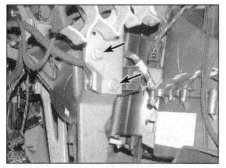

26.17b . . . and the right-hand bolts (arrowed) (LHD model shown)

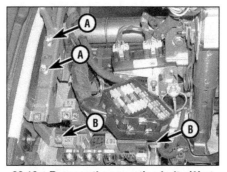

26.18a Remove the mounting bolts (A) at the left-hand end of the beam, and the fuse/relay box mounting bolts (B) – there are two bolts at the far right end of the beam also (LHD model shown)

26.18b With all fasteners and electrical harness removed, the beam can be pulled back for access to heating/air conditioning components

## Scuttle reinforcement beam

**14** With the instrument panel removed, the cowl reinforcement beam can be removed if necessary for other repair procedures, such as heating/air-conditioning work.

 *Warning: This is a difficult job for the home mechanic and involves safety-related critical fasteners.*

**15** Many electrical harnesses and connectors are attached with clips to the beam. Detach them all, taking notes and marking items with masking tape and marking pen to aid in reassembly.

**16** Under the centre of the dash, remove the bolts securing the beam to the brace from the bulkhead **(see illustration)**.

**17** Also at the centre of the dash, remove the beam-to-floor-bracket bolts **(see illustrations)**.

**18** At each end of the beam, remove the fasteners, then pull the beam away from the scuttle **(see illustrations)**.

**19** Refitting is the reverse of the removal procedure.

## 27 Seats – removal and refitting

 *Warning: The models covered by this manual are equipped with Supplemental Restraint Systems*

*(SRS), more commonly known as airbags. Always disable the airbag system before working in the vicinity of any airbag system components to avoid the possibility of accidental deployment of the airbags, which could cause personal injury (see Chapter 12).*

### Front

**1** The front seats on some models are equipped with side-impact airbags at the upper outside of the seatback. Refer to

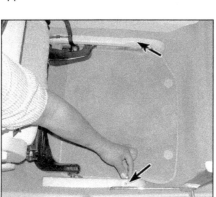

27.2a Remove the plastic buttons in the seat track covers, then remove the screws (arrowed) and the covers

Chapter 12 to disable the airbag system before working on front seats.

**2** Slide the seat forward and remove the seat track covers, move the seat rearward and remove the front seat track bolts and unplug any electrical connectors attached to the seat **(see illustrations)**.

**3** Slide the seat all the way to the back of the tracks and off. Remove the seat from the vehicle.

**4** Refitting is the reverse of removal.

### Rear

**5** Remove the seat bottom cushion by

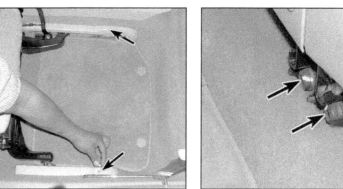

27.2b Remove the front seat front mounting bolts (arrowed), then slide the seat all the way back and off the tracks

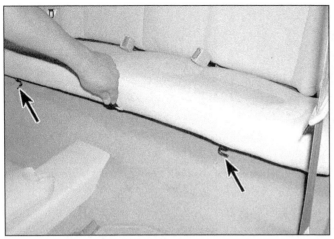

**27.5 Pull up the centre tab of the rear seat cushion to disengage the cushion from the two clips (arrowed)**

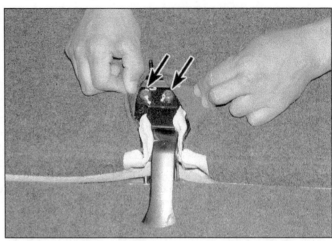

**27.6 Unzip the upholstery, then remove the two bolts (arrowed) at the bottom-centre of the seat back**

pushing in on the front edge of the cushion in the vicinity of the clips, to disengage part of the seat's wire frame from the clips **(see illustration)**. With the clips unhooked, lift up and remove the seat bottom from the vehicle. On later models with two-piece seat bottoms, push each cushion rearward until the seat frame clears the two body clips, then lift the cushion up and out.

6 Fold the seat back down, then remove the two centre bolts **(see illustration)**. Push the spring-loaded hook back to release the seat pivot at each side, then pull out the seat back. On models with two-piece rear seats, prise the connecting rod (one on each back cushion) from its ball stud, then remove the circlip from the lower hinge and prise the pivot pin out to remove the cushion. Repeat for the opposite cushion.

7 Refitting is the reverse of removal. Torque the two seat back bolts to 20 Nm (15 Ft-lbs).

## 28 Sunroof – adjustment

1 The position of the glass panel can be adjusted in the following manner.
2 Open the interior sunshade all the way

back and operate the sunroof until it is tilted open.
3 There are glass-mounting screws on each side of the sunroof opening, inside the vehicle. Remove the plastic covers **(see illustrations)**.
4 Loosen the front screws and lower the sunroof **(see illustration)**. Set the front edge of the glass approximately 1 mm below the surface of the roof when closed. Tighten the front screws.
5 Loosen the rear glass adjustment screws and adjust the glass approximately 1 mm above the roof at the rear. Tighten the rear screws.
6 When the adjustment is correct, tilt the sunroof open and refit the plastic covers over the glass rails.

## 29 Convertible top – general information

**Note:** *This information is general in nature, as it is intended to apply to all vehicle types, years and models.*

## Adjustments

**Note:** *The following are typical adjustments.*

*Some of these adjustments may not be provided for on your vehicle.*

### Latches

The latches secure the convertible top frame to the upper edge of the windshield frame. If the latches are too loose, the top will rattle and move side to side. If the latches are too tight, they will be difficult or impossible to secure. The hooks on some latches are threaded so they can be screwed in or out to tighten or loosen the latch; pliers are often necessary, so make sure you protect the finish of the hook with a rag. Other latches have set-screws that lock the hooks in place – loosen the set-screws (usually with an Allen or Torx key), position the hooks as desired, then tighten the set-screws.

Also keep in mind that a weatherstrip is attached to the front edge of the top. As this weatherstrip deteriorates over time, it will cause the latches and the front edge of the convertible top to become loose. The proper fix for this problem is to replace the deteriorated weatherstrip, which will also reduce wind noise.

### Power-top troubleshooting

Power tops are operated by a hydraulic cylinder that is mounted between the vehicle

**28.3a Unclip and pull out the first sunroof track plastic cover . . .**

**28.3b . . . then the second cover to reveal the tracks**

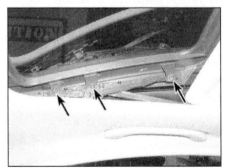

**28.4 The sunroof glass has three screws on each side (arrowed) used to adjust the fit of the glass to the roof**

body (at the left-rear) and the convertible-top framework. The cylinder receives hydraulic pressure from an electric motor/pump assembly that is located in the luggage compartment. When the switch is pressed to raise the top, the motor drives the pump in a direction that sends hydraulic pressure to the bottom end of each hydraulic cylinder, driving the pistons out of the cylinders, which raises the top. When the switch is pressed to lower the top, the motor turns in the opposite direction, sending hydraulic pressure to the top of each cylinder, driving the pistons down and lowering the top.

As a first step in troubleshooting, listen for the whirring sound of the motor as the switch is pressed. If there is no sound from the motor, proceed to *Electrical Troubleshooting*. If you can hear the motor running but the top does not raise, proceed to *Hydraulic/ mechanical troubleshooting*.

### Hydraulic/mechanical troubleshooting

Mechanical and hydraulic problems will cause the top to not open (or close) or to get stuck part-way through the process. If the motor is operating normally, there are generally two possible causes for these problems:
1) A hydraulic system malfunction (low fluid level, air in the system, inadequate pump pressure)
2) A mechanical binding in the top framework.

### Hydraulic system fluid level check

Locate the hydraulic motor/pump attached to the floor in the luggage compartment. The motor/pump is usually a canister-shaped assembly, approximately 12 in long. It will have an electrical connector and hoses attached to it. On the side or end of the motor/pump assembly will be a screw-type check plug. The fluid level is seen through the side of the reservoir. The level should be between Min and Max marks. If necessary, add fluid through the check-plug hole to bring the fluid level to normal, but do not exceed the Max mark.

Check your owner's manual for specific fluid recommendations, but generally, DEXRON III Automatic Transmission Fluid (ATF) is used. If you find a low fluid level, check for leaks at the pump, hoses and hydraulic cylinders. **Note:** *The fluid level should only be checked when the top is in the open position.*

### Hydraulic system bleeding

Air can get into the hydraulic system through leaks and if the fluid level is too low. Air in the system will generally cause excess noise and, in extreme cases, will cause the top to raise or lower only part-way.

To bleed the hydraulic system, first check the fluid level, then start the engine and raise and lower the top. If the fluid has excessive air, the top might not raise or lower, so you will need an assistant to hold the switch while you raise and lower the top slowly by hand. Raise and lower the top several times to work out all the air. Check the fluid level again, since it will likely drop as the air is expelled.

### Checking for binding

If the hydraulic system seems to be operating properly, disconnect the hydraulic cylinders from the top framework and operate the top by hand. The top should go up and down smoothly, without excessive effort.

If the top binds during manual operation, make sure all adjustments are correct and spray penetrating lubricant on all framework joints.

If the top is operating smoothly during manual operation but will not raise properly with the hydraulic cylinders connected, suspect a pump/motor assembly that is not providing adequate pressure.

### Electrical troubleshooting

If you cannot hear the motor running when the switch is pressed, first check for blown fuses and fusible links. If the fuses and fusible links are all OK, disconnect the electrical connector at the motor. Connect a 12-volt test-light to ground and probe each terminal of the disconnected wiring-harness connector while an assistant operates the switch. There should be power (light will illuminate) at one terminal with the switch in the TOP UP position and power at the other terminal with the switch in the TOP DOWN position.

If there is power, but the motor does not operate, check the ground circuit. On most models, there is a third wire from the motor that is attached to ground somewhere near the motor. It is common for this ground connection to become loose or corroded, causing the motor to stop functioning. If the motor is receiving power and has a good ground, but it is still not functioning, the motor itself is the problem. **Note:** *On some vehicles there is no separate ground connection. A*

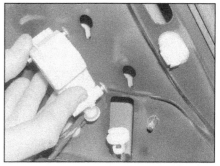

**30.3 Loosen the retaining screws, and remove the locking motor**

*relay in the system alternately grounds one wire and powers the other, depending on switch position. On models with this type of system, check for a solid ground at the relay.*

If there is no power at the motor, check for power at the three switch terminals by backprobing with the electrical connector still attached. There should be power at one of the switch terminals with the switch in the neutral position, and power at two of the terminals with the switch in either the TOP UP or TOP DOWN position. If there is no power at the switch, the problem lies in the wiring between the battery and the switch. If there is power at only one terminal in the TOP UP or TOP DOWN position, the switch is bad. If the switch tests are OK, the problem lies in the relay(s) (if equipped) or the wiring.

### 30 Fuel filler cap lock motor – removal and refitting

#### *Removal*

1 Remove the relevant rear luggage compartment side trim panels.
2 Disconnect the wiring connector and operating rod from the motor.
3 Using a suitable spanner/pliers loosen the retaining screws in a clockwise direction, and remove by sliding the lock motor out of the elongated holes in the body **(see illustration)**.

#### *Refitting*

4 Refitting is the reverse of removal. On completion, check the operation of the filler cap lock motor.

**Notes**

# Chapter 12
## Chassis electrical system

## Contents

## Degrees of difficulty

| Easy, suitable for novice with little experience | | Fairly easy, suitable for beginner with some experience | | Fairly difficult, suitable for competent DIY mechanic | | Difficult, suitable for experienced DIY mechanic | | Very difficult, suitable for expert DIY or professional | |
|---|---|---|---|---|---|---|---|---|---|

## 1 General information

The electrical system is a 12 volt, negative earth type. Power for the lights and all electrical accessories is supplied by a lead-acid type battery that is charged by the alternator.

This Chapter covers repair and service procedures for the various electrical components not associated with the engine. Information on the battery, alternator, ignition system and starter motor can be found in Chapter 5.

It should be noted that when portions of the electrical system are serviced, the negative cable should be disconnected from the battery to prevent electrical shorts and/or fires.

*Caution 1: These models are equipped with an anti-theft radio. Before performing a procedure that requires disconnecting the battery, make sure you have the proper activation code.*

*Caution 2: Disconnecting the battery can cause driveability problems that require a scan tool to remedy. See Chapter 5 for the use of an auxiliary voltage input device ('memory-saver') before disconnecting the battery.*

 *Warning: Do not use a memory-saving device to preserve the ECM's memory when working on or near airbag system components.*

## 2 Electrical troubleshooting – general information

A typical electrical circuit consists of an electrical component, any switches, relays, motors, fuses, fusible links or circuit breakers related to that component, and the wiring and connectors that link the component to both the battery and the chassis. To help you pinpoint an electrical circuit problem, wiring diagrams are included at the end of this Chapter.

Before tackling any troublesome electrical circuit, first study the appropriate wiring diagrams to get a complete understanding of what makes up that individual circuit. Trouble spots, for instance, can often be narrowed down by noting if other components related to the circuit are operating properly. If several components or circuits fail at one time, chances are the problem is in a fuse or earth connection, because several circuits are often routed through the same fuse and earth connections.

Electrical problems usually stem from simple causes, such as loose or corroded connections, a blown fuse, a melted fusible link or a failed relay. Visually inspect the condition of all fuses, wires and connections in a problem circuit before troubleshooting the circuit.

If test equipment and instruments are going to be utilised, use the diagrams to plan ahead of time where you will make the necessary connections in order to accurately pinpoint the trouble spot.

The basic tools needed for electrical troubleshooting include a circuit tester or voltmeter (a 12 volt bulb with a set of test leads can also be used), a continuity tester, which includes a bulb, battery and set of test leads, and a jumper wire, preferably with a circuit breaker incorporated, which can be used to bypass electrical components **(see illustrations)**. Before attempting to locate a problem with test instruments, use the wiring diagram(s) to decide where to make the connections.

### Voltage checks

Voltage checks should be performed if a circuit is not functioning properly. Connect one lead of a circuit tester to either the negative battery terminal or a known good earth. Connect the other lead to a connector in the circuit being tested, preferably nearest to the battery or fuse **(see illustration)**. If the bulb of the tester lights, voltage is present, which means that the part of the circuit between the connector and the battery is problem free. Continue checking the rest of the circuit in the same fashion. When you reach a point at which no voltage is present, the problem lies between that point and the last test point with voltage. Most of the time the problem can be traced to a loose connection. **Note:** *Keep in mind that some circuits receive voltage only when the ignition key is in the Accessory or Run position.*

### Finding a short

One method of finding shorts in a live circuit is to remove the fuse and connect a test light in place of the fuse terminals (fabricate two jumper wires with small spade terminals, plug the jumper wires into the fusebox and connect the test light). There should be voltage present in the circuit. Move the suspected wiring harness from side-to-side while watching the test light. If the bulb goes off, there is a short to earth somewhere in that area, probably where the insulation has rubbed through.

### Earth check

Perform an earth test to check whether a component is properly earthed. Disconnect the battery and connect one lead of a continuity tester or multimeter (set to the ohms scale), to a known good earth. Connect the other lead to the wire or earth connection being tested. If the resistance is low (less than 5 ohms), the earth is good. If the bulb on a self-powered test light does not go on, the earth is not good.

### Continuity check

A continuity check is done to determine if there are any breaks in a circuit – if it is passing electricity properly. With the circuit off (no power in the circuit), a self-powered continuity tester or multimeter can be used to check the circuit. Connect the test leads to

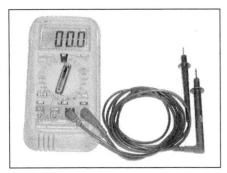

**2.5a The most useful tool for electrical troubleshooting is a digital multimeter that can check volts and amps, and test continuity**

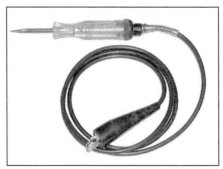

**2.5b A simple test light is very handy, especially when testing for voltage**

**2.6 In use, a basic test light's lead is clipped to a known good earth, then the pointed probe can test connectors, wires or electrical sockets – if the bulb lights, the circuit being tested has battery voltage**

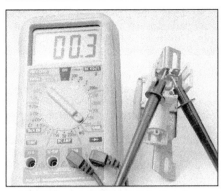

**2.9 With a multimeter set to the ohms scale, resistance can be checked across two terminals – when checking for continuity, a low reading indicates continuity, a high reading or infinity indicates lack of continuity**

**2.15 To backprobe a connector, insert a small, sharp probe (such as a straight pin) into the back of the connector alongside the desired wire until it contacts the metal terminal inside; connect your meter leads to the probes – this allows you to test a functioning circuit**

both ends of the circuit (or to the 'power' end and a good earth), and if the test light comes on the circuit is passing current properly **(see illustration)**. If the resistance is low (less than 5 ohms), there is continuity; if the reading is 10 000 ohms or higher, there is a break somewhere in the circuit. The same procedure can be used to test a switch, by connecting the continuity tester to the switch terminals. With the switch turned On, the test light should come on (or low resistance should be indicated on a meter).

### Finding an open circuit

When diagnosing for possible open circuits, it is often difficult to locate them by sight because the connectors hide oxidation or terminal misalignment. Merely wiggling a connector on a sensor or in the wiring harness may correct the open circuit condition. Remember this when an open circuit is indicated when troubleshooting a circuit. Intermittent problems may also be caused by oxidised or loose connections.

Electrical troubleshooting is simple if you keep in mind that all electrical circuits are basically electricity running from the battery, through the wires, switches, relays, fuses and fusible links to each electrical component (light bulb, motor, etc) and to earth, from which it is passed back to the battery. Any electrical problem is an interruption in the flow of electricity to and from the battery.

### Connectors

Most electrical connections on these vehicles are made with multi-pin plastic connectors. The mating halves of many connectors are secured with locking clips moulded into the plastic connector shells. The mating halves of large connectors, such as some of those under the instrument panel, are held together by a bolt through the centre of the connector.

To separate a connector with locking clips, use a small screwdriver to prise the clips apart carefully, then separate the connector halves. Pull only on the shell, never pull on the wiring harness as you may damage the individual wires and terminals inside the connectors. Look at the connector closely before trying to separate the halves. Often the locking clips

are engaged in a way that is not immediately clear. Additionally, many connectors have more than one set of clips.

Each pair of connector terminals has a male half and a female half. When you look at the end view of a connector in a diagram, be sure to understand whether the view shows the harness side or the component side of the connector. Connector halves are mirror images of each other, and a terminal shown on the right side end-view of one half will be on the left side end view of the other half.

It is often necessary to take circuit voltage measurements with a connector connected. Whenever possible, carefully insert a small straight pin (not your meter probe) into the rear of the connector shell to contact the terminal inside, then clip your meter lead to the pin. This kind of connection is called 'backprobing' **(see illustration)**. When inserting a test probe into a male terminal, be careful not to distort the terminal opening. Doing so can lead to a poor connection and corrosion at that terminal later. Using the small straight pin instead of a meter probe results in less chance of deforming the terminal connector.

### 3  Fuses – general information

The electrical circuits of the vehicle are protected by a combination of fuses, circuit breakers and fusible links. The interior fuse/relay panel is located at the left end of the instrument panel, while the main fuse/relay panel is in the engine compartment **(see illustrations)**.

Each of the fuses is designed to protect a specific circuit, and the various circuits are identified on the fuse panel itself.

Several sizes of fuses are employed in the fuse blocks. There are small, medium and large sizes of the same design, all with the same blade terminal design, as well as five

**3.1a The main fuse/relay box is at the left-hand end of the instrument panel, behind the end cover – the inside of the cover has a legend to identify the fuses and relays**

**3.1b The under-dash fuse/relay panel is located under the sound insulator at the left-hand end of the instrument panel – this panel contains relays (A), fuses (B) and circuit breakers if equipped**

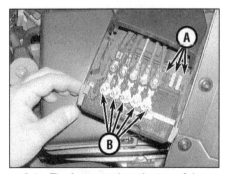

**3.1c The fuse panel on the top of the battery contains large capacity fuses – three are standard type 30-amp (A), and there are five metal fuses (B)**

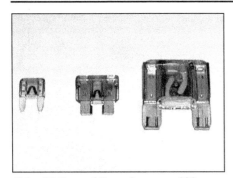

**3.3a All three of these fuse are of 30-amp rating, yet are different sizes. Be sure to get the right amperage and size when purchasing replacement fuses**

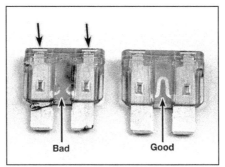

**3.3b When a fuse blows, the element between the terminal melts – the fuse on the left is blown, the one on the right is good – these fuses can be tested on top (arrowed) with a test light without removing the fuse**

'metal' fuses located in the engine compartment fuse panel **(see illustration)**. The medium and large fuses can be removed with your fingers, but the small fuses require the use of pliers or the small plastic fuse-puller tool found in most fuse boxes. The metal fuses are for heavy loads, and if the metal strip melts due to an overload, it is easily seen, although the battery should be disconnected while renewing this type fuse (see the **Cautions** in Section 1). If an electrical component fails, always check the fuse first. The best way to check the fuses is with a test light. Check for power at the exposed terminal tips of each fuse **(see illustration)**. If power is present at one side of the fuse but not the other, the fuse is blown. A blown fuse can also be identified by visually inspecting it.

Be sure to renew blown fuses with the correct type. Fuses (of the same physical size) of different ratings may be physically interchangeable, but only fuses of the proper rating should be used. Renewing a fuse with one of a higher or lower value than specified is

not recommended. Each electrical circuit needs a specific amount of protection. The amperage value of each fuse is moulded into the top of the fuse body.

If the renewal fuse immediately fails, don't renew it again until the cause of the problem is isolated and corrected. In most cases, this will be a short circuit in the wiring caused by a broken or deteriorated wire.

## 4 Circuit breakers – general information and testing

Circuit breakers protect certain circuits, such as the power windows or heated seats. Depending on the vehicle's accessories, there may be one or two 25 amp circuit breakers, located in the under-dash fuse/relay box under the driver's end of the dashboard **(see illustration 3.1b)**.

Because the circuit breakers reset automatically, an electrical overload in a circuit-breaker-protected system will cause the circuit to fail momentarily, then come back on. If the circuit does not come back on, check it immediately.

For a basic check, pull the circuit breaker up out of its socket on the fuse panel, but just far enough to probe with a voltmeter. The breaker should still contact the sockets.

With the voltmeter negative lead on a good chassis earth, touch each end prong of the circuit breaker with the positive meter probe. There should be battery voltage at each end. If there is battery voltage only at one end, the circuit breaker must be renewed.

## 5 Relays – general information and testing

### General information

1 Several electrical accessories in the vehicle, such as the fuel injection system, horns, starter, and fog lights use relays to transmit the electrical signal to the component. Relays use a low-current circuit (the control circuit) to open and close a high-current circuit (the power circuit). If the relay is defective, that component will not operate properly. Most relays are mounted in the under-dash fuse/relay box **(see illustration 3.1b)**. If a faulty relay is suspected, it can be removed and tested using the procedure below or by a dealer service department or a garage. Defective relays must be renewed as a unit.

### Testing

2 Most of the relays used in these vehicles are of a type often called 'ISO' relays, which refers to the International Standards Organisation. The terminals of ISO relays are numbered to indicate their usual circuit connections and functions. There are two basic layouts of terminals on the relays used in the covered vehicles **(see illustrations)**.
3 Refer to the wiring diagram for the circuit to determine the proper connections for the

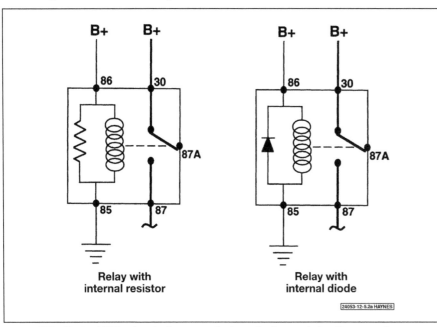

**Relay with internal resistor**

**Relay with internal diode**

24053-12-5.2a HAYNES

**5.2a Typical ISO relay designs, terminal numbering and circuit connections**

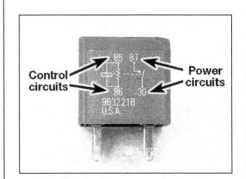

**5.2b Most relays are marked on the outside to easily identify the control circuit and power circuits – this one is of the four-terminal type**

relay you're testing. If you can't determine the correct connection from the wiring diagrams, however, you may be able to determine the test connections from the information that follows.

**4** Two of the terminals are the relay control circuit and connect to the relay coil. The other relay terminals are the power circuit. When the relay is energised, the coil creates a magnetic field that closes the larger contacts of the power circuit to provide power to the circuit loads.

**5** Terminals 85 and 86 are normally the control circuit. If the relay contains a diode, terminal 86 must be connected to battery positive (B+) voltage and terminal 85 to earth. If the relay contains a resistor, terminals 85 and 86 can be connected in either direction with respect to B+ and earth.

**6** Terminal 30 is normally connected to the battery voltage (B+) source for the circuit loads. Terminal 87 is connected to the earth side of the circuit, either directly or through a load. If the relay has several alternate terminals for load or earth connections, they usually are numbered 87A, 87B, 87C, and so on.

**7** Use an ohmmeter to check continuity through the relay control coil.

a) Connect the meter according to the polarity shown in illustration 5.2a for one check; then reverse the ohmmeter leads and check continuity in the other direction.

b) If the relay contains a resistor, resistance will be indicated on the meter, and should be the same value with the ohmmeter in either direction.

c) If the relay contains a diode, resistance should be higher with the ohmmeter in the forward polarity direction than with the meter leads reversed.

d) If the ohmmeter shows infinite resistance in both directions, renew the relay.

**8** Remove the relay from the vehicle and use the ohmmeter to check for continuity between the relay power circuit terminals. There should be no continuity between terminal 30 and 87 with the relay de-energised.

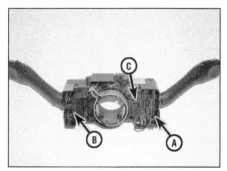

**7.3 Multi-function switch harness connectors: (A) is used for the direction indicators and headlight dimming, (B) for the wash-wipe functions, and (C) for the cruise control**

**9** Connect a fused jumper wire to terminal 86 and the positive battery terminal. Connect another jumper wire between terminal 85 and earth. When the connections are made, the relay should click.

**10** With the jumper wires connected, check for continuity between the power circuit terminals. Now, there should be continuity between terminals 30 and 87.

**11** If the relay fails any of the above tests, renew it.

### 6  Direction indicator and hazard flashers – testing and renewal
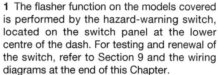

**1** The flasher function on the models covered is performed by the hazard-warning switch, located on the switch panel at the lower centre of the dash. For testing and renewal of the switch, refer to Section 9 and the wiring diagrams at the end of this Chapter.

**2** When the flasher unit is functioning properly, an audible click may be heard during its operation. If the direction indicator on one side of the vehicle flashes much more rapidly than normal, a faulty direction indicator bulb is indicated.

**3** If both direction indicators fail to blink, the problem may be due to a blown fuse, a faulty flasher unit switch, or a loose or open connection. If a quick check of the fusebox indicates that the direction indicator fuse has blown, check the wiring for a short before refitting a new fuse.

**4** If the flasher switch is not the problem, refer to Section 7 and test the direction indicator portion of the multi-function switch.

### 7  Steering column switches – testing and renewal

⚠ *Warning: The models covered by this manual are equipped with Supplemental Restraint Systems (SRS), more commonly known as airbags. Always disable the airbag system before working in the vicinity of any airbag system components to avoid*

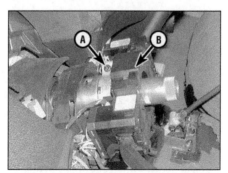

**7.6 Remove the Allen bolt (A) at the back of the multi-function switch (B)**

*the possibility of accidental deployment of the airbags, which could cause personal injury (see Section 26).*

## Multi-function switch

**1** The multi-function switch is located on the top of the steering column. It incorporates into one switch the direction indicator, headlight dimmer, windscreen wiper/washer and, if applicable, cruise control functions. **Note:** *The following checks can be made with simple equipment, but thorough testing of the systems controlled by the Multi-function switch can only be made at a dealer or other garage with a scan diagnosis tool.*

### Testing

**2** Remove the steering column covers and the knee bolster for access (see Chapter 11, Sections 25 and 24). Follow the wiring diagrams at the end of this Chapter to determine which terminals supply the left and right direction indicator circuits, the cruise control and the headlight dimming systems.

**3** Use a test light to check for power at the designated terminals with the switch in each position. Look at the wiring diagrams at the end of this Chapter to see how power and earth are routed. If any portion of the Multi-function switch fails the tests, the switch must be renewed as a unit. The 12-pin connector handles the direction indicators, headlight dimmer and sidelights, the 6-pin and 8-pin connectors control the wipe/wash functions, and the cruise control connector is the 10-pin connector **(see illustration)**.

### Renewal

**4** Remove the steering wheel (see Chapter 10).

**5** Remove the steering column covers (see Chapter 11).

**6** Remove the Allen bolt at the rear of the Multi-function switch **(see illustration)**.

**7** Pull the Multi-function switch out from the steering column enough to disconnect the electrical connectors.

**8** Refitting is the reverse of removal.

### 8  Ignition switch and key lock cylinder – testing and renewal

⚠ *Warning: The models covered by this manual are equipped with Supplemental Restraint Systems (SRS), more commonly known as airbags. Always disable the airbag system before working in the vicinity of any airbag system components to avoid the possibility of accidental deployment of the airbags, which could cause personal injury (see Section 26).*

**1** The ignition switch, located under the steering column (switch on the left, key lock cylinder on the right), is comprised of a cast-metal housing, an ignition lock cylinder and an electrical component, the switch device.

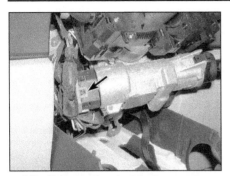

**8.7a Remove the electrical connector (arrowed) from the ignition switch**

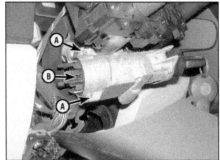

**8.7b With the connector off, remove the two screws (A) securing the switch (B) to the housing**

**8.8 Depress the retainer with a straightened paper clip (arrowed) and withdraw the cylinder by holding the key**

### Testing

2 Access the switch and disconnect the electrical connector from it (see Steps 6 and 7).

3 Backprobe the wires from the switch with an ohmmeter. Power is supplied to the switch through the two red wires (attached to the terminals marked 30 on the back of the switch). Check for continuity between the red and other wires in different switch positions. With the switch Off, there should be no continuity. With the switch in Run, there should be continuity at the black/red and the black wires, and in the Start position, only at the red/black and brown/red wires.

4 If the switch does not have the correct continuity, renew it.

### Renewal

5 Disconnect the negative battery cable (see the **Cautions** in Section 1).

6 Remove the steering column covers (see Chapter 11). On models with automatic transmissions, the gearchange linkage must be in Park before removing/refitting the ignition switch.

7 Disconnect the large electrical connector on the left side of the switch, then remove the two switch mounting screws and pull the switch out of the housing **(see illustrations)**. **Note:** *The screw heads may be coated with a special 'locking' coating. You'll have to chip this off to remove the screws.*

8 To remove the key lock cylinder, place the key in the lock and rotate clockwise to the

Run position. Insert the straightened end of a large paper clip into the hole in the cylinder and pull the key and lock cylinder from the housing **(see illustration)**.

9 When refitting the cylinder, align the cylinder as it was (still in Run position with the key in), then push the cylinder in until it snaps in position. Turn the key to the Lock position and remove the key.

10 The remainder of refitting is the reverse of removal.

### 9 Instrument panel switches – testing and renewal

> **Warning: The models covered by this manual are equipped with Supplemental Restraint Systems (SRS), more commonly known as airbags. Always disable the airbag system before working in the vicinity of any airbag system components to avoid the possibility of accidental deployment of the airbags, which could cause personal injury (see Section 26).**

### Headlight switch

#### Testing

1 The headlight switch must be removed from the instrument panel for testing. See Steps 4 and 5 for removal.

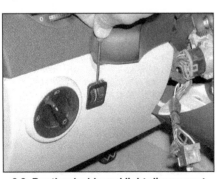

**9.8 Pry the dashboard light dimmer out with a flat-bladed lever (LHD model shown)**

2 Using an ohmmeter or self-powered continuity tester, check the switch for proper continuity between the terminals. Refer to the wiring diagrams at the end of this Chapter for the wire colours and circuits. There should be continuity between the power side and the lighting side when the switch is in the indicated position. If the switch fails any of the tests, renew the switch.

#### Renewal

3 Disconnect the negative cable at the battery (see Chapter 5). See the **Cautions** in Section 1.

4 Turn the headlight switch knob anti-clockwise until it stops. Push in on the switch and twist it to the right (clockwise) then withdraw it from the instrument panel.

5 Pull the switch out far enough to disconnect the electrical connector.

6 Refitting is the reverse of removal.

### Dash light dimmer switch

7 The dimmer is located just to the right of the headlight switch.

8 Use a screwdriver or a trim tool to prise the switch housing out of the instrument panel **(see illustration)**.

9 Apply battery voltage to the input side of the switch (see the wiring diagrams at the end of this Chapter), and use a digital ohmmeter to check for resistance on the output side. If the resistance doesn't vary as the knob is turned, renew the switch.

10 Refitting is the reverse of removal.

### On/Off switches

11 Depending on the options of the vehicle, there may be one or more switches on the instrument panel, including seat heaters, hazard flasher and rear window defogger.

12 All of the above-mentioned switches are located in the switch panel at the centre of the dashboard, just below the radio and heater controls.

13 All of the switches need to be removed for testing, and all are removed the same way. Use a screwdriver or trim tool to prise behind the lip of the switches to release them from the switch panel, then pull them out far enough to disconnect the electrical connector **(see illustration)**.

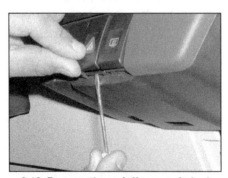

**9.13 Remove the on/off type switched (seat heater switch shown) by prying behind the switch lip and pulling the switch out of the instrument panel**

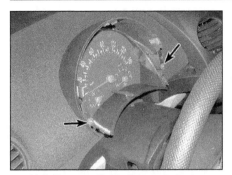

**11.4  Remove the instrument cluster mounting screws (arrowed)**

**11.5  Pull the cluster out enough to disconnect the electrical connectors (arrow indicates one)**

**14** With simple on/off switches, use an ohmmeter or self-powered continuity tester to check the switch for proper continuity between the terminals. Refer to the wiring diagrams at the end of this Chapter for input and output terminals and wire colours. There should be continuity between input and output terminals only when the switch is engaged. If any switch fails the test, renew the switch.

gauge grounded, check for voltage at the other terminal of the gauge (the brown/white wire). There should not be voltage.
**4** If the problem is in the gauge panel itself, the instrument cluster must be renewed (it is not user serviceable). See your dealer for a new or rebuilt instrument cluster. **Note:** *Problems within the instrument cluster, including the fuel gauge, will set DTCs (Diagnostic Trouble Codes) that can be retrieved with a scan tool.*

**5** Pull the cluster out enough to disengage the two large electrical connectors at the back, then pull the cluster out, tilting the bottom out first **(see illustration)**.
**6** Refitting is the reverse of removal.

## 10 Fuel gauge – testing

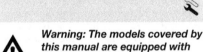

**Warning: The models covered by this manual are equipped with Supplemental Restraint Systems (SRS), more commonly known as airbags. Always disable the airbag system before working in the vicinity of any airbag system components to avoid the possibility of accidental deployment of the airbags, which could cause personal injury (see Section 26).**
**Note:** *This procedure applies to conventional analogue type gauges (NON-digital) only.*
**1** All tests below require the ignition switch to be turned to the Off position before testing.
**2** If the gauge pointer does not move from the empty position, check the fuse. If the fuse is OK, locate the sender unit for the circuit (see Chapter 4A for fuel level sender unit location). Connect the sender unit connector to earth with a jumper wire.
**3** Turn the ignition key On momentarily. If the pointer goes to the full position, renew the sender unit. **Note:** *Turn the key Off right away; grounding the sender unit for too long could damage the gauge.* If the pointer stays in same position, use a jumper wire to earth the sender unit terminal on the back of the instrument cluster (violet/black wire). Refer to the wiring diagrams at the end of this Chapter and refer to Section 11 for access to the connector at the back of the instrument cluster. If the pointer moves, the problem lies in the wiring between the gauge and the sender unit. If the pointer does not move with the sending unit terminal on the back of the

## 11 Instrument cluster – removal and refitting

**Warning: The models covered by this manual are equipped with Supplemental Restraint Systems (SRS), more commonly known as airbags. Always disable the airbag system before working in the vicinity of any airbag system components to avoid the possibility of accidental deployment of the airbags, which could cause personal injury (see Section 26).**
**1** Disconnect the negative cable from the battery (see Chapter 5). See **Cautions** in Section 1.
**2** Lower the steering column to the bottom of its range, and pull it out as far as it will go.
**3** Remove the instrument cluster bezel (see Chapter 11, Section 24).
**4** Remove the screws securing the cluster to the instrument panel **(see illustration)**.

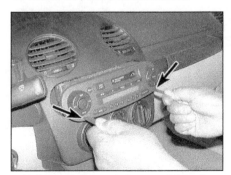

**12.3a  Push the tools (arrowed) into the slots and pull the radio out**

## 12 Radio and speakers – removal and refitting

**Warning: The models covered by this manual are equipped with Supplemental Restraint Systems (SRS), more commonly known as airbags. Always disable the airbag system before working in the vicinity of any airbag system components to avoid the possibility of accidental deployment of the airbags, which could cause personal injury (see Section 26).**
**Note:** *The audio system is part of the diagnostic network of the vehicle. Any problems with the radio, aerial or speakers may set a DTC (Diagnostic Trouble Code) that can be retrieved with a scan tool.*

### Radio
**1** Refer to Chapter 5 and disconnect the negative battery cable. Refer to the **Cautions** in Section 1.
**2** Two special tools, available at motor factors must be used to remove the VW radio.
**3** Push the two tools into the slots on either side of the radio, pull the radio out of the instrument panel, disconnect the connectors, then remove it from the vehicle **(see illustrations)**.
**4** Refitting is the reverse of removal. To disengage the plastic tools from the radio before refitting, depress the lugs on the side of the radio.

### Speakers
**5** The are small tweeter speakers in each of the front 'A' pillars at either side of the windscreen. These speakers are part of the trim panel for the 'A' pillar, and if found defective, the pillar trim/speaker must be renewed as a unit. The remaining speakers

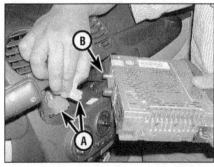

**12.3b  Disconnect the two connectors (A) from the back of the radio, then disconnect the earth wire and the aerial cable (B)**

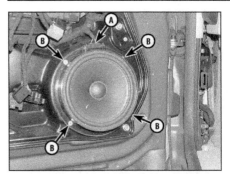

**12.7  To remove a door or rear speaker, disconnect the connector (A), then drill out the rivets (B)**

**13.1  The aerial mast can be unscrewed from its base by twisting it by hand**

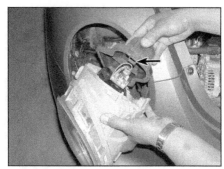

**14.2a  Release the clip (arrowed) at the top and pull back the bulbholder cover**

include one in each door and one in each quarter panel.

**6** To remove the door or quarter-panel speakers, remove the interior trim panel first (see Chapter 11).

**7** Disconnect the electrical connector at the speaker, then drill out the rivets securing it to the door carrier **(see illustration)**.

**8** Refitting is the reverse of the removal procedure. Self-tapping screws may be used to renew the speaker mounting rivets.

## 13  Aerial – removal and refitting

**Note:** *On convertible models, the radio aerial is a 'grid type' embedded in the top of the windscreen. It cannot be repaired or renewed without renewing the windscreen.*

**1** Grip the base of the aerial mast firmly and twist to unscrew it from the mounting base **(see illustration)**.

**2** Refitting of the aerial mast is the reverse of the removal procedure.

**3** If the base or the cable itself must be renewed, the headliner must be removed to access the nut on the bottom of the aerial

base, on the interior side. This is a complex job for the home mechanic, and should be left to a dealer or professional auto stereo shop.

## 14  Headlight bulb – renewal

⚠ *Warning: Halogen bulbs are gas-filled and under pressure and may shatter if the surface is scratched or the bulb is dropped. Wear eye protection and handle the bulbs carefully, grasping only the base whenever possible. Don't touch the surface of the bulb with your fingers because the oil from your skin could cause it to overheat and fail prematurely. If you do touch the bulb surface, clean it with rubbing alcohol or methylated spirit.*

**1** Refer to Section 16 and remove the headlight housing.

**2** Remove the retaining clip to remove the upper (low beam) or lower (high beam) bulbholder from the back of the headlight housing **(see illustrations)**. Remove the old bulb from the holder.

**3** Handling the new bulb only with gloves or a clean rag, insert the new bulb in the holder.

**4** Refitting of the housing is the reverse of the removal procedure.

## 15  Headlights and fog lights – adjustment

⚠ *Warning: The headlights must be aimed correctly. If adjusted incorrectly, they could temporarily blind the driver of an oncoming vehicle and cause an accident, or seriously reduce your ability to see the road. The headlights should be checked for proper aim every 12 months and any time a new headlight is fitted or front-end bodywork is performed. The following procedure is only an interim step to provide temporary adjustment until the headlights can be adjusted by a properly-equipped workshop.*

### Headlights

**1** These models are equipped with headlight housings with two adjustment screws, one controlling left-and-right movement and one for up-and-down movement **(see illustration)**. A 6 mm Allen key is used on the screws. The type with a ball-end works best.

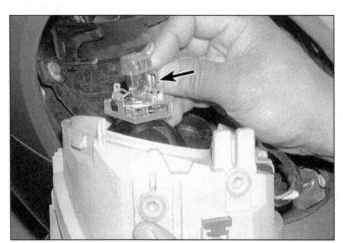

**14.2b  Remove the retaining clip (arrowed), then pull out the headlight bulbholder (dip beam shown, main beam is below this on the housing)**

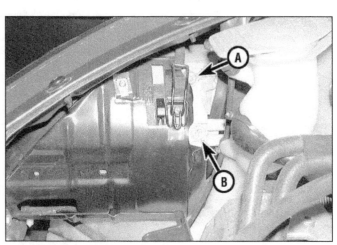

**15.1  Open the bonnet and adjust the headlight alignment with these screws – (A) is the vertical adjuster, (B) is the horizontal adjuster**

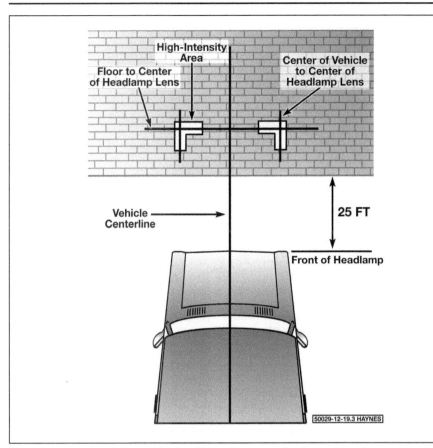

15.2  Headlight adjustment details

15.11  Turn this screw (arrowed) in the grille area to adjust the aim of the fog lights

**2** There are several methods of adjusting the headlights. The simplest method requires an open area with a blank wall and a level floor **(see illustration)**.
**3** Position masking tape vertically on the wall in reference to the vehicle centreline and the centrelines of both headlights.
**4** Position a horizontal tape line in reference to the centreline of all the headlights. **Note:** *It may be easier to position the tape on the wall with the vehicle parked only a few centimetres away.*
**5** Adjustment should be made with the

vehicle parked 8 m from the wall, sitting level, the fuel tank half-full and no unusually heavy load in the vehicle.
**6** Starting with the low beam adjustment, position the high intensity zone so it is 50 mm below the horizontal line and 50 mm to the side of the vertical headlight line away from oncoming traffic. Twist the adjustment screws until the desired level has been achieved.
**7** With the high beams on, the high intensity zone should be vertically centred with the exact centre just below the horizontal line. **Note:** *It may not be possible to position the headlight aim exactly for both high and low beams. If a compromise must be made, keep in mind that the low beams are the most used and have the greatest effect on driver safety.*

16.3  Align the headlight housing ribs with the tracks (arrowed) in the body

**8** Have the headlights adjusted by a dealer service department or suitably-equipped workshop at the earliest opportunity.

### *Fog lights*

**9** Some models have optional fog lights that can be aimed just like headlights **(see illustration 15.2)**.
**10** Tape a horizontal line on the wall that represents the height of the fog lights, and another tape line 100 mm below that line. Park the vehicle 8 m from the wall.
**11** Using the adjusting screws on the fog lights, adjust the pattern on the wall so that the top of the fog light beam meets the lower line on the wall, and that the beam is centred horizontally in front of the lights **(see illustration)**.

### 16  Headlight housing – renewal

**1** Open the bonnet and pull up the release lever at the back of the headlight housing **(see illustration)**. The headlight housing slides in and out of the body in tracks.
**2** Pull the headlight housing far enough forward to disconnect the electrical connectors, then slide the headlight housing all the way out.
**3** To refit the housing, slide it back in, aligning the ridges on each side with the two tracks in the body **(see illustration)**.
**4** When the housing is in far enough, reach through from inside the engine compartment to reattach the electrical connectors. The remainder of refitting is the reverse of the removal procedure. Refer to Section 15 for aiming procedures after the headlight housing is fitted.

### 17  Bulb renewal

 *Warning: Bulbs can remain hot for twenty minutes after they're turned off. Be sure bulbs are off and cool before you touch them.*

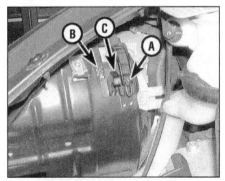

16.1  Release the spring clamp (A), depress the tab (B), then rotate the headlight housing release lever (C) upward and pull the housing forward enough to disconnect the electrical connectors

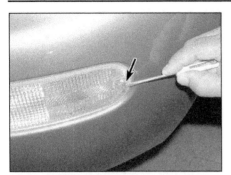

**17.1 Pry back the plastic cover, then remove the screw (arrowed) and swing the direction indicator housing out away from the vehicle**

**17.3 Pull out the bulbholder for the direction indicator lamp and replace the bulb**

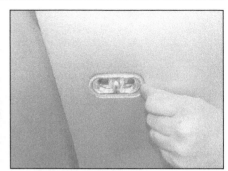

**17.5a Push the repeater in the direction of the spring clip . . .**

### Front direction indicator

**Note:** *Front direction indicator lights on 1998 models are only on the front bumpers, 1999 models have additional side repeaters on the sides of the windscreen scuttle, and later models have side repeaters located in the exterior door mirrors.*

1 Remove the screw securing one end of the direction indicator unit, then swing the unit away from the vehicle **(see illustration).**

2 Disconnect the electrical connectors.

3 Each bulb is renewed by twisting the bulbholder out **(see illustration).**

### Direction indicator side repeater

#### Body-mounted

4 Great care must be taken when removing the direction indicator side repeater, as it is only possible to be removed in one direction, and it is not possible to determine which end of the repeater the spring clip or mounting sits. Consequently, there is a high risk of damaging the vehicle paintwork.

5 Carefully push the repeater sideways in the direction of the spring clip. Once the spring clip is compressed, it should be possible to ease the mounting end of the repeater out of

the aperture, and manoeuvre the assembly from the wing **(see illustrations).**

6 Pull the rubber bulbholder from the repeater. The bulb is a push-fit in the holder **(see illustrations).**

7 Refitting is a reversal of removal.

#### Mirror-mounted

8 Remove the mirror glass as described in Chapter 11.

9 Using a screwdriver, carefully release the surround from inside the mirror housing, starting at the upper, inner corner **(see illustrations).**

10 Disconnect the side repeater wiring from the mirror base unit **(see illustration).**

**17.5b . . . and ease the side repeater from the aperture**

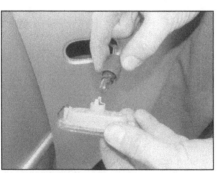

**17.6a Pull the bulb from the holder . . .**

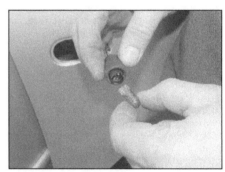

**17.6b . . . then pull out the wedge-type bulb**

**17.9a Use a screwdriver to release the surround . . .**

**17.9b . . . then remove it from inside the mirror housing**

**17.10 Disconnect the wiring . . .**

17.11 . . . release the housing upper clip . . .

17.12a . . . then withdraw the housing . . .

17.12b . . . noting the location slot on the inner end of the housing

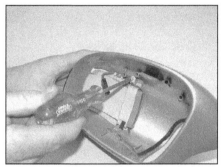

17.13a Undo the screw . . .

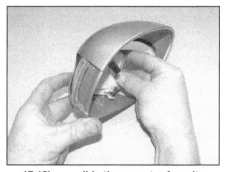

17.13b . . . slide the repeater from its aperture . . .

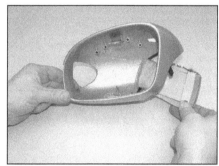

17.13c . . . and withdraw from the housing

**11** Using a screwdriver, release the upper clip securing the housing to the rear of the mirror bracket **(see illustration)**.
**12** Unhook the bottom of the housing from the base unit, then lift it upwards noting that the inner end of the housing locates on a vertical extension. Withdraw the housing from the base unit **(see illustrations)**.
**13** With the housing on the bench, undo the screw and slide the side repeater inwards from the aperture **(see illustration)**.

### Front fog lights

**14** Raise the front of the vehicle and support it securely on axle stands.
**15** From behind the grille area, grasp the back of the fog light housing and twist it anti-clockwise **(see illustration)**.
**16** Pull the black plastic housing away from the fog light until you have access to the metal clip securing the bulbholder **(see illustration)**.
**17** Refit the new bulb in the holder and secure it in the fog light housing with the clip.
**18** The remainder of refitting is the reverse of removal.

### Tail/stop/indicator lights

**19** On all models, these rear lights are all in one housing, mounted on the rear wings.
**20** Remove the trim panel at the rear of the luggage area. Remove the plastic nut securing the taillight housing **(see illustration)**.
**21** Pull the taillight housing out and disconnect the electrical connectors. Twist the bulbholders anti-clockwise to remove them for bulb renewal **(see illustration)**.

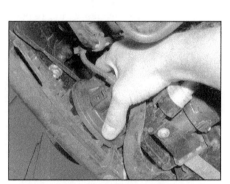

17.15 Twist the fog light housing anti-clockwise to disengage it from the light

17.16 With the back housing pulled to the side, release the clip (arrowed) and pull out the bulbholder

17.20 Remove the plastic trim cover in the boot to access the taillight housing mounting nut (arrowed)

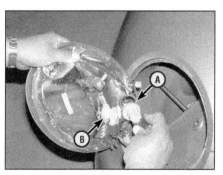

17.21 Rotate the bulbholder and pull it out to remove it – upper bulb (A) is for the direction indicators, (B) is for the brake/taillight bulb

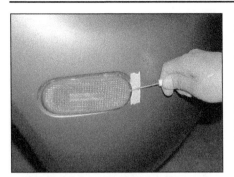

**17.24 Mask the body to protect the paint, then use a small screwdriver to release the rear side-marker lights**

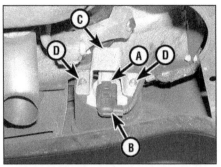

**17.28 Reversing light mounting details**

A  Bulb housing
B  Electrical connector
C  Guard bracket
D  Lens mounting nuts

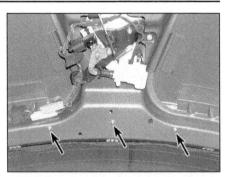

**17.32 Remove the screws (arrowed) and pull the high-level brake light housing out**

22  Refitting is the reverse of removal. Make sure the washer and spacer are in place before refitting the plastic nut on the housing.

### Rear side-marker lights

23  Where fitted, the side-marker lights are in the lower portion of each rear wing. Remove the plastic rear wheelarch liner.
24  Use a small screwdriver to depress the tab on the back of the side-marker light housing and push the light housing to the outside **(see illustration)**.
25  Twist the bulbholder anti-clockwise to remove it and renew the bulb.
26  Refitting is the reverse of the removal

procedure. Make sure the hook end of the light housing goes in first, then snap the housing in place until the tab is engaged.

### Reversing lights

27  The reversing light is located at the bottom of the rear bumper cover.
28  Remove the nuts on the rear of the bumper cover, remove the heat shield, and pull out the light housing **(see illustration)**.
29  Twist the bulbholder anti-clockwise to remove for bulb renewal.
30  Refitting is the reverse of the removal procedure.

### High-level brake light

31  Refer to Chapter 11, Section 22, and remove the inner trim panel from the rear hatch.
32  Remove the three screws for the high-level brake light **(see illustration)**.
33  Pull the housing from the hatch and disconnect the electrical connector **(see illustration)**. Twist the bulbholders anti-clockwise, then renew the bulbs.
34  Refitting is the reverse of the removal procedure. Make sure the gasket on the back of the housing is intact, or a water leak could develop.

### Number plate bulb

35  Use a small screwdriver to depress the clip at the top of the number plate light, then tilt and pull out the light housing **(see illustration)**.
36  Remove the bulbholder from the rear to renew the bulb.
37  Refitting is the reverse of removal.

### Instrument cluster lights

38  On the covered models, the instrument cluster is illuminated by LEDs that are part of the printed circuit board. Thus, there are no user-reneweable bulbs behind the instrument cluster.

### Overhead light

39  On all models, use a small screwdriver to prise the reading light from the bottom of the interior rear-view mirror, then remove the bulb **(see illustration)**.
40  Refitting is the reverse of removal.

### Courtesy lights

41  Prise the light out of the headlining carefully with a small screwdriver, then renew the bulb by pulling it straight out **(see illustration)**.
42  Refitting is the reverse of removal.

### Luggage compartment light

43  Use a small screwdriver to prise the

**17.33 Disconnect the electrical connector from the back of the high-level brake light**

**17.35 Use a small screwdriver to depress the clip securing the number plate to the rear bumper cover**

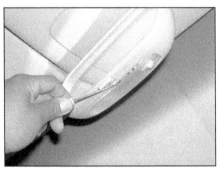

**17.39 Remove the overhead light from the interior rear view mirror**

**17.41 Pry the courtesy light from the headlining, then replace the bulb from the rear**

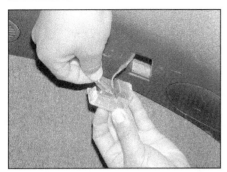

**17.43 Remove the bulb from the back of the luggage compartment light**

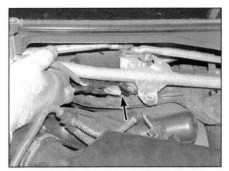

**18.2 Refer to the wiring diagrams and check for proper earth and voltage at the wiper motor connector (arrowed)**

luggage compartment light out of the luggage compartment lining, then remove the bulb from the holder **(see illustration).**

### Rear fog light

**44** The fog light is located in the rear bumper cover.
**45** Remove the right-rear cover next to the wheelarch.
**46** Reach behind the bumper and undo the two retaining nuts.
**47** Disconnect the wiring plug, and remove the fog light.
**48** Twist the bulbholder anti-clockwise to remove the bulb.
**49** Refitting is the reverse of removal.

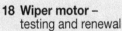

## 18 Wiper motor – testing and renewal

### Wiper motor circuit testing

**Note:** *Refer to the wiring diagrams for wire colours and locations in the following checks. When checking for voltage, probe a grounded 12 volt test light to each terminal at a connector until it lights; this verifies voltage (power) at the terminal. If the following checks fail to locate the problem, have the system*

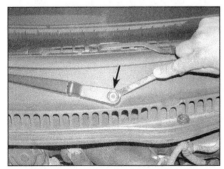

**18.7 Lift the cover, then use a spanner to remove the nut (arrowed) on the wiper shaft, then grasp the wiper arm and use a rocking motion to detach it from the shaft**

*diagnosed by a dealer service department or other properly-equipped repair facility.*
**1** If the wipers work slowly, make sure the battery is in good condition and has a strong charge (see Chapter 5). If the battery is in good condition, remove the wiper motor (see below) and operate the wiper arms by hand. Check for binding linkage and pivots. Lubricate or repair the linkage or pivots as necessary. Refit the wiper motor. If the wipers still operate slowly, check for loose or corroded connections, especially the earth connection. If all connections look OK, renew the motor.
**2** If the wipers fail to operate when activated, check the fuse. If the fuse is OK, connect a jumper wire between the wiper motor's earth terminal and earth, then retest. If the motor works now, repair the earth connection. If the motor still doesn't work, turn the wiper switch to the HI position and check for voltage at the motor **(see illustration)**. *Note: The scuttle cover and plenum panel will have to be removed (see Chapter 11) to access the electrical connector.*
**3** If there's voltage at the connector, remove the motor and check it off the vehicle with fused jumper wires from the battery. If the motor now works, check for binding linkage (see Step 1 above). If the motor still doesn't work, renew it. If there's no voltage to the motor, check for voltage at the wiper control

**18.9 The wiper linkage mounting bolts (arrowed) can be removed even with the plenum panel in place, but the plenum panel must be removed to take out the motor/linkage**

relays. If there's voltage at the wiper control relays and no voltage at the wiper motor, check the switch for continuity (see Section 7). If the switch is OK, the wiper control relay is probably defective. See Section 5 for relay testing.
**4** If the interval (delay) function is inoperative, check the continuity of all the wiring between the switch and wiper control module.
**5** If the wipers stop at the position they're in when the switch is turned off (fail to park), check for voltage at the park feed wire of the wiper motor connector when the wiper switch is Off but the ignition is On. If no voltage is present, check for an open circuit between the wiper motor and the fuse panel.

### Renewal

**6** Disconnect the negative cable from the battery (see Chapter 5). Refer to the **Cautions** in Section 1.
**7** Mark the positions of the wiper arms on the windscreen, then remove the wiper arms **(see illustration)**. **Note:** *Disconnect the washer hose from the wiper arm.*
**8** Remove the scuttle cover (see Chapter 11).
**9** Remove the wiper motor/linkage mounting bolts **(see illustration)**.
**10** Remove the assembly, disconnect the electrical connector and unbolt the motor from the linkage **(see illustration)**.
**11** Refitting is the reverse of removal.

## 19 Horn – testing and renewal

### Testing

**1** Remove the cover from the under-dash fuse/relay box **(see illustration 3.1b)** and check the relay (see Section 5). Check the horn fuse in the fuse/relay panel at the driver's end of the instrument panel.

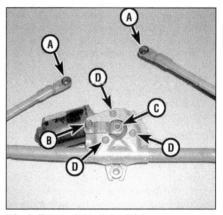

**18.10 Remove the links (A) from the motor arm stud (B), then remove the motor arm nut (C) and remove the motor-to-linkage mounting bolts (D)**

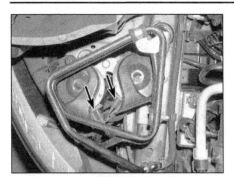

19.2 Disconnect the horn connectors (arrowed) – shown here from below and behind the front bumper

2 Disconnect the electrical connectors from the horns **(see illustration)**. There are two horns, located in the left front wheel arch, just behind the front bumper cover.

3 Have an assistant press the horn button and use a voltmeter to make sure there is battery voltage at the voltage supply wire terminal to the horns (see the wiring diagrams at the end of this Chapter). If the relay is good and there's no voltage at the horn, the wire (which leads to the relay) has a fault.

4 Use an ohmmeter to measure the resistance between the wiring connector brown wire and a good earth. There should be less than 5.0 ohms. If not, repair the fault in the earth circuit.

5 If there's voltage at the horn and the wiring circuits are good, the horn is faulty and must be renewed.

### Renewal

6 Disconnect the electrical connectors, remove the mounting bolts and detach the horns **(see illustration 19.2)**.

7 Refitting is the reverse of removal.

### 20 Rear window heater – testing and repair

1 The rear window heater consists of a number of horizontal heating elements baked onto the inside surface of the glass. Power is supplied through a large fuse from the under bonnet fuse/relay box in the engine compartment. The heater is controlled by the instrument panel switch.

2 Small breaks in the element can be repaired without removing the rear window.

### Testing

3 Turn the ignition switch and heater switch to the On position.

4 Using a voltmeter, place the positive probe against the heater grid positive terminal and the negative probe against the earth terminal. If battery voltage is not indicated, check the fuse, heater switch, heater relay and related wiring. If voltage is indicated, but all or part of the heater doesn't heat, proceed with the following tests.

20.5 When measuring the voltage at the heated rear window grid, wrap a piece of aluminium foil around the positive probe of the voltmeter and press the foil against the wire with your finger

5 When measuring voltage during the next two tests, wrap a piece of aluminium foil around the tip of the voltmeter positive probe and press the foil against the heating element with your finger **(see illustration)**. Place the negative probe on the heater grid earth terminal.

6 Check the voltage at the centre of each heating element **(see illustration)**. If the voltage is 5 to 6 volts, the element is okay (there is no break). If the voltage is 0 volts, the element is broken between the centre of the element and the positive end. If the voltage is 10 to 12 volts the element is broken between the centre of the element and the earth side. Check each heating element.

7 If none of the elements are broken, connect the negative probe to a good chassis earth. The voltage reading should stay the same, if it doesn't the earth connection is bad.

8 To find the break, place the voltmeter negative probe against the heater earth terminal. Place the voltmeter positive probe with the foil strip against the heating element at the positive side and slide it toward the negative side. The point at which the voltmeter deflects from several volts to zero is

20.8 To find a break, place the voltmeter negative lead against the heated rear window earth terminal, place the voltmeter positive lead with the foil strip against the heat wire at the positive terminal end and slide it toward the negative terminal end – the point at which the voltmeter deflects from several volts to zero volts is the point at which the wire is broken

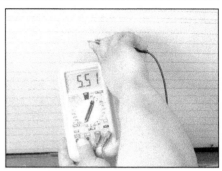

20.6 To determine if a hearing element has broken, check the voltage at the centre of each element – if the voltage is 6 volts, the element is unbroken

the point where the heating element is broken **(see illustration)**.

### Repair

9 Repair the break in the element using a repair kit specifically for this purpose. The kit includes conductive plastic epoxy.

10 Before repairing a break, turn off the system and allow it to cool for a few minutes.

11 Lightly buff the element area with fine steel wool; then clean it thoroughly with rubbing alcohol.

12 Use masking tape to mask off the area being repaired.

13 Thoroughly mix the epoxy, following the kit instructions.

14 Apply the epoxy material to the slit in the masking tape, overlapping the undamaged area about 20 mm on either end **(see illustration)**.

15 Allow the repair to cure for 24 hours before removing the tape and using the system.

### 21 Cruise control system – description and testing

1 The New Beetle has an unusual cruise control system. Instead of having a separate cruise control module, the input from the

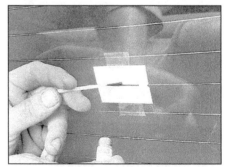

20.14 To use a heated rear window repair kit, apply masking to the inside of the window at the damaged area, then brush on the special conductive coating

vehicle speed sensor and cruise control switches at the steering column is directed to the Engine Control Module (ECM), which controls vehicle speed electronically through the electronic throttle control module on the throttle body. Some features of the system require special testers and diagnostic procedures that are beyond the scope of the home mechanic. Listed below are some general procedures that may be used to locate common problems.

2  Check fuses 5, 13 and 43 in the main fuse/relay box at the driver's end of the instrument panel (see Section 3).

3  The brake pedal position (BPP) switch (or brake light switch) deactivates the cruise control system. Have an assistant press the brake pedal while you check the brake light operation.

4  If the brake lights do not operate properly, correct the problem and retest the cruise control.

5  The cruise control system uses information from the Vehicle Speed Sensor, which is located in the transmission. To test the speed sensor, see Chapter 6A.

6  The testing of the cruise control switch mounted in the Multi-function switch is covered in Section 7.

7  The functioning of the throttle control module is key to the cruise control operation, so refer to Chapter 6A for a description and information about any tests for this device.

8  Test drive the vehicle to determine if the cruise control is now working. If it isn't, take it to a dealer service department or an automotive electrical specialist for further diagnosis.

## 22 Power window system – description and testing

1  The power window system operates electric motors, mounted in the doors, which lower and raise the windows. The system consists of the control switches, the motors, regulators, glass mechanisms and associated wiring.

2  The power windows can be lowered and raised from the master control switch by the driver or by the switch located at the passenger window. Each window has a separate motor that is reversible. The position of the control switch determines the polarity and therefore the direction of operation.

3  The circuit is protected by fuses and a circuit breaker. Check the number 5 fuse in the fuse panel at the drivers' end of the instrument panel, and the 30 amp fuse at the top of the fuse/relay panel near the base of the steering column. The circuit breaker (the one with the red connector) is at the bottom of the fuse/relay panel. See Section 4 for testing of circuit breakers. Each motor is also equipped with an internal circuit breaker; this prevents one stuck window from disabling the whole system.

4  The power window system will only operate when the ignition switch is On. In addition, many models have a window lockout switch at the master control switch which, when activated, disables the switch at the passenger's window also. Always check these items before troubleshooting a window problem.

5  These procedures are general in nature, so if you can't find the problem using them, take the vehicle to a dealer service department or other properly-equipped repair facility.

6  Check the wiring between the switches and fuse panel for continuity. Repair the wiring, if necessary.

7  If the passenger window is inoperative from the master control switch, try the other control switch at the passenger window.

8  If the same window works from one switch, but not the other, check the switch for continuity.

9  If the switch tests OK, check for a short or open in the circuit between the affected switch and the window motor.

10  If one window is inoperative from both switches, use a flat-bladed trim tool to prise up and remove the switch panel from the affected door. Check for voltage at the switch **(see illustrations)** and at the motor (refer to Chapter 11 for door trim panel removal) while the switch is operated.

11  If voltage is reaching the motor, disconnect the glass from the regulator (see Chapter 11). Move the window up and down by hand while checking for binding and damage. Also check for binding and damage to the regulator. If the regulator is not damaged and the window moves up and down smoothly, renew the motor. If there's binding or damage, lubricate, repair or renew parts, as necessary.

12  If voltage isn't reaching the motor, check the wiring in the circuit for continuity between the switches and motors. You'll need to consult the wiring diagram at the end of this Chapter.

13  Test the windows after you are done to confirm proper repairs. **Note:** *This system is governed by the Central Comfort Control Module, which is located under the end of the instrument panel, just above the foot pedals. Problems within this module must be diagnosed by a technician with the manufacturer's scan tool. If you have eliminated the obvious causes of a problem, have the vehicle checked at a dealership.*

## 23 Power door lock and keyless entry system – description and testing

1  The power door lock system operates the door lock actuators mounted in each door. The system consists of the switches, actuators, relays and associated wiring. Diagnosis can usually be limited to simple checks of the wiring connections and actuators for minor faults that can be easily repaired.

2  Power door lock systems are operated by bi-directional solenoids located in the doors. The lock switches have two operating positions: Lock and Unlock. These switches activate a relay, which in turn connects voltage to the door lock solenoids. Depending on which way the relay is activated, it reverses polarity, allowing the two sides of the circuit to be used alternately as the feed (positive) and earth side.

3  Some models may have keyless entry, electronic control modules and anti-theft systems incorporated into the power locks. If you are unable to locate the trouble using the following general steps, consult your dealer service department.

4  Always check the circuit protection first. Refer to the wiring diagrams at the end of this Chapter. Check the two fuses at the upper right of the under-dash fuse/relay panel located near the base of the steering column.

5  Operate the door lock switches in both directions (Lock and Unlock) with the engine off. Listen for the faint click of the relay operating.

6  If there's no click, check for voltage at the switches. If no voltage is present, check the wiring between the fuse panel and the switches for shorts and opens.

7  If voltage is present but no click is heard, test the switch for continuity. Renew it if there's not continuity in both switch positions.

**22.10a  Use a flat-bladed too to pry the door switched from the door panel**

**22.10b  Pry up the driver's door switch assembly from the door panel and backprobe the connector**

23.10 To test a door lock solenoid, check that power is getting to the solenoid connector (arrowed) while the switch is operated

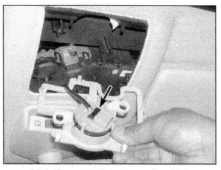

25.4 Remove the sunroof switch connector (arrowed) and check the switch for continuity

25.6 Use a trim tool to pry down the switch panel from the headlining

To remove the switch, use a flat-bladed trim tool to prise out the door/window switch assembly.

8 If the switch has continuity but the relay doesn't click, check the wiring between the switch and relay for continuity. Repair the wiring if there's no continuity.

9 If the relay is receiving voltage from the switch but is not sending voltage to the solenoids, check for a bad earth at the relay case. If the relay case is earthing properly, renew the relay. Relay tests are described in Section 5.

10 If only one lock solenoid operates, remove the trim panel from the affected door (see Chapter 11) and check for voltage at the solenoid while the lock switch is operated (see illustration). One of the wires should have voltage in the Lock position; the other should have voltage in the Unlock position.

11 If the inoperative solenoid is receiving voltage, renew the solenoid.

12 If the inoperative solenoid isn't receiving voltage, check for an open or short in the wire between the lock solenoid and the relay.

Note: It's common for wires to break in the portion of the harness between the body and door (opening and closing the door fatigues and eventually breaks the wires).

Note: This system is governed by the Central Comfort Control Module, which is located under the end of the instrument panel, just above the foot pedals. Problems within this module must be diagnosed by a technician with a factory scan tool. If you have eliminated the obvious causes of a problem, have the vehicle checked at a dealership.

### Keyless entry system

13 The keyless entry system consists of a remote control transmitter that sends a coded infrared signal to a receiver, which then operates the door-lock system.

14 Renew the battery when the transmitter doesn't operate the locks at a distance of 3 m. Normal range should be about 10 m.

15 Use a small screwdriver to carefully separate the case halves.

16 Renew the two (3 volt) CR2016 lithium batteries.

17 Snap the case halves together.

## 24 Electric rear view mirrors – description and testing

1 The electric rear view mirrors use two motors to move the glass; one for up and down adjustments and one for left-right adjustments.

2 The control switch has a selector portion that sends voltage to the left or right side mirror. With the ignition ACC position and the engine Off, roll down the windows and operate the mirror control switch through all functions (left-right and up-down) for both the left and right side mirrors. Note: On some models, the mirrors are also heated electrically, by turning the outside mirror 'joystick' control to the 'heat' position, which is between the left and right positions.

3 Listen carefully for the sound of the electric motors running in the mirrors.

4 If the motors can be heard but the mirror glass doesn't move, there's probably a problem with the drive mechanism inside the mirror. Power mirrors have no user-serviceable parts inside, a defective mirror must be renewed as a unit (see Chapter 11).

5 If the mirrors don't operate and no sound comes from the mirrors, check the Comfort system fuse in the fuse panel at the driver's end of the instrument panel.

6 If the fuses are OK, remove the switch panel for access to the back of the mirror control switch without disconnecting the wires attached to it. Turn the ignition On and check for voltage at the switch. There should be voltage at one terminal. If there's no voltage at the switch, check for an open or short in the wiring between the fuse panel and the switch.

7 If there's voltage at the switch, disconnect it. Check the switch for continuity in all its operating positions. If the switch does not have continuity, renew it.

8 Locate the wire going from the switch to earth. Leaving the switch connected, connect a jumper wire between this wire and earth. If the mirror works normally with this wire in place, repair the faulty earth connection.

9 If the mirror still doesn't work, remove the mirror and check the wires at the mirror for voltage. Check with ignition On and the mirror selector switch on the appropriate side. Operate the mirror switch in all its positions. There should be voltage at one of the switch-to-mirror wires in each switch position (except the neutral 'off' position).

10 If voltage is absent in each switch position, check the wiring between the mirror and control switch for opens and shorts.

11 If there's voltage, remove the mirror and test it off the vehicle with jumper wires. Renew the mirror if it fails this test. Note: This system is governed by the Central Comfort Control Module, which is located under the end of the instrument panel, just above the foot pedals. Problems within this module must be diagnosed by a technician with the manufacturer's scan tool. If you have eliminated the obvious causes of a problem, have the vehicle checked at a dealership.

## 25 Sunroof switch – testing and renewal

1 The sunroof switch is located in a panel in the headlining, above the rear view mirror. The switch is accessible, but the sunroof module and drive can only be accessed by removing the vehicle headlining, which is a job for a dealership service department or other properly-equipped repair facility.

2 To check the switch, the panel must be pulled down (see Steps 6 and 7).

3 Refer to Sections 3 and 5 and check the fuse and relay first.

4 Disconnect the electrical connector on the back of the sunroof switch and check for continuity (see illustration).

5 With the switch Off, there should be no continuity between terminal 2 and 4 or 5. With the switch turned either to Open or Closed, there should be continuity from terminal 2 with 4 in one direction, and 5 in the other direction. If the switch fails the tests, renew the switch.

### Renewal

6 Pull down the sunroof switch panel from the headlining (see illustration).

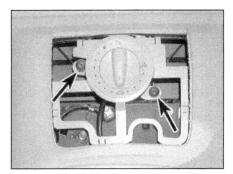

**25.7 Remove the screws (arrowed), pull down the switch frame, and disconnect the two clips on the back securing the switch**

**25.9 Use the emergency sunroof crank handle in the hole in the drive (arrowed)**

**26.1 The airbag control module is located on the floor ahead of the console – do not tamper with the yellow connectors attached to it**

**7** Remove the two screws and pull down the switch and its frame **(see illustration)**.
**8** The switch can be removed from the frame by disconnecting the electrical connector **(see illustration 25.4)** and releasing the two clips at the back of the switch.
**9** In case of sunroof switch or module failure, the sunroof can be operated manually. A crank handle is snapped into clips on the back of the switch panel. Use the crank handle in the hole in the sunroof drive to open or close the sunroof **(see illustration)**.

## 26 Airbag system –
general information

**1** These models are equipped with a Supplemental Restraint System (SRS), more commonly known as airbags, designed to protect the driver and front seat passenger from serious injury in the event of a head-on or frontal collision. All models have a sensing/diagnostic control unit, located on the floor under the centre of the instrument panel, next to the bulkhead **(see illustration)**.

 *Warning: If your vehicle is ever involved in a flood, or the interior carpeting is soaked for any reason, disconnect the battery and do not start the vehicle until the airbag system can be checked by your dealer. If the SRS system is subjected to flooding, the airbags could go off upon starting the vehicle, even without an accident taking place.*

### Airbag modules

**2** The airbag modules consist of a housing incorporating the cushion (airbag) and inflator unit. The inflator assembly is mounted on the back of the housing over a hole through which gas is expelled, inflating the bag almost instantaneously when an electrical signal is sent from the system. The specially-wound wire on the driver's side that carries this signal to the driver's module is called a spiral cable. The spiral cable is a flat, ribbon-like electrically conductive tape that is wound many times so that it can transmit an electrical signal regardless of steering wheel position. Airbag modules are located in the

steering wheel, on the passenger side above the glovebox, and at the upper side of each front seat (side-impact airbags).

### Sensing/diagnostic control unit and sensors

**3** The sensing/diagnostic control unit contains an on-board microprocessor which monitors the operation of the system, and also contains a crash sensor. It checks this system every time the vehicle is started, causing the 'AIRBAG' light to illuminate for five seconds, then go off, if the system is operating properly. If there is a fault in the system, the light may not come on at all, the light will go on and continue, either illuminated steadily or blinking, and the unit will store fault codes indicating the nature of the fault.

### Operation

**4** For the airbag(s) to deploy, one or both impact sensors and the crash sensor must be activated. When this condition occurs, the circuit to the airbag inflator is closed and the airbag inflates. If the battery is destroyed by the impact, or is too low to power the inflator, a back-up power unit inside the SRS system provides power.

### Self-diagnosis system

**5** A self-diagnosis circuit in the SRS unit displays a light on the instrument panel when the ignition switch is turned to the On position. If the system is operating normally, the light should go out after about five seconds. If the light doesn't come on, or doesn't go out after a short time, or if it comes on while you're driving the vehicle, or if it blinks at any time, there's a malfunction in the SRS system. Have it inspected and repaired as soon as possible. Do not attempt to troubleshoot or service the SRS system yourself. Even a small mistake could cause the SRS system to malfunction when you need it.

### Servicing components near the SRS system

**6** There are times when you need to remove the steering wheel, radio or service other components on or near the dashboard. At these times, you'll be working around components and wire harnesses for the SRS

system. The SRS wiring harnesses are easy to identify: They're all covered with a bright yellow conduit. Do not unplug the connectors for these wires. And do not use electrical test equipment on airbag system wires; it could cause the airbag(s) to deploy. *ALWAYS DISABLE THE SRS SYSTEM BEFORE WORKING NEAR THE SRS SYSTEM COMPONENTS OR RELATED WIRING.*

### Disabling the SRS system

 *Warning: Any time you are working in the vicinity of airbag wiring or components, DISABLE THE SRS SYSTEM.*

**7** To disable the airbag system, perform the following steps:
a) *Turn the steering wheel to the straight-ahead position and turn the ignition switch to the Lock position, then remove the key.*
b) *Disconnect the negative battery cable (see Chapter 5). Refer to the Cautions in Section 1 of this Chapter.*
c) *Wait at least two minutes for the backup power supply to be depleted before beginning work.*
d) *Remove the driver's knee bolster (see Chapter 11, Section 24) and disconnect the driver's airbag connector at the steering column (see Chapter 10).*
e) *Open and drop the glovebox door (see Chapter 11, Section 24) and disconnect the connector to the passenger airbag (see illustration).*

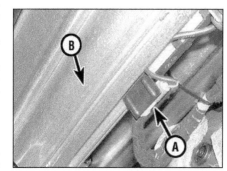

**26.7 Disconnect the connector (A) from the passenger airbag (B), below the right-hand side of the dash**

### Enabling the system

**8** To enable the airbag system, perform the following steps:
  a) *Turn the ignition switch to the Lock position and remove the key.*
  b) *Reconnect the passenger and driver's airbag connectors, making sure the CPA (Connector Positive Assurance) clips are in place so the connectors can't accidentally disengage.*
  c) *Connect the battery cable.*
  d) *With your body out of the path of the airbag, turn the ignition switch to the On position. Confirm that the airbag warning light glows for 5 seconds, then goes out, indicating the system is functioning properly.*

### Removal and refitting

#### Driver's side airbag

**9** Refer to Chapter 10, Section 15, for removal and refitting of the driver's side airbag.

#### Passenger side airbag

**10** Disable the airbag system, see the **Warning** above.

**11** Remove the glovebox and its dash panel (see Chapter 11, Section 24).

**12** From under the instrument panel, disconnect the passenger airbag connector **(see illustration 26.7)**.

**13** The instrument panel must be removed for access to the passenger airbag mounting screws (see Chapter 11). **Note:** *This is a difficult job for the home mechanic, involving tedious dismantling and many electrical connections to keep track of.*

**14** Remove the screws and gently prise the airbag module from the brackets on the cowl support beam.

 *Warning: Whenever handling an airbag module, always carry the airbag module with the trim panel side facing away from your body. Place the airbag module in a safe location with the trim panel side facing up.*
*Caution: The airbag assembly is heavier than it looks, use both hands when removing it from the dash.*

**15** Refitting is the reverse of the removal procedure.

#### Seat belt pre-tensioners

**16** All models are equipped with pyrotechnic (explosive) units in the front seat belt retracting mechanisms for both the lap and shoulder belts. During an impact that would trigger the airbag system, the airbag control unit also triggers the seat belt pre-tensioners. When the pyrotechnic charges go off, they accelerate the retractors to instantly take up any slack in the seat belt system to more fully prepare the driver and front seat passenger for impact.

**17** The airbag system should be disabled anytime work is done to or around the seats or the body 'B' pillars.
*Caution: Never strike the pillars or floor with a hammer or impact-driver tool unless the system is disabled.*

### 27 Wiring diagrams – general information

Since it isn't possible to include all wiring diagrams for every year and model covered by this manual, the following diagrams are those that are typical and most commonly needed.

Prior to troubleshooting any circuits, check the fuse and circuit breakers (if applicable) to make sure they're in good condition. Make sure the battery is properly charged and check the cable connections (see Chapter 1).

When checking a circuit, make sure that all connectors are clean, with no broken or loose terminals. When disconnecting a connector, do not pull on the wires. Pull only on the connector housings themselves.

## VW Beetle wiring diagrams

**Diagram 1**

### Key to symbols

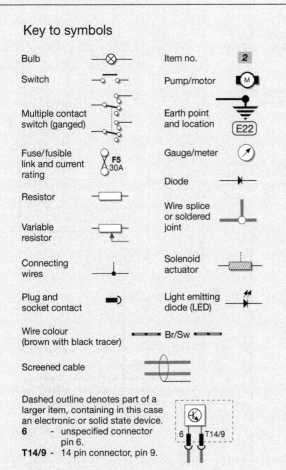

| | |
|---|---|
| Bulb | —⊗— |
| Switch | —o͟ o— |
| Multiple contact switch (ganged) | |
| Fuse/fusible link and current rating | F5 30A |
| Resistor | —▭— |
| Variable resistor | |
| Connecting wires | |
| Plug and socket contact | ▬ |
| Wire colour (brown with black tracer) | Br/Sw |
| Screened cable | |

| | |
|---|---|
| Item no. | **2** |
| Pump/motor | Ⓜ |
| Earth point and location | (E22) |
| Gauge/meter | |
| Diode | —▶|— |
| Wire splice or soldered joint | |
| Solenoid actuator | |
| Light emitting diode (LED) | |

Dashed outline denotes part of a larger item, containing in this case an electronic or solid state device.
**6** - unspecified connector pin 6.
**T14/9** - 14 pin connector, pin 9.

### Key to circuits

| | |
|---|---|
| Diagram 1 | Information for wiring diagrams |
| Diagram 2 | Starting, charging and engine cooling fan |
| Diagram 3 | Simos (1.6) engine management part 1 of 2 |
| Diagram 4 | Simos (1.6) engine management part 2 of 2 |
| Diagram 5 | Motronic (1.8) engine management part 1 of 2 |
| Diagram 6 | Motronic (1.8) engine management part 2 of 2 |
| Diagram 7 | Motronic (2.0) engine management part 1 of 2 |
| Diagram 8 | Motronic (2.0) engine management part 2 of 2 |
| Diagram 9 | Turbo Diesel (1.9) engine management part 1 of 2 |
| Diagram 10 | Turbo Diesel (1.9) engine management part 2 of 2 |
| Diagram 11 | Instrument cluster |
| Diagram 12 | Side, tail & number plate light, headlights and headlight levelling |
| Diagram 13 | Stop & reversing lights, direction indicators & hazard warning lights |
| Diagram 14 | Rear foglight, tank flap release, cigar lighter & accessories socket, clock & interior lighting |
| Diagram 15 | Twin horns, heater blower, heated rear window, wash/wipe |
| Diagram 16 | Diagnostic connector, rear foglight control, airbags, trailer socket |
| Diagram 17 | Heated seats, audio system |
| Diagram 18 | Automatic transmission |
| Diagram 19 | Typical air conditioning system |
| Diagram 20 | Typical ABS system, daytime driving lights |
| Diagram 21 | Typical convenience system part 1 of 2 |
| Diagram 22 | Typical convenience system part 2 of 2 |

### Earth locations

| | |
|---|---|
| E1 | Earthing strap, battery to body |
| E2 | Earthing strap, gearbox to body |
| E3 | LH engine compartment |
| E4 | In centre of plenum chamber |
| E5 | Next to steering column |
| E6 | On right of plenum chamber |
| E7 | On cylinder head |
| E8 | In plenum chamber |
| E9 | On rear left pillar |
| E10 | On left in luggage compartment |
| E11 | Lower LH 'A' pillar |
| E12 | On driver's seat |
| E13 | On passenger's seat |
| E14 | Behind center of dash panel |
| E15 | Lower RH 'A' pillar |

### Fuse holder

| Fuse | Rating | Circuit protected |
|---|---|---|
| F1 | 10A | Heated windscreen washer jets |
| F2 | 10A | Direction indicators |
| F3 | 5A | Headlight levelling |
| F4 | 5A | Number plate lights |
| F5 | 7.5A | Convenience system, cruise control system, Climatronic, control unit for driver's and front passenger's heated seats |
| F6 | 5A | Central locking |
| F7 | 10A | Reversing lights |
| F8 | 5A | Telephone system |
| F9 | 5A | Anti-lock brakes |
| F10 | 10A | Engine management system - petrol |
| F11 | 5A | Instrument cluster, selector lever lock solenoid |
| F12 | 7.5A | Voltage supply for self-diagnosis, telephone system |
| F13 | 10A | Stop lights, glove box illumination |
| F14 | 10A | Interior lights, central locking |
| F15 | 5A | Instrument cluster, central locking |
| F16 | 10A | Engine management - petrol |
| F17 | - | Spare |
| F18 | 10A | RH main beam |
| F19 | 10A | LH main beam |
| F20 | 10A | RH dipped beam, headlight levelling |
| F21 | 10A | LH dipped beam |
| F22 | 5A | RH side lights |
| F23 | 5A | LH side lights |
| F24 | 20A | Windscreen wiper system |
| F25 | 25A | Heater blower, air recirculating system, air conditioning, Climatronic |
| F26 | 25A | Heated rear window, heated mirrors (without electric windows) |
| F27 | - | Spare |
| F28 | 15A | Fuel pump |
| F29 | 15A | Engine management - petrol |
| | 10A | Engine management - Diesel |
| F30 | 20A | Sunroof |
| F31 | 20A | Automatic gearbox |
| F32 | 10A | Engine management fuel injectors |
| | 15A | Engine management - Diesel |
| F33 | - | Spare |
| F34 | 10A | Engine management |
| F35 | 30A | Trailer socket |
| F36 | 15A | Front and rear foglights |
| F37 | 10A | 'S' contact |
| F38 | 15A | Luggage compartment light, central locking |
| F39 | 15A | Hazard warning lights |
| F40 | 20A | Dual tone horn |
| F41 | 15A | Cigar lighter |
| F42 | 25A | Radio |
| F43 | 10A | Engine management |
| F44 | 15A | Heated seats |

H32170

## Wire colours

**Ws** White   **Gr** Grey
**Br** Brown   **Sw** Black
**Bl** Blue   **Li** Lilac
**Ro** Red   **Gn** Green
**Ge** Yellow

\* See also diagram 19
  air conditioning

## Key to items

1 Battery
2 Ignition switch
3 Battery fuse holder
4 Relay plate
5 Starter motor
6 Alternator
7 Engine cooling fan
8 Engine cooling fan thermal switch
9 Fuse holder
10 Engine cooling fan control unit
11 RH cooling fan
12 Engine cooling fan 3rd speed relay
13 Engine cooling fan 3rd speed thermal switch

**Diagram 2**

H32171

### Starting (manual transmission) and charging

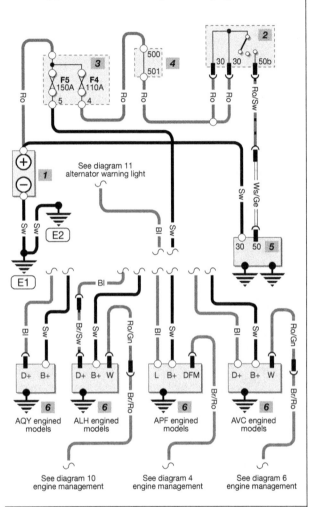

### Engine cooling fan - twin speed

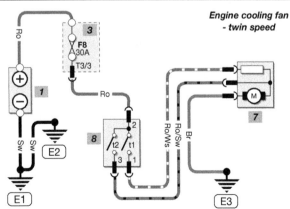

### Engine cooling fan - triple speed

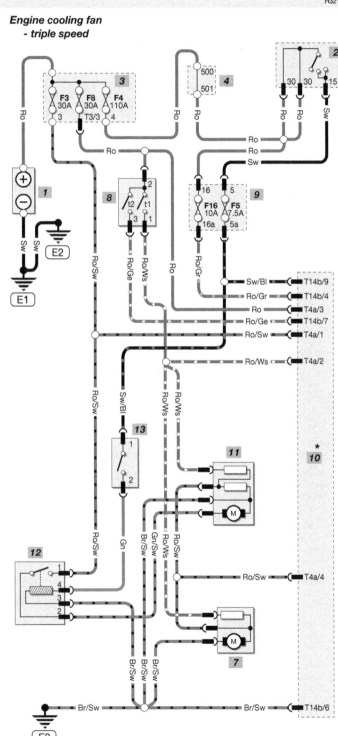

## Wire colours

**Ws** White **Gr** Grey
**Br** Brown **Sw** Black
**Bl** Blue **Li** Lilac
**Ro** Red **Gn** Green
**Ge** Yellow

## Key to items

1  Battery
2  Ignition switch
3  Battery fuse holder
4  Relay plate
9  Fuse holder
15  Fuel pump relay
16  Ignition coil
17  Spark plugs
18  Main relay
19  EGR solenoid valve/EGR potentiometer
20  Crankcase breather heater
21  Secondary air pump
22  Secondary air pump relay
23  Fuel pump/fuel gauge sender unit
24  Inlet manifold change-over valve
25  Fuel injector
26  Engine management control unit
27  Air mass meter
28  Canister purge solenoid valve
29  Oxygen sensor (before catalyst)
30  Oxygen sensor (after catalyst)

**Diagram 3**

H32172

*1.6 Litre/74 kW Simos engine management system (engine code APF) - part 1 of 2*

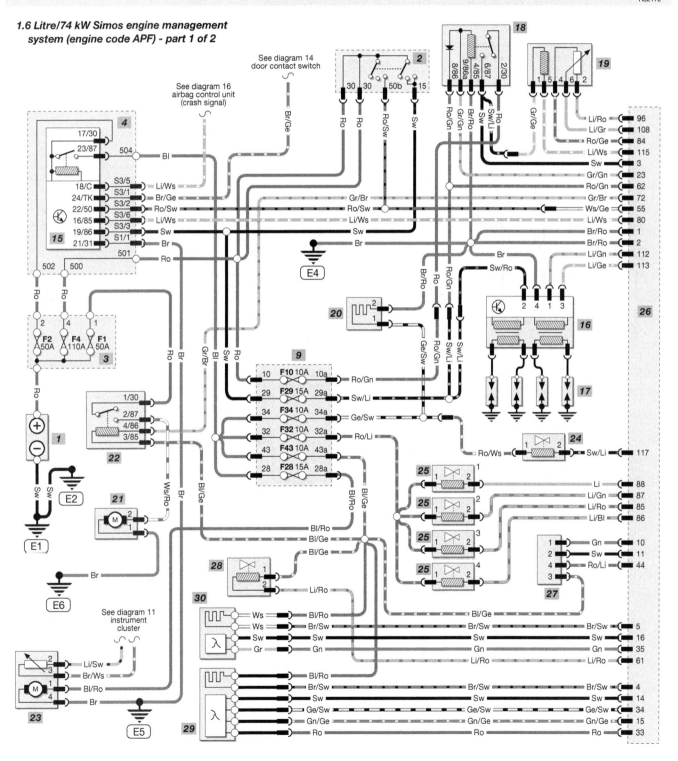

## Wire colours

**Ws** White  **Gr** Grey
**Br** Brown  **Sw** Black
**Bl** Blue  **Li** Lilac
**Ro** Red  **Gn** Green
**Ge** Yellow

## Key to items

1  Battery
2  Ignition switch
3  Battery fuse holder
4  Relay plate
9  Fuse holder
26  Engine management control unit
31  Brake pedal switch/stop light switch
   (models with cruise control)
32  Clutch switch (models with cruise
   control)

33  Cruise control switch
   a = cruise control switch
   b = cruise control SET switch
34  Coolant temperature sensor
35  Knock sensor
36  Throttle valve assembly
   a = throttle valve positioner
   b = throttle valve positioner
     potentiometer
   c = throttle potentiometer

37  Power steering pressure switch
38  Engine speed sensor
39  Accelerator pedal position sensor
40  Camshaft position sensor

## Diagram 4

H32173

*1.6 Litre/74 kW Simos engine management system (engine code APF) - part 2 of 2*

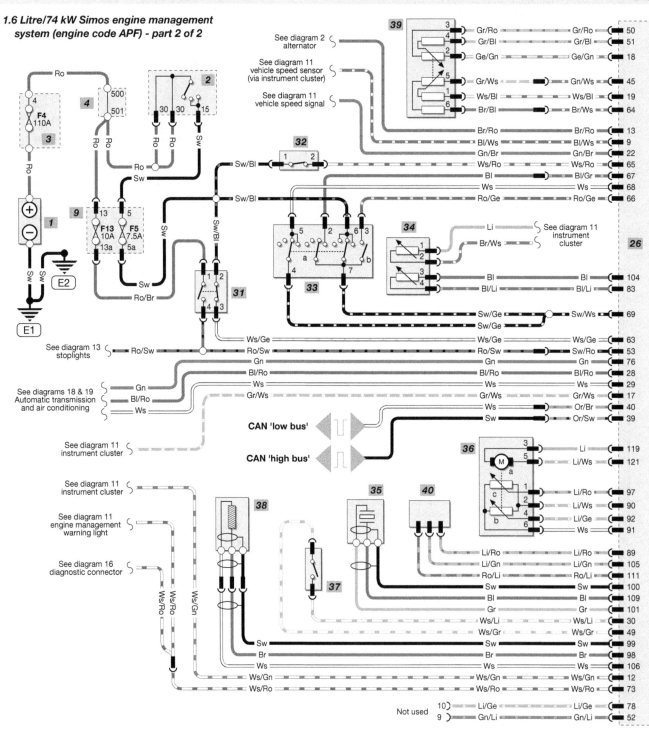

## Wire colours

| | | | |
|---|---|---|---|
| **Ws** | White | **Gr** | Grey |
| **Br** | Brown | **Sw** | Black |
| **Bl** | Blue | **Li** | Lilac |
| **Ro** | Red | **Gn** | Green |
| **Ge** | Yellow | | |

## Key to items

| | |
|---|---|
| 1 | Battery |
| 2 | Ignition switch |
| 3 | Battery fuse holder |
| 4 | Relay plate |
| 9 | Fuse holder |
| 15 | Fuel pump relay |
| 16 | Ignition coil |
| 17 | Spark plugs |
| 23 | Fuel pump/fuel gauge sender unit |
| 25 | Fuel injector |
| 26 | Engine management control unit |
| 27 | Air mass meter |
| 28 | Canister purge solenoid valve |
| 29 | Oxygen sensor (before catalyst) |
| 30 | Oxygen sensor (after catalyst) |
| 45 | Fuel system diagnosis pump |
| 46 | Turbo charger divert valve |
| 47 | Charge pressure control valve |

**Diagram 5**

H32174

### 1.8 Litre/110 kW Motronic engine management system (engine code AVC) - part 1 of 2

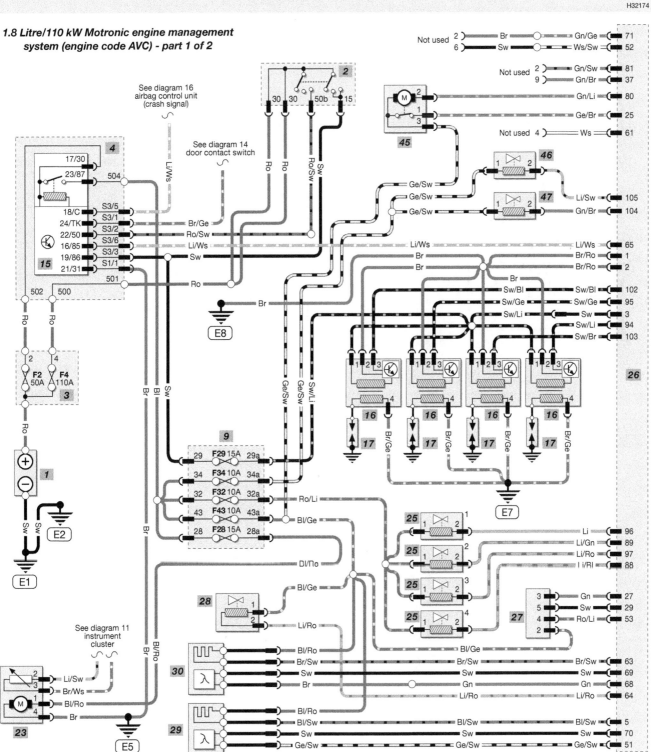

## Wire colours

| | | | |
|---|---|---|---|
| **Ws** | White | **Gr** | Grey |
| **Br** | Brown | **Sw** | Black |
| **Bl** | Blue | **Li** | Lilac |
| **Ro** | Red | **Gn** | Green |
| **Ge** | Yellow | | |

## Key to items

1 Battery
2 Ignition switch
3 Battery fuse holder
4 Relay plate
9 Fuse holder
26 Engine management control unit
31 Brake pedal switch/stop light switch (models with cruise control)
32 Clutch switch (models with cruise control)

33 Cruise control switch
  a = cruise control switch
  b = cruise control SET switch
34 Coolant temperature sensor
35 Knock sensor 1
36 Throttle valve assembly
  a = throttle valve positioner
  b = throttle valve positioner potentiometer
  c = throttle potentiometer

38 Engine speed sensor
39 Accelerator pedal position sensor
40 Camshaft position sensor
41 Knock sensor 2
42 MAP sensor
43 Inlet air temperature sensor

## Diagram 6

H32175

### 1.8 Litre/110 kW Motronic engine management system (engine code AVC) - part 2 of 2

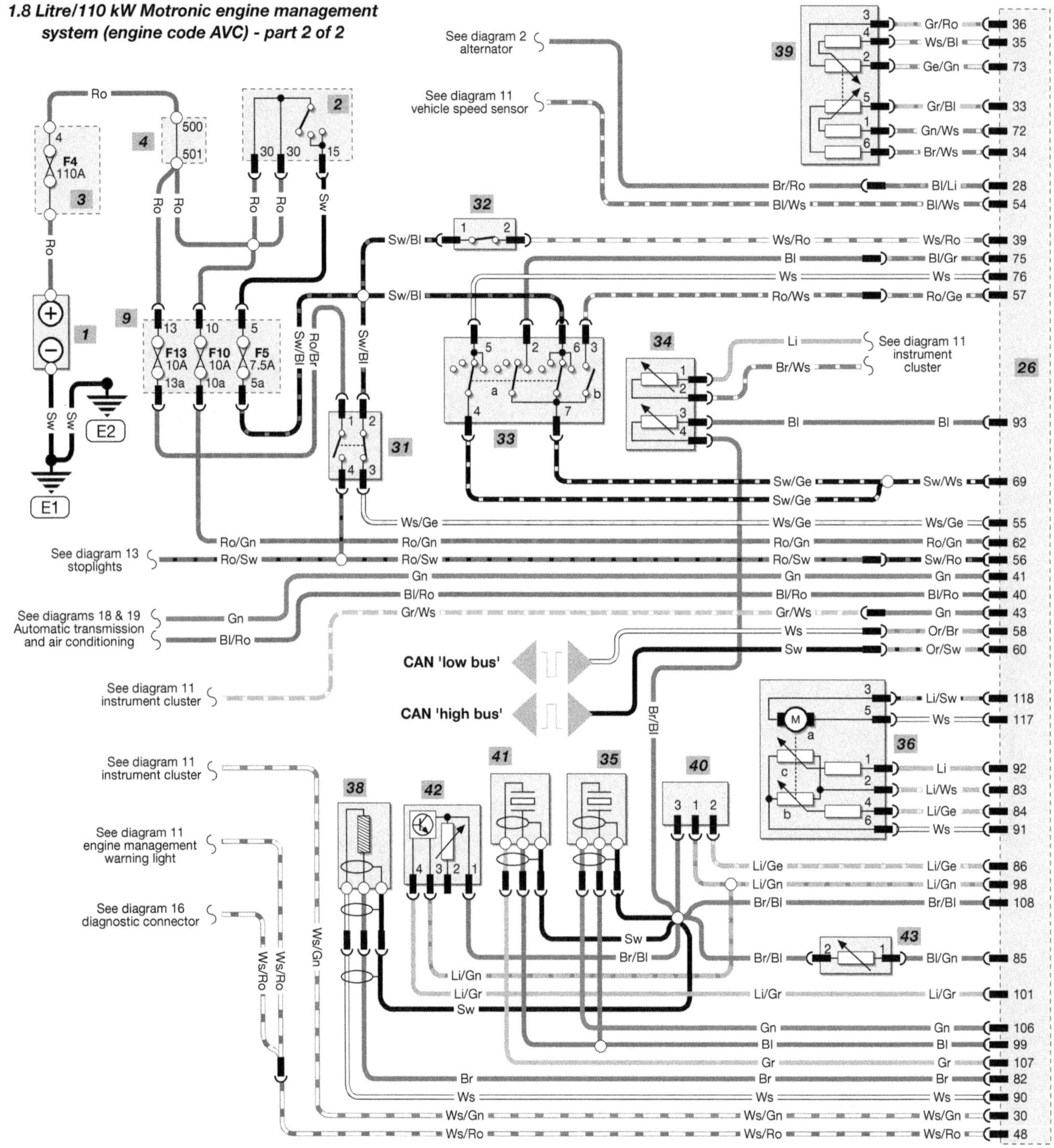

## Wire colours

| | | | |
|---|---|---|---|
| **Ws** | White | **Gr** | Grey |
| **Br** | Brown | **Sw** | Black |
| **Bl** | Blue | **Li** | Lilac |
| **Ro** | Red | **Gn** | Green |
| **Ge** | Yellow | | |

## Key to items

| | | | | | |
|---|---|---|---|---|---|
| 1 | Battery | 17 | Spark plugs | 27 | Air mass meter |
| 2 | Ignition switch | 20 | Crankcase breather heater | 28 | Canister purge solenoid valve |
| 3 | Battery fuse holder | 21 | Secondary air pump | 29 | Oxygen sensor (before catalyst) |
| 4 | Relay plate | 22 | Secondary air pump relay | 30 | Oxygen sensor (after catalyst) |
| 9 | Fuse holder | 23 | Fuel pump/fuel gauge sender unit | 44 | Secondary air inlet valve |
| 15 | Fuel pump relay | 25 | Fuel injector | 45 | Fuel system diagnosis pump |
| 16 | Ignition coil | 26 | Engine management control unit | | |

**Diagram 7**

H32176

### 2.0 Litre/85 kW Motronic engine management system (engine code AQY) - part 1 of 2

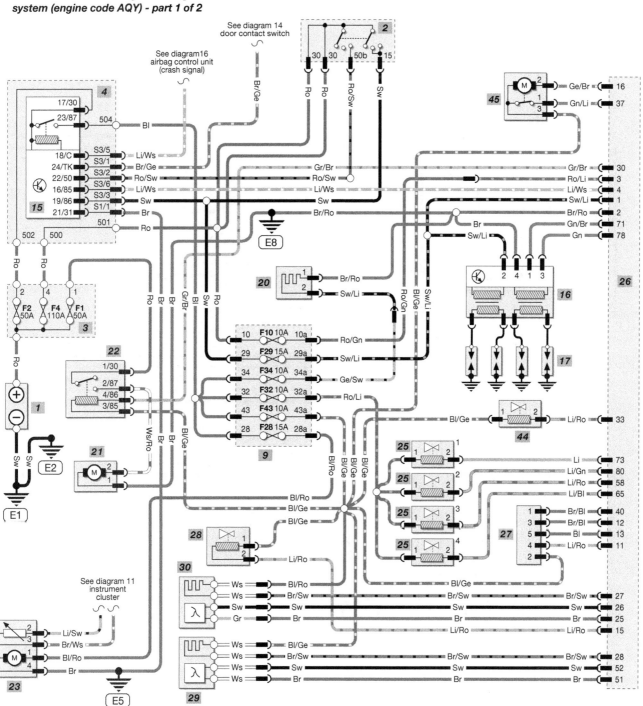

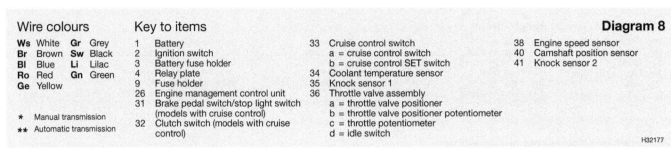

## Wire colours

| | | | |
|---|---|---|---|
| **Ws** | White | **Gr** | Grey |
| **Br** | Brown | **Sw** | Black |
| **Bl** | Blue | **Li** | Lilac |
| **Ro** | Red | **Gn** | Green |
| **Ge** | Yellow | | |

\* Manual transmission
\*\* Automatic transmission

## Key to items

1. Battery
2. Ignition switch
3. Battery fuse holder
4. Relay plate
9. Fuse holder
26. Engine management control unit
31. Brake pedal switch/stop light switch (models with cruise control)
32. Clutch switch (models with cruise control)
33. Cruise control switch
   a = cruise control switch
   b = cruise control SET switch
34. Coolant temperature sensor
35. Knock sensor 1
36. Throttle valve assembly
   a = throttle valve positioner
   b = throttle valve positioner potentiometer
   c = throttle potentiometer
   d = idle switch
38. Engine speed sensor
40. Camshaft position sensor
41. Knock sensor 2

**Diagram 8**

H32177

*2.0 Litre/85 kW Motronic engine management system (engine code AQY) - part 2 of 2*

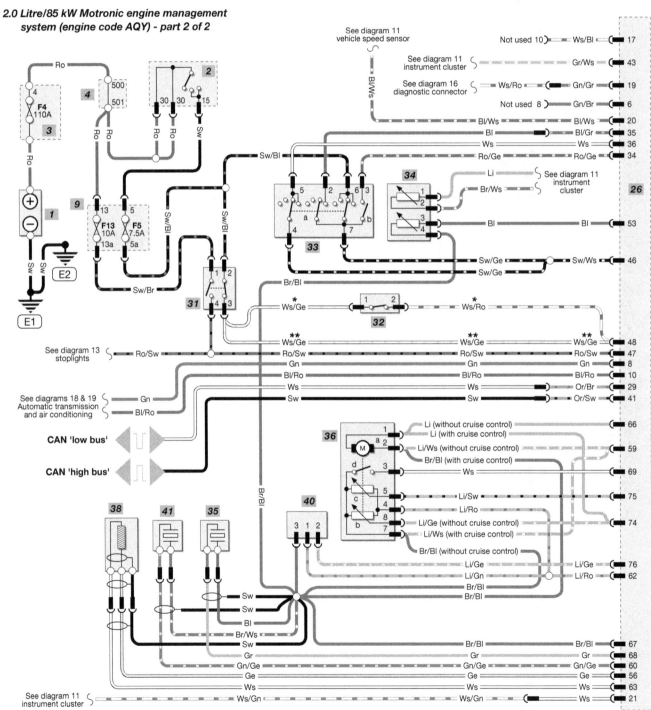

## Wire colours

| | | | |
|---|---|---|---|
| **Ws** | White | **Gr** | Grey |
| **Br** | Brown | **Sw** | Black |
| **Bl** | Blue | **Li** | Lilac |
| **Ro** | Red | **Gn** | Green |
| **Ge** | Yellow | | |

\* Vehicles with crankcase breather elements only

## Key to items

1 Battery
3 Battery fuse holder
4 Relay plate
9 Fuse holder
18 Main relay
24 Inlet manifold changeover valve
26 Engine management control unit
27 Air mass meter
31 Brake pedal switch/stop light switch (models with cruise control)
32 Clutch switch (models with cruise control)
47 Charge pressure control valve
50 EGR recirculation solenoid valve
51 Glow plug relay
52 Glow plugs
53 Coolant heater relay - low heat output (if fitted)
54 Coolant heater relay - high heat output (if fitted)
55 Coolant heater elements (if fitted)
56 Commencement of injection valve
57 Fuel temperature sender
58 Metering adjuster
59 Modulating piston movement sender

## Diagram 9

H32178

**1.9 Litre/66 kW Turbo Diesel engine management system (engine code ALH) - part 1 of 2**

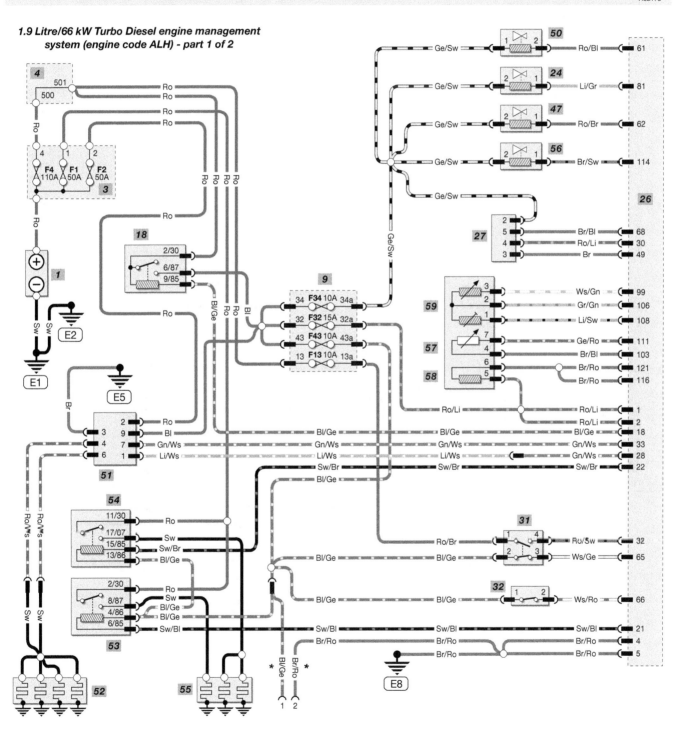

## Wire colours

**Ws** White **Gr** Grey
**Br** Brown **Sw** Black
**Bl** Blue **Li** Lilac
**Ro** Red **Gn** Green
**Ge** Yellow

## Key to items

1 Battery
2 Ignition switch
3 Battery fuse holder
4 Relay plate
9 Fuse holder
26 Engine management control unit

33 Cruise control switch
  a = cruise control switch
  b = cruise control SET switch
34 Coolant temperature sensor
38 Engine speed sensor
60 Accelerator position sensor

61 Kick down switch
62 Idle switch
63 Fuel shut off valve
64 Needle lift sensor

**Diagram 10**

H32179

### 1.9 Litre/66 kW Turbo Diesel engine management system (engine code ALH) - part 2 of 2

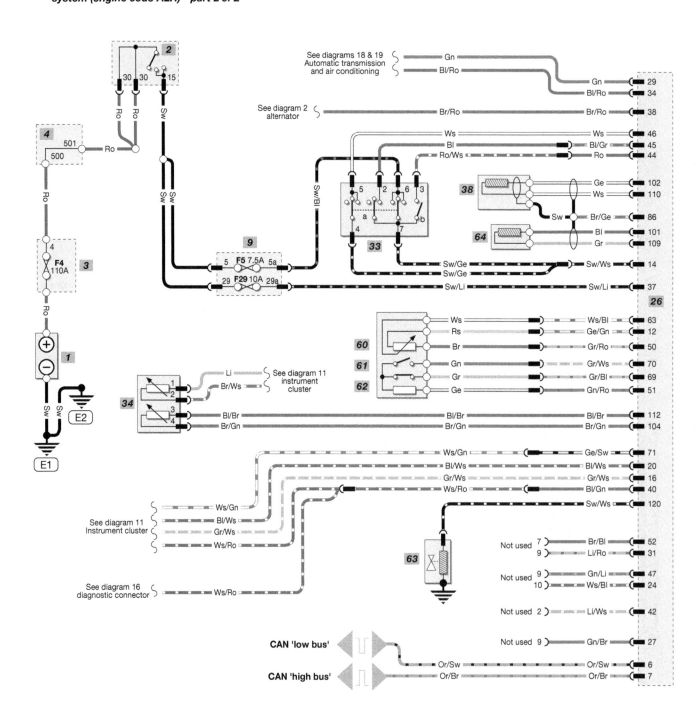

## Wire colours

| | | | |
|---|---|---|---|
| **Ws** | White | **Gr** | Grey |
| **Br** | Brown | **Sw** | Black |
| **Bl** | Blue | **Li** | Lilac |
| **Ro** | Red | **Gn** | Green |
| **Ge** | Yellow | | |

\*      AQY only
\*\*     With flexible service
         indicator display
\*\*\*    APF/ALH only
\*\*\*\*   All other models

## Key to items

1 Battery
2 Ignition switch
3 Battery fuse holder
4 Relay plate
9 Fuse holder
14 Handbrake switch
46 Brake fluid level switch
66 Immobiliser reading coil
67 Oil level/oil temperature sender
68 Speedometer sender unit
69 Oil pressure switch
82 Low coolant sender unit
83 Instrument cluster
    a = immobilizer warning light

83 Instrument cluster continued
    b = low fuel warning light
    c = oil pressure warning light
    d = oil level warning light
    e = alternator warning light
    f = coolant temperature gauge
    g = fuel gauge
    h = lights on warning buzzer
    i = warning buzzer
    j = immobilizer control unit
    k = odometer
    l = speedometer
    m = control/display unit
    n = handbrake warning light

83 Instrument cluster continued
    o = low coolant level/high coolant
        temperature warning light
    p = engine management/glow plug
        warning light
    r = brake system warning light
    s = tachometer
    t = rear foglight warning light
    u = LH indicator
    v = RH indicator
    w = display illumination
    x = main beam warning light
84 LH front pad wear sensor
99 RH front pad wear sensor

**Diagram 11**

H32180

*Instrument cluster*

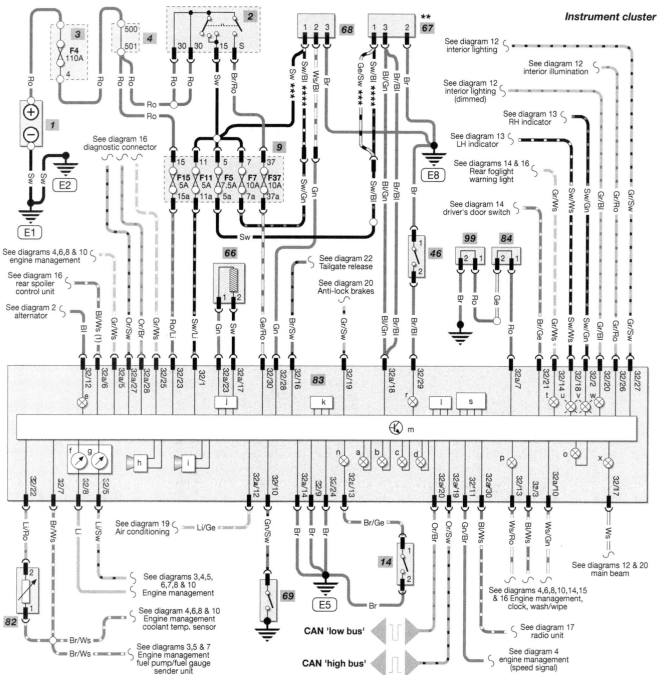

## Wire colours

| | | | |
|---|---|---|---|
| **Ws** | White | **Gr** | Grey |
| **Br** | Brown | **Sw** | Black |
| **Bl** | Blue | **Li** | Lilac |
| **Ro** | Red | **Gn** | Green |
| **Ge** | Yellow | | |

## Key to items

1  Battery
2  Ignition switch
3  Battery fuse holder
4  Relay plate
9  Fuse holder
70  Light switch
   a = side/headlight
71  Multifunction switch
   a = parking light
   b = headlight dipper/flasher
72  Number plate light
73  LH sidelight
74  RH sidelight
75  LH tail light
76  RH tail light
77  LH headlight
78  RH headlight
79  Headlight levelling switch
80  LH headlight levelling motor
81  RH headlight levelling motor

**Diagram 12**

H32181

### Side, tail and number plate lights

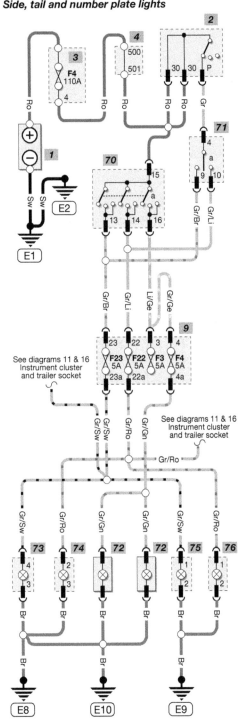

### Headlights and headlight levelling

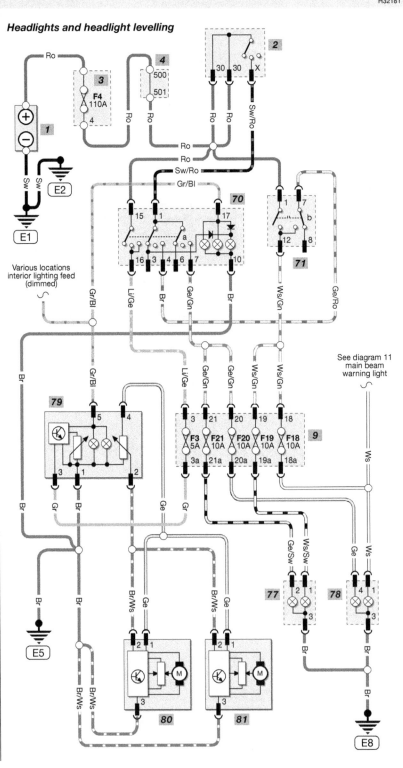

See diagrams 11 & 16
Instrument cluster
and trailer socket

See diagrams 11 & 16
Instrument cluster
and trailer socket

Various locations
interior lighting feed
(dimmed)

See diagram 11
main beam
warning light

## Wire colours

| | | | |
|---|---|---|---|
| **Ws** | White | **Gr** | Grey |
| **Br** | Brown | **Sw** | Black |
| **Bl** | Blue | **Li** | Lilac |
| **Ro** | Red | **Gn** | Green |
| **Ge** | Yellow | | |

## Key to items

| | |
|---|---|
| 1 | Battery |
| 2 | Ignition switch |
| 3 | Battery fuse holder |
| 4 | Relay plate |
| 9 | Fuse holder |
| 31 | Brake pedal switch/stop light switch (models with cruise control) |
| 71 | Multifunction switch<br>c = direction indicators |
| 85 | Stop light switch |
| 86 | Reversing light switch |
| 87 | LH stop light |
| 88 | RH stop light |
| 89 | High level brake light |
| 90 | Reversing light |
| 91 | 'X'contact relay |
| 92 | Direction indicator switch |
| 93 | LH front direction indicator |
| 94 | LH indicator side repeater |
| 95 | LH rear direction indicator |
| 96 | RH front direction indicator |
| 97 | RH indicator side repeater |
| 98 | RH rear direction indicator |

**Diagram 13**

H32182

### Stop and reversing lights

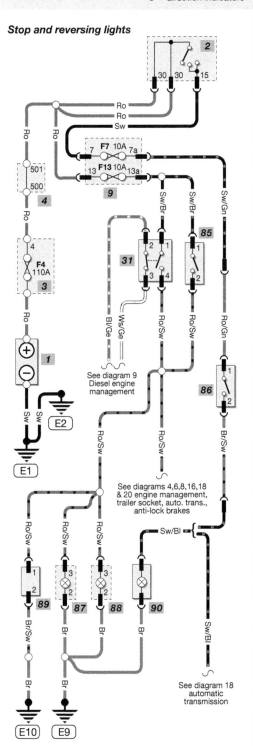

See diagram 9 Diesel engine management

See diagrams 4,6,8,16,18 & 20 engine management, trailer socket, auto. trans., anti-lock brakes

See diagram 18 automatic transmission

### Direction indicator and hazard warning lights

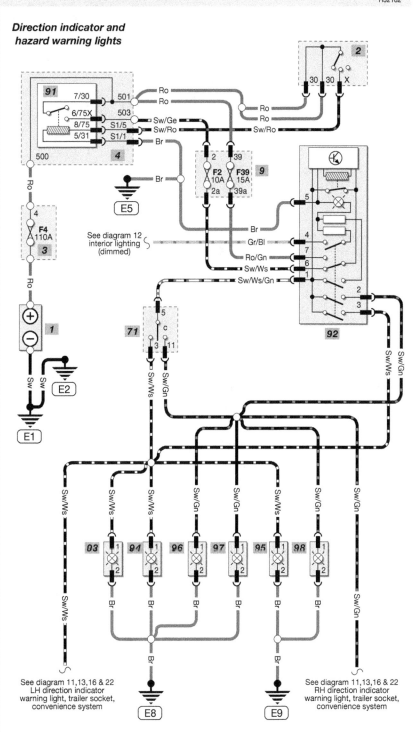

See diagram 12 interior lighting (dimmed)

See diagram 11,13,16 & 22 LH direction indicator warning light, trailer socket, convenience system

See diagram 11,13,16 & 22 RH direction indicator warning light, trailer socket, convenience system

## Wire colours

**Ws** White   **Gr** Grey
**Br** Brown   **Sw** Black
**Bl** Blue   **Li** Lilac
**Ro** Red   **Gn** Green
**Ge** Yellow

## Key to items

| | |
|---|---|
| 1 | Battery |
| 2 | Ignition switch |
| 3 | Battery fuse holder |
| 4 | Relay plate |
| 9 | Fuse holder |
| 70 | Light switch |
| | b = foglight |
| 100 | Rear foglight |
| 101 | Clock/interior light |
| 102 | Glove box light |
| 103 | Glove box light switch |
| 104 | LH rear reading light |
| 105 | RH rear reading light |
| 106 | Luggage compartment light |
| 107 | Luggage compartment light switch |
| 108 | LH door warning light |
| 109 | RH door warning light |
| 110 | Door contact switch |
| 111 | Outside air temp. sensor |
| 112 | Diode |
| 113 | Tank flap release switch |
| 114 | Tank flap release motor |
| 115 | Front cigar lighter |
| 116 | Rear cigar lighter |
| 117 | Accessories socket |
| 118 | Ashtray illumination |

**Diagram 14**

H32183

### Rear foglight

### Tank flap remote release (without convenience system)

### Cigar lighter and accessories socket

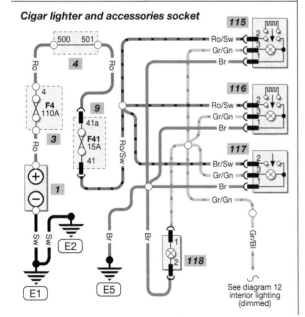

### Clock and interior lighting (without convenience system)

*Note:*
*For models with convenience system see diagrams 21 and 22*

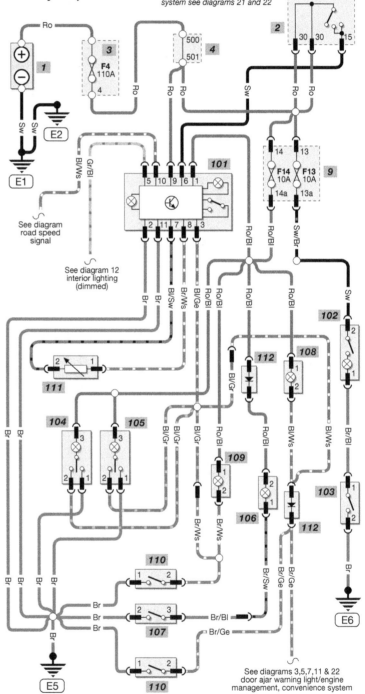

## Wire colours

**Ws** White  **Gr** Grey
**Br** Brown  **Sw** Black
**Bl** Blue  **Li** Lilac
**Ro** Red  **Gn** Green
**Ge** Yellow

## Key to items

1   Battery
2   Ignition switch
3   Battery fuse holder
4   Relay plate
9   Fuse holder
91  'X' contact relay

120 Horn relay
121 Horn switch
122 Horn
123 Heater blower switch
124 Heater blower resistors
125 Fresh/recirculation air flap motor

126 Heater blower motor
127 Heated rear window switch
128 Heated rear window
129 Wash/wipe switch
130 Washer pump
131 Wash/wipe relay

132 Wiper motor
133 Wiper delay rheostat
134 Steering wheel clock spring

**Diagram 15**

H32184

### Twin horns

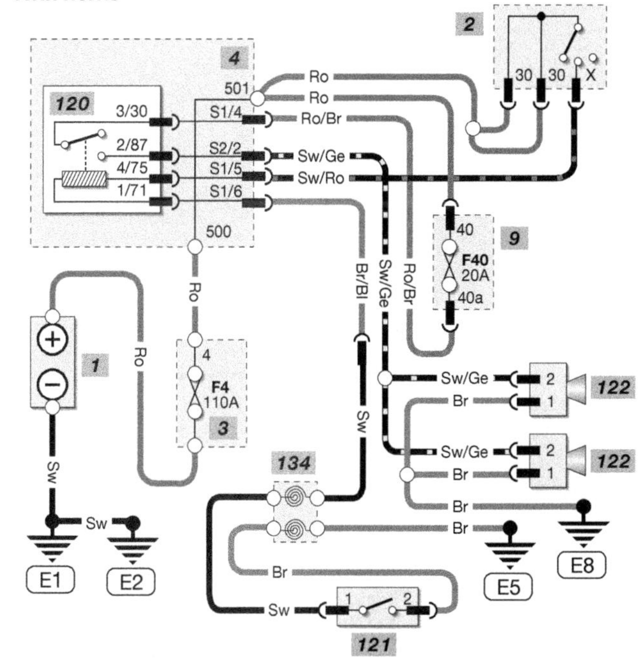

120  3/30  2/87  4/75  1/71
501 Ro
Ro
Ro/Br
S1/4
S2/2  Sw/Ge
S1/5  Sw/Ro
S1/6
500

2  30 30 X

9  40 **F40** 20A 40a

1  + −

3  4 **F4** 110A

134

Ro
Br/Bl
Sw/Ge
Ro/Br
Sw

Sw/Ge  2 1 **122**
Br
Sw/Ge  2 1 **122**
Br
Br
Br

E1  E2  Sw  Sw

Br
Sw  1 2 **121**
E5  E8

### Heater Blower

2  30 30 X 15
E5  Br
Sw

91  7/30 6/75X 8/75 5/31
501 Ro
503
S1/5 Sw/Ge
S1/1 Sw/Ro
500 Br

4

1  + −
3  4 **F4** 110A
Ro  Sw Sw
E2  E1

126  M 2 1
9  25 5 **F25** 25A 25a **F5** 7.5A 5a

See diagram 12
interior lighting
(dimmed)

Sw
Sw/Bl
Ge

124  4 Ge
1 Gn
3 Ws/Sw
2 Bl

123  1 3 4 5 2
Br
Bl/Ge
Ws/Ro

Sw/Bl
Gr/Bl
Sw/Bl

125  M 3 2 1
Br
E11

### Heated rear window

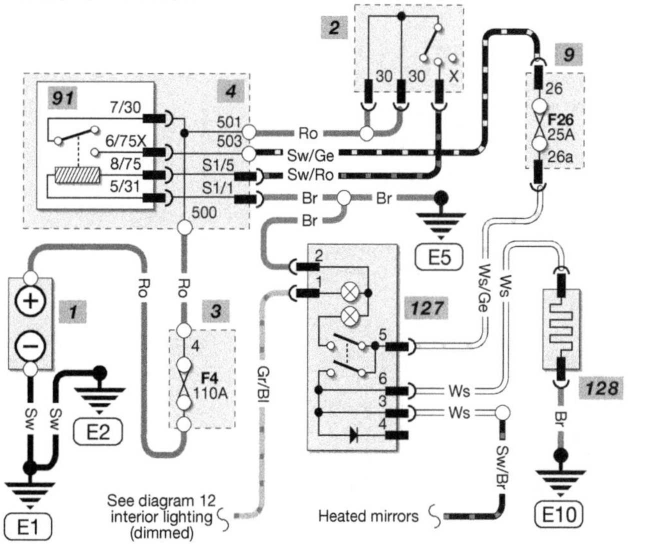

2  30 30 X

91  7/30 6/75X 8/75 5/31
501 Ro
503
S1/5 Sw/Ge
S1/1 Sw/Ro
500 Br
Br

4

9  26 **F26** 25A 26a

1  + −  Sw Sw
E2
E1

3  4 **F4** 110A

Ro
Ro
Gr/Bl

127  2 1 5 6 3 4
Ws
Ws

E5
Ws/Ge
Ws

128

Sw/Br

See diagram 12
interior lighting
(dimmed)

Heated mirrors

E10

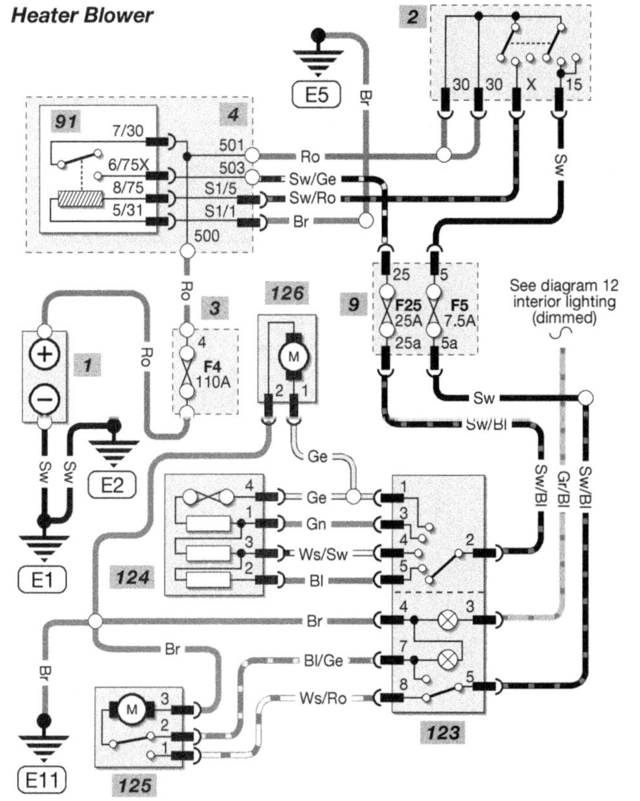

### Wash/wipe

2  30 30 X

91  7/30 6/75X 8/75 5/31
501 Ro
503 Sw/Ge
S1/5 Sw/Ro
S1/1
500 Br

4

Sw/Ge
E5

9  24 **F24** 20A 24a

1  + −  Sw Sw
E2
E1

3  4 **F4** 110A

Ro
Ro

129  5 4 7 3 8 1 2 6

133

Gn/Ws
Gn/Ro
Br/Sw

130  M 1 2

Sw/Gr
Br/Sw
Gn/Ro  Gn/Ro

132  31b 31 53a 53b
M
Gn  Gn/Sw
Br
Sw/Br
Gn/Ge  Gn/Ge
Gn/Sw  Gn

E8

See diagram 11
road speed
signal  Bl/Ws

131  1 4 5 11 7 12 2 8 3 17 13

Gn/Ro Br/Sw Ge/Gn Ws/Gn Gn/Li Br Sw/Gr

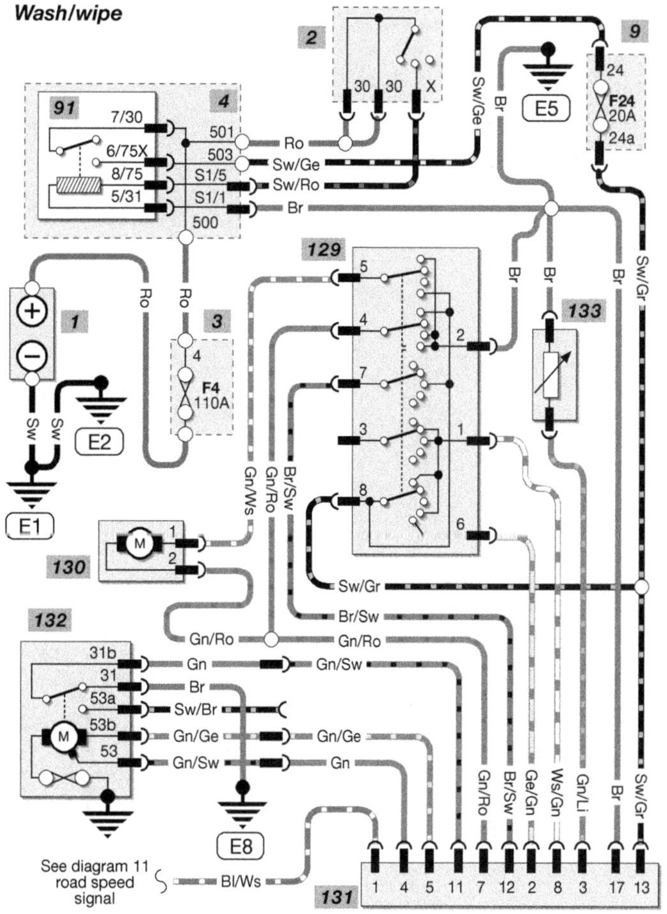

## Wire colours

**Ws** White  **Gr** Grey
**Br** Brown  **Sw** Black
**Bl** Blue  **Li** Lilac
**Ro** Red  **Gn** Green
**Ge** Yellow

\*  Models with sunroof
\*\*  Models without sunroof

## Key to items

1 Battery
2 Ignition switch
3 Battery fuse holder
4 Relay plate
9 Fuse holder
134 Steering wheel clock spring
138 Diagnostic connector
139 Airbag control unit
140 Test socket
141 Driver's airbag
142 Passenger's airbag
143 Driver's side airbag crash sensor
144 Passenger's side airbag crash sensor
145 Driver's side airbag
146 Passenger's side airbag
147 Driver's seatbelt pretensioner
148 Passenger's seatbelt pretensioner
149 Trailer socket
150 Rear foglight switch off switch
(in trailer towing socket)
151 Rear spoiler control unit
152 Rear spoiler adjustment switch

**Diagram 16**

H32185

### Diagnostic connector
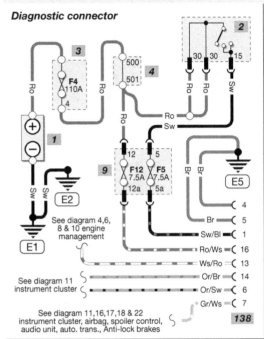

### Rear spoiler control
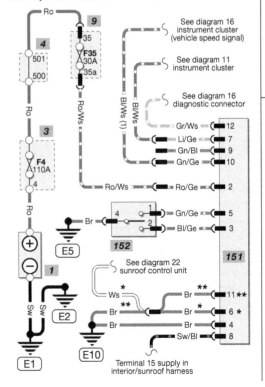

### Airbags
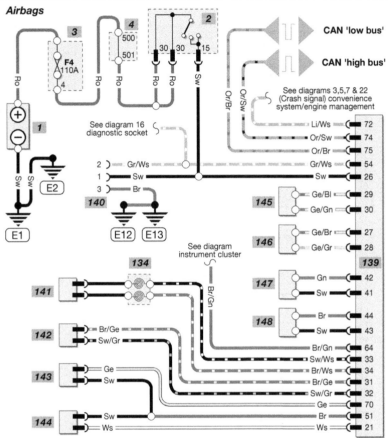

### Trailer socket
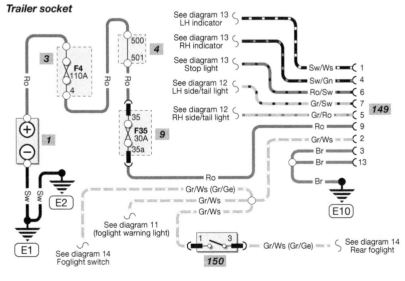

## Wire colours

| | | | |
|---|---|---|---|
| **Ws** | White | **Gr** | Grey |
| **Br** | Brown | **Sw** | Black |
| **Bl** | Blue | **Li** | Lilac |
| **Ro** | Red | **Gn** | Green |
| **Ge** | Yellow | | |

\* Not with CD changer

## Key to items

1 Battery
2 Ignition switch
3 Battery fuse holder
4 Relay plate
9 Fuse holder
155 Driver's heated seat control unit
  a = temperature control
  b = switch illumination
156 Passenger's heated seat control unit
  a = temperature control
  b = switch illumination

157 Driver's heated seat
  a = heating element
  b = temperature sensor
158 Passenger's heated seat
  a = heating element
  b = temperature sensor
159 Driver's seat heated backrest
160 Passenger's seat heated backrest
161 Antenna module
162 Audio unit
163 LH front bass speaker (in door)

164 RH front bass speaker
165 LH front tweeter
166 RH front tweeter
167 LH rear speaker
168 RH rear speaker
169 CD changer

**Diagram 17**

H32186

### Heated seats

### Audio system

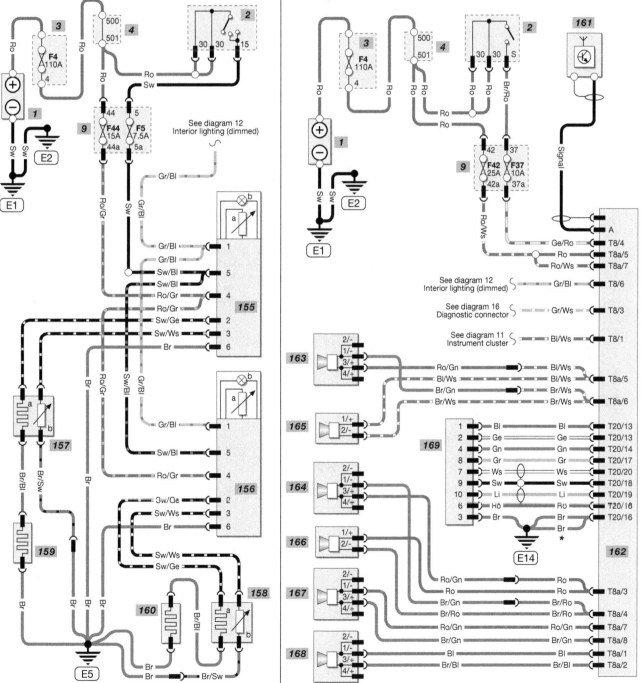

## Wire colours

**Ws** White  **Gr** Grey
**Br** Brown  **Sw** Black
**Bl** Blue    **Li** Lilac
**Ro** Red     **Gn** Green
**Ge** Yellow

## Key to items

1  Battery
2  Ignition switch
3  Battery fuse holder
4  Relay plate
5  Starter motor
9  Fuse holder
175  Starter inhibitor/reversing light relay
176  Selector lever position and scale illumination

177  Multifunction switch
178  Kick down switch
179  Blocking diode
180  Selector lever lock solenoid
181  Automatic transmission ECU
182  Road speed sensor
183  Solenoid valve unit
184  Gearbox speed sensor

**Diagram 18**

H32187

*Automatic transmission*

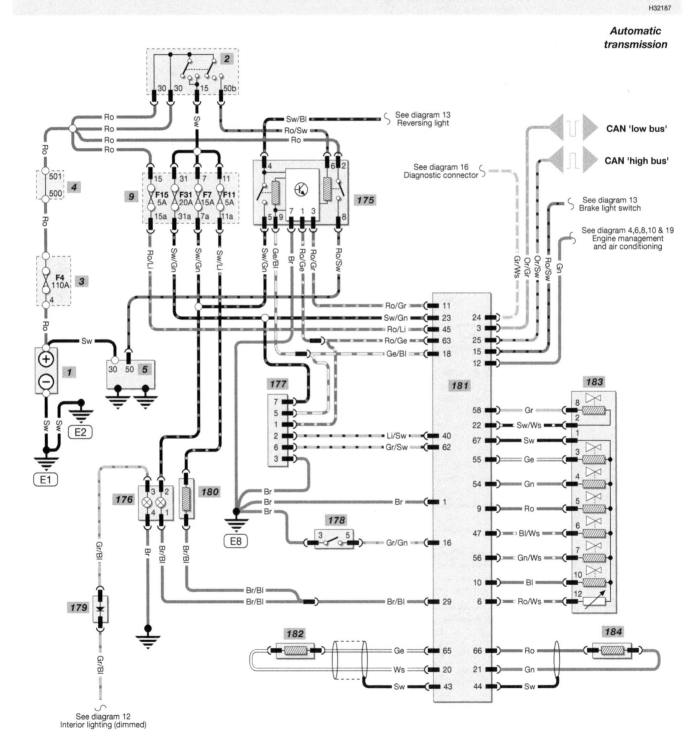

## Wire colours

| | | | |
|---|---|---|---|
| **Ws** | White | **Gr** | Grey |
| **Br** | Brown | **Sw** | Black |
| **Bl** | Blue | **Li** | Lilac |
| **Ro** | Red | **Gn** | Green |
| **Ge** | Yellow | | |

\* See also diagram 2
engine cooling fan -
triple speed

## Key to items

1  Battery
2  Ignition switch
3  Battery fuse holder
4  Relay plate
7  Engine cooling fan
8  Engine cooling fan thermal switch
9  Fuse holder
10  Engine cooling fan control unit
11  RH cooling fan

12  Engine cooling fan 3rd speed relay
13  Engine cooling fan 3rd speed thermal switch
91  'X' contact relay
124  Heater blower resistors
126  Heater blower motor
190  Fresh air/air recirculation flap actuation motor
191  High pressure sensor
192  A/C shut-off thermal switch
193  A/C magnetic clutch solenoid

194  Air conditioning switch
a = fresh air/recirc. flap switch
b = fresh/recirc. air warning light
c = switch illumination
d = A/C system warning light
e = A/C system switch
f = heater blower switch

**Diagram 19**

H32188

## Typical air conditioning system

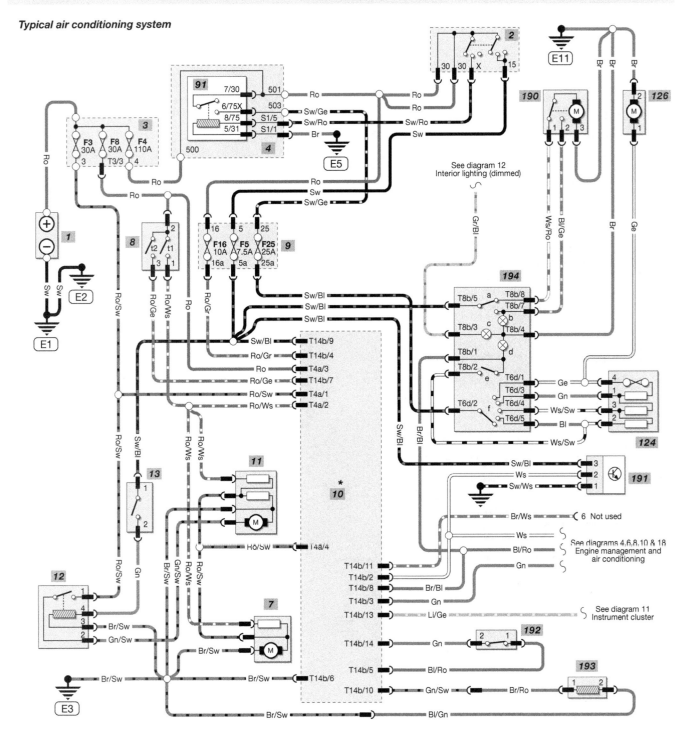

## Wire colours

| **Ws** White | **Gr** Grey |
|---|---|
| **Br** Brown | **Sw** Black |
| **Bl** Blue | **Li** Lilac |
| **Ro** Red | **Gn** Green |
| **Ge** Yellow | |

* Models with Electronic Differential Lock (EDL) only.

## Key to items

1 Battery
2 Ignition switch
3 Battery fuse holder
4 Relay plate
9 Fuse holder
70 Light switch
   a = side light
71 Multifunction switch
   b = headlight dipper/flasher
77 LH headlight
78 RH headlight

79 Headlight levelling switch
80 LH headlight levelling motor
81 RH headlight levelling motor
200 ABS hydraulic pump
201 LH front wheel sensor
202 RH front wheel sensor
203 LH rear wheel sensor
204 RH rear wheel sensor
205 ABS hydraulic unit
   a = control unit
   b = RH rear inlet valve

205 ABS hydraulic unit continued
   c = LH rear inlet valve
   d = RH rear outlet valve
   e = LH rear outlet valve
   f = differential lock valve 1
   g = differential lock valve 2
   h = RH front inlet valve
   i = LH front inlet valve
   j = RH front outlet valve
   k = LH front outlet valve

**Diagram 20**

H32189

**Typical ABS system**

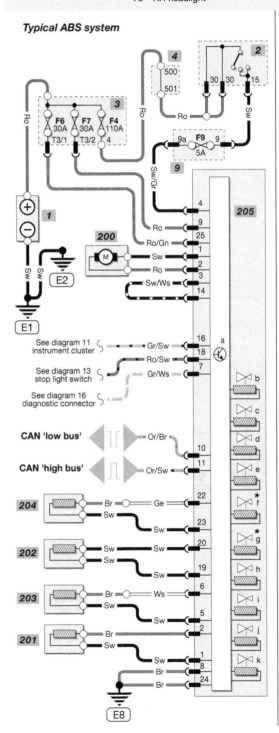

**Daytime driving lights and headlight levelling**

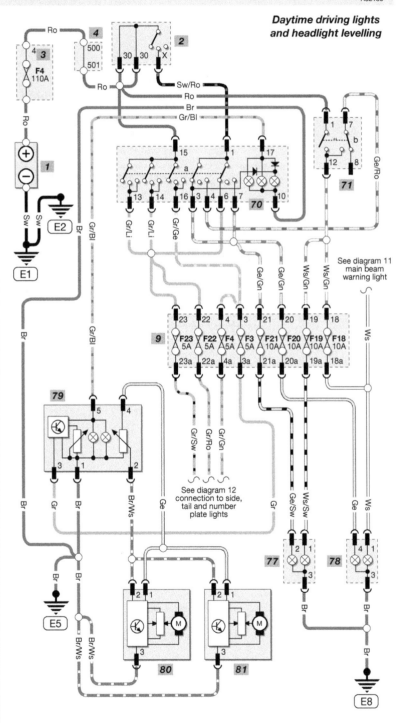

## Wire colours

| | | | |
|---|---|---|---|
| Ws | White | Gr | Grey |
| Br | Brown | Sw | Black |
| Bl | Blue | Li | Lilac |
| Ro | Red | Gn | Green |
| Ge | Yellow | | |

## Key to items

1 Battery
3 Battery fuse holder
4 Relay plate
9 Fuse holder
113 Tank flap release switch
114 Tank flap release motor
210 Fuse for electric window (on additional relay carrier above relay plate)
211 Mirror adjustment switch

212 Front electric window switch
  a = LH window switch
  b = RH window switch
213 Interior locking switch (driver's side)
214 Driver's mirror assembly
215 Warning light for central locking
216 Driver's door control unit

217 Locking unit for central locking (driver's side)
218 Passenger's door control unit
219 Passenger's mirror assembly
220 Locking unit for central locking (passenger's side)
221 Passenger's electric window switch
222 Passenger's interior locking switch

**Diagram 21**

H32190

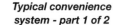

*Typical convenience system - part 1 of 2*

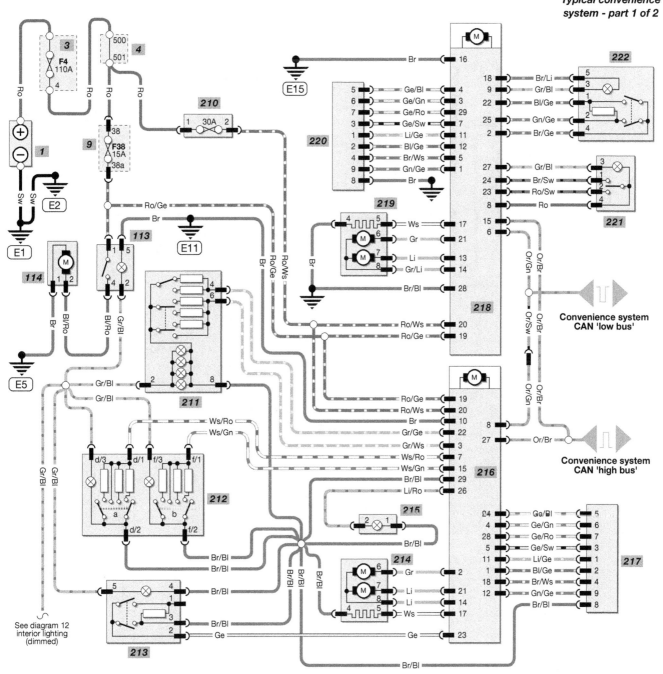

See diagram 12 interior lighting (dimmed)

Convenience system CAN 'low bus'

Convenience system CAN 'high bus'

## Wire colours

**Ws** White    **Gr** Grey
**Br** Brown    **Sw** Black
**Bl** Blue     **Li** Lilac
**Ro** Red     **Gn** Green
**Ge** Yellow

## Key to items

1  Battery
2  Ignition switch
3  Battery fuse holder
4  Relay plate
9  Fuse holder
225  Alarm horn (UK only)
226  Fuse for alarm/immobiliser
227  Fuse for central locking and immobiliser
228  Convenience system central control unit
229  Sunroof control unit
230  Alarm horn (except UK)
231  Tailgate remote release switch

232  RH rear reading light, RH alarm
    ultrasonic sensor
233  Test connector
234  LH vanity mirror illumination
235  RH vanity mirror illumination
236  LH vanity mirror illumination switch
237  RH vanity mirror illumination switch
238  Clock/interior light
239  LH rear reading light, RH alarm
    ultrasonic sensor
240  Interior monitoring switch
241  Luggage compartment light switch

242  Luggage compartment light
243  Blocking diode
244  Tailgate central locking motor
245  Tailate alarm switch

**Diagram 22**

H32191

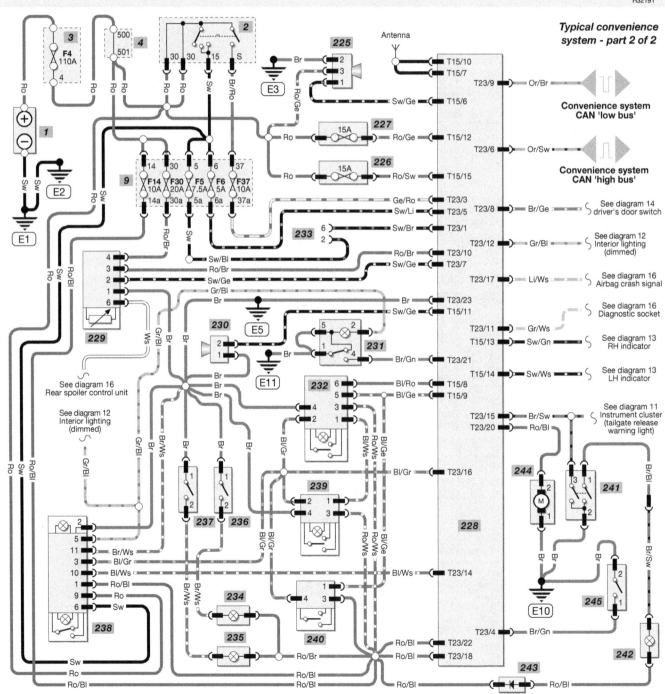

*Typical convenience
system - part 2 of 2*

## A

**ABS (Anti-lock brake system)** A system, usually electronically controlled, that senses incipient wheel lockup during braking and relieves hydraulic pressure at wheels that are about to skid.

**Air bag** An inflatable bag hidden in the steering wheel (driver's side) or the dash or glovebox (passenger side). In a head-on collision, the bags inflate, preventing the driver and front passenger from being thrown forward into the steering wheel or windscreen.

**Air cleaner** A metal or plastic housing, containing a filter element, which removes dust and dirt from the air being drawn into the engine.

**Air filter element** The actual filter in an air cleaner system, usually manufactured from pleated paper and requiring renewal at regular intervals.

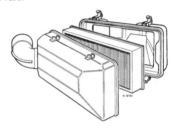

*Air filter*

**Allen key** A hexagonal wrench which fits into a recessed hexagonal hole.

**Alligator clip** A long-nosed spring-loaded metal clip with meshing teeth. Used to make temporary electrical connections.

**Alternator** A component in the electrical system which converts mechanical energy from a drivebelt into electrical energy to charge the battery and to operate the starting system, ignition system and electrical accessories.

**Ampere (amp)** A unit of measurement for the flow of electric current. One amp is the amount of current produced by one volt acting through a resistance of one ohm.

**Anaerobic sealer** A substance used to prevent bolts and screws from loosening. Anaerobic means that it does not require oxygen for activation. The Loctite brand is widely used.

**Antifreeze** A substance (usually ethylene glycol) mixed with water, and added to a vehicle's cooling system, to prevent freezing of the coolant in winter. Antifreeze also contains chemicals to inhibit corrosion and the formation of rust and other deposits that would tend to clog the radiator and coolant passages and reduce cooling efficiency.

**Anti-seize compound** A coating that reduces the risk of seizing on fasteners that are subjected to high temperatures, such as exhaust manifold bolts and nuts.

**Asbestos** A natural fibrous mineral with great heat resistance, commonly used in the composition of brake friction materials.

Asbestos is a health hazard and the dust created by brake systems should never be inhaled or ingested.

**Axle** A shaft on which a wheel revolves, or which revolves with a wheel. Also, a solid beam that connects the two wheels at one end of the vehicle. An axle which also transmits power to the wheels is known as a live axle.

**Axleshaft** A single rotating shaft, on either side of the differential, which delivers power from the final drive assembly to the drive wheels. Also called a driveshaft or a halfshaft.

## B

**Ball bearing** An anti-friction bearing consisting of a hardened inner and outer race with hardened steel balls between two races.

**Bearing** The curved surface on a shaft or in a bore, or the part assembled into either, that permits relative motion between them with minimum wear and friction.

*Bearing*

**Big-end bearing** The bearing in the end of the connecting rod that's attached to the crankshaft.

**Bleed nipple** A valve on a brake wheel cylinder, caliper or other hydraulic component that is opened to purge the hydraulic system of air. Also called a bleed screw.

**Brake bleeding** Procedure for removing air from lines of a hydraulic brake system.

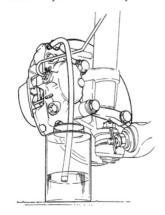

*Brake bleeding*

**Brake disc** The component of a disc brake that rotates with the wheels.

**Brake drum** The component of a drum brake that rotates with the wheels.

**Brake linings** The friction material which contacts the brake disc or drum to retard the vehicle's speed. The linings are bonded or riveted to the brake pads or shoes.

**Brake pads** The replaceable friction pads that pinch the brake disc when the brakes are applied. Brake pads consist of a friction material bonded or riveted to a rigid backing plate.

**Brake shoe** The crescent-shaped carrier to which the brake linings are mounted and which forces the lining against the rotating drum during braking.

**Braking systems** For more information on braking systems, consult the *Haynes Automotive Brake Manual*.

**Breaker bar** A long socket wrench handle providing greater leverage.

**Bulkhead** The insulated partition between the engine and the passenger compartment.

## C

**Caliper** The non-rotating part of a disc-brake assembly that straddles the disc and carries the brake pads. The caliper also contains the hydraulic components that cause the pads to pinch the disc when the brakes are applied. A caliper is also a measuring tool that can be set to measure inside or outside dimensions of an object.

**Camshaft** A rotating shaft on which a series of cam lobes operate the valve mechanisms. The camshaft may be driven by gears, by sprockets and chain or by sprockets and a belt.

**Canister** A container in an evaporative emission control system; contains activated charcoal granules to trap vapours from the fuel system.

*Canister*

**Carburettor** A device which mixes fuel with air in the proper proportions to provide a desired power output from a spark ignition internal combustion engine.

**Castellated** Resembling the parapets along the top of a castle wall. For example, a castellated balljoint stud nut.

**Castor** In wheel alignment, the backward or forward tilt of the steering axis. Castor is positive when the steering axis is inclined rearward at the top.

**Catalytic converter** A silencer-like device in the exhaust system which converts certain pollutants in the exhaust gases into less harmful substances.

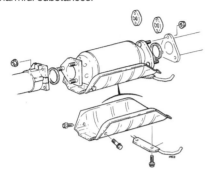

*Catalytic converter*

**Circlip** A ring-shaped clip used to prevent endwise movement of cylindrical parts and shafts. An internal circlip is installed in a groove in a housing; an external circlip fits into a groove on the outside of a cylindrical piece such as a shaft.

**Clearance** The amount of space between two parts. For example, between a piston and a cylinder, between a bearing and a journal, etc.

**Coil spring** A spiral of elastic steel found in various sizes throughout a vehicle, for example as a springing medium in the suspension and in the valve train.

**Compression** Reduction in volume, and increase in pressure and temperature, of a gas, caused by squeezing it into a smaller space.

**Compression ratio** The relationship between cylinder volume when the piston is at top dead centre and cylinder volume when the piston is at bottom dead centre.

**Constant velocity (CV) joint** A type of universal joint that cancels out vibrations caused by driving power being transmitted through an angle.

**Core plug** A disc or cup-shaped metal device inserted in a hole in a casting through which core was removed when the casting was formed. Also known as a freeze plug or expansion plug.

**Crankcase** The lower part of the engine block in which the crankshaft rotates.

**Crankshaft** The main rotating member, or shaft, running the length of the crankcase, with offset "throws" to which the connecting rods are attached.

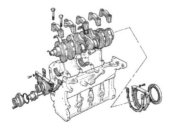

*Crankshaft assembly*

**Crocodile clip** See Alligator clip

## D

**Diagnostic code** Code numbers obtained by accessing the diagnostic mode of an engine management computer. This code can be used to determine the area in the system where a malfunction may be located.

**Disc brake** A brake design incorporating a rotating disc onto which brake pads are squeezed. The resulting friction converts the energy of a moving vehicle into heat.

**Double-overhead cam (DOHC)** An engine that uses two overhead camshafts, usually one for the intake valves and one for the exhaust valves.

**Drivebelt(s)** The belt(s) used to drive accessories such as the alternator, water pump, power steering pump, air conditioning compressor, etc. off the crankshaft pulley.

*Accessory drivebelts*

**Driveshaft** Any shaft used to transmit motion. Commonly used when referring to the axleshafts on a front wheel drive vehicle.

**Drum brake** A type of brake using a drum-shaped metal cylinder attached to the inner surface of the wheel. When the brake pedal is pressed, curved brake shoes with friction linings press against the inside of the drum to slow or stop the vehicle.

## E

**EGR valve** A valve used to introduce exhaust gases into the intake air stream.

**Electronic control unit (ECU)** A computer which controls (for instance) ignition and fuel injection systems, or an anti-lock braking system. For more information refer to the *Haynes Automotive Electrical and Electronic Systems Manual.*

**Electronic Fuel Injection (EFI)** A computer controlled fuel system that distributes fuel through an injector located in each intake port of the engine.

**Emergency brake** A braking system, independent of the main hydraulic system, that can be used to slow or stop the vehicle if the primary brakes fail, or to hold the vehicle stationary even though the brake pedal isn't depressed. It usually consists of a hand lever that actuates either front or rear brakes mechanically through a series of cables and linkages. Also known as a handbrake or parking brake.

**Endfloat** The amount of lengthwise movement between two parts. As applied to a crankshaft, the distance that the crankshaft can move forward and back in the cylinder block.

**Engine management system (EMS)** A computer controlled system which manages the fuel injection and the ignition systems in an integrated fashion.

**Exhaust manifold** A part with several passages through which exhaust gases leave the engine combustion chambers and enter the exhaust pipe.

## F

**Fan clutch** A viscous (fluid) drive coupling device which permits variable engine fan speeds in relation to engine speeds.

**Feeler blade** A thin strip or blade of hardened steel, ground to an exact thickness, used to check or measure clearances between parts.

*Feeler blade*

**Firing order** The order in which the engine cylinders fire, or deliver their power strokes, beginning with the number one cylinder.

**Flywheel** A heavy spinning wheel in which energy is absorbed and stored by means of momentum. On cars, the flywheel is attached to the crankshaft to smooth out firing impulses.

**Free play** The amount of travel before any action takes place. The "looseness" in a linkage, or an assembly of parts, between the initial application of force and actual movement. For example, the distance the brake pedal moves before the pistons in the master cylinder are actuated.

**Fuse** An electrical device which protects a circuit against accidental overload. The typical fuse contains a soft piece of metal which is calibrated to melt at a predetermined current flow (expressed as amps) and break the circuit.

**Fusible link** A circuit protection device consisting of a conductor surrounded by heat-resistant insulation. The conductor is smaller than the wire it protects, so it acts as the weakest link in the circuit. Unlike a blown fuse, a failed fusible link must frequently be cut from the wire for replacement.

# G

**Gap** The distance the spark must travel in jumping from the centre electrode to the side electrode in a spark plug. Also refers to the spacing between the points in a contact breaker assembly in a conventional points-type ignition, or to the distance between the reluctor or rotor and the pickup coil in an electronic ignition.

*Adjusting spark plug gap*

**Gasket** Any thin, soft material - usually cork, cardboard, asbestos or soft metal - installed between two metal surfaces to ensure a good seal. For instance, the cylinder head gasket seals the joint between the block and the cylinder head.

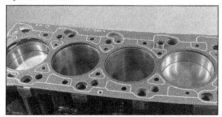
*Gasket*

**Gauge** An instrument panel display used to monitor engine conditions. A gauge with a movable pointer on a dial or a fixed scale is an analogue gauge. A gauge with a numerical readout is called a digital gauge.

# H

**Halfshaft** A rotating shaft that transmits power from the final drive unit to a drive wheel, usually when referring to a live rear axle.

**Harmonic balancer** A device designed to reduce torsion or twisting vibration in the crankshaft. May be incorporated in the crankshaft pulley. Also known as a vibration damper.

**Hone** An abrasive tool for correcting small irregularities or differences in diameter in an engine cylinder, brake cylinder, etc.

**Hydraulic tappet** A tappet that utilises hydraulic pressure from the engine's lubrication system to maintain zero clearance (constant contact with both camshaft and valve stem). Automatically adjusts to variation in valve stem length. Hydraulic tappets also reduce valve noise.

# I

**Ignition timing** The moment at which the spark plug fires, usually expressed in the number of crankshaft degrees before the piston reaches the top of its stroke.

**Inlet manifold** A tube or housing with passages through which flows the air-fuel mixture (carburettor vehicles and vehicles with throttle body injection) or air only (port fuel-injected vehicles) to the port openings in the cylinder head.

# J

**Jump start** Starting the engine of a vehicle with a discharged or weak battery by attaching jump leads from the weak battery to a charged or helper battery.

# L

**Load Sensing Proportioning Valve (LSPV)** A brake hydraulic system control valve that works like a proportioning valve, but also takes into consideration the amount of weight carried by the rear axle.

**Locknut** A nut used to lock an adjustment nut, or other threaded component, in place. For example, a locknut is employed to keep the adjusting nut on the rocker arm in position.

**Lockwasher** A form of washer designed to prevent an attaching nut from working loose.

# M

**MacPherson strut** A type of front suspension system devised by Earle MacPherson at Ford of England. In its original form, a simple lateral link with the anti-roll bar creates the lower control arm. A long strut - an integral coil spring and shock absorber - is mounted between the body and the steering knuckle. Many modern so-called MacPherson strut systems use a conventional lower A-arm and don't rely on the anti-roll bar for location.

**Multimeter** An electrical test instrument with the capability to measure voltage, current and resistance.

# N

**NOx** Oxides of Nitrogen. A common toxic pollutant emitted by petrol and diesel engines at higher temperatures.

# O

**Ohm** The unit of electrical resistance. One volt applied to a resistance of one ohm will produce a current of one amp.

**Ohmmeter** An instrument for measuring electrical resistance.

**O-ring** A type of sealing ring made of a special rubber-like material; in use, the O-ring is compressed into a groove to provide the sealing action.

**Overhead cam (ohc) engine** An engine with the camshaft(s) located on top of the cylinder head(s).

**Overhead valve (ohv) engine** An engine with the valves located in the cylinder head, but with the camshaft located in the engine block.

**Oxygen sensor** A device installed in the engine exhaust manifold, which senses the oxygen content in the exhaust and converts this information into an electric current. Also called a Lambda sensor.

# P

**Phillips screw** A type of screw head having a cross instead of a slot for a corresponding type of screwdriver.

**Plastigage** A thin strip of plastic thread, available in different sizes, used for measuring clearances. For example, a strip of Plastigage is laid across a bearing journal. The parts are assembled and dismantled; the width of the crushed strip indicates the clearance between journal and bearing.

*Plastigage*

**Propeller shaft** The long hollow tube with universal joints at both ends that carries power from the transmission to the differential on front-engined rear wheel drive vehicles.

**Proportioning valve** A hydraulic control valve which limits the amount of pressure to the rear brakes during panic stops to prevent wheel lock-up.

# R

**Rack-and-pinion steering** A steering system with a pinion gear on the end of the steering shaft that mates with a rack (think of a geared wheel opened up and laid flat). When the steering wheel is turned, the pinion turns, moving the rack to the left or right. This movement is transmitted through the track rods to the steering arms at the wheels.

**Radiator** A liquid-to-air heat transfer device designed to reduce the temperature of the coolant in an internal combustion engine cooling system.

**Refrigerant** Any substance used as a heat transfer agent in an air-conditioning system. R-12 has been the principle refrigerant for many years; recently, however, manufacturers have begun using R-134a, a non-CFC substance that is considered less harmful to the ozone in the upper atmosphere.

**Rocker arm** A lever arm that rocks on a shaft or pivots on a stud. In an overhead valve engine, the rocker arm converts the upward movement of the pushrod into a downward movement to open a valve.

**Rotor** In a distributor, the rotating device inside the cap that connects the centre electrode and the outer terminals as it turns, distributing the high voltage from the coil secondary winding to the proper spark plug. Also, that part of an alternator which rotates inside the stator. Also, the rotating assembly of a turbocharger, including the compressor wheel, shaft and turbine wheel.

**Runout** The amount of wobble (in-and-out movement) of a gear or wheel as it's rotated. The amount a shaft rotates "out-of-true." The out-of-round condition of a rotating part.

# S

**Sealant** A liquid or paste used to prevent leakage at a joint. Sometimes used in conjunction with a gasket.

**Sealed beam lamp** An older headlight design which integrates the reflector, lens and filaments into a hermetically-sealed one-piece unit. When a filament burns out or the lens cracks, the entire unit is simply replaced.

**Serpentine drivebelt** A single, long, wide accessory drivebelt that's used on some newer vehicles to drive all the accessories, instead of a series of smaller, shorter belts. Serpentine drivebelts are usually tensioned by an automatic tensioner.

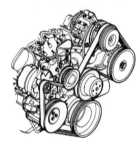

*Serpentine drivebelt*

**Shim** Thin spacer, commonly used to adjust the clearance or relative positions between two parts. For example, shims inserted into or under bucket tappets control valve clearances. Clearance is adjusted by changing the thickness of the shim.

**Slide hammer** A special puller that screws into or hooks onto a component such as a shaft or bearing; a heavy sliding handle on the shaft bottoms against the end of the shaft to knock the component free.

**Sprocket** A tooth or projection on the periphery of a wheel, shaped to engage with a chain or drivebelt. Commonly used to refer to the sprocket wheel itself.

**Starter inhibitor switch** On vehicles with an automatic transmission, a switch that prevents starting if the vehicle is not in Neutral or Park.

**Strut** See MacPherson strut.

# T

**Tappet** A cylindrical component which transmits motion from the cam to the valve stem, either directly or via a pushrod and rocker arm. Also called a cam follower.

**Thermostat** A heat-controlled valve that regulates the flow of coolant between the cylinder block and the radiator, so maintaining optimum engine operating temperature. A thermostat is also used in some air cleaners in which the temperature is regulated.

**Thrust bearing** The bearing in the clutch assembly that is moved in to the release levers by clutch pedal action to disengage the clutch. Also referred to as a release bearing.

**Timing belt** A toothed belt which drives the camshaft. Serious engine damage may result if it breaks in service.

**Timing chain** A chain which drives the camshaft.

**Toe-in** The amount the front wheels are closer together at the front than at the rear. On rear wheel drive vehicles, a slight amount of toe-in is usually specified to keep the front wheels running parallel on the road by offsetting other forces that tend to spread the wheels apart.

**Toe-out** The amount the front wheels are closer together at the rear than at the front. On front wheel drive vehicles, a slight amount of toe-out is usually specified.

**Tools** For full information on choosing and using tools, refer to the *Haynes Automotive Tools Manual*.

**Tracer** A stripe of a second colour applied to a wire insulator to distinguish that wire from another one with the same colour insulator.

**Tune-up** A process of accurate and careful adjustments and parts replacement to obtain the best possible engine performance.

**Turbocharger** A centrifugal device, driven by exhaust gases, that pressurises the intake air. Normally used to increase the power output from a given engine displacement, but can also be used primarily to reduce exhaust emissions (as on VW's "Umwelt" Diesel engine).

# U

**Universal joint or U-joint** A double-pivoted connection for transmitting power from a driving to a driven shaft through an angle. A U-joint consists of two Y-shaped yokes and a cross-shaped member called the spider.

# V

**Valve** A device through which the flow of liquid, gas, vacuum, or loose material in bulk may be started, stopped, or regulated by a movable part that opens, shuts, or partially obstructs one or more ports or passageways. A valve is also the movable part of such a device.

**Valve clearance** The clearance between the valve tip (the end of the valve stem) and the rocker arm or tappet. The valve clearance is measured when the valve is closed.

**Vernier caliper** A precision measuring instrument that measures inside and outside dimensions. Not quite as accurate as a micrometer, but more convenient.

**Viscosity** The thickness of a liquid or its resistance to flow.

**Volt** A unit for expressing electrical "pressure" in a circuit. One volt that will produce a current of one ampere through a resistance of one ohm.

# W

**Welding** Various processes used to join metal items by heating the areas to be joined to a molten state and fusing them together. For more information refer to the *Haynes Automotive Welding Manual*.

**Wiring diagram** A drawing portraying the components and wires in a vehicle's electrical system, using standardised symbols. For more information refer to the *Haynes Automotive Electrical and Electronic Systems Manual*.

**Note:** *References throughout this index are in the form* **"Chapter number • Page number"**

# Preserving Our Motoring Heritage

< The Model J Duesenberg Derham Tourster. Only eight of these magnificent cars were ever built – this is the only example to be found outside the United States of America

Almost every car you've ever loved, loathed or desired is gathered under one roof at the Haynes Motor Museum. Over 300 immaculately presented cars and motorbikes represent every aspect of our motoring heritage, from elegant reminders of bygone days, such as the superb Model J Duesenberg to curiosities like the bug-eyed BMW Isetta. There are also many old friends and flames. Perhaps you remember the 1959 Ford Popular that you did your courting in? The magnificent 'Red Collection' is a spectacle of classic sports cars including AC, Alfa Romeo, Austin Healey, Ferrari, Lamborghini, Maserati, MG, Riley, Porsche and Triumph.

## A Perfect Day Out

Each and every vehicle at the Haynes Motor Museum has played its part in the history and culture of Motoring. Today, they make a wonderful spectacle and a great day out for all the family. Bring the kids, bring Mum and Dad, but above all bring your camera to capture those golden memories for ever. You will also find an impressive array of motoring memorabilia, a comfortable 70 seat video cinema and one of the most extensive transport book shops in Britain. The Pit Stop Cafe serves everything from a cup of tea to wholesome, home-made meals or, if you prefer, you can enjoy the large picnic area nestled in the beautiful rural surroundings of Somerset.

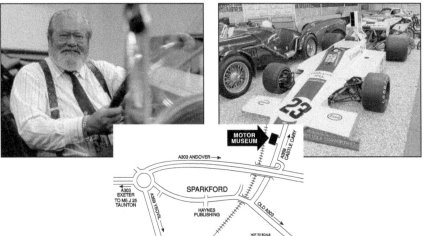

> John Haynes O.B.E., Founder and Chairman of the museum at the wheel of a Haynes Light 12.

< Graham Hill's Lola Cosworth Formula 1 car next to a 1934 Riley Sports.

The Museum is situated on the A359 Yeovil to Frome road at Sparkford, just off the A303 in Somerset. It is about 40 miles south of Bristol, and 25 minutes drive from the M5 intersection at Taunton.
Open 9.30am - 5.30pm (10.00am - 4.00pm Winter) 7 days a week, *except Christmas Day, Boxing Day and New Years Day*
Special rates available for schools, coach parties and outings  Charitable Trust No. 292048